Obesity, Business and Public Policy

Obesity, Business and Public Policy

Edited by

Zoltan J. Acs

McCurdy Distinguished Professor, Merrick School of Business, University of Baltimore, USA

Alan Lyles

Henry A. Rosenberg Professor of Public, Private and Non Profit Partnerships, Yale Gordon College of Liberal Arts, University of Baltimore, USA

In collaboration with Kenneth R. Stanton

Edward Elgar
Cheltenham, UK • Northampton, MA, USA

Published by
Edward Elgar Publishing Limited
Glensanda House
Montpellier Parade
Cheltenham
Glos GL50 1UA
UK

Edward Elgar Publishing, Inc.
William Pratt House
9 Dewey Court
Northampton
Massachusetts 01060
USA

A catalogue record for this book
is available from the British Library

Library of Congress Control Number: 2006934136

ISBN: 978 1 84542 500 5

Printed and bound in Great Britain by MPG Books Ltd, Bodmin, Cornwall

Contents

PART IV   OBESITY AND GOVERNMENT

PART V   LESSONS FROM THE PAST

PART VI   POLICY CONCLUSIONS

Figures

Tables

Contributors

Zoltan J. Acs, University of Baltimore, USA

José Felipé Anderson, University of Baltimore, USA

David B. Audretsch, Indiana University, USA

John Cawley, Cornell University, USA

Ann Cotten, Director, Schaefer Center for Public Policy, University of Baltimore, USA

Dawne DiOrio, Indiana University, USA

Julie Ann Elston, Oregon State University, USA

Stephen J. Gould, City University of New York, USA

Lenneal J. Henderson, Distinguished Professor, School of Public Affairs, University of Baltimore, USA

The Honorable Michael Huckabee, Governor of Arkansas, USA

David T. Levy, University of Baltimore, USA

Alan Lyles, Health Systems Management, University of Baltimore, USA

Marilyn Oblak, Merrick School of Business, University of Baltimore, USA

Kenneth R. Stanton, University of Baltimore, USA

Fiona Sussan, George Mason University, USA

Parke E. Wilde, Tufts University, USA

Foreword

The challenge of communicating a health policy strategy is complicated by the fact that, while many agree on what outcomes are desired, less smoking and exposure to smoke, more people being physically active and eating a nutritious diet, there is great disagreement about how we get there.

It seems that in the past, voices have come primarily from two sides. There are those who oppose any government intrusion into private business decisions and personal behavior. And those on the other side, who whether from a fear of rising health care costs or from a humanitarian motivation, advocate sweeping regulation – and sometimes litigation – in an attempt to regulate personal behavior.

Embarking on my own personal journey to health and dealing with a soaring Medicaid budget, I was forced to face the issue of preventive health in Arkansas. In the process, I've taken some knocks from people on both sides.

Once in office, when you leave the rarefied air of the think tank, you find yourself in a unique environment, restricted by reality, where you're forced to play not with the hand you want, but with the one you're dealt.

When I became governor, the hand I was dealt and the environment I inherited was not unlike those of governors in every other state: too few people had health insurance, too few people were accessing preventive health care and too many people were inactive and overweight, leading the state's Medicaid budget to grow at an unsustainable rate.

Faced with the reality of knowing that the health care system is what it is – a complex combination of private, managed and increasingly subsidized care, we could have dreamt about how great life would be if health care only operated in a true, free market. We could have held a conference on the subject, bringing in the best minds to lecture on the good old days when doctors made house calls and were paid with a chicken. Or, we could acknowledge the facts of where we were at that time in history and choose to act on what we were given.

Like it or not, for good or for bad, more than ever, government is serving as the safety net, catching our most vulnerable citizens as they fall through cracks caused by high insurance costs or jobs that provide no benefits.

In Arkansas, tens of thousands of these citizens were children who, from no fault of their own, had fallen through the cracks – that is until we passed

ARKids First. Since implementing ARKids First, we have reduced the number of uninsured children in Arkansas by 49 percent. That means today, boys and girls whose working parents earn too much to qualify for Medicaid but not enough to pay for private insurance are able to establish a medical home with a family doctor who knows their name. For the first time, many of these children are making regular visits to the dentist and, as a result, when they go to school, they're able to focus on the teacher, not a sore tooth.

Today, few can argue with the success of the program. The simple fact of the matter is that it costs less to prevent illnesses or catch them early than it does for emergency room doctors to serve as a person's only primary care physician.

Likewise, it is much cheaper on state budgets when people are able to prevent illness.

But, this principle leads to complex issues when it comes to how far government can and should go in regulating personal behavior. For some, the economic argument alone is a license to regulate. To others, personal liberty trumps all else.

So, where do we draw the line? Should a crash victim who chose to ride a motorcycle without a helmet be treated in a hospital for months at taxpayers' expense? If we know that high fructose corn syrup is hazardous to our health, do we force merchants to 'card' kids to prevent minors from buying honey buns? Do we arrest parents who smoke and charge them with child endangerment? What about parents who send their kids to school with a Harry Potter lunch pail packed with Twinkies and Cokes? Should we require warning labels to be placed on soft drinks?

These are real questions, and there are real implications to the philosophies that underlie the course we are on. Having asked myself these questions and having considered the relationship between personal responsibility and government regulation, I arrived at several conclusions, and these conclusions have guided my Healthy Arkansas Initiative.

First, from a moral perspective, I believe we are called to be stewards of everything God has given us – whether it is the environment, our finances or our health. For years, I preached about the duty and rewards of stewardship but I failed to apply this principle to my own life when it came to health. Convicted of my own inconsistency, I knew I had to practice stewardship over the body God gave me. Stewardship was not something that someone else could exercise on my behalf nor could anyone force me to exercise it.

Much of the success from Healthy Arkansas will be achieved as we encourage and equip people to practice stewardship over their own lives. We've done this by creating incentives for state employees to exercise and refrain from smoking.

The second conclusion that's driven my health policy is the fact that, in America, people have the right to make choices that some might consider stupid. Americans jump bikes over buses, drive golf carts off cliffs, skateboard down stairs and bungee from bridges. While we can't regulate all behavior, we must promote wise choices in hopes of preventing expensive consequences for which we all have to pay.

To help parents make wise choices for their children, in Arkansas we now measure each school child's Body Mass Index and send it home in a private health report. This report is not intended to be a diagnosis, but it is serving as a way to inform parents when their child may have a problem, whether it's too much weight or too little, and they are given information about local resources where help can be found. Again, we believe that, given the information, people will more often than not make the right choice.

Third, our policies have been tempered by the understanding that Ronald McDonald is not Joe Camel. We have refused to make villains of the food industry for giving us what we demand. This means we have not attempted to regulate what people eat by advocating price controls on unhealthy options or by threatening restaurants with lawsuits. I know this puts me at odds with some of the more vocal public health crusaders, but I believe in the wisdom of the free market and we are already starting to see an evolution of the food industry as consumers begin to demand more healthy options.

Fourth, we recognized an obligation to protect customer and employee safety. If property rights were absolute, the state would have no business enforcing health codes in restaurants to protect our unsuspecting bodies from invaders like *E.coli*. Just as we find it acceptable to protect workers from asbestos, radiation exposure or loud noises, it seems reasonable that we would find it appropriate to protect them from exposure to the toxic fumes of secondhand smoke. Like personal liberty, property rights are tempered when the exercise of those rights puts others in harm's way.

Finally, and this is a truly groundbreaking point, our policies have been driven by the belief that being well is better than being sick. Whether we are talking about our personal budgets or quality of life, it is more fun and less costly to be well.

When I speak at schools, I often ask the kids, 'Who here weighs about 105 pounds?' Several children raise their hands and I ask one of them to come forward. I then hoist them onto my back and begin to walk around the room and I ask, 'Does this look fun? Can you imagine if I had to carry this kid around everywhere I go? Up stairs? Down hills? In 105-degree heat?'

That was me. For years, I was carrying around the equivalent of a small teen-ager and it was literally killing me. When my doctor told me that I had developed type II diabetes and that, unless I made some drastic lifestyle changes, I was entering the last decade of my life, I decided I could no longer avoid responsibility by blaming genetics or my upbringing. I had to act.

And, there was a cost to acting. There was a cost of time and energy – I had to get out of bed extra early each morning to allow time for exercise. Rather than leisurely reading newspapers over the breakfast table, I read the paper over a stationary bike.

There was a financial cost. I entered a program at UAMS (University of Arkansas for Medical Sciences) and consulted with nutritionists. There was a convenience cost. Unhealthy food was always fast and easy to access. It took effort to make and bring my own meals to events. There was a psychological cost as I had to give up foods that I thought I could not live without.

But, the great revelation is that the money I saved by no longer having to take a handful of pills each day to manage my diabetes greatly outweighed the costs. And, my quality of life has improved dramatically – I've run three marathons and I can walk up the stairs of the Capitol without gasping for breath, my joints don't hurt, and I can honestly say that I am enjoying food now more than ever. What I once saw as sacrifice now seems like no sacrifice at all. The rewards greatly outweighed the costs. It's so much better to be well. And this realization has driven my policy.

I am not the first person to advocate a healthy Arkansas or a healthy America. I'm probably not the most effective person, either. I didn't arrive at this agenda having studied it for years in a university or in a hospital residency. Nor did I form conclusions after years of working in, or for, the food industry. My health policy emerged and evolved as I discovered truths about myself, sometimes uncomfortable truths, and as I have been faced with the challenge of managing a budget with health care and Medicaid systems growing at unsustainable rates.

I suspect a lot of policymakers will arrive at health policies through a similar process.

Honorable Michael Huckabee
Governor, State of Arkansas

Preface

This project started in the summer of 2003 when Zoltan J. Acs, Kenneth R. Stanton and two graduate students, Robert Like and Haitham Al-Foraih, started to research the topic of business and obesity. Support for the project came from Dean Anne McCarthy of the Merrick School of Business.

The effects of obesity – once an issue to be settled between doctor and patient – have become practically ubiquitous in North American life. Our culture is awash with mixed messages about 'having it all' and 'bigger is better', not to mention the circus-like atmosphere of weight loss, exercise regimens and proper nutrition. To live in North American society now is to experience everything from an entire television network dedicated to food and food-related news, to constant and occasionally dire warnings about 'good' and 'bad' cholesterol, heart disease, diabetes and a host of other obesity-related ailments. Being overweight is no longer simply a health problem – it is a symptom of a greater cultural shift that shows no sign of abating.

Signs of this change are everywhere, and at the University of Baltimore faculty researchers have taken note of the obesity crisis in the worlds of economics, business and finance, law and public policy. While the current media clamor is focused on the tens of billions[1] of dollars at stake in the behavior modification and medicalization of this issue, under the radar even more important, and occasionally troubling, moves are taking place. Airplane manufacturers and theater designers, for example, are redesigning their products to accommodate larger people. Lawyers who once focused on smoking-related illnesses are turning their attention to the potential culpability of fast food producers in the rise of obesity-related illnesses, especially in younger people. Disability claims related to obesity are on the rise.

The University of Baltimore has established a framework for researching and discussing obesity and its discontents. Faculty analyses from multidisciplinary perspectives provide a portrait of this complex problem, and potential ways to resolve it. UB will examine the web of underlying causes as an 'infrastructure of obesity', resulting from a variety of public policy decisions, economic factors and profit opportunities, in addition to the more obvious health and nutritional aspects of the epidemic. This infrastructure makes it unlikely that a singular solution is possible.

NOTES

*   Some material in the book is taken from an article previously published in a periodical which has been discontinued. Every effort has been made to trace all the copyright holders, but if any have been inadvertantly overlooked the publishers will be pleased to make the necessary arrangements at the first opportunity.

1.   The term 'billion' here and throughout this book refers to the American meaning of a thousand million.

1. Introduction

Zoltan J. Acs and Alan Lyles

Our story begins a long time ago. Hansel and Gretel were walking in the woods. They came across a house made of candy that was inhabited by two witches who ate children. Most children in those days were very thin and had to be fattened up before they would provide a tasty meal, so the witches put Hansel in a cage and made Gretel feed him to fatten him up. A recent cartoon showed a modern-day rendition of the story with two plump children strolling in the woods who come upon the witches' house. The older witch remarks to the other, 'Remember when we used to have to fatten the kids first?'.

Many people have worried about their weight for a long time (Wansink and Huckabee, 2005). But this was not a social issue. Some people were just overweight at least some of the time and most of the costs were internalized, that is, borne by the individual. Over the past 20 years a new trend has emerged – an increase in the prevalence of obesity.[1] Obesity is a state of being that has serious health and economic consequences for both the individual and society at large. While a small percentage of the population has always been obese, the obese fraction of the population started to rise rapidly in the 1970s. Moreover, while obesity used to be a problem predominantly for older people, it has now moved down into the ranks of children.

This rising trend is worrisome because it has significant consequences for individuals, business and society. Obesity leads to debilitating chronic illness (and even early death) for individuals, spiraling health costs and lost productivity for society.[2] While the increasing trend in the prevalence of obesity is not contested, the causes of the increase in obesity, the consequences of the rise in the rate of obesity and its appropriate treatment are issues on which there is much debate.

Moreover what to do about it, if anything, and who should pay for these actions are even more contentious. Is the treatment of obesity a legitimate medical cost that should be borne by insurance? Or is the cost associated with weight control a business investment in its workforce and a government's investment in its populace? Or is it a personal decision for which individuals bear full responsibility? There has been some reticence to intrude on matters regarding weight, although weight has also been termed 'the last socially acceptable form of prejudice'.

The problem is not limited to one or two countries. The World Health Organization (WHO) estimates that in 2000 the number of obese adults stood at over 300 million people. WHO called obesity, 'an escalating global epidemic of overweight and obesity – "globesity" '. That is, the problem is pandemic. While the problem is most acute in the USA and the UK, it affects countries as diverse as China, India and Thailand. What caused this global phenomenon to emerge at this time? What can be done to arrest or even to reverse this dangerous trend? Doing so will require that we consider what must be done to avoid obesity in the first instance, along with who is responsible for treating existing obesity.

For starters let us think about this like an economist. There are demand-side and supply-side issues here. As individuals we demand certain goods and beverages that we consume. For example, these can be raw agricultural commodities like whole potatoes, or we can demand these commodities in a processed form, such as French fries. Some of our demand for food may come in the form of ready-made meals and even fine dining. What economics tells us is that if the price of food falls, the quantity demanded by individuals will increase at the lower price, other things being the same. Second, if either our tastes or income increase this may result in an increase in the demand for food, with the demand curve (if this was represented graphically) shifting to the right (advertising also plays a role in this).

On the supply side, firms are in business to supply us with goods and beverages that they think we are willing and able to purchase. The supply curve represents the different quantities that will be supplied at different prices. The quantity supplied will be an increasing function of the price. The supply curve for food and beverages will be influenced by the cost of producing the food items that are supplied and by technology that might influence the way in which food is produced. If the food-processing technology improves, the supply of food might increase – shifting the supply curve to the right, giving us more food at all levels of existing prices. For example, if the machines that produce hot dogs become more efficient by producing 50 hot dogs per second instead of 10, processors will be able to reduce the cost of supplying hot dogs. A similar result occurs if less expensive substitutes can be used.

This interaction of supply and demand may produce an equilibrial price and quantity of food available to an economy. If the supply curve shifts to the right because of a change in technology, in general the price of food will fall and the quantity supplied and demanded will increase, as long as demand is not inelastic (if individuals only wanted to consume a certain quantity of food no matter what the price, the increased supply could not be sold at any price). However, this is not the case. As the price of food falls, the quantity consumed increases. So as food becomes cheaper, we eat more of it.

Taking a longer view, historically the issue has been one of supply. For centuries the fear was that the supply of food would not keep up with a growing population. In other words the demand curve would shift out faster than the supply curve, leading to the famous Malthusian dilemma. Of course while this situation has been eliminated in most of the developed world, the demand for food still outstrips the supply in certain countries. Most recently a serious famine killed millions in North Korea and many more die in African countries every year.

On the demand side, problems can also occur. In the eighteenth century, during the first industrial revolution, the working class had less to eat than before the industrial revolution – leading to malnutrition, as documented by Charles Dickens. In the nineteenth century a different situation arose. The working class – now with more income – shifted demand from nutritious wholewheat bread to white bread. The reason was that the upper classes ate white bread and it was seen as fashionable. Of course the upper classes also ate meat, which the working classes did not, and the nutritional value of the bread did not matter that much for their health. A public health crisis followed, with the working class being affected by malnutrition.

Today, in the industrialized world, we clearly are not in a Malthusian world (Akst, 2003). In fact, food production is at an all-time high, with the supply curve shifting to the right, in part because of modern technology and farming methods. The price of food is falling and the quantity is increasing. However, we may have some demand issues. Clearly public policy has worked very hard to make sure that families have enough to eat even if they are poor. While hunger still exists it is not viewed as a major problem.[3] However, while the quantity of food has increased and the price has fallen, making it easier for all to afford food, the quality of food has also changed.

The increase in the food supply has been accomplished by a shift to processed food, and in general more unhealthy food; in some ways similar to the way in which the English shifted from wholewheat bread to white bread. This shift seems to be more driven from the supply side of the equation, with food companies producing food of a lower quality that is of less nutritional value and bears greater consequences for public health. A case in point that José Felipé Anderson will make in this book concerns Chicken McNuggets. His argument is that it is not food in the sense that we know it, since you cannot make it at home – rather, it is an industrial product. Finally, the relative price of food, nutritious versus non-nutritious, has emerged as a major factor impacting obesity and health, with nutritious food costing much more than non-nutritious food.

So if Americans are eating more, eating less healthily and getting fatter in the process, should society change the outcome? Let us think about this from the supply-and-demand model again. A demand-side policy would focus on individuals and try to shift the demand curve to the left, reducing demand either by education, advertising or some other policy. In other words, a demand-side policy would try to get the individual to consume less food. A supply-side policy would focus on the availability of food. For example, a supply-side policy might limit the number of places where you can buy food. In other words, a supply-side policy would make food less available. When Americans visited Europe, for example, they used to be surprised that the Europeans had set hours for eating breakfast, lunch and dinner. At other times the restaurants were closed.

The government also has a role to play here by setting rules that allow for the safe functioning of the whole process. For example, the US Department of Agriculture makes sure that the food supply is safe from contaminants and disease, like mad cow disease. The Department of Health in most cities makes sure that restaurants and food establishments are clean. The government can also play a role in setting guidelines on what should be eaten to have a healthy population and thereby regulate the quality of food produced by manufacturers. This final point is important because one of the issues in the obesity debate is both the quantity of food consumed as well as the quality of the food consumed. This is especially an important issue in schools, where concerns about childhood obesity has led to schools trying to improve the quality of their food offerings.

We are then left with three routes to try to address the obesity epidemic: the individual, business and government. Who should play what role in this process? What if the process fails and the obesity epidemic continues to increase? Many have pointed to the strategy employed against tobacco use as one way to address the obesity epidemic. If you will recall, the fight against tobacco started out through advertising appeals to individuals to stop smoking. When this approach failed to stem the rise in tobacco usage, the process shifted to the supply side by trying to limit the availability of tobacco. Finally, when the whole process failed the lawyers took over as a last resort. However, this analogy does not work very well with obesity since everyone has to eat – maybe less but they still have to eat.

So limiting access to food may not be a very practical idea. A more appropriate analogy for thinking about the problem might be driving. The whole driving process is quite complicated but the outlines are simple. In a world with limited public transportation people need to drive get to work, shop and enjoy themselves. Since most people cannot manufacture an automobile by themselves, automobiles are sold by businesses. Finally, most roads are provided by the public sector. The government sets the rules by which the whole process operates. In this process the conditions under which individuals operate is framed by certain regulations. For example, we have a set of rules on how to drive, how fast to drive, how to make turns, how to park, where to park, under what conditions to drive, and so on. These rules need to be learned before one is allowed to drive on one's own.

Thinking systematically about weight control requires that we consider both prevention and treatment once a person has become obese. Since behavioral health change is among the most difficult sustainable changes, we can think of prevention as having both active and passive aspects. With driving, some changes made the highway safer even if the driver was no more vigilant, for example: the use of international signs and symbols to communicate with drivers; moving poles further away from the highway so a car veering off the road would not be as likely to have a collision with the pole; anchoring railguards into the ground to guide a car back on the highway; the use of reflectors to make the lanes and roadway more visible during the night, rain or low visibility; and cutting ruts into the sides of the roads to warn drivers as they started to move off the lane of the roadway. In a related way there can be protective supports to assist people with avoiding the most egregious consequences of their food selections. On the supply side, the government sets rules for what type of cars can be used. While any type of car can be manufactured, they cannot all be driven on the roads. Standards exist for safety, fuel economy, emission standards, braking, airbags, materials, and so on. These rules make sure that the cars and trucks on the road are safe, efficient and compatible with the environment.

Finally, the government establishes the system of checks and balances under which the system should work. If individuals and companies do not work by the rules there exists a system of measures to bring individuals into compliance. Let us take a simple example: if you do not obey the speed limits, most likely you will be given a ticket and required to pay a fine. Repeat offenders will be fined at an accelerating rate and at some point more drastic action might be taken, including suspension of a license to operate the vehicle, sending you back to driving school or even to prison. These rules are necessary to have an orderly society where accident rates are low and fatalities at a minimum. Of course, one also has to consider the problems and time delay in getting drunk-driving laws enforced, and the role of individuals and private advocacy groups such as Mothers Against Drunk Drivers (MADD).

A similar set of rules exists for producers. Auto manufacturers and parts suppliers must meet exacting standards or they will also be fined, or forced to recall their faulty products. For example, cars must meet rigorous standards for crash safety. A passenger must be able to survive a crash at a certain speed if a seat belt is worn and an airbag deploys. The ability of a car to meet these minimum standards will determine if a manufacturer will be allowed to produce and sell an automobile. For example, a manufacturer cannot sell a car without seat belts in order to save money. A manufacturer cannot produce cars without brakes or with less efficient brakes. In the 1970s the Chevrolet Corvair was taken out of production because it was not safe at 'any speed', and it took Detroit years to add airbags to cars.

This system works rather well because of consumer education, manufacturing responsibility and good government regulation. While at times some aspect of this process might break down and the lawyers will have to intervene, these are exceptions and not the rule.

The obesity epidemic is a 'curious' problem. We do have a problem. But the issue is as much one of how to think about it as one of how to fix the problem. Is it a failure of individual responsibility? Is it a failure of corporate responsibility? Is it a failure of regulation? Or is it the unintended consequence of the convergence of separate long-term trends? From a policy point of view, if it is a demand problem – that we just eat too much – the problem can be addressed with traditional demand-side policies. However, if for some reason this does not work, then society might be forced to look at the supply side and consider regulating the food supply more strictly. Let us look at the driving model again as a way of framing the obesity problem.

Put simply, if you are obese, or pre-obese (on the way to becoming obese), while you may think this is free choice it imposes unintended costs on society. These externalities are costs that society has to absorb because you are fat. In the driving analogy, if you are speeding you are putting others at risk at least financially because society has to pay for the health care expenditure from any accident that you might cause. (Note also the continuing debate on motorcycle helmet laws, which uses a similar argument.) Similarly, we estimate that the medical costs of obesity are about $100 billion per year (*The New York Times*, 9 January 2006). If individuals choose to be obese, they should therefore be expected to help cover the cost that they impose on society. A $500-a-year obesity tax (about what you would pay if you smoked a pack of cigarettes a day) levied on the third of the population that is obese would generate $50 billion annually. This is about one half of the additional annual medical cost associated with obesity. On average, treating an obese person cost $1244 more in 2002 than did treating a healthy-weight person.[4] Perhaps the solution could be in the form of higher health insurance premiums, as with smokers. Admittedly, a complication occurs since obesity prevalence is much higher among the poor, who are reliant on publicly funded health care. Similarly, if individuals do not know how to eat a sensible diet (one that does not lead to obesity), perhaps they should be expected to attend nutrition school and relearn how to eat.

Many in society have argued that the fault for the obesity epidemic lies with the businesses that supply us with most of our food. This includes not only the fast food industry, which has been singled out for criticism, but also the soft drink industry, the snack food industry and restaurants. The government is also implicated for the role it has played in contributing to the epidemic. At issue is not just the quantity of food, but the quality of the food supply. As examples, the introduction of inexpensive high-fructose corn syrup in the 1980s, the shift to more processed foods and the increased use of high levels of starch, fats and salts have all played a part in elevating obesity prevalence (*Baltimore Sun*, 5 March 2006, p. 5a).

Finally, the government has not played an active enough role in regulating the whole eating process, from individuals to producers. With the role of advertising increasing, and many consumers relying heavily on information from food producers, consumers may not be able to make informed choices about what and how much to eat. The government can play a much more active role in fighting obesity (*The New York Times*, 11 February 2006).

This book is not about obesity as a medical condition. Nor does it offer a wide-ranging discussion about the health effects of obesity or about the role of the 'right' diet; much of this has been discussed elsewhere. The rapid rise in overweight and obesity over the past two decades has created a debate outside of the medical community about the causes and solutions to this problem. The purpose of this book is to provide a framework for understanding this debate. It offers a framework to address the prevention and treatment of the problem from the perspectives of the individual, business and government.

The starting point of our story is the individual. Individuals make up society and to some extent individuals get obese, not society. So why are we getting fatter? Historically, people grew most of their own food and the distinction between the producers and consumers of food did not exist. Today, businesses provide most of the food that individuals consume, either in the home or outside of the home, unless individuals grow their own. Does business therefore play any role in the obesity epidemic? Finally, the government is supposed to play a role by setting the ground rules by which individuals and businesses operate. The question is how we think about framing this issue. *Obesity, Business and Public Policy* is a multidisciplinary effort to help articulate the problem and frame the debate about obesity. The book is divided into six sections: globalization; the individual; business; government; litigation; and public policy.

The first section examines the obesity problem from a cultural and global perspective. David B. Audretsch and Dawne DiOrio make an argument as to why obesity is also increasing beyond the USA. They suggest that convergence of economic performance in general and economic growth in particular implies convergence in institutions, and social and cultural capital, so obesity is also expected to occur in other developed countries. That is, countries that participate in internationalization cannot pick and choose the institutions that are spreading around the world. Therefore, rising levels of obesity will accompany the spread of globalization as American companies spread the American diet around the world. This would clearly put the blame on the companies and argue for a supply-side solution to the epidemic. On the other hand, is this just a situation of industrialization and rising incomes rather than one of cultural imperialism by the USA?

The second section examines the obesity problem from the perspective of the individual. John H. Cawley provides an overview of the economics of childhood obesity and its relevance for policy. Economics is a useful perspective because it is the study of how people allocate their scarce resources of time and money to maximize their lifetime happiness, and of people's willingness to trade one thing they value (such as future health) for other things they value (such as enjoyment today). The chapter outlines the economic perspective on children's decisions regarding physical activity and nutrition. The chapter also outlines the economic rationales for policy intervention to address childhood obesity and offers the economic perspective on arguments for policy intervention that arise outside of economics. Childhood obesity is one of the most disturbing issues since very few children were obese 20 years ago. Moreover, if individuals are obese as children it is likely that they will be obese as adults.

Lenneal J. Henderson examines obesity, poverty and diversity. What accounts for the trend toward individuals being overweight across age, race and socioeconomic status? If the result is excess weight, are the causes the same? Are the laws of supply and demand universal? To address these causes, must we craft and broadcast the same health and safety messages in public policy, food and drug marketing, and social and cultural institutions, or must we diversify and variegate these messages? If we believe that excess weight reflects socioeconomic status, will an individual, a household or a neighborhood's economic life chances improve with weight control? Given the diversity of the population of the USA, the reality of persistent poverty and the dynamics of geography and space, what are the appropriate policies, corporate and community-level intervention strategies to reduce and prevent obesity?

In the next chapter Cawley discusses the overall correlation between obesity and wages. A review of the literature yields a strong conclusion that in the USA heavier women tend to earn less than women of a healthy weight. The well-documented fact is that obese individuals receive lower wages than non-obese individuals and are therefore assumed to be less productive. However, the direction of causality is not clear. All of the results are no more than correlations, which means that the differences in wages cannot be interpreted as the result of weight.

The third section examines the relationship between obesity and business. We focus on two aspects of the business world that play a major role in the obesity epidemic: communications and marketing, and health insurance. Stephen J. Gould and Fiona Sussan examine the communication and advertising debate on obesity. Obesity is an issue often thought to be a marketing problem in that marketing communications messages about food are conveyed that are said to encourage overeating. However marketing, especially in the form of social marketing, also provides other messages, which concern controlling weight. These messages, moreover, address different consumer self-regulatory, weight-oriented systems respectively: promotional–hot–taste and preventive–cool–nutritional–thin. Hence there are mixed marketing communications messages; hot and cool. By applying these to establish an encompassing framework for marketing programs and policies dealing with these systems and messages (the Weight–Lifestyle Segmentation Framework (WLSF)), three broad market segments are identified, including: Weight Loss Resisters who are the most responsive to hot messages at the expense of cool ones, and Dieters and Health-Conscious Consumers who are more receptive to cool ones. Implications are drawn for creatively turning cool messages into hot ones and for applying the WLSF to the solving of obesity issues (*The New York Times*, 11 February 2006, p. B1).

Alan Lyles and Ann Cotten examine the relationship between weight control, private health insurance and public policies. Obesity has been ruled a disease and therefore many are seeking treatment for the problem. The chapter examines the obesity trends in the USA, national health goals for weight, and relevant private health insurance and public policy trends. Two critical issues raised in this chapter are the related but distinct roles that business and government have in providing access to health care services, and the related but different roles that state and federal government have in this area (*The New York Times*, 17 January 2006).

The fourth section focuses on obesity and the role of government. Zoltan J. Acs, Ann Cotten and Kenneth R. Stanton suggest that much of the difficulty in fighting obesity experienced by the individual can be found in the infrastructure of obesity that has been built up in the USA, and as Audretsch points out, has spread around the world (Stanton and Acs, 2005). This infrastructure includes the investment in fast food restaurants, their processing plants and their marketing budgets. This infrastructure has invaded the schools and cafeterias of the country. This chapter explains the distinct federal and state government roles and the primacy of state government in health matters. Under this structure state public policy experiments are critical in trying to reverse this infrastructure with supply-side policies that limit the availability of unhealthy food (Maryland Department of Health and Mental Hygiene, 2006).

Park E. Wilde examines the role of the US Department of Agriculture in setting dietary guidelines through the food pyramid. The new *Dietary Guidelines for Americans* focus on obesity prevention. They recommend increased consumption of whole grains, fruit, vegetables, fish and low-fat dairy products within a balanced diet where total calories consumed have been moderately reduced. Nevertheless, the best-known and best-funded federally sponsored consumer communications promote increased total consumption of beef, pork and dairy products, including calorically dense foods such as bacon cheeseburgers, barbecue pork ribs, pizza and butter.

The federal government's commodity promotion programs, known as 'checkoff' programs, sponsor these communications. The programs are established by Congress, approved by a majority of the commodity's producers, managed jointly by a producer board and the US Department of Agriculture (USDA) and funded through a tax on the producers. The federal government enforces the collection of hundreds of millions of dollars each year in mandatory assessments, approves the advertising and marketing programs, and defends checkoff communication as the federal government's own message – in legal jargon, as its own 'government speech'. Federal support for promoting fruit and vegetables is small by comparison.

The checkoff programs recently have become identified more clearly as federal programs. Following a recent decision by the US Supreme Court upholding the constitutionality of the checkoff programs, calls for consistency with the *Dietary Guidelines* may get louder. The current inconsistencies in federal communication undermine the effectiveness of the *Dietary Guidelines* as an antidote to the wild private-sector market for information about weight and obesity.

Julie Ann Elston, Kenneth R. Stanton, David T. Levy and Zoltan J. Acs examine if and how tax policies may be used to help fight the obesity epidemic. Their chapter concludes that tax policy in theory may be a more effective weapon against obesity than it was against tobacco, but the problems of developing an implementable tax policy are far from trivial. At least one of the contributing factors to the problem is apparent. The externality arises because the price of calories consumed, faced by the individual, is lower than the social cost of those calories. What is required is a reduction in the quantity of calories that can be obtained at any specific price or alternatively, the price must be somehow increased to reflect the cost to society. The addition of a tax is one means of internalizing the cost. However, the model also shows how the issue might not be the absolute level of prices but the relative price of healthy versus unhealthy food: fresh versus processed; high nutrition versus low nutrition (Sturm and Datar, 2005).

What happens when society – individuals, business and government – cannot come to a solution about a social problem? Take the case of tobacco. After years of trying to deal with the problem through the traditional means of demand- and supply-side policies the problem was given over to the courts to find a solution. Most controversial public policy issues in the USA end up in state or federal courtrooms for resolution. This is an option of last resort, as many lawyers will tell you. Part V of this book examines what happened with tobacco litigation and examines the parallels with obesity. David T. Levy and Marilyn Oblak examine the lessons for obesity control that can be learned from tobacco control. They consider the perspective of the individual, the role of public policy, the role of business and the interrelationship between the individual, business and society. However, if one-third of children are obese and getting fatter, arguments of free choice and free enterprise will not carry the day. People will demand action and the legal system is set up to do just that. The emphasis will shift from looking to individuals to change their eating and exercise habits to looking for fault with the food industry. In fact, no matter how free market oriented one is, it is hard to argue that obesity is free choice. Nobody chooses to be obese. José Felipé Anderson presents the argument from the McDonald's litigation and argues that these types of lawsuits, even if they do not succeed, change behavior; McDonald's is now serving fruit in its restaurants.

The final chapter provides a summary of the book and a framework for thinking about where public policy stands today in the fight against obesity. Zoltan J. Acs, David T. Levy, Lenneal J. Henderson, Alan Lyles and Kenneth R. Stanton provide a framework for thinking about the obesity problem. They focus on the links between the individual, the market and the role of the government. The difficulty of coordinating a solution to the obesity problem is confounded by four factors in the USA: 1) the social structure; 2) federalism; 3) political pluralism; and 4) interest group lobbying. The issue is how to facilitate discourse and consciousness of the social, economic and personal costs of obesity across such vast differences. Rational planning and intervention can achieve significant coordination and collation of complex systems. However, discourse, debate and even public dialectics as methods of radically raising the consciousness of citizens about policy issues through education may be the most important. Indeed for policy mandates and market dynamics to register, they must be interpreted and processed by these systems.

The chapter concludes with a recommendation that the most important point of intervention in the fight against obesity should focus on childhood obesity. While the current generation of adults is overweight and half of the overweight are obese, we have never had a generation of adults that started out obese as children. The implications of a generation that will be obese for most of their lives are frightening.

NOTES

1. See www.hhs.gov/news/press/2002press/20021008b.html.
2. See www.newsinferno.com/archives/923.
3. In 2001 the number of Americans who were food insecure, hungry, or at risk of hunger was 33.6 million, a rise over the figures for 2000, when 33.2 million Americans were food insecure. The number of individuals suffering from hunger rose from 8.5 million in 2000 to 9 million in 2001. The number of food insecure households with children has also risen since 2000, by 10 000, to 6.18 million. See www.secondharvest.org/site_content.asp?s=59.
4. See www.usatoday.com/news/health/2005-06-26-health-spending-obesity-x.htm.

REFERENCES

Akst, Daniel (2003), 'Cheap eats', *The Wilson Quarterly*, **27** (3), 1–6.
Baltimore Sun (2006), 'Scientists souring on soft drinks', 5 March, p. 5a.
Maryland Department of Health and Mental Hygiene (MDHMH) (2006), *The Maryland Nutrition and Physical Activity Plan*, Baltimore, MD: MDHMH.
Stanton, Kenneth and Zoltan J. Acs (2005), 'The infrastructure of obesity and the obesity epidemic', *Applied Health Economics and Health Policy*, **4** (3), 139–46.
Sturm, Robert and A. Datar (2005), 'Body mass index in elementary school children, metropolitan area food prices and food outlet density', *Health Affairs*, **119**, 1059–68.
The New York Times (2006), 'Diabetes and its awful toll quietly emerges as a crises', 9 January, p. 1.
The New York Times (2006), 'Another fad hits the wall', 11 February, A1.
The New York Times (2006), 'Two approaches to the nation's obesity epidemic coming up for review', 17 January, p. C1.
Wansink, Brian and Mike Huckabee (2005), 'De-marketing obesity', *California Management Review*, **47** (4), 6–18.

PART I

Culture, obesity and institutions

2. The spread of obesity

David B. Audretsch and Dawne DiOrio

INTRODUCTION

That more people are becoming obese in the USA is clear. As Cutler et al. (2003, p. 1) point out:

> In the early 1960s, the average American male weighted 168 pounds. Today, he weighs nearly 180 pounds. Over the same time period, the average female weight rose from 142 pounds to 152 pounds. The trends in very high weight are even more striking. In the early 1970s, 14 percent of the population was classified as medically obese. Today, obesity rates are two times higher.

Similarly, Kuchler et al. (2005, p. 1) warn that 'Americans are increasingly overweight, with the number of obese adults and overweight children doubling between the late 1970s and early 2000s'.

It is equally clear that this increase in obesity poses a medical and economic problem. According to Cutler et al.:

> Weights have been rising in the US throughout the twentieth century, but the rise in obesity since 1980 is fundamentally different from past changes. For most of the twentieth century, weights were below levels recommended for maximum longevity (Fogel, 1994), and the increase in weight represented an increase in health, not a decrease. Today, Americans are fatter than medical science recommends, and weights are still increasing. (2003, p. 1)

Cutler et al. provide an analysis of why obesity has increased in the USA, and while their observation that obesity is 'higher in the US than in any other developed country' is true, they also acknowledge that 'many other countries have experienced significant increases in obesity' (2003, p. 1).

The purpose of this chapter is to explain why obesity is diffusing beyond the borders of the USA and spreading across the globe to affect other countries. In the second section of this chapter the diffusion of obesity across national borders is analysed through the framework of convergence theory. In the third section implications for public policy are discussed. Finally, a summary and conclusions are presented. In particular, we find that obesity is in fact spreading beyond American borders and that convergence of lifestyles and technological adoption are conducive to the spread of obesity.

IS OBESITY CONVERGING?

Why should rates of obesity be diffusing beyond America's borders? One lens through which this question can be analysed is by models of economic convergence. An important implication of the Solow (1956) model of economic growth is that each country should predictably converge to a steady-state growth rate. If technology is assumed to be identical across countries, this suggests that as savings rates and population growth rates converge, the levels of income between the countries will also converge (Quah, 1993; Sala-i-Martin, 1996; Barro and Sala-i-Martin, 1992; Bernard and Jones, 1996).

Of course, the key assumption of equalization of technological adoption across countries is restrictive and has been questioned and challenged in the convergence literature. Technology will only diffuse across countries to the degree that knowledge diffuses across countries. The exact mechanisms facilitating such technological and knowledge diffusion have remained a virtual black box, at least in the convergence literature itself.

Do technology and knowledge effortlessly, and without cost, diffuse across countries? According to Landes (1998) they do not. Landes argued that while factors of production explain differences in levels of economic performance across countries, a key part of Solow's unexplained residual is not technological but rather the endowment of cultural capital. Landes takes national culture to be exogenous, and uses differences to explain cross-national variations in economic performance. According to Landes, the requisite diffusion of technology and knowledge for convergence is impeded by barriers to cultural convergence, at least in terms of capacity for absorbing technological advances.

Friedman (2005) agrees that technology and knowledge can only be adapted through cultural convergence. The adoption of cultural capital from best practices is not trivial and certainly not without cost. Friedman quotes his economics tutor Paul Romer as teaching 'Everyone wants economic growth, but nobody wants to change'. The lesson for Friedman being, 'If you want to grow and flourish in a flat world, you better learn how to change and align yourself with it' (2005, p. 139).

Thus, in contrast to Landes, Friedman considers culture to be endogenous to globalization in what he terms to be a flat world. He essentially argues that convergence in economic performance requires convergence (or probably more accurately, cultural tendencies) in institutions and culture:

In my own travels, two aspects of culture have struck me as particularly relevant in the flat world. One is how outward your culture is: To what degree is it open to foreign influences and ideas? How well does it 'glocalize?' . . . The more you have a culture that naturally glocalizes – that is, the more your culture easily absorbs foreign ideas and best practices and melds those with its own traditions – the greater advantage you will have in a flat world.

Thus, convergence in economic performance across countries is not at all automatic, but rather requires the adoption of requisite institutions and cultural capital. As Friedman (2005) argues, this may involve elements of lifestyle that are identified with best practice countries. Since the Second World War, the USA has remained the global leader in terms of per capita income and wealth, and there has been a tendency to adopt American lifestyle patterns, habits, and even institutions. It is virtually undisputed in Germany that whatever is included in the contemporary cultural zeitgeist usually first emerged and became established in the USA five to ten years earlier. Prior to the turn of the millennium, for example, delivery pizza in Germany was generally prohibited. Now it is pervasive in every German city of any consequential size. Prior to the 1980s, fast food was hard to find. Subsequently it became entrenched in the German cultural landscape.

Figure 2.1 shows how Americans have been relying more on meals obtained away from the home, with increased frequency over time. This same trend is reported to be happening across a broad spectrum of European and other OECD (Organization for Economic Cooperation and Development) countries.

Friedman argues that globalization is leading to a profound convergence in institutions and patterns of living:

If I am right about the flattening of the world, it will be remembered as one of those fundamental changes – like the rise of the nation-state or the Industrial Revolution . . . The flattening process is happening at warp speed and directly or indirectly touching a lot more people on the planet at once. (2005, pp. 45–6)

Inherent in globalization is a process of convergence, or actually what Friedman refers to as a triple convergence:

The net result of this convergence was the creation of a global, Web-enabled playing field that allows for multiple forms of collaboration – the sharing of knowledge and work – in real time, without regard to geography, distance, or, in the near future, even language. No, not everyone has access yet to this platform, this playing field, but it is open today to more people in more places on more days in more ways than anything like it ever before in the history of the world. This is what I mean when I say the world has been flattened. It is the complementary convergence . . . (2005, p. 176)

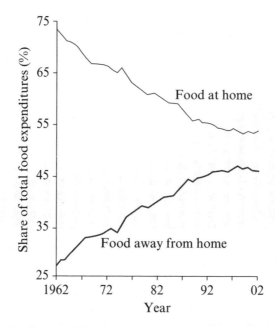

Source: Food consumption (per capita) data system, USDA, Economic Research Service.

Figure 2.1   Americans are eating out more

Of course, to argue that globalization has accelerated the process of convergence in terms of cultural and institutional capital does not at all imply global homogeneity or spatial singularity. Rather, as Florida (2005) suggests, a 'flat world' is not at all incompatible with what he terms as spikes in economic performance, which would indicate heterogeneity rather than homogeneity. The flat world argument of Friedman refers to connectedness and integration, and therefore possibilities open to large parts of the world that had previously been excluded. Just as obesity is not consistently prevalent across regions of the USA or different socioeconomic groups, it is also likely to be characterized by spatial spikes, reflecting perhaps even increased heterogeneity. But isolation and total independence, both in an economic as well as a cultural sense, has become increasingly difficult and rare in Friedman's 'flat world'.

Figure 2.2 shows that obesity has not remained restricted to the USA. Rather, as Cawley et al. (2005) show for Germany, and Grieve (2005) and Bendixen et al. (2004) show for Denmark, obesity is clearly spreading beyond American borders. Similarly, Table 2.1 confirms that obesity is becoming more than an American problem.

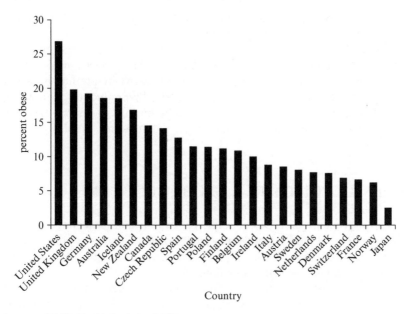

Source: OECD Health Statistics (2000).

Figure 2.2   Obesity in international perspective

Table 2.1   Trends in obesity in selected countries

Country	Age group	Year	% obese (men)	% obese (women)
USA	20–74	1976–80	12	17
		1988–94	20	25
Canada	20–70	1978	7	10
		1988	9	9
England	16–64	1980	6	8
		1991	13	15
Finland	20–75	1978–79	10	10
		1991–93	14	11
Sweden	16–84	1980–81	5	9
		1988–89	5	9
Australia	25–64	1980	9	8
		1989	12	13
Japan	20+	1976	1	3
		1993	2	3

Source: World Health Organization (2000).

We certainly are not arguing that obesity is any more targeted as a cultural goal in Germany, Europe or anywhere else in the world any more than it is in the USA. We are positing that the lifestyle trends, choices and modes of living that have emerged in the USA are emulated to various degrees in other countries, and that just as obesity is a negative by-product of such a lifestyle in the USA, it is diffusing as a negative by-product throughout the world. The spread of obesity is a negative by-product of convergence, not just in terms of economic performance, but in terms of lifestyles and culture.

OBESITY POLICY IN A GLOBAL CONTEXT

If convergence in levels of economic performance implies convergence in lifestyles, culture and institutions – resulting in an increased prevalence of obesity as a negative cultural by-product associated with globalization – are there any implications for public policy?

One school of thought resolutely argues no (Jayachandran, 2005a and 2005b; and Kuchler and Ballenger, 2002). According to Kuchler and Golan (2004) and Kuchler et al. (2004), public policy to reduce or counter obesity is futile and lacks economic and social justification. In particular, Kuchler et al. (2005) argue:

> Action to combat obesity and overweight could come in many forms since many variables influence diet and lifestyle choices. While economics tells us that prices and income shape choices, other factors are important, too. Individuals choose foods based on taste, convenience, family structure and traditions, age, health status, knowledge, and lifestyle. Policy targeted at any of these factors could have some success in reducing obesity and overweight. However, such success is likely to be limited if all other factors remain unchanged. The economic levers available to policymakers to create incentives for individuals to alter diet and lifestyle choices affect only some of the determinants of food choices. (p. 28)

According to Kuchler et al. (2005):

> Weight status – underweight, healthy weight, overweight, or obese – is, for most people, an outcome of personal choices: what and how much to eat and whether and how much to exercise. Changes in habits are possible – recent statistics from the Centers for Disease Control and Prevention (2001) indicate that former smokers now outnumber smokers. Furthermore, habits would not have to change drastically to lead to reclassifying the weight status of most Americans. The American Dietetic Association says that each additional 3,500 calories a person consumes results in an additional pound of body weight. That implies that a person who gave up 100 calories (equivalent to a piece of toast) each day for a year would end up approximately ten pounds lighter at year's end. (p. 33)

The list of policies that could potentially help Americans turn the corner on obesity and overweight is as long as the list of factors that influence an individual's diet and lifestyle choices. The list of unintended consequences stemming from obesity policy is probably longer. Even the most apparently straightforward policy proposal can have surprising effects: mandatory nutrition information at fast food restaurants could lead to reformulations or price promotions that do not necessarily contribute to healthier diets; taxes on snack foods could lead some consumers to substitute equally unhealthy foods for the taxed food; and restrictions on food advertising could ultimately lead to lower prices for food subject to the restrictions. Food policy overflows with unintended consequences. The trick is making sure they do not overwhelm the intended ones.

A radically different public policy stance argues for intervention to try to pre-empt the spread of obesity. The mandate for public policy to curb obesity is rooted in market failure. According to Cutler et al. (2003, p. 112), 'At least some food consumption is almost certainly not rational'. Cutler et al. (2003) provide compelling evidence to suggest that the food consumption of adults is not consistent with the assumption of rationality.

There are two main public policy approaches to impeding or pre-empting the obesity diffusion. The first focuses on the demand side and attempts to reduce the demand for products and lifestyle practices that are conducive to obesity. With this approach the major mechanism for reducing obesity is through reducing the demand for obesity-conducive activities and products. Information, education, labeling, advising, and also taxing products and practices that are conducive to obesity, are the focus of demand-side policies.

By contrast, the second public policy approach focuses on the supply side. The public policy effectively restricts or else raises the cost of supplying obesity-conducive products or for people to engage in obesity-conducive activities. In the USA supply-side policies for public protection have generally been avoided and only used when everything else seems to fail.

One of the most compelling examples of supply-side policy has been the campaign against tobacco. While numerous demand-side policies were undertaken to reduce consumer tastes and preferences for smoking cigarettes (Gruber, 2001; Gruber and Koszeigi, 2001), the urgency and severity of the problem triggered a mandate for supply-side policies. As Paul Krugman (2005, p. A23) points out, 'The obvious model for those hoping to reverse the fattening of America is the campaign against smoking. Before the surgeon general officially condemned smoking in 1964, rising cigarette consumption seemed an unstoppable trend, since then, consumption per capita has fallen more than 50 percent.' However, he warns that:

It may be hard to match that success when it comes to obesity. I'm not talking about the inherent difficulty of the task – getting people to consume fewer calories and/or exercise more may be harder than getting people to stop smoking, but we won't know until we try. I'm talking, instead about how the political winds have shifted. (Krugman, 2005, p. A23)

As Krugman (2005) points out:

Public health activists were successful in taking on smoking in part because at the time corporations didn't know how to play the public opinion game. By today's standards, the political ineptitude of Big Tobacco was awe-inspiring. In a famous interview on *Face the Nation*, the chairman of the board of Philip Morris, confronted with evidence that smoking by mothers leads to low birth weight, replied, Some women would prefer having smaller babies' . . . Today's food industry would never make that kind of mistake. In public, the industry's companies proclaim themselves good guys committed to healthier eating. Meanwhile, they outsource the campaigns against medical researchers and the dissemination of crude anti-anti-obesity propaganda to industry-financed groups like the Center for Consumer Freedom. (p. A23)

In fact, the public policy context has changed considerably since the anti-smoking policies were devised and implemented. As Krugman (2005, p. A23) observes, 'In today's America, proposals to do something about rising obesity rates must contend with a public predisposed to believe that the market is always right and that the government always screws things up.'

According to Krugman: and as the Department of Agriculture concludes, public policy to combat obesity is condemned to fail.

'Americans' rapid weight gain may have nothing to do with market failure. It may be a rational response to changing technology and prices . . . If consumers willingly trade off increased adiposity for working indoors and spending less time in the kitchen as well as for manageable weight-related health problems, then markets are not failing'. (2005, p. A23)

Krugman concludes that:

Above all, we need to put aside our anti-government prejudices and realize that the history of government interventions on behalf of public health, from the construction of sewer systems to the campaign against smoking is one of consistent, life-enhancing success. Obesity is America's fastest-growing health problem; let's do something about it. (2005, p. 2)

As obesity diffuses beyond the American borders, Krugman's plea becomes relevant for countries that previously seemed to remain insulated from widespread problems with obesity. Demand-side policies do not seem to be adequate to significantly keep obesity restrained. Rather, the promise of public policy in curbing obesity lies in supply-side approaches.

CONCLUSIONS

While the problem of widespread obesity first became prevalent in the USA, America is losing its monopoly. Rather, as this chapter makes clear, obesity is clearly diffusing beyond the borders of the USA and is becoming an affliction throughout the industrialized and developed world.

This chapter has suggested that perhaps the spread of obesity has been, if not inevitable, at least to be expected. If obesity has at least some connection to a cultural basis in the USA, it would be expected that this problem would not remain solely an American phenomenon.

Rather, the process of convergence in economic performance in general, and economic growth in particular, is facilitated by a concomitant process of convergence in institutions and cultural capital. To facilitate the absorption of the requisite knowledge and technology underlying economic convergence, cultural practices, norms, and lifestyles also converge. A negative by-product of the social and cultural convergence needed to facilitate economic convergence is obesity.

Countries hoping to enjoy a high economic performance, including a convergence toward the highest standards of living in the world, while remaining immune to obesity should expect a rude awakening. The USSR's failed policy of achieving economic parity while avoiding cultural and social convergence illustrates the difficulty of separating economic convergence from institutional, social and cultural convergence. Rather, as obesity diffuses beyond the American countries, nations would be well advised to start preparing public policies to combat obesity.

REFERENCES

Barro, Robert J. and Xavier Sala-i-Martin (1992), 'Convergence', *Journal of Political Economy*, **100** (2), 223–51.

Bendixen, Hanne, Claus Holst, Thorkild I.A. Sorensen, Anne Raben, Else Marie Bartels and Arne Astrup (2004), 'Major increase in prevalence of overweight and obesity between 1987 and 2001 among Danish adults', *Obesity Research*, **12**, 1464–72.

Berg, C., A. Rosengren, N. Aires, G. Lappas, K. Toren, D. Thelle and L. Lissner (2005), 'Trends in overweight and obesity from 1985 to 2002 in Goteborg, West Sweden', *International Journal of Obesity*, **29** (8) (August), 916–24.

Bernard, Andrew B. and Charles I. Jones (1996), 'Technology and convergence', *Economic Journal*, **106**, 1037–44.

Cawley, John, Markus Grabka and Dean R. Lillard (2005), 'A comparison of the relationship between obesity and earnings in the US and Germany', *Schmollers Jahrbuch*, **125** (1), 119–29.

Centers for Disease Control (2001), *Health, United States*, Atlanta: Centers for Disease Control and Prevention.

Cutler, David M., Edward L. Glaeser and Jesse M. Shapiro (2003), 'Why have Americans become more obese?', *Journal of Economic Perspectives*, **17** (3), 93–118.

Florida, Richard (2005), *The Flight of the Creative Class*, New York: HarperCollins.

Fogel, Robert W. (1994), 'Economic growth, population theory and physiology: the bearing of long-term processes on the making of economic policy', *American Economic Review*, **84** (3), 369–95.

Friedman, Thomas L. (2005), *The World Is Flat*, New York: Farrar, Strauss and Giroux.

Grieve, Jane (2005), 'Obesity and labor market outcomes, new Danish evidence', unpublished manuscript, Cornell University and Aahus School of Business, Denmark.

Gruber, Johnathan (2001), 'Tobacco at the crossroads: the past and future of smoking regulation in the US', *Journal of Economic Perspectives*, **15** (2), 193–212.

Gruber, Johnathan and Botaond Koszeigi (2001), 'Is addiction "rational"? Theory and Evidence', *Quarterly Journal of Economics*, **66**, 1261–303.

Jayachandran N. Variyam (2005a), 'Nutrition labeling in the food-away-from-home sector: an economic assessment', ERR-4, USDA, Economic Research Service (April).

Jayachandran N. Variyam (2005b), 'The price is right: economics and the rise in obesity', *Amber Waves: The Economics of Food, Farming, Natural Resources and Rural America*, USDA, Economic Research Service, **3** (1) (February).

Krugman, Paul (2005), 'Free to Choose Obesity?' *The New York Times*, 12 July.

Kuchler, Fred and Nicole Ballenger (2002), 'Societal costs of obesity: how can we assess when federal interventions will pay?', *Food Review*, USDA, Economic Research Service, **25** (3), 21–7.

Kuchler, Fred and Elise Golan (2004), 'Is there a role for government in reducing the prevalence of overweight and obesity?', *Choices* (Fall, 3rd quarter), 41–5.

Kuchler, Fred, Abebayehu Tegene and J. Michael Harris (2004), 'Taxing snack foods: what to expect for diet and tax revenues', AIB-747-08, USDA, Economic Research Service.

Kuchler, Fred, Elise Golan, Jayachandran N. Variyam and Steven R. Crutchfield (2005), 'Obesity policy and the law of unintended consequences', *Amber Waves: The Economics of Food, Farming, Natural Resources and Rural America* (June), see www.ers.usda.gov/AmberWaves/June05/Features/ObesityPolicy.htm.

Landes, David S. (1998), *The Wealth and Poverty of Nations: Why Some are So Rich and Some So Poor*, New York: W.W. Norton & Company.

Macdonald, Sharon M., Bruce A. Reeder, Yue Chen and Jean-Pierre Despres (1997), 'Obesity in Canada', *Canadian Medical Association Journal*, **157** (1S) (July), 3S–9S.

Quah, Danny (1993), 'Galton's fallacy and tests of the convergence hypothesis', *Scandinavian Journal of Economics*, **95** (4), 427–43.

Sala-i-Martin, Xavier (1996), 'The classical approach to convergence analysis', *Economic Journal*, **106**, 1019–36.

Solow, Robert M. (1956), 'A contribution to the theory of economic growth', *Quarterly Journal of Economics*, **70**, 65–94.

PART II

Obesity and the individual

3. The economics of childhood obesity policy

John Cawley[1]

INTRODUCTION

Since the early 1970s, the prevalence of overweight (defined by the Centers for Disease Control and Prevention as a body mass index above the historic 95th percentile for age) has more than doubled among children aged 2–5 years, almost quadrupled for children aged 6–11 years and more than doubled among adolescents aged 12–19 years. During 1999–2000 the prevalence of overweight was 11.6 percent among children aged 6–23 months, 10.4 percent among those aged 2–5 years, 15.3 percent among those aged 6–11, and 15.5 percent among those aged 12–19 (Ogden et al., 2002). (For more information on the prevalence of overweight among children and adolescents, see the chapter by Henderson in this volume.)

Childhood obesity is associated with severe health consequences, including asthma, hypertension, type II diabetes and cardiovascular disease – leading medical authorities to declare the rise in childhood obesity a public health crisis (Ebbeling et al. 2002; Kimm and Obarzanek, 2002). In addition to the impact on physical health, obesity also imposes on children the psychosocial costs of stigma, depression and low self-esteem (Puhl and Brownell, 2002; Strauss, 2000).

While the prevalence of adult obesity has also risen considerably since 1980 (Flegal et al., 2002), this chapter focuses on childhood obesity because it is of greater policy interest. With adults there is an assumption of consumer sovereignty. In contrast children are generally accepted to be unable to weigh the future consequences of their actions, so governments regulate the decisions of children more tightly than those of adults. Moreover, when children are in school, the government acts *in loco parentis*; for this reason it is important to consider how school policies (such as the composition of school lunches) affect childhood obesity. There are also practical reasons for focusing on childhood obesity. Childhood and adolescent overweight are likely to persist into adulthood, suggesting that the best way to prevent adult obesity in the future is to prevent childhood obesity today (US DHHS, 2000a, 2001; Bouchard, 1997).

For issues like childhood obesity, that involve a host of influences, it is likely that no single discipline or viewpoint has all of the answers to the important questions. There is much to learn from many disciplines, such as sociology, epidemiology, psychology and economics. This chapter is dedicated to outlining the insights into childhood obesity that are provided by one discipline: economics.

Economics is useful for studying people's decisions about their physical activity and nutrition because it is the study of how people allocate their scarce resources of time and money in order to maximize their lifetime happiness. The economic framework can answer the following questions. Should policymakers care about childhood obesity? That is, is government action justified? If it is justified, what is the appropriate course of action? How can we evaluate the success of any such interventions to affect childhood obesity? What is the 'right' level of childhood obesity for American society? The economic perspective on all of these questions will be provided and discussed in this chapter.

The first section details the economic view of nutrition and physical activity, starting with a framework for the behavior of adults, and then extending it to cover the decisions of children. The second section reviews and evaluates the literature on the economic aspects of childhood obesity. Special considerations for low-income and minority children are discussed when appropriate. The third section outlines the economic rationales for government intervention. In short, economics supports intervention only in the case of market failure. Several market failures appear to exist in markets that affect nutrition and physical activity, and specific policies are discussed. The fourth section provides an economic perspective on rationales for government intervention that arise outside of economics. The final section assesses the greatest research needs and opportunities in childhood obesity.

ECONOMIC FRAMEWORK FOR UNDERSTANDING CHILDHOOD OBESITY

This section presents an economic framework for understanding childhood obesity that is a simplification of more technical and mathematical economic models of calorie intake, expenditure and body weight available elsewhere (Cawley, 1999; Lakdawalla and Philipson, 2002; Chou et al., 2004; Rashad et al., 2003; Cutler et al., 2003). First a framework for adults is presented, and then it is modified to the special circumstances of children.

In an economic framework of diet, physical activity and weight individuals are assumed to maximize their utility (such as happiness or welfare) subject to the constraints of time, budget and biology. Utility can be thought of as a function of a person's weight, their health, the foods they eat, the activities they pursue and other commodities. People cannot directly choose their weight and health, but they can indirectly alter them through physical activity and diet.

The time constraint is that there are only 24 hours in the day; if one wishes to exercise more, that time must come from somewhere: either time previously spent working for pay, doing chores at home or on some other activity. The budget constraint reflects the fact that people have a limited amount of money at their disposal that they can allocate between competing ends, such as buying vegetables or fast food. The biological constraint simply states that when caloric intake is high relative to calorie expenditure, weight will rise. If calorie intake is less than calorie expenditure, weight will fall. Obesity, then, is not caused by any particular food item or any particular activity but simply by an energy imbalance: more calories ingested than expended.

Individuals' decisions about eating and time allocation reflect both the immediate and the future marginal costs and benefits. For fast food consumption, for example, the marginal benefits include the instantaneous pleasure of eating, and the marginal costs include the monetary cost of buying the food, the utility loss from higher future weight and the utility loss from any future adverse health consequences. Individuals typically assign less importance to outcomes in the distant future than to those in the present; for this reason individuals may assign little importance to future health consequences when deciding how much time to spend exercising, or when deciding how many calories to consume.

Although we do not know exactly how each individual's utility varies with health, weight, calorie intake or various activities, it is possible to make a few generalizations about the trade-offs that each person faces.

When an individual has optimally allocated his resources, he or she will satisfy what is called the 'last dollar' rule. The optimal allocation of money will be such that the individual will receive an equal increment of net utility for the last dollar spent on each type of food and on all other goods. If, hypothetically, a person received higher marginal net utility from the last dollar he spent on candy bars than from the last dollar he spent on rice, he or she could increase their utility by spending less money on rice and more money on candy bars until the last dollar rule is satisfied. The last dollar rule is useful for considering causes of the recent rise in obesity. For example, if the price of fast food fell relative to the prices of all other foods, then we would expect individuals to reallocate their budgets in order to buy more fast food and less of other goods, until the last dollar rule is again satisfied. Similarly, if prices of home entertainment electronics (such as video games and big-screen TVs) fell relative to the prices of all other goods, we would expect people to reallocate their budgets in order to buy more of such goods until the last dollar spent on those goods provides the same utility as the last dollar spent on other goods and services.

When a person has optimally allocated their money and time, he or she will receive an equal increment of utility for the last hour spent in each activity, net of the utility costs associated with engaging in this activity: this is called the 'last hour' rule, which is for time what the last dollar rule is for money. If, hypothetically, a person received a larger increment of net utility from the last hour of sedentary leisure than for the last hour spent at all other activities, then the individual could increase his or her utility by spending more time at sedentary leisure and less time at all other activities until the last hour rule is satisfied. The last hour rule is also useful for considering causes of the recent rise in obesity. For example, if the marginal utility provided by an hour of sedentary entertainment rose (such as because of increasing numbers of television channels and the rise of home video games) and the marginal utility of all other activities remained constant, then the framework predicts that individuals would reallocate their time in order to spend more time in sedentary pursuits.

In this framework, when individuals are deciding whether to eat large amounts of saturated fat, skip vegetables or be sedentary, they act as if they weigh the utility benefits of the behavior (for example taste or relaxation) against the welfare losses of the behavior (that is higher risk of morbidity and mortality). People care about their health, but health is only one of many things that people value. Economists accept that people may rationally accept worse health or a higher risk of mortality in exchange for immediate pleasure.

When considering how to extend the framework described above (which applies to adults) to children, one must include considerations of how parents intervene and impose solutions for children, and the constrained maximization problem faced by the child's parents. Parents have some power to compel their children to allocate time in certain ways; in terms of the economic framework, parents can impose constraints on a child's behavior. For example, a parent can insist that a child go outside and play instead of sitting and watching television. Parents can deny children certain foods (although they seem to have limited ability to compel children to eat specific foods). In short, parents can attempt to impose on children the solution that they think is best.

Children are faced with what economists call the principal-agent problem: the utility of children (the principals) is affected by the decisions of the agents (the parents), so children seek strategies to influence the behavior of the parents. For example, a child may use the strategy of throwing a tantrum at the supermarket checkout line in order to get a candy bar. A recent study by the Center for Science in the Public Interest entitled 'Pestering parents: how food companies market obesity to children' reviews studies that find that commercials lead to increased requests by children for specific foods, which in turn leads both to parents acceding to the requests and to increased parent–child conflict (CSPI, 2003).

Children are affected by how their parents choose to allocate their time. Parents face constrained maximization problems themselves, and if parents choose to feed the family at fast food outlets because they would rather spend less time cooking and more time at work, the health and weight of the children may potentially be affected.

In response to the rise in childhood obesity some have argued that parents should do more to monitor their children's eating, engage them in active recreation, prepare more home-cooked dinners and have more family dinners. However, just saying that parents should do these things is not likely to have any effect; parents are allocating their time in response to the incentives and trade-offs that they face. For example, the welfare reforms enacted in 1996 increase the incentives for single mothers to work and increase the disincentives for single mothers to stay home with their children and not work. Calling for low-income parents to spend more time preparing home-cooked meals may have no effect if the reason that low-income single mothers spend their time the way they do is to satisfy the work requirements of public assistance programs. If policymakers want to change the way that parents spend their time, they must create incentives for such changes.

ECONOMIC EXPLANATIONS FOR CHILDHOOD OBESITY

The economic framework provides insight into the causes of childhood obesity. This section first considers economic explanations for cross-sectional variation in childhood obesity, and then considers economic explanations for the recent rise in childhood obesity.

Economic Explanations for Cross-Sectional Variation in Childhood Obesity

Why are some children overweight but not others? One answer, based on the economic framework, is that some children have different ideal weights than others. Children may differ in their ideal weights because they have different preferences or face different constraints or trade-offs.

However, when the economic framework is applied to children, one must take into account that children are not perfectly rational. For example, there is abundant evidence that children are incapable of weighing the future consequences of their actions. The higher prevalence of anorexia and bulimia among teens than adults (Beumont, 2002) strongly suggests that teens may not be rational when making decisions about diet and exercise. Children may have poor information about the future health consequences of a calorie-rich diet or a sedentary lifestyle. Even if they have full information about the future consequences of their actions, they may assign little importance to events that occur in the distant future.

The relatively young field of behavioral economics studies departures from rationality, such as time-inconsistent preferences. A person with time-inconsistent preferences would like to be able to commit to the strategy that maximizes happiness in the long term, but consistently succumbs to temptation and chooses the short-term strategy over the long-term one (Laibson, 2001). This pattern of behavior is observed in people who express a strong preference for weight loss but are unable to stick to a diet or exercise regimen. People with time-inconsistent preferences seek ways of pre-committing to their long-term strategy; that is, they try to lock in a future course of action to prevent their succumbing to temptation later. For example, a person might publicly announce a New Year's resolution to lose weight, hoping that peer pressure will help them stick to the diet. Another example is that some people check into weight loss clinics in order to avoid the temptation they would face if they stayed at home. Differences between people in self-control and the degree of time-inconsistent preferences they exhibit likely explain some of the variation in weight between individuals.

Other explanations for disparities in weight among children focus on the decisions of parents. Parents in low-income families may be more likely to purchase high-fat instead of vitamin-rich foods. The reason is that on a per calorie basis, energy-dense foods (those containing fats and sugars) are cheap, whereas foods low in energy density, like fresh fruit and vegetables, are much more expensive (Drewnowski and Specter, 2004). Thus, parents face the trade-off of buying cheap high-fat food and more of all other goods, or expensive low-fat food and fewer of all other goods. For high-income families this trade-off may not be a painful one but for low-income families purchasing expensive low-fat foods might force very difficult trade-offs, like not paying the rent. However, most studies have found little, if any, correlation between socioeconomic status and obesity for children of either gender (Troiano and Flegal, 1998; Sobal and Stunkard, 1989).

Disparities in weight among children may also be due to how parents choose to spend their time. Anderson et al. (2003) studied data from the National Longitudinal Survey of Youth and concluded that mothers who work more hours per week over their children's lives are more likely to have an overweight child. They found that this relationship exists only among families of higher socioeconomic status. They did not specify the mechanism for this effect, but discussed the possibilities that mothers are less able to monitor the exercise and food intake of their children if they are working a greater number of hours outside the home, and that childcare providers may offer children food that is high in calories and low in nutrients. The authors emphasized that they do not find this relationship among families of low socioeconomic status, among whom childhood obesity may be most common. Takahashi et al. (1999) studied a sample of 3-year-old Japanese children and also found a positive correlation between maternal employment and the probability of overweight children. In contrast, Johnson et al. (1992) studied American children aged 2–5 years old and found no significant correlation between maternal employment and nutrient intake.

Other factors that may partially explain cross-sectional differences in obesity are habit formation and addiction. The economic model presented in the first section of this chapter can be altered to incorporate habits or addiction by allowing the utility derived from current eating to be a function of how much one has tended to eat historically. Exercise has addictive aspects in that it is more enjoyable the more one has done it recently. Conversely, if one has been sedentary recently, exercising can be very unpleasant. (Consider the difference in enjoyment of two people running a race, one of whom has trained for the race and one of whom has not.)

Some evidence suggests that the consumption of calories may be addictive. At first, it might seem odd to describe calories as potentially addictive. However, the assumption that eating patterns are addictive appears in many diverse literatures, including economics (Becker and Murphy, 1988; Dockner and Feichtinger, 1993), sociology (Riessman and Carroll, 1997), psychology (Kayloe, 1993; Jansen et al., 1989; Orford, 1985), psychotherapy (Pipher, 1994), as well as general social science (Elster, 1999a, 1999b; Elster and Skog, 1999). Biology has yielded evidence that consumption of calories may be addictive; eating, like the intake of amphetamines and cocaine, is associated with a rise in the level of dopamine in the brains of rats (Hernandez and Hoebel, 1988). Heien and Durham (1991) and Naik and Moore (1996) find that patterns of household food expenditures yield strong evidence in favor of economic models of habit formation. Cawley (1999) tests an economic model of addiction (Becker and Murphy, 1988) and finds that patterns of weight over time are consistent with the hypothesis that the consumption of net calories (intake minus expenditure) is addictive.

The finding that calories may be addictive emphasizes the importance of preventing childhood obesity. The model of rational addiction implies that 'baby fat' is not necessarily something people grow out of; rather, it may reflect early habit formation. In fact, childhood and adult obesity are highly correlated: a review of eight studies finds that one-third of obese preschool children and one-half of obese grade school children become obese adults (Bouchard, 1997). The risk of obesity in adulthood is twice as high for obese as non-obese children (ibid.). This implies that the recent rise in the prevalence of childhood obesity may, as today's children age, lead to even higher rates of adult obesity in the future. If calories are addictive, the most effective way to prevent adult obesity may be to prevent childhood obesity. The recognition that nicotine is addictive led to a similar focus on preventing habit formation among youths.

Economic Explanations for the Recent Rise in Childhood Obesity

The economic view is that changes in dietary patterns and physical activity are driven by changes in the incentives that people face, rather than by changes in their genetics, preferences or willpower. One important change in incentives is the decline in the real price of food since the 1970s (Cawley, 1999); downward-sloping demand curves imply that for all normal goods, a fall in price will result in a greater quantity demanded. Lakdawalla and Philipson (2002) attribute 40 percent of the recent rise in weight to lower food prices. One might be concerned that children have firm preferences for specific foods and are not swayed by changes in price. However, evidence from recent experiments indicates that even schoolchildren are sensitive to changes in the relative prices of high-fat and low-fat foods (French et al., 1997; French et al., 2001; Hannan et al., 2002).

Another important change in the last three decades is the dramatic increase in the percentage of married women with young children who participate in the labor force. Anderson et al. (2003) calculate that the increase in mothers' average weekly hours of work in the past three decades explains between 12 and 35 percent of the increase in the prevalence of childhood obesity in high-SES (socioeconomic status) families.

When technological changes increase the utility to be derived from sedentary leisure, we can expect people to spend more time in sedentary leisure. Sturm (2003) documents a surge in sales of devices that make sedentary leisure more enjoyable, such as big-screen televisions, which he attributes to technological improvements. This may have contributed to the increase in childhood obesity, for Gortmaker et al. (1996) and Dietz and Gortmaker (1985) find a positive correlation between television viewing and overweight among children. However, this correlation may be due to unobserved heterogeneity: the fact that families in which children watch a lot of TV are different in many ways from families in which children watch little TV. Reading is just as sedentary as watching TV, but because reading is probably more common among high socioeconomic status children it probably has less of a correlation with childhood obesity.

The few economic studies of the recent rise in obesity to date mostly study data on adults; however, these studies provide insights into the recent rise in obesity among children. Cutler et al. (2003) argue that the recent rise in obesity is due to technological innovations that made it possible for food to be mass prepared far from the place of consumption and consumed with lower time costs of preparation and cleaning. They support their argument with a variety of data that show that consumption of mass-produced foods increased the most, that people with the greatest ability to take advantage of these technological changes had the greatest increase in weight, and that obesity across countries is correlated with access to processed food.

Chou et al. (2003) studied data for 1984–1999 from the Behavioral Risk Factor Surveillance System and found that the number of fast food outlets in an area is correlated with a rise in obesity. However, it is not clear whether the increase in the number of such outlets is the cause of the rise in obesity or the effect of changing consumption patterns. The authors also found that weight is positively correlated with the local price of cigarettes; the magnitude of its effect on weight is equivalent to that of the price of groceries. As a result of the fact that smoking can suppress the appetite, an unanticipated consequence of the anti-smoking campaign may have been to raise calorie consumption and therefore body weights. (However, the authors find no correlation for weight with clean indoor air laws that restrict smoking.) The link between reduced smoking and weight is relevant for youths; Cawley et al. (2004) found that teenagers who initiated heavy smoking in the previous two years gained less weight over those two years than those who continued to abstain. Thus, decreases in youth smoking may have contributed to the rise in overweight.

Note that some of the trends that may have led to the rise in obesity are ones that we do not want to reverse; for example, the trends toward cheaper food, more widespread computer use, women in the labor force and decreased smoking among youths. It is not practical or desirable to lower childhood obesity by turning back the clock or reversing these trends; instead, society must find ways of addressing the deleterious side effects of technological change (Philipson, 2001; Rashad and Grossman, 2004).

The evidence presented earlier that calories may be addictive is not, in isolation, an explanation for the recent rise in obesity but it does help explain why people might respond dramatically to changes in the money or time cost of eating or being obese. One interesting insight from the addiction model is that, because it assumes that people are forward looking and respond today to anticipated future changes, part of the rise in obesity may be due to expectations of *future* changes in the economy and society. For example, parents might assume that there will be further innovation in anti-obesity and cholesterol-busting pharmaceuticals, lowering the lifetime cost of obesity, and for that reason invest less in maintaining healthy weight in their family.

While most economists argue that the rise in obesity is due to changes in prices or trade-offs, Komlos et al. (2004) argue that it may be due to changes in time preference: specifically, an increasing focus on short-term gratification at the expense of long-term well-being. In support of this hypothesis, the authors offer suggestive evidence: falling savings and rising indebtedness in the USA over the same period that obesity rose, and a correlation in savings rate and prevalence of obesity across developed countries.

In summary, differences among people in the economic trade-offs that they face partly explain cross-sectional differences in childhood obesity, and changes in the relative costs or benefits of certain foods or activities partly explain the recent rise in childhood obesity.

ECONOMIC RATIONALES FOR MARKET INTERVENTIONS

Calorie consumption and physical activity are determined by preferences, incentives, trade-offs and constraints. Individuals likely differ in their preferred body weight and their willingness to trade long-term health for immediate enjoyment. What, then, determines whether and how the government should intervene to change consumers' decisions? Economics supports government intervention only to correct market failure. This is a useful rule because it respects consumer sovereignty, makes clear when government intervention is justified and implies an easy method of measuring the success of such interventions. It respects consumer sovereignty because it assumes that, in the absence of any market failure, consumers should be left alone to make their own decisions. It makes clear when government intervention is justified because there are specific market failures one can look for; such as lack of information, externalities, adverse selection and failures of rationality – each of which will be addressed here.

The rule implies an easy method of measuring the success of interventions: the extent to which the market failure has been corrected. For example, suppose that the market failure is a lack of information, and to fix that market failure policymakers pass a law requiring that restaurants provide information on the nutritional and caloric content of their food. One would evaluate the success of this intervention by how well it supplied consumers with the information they previously lacked. Note that the success of the intervention is not judged by whether it led consumers to change their diets or their weight.

An important advantage of the economic framework of obesity is that it has a clear goal: to eliminate market failures. It is unclear what the goals are of other frameworks for thinking about obesity. Do they want to completely eliminate childhood obesity? This is unrealistic and likely impossible because of genetic variation in weight. Or do they want to reduce it to some arbitrary level? For example, one of the Healthy People 2010 goals is to reduce the proportion of children aged 6–11 years old who are overweight or obese to 5 percent by 2010 (US DHHS, 2000a). This begs the question: why 5 percent? Are we sure we can reduce it below 6 percent? Can it not be brought to 4 percent? Is 5 percent the 'natural' rate of obesity in a population, determined by genetics? The arbitrariness of obesity goals for children is a weakness of other conceptual frameworks (and of arguments that are ad hoc and not based on any explicit framework). The economic framework implies that the 'right' level of obesity in the USA is whatever level exists after market failures have been corrected. The goal is not a specific level of obesity, but a well-functioning process for making decisions about nutrition and physical activity.

Once an appropriate goal has been chosen (for example, to provide information that is missing in the market for prepared foods), society should achieve the goal in the most cost-effective way. There will be a large number of possible interventions to achieve each goal, and the intervention that gives the most 'bang for the buck' should be chosen. This will ensure that the scarce resources allocated to obesity prevention have the largest possible impact.

In the absence of market failure, the operation of free markets maximizes social welfare. However, market failure is not uncommon, and in such cases free markets do not maximize social welfare and economists recommend policy interventions to reduce the inefficiency caused by the market failures. The remainder of this section discusses the market failures that may affect diet and physical activity: information deficits, externalities, adverse selection and failures of consumer rationality.

This chapter does not address the challenges to the passage of legislation and implementation of policy. For such a discussion see Chapter 4 where Henderson addresses the political and other challenges to the development and implementation of anti-obesity policies.

Providing Public Goods Like Information

Free markets tend to under-provide objective information. The reason is that once someone pays to create information, it can be freely distributed among consumers beyond the control of the producer; in the argot of economics, information is a non-excludable public good.

Consumers are forced to make decisions about their calorie intake and expenditure with imperfect information. Body weight is determined by energy balance: the calories consumed relative to the calories expended. However, it is very difficult to measure energy in and energy out. For example, consumers have very little information about the calorie content of the foods they eat in restaurants. Moreover, consumers lack information about the consequences of their actions; for example, the health harms associated with various levels of inactivity, foods, or body weights (it could be argued that even experts lack perfect information on these questions). In addition, what is known is often complex. It is difficult for the average consumer to comprehend, for example, the information embedded in an infant body mass index (BMI) growth chart.

The public good aspect of information implies that there is an economic rationale for governments to sponsor the production and dissemination of information. The government of the USA supplies information about physical activity, nutrition and weight through National Institutes of Health (NIH) reports for doctors and patients, Surgeon General's Reports and the US Department of Agriculture's Dietary Guidelines and Food Pyramid. However, government education campaigns may be drowned out by food industry advertising. For example, in 1996 the advertising budget for McDonald's was $599 million while that for the National Cancer Institute's 5-A-Day promotion of fruit and vegetable consumption was less than $1 million (Vanchieri, 1998). (For more information on food marketing, see Chapter 6.)

If information is costly to use, the economic framework implies that consumers will use information to the extent that its marginal benefits equal its marginal costs. For example, information may be time-consuming to use: when choosing what to drink, a consumer needs to know not just the calorie content of one can of soda but also how it compares to other beverage options, which can be time-consuming to determine. Because processing the information needed to make a large number of comparisons can be costly, people have been found to ignore information; for example, on health insurance plan options (Farley et al., 2002). It has also been found that adding investment options to retirement plans can actually lower the fraction of people who participate (Iyengar et al., 2004), suggesting that at some level of information complexity consumers refuse to process the information. These findings suggest that the market failure caused by a lack of information regarding the calorie content of purchased foods may not be resolved by simply providing more information, but may require finding ways to present information so that consumers may process it more quickly and easily.

In addition to creating and disseminating information, there is an economic rationale for government regulation to ensure that privately disseminated information is accurate. One notable example of such regulation is the labeling of pre-packaged food. Evidence suggests that consumers respond to nutritional information. For example, Reger et al., (1999) document the effectiveness of a media campaign to convince people to shift from whole-fat to low-fat milk. Mathios (2000) documents a shift away from high-fat towards low-fat salad dressing after product labels were compelled to reveal fat content. However, a large proportion of food consumed, including most restaurant food, does not carry this information. Mathios (1998) reviews the literature which finds that, after the US government allowed food companies to include the health benefits of their products in their advertisements, there was an increase in consumer knowledge of diet–disease relationships and improvements in the composition of diet in the USA; however, while these changes occurred simultaneously with the regulatory change, it is not possible to prove that they were caused by the regulatory change.

Misleading advertising is rampant in the weight-loss industry (Cleland et al., 2002). The Federal Trade Commission has filed 80 cases in the past ten years against the weight-loss industry for deceptive advertising – more than were filed against this industry in the previous seven decades combined (Beales, 2002). Consumers who are fooled by such deceptive advertising not only lose the money they spent on the weight-loss products but also pay the opportunity cost of not pursuing other, possibly much more effective, methods of weight loss and exercise. Consumers repeatedly fooled by deceptive advertising may become discouraged and abandon attempts at weight loss or exercise altogether.

To provide consumers with the information they need to make informed decisions about nutrition and physical activity, policymakers could do the following: require nutrition labels that enable people to quickly and easily make relevant comparisons; design school curricula to teach children to become better informed and healthy consumers; engage in more vigorous prosecution of the misleading advertising of food and exercise products; provide parents with information on diet and physical activity for children; and determine what if any information gaps lie with physicians and seek to fill those gaps.

External Costs

Economists classify the costs of producing or consuming a good or service that are borne by consumers and producers as 'internal' costs, while those imposed on other people in society are classified as 'external' costs. A RAND study calculated that the external costs imposed on society by people with a sedentary lifestyle may be greater than those imposed by smokers (Keeler et al., 1989; Manning et al., 1991). More recent evidence presented in Finkelstein et al. (2003) is consistent with large lifetime external costs of overweight and obesity. These external costs are largely imposed through health and life insurance. To the extent that health insurance premiums imperfectly adjust for the fact that obese and sedentary individuals tend to be sicker and therefore have higher health care expenditures, external costs are imposed on other members of the health insurance pool in the form of higher premiums. Likewise, to the extent that term life insurance premiums imperfectly adjust for the fact that obese and sedentary individuals face higher risks of mortality, external costs are also imposed on other members of the life insurance pool in the form of higher premiums. Other possible external costs imposed by obese and sedentary individuals include greater charges to disability insurance and Medicaid.

On the other hand, to the extent that obese or sedentary individuals participate in defined-benefit pension plans and tend to die younger than lighter or more active people, they generate positive externalities because they die before they can collect their full share of pension benefits. Likewise, obese individuals may on average draw fewer social security benefits.

Broadly speaking, two strategies could be used to 'internalize' the external costs of a sedentary lifestyle or obesity. The government could tax the problem, or it could subsidize the solution.

Some have proposed taxes on 'junk' foods, but this would be unsatisfactory for several reasons. First, classifying foods as healthy or unhealthy is not meaningful. The key to preventing obesity is energy balance: the balance between calorie intake and calorie expenditure. For this reason, there are no such things as 'junk' food and 'healthy' food. If one is starving, virtually any food is 'healthy' food. If one is morbidly obese, virtually any food is 'unhealthy' in that it leads to greater energy imbalance. Once one recognizes that there is no meaningful distinction among foods as being healthy or unhealthy, it becomes apparent that it is impossible to decide which foods should be taxed and which foods should be subsidized in order to promote energy balance. The most common way of consuming potatoes is as French fries and the most common way of consuming tomatoes is as ketchup; subsidies for growing potatoes and tomatoes may therefore lower the cost of, and increase the consumption of, French fries with ketchup. There is therefore no distinct category of foods that should be taxed and no distinct category of foods that should be subsidized in order to prevent obesity.

Taxes on calorie consumption are also unattractive because low-income families spend a greater fraction of their income on food than do higher-income families. For this reason, taxes on foods are regressive; that is, all harder on low-income than high-income families. Also, taxes on obesity per se are likely to be politically unacceptable.

For these reasons, it is preferable to subsidize physical activity than to tax calorie consumption, sedentary lifestyles or obesity. Manning et al. (1991, p. 23) write: '[S]ociety can tax people for "wrongful consumption" – per unit of substance consumed. It is hard to imagine how they can be taxed for not doing the "right" thing. They could, however, be "rewarded" for doing it'. Subsidies for physical activity do not rely on a false distinction between good foods and bad foods, they do not impose costs disproportionately on the poor, and are relatively uncontroversial compared to taxes on certain body types or lifestyles. Given the evidence on negative externalities of obesity and sedentary lifestyles, subsidies for physical activity seem justified.

However, there remains the practical issue of how to use subsidies to stimulate physical activity in children. Research indicates that children's physical activity appears uncorrelated with the availability of local facilities (Zakarian et al., 1994) or with neighborhood safety (Sallis, 1999).

Adverse Selection

Economics also accepts a role for government action to address market failures caused by adverse selection. The fear of adverse selection may lead health insurers to refuse to cover treatment for obesity. The problem is rooted in the fact that obesity treatment is so discretionary on the part of the patient. Health insurers may fear that if they alone offer reimbursement for obesity treatment, then they will attract as applicants those who are most likely to seek obesity treatment. The health insurer may not be able to identify the applicants who intend to use a lot of weight-loss services and therefore the insurer cannot charge such people a higher premium. If the insurance company sets the part of its premium due to expenditures on weight-loss services according to average use, the health insurance policy will be unattractive to people who do not intend to use weight-loss services, and very attractive to those who do.

In general in such a situation, a 'premium death spiral' can result, in which the customers with low utilization cancel their insurance because of its cost, premiums rise, the next-lowest-utilization customers cancel their insurance because of its higher cost and the shrinking insurance pool increasingly consists of high-utilization people. Wary of initiating this chain of events, insurers often decline to cover any kind of discretionary expenditure (including weight-loss treatments but also mental health services, substance abuse treatment, chiropractic services and maternity stays). To avoid this problem, states often mandate that certain benefits be included in health insurance plans.

Coverage of obesity treatments varies among private health insurance plans (American Obesity Association, 2002). To the extent that fear of adverse selection leads insurers to refuse to cover treatments for weight loss, there may be a role for government to require that health insurers cover such treatments. State governments have intervened in health insurance markets many times in the past three decades. Between 1970 and 2002 the number of state-mandated benefits rose 25-fold; as of January 2002 there were 1260 state-mandated health insurance benefits (Bunce, 2002).

The government could also expand publicly provided insurance to cover treatment of weight loss. Medicaid coverage of anti-obesity pharmaceuticals and surgical treatments for obesity are determined on a state-by-state basis (American Obesity Association, 2002). The Medicare Coverage Issues Manual states that 'obesity is not considered an illness . . .' and notes that Medicare covers treatment for obesity only if obesity is caused by a recognized illness or is aggravating a recognized illness (US DHHS, 2000b, sections 35–26).

However, the extent to which adverse selection truly impedes the functioning of health insurance markets is unclear (Cardon and Hendel, 2001). To minimize adverse selection, insurers engage in the process of underwriting to refine their estimates of the expected expenses associated with each applicant. In fact, the first study of body weight and mortality was conducted in 1942 by the Metropolitan Life Insurance Company to more accurately assess the mortality risk of those applying for life insurance coverage. For this reason it is not clear to what extent the failure of certain health insurance plans to cover obesity can be attributed to insurer concerns about adverse selection.

Failures of Rationality

The fourth issue of market failure that affects diet and physical activity is that decision-makers may be less than perfectly rational. One does not judge whether an individual is rational based on whether one agrees with his action but by whether the individual is capable of acting in his own interest (in economics jargon, maximizing his utility).

It is widely accepted that children are unable to take into account the future consequences of their actions. While society may trust adults to accurately weigh the costs and benefits of a high-calorie diet or a sedentary lifestyle, we may wish to intervene for paternalistic reasons to influence the decisions of children. There is an abundance of precedents for treating children differently than adults on the basis of their inability to make responsible decisions: cigarette and alcohol sales to minors are banned; those under age 16 may not drive; and those under 18 may not vote.

Time-inconsistent preferences, which are characterized by the tendency to succumb to the temptation to accept immediate gratification at the expense of long-term best interest, seem to be fairly common, especially among children. Cutler et al. (2003) show that under the assumption of time-inconsistent preferences, recent technological changes that lowered the cost of food could have led to increases in consumption that lowered social welfare. When preferences are time inconsistent, the optimal 'sin tax', one which forces the consumer to pay the full cost of their behavior, should reflect not only all of the external costs to society but also some of the internal costs. The logic is that time-inconsistent individuals may be grateful for the tax, because it forces them to do what they would like, but are unable, to do unassisted: take into account today the future consequences of their actions (Gruber and Mullainathan, 2002). However, as described under the External Costs section, sin taxes on food are impractical and those on obesity are undesirable.

Some have advocated that advertising to children be regulated because children, being less than fully rational, are too vulnerable to marketing (Nestle, 2002; Schlosser, 2001). However, Congress has historically tolerated very little regulation of commercial speech. A cautionary tale for those who urge greater regulation of food advertising to children is the 1979 'KidVid' episode in which the Federal Trade Commission (FTC) sought to regulate the television advertising of sugary cereals to children under the age of 13 (interestingly, not because of obesity but because of tooth decay). Congress responded firmly to defend commercial speech and limit the FTC's power; as a result, the FTC had to struggle just for reauthorization (Engle, 2003). One example of the American government shielding children from advertising is the 1992 Telephone Disclosure and Dispute Resolution Act, which empowered the FTC to issue what is known as the '900 Number' rule. This rule bans advertising of 1-900 phone numbers to children under the age of 12 and requires that advertising directed to children under the age of 18 include the warning that children need their parents' permission to use the service. (When 1-900 numbers first were marketed, some unscrupulous entrepreneurs encouraged children to call the numbers to talk to their favorite cartoon characters, Santa Claus or the Easter Bunny.)

A difficulty with a ban on advertising to children is that it would impede firms marketing low-energy-dense foods to kids from seizing market share away from firms marketing energy-dense foods. It would also prevent the physical activity industry from encouraging children to buy sporting equipment and shoes that might lead them to be more active. Such a ban might also be easy to circumvent through product placements in television shows, movies and books, and through advertising that does not rely on media (such as on vending machines, sponsoring concert series, or NASCAR).

There is evidence of other failures of rationality. For example, a recent study finds that people tend to consume more calories when they are given larger portions (Rolls et al., 2002). This is particularly interesting in light of the finding that portion sizes have increased over the last 20 years (Nielsen and Popkin, 2003; Young and Nestle, 2002).

While it is probably politically infeasible to restrict the choices of American children and youth in their homes, it is easier to justify regulating children's choices in school. At school the government, through teachers, acts *in loco parentis* – in place of the parents. Teachers and administrators are allowed to regulate children's behavior and even discipline them. For this reason, it may be acceptable for schools to regulate children's choices as regard calorie intake and calorie expenditure. For example, states could mandate that all schools must remove vending machines dispersing soda and candy. As described in the External Costs section, there is no meaningful distinction among foods as being healthy and unhealthy, and for this reason it is somewhat arbitrary where the line should be drawn as to what foods should be allowed in schools and which should be banned. Because children are not generally capable of choosing foods to achieve energy balance, energy-dense foods such as non-diet sodas and candy may be the most likely to lead to energy imbalance and subsequent obesity. Advertising of energy-dense foods could likewise be banned in schools. School meals could be reconfigured to consist of low-energy dense foods that facilitate energy balance, and the portions served should take into account the portion size effect observed in the research literature.

By this same logic, schools can mandate certain levels of physical activity. Schools could conduct meaningful physical education classes that involve physical activity and nutrition classes that train students to become educated consumers. If children are determined to be not fully rational, they should not simply be shielded from advertising but taught how to understand it and put it in context so that later they can act as educated consumers.

ECONOMIC PERSPECTIVE ON OTHER RATIONALES FOR POLICY INTERVENTION

The previous section outlined the policy interventions that are justified by the economic framework. This section briefly provides the economic perspective on rationales for intervention that are motivated by non-economic considerations.

Fairness/Equity

Distributional considerations such as fairness and equity are outside the realm of economics, which focuses only on economic efficiency. In other words, economists focus on maximizing the size of the economic pie and leave to others the work of determining how big a slice of pie each person gets.

However, there are distributional issues in obesity. While there is little, if any, correlation between socioeconomic status and obesity for children of either gender (Troiano and Flegal, 1998; Sobal and Stunkard, 1989), obesity in the USA is a particularly significant problem among adult female members of disadvantaged minority groups (Fontaine and Bartlett, 2002; Sobal and Stunkard, 1989). Data from 1999–2000 reveal that 49.7 percent of African-American women and 39.7 percent of Mexican-American women are obese, compared to 30.1 percent of non-Hispanic white American women (Flegal et al., 2002). Compared to Caucasian Americans, African-Americans and Hispanics may receive less disutility from heaviness (Brown and Bentley-Condit, 1998; Stearns, 1997). African-American and Hispanic women report larger ideal body sizes than Caucasian women, and African-American men are more likely than Caucasian males to report a willingness to date heavy women (Powell and Kahn, 1995). Given the correlation of obesity with morbidity and mortality, socioeconomic disparities in obesity among women threaten to worsen socioeconomic inequities in health in the USA.

Inequities also exist with respect to diet and physical activity. Grocery stores in poorer, African-American neighborhoods are less likely to sell low-fat foods and tend to stock a smaller variety and worse quality of fresh fruits and vegetables than those in wealthier neighborhoods with fewer minorities (Sloane et al., 2003). Safe environments for physical activity are more difficult to find in poor inner-city neighborhoods than in wealthier suburbs. To some, these disparities may justify policy intervention on grounds of equity.

Paternalistic or Puritanical Desire to Change Other People's Behavior

Throughout American history there have been calls to regulate what is ostensibly private behavior (Kersh and Morone, 2002), even when there are few discernible externalities and no evidence of other market failures. Some of the proposals to encourage obese people to restrict their diets, exercise more or achieve healthy weight may partly be influenced by puritanical disgust for sloth and gluttony.

This puritanical disgust for certain lifestyles or values may lead to criticism of certain foods or activities, not because those foods or activities are important contributors to obesity but because they are symbolic of values of which the public disapproves. For example, studies have found that television watching among children is correlated with obesity. However, this may be due to the fact that families in which children watch a lot of TV are different in many ways from families in which children watch very little TV. For example, those that watch a lot of TV may be poorer, more likely to be headed by a single parent and more likely to be headed by parents without college degrees. While reading is about as sedentary as watching TV, no one has attributed childhood obesity to reading. TV is an easier target, because it represents a lifestyle or set of values of which some people disapprove.

Disagreement with others' lifestyles may also lead to calls for parents to simply change their behavior – to stay at home more with their children, for example. Such calls ignore the fact that parents allocate their time based on the trade-offs and incentives that they face. Telling parents to do more to avoid childhood obesity, without making it easier for them to do so, is unrealistic and likely to be ineffectual. For example, the previously mentioned welfare reform of 1996 increased the disincentives for single mothers to stay home with their children and increased the incentives for them to work. Telling single mothers that they really should have more dinners prepared from scratch and eaten around the table with the family is to be unsympathetic to the economic realities that such women face. For this reason, policies that seek to change parental behavior should not rely on persuasion but on changing the incentives and trade-offs that have led to the present allocation of time.

Land Use and Neighborhood Design

Some claim that new suburbs and developments contribute to obesity because they lack sidewalks and nearby stores to which one could walk (Ewing et al., 2003) or because they are associated with longer commutes (Frank et al., 2004). However, children's physical activity appears uncorrelated with the availability of local facilities (Zakarian, 1994) and with safety (Sallis, 1999).

In the context of the economic framework, one might argue that the suburban housing market under-provides public goods like sidewalks. However, the public goods argument appears weak because the developers of these suburbs do provide many public goods, such as green spaces, trails, swimming pools and health clubs. Another explanation for the lack of sidewalks in newer developments is that residents do not value sidewalks as much as they cost to build.

Causation between urban design and obesity has not been established. People are not randomly assigned to neighborhoods; people choose where they live. In particular, people are not trapped in new suburbs due to poverty or discrimination; they voluntarily move there. In fact, the new suburbs that lack sidewalks tend to be the desired homes of the relatively affluent.

Policymakers should be wary of recommendations to change zoning laws or build sidewalks because they would be very costly to society and there is no proof that they solve a market failure or would even increase physical activity.

Opposition to the Food Industry

Recent best-selling books have attacked the food industry for selling high-fat foods (Nestle, 2002; Brownell and Horgen, 2004). However, Adam Smith wrote in *The Wealth of Nations*, 'It is not from the benevolence of the butcher, the brewer, or the baker, that we expect our dinner, but from their regard to their own interest' (Smith, [1776] 1976). Likewise, it is not from the malevolence of the butcher that we are sold sausage, the malevolence of the brewer that we are sold soda pop, or the malevolence of the baker that we are sold dessert. Industry produces and sells the goods or services that yield the highest profit. This is not a bad thing for society, as industry's desire to earn profit leads it to sell the items that satisfy consumers' desires. The fact that American industry sells a lot of high-fat foods and not very many abdominal exercise machines is not evidence that industry is evil and is attempting to fatten the American people, but is a reflection of a consumer sentiment that high-fat foods are tasty and exercising can be a chore.

This raises a point that has not been sufficiently appreciated in the debate over the recent rise in obesity: to the extent that consumers want to be more physically active, eat healthier foods and weigh less, private industry has a profit incentive to help them do it. For example, the success of diet carbonated beverages and the recent development of Olestra indicates that the food industry is seeking ways to increase profit by decreasing the impact of their products on body weight. Moreover, the pharmaceutical industry is developing drugs to help alleviate obesity. Annual sales of anti-obesity drugs totaled $426 million in 2000 in the USA; this market is expected to grow to $1.3 billion by the year 2010 (Farrigan and Pang, 2002). Even simple changes in preparation or packaging can have a large impact on consumer behavior. The market for pre-washed lettuce did not exist 30 years ago; today it is a multi-billion-dollar industry. Such simple innovations that accommodate consumers' preferences to spend less time preparing meals facilitate consumers eating less energy-dense meals. The enormous profit incentive to develop tasty low-calorie foods that are easy to prepare, and efficient and enjoyable exercise equipment, is a reason for optimism that private markets can help consumers achieve their goals with respect to exercise, nutrition and weight.

Some have called for subsidies for industry to develop healthy foods and encourage exercise. Unless one can demonstrate positive externalities to these research programs or products, subsidies to industry are unnecessary and unjustified. Industry has the profit incentive to innovate; they do not need additional incentives from the government.

DATA AND RESEARCH NEEDS

This section notes where more data and research are needed. In brief, we need better information on: children's resources and how they spend them; the components of children's energy balance equations; the extent to which there exist market failures as regard nutrition and physical activity; the cost-effectiveness of interventions to repair such market failures; and the extent to which farm policy in the USA has the unintended consequence of increasing childhood obesity.

More data is needed simply to understand what resources children have access to and how they spend them. Data should be consistently collected on how children spend one important resource: their time. In particular, it will be important to know how much of their time is spent being active as opposed to sedentary. Interesting changes in how American adults spend their time have been documented using the Americans' Use of Time Project, in which respondents keep time diaries (Robinson and Godbey, 1997; Sturm, 2003). However, children younger than 18 were not surveyed in this project and there is little data on how children's use of time has changed in the last few decades.

Another important resource is disposable income (from, for instance, allowances, gifts and wages). Surveys of both parents and children would be useful in understanding the disposable income that children enjoy, how it is spent and how it changes over time.

Data on the components of energy balance is also needed. Data needs to be collected on the number of calories consumed by children in order to determine how energy intake is changing over time. Data on calorie expenditure should be recorded when data is collected on how children spend their time. A difficulty with collecting this data is that calorie intake and expenditure are notoriously hard to measure.

Research is needed to determine the extent to which there exist market failures; this information is critical because proof of such failures represent economic justification for government intervention. Another gap in the research that urgently needs to be filled concerns the lack of cost-effectiveness studies of anti-obesity programs. Cost–benefit and cost-effectiveness studies are useful because a comparison of them will indicate which program is the cheapest method of achieving a certain goal and will also determine whether spending money on preventing or treating child-hood obesity is the best use of society's scarce resources (Ganz, 2003; Kuchler and Ballenger, 2002; Martin et al., 2000). The Centers for Disease Control is currently making an effort to fill this gap with its Project MOVE (Measurement of the Value of Exercise), which is calculating the cost-effectiveness using published data of previous interventions, but there is need for prospective cost-effectiveness studies of new interventions to affect children's nutrition and physical activity.

Perhaps the only cost-effectiveness study of an anti-obesity program for children is that conducted by Wang et al. (2003), which used a randomized design and found that Project Health, a school-based intervention to reduce obesity in middle-school children by encouraging a decrease in tele-vision viewing and high-fat foods and an increase in physical activity and intake of fruits and vegetables, cost $4305 per quality-adjusted life year (QALY) saved. One alternative to an obesity prevention program targeted at children is to do nothing and either pay the health care costs of the obese or pay for obesity treatment of adults. One cost-effectiveness study con-cluded that bariatric surgery cost $4004 to $3928 per QALY saved (Van Gemert, 1999). A comparison of the costs per QALY saved by Project Health and those of bariatric surgery suggests that societal resources should be targeted toward bariatric surgery rather than obesity prevention, although the costs per QALY are close. However, there are other options than simply Project Health and bariatric surgery, and further studies are needed to determine the cost effectiveness of these other programs, treat-ments and opportunities.

Research is needed to determine what information consumers lack, and how that information can be best communicated. For example, to what extent would parents and children respond to additional information about the calorie content of prepared and restaurant foods? How could such information be conveyed so that it is easy to use? It would also be useful to know whether the move toward managed care and capitation of physician reimbursement per patient has led physicians to spend less time counseling their patients on nutrition and the maintenance of healthy weight; if so, attempts to provide information to children and parents through physicians may not be effective.

With respect to externalities, calculations are needed of the external costs of calorie consumption, sedentary lifestyle and obesity *in children*. More research is needed on the extent to which individual behavior responds to subsidized opportunities for physical activity. Public works projects can be expensive, and if people are not responsive to such opportunities the projects may not be cost effective.

It is unclear the extent to which adverse selection truly impedes the functioning of insurance markets. Research should examine the extent to which the failure of certain health insurance plans to cover obesity treatments can be attributed to insurer concerns about adverse selection; it is possible that it is instead due to individuals assigning little value to, and therefore being unwilling to pay for insurance that covers, nutrition counseling and weight-loss treatments.

In general, many recently proposed interventions involve altering the environment in schools. An important research need is to understand whether children would engage in offsetting behavior. That is, if soda and candy vending machines are removed from schools, do children increase their consumption of these items outside of school, with no net change in calorie intake? Analogously, if more rigorous physical activity requirements are imposed in schools, how will this affect children's calorie expenditure outside of school? What matters for energy balance isn't calorie consumption and expenditure in school alone, but overall.

Another research need is to better understand how farm policy in the USA, which is designed primarily to increase profits for farmers, affects childhood obesity. Some aspects of farm policy could be said to decrease calorie consumption. For example, the USA imposes quotas on sugar imports; as a result, the price of sugar in the USA is considerably higher than the world price. The law of demand implies that this higher price results in a lower quantity of sugar demanded in the USA.

However, in other ways farm policy may unintentionally contribute to childhood obesity (Pollan, 2003). For example, price supports lead to excess supply. If this excess supply were sold on the open market it would cause the prices to fall, defeating the purpose of the farm programs. To support the price, the government buys the excess and distributes it through the US Department of Agriculture's Schools / Child Nutrition Commodities Program, which sells the excess products at low prices to school districts for the National School Lunch Program, the Child and Adult Care Food Program and the Summer Food Service Program. The foods that the program distributes are not chosen because they are the healthiest for children, but because they are in surplus as a result of programs to increase profits for farmers; in most cases the commodities involved are energy-dense, such as beef, pork, and cheese.

Government 'checkoff' programs may also contribute to obesity. The government of the USA requires producers of commodities that enjoy price supports to contribute a fixed amount of money per unit sold into a fund that is used for commodity-specific advertising and research. The intention of this program is to increase consumer demand for the commodity, leaving less excess supply for the government to purchase at the taxpayers' expense. It is the money raised by check-off programs that pays for such advertising campaigns as: 'Got Milk?', 'Milk Moustache', 'Ahh – The Power of Cheese', 'California Raisins', 'Beef – It's What's For Dinner', and 'Pork – The Other White Meat'.

Interestingly, check-off funds are also used to increase the sale of commodities through fast food outlets. The Pork Board's 2003 *Checkoff Timeline Brochure* reports: '1989: Technology developed with producer Checkoff funds is used by McDonald's nationally to market The McRib pork sandwich.' It continues: '2002: Through the Pork Checkoff, pork items are added to menus at Taco Bell, TGI Friday's, McDonald's, Burger King, Applebee's and other restaurants across America' (Pork Board, 2003). A press release from the Dairy Checkoff program touts their success in providing Pizza Hut with menu development and market research for bringing to market the 'Insider Pizza', which uses one pound of cheese per pizza (Dairy Management Inc., 2002). Research is needed to determine the extent to which these government-mandated expenditures on advertising energy-dense foods contribute to childhood obesity.

SUMMARY

This chapter describes the economic perspective on children's decisions regarding physical activity and nutrition. It attributes cross-sectional differences in childhood obesity to differing incentives and trade-offs faced by different families, and attributes the recent increase in childhood obesity to changes over time in the costs and benefits of certain foods and activities.

Market failure is the economic rationale for policy intervention. Relevant market failures include: lack of information; external costs of obesity and sedentary lifestyles; adverse selection impeding insurance markets; and children being imperfectly rational. This chapter also offers the economic perspective on arguments for policy interventions that arise outside of economics, such as those motivated by issues of equity, paternalism, land use and opposition to the food industry. Needs for better data and more research on issues relating to childhood obesity are identified. Given how much is still unknown, this is undoubtedly an area in which researchers, foundations and the government can make tremendous contributions.

NOTE

1. I thank Laura Leviton, Dean Lillard, Tracy Orleans and the Robert Wood Johnson Foundation working group on childhood obesity for their helpful comments and suggestions.

REFERENCES

Acs, Zoltan, Lenneal Henderson, David T. Levy, Alan Lyles and Kenneth R. Stanton (2006), 'A policy framework for obesity management', Chapter 13, this volume.

American Obesity Association (2002), 'Health insurance coverage', accessed at www.obesity.org/treatment/health.shtml.

Anderson, P.M., K.F. Butcher and P.B. Levine (2003), 'Maternal employment and overweight children', *Journal of Health Economics*, **22**, 477–504.

Beales, J.H. (2002), 'Prepared statement of the Federal Trade Commission before the Committee on Government Affairs', Federal Trade Commission press release, 8 October.

Becker, Gary S. and Kevin Murphy (1988), 'A theory of rational addiction', *Journal of Political Economy*, **96** (4), 675–700.

Beumont, Pierre J. (2002), 'Clinical presentation of anorexia nervosa and bulimia nervosa', in Christopher G. Fairburn and Kelly D. Brownell (eds), *Eating Disorders and Obesity: A Comprehensive Handbook*, 2nd Edition, New York: Guilford Press.

Bouchard, Claude (1997), 'Obesity in adulthood – the importance of childhood and parental obesity', *New England Journal of Medicine*, **337** (13), 926–7.

Brown, Peter J. and Vicki K. Bentley-Condit (1998), 'Culture, evolution and obesity', in George A. Bray, Claude Bouchard and W.P.T. James (eds), *Handbook of Obesity*, New York: Marcel Dekker.

Brownell, Kelly D. and Katherine B. Horgen (2004), *Food Fight: The Inside Story of the Food Industry, America's Obesity Crisis and What We Can Do About It*, New York: Contemporary Books.

Bunce, Victoria (2002), 'Mandated health insurance benefits', *Council for Affordable Health Insurance*, **5** (1).

Cardon, James H. and Igal Hendel (2001), 'Asymmetric information in health insurance: evidence from the National Medical Expenditure Survey', *RAND Journal of Economics*, **32** (3), 408–27.

Cawley, John (1999), 'Rational addiction, the consumption of calories and body weight', Ph.D. dissertation, Department of Economics, University of Chicago.

Cawley, John, Sara Markowitz and John Tauras (2004), 'Lighting up and slimming down: the effects of body weight and cigarette prices on adolescent smoking initiation', *Journal of Health Economics*, **23** (2), 293–311.

Center for Science in the Public Interest (CSPI) (2003), 'Pestering parents: how food companies market obesity to children', Washington, DC: CSPI.

Chou, Shin-Yi, Michael Grossman and Henry Saffer (2004), 'An economic analysis of adult obesity: results from the behavioral risk factor surveillance system', *Journal of Health Economics*, **23** (3), 565–87.

Cleland, R.L., W.C. Gross, L.D. Koss, M. Daynard and K.M. Muoio (2002), 'Weight loss advertising: an analysis of current trends', Federal Trade Commission staff report, September.

Cutler, D.M., E.L. Glaeser and J.M. Shapiro (2003), 'Why have Americans become more obese?', *Journal of Economic Perspectives*, **17** (3), 93–118.

Dairy Management, Inc. (2002), 'Pizza Hut summer of cheese showcases power of dairy checkoff partnerships', accessed at www.dairycheckoff.com/news/release-070902.asp.

Dietz, W.H. and S.L. Gortmaker (1985), 'Do we fatten our children at the television set? Obesity and television viewing in children and adolescents', *Pediatrics*, **75** (5), 807–12.

Dockner, Engelbert J. and Gustav Feichtinger (1993), 'Cyclical consumption patterns and rational addiction', *American Economic Review*, **83** (1), 256–63.

Drewnowski, Adam and S.E. Specter (2004), 'Poverty and obesity: the role of energy density and energy costs', *American Journal of Clinical Nutrition*, **79** (1), 6–16.

Ebbeling, Cara B., Dorota B. Pawlak and David S. Ludwig (2002), 'Childhood obesity: Public health crisis, common sense cure', *Lancet*, **360**, 473–82.

Elster, Jon (1999a), *Strong Feelings: Emotion, Addiction and Human Behavior*, Cambridge, MA: MIT Press.

Elster, Jon (1999b), *Addiction: Entries and Exits*, New York: Russell Sage Foundation.

Elster, Jon and Ole-Jorgen Skog (1999), *Getting Hooked: Rationality and Addiction*, New York: Cambridge University Press.

Engle, Mary (2003), Testimony before the Institute of Medicine Committee on Prevention of Obesity in Children and Youth, 9 December, Washington, DC.

Ewing R., T. Schmid, R. Killingsworth, A. Zlot and S. Raudenbush (2003), 'The relationship between urban sprawl and physical activity, obesity and morbidity', *American Journal of Health Promotion*, **18** (1), 47–57.

Farley, D.O., P.F. Short, M.N. Elliott, D.E. Kanouse, J.A. Brown and R.D. Hays (2002), 'Effects of CAHPS health plan performance information on plan choices by New Jersey Medicaid beneficiaries', *Health Services Research*, **37** (4), 985–1007.

Farrigan, C. and K. Pang (2002), 'Obesity market overview', *Nature Reviews/Drug Discovery*, **1**, 257–8.

Finkelstein E., I. Fiebelkorn and G. Wang (2003), 'National medical spending attributable to overweight and obesity: how much and who's paying?', *Health Affairs Web Exclusive*, 14 May.

Flegal, K.M., M.D. Carroll, C.L. Ogden and C.L. Johnson (2002), 'Prevalence and trends in obesity among US adults, 1999–2000', *Journal of the American Medical Association*, **288** (14), 1723–7.

Fontaine, K. and S. Bartlet (2000), 'Access and use of medical care among obese persons', *Obesity Research*, **8**, 403–6.

Frank, Lawrence, Martin Andresen and Tom Schmid (2004), 'Obesity relationships with community design, physical activity and time spent in cars', *American Journal of Preventive Medicine*, **27** (2) (August), 87–96.

French, S.A., R.W. Jeffery, M. Story, P. Hannan and M.P. Snyder (1997), 'A pricing strategy to promote low-fat snack choices through vending machines', *American Journal of Public Health*, **87** (5), 849–51.

French S.A., R.W. Jeffery, M. Story , K.K. Breitlow, J.S. Baxter, P. Hannan and M.P. Snyder (2001), 'Pricing and promotion effects on low-fat vending snack purchases: the CHIPS study', *American Journal of Public Health*, **91**, 112–17.

Ganz, Michael L. (2003), 'The economic evaluation of obesity interventions: its time has come', *Obesity Research*, **11** (11), 1275–7.

Gortmaker, S.L., A. Must, A.M. Sobol, K. Peterson, G.A. Colditz and W.H. Dietz (1996), 'Television viewing as a cause of increased obesity among children in the United States, 1986–1990', *Archives of Pediatrics and Adolescent Medicine*, **150** (4), 356–62.

Gould, Steven J. and Fiona Sussan (2006), 'Mixed messages in marketing communications about food and obesity', Chapter 6, this volume.

Gruber, J. and S. Mullainathan (2002), 'Do cigarette taxes make smokers happier?', National Bureau of Economic Research working paper no. 8872, Cambridge, MA.

Hannan, P., S.A. French, M. Story and J.A. Fulkerson (2002), 'A pricing strategy to promote sales of lower fat foods in high school cafeterias: acceptability and sensitivity analysis', *American Journal of Health Promotion*, **17** (1), 1–6.

Heien, Dale and Cathy Durham (1991), 'A test of the habit formation hypothesis using household data', *Review of Economics and Statistics*, **73** (2), 189–99.

Henderson, Lenneal J. (2006), 'Obesity, poverty, and diversity: theoretical and strategic challenges', Chapter 4, this volume.

Hernandez, Luis and Bartley G. Hoebel (1988), 'Food reward and cocaine increase extracellular dopamine in the nucleus accumbens as measured by microdialysis', *Life Sciences*, **42** (18), 1705–12.

Iyengar, S.S., W. Jiang and G. Huberman (2004), 'How much choice is too much? Determinants of individual contributions in 401(k) retirement plans', in O.S. Mitchell and S.P. Utkus (eds), *Developments in Decision-Making Under Uncertainty: Implications for Retirement Plan Design and Plan Sponsors*, Oxford: Oxford University Press.

Jansen, Anita, Jacqueline Klaver, Harald Merckelbach and Marcel van den Hout (1989), 'Restrained eaters are rapidly habituating sensation seekers', *Behaviour Research and Therapy*, **27** (3), 247–52.

Johnson, R.K., H. Smiciklas-Wright, A.C. Crouter and F.K. Willits (1992), 'Maternal employment and the quality of young children's diets – empirical evidence based on the 1987–1988 Nationwide Food Consumption survey', *Pediatrics*, **90** (2, part 1), 245–9.

Kayloe, Judith C. (1993), 'Food addiction', *Psychotherapy*, **30** (2), 269–75.

Keeler, E.G., W.G. Manning, J.P. Newhorse, E.M. Sloss and J. Wasserman (1989), 'The external cost of a sedentary life style', *American Journal of Public Health*, **79** (8), 975–81.

Kersh, R. and J. Morone (2002), 'The politics of obesity: seven steps to government action', *Health Affairs*, **21** (6), 142–53.

Kimm, S.Y.S. and E. Obarzanek (2002), 'Childhood obesity: A new pandemic of the new millennium', *Pediatrics*, **110** (5), 1003–7.

Komlos, John, Patricia K. Smith and Barry Bogin (2004), 'Obesity and the rate of time preference: is there a connection?', *Journal of Biosocial Science*, **36**, 209–19.

Kuchler, Fred and Nicole Ballenger (2002), 'Societal costs of obesity: how can we assess when federal interventions will pay?', *FoodReview*, **25** (3), 33–7.

Lakdawalla, D. and T. Philipson (2002), 'The growth of obesity and technological change: a theoretical and empirical examination', National Bureau of Economic Research working paper no. 8946, Cambridge, MA.

Laibson, David (2001), 'A cue-theory of consumption', *Quarterly Journal of Economics*, **116** (1), 81–119.

Manning, W.G., E.G. Keeler, Joseph P. Newhorse, E. Sloss and J. Wasserman (1991), *The Costs of Poor Health Habits*, Cambridge, MA: Harvard University Press.

Martin, Louis F., Alex Robinson and Barbara J. Moore (2000), 'Socioeconomic issues affecting the treatment of obesity in the new millenium', *Pharmacoeconomics*, **18** (4), 335–53.

Mathios, Alan D. (1998), 'Economic perspectives on the dissemination of science-based information to consumers', *Journal of Consumer Policy*, **21**, 221–55.

Mathios, Alan (2000), 'The impact of mandatory disclosure laws on product choices. An analysis of the salad dressing market', *Journal of Law and Economics*, **43** (2), 651–77.

Naik, Narayan Y. and Michael J. Moore (1996), 'Habit formation and intertemporal substitution in individual food consumption', *Review of Economics and Statistics*, **78** (2), 321–8.

Nestle, Marion (2002), *Food Politics: How the Food Industry Influences Nutrition and Health*, Berkeley, CA: University of California Press.

Nielsen, S.J. and B.M. Popkin (2003), 'Patterns and trends in food portion sizes, 1977–1998', *Journal of the American Medical Association*, **289**, 450–3.

Ogden, Cynthia L., Katherine M. Flegal, Margaret D. Carroll and Clifford L. Johnson (2002), 'Prevalence and trends in overweight among US children and adolescents, 1999–2000', *Journal of the American Medical Association*, **288** (14), 1728–32.

Orford, Jim (1985), *Excessive Appetites; A Psychological View of Addictions*, New York: John Wiley and Sons.

Philipson, T. (2001), 'The world-wide growth of obesity: an economic research agenda', *Health Economics*, **10**, 1–7.

Pipher, Mary (1994), *Reviving Ophelia: Saving the Selves of Adolescent Girls*, New York: Ballantine.

Pollan, Michael (2003), 'The (agri)cultural contradictions of obesity', *The New York Times Magazine*, 12 October.

Pork Board, The (2003), *2003 checkoff timeline brochure*, www.porkboard.org/docs/checkoff%20timeline%20bro2003.pdf

Powell, A.D. and A.S. Kahn (1995), 'Racial differences in women's desires to be thin', *International Journal of Eating Disorders*, **17**, 191–5.

Puhl, Rebecca and Kelly D. Brownell (2002), 'Stigma, discrimination and obesity', in C.G. Fairburn and K.D. Brownell (eds), *Eating Disorders and Obesity: A Comprehensive Handbook*, New York: Guilford Press.

Rashad, I. and Michael Grossman (forthcoming), 'A realistic look at obesity', *The Public Interest*.

Rashad, Inas, Michael Grossman and S.-Y. Chou (2006), 'A structural estimation of caloric intake, exercise, smoking and obesity', *Quarterly Review of Economics and Finance*, **46**, 268–83.

Reger, B., M.G. Wootan and S. Booth-Butterfield (1999), 'Using mass media to promote healthy eating: a community-based demonstration project', *Preventive Medicine*, **29**, 414–21.

Riessman, Frank and David Carroll (1997), 'A new view of addiction: simple and complex', *Social Policy*, **27** (2), 36–46.

Robinson, John P. and Geoffrey Godbey (1997), *Time for Life: The Surprising Ways Americans Use Their Time*, University Park, PA: Pennsylvania State University Press.

Sallis, J.F., J.E. Alcaraz, T.L. McKenzie and M.F. Hovell (1999), 'Predictors of change in children's physical activity over 20 months: variations by gender and level of adiposity', *American Journal of Preventive Medicine*, **16** (3), 222–9.

Schlosser, E. (2001), *Fast Food Nation: The Dark Side of the All-American Meal*, New York: Houghton Mifflin.

Sloane, D.C., A.L. Diamant, L.B. Lewis, A.K. Yancey, G. Flynn, L.M. Nascimento, W.J. McCarthy, J.J. Guinyard, M.R. Cousineau and REACH Coalition of the African American Building a Legacy of Health Project (2003), 'Improving the nutritional resource environment for healthy living through community-based participatory research', *Journal of General Internal Medicine*, **18** (7), 568–75.

Smith, Adam (1776), *An Inquiry Into the Nature and Causes of the Wealth of Nations*, reprinted 1976. Indianapolis: Liberty Classics.

Sobal, J. and A.J. Stunkard (1989), 'Socioeconomic status and obesity: a review of the literature', *Psychological Bulletin*, **105**, 260–75.

Stearns, P.N. (1997), *Fat History: Bodies and Beauty in the Modern West*, New York: New York University Press.

Strauss, Richard S. (2000), 'Childhood obesity and self-esteem', *Pediatrics*, **105** (1), e15–e20.

Sturm, R. (2003), 'The economics of physical activity: societal trends and rationales for interventions', unpublished manuscript, RAND Corporation.

Takahashi, E., K. Yoshida, H. Sugimori, K. Miyakawa, M. Izuno, T. Yamagami and S. Kagamimori (1999), 'Influence factors on the development of obesity in three-year-old children based on the Toyama study', *Preventive Medicine*, **28** (3), 293–6.

Troiano, R.P. and K.M. Flegal (1998), 'Overweight children and adolescents: description, epidemiology and demographics', *Pediatrics*, **101** (3), 497–504.

US Department of Health and Human Services (2000a), *Healthy People 2010: Understanding and Improving Health*, 2nd edn, Washington, DC: US Government Printing Office.

US Department of Health and Human Services (2000b), *Medicare Coverage Issues Manual*, 29 August, Washington, DC: US Government Printing Office.

US Department of Health and Human Services (2001), *The Surgeon General's Call to Action to Prevent and Decrease Overweight and Obesity*, Washington, DC: US Government Printing Office.

van Gemert, W.G., E.M. Adang, M. Kop, G. Vos, J.W. Greve and P.B. Soeters (1999), 'A prospective cost-effectiveness analysis of vertical banded gastroplasty for the treatment of morbid obesity', *Obesity Surgery*, **9**, 484–91.

Vanchieri, C. (1998), 'Lessons from the tobacco wars edify nutrition war tactics', *Journal of the National Cancer Institute*, **90** (6), 420–2.

Wang, Li Yan, Q. Yang, R. Lowry and H. Wechsler (2003), 'Economic analysis of a school-based obesity prevention program', *Obesity Research*, **11** (11), 1313–24.

Young, L.R. and M. Nestle (2002), 'The contribution of expanding portion sizes to the US obesity epidemic', *American Journal of Public Health*, **92** (2), 248–9.

Zakarian, J.M., M.F. Hovell, C.R. Hofstetter, J.F. Sallis and K.J. Keating (1994), 'Correlates of vigorous exercise in a predominantly low SES and minority high school population', *Preventive Medicine*, **23**, 314–21.

4. Obesity, poverty and diversity: theoretical and strategic challenges

Lenneal J. Henderson

INTRODUCTION

According to the Centers for Disease Control (CDC), everyone is becoming fatter, or, to use the polite word, 'obese'. What accounts for the trend toward overweight individuals across age, race and socioeconomic status? If the result is excess weight, are the causes the same? Are the laws of supply and demand universal? To address these causes, must we craft and broadcast the same health and safety messages in public policy, food and drug marketing, and social and cultural institutions – or must we diversify and variegate these messages? If we believe that excess weight reflects socioeconomic status, will an individual, a household or a neighborhood's economic life chances improve with weight control? Given the diversity of the population in the USA, the reality of persistent poverty and the dynamics of geography and space, what are the appropriate policy, corporate and community-level intervention strategies to reduce and prevent obesity? These are among the interrelated questions driving this chapter.

The quality of the evidence purporting the link obesity to race, gender, ethnicity and income is a salient analytical and public policy issue. Medical evidence of the adverse consequences of obesity abounds. Less clear is how the curious admixture of race, culture, income and geographic location cast themselves over the shadows of mental, behavioral and medical explanations for obesity. First, we review samples of existing evidence linking the medically obese to their race, ethnicity, gender and geographic location. Second, we raise questions about the relationship of who we are to the varieties of institutional experiences we have, as it influences what we eat and drink. Finally, we ask whether the theoretical frames of reference and tools we use are capable of advancing our understanding of the no doubt complex interaction of sociological diversity and obesity. It is essential to expand the scope of salient health crises like obesity to include not only the function of individual traits but also the characteristics of the environments in which people live. Boardman and his colleagues refer to this phenomenon as health, place and race (Boardman et al., 2004).

DEFINITIONS

Consensus exists on the biomedical definition of obesity. Central is the Body Mass Index (BMI). According to Patricia Crawford and her colleagues, 'regardless of gender, adults with a Body Mass Index (BMI) between 25 and 30 are described as overweight, and with a BMI of over 30 as obese' (Crawford et al., 2003). BMI is calculated by dividing weight (in kilograms) by height (in meters) squared. Children who are at or above the 95th percentile of BMI, using CDC standards, are considered overweight.

Whether child or adult, overweight and obesity are risk factors for: diabetes; heart disease; stroke; hypertension; gallbladder disease; high blood cholesterol; complications with pregnancy; infertility; menstrual irregularities; increased surgical risk; osteoarthritis; sleep apnea and other respiratory problems; several forms of cancer including uterine, breast, colorectal, kidney and liver; stress incontinence (urine leakage caused by weak pelvic floor muscles); and psychological disorders such as depression. These are the medical parameters of overweight and obesity.

However, there is less consensus in the research and professional literatures on the psychosomatic and cultural aspects of obesity. These dimensions begin but go beyond core medical definitions. They are operationalized in the behavior of racial, ethnic, and age groups, and of women and men. Am I fat? Who says so? Is it OK in my family? My community? My world?

These questions are as much an artifact of family, institutional and cultural socialization as raw indicators such as BMI. They are not only artifacts of culture but, as immigrants come and progress through generations in the USA, they may affect differential levels of the acculturation of the supply and demand behaviors and dynamics. Vanessa Smith Castro has advanced theories of acculturation inclusive of socialization, behavior modification and cultural adaptation (Castro 2003). Definitions of obesity absent a cultural context may inadvertently omit these cultural and acculturation elements.

The challenge is to establish and to engender overweight and obesity definitions that include both physiological and anatomical dimensions *and* socioeconomic and sociocultural dimensions. Once met, this challenge facilitates the use of integrated definitions that enable both quantitative and qualitative metrics for both defining obesity supply and demand and cultural preferences that influence strategic interventions, and the efficacy of such interventions.

THE CONTEXT

Once definitions are operationalized to include quantitative measures such as BMI and socioeconomic and cultural behaviors, comparisons among varied racial, ethnic, socioeconomic, gender and generational populations are possible and more useful. For example, white males increased the proportion of their overweight population from 61.6 percent in 1994 to 69.5 percent in 2002 and their obese population from 20.7 percent in 1994 to 28.7 percent in 2002. White females increased the proportion of their overweight population from 47.2 percent in 1994 to 57 percent in 2002 and obesity from 23.3 percent in 1994 to 31.3 percent in 2002 (NIH, 2004b).

However, black males increased the relative proportions of their overweight and obese population from 58 and 21.3 percent in 1994 to 62 and 27 percent in 2002; and black females increased their respective proportions from 68.5 percent and 39.1 percent in 2002 to 39.1 percent and 46.6 percent in 2002! For Mexican American males the 1994 percentages were 69.4 percent in 1994 and 74.1 percent in 2002 for being overweight and 24.4 percent and 29.0 percent for being obese in 1994 and 2002. For Mexican American females, the numbers were 69.6 percent overweight in 1994 and 71.4 percent in 2002, and 36.1 percent and 38.9 percent obese in 1994 and 2002 (NIH, 2004b).[1]

The higher gender correlate suggests that females are more likely to be obese than males, regardless of race, ethnicity or socioeconomic status. A closer look at the gender correlate suggests that women with incomes at or above $100 000 per annum are slightly less likely to be obese than those earning less than $30 000. However, intervening variables like the number of children women bear, the educational background of women and the occupations and professions they pursue are all essential to generating plausible explanations for the relationship between gender and obesity. In addition, variations in cultural and institutional practices may explain food and nutritional practices and even the self-image concept of various populations. These in turn may provide insight into weight and obesity disparities by racial, cultural and generational group. A related contextual issue is the socioeconomic status of various populations. Poverty, particularly among larger families, is often associated with poor nutrition and the selection of food and drink that is low in nutrients and high in calories.

The University of California Cooperative Extension Body Weight and Health Workgroup Study of 561 Latino mothers and their young children raises issues of food security. Food security is defined as access by all people at all times to enough food for an active, healthy life. It includes at a minimum: first, the ready availability of nutritionally adequate and safe food; and second, an assured ability to acquire acceptable food in socially

*Table 4.1   Disparities in prevalence of overweight among children in
the USA*

Age distribution	Non-Hispanic whites (%)	Non-Hispanic blacks (%)	Mexican Americans* (%)
Preschoolers	8.6	8.8	13.1
Ages 6–11	13.5	19.8	21.8
Ages 12–19	13.7	21.1	22.5

Note: * Data for Mexican Americans are as reported by government agencies or specific studies. There is limited data for other Hispanic groups.

Source: Robert Wood Johnson Foundation, (2005), p. 7.

acceptable ways, such as without resorting to emergency food supplies, scavenging, stealing or other coping strategies (Crawford et al., 2003).

As Table 4.1 indicates, there are clear disparities in the rates of obesity among white and non-white children. These disparities become even more pronounced as children transition from preschool age to 6–12 years old. By the time they reach puberty and their late teens, racial differences in obesity become greater, particularly in the Mexican American population. Clearly these differences are attributable to family life and lifestyle, income, the activity patterns of children and experiences in school.

Another key correlate of obesity is geographic location. Whether individuals live in central cities, suburbs or rural areas is a significant dimension of the sociology and economics of diversity. Using data from 1990–1994 National Health Interview Survey, Jason Boardman and his colleagues estimate the independent association of three residential characteristics – race, class and health – on the risk that an individual will be obese. They pay particular attention to the possibility that neighborhood-level racial composition, poverty rates and obesity prevalence are positively associated with risk of obesity among adults (Boardman et al., 2004).

Moreover, as Thompson et al. (2002) propose, 'race may be a proxy for a social experience in which members of a racial group are more often exposed to chronic social and environmental stressors due to racial group status'. Social experience includes participation in faith, educational, occupational and recreational institutions and activities that promote varieties of food and drink cultures and behaviors. Combined with the peculiarities of the individual's behavior and exposure to mass media, the unique configuration of faith, cultural, educational and other institutions in the community and the recreational infrastructure available to community residents, social experience reflects a variation in obesity propensity.

These propensities result in structures of economic demand for food and beverage products that have both diverse household and diverse institutional sources. Household demand structures for obesity-inducing products and retail distribution chains are reinforced by geographically accessible commercial institutions such as fast food and convenience store chains, restaurants, faith institutions, and the lunchrooms and vending areas of local public and private employers. These household and institutional structures display significant variations in their histories, cultural orientations and ways of seeing and knowing health and lifestyle.

In addition, using data from the 1998 Medical Expenditure Panel Survey and the 1996 and 1997 National Health Inter-Surveys, the direct and indirect costs of obesity have been documented by Finkelstein and his colleagues. In the aggregate, these expenditures accounted for 9.1 percent of total annual medical expenditures in the USA in 1998 and were calculated to be as high as $78.5 billion (in 1998). Medicare and Medicaid financed approximately one half of these costs and more than 40 percent of Medicare and Medicaid recipients were non-white and/or poor (Finkelstein et al., 2003). Consequently, the socioeconomic impact of obesity is costly not only to non-white, low-income and senior households but also to the health care institutions, particularly those that are funded by the public sector. These costs are reflected in the budgets of the federal and state governments and therefore in taxation. All taxpayers bear the burden of such costs and therefore have a stake in obesity prevention and reduction strategies for all citizens, particularly those least fortunate and at high-risk.

Moreover, as indicated by *A Nation at Risk*, the health-related economic cost of obesity and its associated ailments represents more than 5 percent of total medical costs and is associated with escalating costs of health care insurance for large and small businesses. As BMI increased, so did the number of sick days, medical claims and healthcare costs (Robert Wood Johnson Foundation, 2005).

For example, commenting on a study by Powell et al. (2004), Risa Lavizzo-Mourey (Ascribe Newswire, 2004) observes that an obesity reduction and prevention strategy requires a healthier lifestyle but concedes the following:

- Communities with higher percentages of African American populations are likely to have fewer available sports areas, parks and green spaces, public pools and beaches.
- Moving from a high poverty area (10 percent poverty rate) to a low poverty area (1 percent rate) is associated with a 50 percent increase in the overall availability of physical activity opportunities.

- Fifty-seven percent of communities with a 1 percent poverty rate are likely to have bike paths, while only 9 percent of communities with a 10 percent poverty rate are likely to have such facilities.
- The juncture of race, place, and poverty cultivates a growing culture of overweight and obesity.

Drewnowski and Specter (2004) argue that there is no question that the rates of obesity and type two diabetes in the USA follow a socioeconomic gradient, such that the burden of disease falls disproportionately on people with limited resources, racial–ethnic minorities and the poor. Among women, higher obesity rates tend to be associated with low incomes and low education levels.

However, in its national study the Robert Wood Johnson Foundation (2005, p. 11) argues that, 'while personal choices play a role in the rise of obesity, they alone are not responsible for the epidemic we face today'. Many children and adults are socialized into lifestyles, eating habits, nutritional behavior and product demand patterns that pour unhealthy foods into homes, workplaces, recreational sites, schools and streets. There are many fast food restaurants featuring foods high in saturated fats, carbohydrates, sodium and sugar, and few stores selling nutritious foods, vitamin supplements or healthy literature. Many in poorer neighborhoods cannot afford healthy foods, memberships of health clubs or participation in organized sports or physical fitness activities.

These patterns strongly suggest the issues of diversity and poverty in overweight and obesity are as institutional as they are individual or household-related. Indeed, a key unit of analysis in the diagnosis and treatment of obesity and the supply-and-demand dynamics contributing to demographic, cultural and socioeconomic diversity is the interaction of institutions, households and individuals to create unhealthy patterns of consumption leading to weight problems. Key institutions like churches, mosques, synagogues, temples, schools, social clubs, civil rights organizations, cultural organizations and community-based institutions are key ingredients to decoding the laws of supply and demand in non-white, poor, female-headed and senior households.

For example, as Table 4.2 indicates, overweight and obese individuals pervade the population of the USA. When gender, race and age are considered together, 65.1 percent of the population of the USA is overweight and obese, and 30.4 percent are obese. However, black and Mexican American females are most prone to both be overweight and obese. Among black females, 77.2 percent are overweight and obese, and 49 percent are obese. Among Mexican American females, 71.7 percent are overweight and obese, and 38.4 percent are obese. When combined with higher fertility

Table 4.2   Prevalence of overweight and obesity in adults aged 20 and older in the USA

Gender and ethnicity	Overweight and obesity (%)	Obesity (%)
Total population	65.2	30.4
Total males	68.8	27.6
Total females	61.6	33.2
Non-Hispanic white males	69.4	28.2
Non-Hispanic white females	57.2	30.7
Non-Hispanic black males	62.9	27.9
Non-Hispanic black females	77.2	49.0
Mexican American* males	73.1	27.3
Mexican American* females	71.7	38.4

Note: * Data for Mexican Americans are as reported by government agencies or specific studies. There is limited data for other Hispanic groups.

Source: Robert Wood Johnson Foundation, (2005), p. 4.

rates among black and Mexican American females, these data suggest that weight and child-bearing activities must be considered with income and nutritional practices to account for disparities in weight and obesity.

Further examination of the varieties of institutional circulation and socialization in the experience may extend the epistemology of obesity to include how attitudes, perceptions, self-image and socialization are formulated and sustained. The church dinner, the school lunch or prom, the community cookout, the local banquet, donations of foodstuffs for the poor, the clearance sale at the neighborhood store or chain, and the candy and sodas at the checkout counters all have institutional roots and supply and demand characteristics. Ethnographic studies of racial and ethnic communities identify the institution as the mediating influence in the laws of local supply and demand for poor, racial or ethnic communities. These institutions are geographically located in strategic proximity to households and individuals in or near communities. They display an amazing variety of cultural forms, organizational structures, governance arrangements, media and communication modes and, most of all, influences on the attitudes, perceptions and behaviors of their members, clients and constituents. Whether old or young, white or non-white, male or female, rich or poor, the nature and quality of participation or exposure to local, regional or national institutions is an essential part of the socialization of norms and values about nutrition, weight and health.

Lack of exposure to key institutions or conflict with these institutions is also essential. This is particularly true of children and adults at opposite

Obesity and the individual

ends of the age spectrum. Aside from their families and legal guardians, children under the age of 18 are exposed primarily to the school and may have conflicts with the school arising from their behavior, poor academic performance or low quality of contact with school teachers, counselors and health professionals. Some may belong to faith institutions, others to youth organizations. However, some are at risk of exposure to juvenile justice institutions, particularly non-white and low-income youth.

At the opposite end of the age spectrum, seniors who fail to join and participate in social, cultural or community organizations after retirement may suffer a kind of institutional isolation, even from the family. This isolation may deprive them of nutritional and health information. They may lack the information needed to address overweight and obesity. Indeed, some may take the view that their appearance and health is not as central a concern as it was when they were younger and in the workforce. Consequently, their consumer behavior changes, their social channels to key institutional sources of health information and motivation decline and their risk of suffering diseases arising from weight increase.

Continuing with the issue of diversity across generations, the issue of weight and obesity in children is clearly both an issue of racial/ethnic diversity and intergenerational diversity. Table 4.3 indicates that non-white children and adolescents are significantly more likely to be overweight and obese than white children and adolescents. These differences are particularly substantial for non-white females in the 12–19-year-old category. At this stage, the gap between white and non-white females begins and

Table 4.3   *Combined percentage of children and teens considered overweight or at risk of being overweight in the USA*

Gender and age	Average for all groups (%)	Non-Hispanic whites (%)	Non-Hispanic blacks (%)	Mexican Americans* (%)
Males aged 2–5	23.4	21.7	20.9	27.6
Females aged 2–5	23.5	20.0	25.6	25.0
Males aged 6–11	34.3	29.3	29.7	43.9
Females aged 6–11	33.1	27.7	37.9	33.8
Males aged 12–19	34.4	29.2	32.1	41.9
Females aged 12–19	35.9	26.5	41.9	39.3

Note: * Data for Mexican Americans are as reported by government agencies or specific studies. There is limited data for other Hispanic groups.

Source: Robert Wood Johnson Foundation, (2005), p. 3.

continues into the adult age categories. The question is how schools and social, recreational, health care and faith institutions influence these trends. A more ominous issue is the extent to which disconnection from those institutions and with key health norms, values and information may encourage demand for food and drink in these age and gender cohorts. An absence of balance between family, peer and institutional exposure as young women mature, particularly at the level of race, ethnicity or socioeconomic status, may contribute to unhealthy behaviors and obesity. An absence of health care due to an inability of parents or legal guardians to obtain health insurance or to pay directly for such care may deprive youth of critical health care information and motivation.

Moreover, aside from these characteristics of neighborhood and community, there is a mental health dimension to obesity in non-white and poor communities. Pi-Sunyer (2000) has referred to this as 'the pathogenesis of obesity' (Pi-Sunyer, 2000). This pathogenesis includes mental stressors arising from inter- and intra-racial conflict, stressful socioeconomic conditions, pediatric or geriatric conditions, absence of exposure to green space environments, and lack of educational and occupational attainment. These symptoms of mental health are associated with the geography of race, space, place, age and poverty. They are often transmitted across generations, particularly amongst those on public assistance, receiving Medicaid or incarcerated. The mental health environment creates a complex of precipitated dynamics that produce a disproportionate propensity to be overweight in non-white and poor children, and adults. As Tables 4.1 and 4.3 suggest, the pediatric anxiety and mental dispositions of children, and their often psychologically challenging transition to adolescence and young adult status, produce mental states that often contributed to excessive food intake, scant physical exercise, sedentary activity patterns and poor nutrition. Conversely, the physical and mental decline among those who are aging contribute significantly to the problems of weight, self-image and pursuit of healthy norms.

The American Indian and Alaskan Native population is approximately 2.5 million in the USA. Fifty percent of American Indians live in urban areas and one-third live on reservations or historic trust lands. According to Khan (2003), over 60 percent of American Indian women less than 60 years of age are likely to be overweight or obese; 40 percent of school-age American Indians were obese in 1990; among preschool and school-age children the rates of obesity and overweight are three times those of other children in the USA; and 80 percent of American Indian women in Arizona and 67 percent of men were overweight, according to researchers from the Strong Heart Study in 1995 (Khan, 2003; Knowler et al., 1991; Indian Health Service Report to Congress, 2001).

Poverty and hunger are egregious dimensions of 'the pathogenesis of obesity'. According to Alison Leff:

> Low-income and minority persons are more likely to suffer from food insecurity. Food insecurity affects 35 percent of low-income households. According to the US Agriculture Department's (USDA) Food and Nutrition Service (FNS), a household's chances of being hungry or food-insecure decrease as income rises. African American and Hispanic households face food insecurity and hunger rates three times as high as those of white households. (Leff, 2002, p. 39).

The two principal public policy responses to these challenges are the Food Stamp Program and the Women, Infants and Children (WIC) Program and school feeding program. There are 17 million Food Stamp recipients, 46 percent of whom are white, 33 percent African American and 17 percent Hispanic. According to Leff (2002), in 2000 WIC provided nutritious foods and nutrition services for approximately 7.2 million pregnant low-income women and their infants and children each month. The National School Lunch Program serves more than 27 million meals every school day, in 95 percent of the nation's public and private schools (Leff, 2002). Consequently, public policy programming is part of the institutional complex of influence on the nutritional choices of eligible households.

THE CONCEPT

Beyond Health Disparity Models

Given the racial, ethnic, socioeconomic, gender, age and geographical characteristics of the obesity issue, it is essential to consider a conceptual frame of reference that both adequately categorizes obesity and these diverse dynamics and allows careful and systematic inquiry into the household, institutional and cultural elements that produce variation in the causes, consumer behavior and institutional factors contributing to obesity. The results of these inquiries contribute to the design, testing and implementation of policy, corporate, faith, school, health care and other interventions designed to prevent and reduce the incidence and impact of obesity.

Current health disparity models are confined to two sets of variables: purely medical indices of health disparity (measured, for example, by variations in BMI); and disparities in health care access and cost. Both are essential to inquiries and interventions of diversity in poor, non-white, young or old or female-headed households and institutions. However, disparity models often understate or ignore key cultural and community institutional dynamics in populations at risk. These dynamics are essential to both explaining dis-

Table 4.4   Key conceptual characteristics of diversity and obesity

Race	Ethnicity	Age	Gender	Geographic location
Physical attributes	Cultural orientation/ institutions	Gerontology/ geriatric dynamics and health	Fertility	Urban/rural/ suburban
Mental state/stress	Mental/ perceptual frame of reference	Mental acuity	Mental state	Link between physical character of local and mental state
Socio-economic correlates	Socio-economic characteristics	Financial health	Financial self-sufficiency	Socioeconomic character of the community
Nutritional preferences	Cultural/ nutritional preferences/ lifestyle	Nutritional needs/ preferences	Nutritional needs/ preferences	Nutritional access and availability

parities in BMI and associated health risks and accounting for the poorer access and affordability of health care in communities at risk.

Table 4.4 provides a matrix of many of these key diversity characteristics. These elements result from a review and critique of the interdisciplinary literature on obesity, poverty and cultural diversity. Racial, ethnic, age, gender and geographic location are said by the obesity literature to be related to mental, cultural, socioeconomic variables capable of explaining nutritional preferences. These preferences are reflected in the individual, household and institutional demand patterns of non-whites, the poor and others at risk. These preferences generate caloric consumption patterns that produce obesity propensities. These propensities create lifestyle stress points that at-risk populations seek to accommodate through poorer dietary choices. These choices in turn exacerbate socioeconomic and household financial stresses that in turn produce and reify obesity tendencies by class, race, age, gender and geographic location. Geographic location includes commercial and retail infrastructure in or near communities with substantial or dominant at-risk populations that make fast food, high fat, sodium and sugar products disproportionately available in these communities.

Demand for weight-inducing food appears to be inelastic and influenced little by price increases. Demand patterns are also reified by institutional socialization reflected in faith, restaurant, educational, media, food store, recreational, and even occupational and professional lifestyle and food service patterns. One only has to peruse recent issues of ethnically oriented newspapers, magazines and cable stations to notice advertisements, promotions and lifestyle images that induce food and drink behaviors resulting in weight and obesity problems.

Key Components of Behavior Modification to Prevent and Reduce Obesity

Only recently have these cultural and special population media sources joined public, health care and insurance companies in campaigns to combat obesity. The American Association of Retired Persons (AARP) and a variety of state and local public and non-profit senior agencies have increased the decibel level of messages about weight control, nutrition, exercise and other lifestyle adjustments. Parallel messages are sent to racial, ethnic and neighborhood populations with varying degrees of efficacy. Women and men are also inundated with messages about exercise, weight control and nutrition, often including the need to model food and drink behaviors for their children. The data in Tables 4.1, 4.2 and 4.3 suggest that these messages have mixed results (and minimal results in the combined categories of gender, geographic location and race/ethnicity). These characteristics combine to create significant variations in the nature of weight and obesity as an issue, problem and policy challenge.

The challenges of modifying individual, household and institutional behavior across USA, particularly across variations in the population, include at three components. First, an alteration in health norms, values and ethics is imperative. Nutrition and health are not simply medical phenomena but essential elements of personal, household, institutional and community ethics. As with smoking, irresponsible sexual behavior or alcoholism, obesity and its legion of ill-health effects plagues families, institutions and communities. Messages from faith and other institutions, regardless of cultural orientation, increasingly stress the ethical dimension of obesity control.

Second, changes to consumer behavior, particularly in populations at risk, are essential. Changes in the supply and demand patterns affecting poor, non-white and older populations is an indispensable aspect of obesity prevention and reduction. Faith, business (small and large), school, community and policy institutions close to diverse populations are in a strategic position to influence consumer demand patterns. Their first task is to alter their own consumer demand by responsibly purchasing health food, drink and pharmaceutical products.

Third, the construction of health-oriented alliances and coalitions between diverse and majority populations is essential. Corporate, media and public policy strategies that cultivate alliances and coalitions with the complex of institutions closest to populations at risk are likely to find resources able to sustain messages and themes long after the corporation or the public agency are gone.

Another significance of Table 4.4 is its utility as a framework for both defining public policy strategic needs and as a source of criteria for evaluating the efficacy of public policy in altering supply and demand dynamics resulting in overweight and obesity. Federal initiatives such as the Health Disparities Center of the National Institutes of Health, the Obesity Project of the federal Food and Drug Administration (FDA) and nutritional imperatives of the US Department of Agriculture emphasize the strategic importance of incorporating diverse messages, institutions and geographic locations in obesity prevention and reduction policy. We will return to this issue later in this chapter.

However, the dynamics captured in the Table 4.4 matrix represent both a challenge and an opportunity to address obesity. The challenge is how to fashion an effective set of policies, including income-building and wealth, behavior modification, lifestyle changes, nutritional literacy, health care cost and access, and family policy to achieve obesity reduction and prevention objectives. The opportunity is that key faith, educational, advocacy, business and other institutions endemic to the geographical locations and cultural preferences can be important points of access to non-white and poor populations in cities, suburbs and rural areas alike. Despite variations in their levels of viability, outreach and efficacy, these institutions are key intermediaries with diverse and poor individuals, households and communities.

THE CASES

To amplify this opportunity, we examine three distinct cases of obesity prevention and reduction interventions. These interventions represent the life cycle of efforts to address and reduce obesity, from the diagnosis of obesity problems through the design, development, testing, implementation and evaluation of public, corporate and non-profit obesity and obesity-related programs. These cases also reflect a continuum of emphases, from demand-side interventions designed to change lifestyles and curb demand for obesity-inducing food and beverage products, to supply-side efforts to change the mix of products available to consumers (including the 'green menus' of fast food chains, expansion of healthy school lunch programs and exercise and nutritional supplements for senior populations).

Case 1: The University of California Cooperative Extension Body Weight and Health Workgroup

As a state institution, the University of California Cooperative Extension Service (UCCE) developed an alliance with several Latino community and professional organizations to address obesity among Latino mothers and children. The alliance included both a study component and an action component. The study component included 561 low-income Latino mothers and children, and focused on issues of family food insecurity, weight and obesity. Using the 1997–8 National Health Interview Survey (NHIS) sample of 68 556 adults as context, the UCCE study was also focused on the design of prospective interventions to address food insecurity and obesity.

The action component involved the development of relationships with health professionals and policymakers in six counties. Through workshops and intensives, and through the deliberate inclusion of Latino community-based educational, cultural and advocacy organizations, the six counties designed education interventions targeting food-insecure, low-income Latino families. Specifically food assistance programs, relationships with the food industry, and before-, during- and after-school initiatives were developed by the coalition. These efforts were aimed at working on both the supply and demand side of the food and nutrition equation. Also essential to the coalition was the development of community advocacy capacity. UCCE believes that, 'community groups can advocate for safe and clean neighborhoods conducive to physical activity, recreation, including sidewalks, crosswalks, bicycle, and walking paths, parks and open spaces; physical education and nutrition in schools; and smaller portions and more healthful foods in restaurants' (Crawford et al. 2003, p. 17).

Key to the efficacy of this coalition was the use of a multi-level and multi-sector strategy to modify consumer nutritional behavior among Latino mothers. Public policy, negotiation with food manufacturers and distributors, and relationships with schools and health care providers were all ingredients of the process. Moreover, the UCCE case illustrates the value of an action–research strategy in health promotion in culturally diverse settings. Staff skills included bilingual capability, outreach skills, advocacy capability and a combination of other professional skills.

Case 2: A Pilot Church-Based Weight Loss Program for African American Adults Using Church Members as Health Educators

Kennedy and her colleagues (2005) report the results of a six-month, church-based pilot intervention to promote weight loss and to improve the health of African American adult participants. They used a randomized trial design without a control group, and eligible church members were randomized into two groups: an intervention delivered in the group setting and an intervention delivered in the individual setting. The church was based in Baton Rouge, Louisiana and the team of scholar-practitioners managing both the intervention and the study were based at Southern University and Agricultural & Mechanical College, also in Baton Rouge. Forty church members were enrolled in the study and two trained church members, without specialization in obesity treatment, conducted the study. The program retention rate was 90 percent and, after six months, a modest but significant mean weight loss of 3.3 kg was reported. The mean weight losses in the individual and group interventions were 3.4 kg and 3.1 kg, respectively. The mean body fat loss was 2.1 kg and 1.9 kg, respectively.

Although the primary outcome measure was weight loss, the intervention also measured its success in involving a church in the obesity reduction strategy. The study team concluded that, 'A church setting may provide an effective delivery mechanism for a health and nutrition program. Church members may be trained to conduct a weight control program. Both interventions (individual and group) were effective in inducing weight loss' (Kennedy et al., 2005, p. 373).

As a Historically Black College and University (HBCU), the Southern University collaboration with a local black church illustrates three interrelated values in obesity prevention and reduction strategy:

1. The interplay of research and action in obesity prevention and reduction strategy. Research not only suggests the feasibility and parameters of key strategic interventions but also the best methods of evaluating the efficacy of these interventions. Conversely, experience with intervention defines the next sequence of research questions and agendas;
2. The utility of cultural legitimacy in a familiar institution. The trust still accorded the black church in the black community establishes its role as a core part of the alliance with health care scholars and professionals in addressing obesity and other health challenges in black communities; and
3. Capacity-building within institutions close to populations at risk. The training and capacity-building of church members in the pilot study clearly indicates that capacity-building is a sound method of building health care infrastructure in local communities.

Case 3: The Urban Nutrition Initiative in West Philadelphia

Given the interplay of racial, ethnic, age, gender, socioeconomic and geographic variables with issues of obesity, the Urban Nutrition Initiative at the University of Pennsylvania's Department of Anthropology involves the use of service learning to address key community issues and needs. According to Johnston and his colleagues (2004), the basic components of service learning (self-discovery, reflection, and values clarification) are integrated with the values, frameworks and research processes of anthropology to conduct a nutritional needs assessment in the racially-diverse and low-income neighborhoods of West Philadelphia that served as the basis for a Participatory Action Research (PAR) Project with a coalition of community-based organizations and institutions. The needs assessment covered the period 1970–97 and included some 396 obese women. It examined closely the dietary habits and recalls of young women aged 11–14 and critically reviewed the mean servings of fruits and vegetables per day for 11–14-year-old African American school students both at home and in school. The PAR included schools from kindergarten to high school levels and a variety of culturally-sensitive community-based health care and advocacy organizations.

The Initiative help to create and sustain a curriculum that focused on: improving community health and increasing educational skills and abilities; working with students to train them as agents of change in dietary and lifestyle habits; the development of school gardens maintained by students as part of their studies; after-school fruit and vegetable stands that sell to school, students, staff, parents and other community members; urban agriculture and micro-business development for high school students; and a farmers' market open on weekends (with a winter buying club in the off-season). These programs continued into the summer months. As with the black church project, the emphasis in this initiative was community capacity-building and sustainability to meet nutritional needs. By citing the Initiative in the Department of Anthropology, undergraduate and graduate students and senior scholars were able to mobilize the subdisciplines of urban, cultural, biomedical and physical anthropology to support the research and evaluation of the initiative (Johnston et al., 2004; Harris and Bronner, 2001).

THE LESSONS OF STRATEGIC ALTERNATIVES

These three cases provide an appreciative look at the possibilities of linking the traditional disparity and medical measures of obesity to culturally and demographically sensitive measures and assessments of obesity prevention and reduction strategies. Given key racial, ethnic, socioeconomic, gender and generational differences in obesity definitions, understanding and behaviors, obesity prevention and reduction strategies work from a

Table 4.5   Levels of strategy for obesity prevention and reduction in diverse and poor populations

Scale	Scope	Skills	Strategies
Macro-level	Nutrition focus	Cultural competence to transcend language, cultural variety, gender and generation	Use of diverse media and collaboration with diverse advocacy institutions
Meso-level	Cost reduction focus	State-level coordination to address disparities in information, care and behavior outreach skills	Statewide strategic planning inclusive of obesity action elements and performance measures across diverse populations
Micro-level	Community-based health intensives	Individual/household level intervention Health education skills and outreach	Community cross-cultural and intergenerational coalitions

common base of media, public policy, education and faith elements but must be sufficiently variegated to account for cultural, generational and gender variations in obesity behavior and behavior modification possibilities. A 'one size fits all' strategy simply is not working. As Table 4.5 indicates, intervention strategies are comprised of scale, scope, skills and strategic elements (NIH, 2004a). These elements take into account the geographic and demographic scale, policy scope, multidisciplinary skill and multifaceted strategic capability necessary to craft and sustain obesity interventions in hyper-diverse national, regional, local and institutional settings.

NOTE

1.   Body Mass Index (BMI) adjusted. These data include correlates for: gender 0.66; income 0.51 literacy/education 0.77; and geographic location 0.68 (inner city, rural, suburban).

REFERENCES

Ascribe Newswire (2006), 'Low-income, minority populations lack places for physical activity; study finds race, ethnicity, economic status play role in access to physical activity settings', accessed 14th August at www.ascribe.org.

Boardman, Jason D., Jarron M. Saint Onge, Richard G. Rogers, Justin T. Denny, (2004), 'Race differentials in obesity: the impact of place', Research Program on Population Processes working paper POP2004–0005.

Castro, Vanessa Smith (2003), *Acculturation and Psychological Adaptation*, Westport, CT: Greenwood Press.

Crawford, Patricia B., Marilyn S. Townsend, Diane L. Metz, Dorothy Smith, Gloria Espinosa-Hall, Susan S. Donohue, Anna Olivares, and Lucia L. Kaiser (2003), 'How can Californians be overweight and hungry?' *California Agriculture*, **58**, (1), 12–18.

Drewnowski, Adam and S.E. Specter, (2004) 'Poverty and obesity: the role of energy density costs', *American Journal of Clinical Nutrition*, **79**, (6), 6–16.

Finkelstein, Eric A., Ian C. Fiebelkom and Guijing Wang (2003), 'National medical spending attributable to overweight and obesity: how much, and who's paying?', *Health Affairs: The Policy Journal of the Health Sphere*, 14 May.

Harris, E. and Y. Bronner (2001), *Food Counts in the African American Community: Chartbook 2001*, Baltimore, MD: Morgan State University.

Henderson, Karla A. and Barbara E. Ainsworth (2003), 'A synthesis of perceptions about physical activity among older African American and American Indian women', *American Journal of Public Health*, **93**, (2), 254–60.

Indian Health Service Report to Congress (2001), 'Obesity prevention and control for American Indians and Alaska natives', presentation to the President of the USA and to Congress by the Secretary of Health and Human Services with the assistance of the Indian Health Service and the American Indian and Alaska Native People.

Johnston, Francis E., Ira Harkavy, Frances Barg, Danny Gerber and Jennifer Rulf (2004), 'The urban nutrition initiative: bringing academically-based community service to the University of Pennsylvania's Department of Anthropology', *Urban Nutrition Initiative Net.*, 1–12, accessed at www.urbannutrition.org/UNI/documents/files/service learning.html.

Khan, Zainab (2003), 'The association of race, socioeconomic status, and health insurance status with the prevalence of overweight among children and adolescents, accessed at www.ajph.or/cgi/reprint/93/12/2105.

Kennedy, Betty M., Paeratakul Sahasporn, Catherine M. Champagne, Donna H. Ryan, David W. Harsha, Bernestine McGee, Glenda Johnson, Farzad Deyhim, William Forsythe and Margaret L. Bogle (2005) 'A pilot church-based weight loss program for African American adults using church members as health educators: a comparison of individual and group intervention', *Ethnicity and Disease*, **15**, (3), 373–8.

Knowler, W.C., D.J. Pettitt, M.F. Saad, M.A. Charles, R.G. Nelson, B.V. Howard, C. Bogardus and P.H. Bennett (1991), 'Obesity in the Pima Indians: its magnitude and relationship with diabetes', *The American Journal of Clinical Nutrition*, **53**, 1543S–51S.

Leff, Alison (2002), 'Race, poverty and hunger', *Poverty and Race Research Action Council Bulletin*, Spring.

National Conference of State Legislatures (NCST) (2005), *Childhood Obesity: 2005 Update and Overview of Policy Options*, Washington, DC: NCST.

National Institutes of Health (NIH) (2004a) *Strategic Plan for NIH Obesity Research*, August, Washington, DC: NIH Obesity Research Task Force.

National Institutes of Health (NIH) (2004b), *Obesity in the US*, pp. 12–14.

Pi-Sunyer, F.X. (2000), 'Obesity research and the new century', *Obesity Research*, 8(1).

Powell, L.M., S. Slater and F.J. Chaloupka (2004), 'The relationship between community physical activity settings and race, ethnicity and socioeconomic status', *Evidence-Based Preventive Medicine*, **1** (2), 135–44.

Robert Wood Johnson Foundation (RWJF) (2005), *A Nation At Risk: Obesity in the United States: A Statistical Sourcebook*, May, Washington, DC: RWJF.

Thompson, Hayley S., Thomas W. Kamarck and Stephen B. Manuck (2002) 'The association between racial identity and hypertension in African American adults: elevated resting and ambulatory blood pressure as outcomes', *Ethnicity and Disease*, **12**, (1) (winter) 20–8.

5. The labor market impact of obesity

John H. Cawley[1]

The prevalence of obesity in the USA has risen dramatically in the last several decades. Obesity, defined as when a person has a body mass index (BMI) of 30 or higher, rose from 15 percent of the population during 1976–80 to 30.4 percent during the period 1999–2002 (Flegal et al., 2002; Hedley et al., 2004). This trend has generated tremendous interest in better understanding the consequences of obesity: medical, social and economic. This chapter describes obesity's impact on one important economic outcome: wages.

In particular, this chapter will discuss the overall correlation between obesity and wages. It describes how we can measure the causal impact of weight on wages, and what such estimates of the causal impact indicate. It explores explanations for the differences across gender and race in the relationship between weight and wages, and concludes by expanding the review to studies of countries outside the USA.

A review of the literature yields a strong conclusion: in the USA, heavier women tend to earn less than healthy-weight women. Two studies calculate that obese white females tend to earn 12 percent lower wages than healthy-weight women (Cawley, 2004; Averett and Korenman, 1996). Obese black females tend to earn 6.1 percent less than healthy-weight black females, and obese Hispanic females tend to earn 8.2 percent less than healthy-weight Hispanic females (Cawley, 2004). Only for white females is being overweight (having a BMI greater than or equal to 25 but less than 30) associated with lower wages; specifically, overweight white females tend to earn 4.5 percent less than healthy-weight white females.

Results for Hispanic men are similar to those for Hispanic women and black women: the obese (but not the overweight) tended to earn significantly less (for Hispanic men, 6.6 percent less) than those of healthy weight.[2] However, obese white men and obese black men earned no less than those of healthy weight (Cawley, 2004). In fact, overweight status was associated with 3.9 percent *higher* wages among white men. This is consistent with the findings of a 1980 study, which documented that heavier men (of all races combined) earn more (McLean and Moon, 1980).[3]

All of the results just described are no more than correlations, which means that the differences in wages cannot be interpreted as the *result* of weight. For example, there are three theories that are consistent with the pattern that, among women and Hispanic men, heavier individuals tend to earn less. The first theory is that weight does indeed affect labor market outcomes. However, another plausible theory is that the reverse is true: poor labor market outcomes cause obesity. This could happen because lower-income people tend to live in poorer areas in which nutritious foods are harder to find and in which stores tend to sell energy-dense, fattening foods (Morland et al., 2002). A third theory consistent with these correlations is that something that the researchers did not observe caused both obesity and poor labor market outcomes for women and Hispanic men. For example, perhaps the truly important characteristic is a willingness to delay gratification. Those who are willing to do so may be the type of people who resist overeating and stay in shape, and also invest in marketable skills and work harder than others. Even if obesity doesn't cause lower wages, an unobserved characteristic like willingness to delay gratification could create a correlation between obesity and low wages. Because all three of these theories are consistent with what we observe, the basic correlations should never be interpreted as measuring the causal impact of obesity on wages.

So how can we measure the causal impact of obesity on wages? In social science as well as in medicine, the most convincing way to measure the causal impact of something is through a randomized controlled trial. As a hypothetical scenario, assume that we pay 10 000 subjects to be part of our experiment to answer the question 'Does obesity impact wages?' The first step would be to weigh each individual and record their wages. We would then randomly divide them in half: 5000 would be in a control group, and we would do nothing to them. The other 5000 would serve as our treatment group: we would increase the weight of each person in the treatment group until they were obese by increasing their caloric intakes or reducing their caloric expenditure (exercise). After 'treating' these individuals in the treatment group, we would record again the wages for members of both groups. We could then compare how the experimentally induced obesity for each person in the treatment group changed wages among the people in the group; we would compare this change to any change in wages among the control group to eliminate the influence of any economy-wide changes in wages during the study (for example, as a result of a recession). Such a randomized controlled trial would be the most convincing way of measuring the causal impact of obesity on wages.

Such a study, however, will never be conducted; it would obviously be unethical and unsafe – even small changes in weight are associated with changes in health (US DHHS, 2001). So we must find a way to scientifically

measure the impact of obesity on labor market outcomes without con-
ducting a randomized trial. Fortunately, there is another method available:
the method of instrumental variables (IV). IV is possible when you can find
a 'natural' experiment: in our case, some variation in weight that people
didn't choose. Remember that the reason we can't trust correlations in the
first place is because people have some control over their weight and these
differences in weight may be due to unobserved variables (like willingness
to delay gratification) that may also affect wages. What we want is some
variation in weight that was imposed on people by forces beyond their
control – because that variation will be uncorrelated with any unobserved
characteristics that might also be correlated with wages.

For example, suppose we wanted to study the impact of military service
on the probability of clinical depression at the age of 40. We can't simply
compare those who served in the military to those who didn't because the
US military has been an all-volunteer force since 1973; those who served in
the military are those who chose to serve and are therefore likely to be ambi-
tious, hardworking people who may be especially unlikely to become
depressed (in this case, the critical unobserved variable is propensity to
become depressed). A randomized trial could answer this question; our
treatment group would be forced to join the military and our control group
would not enlist. We could then compare the probability of depression in
the two groups at the age of 40 to answer our research question.

However, this isn't feasible because researchers don't have the power to
force people to join the military. Does that mean we cannot answer this
research question? No – it simply means that we must look for a natural
experiment, some variation in military enlistment that was beyond the
control of the individuals themselves. And in fact, such a natural experiment exists. Prior to the end of the draft in 1973, men in the USA were
assigned a draft number based on their date of birth. Government officials
would randomly select draft numbers, and all those with the selected draft
numbers were 'drafted' and were subject to mandatory enlistment in the
military. This is a perfect example of a natural experiment: it was not initiated by a researcher but it randomly assigns people into the treatment
group (those who were drafted) and the control group (those not drafted).
By comparing the probability of depression at the age of 40 among those
who were randomly drafted and those who were randomly not drafted, we
can answer our research question.

For our purposes, the key question is: can we find variation in weight that
is randomly assigned, that is, imposed on individuals beyond their control?
One study found such variation in our own genes (Cawley, 2004). Our genes
are randomly assigned to us before we are born, and genes endow some
people with a propensity to obesity and endow others with a propensity to

leanness. As long as the genes that are associated with a predisposition to obesity are not the same genes that are associated with a predisposition to important unobserved characteristics like willingness to delay gratification, genes represent an excellent natural experiment.

However, how can this natural experiment be studied? That is, how can we determine who has a genetic predisposition to obesity? Some obese individuals may have had a strong predisposition toward fatness and remain obese despite intense exercise and disciplined dieting, but other obese individuals may have no genetic predisposition to the condition and may be obese because of high caloric intake. However, we can't tell which obese individuals fall into the former category and which into the latter. What makes it possible to study the genetic natural experiment is the fact that siblings are expected to share half of their genes, on average. Thus, with a dataset of siblings one can interpret the similarity in weight between siblings as the result of their shared genes – and it is these genes that represent our 'treatment'.

One might be concerned that the similarity in weight between siblings is due to their common environment – being raised in the same household, eating similar foods – but research in behavioral genetics indicates that all of the similarity between family members is due to genetics: in other words, that there is no common household environment effect on weight. Adoption studies have consistently found that the correlation in weight between a child and its biological parents is the same for adopted children as for biological children (Vogler et al., 1995; Stunkard et al., 1986). Other studies have found that the weights of unrelated adopted siblings are uncorrelated (Grilo and Pogue-Geile, 1991). Studies of twins reared apart (which, not surprisingly, generally involve small samples) also find no effect of a shared family environment on weight: there is no significant difference between the correlation in weight of twins reared together and twins reared apart (Price and Gottesman, 1991; Maes et al., 1997). In summary, Grilo and Pogue-Geile (1991), in a comprehensive review of studies of the genetic and environmental influences on weight and obesity, conclude that '[E]xperiences that are shared among family members appear largely irrelevant in determining individual differences in weight and obesity'. As a result of this surprising but consistent finding, the similarity in weight between siblings can be attributed to genetics and thus provides us with the natural experiment we need to identify the causal impact of weight on labor market outcomes.

When the genetic variation in weight is exploited as a natural experiment using the econometric method of instrumental variables (IV), two remarkable results appear. First, for white females the causal impact of weight on wages (as measured using the natural experiment of genetics) is actually larger than the overall correlation suggests. While the overall correlation suggests that a gain of 20 pounds is associated with 3.2 percent lower wages for white females, our natural experiment indicates that the true effect of an extra 20 pounds of weight is to lower wages by 5.6 percent. The second important finding from our natural experiment is that the correlations of weight with wages among black males and females, Hispanic males and females, and white males, are essentially zero.

One important conclusion that is apparent from the results described here is that there are some dramatic differences across gender and race in both the correlations between weight and wages and the causal impact of weight on wages. This raises an interesting question: why isn't the impact of obesity on labor market outcomes the same for everyone? Why does weight lower wages only for white females?

Let us start by considering why the impact of weight on wages might be different for women than men. In general, the social stigma of obesity is greater for women than for men (Sobal, 2004). In addition, more men than women may be in blue-collar occupations in which additional mass is helpful if it lends strength or reflects additional muscle. (One limitation of the current definition of obesity is that it does not distinguish between muscle and fat.)

Next let us consider why weight lowers wages for white females but not for black or Hispanic females. A recent study of a sample of current and former welfare recipients found that the black females in the sample were no more likely to be morbidly obese than black females nationally, but the white females in the sample were *three times more likely* to be morbidly obese than white females nationally (Cawley and Danziger, 2005). This finding is consistent with the results from our natural experiment: if only white females, but not black females, suffer labor market disadvantage from obesity, then we would expect the white females on welfare to be more obese than average, but the black females on welfare to be no more obese than average.

Why, though, should obesity lower wages for white females but not black or Hispanic females? One possibility is that employment discrimination on the basis of weight is more punitive towards white women than black or Hispanic women. In general, there is substantial evidence of weight-based discrimination in employment, for people of both genders and all races and ethnicities. Researchers have tested for weight-based discrimination in laboratory settings. Participants are asked to make hiring or promotion decisions on the basis of materials that include photographs, videotapes or descriptions indicating the worker's weight. The weights of the hypothetical workers are manipulated to determine the extent to which hiring decisions are affected by discrimination against the obese. Reviews of this research (Puhl and Brownell, 2001; Roehling, 1999) document weight-based discrimination at every stage of employment, from the hiring decision through to wage-setting and promotion. Roehling (1999) even found that weight explains a greater proportion of the variance in hiring decisions than race or gender. A recent reflection of such sentiment is found in the 2003 Gallup Consumption Habits Survey, in which 20 percent of respondents answered that they would be less likely to hire a job applicant if they learned that the applicant was overweight (Gallup, 2003).[4]

These findings suggest that there is employment discrimination against obese persons of all races and ethnicities. But might this discrimination for some reason be more punitive against white females than black or Hispanic females? The prevalence of obesity among women varies dramatically by race: it is 30.7 percent for white females, 38.4 percent for Hispanic females, and 49.0 percent among black females (Hedley et al., 2004). These different rates of obesity may lead to different expectations about appearance; since obesity is rarer among white females, they may suffer greater employment discrimination for it. In the study of current and former welfare recipients described earlier, the women were asked whether at their current or most recent job they were discriminated against because of their weight. Such discrimination was reported by 5.2 percent of obese white respondents and 2.8 percent of obese African American respondents (Cawley and Danziger, 2005). This difference was not statistically significant given the small sample size, but the point estimate of the difference is consistent with harsher weight-based employment discrimination against white females than black females.

Another possible explanation for why weight lowers the wages of white females but not black or Hispanic females is that obesity has a more adverse impact on the self-esteem of white females than on that of other females, and low self-esteem worsens labor market outcomes. Obesity may harm self-esteem because research indicates that obese people (especially women) are stigmatized (Sobal, 2004) and obese individuals have a more difficult time forming and maintaining romantic relationships than their thinner counterparts (Halpern et al., 1999). Obesity may have a more adverse impact on the self-esteem of white females than on that of black females who report perceiving higher weight as a signal of power and stability (Brown and Bentley-Condit, 1998; Stearns, 1997). However, when studies have controlled for differences in self-esteem, they continue to find different correlations of weight with wages (Cawley, 2003; Averett and Korenman, 1999). Thus, self-esteem (as measured in these data) does not account for the difference in outcomes across race and gender. In brief, the reason for this discrepancy across race and gender in the impact of obesity on wages is not well understood and this interesting pattern remains to be definitively answered.

All of the results described so far have been based on data from the USA. How does obesity impact wages in other countries? Is there a universal pattern across countries or does it vary with cultural and labor market institutions? Published studies exist for England, Scotland and Wales (Sargent and Blanchflower, 1994), Finland (Sarlio-Lahteenkorva and Lahelma, 1999) and Germany (Cawley et al., 2005).[5] There are also preliminary estimates for Denmark (Greve, 2005) and China (Shimokawa, 2005).

In England, Scotland and Wales obesity[6] at the age of 16 is associated with 5.3 percent lower hourly earnings at the age of 23 for women, but with no significant difference in hourly earnings for men (Sargent and Blanchflower, 1994).

In Finland, obese women were found to be 50 to 70 percent more likely to be in the lowest fifth of disposable household income, to have less than half the median earnings, and to be in the lowest fifth of after-tax income. Obese men were no more likely than healthy-weight men to have a low income.

In Germany, obesity is associated with 3.5 percent lower wages for men and 19.5 percent lower wages for women (Cawley et al., 2005). Overweight is not associated with lower wages for men but is associated with 8.6 percent lower wages for women. We also have evidence from Germany on the causal impact of obesity (estimated using genetics as a natural experiment); these results indicate that it is impossible to reject the hypothesis of no causal impact of weight on wages in Germany. However, the sample sizes are small (930 men, 553 women) so only a very large effect could have been detected (ibid.).

While those are the only published studies on this question that use data from outside the USA, as previously mentioned there are preliminary studies examining this question for Denmark (Greve, 2005) and China (Shimokawa, 2005). In Denmark, obesity is associated with no difference in wages for either men or women (Greve, 2005). However, for men there is evidence of a positive correlation between overweight and one measure of wages but not others.

In China, obesity is associated with no difference in wages for either men or women (Shimokawa, 2005). In China, the important correlation of weight with wages concerns the underweight: being underweight is associated with 5.6 percent lower wages for males, and 6.8 percent lower wages for females. The China study also provides evidence on the causal impact of obesity (also estimated using genetics as a natural experiment); these results indicate that it is impossible to reject the hypothesis of no causal impact of weight on wages in China.

The correlation between obesity and wages may depend in part on how common obesity is in that society. The prevalence of obesity varies considerably across the countries studied (see Chapter 2, Figure 2.2).

In the USA, data on obesity is collected regularly through the National Health and Nutrition Examination Surveys (NHANES). The most recent NHANES data, which was collected between 1999 and 2002, indicates that the prevalence of obesity in the USA was 27.6 percent for men and 33.2 percent for women (Hedley et al., 2004).

The USA is unusual in regularly collecting data on obesity, so it is difficult to compare obesity prevalence across countries in a single year. The prevalence of obesity in Denmark in 2001 was 11.8 percent among men and 12.5 percent among women (Bendixen et al., 2004). The prevalence of obesity in England in 2003 was 22.2 percent for men and 23 percent for women (International Obesity Task Force, 2005). In Germany during 2002, the prevalence of obesity was 22.5 percent for men and 23.3 percent for women (ibid.). The prevalence of obesity in Finland in 1997 was 19.8 percent among men and 19.4 percent among women (Lahti-Koski et al. 1999; International Obesity Task Force, 2005). Interestingly, the prevalence of overweight in both Finland and Germany exceeds that in the USA (International Obesity Task Force, 2005). The prevalence of obesity in China is far lower than in any of the previously discussed countries; a 2002 survey calculated that the obesity rate for men and women combined was 7.1 percent (*People's Daily Online*, 2004). (For more information on trends in obesity worldwide, see Chapter 2.)

Taken together, the results from outside the USA suggest that the correlation of obesity with wages varies across countries and cultures. Obesity is associated with lower wages for women in England, Scotland, Wales, Finland and Germany, but not Denmark or China. In all of these countries except Germany, obesity among men is uncorrelated with income or earnings. In the two countries outside the USA for which it was possible to test for a causal impact of obesity on wages, Germany and China, no evidence of a causal impact was found for either men or women.

So what are the fruitful areas for future research? A key unresolved question is what causes the differences across race and gender in the impact of obesity on wages in the USA. Another priority is to conduct studies of the labor market impact of obesity in additional countries in order to determine the extent to which these impacts vary across countries, cultures and levels of development. In recent years the prevalence of obesity has increased in many countries (WHO/FAO Expert Consultation on Diet, Nutrition and the Prevention of Chronic Diseases, 2002), and understanding the economic consequences of obesity is of worldwide interest.

NOTES

1. I thank Zoltan Acs for encouraging me to write this chapter, and I thank my co-authors of the research I describe in it: Sheldon Danziger, Markus Grabka and Dean Lillard.
2. Each of the results described in this chapter are derived from regression models in which the economic outcome (wages or earnings or income) is regressed on weight and other factors that are correlated with economic outcomes and may also be correlated with weight, such as education, marital status, local labor market conditions and race/ethnicity.
3. This chapter is concerned with the impact of excess weight on labor market performance, but there are also interesting correlations of underweight status (having a BMI of 18.5 or less) with wages. For white and Hispanic females, being underweight is not associated with lower wages than for those of healthy weight, but for black women being underweight is associated with 5.6 percent lower wages. Being underweight is associated with 14 percent lower wages for white men and 9.9 percent lower wages for black men, but is not associated with lower wages for Hispanic men.
4. The consistent laboratory findings of employment discrimination against the obese raise the question of why overweight status is correlated with *higher* wages for white males and black males. Two researchers who noticed the positive correlation between weight and wages among men attributed it to what they called a 'portly banker' effect: 'Large size may generate a "non-verbal signal" of power, strength or capability which commands respect . . .' (McLean and Moon, 1980, p. 1009). However, the results from our genetic natural experiment offer no support for a portly banker effect, as there is no detectable causal effect of weight on wages for white men or black men.
5. There are also studies of other countries that simply compare obesity rates across income categories but those are less interesting because they do not control for education, marital status and other factors that may be correlated with both obesity and income. The studies described here are those that use regression analysis to control for factors such as education, marital status and race/ethnicity.
6. In the study of England, Scotland and Wales, obesity was defined as having a BMI at the 90th percentile or greater; every other study described in this chapter uses the official definition of obesity of the National Institutes of Health and the World Health Organization, which is that of having a BMI of 30 or higher.

REFERENCES

Audretsch, David B. and Dawne DiOrio (2006), 'The spread of obesity,' Chapter 2, this volume.

Averett, Susan and Sanders Korenman (1996), 'The economic reality of the beauty myth', *Journal of Human Resources*, **31** (2), 304–30.

Averett, Susan and Sanders Korenman (1999), 'Black–white differences in social and economic consequences of obesity', *International Journal of Obesity*, **23**, 166–73.

Bendixen, Hanne, Claus Holst, Thorkild I.A. Sorensen, Anne Raben, Else Marie Bartels and Arne Astrup (2004), 'Major increase in prevalence of overweight and obesity between 1987 and 2001 among Danish adults', *Obesity Research*, **12**, 1464–72.

Brown, Peter J. and Vicki K. Bentley-Condit (1998), 'Culture, evolution and obesity', in George A. Bray, Claude Bouchard and W.P.T. James (eds), *Handbook of Obesity*, New York: Marcel Dekker.

Cawley, John (2003), 'What explains race and gender differences in the relationship between obesity and wages?', *Gender Issues*, **21** (3), 30–49.

Cawley, John (2004), 'The impact of obesity on wages', *Journal of Human Resources*, **39** (2), 451–74.

Cawley, John and Sheldon Danziger (2005), 'Morbid obesity and the transition from welfare to work', *Journal of Policy Analysis and Management*, **24** (4), 1–17.

Cawley, John, Markus Grabka and Dean R. Lillard (2005), 'A comparison of the relationship between obesity and earnings in the US and Germany', *Journal of Applied Social Science Studies*, (Schmollers Jahrbuch), **125** (1), 119–29.

Flegal, K.M., M.D. Carroll, C.L. Ogden and C.L. Johnson (2002), 'Prevalence and trends in obesity among US adults, 1999–2000', *Journal of the American Medical Association*, **288** (14), 1723–7.

Gallup Organization (2003), 'Poll analyses: smoking edges out obesity as employment liability', 7 August.

Greve, Jane (2005), 'Obesity and labor market outcomes: new Danish evidence', unpublished manuscript, Cornell University and Aahus School of Business, Denmark.

Grilo, Carlos M. and Michael F. Pogue-Geile (1991), 'The nature of environmental influences on weight and obesity: a behavioral genetic analysis', *Psychological Bulletin*, **110** (3), 520–37.

Halpern, Carolyn Tucker, J. Richard Udry, Benjamin Campbell and Chirayath Suchindran (1999), 'Effects of body fat on weight concerns, dating and sexual activity: a longitudinal analysis of black and white adolescent girls', *Developmental Psychology*, **35** (3), 721–36.

Hedley, A.A., C.L. Ogden, C.L. Johnson, M.D. Carroll, L.R. Curtin and K.M. Flegal (2004), 'Prevalence of overweight and obesity among US children, adolescents and adults, 1999–2002', *Journal of the American Medical Association*, **291** (23), 2847–50.

International Obesity Task Force (2005), 'EU platform on diet, physical activity and health', www.iotf.org/media/euobesity3.pdf, 15 March.

Lahti-Koski, Marjaana, Pirjo Pietinen, Satu Mannist and Erkki Vartiainen (1999), 'Trends in body mass index and prevalence of obesity among adults in Finland from 1982 to 1997', in H. Mykkänen, (ed.), www.iaso.org/affiliates/finland2.htm.

Maes, Hermine, H.M. McNeale and L.J. Eaves (1997), 'Genetic and environmental factors in relative body weight and human adiposity', *Behavior Genetics*, **27** (4), 325–51.

McLean, Robert A. and Marilyn Moon (1980), 'Health, obesity and earnings', *American Journal of Public Health*, **70** (9), 1006–9.

Morland, Kimberly, Steve Wing, Ana Diez Roux and Charles Poole (2002), 'Neighborhood characteristics associated with the location of food stores and food service places', *American Journal of Preventive Medicine*, **22** (1), 23–9.

People's Daily Online (2004), 'Obesity rate doubles in China in ten years', http://english.people.com.cn/200410/13/eng20041013_160062.html, 13 October.

Price, R. Arlen and Irving I. Gottesman (1991), 'Body fat in identical twins reared apart: roles for genes and environment', *Behavior Genetics*, **21** (1), 1–7.

Puhl, R. and K.D. Brownell (2001), 'Bias, discrimination and obesity', *Obesity Research*, **9** (12), 788–805.

Roehling, M.V. (1999), 'Weight-based discrimination in employment: psychological and legal aspects', *Personnel Psychology*, **52** (4), 969–1016.

Sargent, J.D. and D.G. Blanchflower (1994), 'Obesity and stature in adolescence and earnings in young adulthood: analysis of a British birth cohort', *Archives of Pediatrics and Adolescent Medicine*, **148** (7), 681–7.

Sarlio-Lahteenkorva, Sirpa and Eero Lahelma (1999), 'The association of body mass index with social and economic disadvantage in women and men', *International Journal of Epidemiology*, **28** (3), 445–9.

Shimokawa, Satoru (2005), 'Are there negative wage effects of obesity in China?', Unpublished manuscript, Cornell University.

Sobal, Jeffery (2004), 'Sociological analysis of the stigmatization of obesity', in John Germov and Lauren Williams, *A Sociology of Food and Nutrition: The Social Appetite*, 2nd edn, Melbourne: John Wiley, pp. 83–402.

Stearns, P.N. (1997), *Fat History: Bodies and Beauty in the Modern West*, New York: New York University Press.

Stunkard, A.J., T.I.A. Sorensen, C. Hanis, T.W. Teasdale, R. Chakraborty, W.J. Schull and F. Schulsinger (1986), 'An adoption study of human obesity', *New England Journal of Medicine*, **314** (4), 193–8.

US Department of Health and Human Services (2001), *The Surgeon General's Call to Action to Prevent and Decrease Overweight and Obesity*, Washington, DC: US Government Printing Office.

Vogler, G.P., T.I.A. Sorensen, A.J. Stunkard, M.R. Srinivasan and D.C. Rao (1995), 'Influences of genes and shared family environment on adult body mass index assessed in an adoption study by a comprehensive path model', *International Journal of Obesity*, **19**, 40–5.

WHO/FAO Expert Consultation on Diet, Nutrition and the Prevention of Chronic Diseases (2002), 'Diet, nutrition and the prevention of chronic diseases: report of a joint WHO/FAO expert consultation', Geneva, Switzerland: World Health Organization.

PART III

Obesity and business

6. Mixed messages in marketing communications about food and obesity

Stephen J. Gould and Fiona Sussan

INTRODUCTION

Obesity has been declared a public health epidemic by the Centers for Disease Control (CDC) (Seiders and Petty, 2004). Moreover, it is not only a major health issue in the USA, but also worldwide due to economic, social and cultural convergence (Audretsch and DiOrio, 2006). However, even with this widespread recognition of the problems obesity presents, it remains a highly charged social issue bringing to bear a variety of cross-currents and competing interests, especially when marketing factors are considered.

In particular, this chapter focuses on the various currents of understandings; business interests and consumer behaviors related to food (and beverage) marketing; other product or services marketers (such as health clubs or diet supplement marketers); social marketers (such as governmental agencies and non-profit organizations); health care providers; and marketing communications. Food marketers promote the foods whether unhealthy or healthy while social marketers, other product marketers, and even the food marketers themselves, offer ideas about controlling or losing weight. Both types of marketers use marketing communications, which for our purposes here largely involve using advertising and publicity, to get their messages across to targeted consumers. To set the stage for considering these issues, it is necessary to take a step back and look at some of the underlying dynamics of obesity that drive them.

One facet that needs to be considered involves the idea of genetic heritage versus cultural factors, self-care and self-responsibility, and related processes of self-regulation (Cottam, 2004). As in many issues involving nature and nurture, there is evidence involving both our genetic makeup and controllable behaviors that result in varying degrees of weight beyond what is thought to be healthy. Nonetheless, obesity is said to be a preventable cause of mortality and morbidity, and in this status is the second leading cause of death in the USA (Wee et al., 2005). Given our focus on marketing issues, we will deal here with issues of individual behavioral and psychological self-regulation, which means the sphere where people are in control of, or at least could control, their actions with respect to their weight, such as avoiding overeating and/or engaging in exercise. Thus, while genetic heritage and DNA cast a huge shadow over the obesity issue, we mention them here only to locate the self-responsibility domain.

Therefore, given that most obese consumers bear at least some, if not total responsibility for their overweight, it then becomes a matter of discussing how their own attitudes, behaviors and decisions are implicated in their conditions. Here, we look at this responsibility in terms of the psychological construct of self-regulation, which means that consumers to varying degrees interact with their bodies to modulate their weight up, down or just to maintain it. For example, overeating may be viewed as a matter of self-regulation failure in which consumers lose their ability to control it in various situations (Bandura and Vohs, 2003). We further amplify that perspective by considering how marketing and social marketing interact with consumers to play to their self-regulatory tendencies. For example, the media and their variety of mixed messages may promote overeating or through other messages emphasizing thinness go to the other extreme and lead to eating disorders (Harrison and Cantor, 1997). Thus, while the emphasis in this chapter is on the marketing and marketing communications associated with obesity, it is necessary to point out the other side of the coin in making the case for the vast cross-currents of mixed messages that permeate the ecology of consumer behavior, food, weight, lifestyles and marketing.

THE SELF-REGULATION FRAMEWORK FOR MARKETING AND MARKETING COMMUNICATIONS CONCERNING OBESITY

In general, consumer psychology can be framed in terms of the broad historic and dichotomous constructs of approach–avoidance, pleasure–pain and risk seeking–risk aversion. A current theoretical approach that captures these dimensions, in terms of considering how behavior is driven by them, is self-regulation. Self-regulation may be construed in any number of ways (Bandura and Vohs, 2003) but here we follow the work of Higgins (1997) and apply his two-pronged or dual-process approach to the issue. Consumers act in either promotion or prevention modes in various situa-

Table 6.1   *Promotion (hot) versus prevention (cool) system of the*
                 self-regulation of weight and overeating

Promotion–hot–taste	Prevention–cool–nutrition/thin
Approach	Avoidance
Pleasure	Pain
Emotional	Cognitive
Eat as much and as well as desired	Restrain eating
Taste, food and beverage marketing communications appeals to this system	Social and other weight control marketing communications appeals to this system

tions. Promotion is expansive and pleasure seeking while prevention is constrictive and painful. Table 6.1 shows the two sides of this self-regulation process as they are hypothesized to operate.

These two modes of promotion and prevention may also be related in parallel fashion to a self-regulatory framework which has been called a hot–cool system by Metcalfe and Mischel (1999). In this system, hot relates to the emotions and senses and is stimulus-driven while the cool system is more cognitive and emotionally neutral. In terms of behavior, the hot system is what consumers respond to in terms of pleasure and the cool system is more likely to be the one in which one is seeking to engage in control and is tied into delayed gratification. A related formulation concerns time-inconsistent preferences in which desire in the present competes with willpower oriented to the future (Hoch and Loewenstein, 1991). In terms of obesity, and especially overeating, the hot system is the one that operates promotionally to pleasure cues while the cool system is the one involved preventively in avoiding or tempering overeating.

When the former dominates in a food situation, the consumer will tend to overeat even if she or he is aware of the consequences posed by the cool system. Of course, awareness itself is an issue and consumers will possess varying degrees of knowledge and awareness of the nature and health consequences of obesity in their lives. Some will have a great deal of such awareness and some much less, if not next to none. Other things being equal, it is likely that those who possess greater degrees of awareness will be more responsive to cool messages, but the very fact of mixed messages reflects the ambivalence many consumers (even relatively aware and knowledgeable ones) may experience.

Thus, the marketing and marketing communications side of self-regulation is also double-pronged. In this sense, marketers of fat-inducing products play on consumers' tendencies for expansive promotion and hot messages, while marketers offering diet or otherwise healthy products aim at prevention. Social marketers who target certain individuals with the aim of changing their ideas and practices (Bloom and Novelli, 1981) are also players in this promotion–prevention ecology, largely on the prevention side. For instance, such social marketers as government agencies charged with health and medical regulation, and others, seek to reduce obesity through messages about eating healthily and exercising. Bloom and Novelli note that profit-driven organizations may also be said to engage in social marketing when they aim to change consumers' behavior in terms of some responsible activity, and therefore it could be said that marketers who encourage sensible eating or other healthy behaviors related to obesity (such as use of exercise products or health clubs) are engaging in social marketing. However, when we use the term social marketing here it will largely refer to non-profit (and in most cases governmental) entities, so that we can distinguish for-profit products and messages aimed at dieting and healthy eating from their non-profit counterparts.

As posed by Wansink and Huckabee (2005), the self-regulation issue may also be construed as a trade-off between taste and nutrition. Taste is sensual and 'hot' while nutrition is cognitive and 'cool'. In the approach taken here, it is necessary to modify their formulation: weight control may be seen as a matter of nutrition or as a matter of thinness so that it has two channels – see the next section where dieting and health-conscious consumers are identified as separate segments. Moreover, taste and nutrition can be expanded as concepts to fully account for their effects. In that regard, while taste by itself is an immediately available sense that consumers draw on to make food decisions, it is also surrounded by a 'culture of taste' which serves to reinforce that consumers indulge in tasty foods and drink even if they are attempting to resist doing so.

This culture, while bearing the imprints of psychosocial variables and reflecting marketing inputs such as advertising and tasty products, is also a product of peer pressure. For instance, during the holidays, it is difficult for consumers to resist overindulging – it is almost anti-social, if not un-American. While there is also a 'culture of nutrition', it is often weak by comparison. The culture of thinness must also compete with the culture of taste and seems to be a constant war in the 'battle of the bulge'. While it involves many cool aspects in terms of involving effort and prevention, and cognitive aspects in terms of thinking about diets, calories, 'carbs', and the like, it has some characteristics of hotness in terms of appealing to appearance and related aspects of attractiveness, youthfulness and sexual appeal, thus making it a bit easier to communicate than nutrition per se. Still, taste is the hottest system and thinness remains a more difficult, cool system overall.

Given the links between the two systems, the promotional–hot and preventive–cool relationship may be subverted. For example, Thompson (2004) suggests that an advertisement for Herbal Phen Fuel addresses the issue that while obesity may prevent one from attaining a certain natural state of balance, dieting may also limit vitality, in that it involves a reduction in caloric intake. Clearly the latter is cool though the former has elements of both hot and cool. The claim is made for Herbal Phen Fuel that it can increase energy while reducing weight. This is how many diet products must appeal to consumers: by making the preventive, cool product or behavior into a hot one, such as claiming to provide an energy boost or as many others do by making diet or healthy products tasty.

As will be seen, this idea of taking the mixed messages of 'hot' and 'cool' and rendering or transforming the cool into something hot is perhaps the best way of applying marketing to the problems of overeating and obesity. Thus, somewhat paradoxically, the mixed messages are not lost or abandoned, especially since they reflect the promotional and preventive aspects of life we all share, but instead they are integrated in a way that the cool becomes hot.

Figure 6.1 illustrates responses to mixed marketing messages. Consumers respond to messages which are promotional or preventive in terms of their hot and cool systems. Both systems may be activated; as when, for instance, temptation arises and thoughts and emotions lending themselves both to giving in and resisting arise. Of course, one or the other system may be so dominant that the other plays no role, but probably in most cases both systems are activated and compete with one another. The consumer makes a choice and engages in one of these two behaviors. For many, the choice follows the hot one and that helps to explain in large part why there is an obesity problem, though many factors may interact in its development.

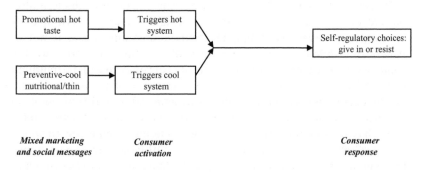

| Promotional hot taste | → | Triggers hot system | |
| Preventive-cool nutritional/thin | → | Triggers cool system | → Self-regulatory choices: give in or resist |

Mixed marketing and social messages   *Consumer activation*   *Consumer response*

Figure 6.1 Promotion (hot) versus prevention (cool) self-regulation of weight and eating

For example, to assess the psychosocial, cultural and marketing impacts on the hot system, consider brands and blind taste testing. Brand names are thought to have such strong placebo effects, as established by marketing and these other impacting variables, that to isolate pure taste effects marketers use blind taste tests. With respect to the taste system and overweight, this means that it is taste plus branding and related cultural understandings of what foods and beverages should be consumed (and when) that drive overindulgence. Thus, while taste and nutrition–thinness are important delimiters of the obesity issue and the hot and cool systems, it is important to note their embedding and reinforcement in well-established and competing cultural systems.

Relatedly, both marketers and consumers must make a lot more effort in applying the nutrition/thinness–prevention–cool system than the fast taste–promotion–hot system. In that regard, Wansink and Huckabee (2005) suggest that people seek out the most convenient solutions, with respect to eating as well as many other things: something they refer to as the law of least effort. This idea may also be tied into decision theory where, for instance, consumers will demonstrate a preference for things that are easier to evaluate (Hsee, 1996). In this case, taste as a sense is so immediate and tangible that it requires less effort to evaluate or interpret relative to a calorie evaluation, which is more intangible and cognitive and can easily be rationalized away. Indeed, in a recent survey only 12 percent of consumers responded that nutrition was a factor in their food purchases (C.J. Thompson, 2004; S. Thompson, 2005). Thus, the extra effort for marketers lies in having to create and convey the much more complex cognitive message about weight control.

Another aspect of the 'least effort' law or hypothesis is that even if consumers try to achieve weight maintenance and reject overeating, their efforts must be construed in terms of goals that they may or may not achieve (Bagozzi and Warshaw, 1990). For instance, in some circumstances a consumer may think, 'This goal of weight loss is so difficult and I may not even achieve it so I might as well give up, at least at today's holiday party'. Some aspects of this may reflect motivation while others may reflect an inability to lose weight, either because of genetic reasons or because of a lack of knowledge, control or the resources necessary to engage in weight loss practices (cf. Moorman and Matulich, 1993).

Thus, while there are many influences on obesity, the factors identified in this section provide a central framework for considering them and also for relating them to marketing and marketing communications. In summary, what emerges is a bifurcated framework involving the promotional–hot–taste and preventive–cool–nutrition, thinness systems. These systems provide a theoretical basis for the cross-currents and mixed messages that marketing provides consumers. In the next section this framework is applied in the context of marketing segmentation to consider how different consumers respond to the promotional and preventive aspects of obesity.

MARKET SEGMENTS FOR OBESITY

Market segmentation is a broadly applied practice and concept in both marketing and marketing communications in which groups of consumers are distinguished from one another on the basis of different variables relevant to their buying or product-use decisions (for example, that younger consumers are more frequent movie attendees than older consumers). Marketers use this approach to target particular consumer segments with marketing programs and communications geared specifically towards them. With respect to obesity, this means that various consumers are segmented so that they will respond differently to hot and cool messages, thus rendering the task of dealing with obesity a far more complex issue than a one-size-fits all approach would suggest. In marketing, the latter is often referred to as a mass marketing approach and in most cases, with a few exceptions for widely diffused and popular products, is regarded as less effective and sophisticated than targeted marketing with segmentation in which appropriate groups of consumers are addressed.

There is probably also a serious asymmetry in this regard between food and beverage marketers on the one hand and social marketers on the other. The former are probably more aware of targeted marketing, better at it, and have more resources at their disposal to apply it. Moreover, they also have the distinct advantage of being able to provide hot-system products and utilize hot advertising messages while social marketers are necessarily forced to provide cool, cognitive messages. Nutritional or thinness-oriented product marketers (some of whom may paradoxically also simultaneously market unhealthy taste products, though perhaps with different brand names) are likely to be somewhere in the middle in terms of approach, in that they may also be sophisticated users of segmentation while having to communicate largely cool messages.

The segmentation framework that emerges, which we label the Weight–Lifestyle Segmentation Framework (WLSF), revolves around three main lifestyle aspects of obesity that can be identified among all adult consumers dealing with weight issues, each with their own receptivities to hot and cold messages. In fact, it is based on their motivational and lifestyle approach to such weight issues. Motivation is a particularly important if complex variable in driving consumers' preventive health behavior (Moorman and Matulich, 1993) and here can be seen to underlie the development of the three lifestyle segments.

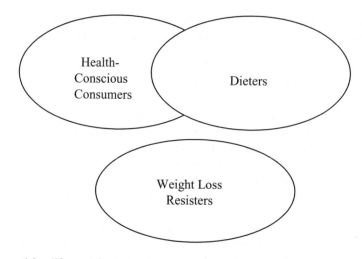

Figure 6.2   The weight–lifestyle segmentation framework

These three weight–lifestyle segments, as shown in Figure 6.2, are: Dieters; Health-Conscious Consumers; and Weight Loss Resisters. The first two segments deal with, or attempt to deal with, weight control and/or loss and resist overeating while the third segment either resists doing anything about their weight, gives in to temptation relatively easily, and/or may not even recognize that there is a problem (that is, they lack awareness or knowledge to varying degrees or counterargue that knowledge with other views to make weight or overweight a positive – such as finding body weight attractive).

Children may be seen as a special, vulnerable class of all the segments, depending on their parents and other factors (though when dealt with alone, their natural tendency and fit would be in the 'Resisters' segment since they generally lack the knowledge or motivation to deal with dieting or health) (cf. Seiders and Petty, 2004). In that regard, a recent report by the Institute of Medicine of the National Academies examined 120 studies relating television advertising and overweight children and found that, indeed, such advertising influenced the food preferences of children under 12 for unhealthy foods (Burros, 2005). Thus, children are a classic target for hot marketing and much government regulation and policy aims at restricting their exposure to advertising for fatty products and restricting the availability of unhealthy and fatty foods in schools (Seiders and Petty, 2004).

Dieters and Health-Conscious Consumers have the motivation to lose weight, but with different motivations and different perceptions of the symptomatology of obesity and remedies for weight control (cf. Gould et al., 1997). Dieters generally are concerned with appearance and see food in terms of increasing or decreasing thinness; Health-Conscious Consumers, on the other hand, focus on health reasons for weight control, such as preventing obesity-correlated heart disease and stroke, and see food as providing more or less nutrition.

These two motivations are not mutually exclusive and thus, as illustrated in Figure 6.2, they may overlap so that some consumers are in both segments (though generally depending on how easy it is to identify and reach these consumers with separate communications, they may be viewed as two distinct and separate segments). They are also likely to be 'scientific' about their weight (Gould, 1988) and in fact will often pay close attention to developments in the field of dieting and/or health through the media or word-of-mouth networks and try many things in a self-experimental manner to control their weight (cf. Gould et al., 1993).

Within these three broad framing segments, there are any number of segmentation variables that might apply, ranging from various demographics to psychographic or lifestyle variables (that is, activities, interests and opinions), perceptions of obesity and body image, differences in health status and perceptions, and the relative degrees of obesity a consumer may present medically and also perceive that he or she presents. To use these segments wisely, the particular situation presented to the marketer or social marketer should dictate which variables are used. For example, there may be differences in how Caucasian, African American and Latino consumers view obesity and respond to communications about it. Indeed, minorities are said to account for a disproportionate frequency of the obesity in the USA (Wee et al., 2005) and their attitudes toward body image and weight can often differ from those of majority Americans (see for example Goodman, 2002). Thus, among Weight Loss Resisters, for instance, there will be further segmentation divisions, here reflecting ethnicity, which can help target specific consumers further and more effectively. In addition, other variables such as gender have their own effects and likely interact with ethnicity.

Moreover, marketers must make sure that claims and messages about food should not only be targeted to the appropriate consumer but should also reflect the knowledge, motivation and interest level of this segment in order to be effective (Wansink and Cheney, 2005). Here, since all these variables will often be situational, we cannot provide a one-size-fits-all scenario. In fact it would be highly inappropriate. But what can be done is the provision of this broad three-segment framework in which the other segmentation schemes may be situated or benchmarked, and to which promotion and prevention may be related.

As indicated above, another issue to be assessed when considering segmentation and behavior is that there may be differences in perceptions of objective weight standards as medical practitioners and scientists promulgate them, and consumers present them, versus subjective standards as consumers perceive them. Thus, consumers may be overweight by the standards of medical science while not perceiving themselves as such, or may believe culturally that 'thinness' is not desirable. Weight Loss Resisters might be of particular note in this case, since some of them may not perceive any problems with their weight, reflecting differences in awareness discussed above, even though health care providers might find that such problems exist. Of course on the other hand, some consumers may also perceive themselves as overweight though they are not by medical standards (for example bulimics or anorexics).

In this regard, health care providers may differ from marketers in how they perceive and deal with overweight consumers. The providers deal with individual consumers as patients in terms of their own specific personal needs and practices. Moreover, in public health it may be that aside from community-wide measures, while helpful and necessary, other measures which identify those who are particularly prone to engage in behaviors conducive to obesity would be most effective (VanItalle and Stunkard, 1990). Marketers on the other hand, even those applying sophisticated segmentation schemes, still must deal with large groups of consumers rather than individuals, though perhaps their approaches can be useful for public health agencies. Continuing or future advances in customization, such as the continuing development of the Internet as a one-to-one tool for marketing communications, may permit some degree of individualized targeting, but it is necessary for now to more predominantly position marketing as a group-oriented approach (especially social marketing in this regard, as a complement or an adjunct to more individualized health care and medical practice).

Thus, this market segment framework may be applied by considering the main motivations of those identified as having weight issues, identifying subsegments within them as relevant (subsegments based on gender, ethnicity or eating habits, for example) and constructing marketing programs and communications aimed at them. As proposed here, it is assumed that for most communications the broad segments are quite necessary but probably not sufficient in most cases to target specific consumers. Further strategic implications of this segmentation formulation are drawn in the next section.

IMPLICATIONS FOR MANAGERIAL AND POLICY STRATEGY

The WLSF can be viewed in broad terms from a strategic perspective that suggests how policymakers and marketers can position consumers and their segments *vis-à-vis* one another, as well as recognizing their distinct characters and autonomy. Reflecting motivations concerning weight and obesity as a basis for these lifestyle segments, broadly construed the segments may be seen as a hierarchy with a flow from the least health-oriented to the most. The least health-oriented segment is that of the Weight Loss Resisters while Health-Conscious Consumers are the most health-oriented, with Dieters generally in the middle.

Consistent with marketing theory and practice regarding market segments, and especially the dynamics of marketing-induced change, it would be desirable for Weight Loss Resisters to be converted at a minimum to Dieters, if not to the Health-Conscious segment. Similarly, Dieters would ideally be converted to the Health-Conscious Consumer segment. This progression reflects to a large degree the view that obesity is only one, albeit major, health issue among many and that it would be highly desirable for consumers to be so conscious. However, since the focus is on obesity here, it would seem that the most important single strategic implication is to focus on Weight Loss Resisters and convert them at a minimum to Dieters. The other two segments already acknowledge the issue and are taking steps to deal with it. This is not to say that there are not issues for them that can be addressed by strategic policy and marketing (for example: Dieters eating 'lite' though not necessarily healthy foods or going overboard the other away in extreme behaviors of anorexia and bulimia; and further refinements of health information and services for even Health-Conscious Consumers). Rather our focus is to project that the Weight Loss Resisters segment is perhaps the most crucial in terms of social and health cost, and at the same time the most perplexing.

Thus, with respect to self-regulation in terms of promotion and prevention, Weight Loss Resisters have a promotional and hot perspective that for the most part does not allow them to take into account any preventive self-regulation whatsoever. On the other hand, Dieters and Health-Conscious Consumers are able to frame their weight issues in terms of a cooler system of preventive measures. So depending on the segment, marketing programs and communications will require different strategies. To be sure, all segments respond to promotional or hot communications in terms of having fun and enjoying food and life. But Weight Loss Resisters have a relatively undeveloped cool–preventive system for countering hot messages. On the other hand, Dieters and Health-Conscious Consumers have a countervailing system, which at a minimum allows them to respond to preventive weight control messages. It should be noted that even in their prevention there is a promotion side, in that messages aimed at them invoke hot elements, such as the energy mentioned in the Herbal Phen Fuel example raised earlier. For example, Dieters are told if they engage in weight control that they will have a pleasing, attractive appearance and Health-Conscious

Consumers are shown being able to engage in various activities free of disease or worry about it.

What further can marketers and social marketers do? A key issue in diffusion of innovations research, which marketers apply in terms of new ideas and products, concerns compatibility: change must be compatible with consumers' lives or they will not adopt it. In the present context, that refers to rendering obesity-reducing messages and practices in ways that are compatible with consumers' lifestyles. This is much easier for Dieters and Health-Conscious consumers than for the Weight Loss Resister segment since weight reduction is already compatible with their lifestyles to varying degrees, and is often opposed to the lifestyles of Weight Loss Resisters. Moreover, since we have identified a number of variables which suggest that not all consumers share the same lifestyles or respond to the same messages, then policy implications must be more finely granulated than a mass approach might allow.

In this, it is likely that promotional marketers selling taste to the hot system have a distinct asymmetric and perhaps built-in advantage in that they are oriented toward segmentation and consumer differences, and thereby effective marketing communications, while the government is often constrained by its own inertia, lack of understanding of segmentation and political constraints that may inhibit specific responses to particular groups. The quality of the social marketing of the governmental cool system never seems a match for the hot system of corporate marketing. If anything, the best marketing communications and product development aimed at combating obesity probably, and ironically, comes from marketers who take the cool proposition of dieting and turn it into a promotional–hot one. This is similar to the win–win proposition of Wansink and Huckabee (2005) in which consumers can still get tasty products while certain drivers of obesity are reversed.

In any case, given the asymmetry between marketers and social marketers in government and other non-profit organizations, it behooves the latter to engage in education and information-providing measures, both to consumers and food marketers themselves. Food and beverage marketers themselves, however, will bear the brunt of the communications and product offerings and thus will do the most 'hot' marketing in the interest of the cool system. Governments and their agencies can take such measures as mandating the improvement of labeling, regulating the fat and health content of food to varying degrees, regulating school lunchroom diets, encouraging and/or funding research on obesity and seeking to improve dietary education, among other things.

However these measures, while necessary and helpful, will not solve the problem by themselves. These are cool and often unobtrusive measures that do not surface or register in the hot–promotional world of the everyday consumer, especially Weight Loss Resisters. Social marketers, need to develop ways to make cool messages hotter. Nonetheless, it is the food and beverage marketers, along with others such as work-out clubs and exercise equipment manufacturers, who best address this world. Thus, perhaps a most productive avenue for social marketers would be to partner with appropriate food and other product or services marketers in creating marketing programs, marketing communications and educational programs concerned with weight control.

This consumer self-regulation and segmentation approach can also be extended on a worldwide basis. In this regard, the convergence issues raised by Audretsch and DiOrio in Chapter 2 are at issue not only in spreading obesity but also in the need for regulation to keep pace. For example, it has been suggested that the European Union is behind the USA in dealing with its own obesity epidemic and needs to catch up in dealing with this spreading problem (Meller, 2005). What this suggests, moreover, is that there are different stages in developing measures for dealing with obesity. For instance, Wansink and Huckabee (2005) suggest there are three stages of how the food industry deals with obesity: first, denial, in which it denies any responsibility for the problem; second, recognizing consumers' sovereignty and letting the consumer decide; and third, win–win situations in which marketers create products that allow consumers to enjoy their food while consuming less calories (such as by reducing the volume or portion of a food consumed in a given situation).

In this regard, it is likely that European companies, and particularly their counterparts in government, are trying to move beyond the 'no responsibility stage', though in this case the threat of regulation looms. In any case, while countries and regions may learn from each other and transfer knowledge, the segmentation perspective taken here is that solutions must as much be local as they are global. For instance, consumers in the USA may be inured to messages that would have a sparkling sense of novelty in Europe. Furthermore, given the earlier stage of dealing with this issue, there are presumably more consumers drawn to hot taste messages who may be found in the Weight Loss Resister category in Europe.

CONCLUSION

This chapter has dealt with the marketing and social marketing implications for dealing with consumers' obesity and weight control issues. Several points should be emphasized. First, marketing as a practice is neutral in itself; much as fire, for instance, can be used to cook food or to commit an act of arson. On the one hand, food and beverage marketers often are blamed for encouraging consumers to over-consume, in terms of the messages and products they provide. On the other hand, social marketers, and even many food and beverage marketers, try to appeal to consumers' needs to control their weight by offering less fatty products and messages that encourage consumers to consume less. Marketers offering consumer exercise products and clubs can also be helpful. Thus, marketing as a tool can be applied in either way.

Second, marketing interacts with the complex self-regulatory and segmentation aspects of consumption. So even if food and beverage marketers may bear some responsibility for the obesity epidemic, they are nonetheless actors in a complex cultural dynamic. Social marketers in an ironic sort of way also bear some responsibility in that they have not been able to refine their skills or acquire the resources to compete with product marketers. In this regard, it has been suggested that social marketers educate consumers while pushing food and beverage marketers to provide better products and communicate more healthful messages. Given the fact that people in the USA and much of the rest of the world, especially the developed world, live in capitalist societies that drive this reliance on product marketers, it seems that these same marketers are much better equipped to create and deliver the messages and products required for the task of communicating weight control messages, if they so choose. To wit, they can appeal to the preventive–cool needs of consumers by adding the necessary elements of promotional–hot communications to make weight loss hot. Paradoxically, this approach takes advantage of the mixed messages currently in the system. It does so not by getting rid of them entirely, since they necessarily exist because of the promotional–preventive trade-off of much if not all human activity, but instead creatively manages them so that what is 'cool' is related to or rendered as 'hot'. However this creative rendering as hot is performed in practice, and given all the variations that arise, the idea of it constitutes the main thought and contribution of this chapter.

Third, the idea of marketing segmentation is one way to address all the variations that occur. Here, the market for obesity ideas and product targeting has been conceived in terms of the WLSF and its three broad segments: Dieters, Health-Conscious Consumers and Weight Loss Resisters. This broad formulation reflects the motivations and lifestyles of consumers and can be used to drive marketing programs. Nonetheless, however necessary they are to consider and frame the issues of obesity, they also must be fine-tooled and granulated in a way that reflects other segmentation variables. These include including demographics and psychographic lifestyle variables that may be found within these broader three segments and which further subdivide them in ways that make product and message marketing even better targeted and more cost effective. Moreover, targeting within these segments also helps to minimize the effects of counterproductive mixed messages being delivered, in that the appropriate segments will receive the appropriate messages and those outside the segments will as much as possible be spared.

In this regard the use of media such as television, the Internet and print (magazines and newspapers) is a cost that is best reduced when only targeted consumers are in the audience, and non-targeted consumers are excluded as much as possible. For instance, the identification of dayparts (such as morning or primetime) and television channels or magazines aimed at one or another of Dieters or Health-Conscious Consumers would be most effective. Weight Loss Resisters might require different media strategies since they are not such an easy group to target on such a basis. However, they could be reached through media that target other related characteristics as well, such as magazines or television channels aimed at specific gender, ethnic and lifestyle groups with large numbers of Weight Loss Resisters, rather than self-contained weight-oriented segments.

Targeting particular segments also enhances the creativity of messages delivered and the development of the product/service offerings provided by marketers of all types gearing their efforts in terms of particular consumers. A message to Dieters will generally appeal on terms of appearance and looks while one to Health-Conscious Consumers will mention increased health and the prevention of various health problems. To be sure, there will be other specifics related to the subsegments that need to be considered, such as differences among younger and older dieters, for instance, whose issues and needs in terms of dieting may differ. Weight Loss Resisters again will probably require the greatest attention to subsegments and perhaps the greatest efforts in terms of creativity since they are the most intractable and diffuse segment. Moreover, there is a two-staged process or two-pronged appeal that is required to reach them. Whereas the other two segments are already convinced to varying degrees that is it desirable or necessary to engage in weight control and/or loss, the Weight Loss Resisters are generally not. In their case, it is first necessary to convince them that weight control is something they should do. Only after that can more specific measures be addressed to them. This is not to say that at times creative messages addressing both aspects simultaneously could not be designed but rather it is to recognize that a long-term campaign (rather than one-time messages) must be created to reach and persuade this segment of consumers.

Finally as evidenced by this book overall, marketing is but one of many disciplines and subdisciplines dealing with obesity. In designing marketing programs, food, social and other involved marketers can build on the research in related fields in terms of: the psychophysiological, psychological and health aspects of obesity; consumers' food habits, preferences, practices and rituals in sociological, cultural and anthropological terms; and the economic costs and trade-offs, among others. Informed by these perspectives marketers can develop products and messages that are appropriate to the problem.

At the same time, marketing in its various aspects and roles can inform these other disciplines by providing input and feedback concerning how consumers are dealing with obesity and in particular regarding what product or services they are using and what messages they are being persuaded by and are responding to. In particular, marketing practitioners and academics both have much to offer in providing understandings of consumer weight-salient behavior and in how to design marketing programs that address consumers' needs and wants with respect to obesity in effective ways. While everyone in the obesity field will likely acknowledge the need for a multidisciplinary approach to studying weight control and developing appropriate behavioral programs, there is probably less acknowledgment of the positive contribution that marketing can make within that approach; no doubt this is in part because marketing is viewed, in negative terms, with some justification, as part of the problem. Hopefully, this chapter provides a step towards modifying that view.

REFERENCES

Audretsch, David B. and Dawne DiOrio (2006), 'The spread of obesity', Chapter 2, this volume.

Bagozzi, R.P. and P.R. Warshaw (1990), 'Trying to consume', *Journal of Consumer Research,* **17** (2), 127–40.

Bandura, Roy F. and Kathleen D, Vohs (2003), 'Self-regulation and the executive function of the self,' in Mark R. Leary and June Price Tangney (eds), *Handbook of Self and Identity*, New York and London: The Guilford Press, pp. 197–217.

Bloom, P.N. and W.D. Novelli (1981), 'Problems and challenges in social marketing', *Journal of Marketing*, **45** (2), 79–88.

Burros, M. (2005), 'Federal advisory group calls for change in food marketing to children', *The New York Times*, 7 December, p. C4.

Cottam, R. (2004), 'Obesity and culture', *Lancet*, **364** (9441), 1202–3.

Goodman, J.R. (2002), 'Flabless is fabulous: how Latina and Anglo women read and incorporate the excessively thin body idea into everyday experience', *Journalism and Mass Communication Quarterly*, **79** (3), 712–27.

Gould, Stephen J. (1988), 'Consumer attitudes toward health and health care: a differential perspective,' *Journal of Consumer Affairs*, **22** (Summer), 96–118.

Gould, S.J., J.M. Considine and L.S. Oakes (1993), 'Consumer illness careers: an investigation of allergy sufferers and their universe of medical choices', *Journal of Health Care Marketing*, **13** (2), 34–48.

Gould, S.J., L.S. Oakes and J.M. Considine (1997), 'Profiling pharmaceutical allergy medications by symptoms and their relief: a study of consumer perceptions', *Journal of Business Research*, **40** (3), 199–206.

Harrison, K. and J. Cantor (1997), 'The relationship between media consumption and eating disorders', *Journal of Communication*, **47** (1), 40–67.

Higgins, E.T. (1997), 'Beyond pleasure and pain', *American Psychologist*, **52** (12), 1280–1300.

Hoch, S.J. and G.F. Loewenstein (1991), 'Time-inconsistent preferences and consumer self-control', *Journal of Consumer Research*, **17** (4), 492–507.

Hsee, C.K. (1996), 'The evaluability hypothesis: an explanation for preference reversals between joint and separate evaluations of alternatives', *Organizational Behavior and Human Decision Processes*, **67** (3), 247–57.

Moorman, C. and E. Matulich (1993), 'A model of consumers' preventive health behaviors: the role of health motivation and/health ability', *Journal of Consumer Research*, **20** (2), 208–28.

Meller, P. (2005), 'Europe's turn to wrestle with obesity', *The New York Times*, 24 November, p. C5.

Metcalfe, J. and W. Mischel (1999), 'A hot/cool system of delay of gratification: dynamics of willpower', *Psychological Review*, **106** (91), 3–19.

Seiders, K. and R.D. Petty (2004), 'Obesity and the role of food marketing', *Journal of Public Policy and Marketing*, **23** (2), 153–69.

Thompson, C.J. (2004), 'Marketplace mythology and discourses of power', *Journal of Consumer Research*, **31** (1), 162–80.

Thompson, S. (2005), 'Food industry struggle to meet public's health needs', accessed 30 November at www.adage.com/news.cms?newsid=46970.

Vanitallie, T.B. and A.J. Stunkard (1990), 'Using nature to understand nurture', *American Journal of Public Health*, **80** (6), 657–8.

Wansink, B. and M.M. Cheney (2005), 'Leveraging FDA health claims', *Journal of Consumer Affairs*, **39** (2), 386–98.

Wansink, B. and M. Huckabee (2005), 'De-marketing obesity', *California Management Review*, **47** (4), 6–18.

Wee, Christina C., R.L. Phillips, A.T.R. Legedza, R.E. Davis, J.R. Soukup, G.A. Colditz and M.B. Hamel (2005), 'Healthcare expenditures associated with overweight and obesity among adults', *American Journal of Public Health*, **95** (1), 159–65.

7. Weight control, private health insurance and public policies

Alan Lyles and Ann Cotten

American social life, in and out of the house, is often built around eating.

J.E. Tillotson (2004)

OVERVIEW

Given the critical function that employment-based health insurance has on the provision of health care in the USA, this chapter focuses on employers in their role as primary providers of private health insurance, the public sector's role as regulator of insurers and employers, and the options available to both groups for preventing and treating obesity. To understand how public policy can influence obesity prevention and treatment through the health care system, the factors that shaped the evolution of the current private insurance system will also be discussed. While the public policies that influence the availability and content of private health insurance are considered, the public programs that provide health benefits to poor, disadvantaged and elderly populations, such as the Medicare and Medicaid programs, are beyond the scope of this chapter.

Obesity represents a major cost to insurers and to the public. Fifty-three percent of adults in private insurance plans are overweight or obese – a level comparable to that of other insurance categories (Finkelstein et al., 2003). Medicaid, however, has the largest percentage of obese enrollees, at 27.4 percent (versus a range of 17.0–18.8 percent for others). The aggregate financial impact of excess weight varied by insurer – costing private insurers 8.2 percent of their spending – for obesity alone was recently estimated at $9.5–16.1 billion. Public payors had a similar experience: Medicaid at 8.8 percent (for obesity, $2.7–10.7 billion) and Medicare at 11.1 percent (for obesity, $10.8–13.8 billion). Taken together, obesity and excess weight produce a global mean excess health cost of $395 per person compared to those not overweight (Finkelstein et al., 2003).

The use of medical services is strongly influenced by having health insurance and by its provision or exclusion of specific benefits. In the USA universal health insurance does not exist. Instead, private health insurance is the most prevalent form of insurance and is most often obtained through employment, giving business a direct interest in this growing and difficult-to-control cost. To control costs, private insurance policies have generally excluded preventive medicine and weight loss services. Paradoxically, employers have begun to promote prevention and wellness based on evidence that untreated obesity is associated with lost productivity and large additional health care costs.

Even for those with health insurance, it is difficult to determine which services to request or to accept. Medical costs and the knowledge required for informed decisions put the individual patient at a disadvantage in making truly independent decisions. Unlike other goods and services, the demand for medical care has unique features that influence business and regulatory health benefit decisions:

1. The patient is not the ultimate determiner of which medical services are consumed – both physicians and patients determine whether, which and how much of specific medical services will be used.
2. The recipient of health care usually does not bear the full cost: third payors (employers and insurance companies) are responsible for much of it.
3. Regulation of health care and health insurance distorts the costs of care and the traditional relationship between supply and demand.

The health care market's inflationary structure and its resistance to change prompted businesses to form coalitions that would leverage their health care purchasing power. The mandates of these coalitions include controlling costs, improving quality and promoting efficient delivery of appropriate medical care. Cost pressures are still paramount and high deductible health insurance policies are increasingly used to shift a larger portion of health care costs to employees. Since high deductible amounts require first dollar out-of-pocket payments, even for insured services, employees may delay or reduce the use of covered services until their condition is more serious and more costly. To counteract this disincentive to seek preventive care, employers are instituting benefit innovations that emphasize health promotion, wellness and weight loss. Employers as a group are undergoing a fundamental shift from viewing health expenses as essentially a cost to be controlled to an investment to be optimized.

Employers are no longer passive payors – the business sector has become a force in health services market reform; however, the foundation for durable solutions requires both market discipline and regulation. States regulate health care and are responsible for oversight of health insurance, but federal law sometimes unintentionally thwarts state regulations. For example, one federal law, originally intended to preserve workers' pensions, has had the unintended and perverse result of allowing employers to pre-empt state mandates by self-insuring. Thus, state mandates to correct health insurance market failures for specific treatments and/or populations, such as bariatric services, may actually reduce the number of firms offering health insurance benefits to their employees.

How can the public and private sectors work together to address obesity through the health care system? The remainder of this chapter will discuss the USA's national health goals for weight control, the main clinical treatment options for obesity and the history of private health insurance. It specifically addresses the role(s) of business and of public policies in creating the private insurers' view of preventative care and the ways in which public policy can influence the private sector to promote obesity prevention and treatment. Finally, business's innovations in health promotion and wellness are presented as examples of private sector leadership in the prevention and management of obesity and its related costs.

OBESITY AND THE HEALTH OF THE PUBLIC

In the USA, life expectancy at birth increased from 47.3 years in 1900 to 68.2 years by 1950, and 77.0 years by 2000 (NCHS, 2004). Initial increases in life expectancy resulted from improvements in sanitation and hygiene, but subsequent increases reflected improved nutrition, the availability and use of antibiotics and newer medical technologies. With increasing longevity, however, medical priorities have shifted from treating acute and infectious illness to managing chronic conditions. Environment and genes play a significant role in the development of chronic conditions, but '*overnutrition*' (Nestle, 2002) and a sedentary lifestyle now explain a growing proportion of medical need and of treatment outcomes – leading to speculation that the gains in life expectancy from scientific advances may erode with the increasing prevalence of obesity (Olshansky et al., 2005).

In 1985 the National Institutes of Health (NIH) Consensus Development Program Panel on 'Health Implications of Obesity' concluded that credible evidence linked obesity to health hazards and that obesity should be treated under a physician's supervision.[1] The Panel also noted that excess weight below the threshold for an obesity diagnosis could contribute to medical risks – particularly for people with co-morbid illness (NIH Consensus Development Program, Obesity Consensus, 1985). The challenge for the nation and for employers was then to set specific goals to align their disparate programs related to health and weight control, so that they reinforced one another. Relying on its review of the then available evidence, the Obesity Consensus Panel stressed the need for an applied research agenda that included both study of the underlying pathophysiology of obesity and of its prevention.

National Health Goals

Obesity is a major source of avoidable morbidity and mortality in the USA, exceeding the consequences of smoking and of problem drinking (Sturm, 2002). Unfortunately, mixed public–private health care funding for medical care in the USA produces inconsistent coverage for similar conditions and treatments, and priorities that may not reinforce one another. To set common priorities and measurable goals, the Surgeon General of the USA issued a 1979 report assessing the nation's health. Subsequent Surgeons General have continued this practice, making explicit national health objectives and assessing progress against these goals with *Healthy People 2000*, and most recently with *Healthy People 2010* (USDHHS, 2000a). These national objectives were not established by agencies within the government, but through the collective efforts of more than 600 national organizations. These provide an explicit, consistent set of health priorities to align otherwise independent public and private priorities.

The ten highest Healthy People priorities have been further identified as Leading Health Indicators, selected on their ability to motivate action, the availability of data to measure progress, and their importance as public health issues (USDHHS, 2000b) The first two Leading Health Indicators are, first, Physical Inactivity and, second, Overweight and Obesity. Progress, or the failure to achieve progress, becomes apparent since each indicator has a target, a baseline and a data source for monitoring progress. As indicated by *Data 2010* (USDHHS, 2006), progress on these national objectives has been elusive – with all measures moving in the wrong direction:

Objective 19-1: Increase the proportion of adults who are at a healthy weight
Forty-two percent of Americans had a healthy weight at baseline (1988–94) and the target for 2010 is 60 percent. This indicator dropped to 34 percent in 2000 and to just 12 percent for persons with diabetes.

Objective 19-2: Reduce the proportion of adults who are obese
Twenty-three percent of Americans were obese at baseline (1988–94), with the target for 2010 equal to 15 percent. This indicator increased to 31 percent overall in 2000 and soared to 62 percent for persons with diabetes.

Objective 19-3: Reduce the proportion of children and adolescents who are overweight or obese
Eleven percent of American children under 18 were obese at baseline (1988–94), with the target of 5 percent in 2010. This indicator increased to 15 percent in 2000.

Americans' increasing corpulence led the Surgeon General to issue a separate, additional *Call to Action* in 2001 for the prevention and treatment of obesity. The Surgeon General's report strove to '*develop and enhance . . . public–private partnerships to help implement this vision*' (USDHHS, 2001).

Overweight and obese adults are an emergency, but excess weight in children and young adults is an ethical, medical and economic crisis. Their average weight gain portends large costs for employers who may provide their future health insurance, both as dependents of active workers and as adolescents age into the workforce with physical conditions resembling middle age more than youth. Clearly, identifying and promoting safe, efficacious and cost-effective treatments for obesity will have far-reaching individual, corporate and societal benefits.

Treatment Options, Utilization and Costs

People who confront obesity and excess weight have many options, though few exist with established long term effectiveness and safety. Sustained behavioral change is among the most difficult of medical interventions; motivated behaviors have multiple triggers and influences, with relapse being common. These factors support the reluctance of employers to provide benefits for such services. Americans annually spend approximately $30 billion to lose or control their weight (AOA, 2005). Defining successful long-term weight loss as sustained loss of 5–10 percent of initial body weight, follow-up on a very low-calorie, intensive weight loss program reported that five years after 40 percent of participants had a 5 percent weight loss, and that at seven years after 25 percent had a 10 percent weight loss (Anderson, et al., 1999).

Well-intended commitments to exercise programs represent another, though less common, approach to weight loss and weight maintenance. Approximately 39.4 million people in the USA joined gyms, health spas and clubs in 2003, at an estimated cost of $14.1 billion (*Boston Business Journal*, 2004). However sustained exercise programs may prove difficult, as indicated by a nationwide 2003 survey that documented a mere 29 percent of the respondents reporting favorite pastimes that involved exercise (Taylor, 2003).

Pharmacotherapy
When diet and self-management are inappropriate or unsuccessful, medication and/or surgery may be considered. According to the National Heart

Lung and Blood Institute, bariatric pharmacotherapy may be appropriate to add to a treatment regimen that already includes nutrition, exercise and behavior modification. Pharmacotherapy is recommended for high-risk persons who have a BMI of 27 or greater, or a BMI of 30 or greater if other risk factors are absent (NHLBI, 2000); however, there is no single-decision rule for medication use. As with all medications and procedures, the risks of side-effects from medications must be judged for each individual against the potential health gains from weight loss and the existing risks of untreated obesity.

The history of pharmacotherapy for weight loss has been a disappointing trail of products that began with great promise but subsequently were discovered to have unexpected shortcomings – such as the potential for abuse and addiction, the loss of efficacy during prolonged use, or separately marketed products being used in combinations that then posed substantial risks of serious harm. Nevertheless, the pursuit of pharmacological treatment continues since, first, behavioral change alone is on average unsuccessful for the population, and second, discoveries underlying obesity pathophysiology and motivated behaviors improve the potential for effective, relatively safe products. Currently there are an estimated 100 potential products at different points in pre-marketing testing (Korner and Aroune, 2004).

Eight prescription-only weight loss pharmaceutical products were available in 2002: three-quarters were not to be used for longer than 12 weeks and two had a two-year limit (Encinosa et al., 2005). Of these products, 88 percent (all of the short term and one of the longer term) act by suppressing appetite, while one blocks the amount of fat absorbed from foods. A promising product with a different mechanism of action from those currently marketed is nearing a marketing approval decision by the Food and Drug Administration (FDA).

The relative cost of drug therapy versus bariatric surgery would be compelling if its outcomes were more substantial. A recent meta-analysis assessed nine pharmaceutical products, both those with and without primary indications for the treatment of obesity. Those products provided modest incremental weight loss over diet and exercise: there was less than 5 kg placebo-corrected weight loss at one year, but evidence was lacking on long term-effects and was insufficient for safety conclusions (Zhaoping et al., 2005). Although even this weight loss reduces the health risks associated with obesity, the absolute amount is not encouraging and drop-out rates remain a concern.

In a sample of employee claims in the Medstat 2002 Market Scan Commercial Claims and Encounter Database, in the order of 78 percent of those with a prescription drug benefit had coverage that included bariatric drugs. However, only about 2.4 percent of obese persons with this coverage actually received such medications, and even the two long-term drugs were generally used for less than four months. The average total annual drug payment per patient was small in comparison to surgery: $356 ($29 out of pocket) for one class of drugs and $317 ($38 out of pocket) for the other (Encinosa et al., 2005).

Surgery
Significant weight gain across the spectrum of the population of the USA has not been reversed by innovative surgeries, pharmaceutical products, nutrition or lifestyle options. The discouraging statistics on initial weight loss and relapse rates for those who have lost weight suggest that, for some, surgical intervention may be the only durable treatment. Persons with a BMI of 40 or greater, a condition known as clinically severe obesity, or those with major co-morbidities and a BMI of 35 or greater may be suitable candidates for surgery (NHLBI, 2000).

The main surgical options are binding and gastroplasty without bypass or Roux-en-Y (gastric bypass), and there are several other less frequently performed procedures. These procedures make the stomach smaller and decrease absorption. Of an estimated 11.5 million adults clinically eligible for one of these procedures in 2002, only 0.6 percent actually had bariatric surgery (Table 7.1). Despite this low utilization, the number of bariatric

Table 7.1   Estimates of underutilization of insured bariatric services, 2002

	National	Large employer sample
Insurance coverage and clinically eligible	11 500 000	918 000
Actual use	70 124	21 797
%	0.6	2.4

	Surgery	Pharmaceuticals
Payment %		
Private pay	3.4	
Self-pay	82.9	
Average payments ($US)		
Out of pocket	635	29
Health plan	18 710	275
Total	19 346	304

Source: Encinosa (2005). Based on Hedley, A.A. et al. (2004), 'Prevalence of overweight and obesity among US children, adolescents and adults, 1999–2002', *Journal of the American Medical Association*, **291** (23), 2847–50; and Mokdad, A.H. (2003), 'Prevalence of obesity, diabetes and obesity-related health risk factors, 2001', *Journal of the American Medical Association*, **289** (1), 76–9.

surgeries performed in the USA still increased by 436 percent from 1998 to 2002 (Encinosa et al., 2005). The mortality rate associated with bariatric surgery has decreased from 0.89 inpatient deaths per 100 surgeries in 1998 to 0.32 in 2002; however, statistics on complication rates and trends are not routinely available. Improved safety has not made this a low-cost procedure. Furthermore, the current underutilization indicates a large potential cost exposure for employers should eligibility criteria remain the same and use among those currently eligible for the procedures increase

The average cost across bariatric surgery types was $19 346 in 2002 – primarily due to hospital costs. The preponderance of bariatric surgery payments came from health plans ($18 710) with only 3 percent ($635) on average being paid by the patient out of pocket (see Table 7.1). The extent of insurance coverage may influence the specific services demanded when a surgery is performed. Laparoscopic surgeries cost less overall ($16 600) than did non-laparoscopic ($19 047), but may have been less favored by patients since their out-of-pocket costs were greater with laparoscopic surgery ($1009 vs $576)

HEALTH INSURANCE IN THE USA

The Development of Private Health Insurance

The latter half of the twentieth century presented seemingly limitless possibilities for medical advances. However, the costs for providing access to these treatments exceeded what individuals could afford, and what either the public or the private sectors would assume responsibility for paying. This led to the need for insurance to pool the risk of medical care losses. These risks have been demonstrated recently by the concentration of medical costs: in 1999, 84 percent of non-institutionalized civilians in the USA incurred some health care expenses, but the top 5 percent of these represented 52.4 percent of all health care spending that year, while the bottom 50 percent had just 3.1 percent of the total (NCHS, 2004). The consequence of being uninsured or underinsured can be financial disaster. Approximately 1.5 million filings for personal bankruptcy were made in 2001, affecting an estimated 3.9 million people (1.3 million of whom were under 18 years of age). Illness or injury was cited as the specific reason for bankruptcy by 28 percent, but 54 percent cited medical contributors to their bankruptcy. Thirty-two percent of those with medical bankruptcy were uninsured or had a dependent who was uninsured at the time of the bankruptcy, and 38 percent of those who had a major medical bankruptcy had had an interruption in their health insurance coverage during the two years prior to the filing (Himmelstein et al., 2005).

In the early decades of the twentieth century, few people in the USA had private health insurance. Premiums for mutual accident and sick benefit associations were $47 million in 1930 and, reflecting the malaise of the economy during the Great Depression, declined to $45 million a decade later. Private health insurance evolved slowly, mainly as a negotiated benefit linked to employment. Wage and price freezes during the Second World War, coupled with the growing size of unions and too few domestic workers led to effective labor demands that companies provide improved health benefits. This focus on benefits was further reinforced by the War Labor Board's prohibition on employers' use of higher wages to compete for the available workers, but its acceptance of employers being able to offer enriched worker benefits (Kuttner, 1999). Public policies that froze wages but permitted benefits to grow during the war led to an almost tripling of insurance premiums from their pre-war level, to $111.7 million in 1947 (Statistical Abstract of the United States, 1950). In the robust economy of the early 1950s, favorable tax treatment of health insurance as a fringe benefit stimulated the expansion of employment-based health insurance (Kuttner, 1999).

Since 1998, the annual per capita increase in health care spending has exceeded both the growth in workers' earnings and overall inflation (Figure 7.1, Table 7.3). Cost increases and general economic conditions

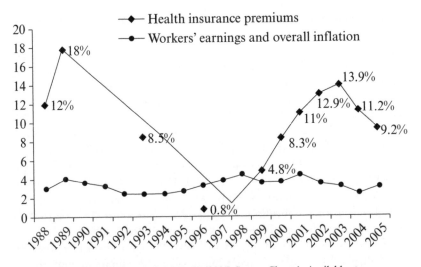

Source: Kaiser Family Foundation/Hewitt (2005) Survey Chart 1. Available at www.kff.org/insurance/7315/sections/upload/7375.pdf.

Figure 7.1   Increases in health insurance premiums compared to other indicators, 1988–2005

have had an impact on health benefits. From a high of 63.6 percent in 2000, the percentage of persons with employment-based private insurance dropped to 60.4 in 2003 (US Census, 2003), and the percentage of persons with *any* private insurance declined from 75.5 percent in 1987 to 68.6 percent in 2003. Forty-five million people in the USA under 65 years of age lacked health insurance in 2003 (Kaiser Family Foundation, 2004a). Employer-sponsored health insurance (ESI) is heavily subsidized when it is offered; in 2004, workers with single coverage paid on average 16 percent of the premium while those with family coverage paid an average of 28 percent. (Kaiser Family Foundation, 2004c).

Although private health insurance in the USA is most often a consequence of employment, not all workers have health insurance. Overall, 18.7 percent of workers between the ages of 18 and 64 were uninsured in 2003. However, being uninsured varies across occupations and industries (for example, 9.8 percent of professionals and managers as a group were uninsured versus 22 percent of workers in wholesale and retail, 35.7 percent in services, 40.7 percent in construction and 46.8 percent in agriculture), and within employment categories (3.2 percent of professionals and managers in public administration lacked insurance but 26.2 percent of those in agriculture were uninsured) (Kaiser Family Foundation, 2003).

While market-based health insurance reflects the confluence of national values and the political history of the USA, its cost is increasingly contrary to US business interests. Global competition with companies that do not have responsibility for the health care costs of active workers, their dependents, or their retirees exacerbates international cost disadvantages for US companies. Consequently, successive health insurance products have been a response to the shortcomings of prior products: from indemnity insurance to managed care, and now from managed care to high deductible health plans.

In a survey of employer cost concerns, 65 percent of large firms identifying benefits that were their greatest cost concerns ranked health insurance first, while salary was second most common (20 percent) (Kaiser Family Foundation, 2002). From the employee's perspective, health insurance was ranked the most important benefit by 60 percent of workers and the second most important by an additional 15 percent – substantially ahead of the next most important, a retirement savings plan (EBRI, 2004a).

Given the importance of employment-based health insurance, the critical challenge for employers has been how to align financial and quality incentives to control costs, provide needed services and discourage inappropriate or discretionary services. Indemnity insurance, also known as fee-for-service, permits the insured individual freedom of choice of providers and pays providers on the units and types of services provided. Indemnity

Table 7.2 *National health expenditures, USA 1970–2003: total, source of*
            payment and percentage of gross domestic product (GDP)

	1970 (%)	1980 (%)	1993 (%)	2003 (%)
Total	100.0	100.0	100.0	100.0
Consumer				
Out of pocket (OOP)	34.3	23.7	16.5	13.7
Private health insurance	21.2	27.7	33.6	35.8
Federal	24.1	29.0	30.9	32.3
State and local	13.7	13.6	13.1	13.3
NHE % GDP	7	8.8	13.3	15.3

Source: Smith et al. (2005).

insurance provided a financial buffer to the insured, but it provided incentives for greater utilization and led to unacceptably high-cost growth – patients and providers were generally insensitive to costs since all of the financial risk was borne by the insurance companies (Table 7.2).

Health care cost containment actions by employers during 1993–6 focused on channeling employees from fee-for-service indemnity plans into managed care plans, restricting choice – of provider and of drugs – and raising the amounts employees must share in the costs (Kuttner, 1999).

Managed care held the promise of restraining cost increases with an emphasis on primary care and fixed prospective payment (capitation) for a specified set of covered services. Capitation changed the incentive to provide more services by paying on the basis of plan membership rather than for services actually provided to patients. These actions briefly restrained costs, however, they have not been a long-term solution (Figure 7.1). The restrictions under managed care led to a patient backlash and more insurance products offering greater choice – but at a higher premium.

Private health insurance relies on premiums, procedures, exclusions, benefit design and patient cost-sharing collectively to influence the type and amount of medical services that are actually used. Through deductibles (the amount that the insured must pay before the insurance benefit applies), co-insurance (the percentage of a covered service that the insured must still pay out of pocket once the deductible has been met) and co-payments (fixed amounts that the insured must pay per unit of covered service), insurance benefits can elicit price sensitivity, even with indemnity insurance. These also directly lower the health plan's cost by the amount that is transferred directly to the patient. Therefore, the decision to provide coverage of bariatric services as a category is just the beginning – it is as important for insurers to determine the criteria that qualify a candidate for services and the cost that they must share. Cost-sharing arrangements can have far-reaching implications for the broader economy, as shown by a medical bankruptcy where '. . . many of the insured debtors blamed high co-payments and deductibles for their financial ruin' (Himmelstein et al., 2005).

To manage the relentless health care cost squeeze, employers are changing the health insurance options for their employees – emphasizing high deductible plans that require more substantial cost-sharing by employees. It is a difficult balance between cost management and retaining a strong, competitive workforce. Employers who passed premium increases on to their employees have experienced other problems – 44 percent of them who increased the amount that employees had to pay said in a 2002 survey that it had been 'somewhat' to 'much harder' to attract and to retain qualified workers, compared to 28 percent of those who did not increase employee payments (Kaiser Family Foundation, 2002). In a 2004 survey, only 10 percent of employers offered high deductible plans (20 percent of those with more than 500 employers) (Kaiser Family Foundation, 2004c) but this is expected to increase now that the IRS has provided tax incentives for such plans.

Asset-based insurance options such as Health Savings Accounts (HSAs) are now available to persons in high deductible health plans (those with a self-only deductible of not less than $1000 and family deductibles of not less than $2000) To encourage employees to be selective in demanding services and in their costs, unused amounts carry forward from year-to-year and the employee owns the HSA, retaining access to it even after leaving their employer (EBRI, 2004b).

THE RISE OF EMPLOYER COALITIONS

The growth of private health insurance and public benefit programs introduced powerful third parties into the patient–physician relationship: health services providers began to be paid more often by third parties than by the patients themselves. Hospital and physician services paid by insurance benefits rose quickly – from $992 million in 1950 to $2.5 billion in 1955, and to $3.88 billion in 1958 (Statistical Abstract of the United States, 1960). By 1970 individuals were still paying for more than a third of the National Health Expenditures (NHE) out of pocket, and paid 62 percent more than the NHE payments through private health insurance (Smith et al., 2005). By 2003 individual out-of-pocket payments had dropped to 13.7 percent of the total and were down to just 38 percent of private health insurance payments. These increases produced powerful, continuing demands for cost control both from government programs and from the private sector.

Through the creation of business coalitions, employers have sought more influence over the health care sector. These coalitions introduced fiscal discipline and restructured the perverse financial incentives in the market. The National Business Group on Health (NBGH), a coalition of coalitions, has an approximate membership of 90 employer coalitions, consisting of about 7000 companies (NBGH, 2005). Begun in 1974 as the Washington Business Group on Health, the National Business Group on Health (NBGH) is comprised of more than 220 large employers, representing over 45 million covered workers and their dependents. The NBGH's primary mission and main objectives are to support members in identifying business solutions for health benefits and to influence health policy.

Although logical, business coalitions throughout the 1980s were generally not effective in concentrating individual employers' purchasing power to influence health care costs and delivery, due to differences in the benefits offered, in union relations and in the terms of their contracts. The presence of health care providers, and drug and device manufacturers among coalition members further impeded the development of a consensus on the causes and preferred solutions to employee health care cost containment. High year-on-year health care cost increases (18.6 percent in 1988, 16.7 percent in 1989 and 17.1 percent in 1990) provided the incentive for employers to make their coalitions more powerful (Bodenheimer and Sullivan, 1998).

The California Public Employees Retirement System (CALPERS) was among the early health benefit providers to pressure insurers and health care providers to restrain cost increases. Using the strength of approximately one million members, CALPERS limited health care cost increases to 0.4 percent in 1993, 0.7 percent in 1994 and 5.4 percent in 1995 (Bodenheimer and Sullivan, 1998) – periods in which overall health insurance premium increases were 8.0 percent, 4.8 percent and 2.1 percent respectively (Strunk et al., 2002) The Pacific Business Group on Health, consisting of 11 companies representing about 300 000 employees, followed CALPERS' example and their 1995 Health Maintenance Organization (HMO) premiums were 9.2 percent *below* those of 1994 (Bodenheimer and Sullivan, 1998).

The Leapfrog group consists of more than 170 health care purchasers who pay approximately $67 billion for the health benefits of 36 million people across the USA. It was organized in 2000 to 'mobilize employer purchasing power to alert America's health industry that big leaps in health care safety, quality and customer value . . . [would] be recognized and rewarded'. Two of Leapfrog's key purchasing principles are: '1) educating and informing enrollees about the safety, quality and affordability of health care and the importance of comparing the care health providers give, and 2) recognizing and rewarding health care providers for major advances in the safety, quality and affordability of their care' (Leapfrog Group, 2005).

Over time a mixed model of personal, private and public financing for health expenditures emerged, though with significant gaps and exclusions, and with most private health insurance being linked to employment. Contrary to the health interest of employees and the financial interest of employers, services to prevent obesity, achieve weight loss and maintain weight once an excess has been lost have generally been categorical exclusions. It is ironic that the evolution of private health insurance and the concomitant efforts to control short-term costs have resulted in the sequelae of obesity being a more frequently covered benefit than obesity itself.

A Shift in Focus

Obesity added $272 per capita to health care spending in 1987; that is, $3.6 billion or 2 percent of total private insurance spending. This is an impressive amount but nothing close to the change owing to obesity by 2002: $1 244 per capita, equal to 11.6 percent of total private insurance spending, or $36.5 billion (Thorpe et al., 2004b) Health care expenditures, which have produced a resurgence in premium increases each year since 1996 (Figure 7.1), are concentrated in specific areas. An estimated 43–61 percent of the rise in private health insurance spending between 1987 and 2002 was due to 15 conditions and of these five accounted for 31 percent of it (Thorpe et al., 2004b) Obesity is associated with an increased relative risk for at least

Table 7.3   Per capita growth in health care spending and GDP (1998–2004)

	Hospital in-patient	Hospital out-patient	Physician	Prescription drugs	All services	GDP
Jan–Jun '98	(1.1)	7.9	4.0	13.1	4.6	4.1
Jul–Dec '98	0.8	7.2	5.5	15.0	5.9	4.1
Jan–Jun '99	1.9	10.4	6.4	17.2	7.6	4.6
Jul–Dec '99	1.3	9.9	3.7	19.5	6.6	4.9
Jan–Jun '00	3.1	8.1	6.0	15.3	7.1	5.4
Jul–Dec '00	5.1	11.5	6.6	13.7	8.4	4.1
Jan–Jun '01	7.9	15.1	6.2	15.3	9.9	2.5
Jul–Dec '01	9.5	14.1	7.1	12.4	10.0	1.7
Jan–Jun '02	9.3	12.6	5.9	13.0	9.3	2.1
Jul–Dec '02	7.3	13.4	7.4	13.4	9.8	2.9
Jan–Jun '03	6.0	11.7	5.7	8.5	7.6	3.0
Jul–Dec '03	6.4	10.5	5.4	9.6	7.6	4.8
Jan–Jun '04	5.1	11.4	5.7	8.8	7.5	5.9

Source: Center for Studying Health System Change (2004).

four of these high-cost conditions (diabetes, hypertension, heart disease and cancer).

The active promotion of wellness has been a recent innovation in employee benefits and employment-based health insurance. This approach is a transition from the employers' managing of health insurance benefit costs from the supply side, to promoting prevention and wellness that manages the demand for care (through a reduction in obesity-related diseases) as both productivity enhancers and as cost controls. To develop and disseminate evidence on the costs of obesity and effective strategies to address the condition, the NBGH established the Institute on the Costs and Health Effects of Obesity in 2003. The Institute's four main objectives are to:

1. Serve as a reliable source for large employers on the health and cost repercussion of obesity and related chronic conditions;
2. Provide employer tool kits to jumpstart efforts to offer employees health options and information;
3. Propose innovative solutions that large employers can implement to control costs related to obesity. This will include identifying effective strategies to decrease the incidence of obesity . . . among the US Workforce; and
4. Develop and disseminate clear messages stressing obesity's preventable nature as well as messages that communicate obesity as a health and well-being issue, as opposed to a cosmetic and beauty issue. (NGBH, 2005)

The Institute's *Guide to Starting a Weight-Management Program in Your Company* stresses both the positive impact on employee relations and that the results of such programs can be measured, that is, that there can be a business case for them. Since 2003 the Institute has convened an annual Obesity Summit to identify lessons learned and disseminate results from corporate members. It has also developed and made available to members an Obesity Cost Calculator – to assist them in identifying the extent of obesity-related costs in their own companies.

Recent increases in bariatric surgery expenditures are a resulting in greater emphasis on prevention and wellness programs, but also more restrictive criteria to qualify for the surgery. As of 30 November 2004, Blue Cross and Blue Shield of Alabama's guidelines for coverage determinations required both a medical record documentation of severe obesity for three years prior to the requested surgery and participation in a *physician monitored* weight loss program for at least the six months prior to the requested surgery (Velasco, 2005). Other Alabama insurers only cover bariatric surgery in products for self-insured employers who have elected to offer that coverage.

PUBLIC POLICIES

The absence of universal health insurance in the USA makes it critical that national health priorities, public policies and programs complement market-based private health insurance. The private sector strengths of innovation in health insurance options and programs, payment systems and efficiency complement the public sector's role as regulator, standard setter and enforcer. Through appropriate execution of these roles, public policies can be designed to address societal interests related to health insurance and to provide a safety net for those most in need.

Several types of public policies have influenced the existence and features of private health insurance. These policies address: federal-state jurisdictions over employer's health care insurance; market failure(s); incentives that rely on market mechanisms; and information asymmetries – between producers and consumers, and between patients and providers.

Federal versus state jurisdiction over health insurance as an employment benefit has been influenced most by a law originally intended to secure workers' pensions. The Employee Retirement Income Security Act (ERISA) of 1974 is a federal law that provided protections for employee benefits, established national standards (mainly for pensions) and created incentives for private employers to offer benefits voluntarily (USDOLa). ERISA established criteria that permits employers to self-insure and thus remove (pre-empt) themselves from state health coverage mandates. This was a small matter in 1974 when the law was passed, since few employers were self-insured. Subsequent expansion of the numbers of large, and then small, employers who self-insure for health insurance has made this opportunity to pre-empt state mandates a significant factor in employers' decisions.

However, mandates represent one policy response to market failure. Mandates only have the potential to rectify insurance product market failures if employers do not decide to drop the health insurance benefit altogether, or become self-insured and remove themselves from state regulatory oversight. Insurance products must be priced competitively and that may result in adverse selection if a product appeals to sicker-than-average members of the population. Consequently, health services for which there may be evidence both of need and effectiveness may not be available generally if the premiums for products that include them are priced based on attracting greater numbers of high use/high cost enrollees. Three major insurers (Florida BlueCross/BlueShield plans, Humana, and Cigna) are beginning to drop their coverage of gastric by-pass surgery (Larkin, 2004). As health insurers responded to market preferences for lower premiums by offering products that selectively excluded services or conditions, states perceived some of these as market failures and have sought to rectify the situation by mandating coverage of specific services and/or populations.

Mandates have ranged from mandatory inclusion (that is, requiring specific populations, services, providers or conditions be covered); to mandatory options that require policies to have those offered; to high-risk insurance pools for the medically uninsurable; and specific operational features of managed care plans, such as freedom of choice of providers and minimum lengths of inpatient stay for labor and delivery (Jensen and Morrisey, 1999).

Some states are moving to mandate insurance coverage for bariatric surgery. For example, Maryland and Virginia mandate coverage for techniques to treat obesity that are recognized by the NIH as being effective (Maryland Code and Virginia Code), and Indiana mandates coverage for non-experimental surgical treatment for obesity that has persisted for 5 years, and for which non-surgical treatment supervised by a doctor has been unsuccessful for at least 18 months (Indiana Code). Other state legislatures have considered laws that would mandate coverage under certain conditions, such as exceeding a specific BMI and having a physician attest to the medical necessity of the procedure for a specific person (Gillespie, 2005).

Another market failure arises as an artifact of employment-based health insurance: gaps in health insurance coverage can occur during employment changes. The Consolidated Omnibus Budget Reconciliation Act of 1986 (COBRA) was designed to assist workers who lost health insurance coverage due to termination, change of employment or other qualifying factors. COBRA permits continuation of coverage for up to18 months for employees whose insurance would otherwise have ended. This extension permits qualified beneficiaries (former employees and their dependents) to continue to obtain their insurance at the employer's group rate (USDOLb) While this policy appears to resolve a large gap in employment-based health insurance, it exposes the former employee paying the COBRA premium to larger out-of-pocket costs since the employer is no longer paying its substantial subsidization of the premium.

Incentives are an alternative to mandates and requirements. Through tax policy, the federal government subsidizes weight management efforts. Specifically, the IRS allows the costs associated with the treatment of obesity as a disease to be deducted as a medical expense for those who itemize deductions (IRS, 2003) Additionally, the IRS allows expenses associated with weight loss programs as a treatment for a specific disease (including obesity) to be treated as allowable medical expenses for the purposes of Health Savings Accounts, Archer Medical Savings Accounts, Medicare Advantage Medical Savings Accounts, Flexible Spending Arrangements and Health Reimbursement Accounts (IRS, 2004a). While the IRS allows taxpayers to deduct expenses paid for the 'diagnosis, cure, mitigation, treatment, or prevention of . . .' disease, some expenses for obesity prevention, such as health club dues and diet foods, are still not deductible (IRS, 2004b). The IRS's classification of obesity as a disease and the regulations specifying the types of weight loss services that would be deductible was an important development in acknowledging the medical appropriateness of treatment for a physician-diagnosed condition.

However, the federal government does recognize the importance of preventing obesity and starting with tax years beginning after 31 December 2003, a preventive care safe harbor was created that allows high deductible health plans to provide preventive care services, including weight loss treatment, without a deductible or with a deductible below the plan minimum (IRS, 2004b). High deductible health insurance plans with HSAs have the potential to do more harm than good. Such arrangements potentially segment the market between healthy and ill employees. If that occurs, then premiums for alternative types of insurance for the sick would quickly become more costly – and possibly unaffordable to those who need it the most.

Effectively functioning markets require full, or at least adequate, information to be available to consumers so that they can make an informed choice. The federal government has approached this need in two main ways' by developing nutrition recommendations and requiring content labels on foods.

Policies reflect the problems of the time in which they were adopted, and for different government agencies may also arise from their particular mandates; for example those of the US Department of Agriculture versus those of the Department of Health and Human Services – the former concerns the business of agriculture while the latter concerns the health of the public. The focus of the first half of the twentieth century concerned diseases arising from nutrient deficiency, followed for the next 30 years by policies to implement findings on nutrition's contribution to population health risks for hypertension and cardiovascular disease. The 'eat more' message became 'eat differently' and currently it is to 'eat less'; however, existing and transitional policies concerning agricultural production, processed and fast foods are not consistently linked to nutritional health, nor are they responding to these changes (Nestle, 2002).

Dietary Guidelines, begun under the US Department of Agriculture and Department of Health and Human Services in 1980, and has been updated in numerous subsequent editions. These *Guidelines* are based on the most credible evidence from nutrition research and translated for the lay public. The theme of these guidelines is that effective dietary guidance can support healthy choices and weight control as part of an overall active lifestyle. Their further clarification into hierarchies, for example, the *Food Guide Pyramid* (1992), may facilitate informed individual actions if the public is aware of and understands the hierarchies and how to apply them. For a more complete discussion regarding the inter-agency jurisdictional conflicts, the messages of 'eat less' versus 'moderate intake', and definitions of food groups and serving sizes, see Nestle (2002).

Medicare

The Great Society programs of the 1960s that amended the Social Security Act of 1935 reflected the structure of health insurance benefits at the time. While the Medicare and Medicaid programs created under these amendments fund the provision of treatment of disease, they have had minimal medical coverage of weight loss. The Medicare legislation is sufficiently vague, stating that Medicare will cover only services that are 'reasonable and necessary', and that specific coverage determinations have had to be made, reviewed and clarified since its inception.

Medicare is the nation's largest insurer, providing coverage for just over 41 million people in 2003 (CMS, 2003). Through an October 2004 ruling by the Secretary of the US Department of Health and Human Services, the statement 'obesity is not a disease' has been removed from the *National Coverage Determinations Manual*, clearing the path for obesity treatments to be considered for coverage under Medicare (CMS, 2004). The next step will be for doctors and companies to submit applications to the Centers for Medicare and Medicaid Services for approval of their treatments for obesity. An expert panel (the Medicare Coverage Advisory Committee – MCAC) reviewed the evidence relating to the efficacy and risks of each treatment. An expanded list of surgical treatments was determined to be efficacious and was approved for payment (CMS, 2006). Now that Medicare has expanded coverage of specific interventions for the prevention and treatment of obesity, it is likely that states and private insurers will eventually follow.

HEALTH PROMOTION AND WELLNESS

As an investment, wellness programs and weight management initiatives by employers can encourage employee retention and may increase participating employees' productivity. As an expense, wellness and weight management programs offer the prospect of cost offsets from reduced direct medical needs from some employees with type II diabetes, osteoarthritis and hypertension.

Health risk appraisals for early detection of risk factors and prevention are not new, but employers' use of them to integrate wellness and health promotion is a recent development. For example, St Joseph Occupational Health Services of Bryan, Texas performs an assessment that includes an 11-point Personal Wellness Profile that includes assessments of coronary risk, cancer risk, nutrition, fitness, stress/coping and substance use, to individualize interventions.

In the private sector, increased media coverage of weight gain and obesity has tapped into a consumer audience for information in a form that they can use for their own decisions. The scientific medical literature poses formidable barriers to a lay audience due to its methodology, jargon and apparently conflicting findings. Universities have taken on the roles of translator and disseminator of this literature and its implications for the general public, providing consumer health information through newsletters such as Tufts University's *Health and Nutrition Letter*, the *Harvard Health Newsletter* and Johns Hopkins's *Health After 50*. These publications offer individual subscriptions that provide consumer-oriented information on medical conditions, relevant research results, lifestyle, nutrition, cooking and advice columns in which a vetted expert responds to readers' questions.

As employers accept the connections among poor health, increased medical expenses and diminished productivity, they have become more creative in using the workplace and the health insurance benefit to provide inducements for behavioral change. Incentives for employee participation in weight management programs have included cost reimbursement, paid leave while attending the program, relevant reinforcing magazine subscriptions, recognition of successful employees, identification of role models, provision of healthy foods and portions for work-related consumption, gym memberships (full or partial support) and programs that meet IRS criteria for tax deductibility or pre-tax payment (for example, through Health Savings Accounts under high deductible health plans).

For example, Wellpoint Health Network and Destiny offer 'points' to employees for vaccinations, participation in exercise classes and consultation with a nurse health educator; these points are then redeemable for a range of products or services. A similar approach has been used by PacifiCare Health Systems – where the points may be used for discounts on care or as entry into a drawing for exercise equipment; Lumenos offers a $100 deposit to an employee's health account for completion of a health questionnaire; and others, such as Anthem, provide discounts for the Jenny Craig weight loss program (Bennett, 2003; Dubose, 2004).

Health plans and some employers have begun to focus specifically on weight loss. BlueCross/BlueShield insurance plans in South Carolina and Vermont, as well as the national Pep Boys chain, include a national weight loss program based on that program's geographic availability and that it customizes the plan for each individual enrollee (Berk, 2004).

These are the actions of innovators, not yet broadly disseminated. To enhance the spread of effective innovations, the NBGH sponsors the Annual Best Employers for Healthy Lifestyles Awards: 22 companies were recognized in 2005. Employer's initiatives vary in breadth (Baptist Health South Florida uses six domains in its program: physical, intellectual, emotional and spiritual, social, occupational and environmental), focus (IBM's Virtual Fitness Center reflects the central role of 'physical activity to help employees gain immediate benefits'; Occidental Oil and Gas Corporation's program stresses 'prevention and health risk reduction . . . [with employee] access to personal health coaching, . . . lifestyle programs via Internet and corporate intranet, individual and work site physical activity and wellness challenges . . . health and fitness recognition awards, . . . and participation incentives'), integration with other activities (for example, Union Pacific Railroad's Health Track is integrated into 'the Safety Programs, Operating Work Units, and Healthcare Benefits'), and incentives (NBGH, 2006).

Features of award-winning corporate initiatives include: emphasizing the cumulative impact of modest changes; online and in-person speakers; prizes that include a spa vacation or gym membership; Weight Watchers at Work meetings; healthy food options in vending machines and company cafeterias; step counting programs/pedometer gifts, and and on-site fitness centers.

Changing employee behavior poses a formidable challenge to employers. Of employees participating in a 2003 national survey, 25 percent reported that employers provided access to wellness programs. Only 9 percent of all employees participated in these programs, but of those who did participate 99 percent felt that the programs were 'somewhat' (55 percent) to 'very helpful' (44 percent) (Wall Street Journal Online/HarrisInteractive, 2003).

To leverage health benefits even more, some employers are linking changes in deductibles for health insurance to employee behaviors. For example, Benicomp, Inc. paired raising the annual employee deductible from $500 to $2500 with a $500 incentive for each of the following: healthy blood pressure, regular exercise, appropriate BMI and not smoking (Slater, 2003). The net impact of this arrangement is that employees could retain the full amount of the increased cost-sharing by adopting specific healthy behaviors.

DISCUSSION

Americans are now, on average, the fattest people in the world. The full consequences of this have yet to be experienced, both in declines in health and their potential cost consequences.

Investments in the infrastructure of scientific medicine continue to yield advances in the early detection and treatment of disease and its amelioration. Prevention, however, has had a less exalted role, resulting in an evidence base and a payment system that is tilted in favor of the treatment of disease rather than for avoiding the conditions. Access to medical services for prevention or treatment is strongly linked to insurance coverage and/or ability to pay. Bariatric treatment in particular has often been excluded as a covered insurance benefit due to its perceived cosmetic aspect, or due to prejudices that it is not a medical condition but a deficit of willpower or character. Preventive services have been infrequently covered under indemnity insurance – presumably due to their discretionary nature and utilization being less controllable by need or professionals.

Patients between 18 and 54 years of age accounted for 88 percent of bariatric surgeries in 2002 (Encinosa et al., 2005) – a critical fact for employers, legislators and regulators whose decisions will influence the trajectory of these vastly underused procedures. Recent evidence on the scope, scale and costs of excess weight has motivated employers to experiment with initiatives directed to wellness and prevention. As the source of health insurance for most of the working Americans and their dependents, employers are in a uniquely influential role. Whether they view health as an expense or as an investment, strategic design of health care benefits, employee cost-sharing and incentives are essential to avoid the productivity losses and work absences associated with obesity. Recent employee health insurance based on high deductible health plans and the implementation of Health Savings Accounts may discourage employees from making first-dollar expenditures, resulting in deferred attention to health conditions until they advance. For businesses with high deductible health plans, there needs to be sufficient evidence to designate obesity as a chronic condition excluded from having to meet the insured's deductible before the insurance coverage is activated.

Public policy has only recently begun to identify and to address the structural problems of community development, nutrition, inactivity and lifestyle as unintended contributors to the ubiquity of obesity in American life. As the provider of health benefits to 41 million Medicare beneficiaries, and party to Medicaid programs with similar enrollments, the federal government's program decisions can influence private insurance coverage and benefit design. Recently Medicare and IRS decisions provided precedent and incentives for private employers to become engaged in obesity treatment and prevention.

Employers are experiencing a world of global competition and relentless pressures on costs and efficiency. Consequently, as a group they are demanding evidence of the cost-effectiveness, safety and long-term impacts of the bariatric health care they purchase on behalf of their employees. Prevention and wellness programs are, however, becoming widespread and may become the foundation of the private sector's strategy for addressing obesity in American workers and their dependents. These initiatives transcend the medical expense line item and are a strategic, broader investment in their workforce for productivity gains as well as future cost avoidance.

NOTES

* Reprinted with permission of the Center for Studying Health System Change, Washington, DC. www.hschange.org.
1. The National Institutes of Health (NIH) Consensus Development Program convenes independent leading experts, who are neither advocates nor federal employees, to assess the evidence concerning a controversial issue in medical practice (NIH Consensus Program, 2005).

REFERENCES

American Obesity Association (AOA) (2005), *AOA Fact Sheets,* accessed at www.obsity.org/subs/fastfacts/Obesity_Consumer_Protect.shtml.
Anderson, J.W., S. Vichitbandra, W. Qian and R.J. Kryscio (1999), 'Long-term weight maintenance after an intensive weight-loss program', *Journal of the American College of Nutrition,* **18** (6), 620–7.
Bennett, J. (2003), 'HMOs try "frequent jogger points"', *Wall Street Journal,* 25 September.
Berk, CC. (2004), 'Jenny Craig teams with firms, insurers on workers' diet plans', *Wall Street Journal,* 6 October.
Bodenheimer, T. and K. Sullivan (1998),'How large employers are shaping the health care market, *New England Journal of Medicine,* Part 1, **338** (14), 1003–7, Part 2, **338** (15), 1084–7.
Boston Business Journal, (2004), 'Health club,, memberships, sales grew, in 2003', accessed 15 April at http://boston.bizjournals.com/boston/stories/2004/04/12/daily40.html.
Center for Studying Health System Change (2004), 'Tracking health care costs', issue brief no. 91, accessed at: http://www.hschange.org/CONTENT/721/.
CMS (Centers for Medicare and Medicaid Services) (2003), 'Medicare beneficiaries enrolled by state as of July 1, 1999–2003', accessed at www.cms.hhs.gov/statistics/enrollment/stenrtrend99_03.asp.
CMS (2004a), 'Treatment of obesity MM3502', accessed 1 October at www.cms.hhs.gov/medlearn/matters/mmarticles/2004/MM3502.pdf.

CMS (2004b), 'Health savings accounts and other account-based health plans'. Issue brief # 273, accessed September at www.ebri.org/publications/ib/index. cfm?fa=ibDisp&content_id=3504.

CMS (2006), 'Medicare expands national coverage for bariatric surgery procedures', accessed at www.cms.hhs.gov/apps/media/press/release.asp?Counter=1786.

Dubose, J. (2004), 'HealthLeaders research: reviews mixed for consumer-driven plans', accessed 7 January at www.healthleaders.com/news/print.php?contentid= 51398.

EBRI (Employee Benefits Research Institute) (2004a), 'Public attitudes on the US health care system: findings from the health confidence survey', EBRI Issue brief # 275,: accessed November at www.ebri.org/pdf/briefspdf/1104ib3.pdf.

Encinosa, W.E., D.M. Bernard, C.A. Steiner and C.C. Chen (2005), 'Use and costs of bariatric surgery and prescription weight-loss medications', *Health Affairs*, **24** (4), 1039–46.

Finkelstein, E.A., I.C. Fiebelkorn and G. Wang (2003), 'National medical spending attributable to overweight and obesity: how much and who's paying?', *Health Affairs Web Exclusive*, W3-219-226.

Gillespie, N. (2005), 'States consider obesity surgery coverage', *WJLA News*, accessed 22 March at www.wjla.com/news/stories/0305/215302.html.

Himmelstein, D.U., E. Warren, D. Thorne and S. Woolhandler (2005), 'Illness and injury as contributors to bankruptcy', *Health Affairs Web Exclusive*, W5-63–W5-73.

Indiana Code. I.C 27-27-8-14. 1-4. IN STATE 27 – 8 – 14. 1-4

Internal Revenue Service (IRS) (2003), 'Medical and dental expenses (including the health coverage tax credit) for use in preparing 2003 returns', Publication 502, Department of the Treasury. Accessed on 4 March 2004.

IRS (2004a), 'Health savings accounts and other tax-favored health plans', Publication 969, www.irs.gov/pub/irs-pdf/p 969.pdf.

IRS (2004b), 'Internal revenue bulletin no. 2004–15, www.irs.gov/pub/irs-irbs/ irb04-15.pdf.

IRS (2004c), Medical and Dental Expenses (Including the Health Coverage Tax Credit) for use in Preparing 2003 Returns, Publication 502, Section 213 (d) (1), Department of the Treasury, accessed 4 March, 2004, on line.

Jensen, G.A. and M.A. Morrisey (1999), 'Employer-sponsored health insurance and mandated benefit laws', *The Milbank Quarterly*, **77** (4), 425–59.

Kaiser Family Foundation (2002), 'Employer health benefits 2002 annual survey', www.kff.org.

Kaiser Family Foundation (2003), 'Health insurance coverage in America 2003. Data Update', www.kff.org, November 2004. (Table 12: Characteristics of Uninsured Workers, 2003).

Kaiser Family Foundation (2004a), 'The uninsured: a primer', www.kff.org, November.

Kaiser Family Foundation (2004b) 'Employer-sponsored health insurance coverage: sponsorship, eligibility, and participation patterns in 2001', www.kff.org, July.

Kaiser Family Foundation (2004c), 'Employer health benefits 2004 annual survey', www.kff.org.

Korner, J. and L.J. Aroune (2004), 'Pharmacological approaches to weight reduction: therapeutic targets', *Journal of Clinical Endocrinology and Metabolism*, **89** (6), 2616–21.

Kuttner, R. (1999), 'The American health care system: employer-sponsored health coverage', *New England Journal of Medicine*, **340** (3), 248–52.

Larkin, H. (2004), 'Insurance bypass', *Hospitals and Health Networks*. **78** (8), 22, accessed 10 August, 2005, at www.hhnmag.com/hhnmag/hospitalconnect/ search/article.jsp?dcrpath=HHNMAG/PubsNewsArticle/data/0408HHN_ Inbox_ Payment&domain=HHNMAG.

Leapfrog Group (2005), 'Fact sheet: The Leapfrog Group', accessed 31 January, 2006 at www.leapfroggroup.org/media/file/LF_FactSheet_052605.pdf.

Maryland Code, Insurance Section 15-839

National Business Coalition on Health (NBCH) (2005), 'More about NBCH', accessed at www.nbch.org/more.cfm.

National Business Group on Health (NBGH) (2005), 'About the Institute on the costs and health effects of obesity', accessed at www.wbgh.org/healthy/about.cfm.

NBGH (2006), 'Best employer awards', accessed 28 July at www:businessgrouphealth .org/healthyawards.htm.

National Center for Health Statistics (NCHS) (2004), 'Health, United States, 2004. With chartbook on trends in the health of Americans', accessed at www.cdc. gov/nchs/data/hus/hus04trend.pdf#027, Hyattsville, MD.

National Heart Lung Blood Institute (NHLBI) Obesity Education Initiative (2000), 'The practical guide: identification, evaluation, and treatment of over-weight and obesity in adults', NIH Publication Number 00-4084, October, accessed at www.nhlbi.nik.gov/guidelines/obesity/prctgd_b.pdf.

Nestle, M. (2002), *Food Politics: How the Food Industry Influences Nutrition and Health*, Berkley and Los Angeles, CA: University of California Press.

National Institutes of Health (NIH) (2005), Consensus Development Program, accessed 28 July at http://consensus.nih.gov/ABOUTCDP.htm.

NIH Consensus Development Program, 'Health implications of obesity', NIH Consensus Statement Online 1985 Feb 11–13 [cited year, month, day]; **5** (9), 1–7, accessed 31 January, 2006, at http://consensus.nih.gov/1985/1985Obesity049 html.htm.

Olshansky, S.J., D.J. Passaro, R.C. Hershow, J. Layden, B.A. Carnes, J. Brody, L. Hayflick, R.N. Butler, D.B. Allison and D.S. Ludwig (2005), 'A potential decline in life expectancy in the United States in the 21st century', *New England Journal of Medicine*, **352** (11), 1138–45.

Slater, S. (2003), 'New health plan rounds into shape: coverage rewards wellness', *The Journal Gazette*, accessed 1 September at www.benicompadvantage.com/ 2003_09_05_new_health_plan.htm.

Smith, C., C. Cowan, A. Sensenig, A. Catlin and the Health Accounts Team (2005), 'Trends: health care spending slows in 2003'. *Health Affairs*, **24** (1), 185–94.

Strunk, B.C., P.B. Ginsburg and J.R. Gabel (2002), Tracking health care costs: growth accelerates again in 2001', *Health Affairs Web Exclusive*, W299–W310.

Sturm, R. (2002), 'The effects of obesity, smoking, and drinking on medical prob-lems and costs', *Health Affairs*, **21** (2), 245–53.

Taylor, H. (2003), 'Large decline since 1995 in favorite activities which require physical exercise', *The Harris Bulletin*, (72) (1, December), accessed at www. harrisinteractive.com/harris_poll/index.asp?PID=421.

Thorpe, K., C.S. Florence, D.H. Howard and P. Joski (2004a), 'The impact of obesity on rising medical spending', *Health Affairs Web Exclusive*, W4-480–W4-486.

Thorpe, K., C.S. Florence and P. Joski (2004b), 'Which medical conditions account for the rise in medical spending?', *Health Affairs Web Exclusive*, W4-437–W4-445.

Tillotson, J.E. (2004), 'America's obesity: conflicting public policies, industrial economic development, and unintended human consequences', *Annual Review of Nutrition*, 24, 617–43.

US Census (2003), 'Health insurance historical tables: table HI-4 1987-2003', accessed at www.census.gov/hhes/www/hlthins/historic/hihistt4.html.

US Department of Commerce (USDOC) (1950), 'Statistical abstract of the United States. Table 500 mutual, accident and sick benefit associations – financial condition and business transacted: 1901–1948', Washington, DC: US Department of Commerce, accessed at www2.census.gov/prod2/statcomp/documents/1950-06.pdf.

USDOC (1960), 'Statistical abstract of the United States, table 80 private expenditures for medical care and voluntary health insurance: 1950– 1958', accessed at www2.census.gov/prod2/statcomp/documents/1960-02.pdf.

US Department of Health and Human Services (USDHHS) (2000a), *Healthy People 2010: Understanding and Improving Health,* 2nd edn, Washington, DC: US Government Printing Office, accessed at, www.healthypeople.gov/Document/tableofcontents.htm#under.

USDHHS (2000b), 'Healthy people 2010: What are leading health indicators?', accessed 28 July 2006 at, www.healthypeople.gov/LHI/lhiwhat.htm.

USDHHS (2001), 'The Surgeon General's call to action to prevent and decrease overweight and obesity', Rockville, MD: US Public Health Service, Office of the Surgeon General, accessed at www.surgeongeneral.gov/topics/obesity/calltoaction/CalltoAction.pdf.

USDHHS (2006), Data 2010, accessed at http://wonder.cdc.gov/data2010/.

USDHHS (2006), 'Data 2010 . . . the healty people 2010 database', updated June 2006, accessed 28 July 2006 at www.cdc.gov/data2010/obj.htm.

USDHHS (unknown), 'What Are the leading Health Indicators?'.

US Department of Labor (USDOL) (2005a), 'Health plans and benefits: employee retirement income security Act – ERISA', accessed 22 June at www.dol.gov/dol/topic/health-plans/erisa.htm.

USDOL (2005b), 'Employee benefits security administration: COBRA continuation health coverage frequently asked questions, accessed 22 June at www.dol.gov/ebsa/faqs/faq_consumer_cobra.html.

Velasco, A. (2005), 'Insurer limits obesity surgery: rules may mean longer waits for Blue Cross patients', *Birmingham News*, 12 January.

Virginia Code. VA Code Annotated, section 38.2 – 3418.13

Wall Street Journal Online/Harris Interactive Health-Care Poll (2003), 'Only 9% of employees participate in corporate wellness programs', 2 (10), accessed at www.harrisinteractive.com/news/newsletters/wsjhealthnews/WSJOnline_HIHealth-CarePoll2003vol2_iss 10.pdf.

Zhaoping, L., M. Maglione, W. Tu, W. Mojica, D. Arterburn, L.R. Shugarman, L. Milton, M. Suttorp, V. Solomon, P.G. Shekelle and S.C. Movaton (2005), 'Meta-analysis: pharmacologic treatment of obesity', *Annals of Internal Medicine*, 142 (7), 532–46.

PART IV

Obesity and government

8. The infrastructure of obesity

Zoltan J. Acs, Ann Cotten, Kenneth R. Stanton[1]

INTRODUCTION

The accelerating growth rate in obesity prevalence appears very unlikely to slow on its own. Our review of the evidence and surrounding literature suggests that the increase is driven by an infrastructure of obesity that is firmly established, especially in the USA. This infrastructure includes an oversupply in the production of food, an increased supply of processed food, a growing fast food industry and an increasing reliance on urban sprawl. In tandem with the growing supply of cheap foods, marketers have devised increasingly persuasive strategies to encourage greater consumption. They have intensified their advertising of predominantly unhealthy foods and beverages through traditional media, with a noticeably heavy focus on reaching children. However, of greater concern are the strategies of placing soda and snack vending machines in schools. These strategies are very successful in cultivating lifelong habits of shifting to unhealthy diet choices. It is not that this danger is unrecognized but, in many cases, the contracts are sufficiently lucrative for the schools themselves that school administrators strongly resist any suggestions to remove vending machines and other sources of unhealthy foods.

We do not rule out the possibility that the growth rate in obesity prevalence could accelerate even further, nor do we deny that the adoption of healthier lifestyles or other factors could eventually slow the rate. However, the prospect seems unlikely given the scale of the obesity-conducive infrastructure that encourages greater supply, greater consumption and lower energy outputs.

The trend in obesity prevalence over the past few decades is not encouraging. Under the assumption that the growth trends remain relatively stable for the near future, our estimates of the expected prevalence rates and associated costs indicate that the obesity problem warrants prompt attention from policymakers. Unless there is a concerted effort to dismantle the infrastructure, individual efforts to adopt healthier eating and exercise combinations are essentially doomed to fail.

There is considerable urgency for addressing obesity. It is not enough simply to increase awareness of the infrastructure but active steps must be taken to counteract it, or better still, to unravel it. In this vein, there are two primary public policy approaches to impeding the problem: controlling the demand, or controlling the supply. A demand-side policy alters the usage of the product. So far, demand-side approaches to reducing the demand for obesity-conducive activities and products have been favored. Such policies include education, labeling, advertising and taxing products.

By contrast, the second public policy approach focuses on the supply side. Supply-side policies affect the availability of the product. These policies directly restrict supply, or raise the cost of supplying products or activities. In the USA supply-side policies for public protection have generally been avoided and only used when everything else seems to fail. In truth, the current supply-side policies, such as the subsidies extended through the Department of Agriculture and various state-level programs, are structured to have the net effect of encouraging rather than discouraging food production. These subsidies are aspects of the existing infrastructure that must be reversed and state governments have a role in implementing restrictions on the supply.

One of the most compelling examples of the use of restrictive supply-side policy has been the campaign against tobacco. While numerous demand-side policies were undertaken to reduce consumer tastes and preferences for smoking cigarettes, the urgency and severity of the problem triggered a mandate for supply-side policies. It is our view that while the problem is different – the ban on workplace smoking has no obvious counterpart – the similarities are sufficient to warrant a policy shift from demand-side to supply-side policies. The obesity problem is similar to tobacco on several counts. First, both smoking and overeating are linked to serious diseases. Second, both involve changes in body chemistry and in habitual behavior that are difficult to change. Smokers have low rates of success in quitting; likewise, those who are overweight have trouble maintaining an improved diet and exercise regimen. Finally, the effects of individuals' smoking and obesity add to society's medical costs.

In the remainder of this chapter, we will present a simple model of the infrastructure of obesity and document the cost of not addressing the obesity problem, with projections of future obesity rates and associated health care costs. The analysis of the scope of the problem will be followed by an in-depth analysis of public policy prescriptions considered by state legislatures in their attempt to stem the obesity crisis. The chapter will conclude with our recommendations for how the public sector can address these issues.

THE INFRASTRUCTURE OF OBESITY

Many factors have been blamed for the increase in obesity including infrastructure, changing societal patterns, food availability and changes in individual behavior patterns. It is likely that the current problem is the combined result of several of these. When faced with a variety of potential causes for the obesity problem, an important first step is to identify those underlying causes that are the most significant contributors to the problem and are most likely to yield immediate or near-term results when addressed.

At the most elementary level, excess body weight results from individuals consuming more calories than they are expending. On the consumption side, about 10 percent of the energy typically provided by the food consumed is expended in its digestion. Another fraction of that food energy is utilized to keep organs operating and to sustain life functions. That fraction, the basal metabolic rate (BMR) is directly related to body weight. Stated in algebraic terms,

$$BMR = \alpha + \beta W \tag{1}$$

where W is body weight in kilograms. Evidence indicates that the coefficients in this equation are gender specific. Schofield et al. (1985) estimate that α equals 879 for men and 829 for women. Their estimates for β are 11.6 and 8.7, for men and women respectively. The energy that remains after accounting for the energy lost in digestion or maintaining basic bodily functions is available to generate output, or, if not utilized, adds to body weight. On the output side, the amount of energy expended can be stated as

$$ENERGY = \lambda WT \tag{2}$$

where (λ depends on the type of activity, W is the weight in kilograms and T is the amount of time spent in that activity.

It is understood that the excess weight problem is the result of a downward trend in the amount of energy expended through work or leisure, and/or an upward trend in caloric intake. As we indicated above, any corrective actions should be focused on the most influential causes first. That means that we must answer the following questions. Is the weight problem caused primarily by less energy output, as a consequence of the shift toward more sedentary lifestyles? Or is the dominant cause on the input side, as a result of consuming more energy than the human body requires? One piece of evidence that may narrow our search for an answer is that obesity prevalence appears to have jumped upward near the start of the

1980s. A satisfactory theory of the causes of increased obesity ought to explain not just the overall increase, but also the time path of the increase.

Most would agree that there has been a shift away from physical lifestyles, with manual labor-intensive work, to more sedentary lifestyles. However, this does not explain the timing of the increase in obesity and pre-obesity. According to Philipson and Posner (1999), energy output among residents of the USA has not changed much since the 1980s. This evidence points more heavily toward increased caloric intake as the explanation. As documented later in this chapter, caloric intake has increased dramatically and has far surpassed what would be possible to counter by exercising or choosing more physically demanding work. Additionally, the reductions in the cost of producing food due to technological improvements in combination with reductions in the amount of time required to prepare and consume food, are primary explanations for the weight problem (Philipson and Posner, 1999).

As we would expect, a reduction in the price of any good, including food, leads to a greater quantity demanded. Food consumption has increased markedly over the past two decades, and on the supply side improvements in food production technology have greatly reduced the costs of production (Philipson and Posner, 1999). A key reason for this can be found in policy changes of the early 1970s. Responding to commodity price increases, President Richard Nixon ordered his Secretary of Agriculture, Earl Butz, to do whatever was necessary to drive down agricultural commodity prices. The policy of providing forgivable loans to farmers, which allowed them to keep their grain off the market when prices were low, was discontinued and replaced with a system of subsidies (Hannich 2003).[2] Not surprisingly, the result was an increase in the supply of grain.

The US Department of Agriculture constructed estimates of caloric intake for the 1909 to 1999 period. For most of the period, the number of kilocalories consumed per person per day remained quite stable. However, there has been a very noticeable upswing in caloric intake since the late 1970s. During the 1950s and 1960s, the value was in the range of 3200 to 3300 kilocalories per day, but by 1999 it had increased to the 3700 mark. By itself, this creates a significant problem because the additional 300 to 400 kilocalories cannot be easily expended by more strenuous work (USDA, 2000).

Exploring the changes in the types of foods consumed reveals another important aspect of the increase in caloric intake. Whole foods (foods that return a higher proportion of value to the farmer) such as vegetables, fruits and whole grains have come to represent a smaller proportion of calories consumed, while products that are more highly processed (foods that return a lower proportion of value to the farmer) have increased in terms of caloric intake. Similar conclusions are supported by Table 8.1, which shows the distribution of calories by meal and location. Where people eat may

Table 8.1   Caloric intake by meal and location

Meal	Location	Men			Women		
		1977–8	1994–6	Change	1977–8	1994–6	Change
Breakfast	Home	350	328	−22	271	260	−11
	Store	3	14	11	0	7	7
	Restaurant	13	26	13	4	13	9
	Fast food	5	26	21	2	12	10
	School/Work	8	14	6	5	11	6
	Other	*6*	*12*	*6*	*4*	*10*	*6*
	Total	385	420	35	286	313	27
Lunch	Home	331	296	−35	258	239	−19
	Store	5	26	21	2	10	8
	Restaurant	45	51	6	23	36	13
	Fast food	30	103	73	18	46	28
	School/Work	78	61	−17	52	40	−12
	Other	*28*	*30*	*2*	*14*	*26*	*12*
	Total	517	567	50	367	397	30
Dinner	Home	800	630	−170	597	451	−146
	Store	0	15	15	0	9	9
	Restaurant	48	88	40	29	61	32
	Fast food	21	60	39	13	33	20
	School/Work	10	10	0	5	7	2
	Other	*40*	*56*	*16*	*31*	*40*	*9*
	Total	919	859	−60	675	601	−74
Snacks	Home	199	358	159	146	258	112
	Store	7	38	31	5	19	14
	Restaurant	7	27	20	4	11	7
	Fast food	10	18	8	5	11	6
	School/Work	16	19	3	9	14	5
	Other	*22*	*41*	*19*	*17*	*32*	*15*
	Total	261	501	240	186	345	159
Grand Total		2082	2347	265	1514	1656	142

Source: Continuing survey of food intake, US Department of Agriculture.

also play an important role in the obesity epidemic. The pattern is one of an overall increase in calories per day from the late 1970s to the mid-1990s – an increase of 268 for men and 145 for women – even though the calories consumed in the home at dinnertime have been greatly reduced.

The most notable increase in calories appears as snacks, with snacks consumed in the home almost fully offsetting the reduction in calories obtained from dinners at home. Men increased their intake of snacks by 240 calories, 159 of which are comprised of snacks in the home. Women followed with a snack increase of 159 calories with 112 calories from snacks at home.

Increases in calories derived from fast food also show substantial increases, especially for men. Considering only lunch and dinner, men increased their fast food intake by 112 calories. The comparable increase for women was 48 calories. Increases in the production levels of high-fructose corn syrup closely match the time path of the changes in body weight measures. The overall image from this is that more highly processed foods are providing a larger share of our growing caloric intake (Naik and Moore 1996).[3]

The relative prices of leisure and food consumption, that result in changes in lifestyle choices, are also important factors affecting demand. In particular, the value that Americans place on their time has increased, especially for women. Chou et al. (2003) explain that the price changes have caused people to work more, spend less time at home, and to shift away from home-prepared meals to foods that require less preparation time. These changes have been accompanied by an increase in the availability of fast food and other restaurant-prepared meals, at generally lower prices. Their regression analyses of the factors affecting obesity, pre-obesity and BMI – which controlled for gender, race, income level, marital status and age – incorporated explanatory variables such as indicators of the availability and prices for fast food and full service restaurants, and the price of food prepared at home. Although the pattern of increase in the per capita numbers of restaurants is positively correlated with increases in obesity, pre-obesity and increases in BMI, the direction of causality is not resolved by their study.

The increase in the number of restaurants, both fast food and full service, may be driven by the increased demand for their products, rather than the increased supply of restaurants causing the weight problem. Consumers – perhaps to a greater extent in the USA than elsewhere – face a continuous barrage of marketing tricks to encourage excess consumption of unhealthy foods.[4] Not only have fast food restaurants dramatically increased in number, especially in areas close to schools (Austin et al., 2005), but strategies to encourage purchases of junk food have also intensified. The placement of candies, snacks and soda at every checkout counter and the increased availability of unneeded food, even at non-traditional locations for food purchase such as gasoline stations, is strikingly noticeable.

Combining the results of these studies provides some important insights. The trend of reduced food production costs is likely to continue, which encourages increased supply of food in general and more highly processed food in particular. More processed foods have a tendency to be less healthy overall. As the price of less healthy food falls, consumption is likely to increase. This is supported by the US Department of Agriculture's consumption data that show that processed foods are rapidly gaining ground.

One conclusion that can be reached is that the increase in the rate of obesity over the past 20 years has been mostly caused by increased caloric intake rather than reduced caloric expenditure (Cutler et al., 2003). While we cannot be certain that this explanation is right or that it is the entire explanation for the rise in obesity, it is the most plausible given trends in obesity rates.

This caloric increase is today supported by an infrastructure of obesity.[5] The infrastructure is the result of recent investment in the agricultural, food processing, food distribution and food preparation industries that supports the shift to increased caloric intake. The huge investment in food processing cannot easily be reversed, and indeed is increasing. To give an indication of the value of the infrastructure, the total market capitalization of eight drug manufacturing, food processing and marketing companies exceeded $530 billion in 2003 (Brown, 2003). Therefore, reducing the rate of increase in obesity will be very difficult, if not impossible, given the inertia of the current infrastructure.

At the individual level, if any part of the explanation lies in personal failures to make appropriate lifestyle choices, then the situation is more likely to become worse than it currently is. Basically, if the price of eating falls and self-control is not adequate, then excess consumption resulting in increased body weight is the outcome. Unless the current situation is significantly altered we can expect people to eat more of the types of food that increase their weight, resulting in greater prevalence of associated health risks. Increasing exercise, although helpful, will not by itself eliminate the upward trend in body weight measures if the current rate of increase in caloric intake is not slowed. Therefore, the case we have tried to make in this section is that the infrastructure of obesity fuels the epidemic and the prevalence of obesity continues to increase in the USA and around the world (Flegal et al., 2002).

FUTURE TRENDS

Many would agree that obesity has achieved epidemic proportions. But it is important to evaluate how much worse the problem is likely to become. Assuming current growth rates continue, we make here simple projections to forecast obesity prevalence and the level of medical expenditure that is likely to result. Data from the National Health Examination Survey (NHES) and the series of National Health and Nutrition Examination Surveys (NHANES) form the basis of our projections. Table 8.2 shows the

Table 8.2   Prevalence of obesity and overweight among adults in the USA, aged 20–74 years

Study	Time period	% Obese (BMI ≥ 30)	% Overweight (BMI ≥ 25)
NHES I[a]	1960–1962	13.5	45.2
NHANES I[b]	1971–1974	14.4	47.0
NHANES II[b]	1976–1980	14.7	46.4
NHANES III[b]	1988–1994	22.7	55.0
NHANES IV[b]	1999–2000	30.8	64.3

Notes:
a. National Health Examination Survey (NHES).
b. National Health and Nutrition Examination Survey (NHANES).

Source: Centers for Disease Control and Prevention, National Center for Health Statistics, www.cdc.gov/nchs/about/major/nhanes/datalink.htm.

obesity and pre-obesity prevalence measures for adults in the USA of 20 to 74 years of age, for the 1960–2000 period. There is very little change in prevalence from the initial NHES measures in 1960 to the NHANES II survey in 1980. However, for the 22-year period from 1978 (the mid-year of NHANES II) to 2000 (the end year of NHANES IV), the number of pre-obese people grew by 45 percent and the number of obese grew by 120 percent. During this time the average BMI rose by 1.24 kg/m^2, or by 5 percent. This represents a 6 lb gain for the average adult.

The change since 1978 is important because there is an inverse relationship between BMI and strenuous work (Philipson, 2001). As society shifted from agricultural work to industry and then to services, one would expect that BMI would rise as work entailed less exercise. However, this sheds little light on the trend between NHANES II and NHANES IV when the job strenuousness measure was very stable.

The NHANES data were collected through actual measurement and are consequently less likely to be biased than self-reported data. However, they provide very few observations for analysis. Thus, we have also used the self-reported survey data provided by the Center for Disease Control's (CDC's) Behavioral Risk Factor Surveillance System (BRFSS). All states were not always represented in the BRFSS data, but reliable data have been available since 1990. The BRFSS data are taken from the CDC Trend Data Display, employing the median values of state-by-state measures of the prevalence of obesity and pre-obesity for adults 18 years of age and older. Adding these observations to the NHANES data yields 18 observations. Because the BRFSS data are self reported, and the NHANES data survey adults aged 20–74, they are not directly comparable. However, if we assume that any structural differences or self-reporting biases remain relatively stable over time, the time series properties of the BRFSS data are likely to mirror any trend in the overall population.[6]

As expected, the BRFSS obesity prevalence estimates are lower than NHANES estimates. While this could be expected from the inclusion of 18- and 19-year-olds, the differences may also be largely due to self-reporting biases. On the other hand, the pre-obesity prevalence estimates of the BRFSS data appear to be slightly higher than comparable NHANES measures. Taken together, this indicates that people who are actually obese, may misrepresent themselves as lighter or taller in a telephone interview.

Forecasts of obesity prevalence are derived from a simple time-series model, estimated over the 18 observations

$$Obesity\ rate = 3.02098 + 10.6661\ d - 0.17293\ time$$
$$(0.0001)\quad (4.8E-15)(0.0008)$$
$$+\ 0.01509\ time^2$$
$$(4.12E-11) \tag{3}$$

where d is a dummy variable that is set at 0 for observations taken from the BRFSS data and 1 for NHANES data. All of the parameter estimates are highly significant with all p-values (shown in parentheses) smaller than 10^{-3} and an adjusted R-squared of 0.99. Although the coefficient on the first-order time variable is negative, its effect is rapidly dissipated by the positive sign on the quadratic ($time^2$) component.

Since the NHANES data are more reliable, our fitted line was created under that assumption. We set the dummy variable to 1 to create our predicted obesity rates as an extension to the NHANES observations. Figure 8.1 shows the fitted curve and the observed values from the NHANES and BRFSS studies for the period 1960–2002. The model fits the NHANES data quite closely, and in keeping with our assumption, the self-reporting bias in the BRFSS data is stable over time.

The forecasts from the obesity regression are shown in Figure 8.2. If the model reflects the future as well as it represents the existing data, then more than 51 percent of the population will be obese by the year 2016. This is a startling prediction. In the short term, obesity prevalence of well over 40 percent within the next five years is plausible.[7]

Given the magnitude of the percentages, one might be inclined to treat these projections with skepticism. However, there are subsets of the population that have already neared these levels. For example, NHANES (III) data show obesity rates of 36.5 percent for non-Hispanic Black women and 33.3 percent for Mexican American women. Similarly, the rates of

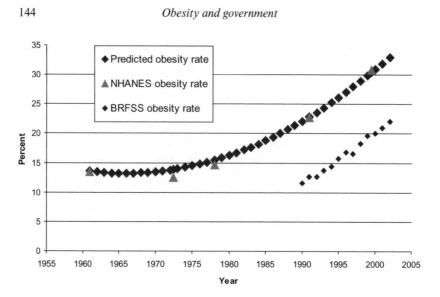

*Figure 8.1   Predicted and observed obesity prevalence in the USA,
1960–2002*

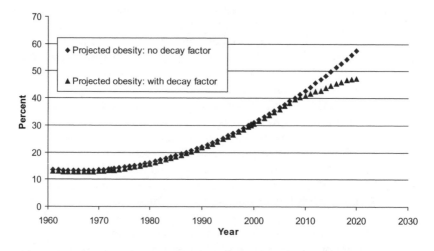

Figure 8.2   Projected obesity prevalence rates in the USA, 1960–2020

combined pre-obesity and obesity among non-Hispanic Black women, and
Mexican-American women were 77.3 percent and 71.9 percent respectively.

To further illustrate the increasing seriousness of the problem we
have plotted the ratio of obesity prevalence relative to the prevalence of
overweight (pre-obesity and obesity combined). From the 1960s until about

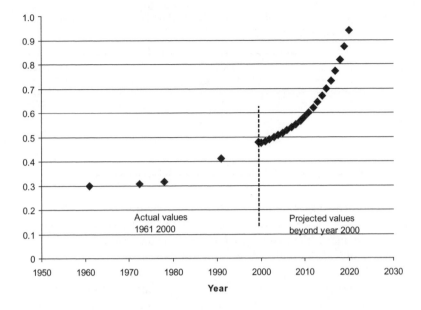

Figure 8.3   Ratio of obese to all overweight: obese/(preobese + obese)

1978, only about 30 percent of all individuals who had BMIs in excess of 25 were obese. By the year 2000, 48 percent of the people who exceeded the BMI cut-off point of 25 were obese. What this is telling us is that not only are the numbers of people with excess weight increasing, but the severity of the excess weight is increasing as well. As shown in Figure 8.3, if the current trends continue, the ratio will exceed 73 percent by 2016.[8]

It will no longer be relevant to debate whether being a few pounds over-weight is associated with significant health risk increases if the obese greatly outnumber those with BMIs between 25 and 30. The important point to be made is that this shift toward higher BMIs will undoubtedly increase the incidence of weight-related health effects and associated costs. Furthermore, this will be accompanied by a far higher rate of morbid obesity (associated with a BMI of 40 or greater), which dramatically reduces life expectancy and increases health care costs.

In order to estimate the expected costs, we merged our prevalence esti-mates and the Census Bureau's population projections to arrive at the numbers expected to be obese and pre-obese. Finkelstein et al. (2003) esti-mated that the incremental health care costs for obese and pre-obese indi-viduals were $732 and $247 per year respectively, across all ages of life. The projections are shown in Table 8.3.[9] By 2010, the costs from obesity alone will approach the amount for obesity and pre-obesity combined in 2000

Table 8.3   *Total direct health care costs attributable to obesity and overweight in the USA (billions of 1998 dollars)*

Year	Obesity (BMI ≥ 30)	Overweight (BMI ≥ 25)
2000	44.56	71.25
2005	55.45	83.51
2010	68.47	95.04
2015	83.75	103.32
2020	100.91	104.50

and could exceed $100 billion by 2020. These figures are not adjusted for inflation and if price inflation in medical expenditures exceeds the consumer price index, the cost in real terms will be understated.

Obesity prevalence is already very high and the associated costs are large. Our projections underscore the severity of the obesity problem. Obesity rates could conceivably reach very high levels in the near future if we don't intervene promptly. If we allow the problem to increase unimpeded the costs will be serious.

PUBLIC POLICY IMPLICATIONS

The policy debate has focused on whether the problem is systemic or one of personal failure. If the latter, the growth rate of obesity can decelerate if we adopt healthier lifestyles. However, our analysis suggests that obesity has become a problem because society – both business and government – has constructed an infrastructure that accommodates unhealthy lifestyles. Because its components are to a large extent systemic, it will be difficult to change. Nonetheless, as we discuss below, there are points in the infrastructure that are logical targets for state policy to address.

Overall public policy is shifting to increase regulation of food supply and distribution. Recent evidence derived from a sample of Organization for Economic Cooperation and Development (OECD) countries suggests that the actual number of food laws – including labeling requirements, preservative tolerances and pesticide regulations – has a positive effect on slowing rates of obesity (Kellman and Guarino, 2000).

The regulatory approach seems to have gained favor at the state level now in the USA, where rising health care costs are driving up state budgets. One attractive method for states to counteract the obesity infrastructure is to reduce the accessibility of less healthy foods within schools. The objective of restricting vending machine access to soda and snack food is to prevent children from making poor dietary choices. The counterpart to restricting the supply of these less healthy foods is to set nutrition standards for the foods and beverages offered through schools. Replacing unhealthy snacks and beverages with more nutritious fare encourages children to develop better eating habits. Similar school-based effort can be directed toward encouraging children to become more physically active and better informed about nutrition. These approaches should reduce obesity rates in children. This has a larger benefit in the long term as these children become parents and set the example of healthier lifestyle choices for their children.

Beyond the schools, restricting access to unhealthy foods is likely to be more difficult. Even seemingly simple steps such as placing taxes on snack foods are exceedingly difficult to implement. However, states should assess the prospects for more general controls such as restrictions on the locations of fast food and other restaurants, vending machines and other access points for less healthy foods and beverages. Other possibilities include controls on advertising similar to the restrictions placed on the promotion of tobacco products.

We have indicated some avenues for policy interventions but what have state governments actually done so far? Second, how do individual states compare to one another in terms of their attempts to address obesity? To examine the prevalence of state legislative responses to the obesity crisis, we collected data for each of the 50 states about state-level efforts to implement obesity control legislation using the LexisNexis and Westlaw databases. The research focused on the following eight types of regulation that have been introduced and in some states, passed:

- Nutrition standards for school-provided foods.
- Controls on the hours of operation and contents of vending machines in schools.
- Standards for the provision of recess and physical education.
- Obesity education programs.
- Requirements for schools to measure students' BMIs.
- Mandatory coverage of obesity treatment in health insurance.
- State support for obesity research.
- Establishment of obesity research commissions to develop solutions.

For the purpose of comparison, we have created a report card for each state, based on efforts to pass obesity control measures. In our report card assessment, successfully passing a law was necessary to obtain an 'A'. However, since introducing legislation at least indicates some awareness and the presence of a will directed to controlling obesity, points were awarded even if the proposed legislation is not currently active. The grade for each state is a composite of the score for each of the eight types of legislation. Most of these efforts attempt to regulate, reduce, and/or better understand obesity.[10]

REPORT CARD RESULTS

Through our research we developed two report cards. The first examined overall efforts to control obesity and the second examined efforts to control childhood obesity. The findings of our research were not encouraging. The majority of states (23) received a 'C'. Based on our scorecard, five states received a failing grade for their efforts in combating the problem, as seen in Figure 8.4. Although California received an 'A' for its attempts to control childhood obesity, not one state received an 'A' for its overall efforts to address the epidemic. A growing number of states (11) have earned a grade of 'B'. The majority of states (23) received a 'C', 11 received a 'D' and 5 received an 'F' for taking no action at all.

Although there is greater awareness of the need to address the obesity problem, it is still the case that some of the states with the most serious obesity prevalence are lagging behind in taking corrective steps. Mississippi has the nation's highest obesity rate, followed by West Virginia and Michigan. Mississippi has passed legislation specifying requirements for

Number in the state shows its rank by Obesity Prevalence
(Mississippi ranks first, with the country's highest obesity rate. Colorado has the lowest obesity rate, ranking 50th.)

Source: Schaefer Center for Public Policy, University of Baltimore. Copyright © A. Cotten, K. Stanton and Z. Acs.

Figure 8.4   State efforts to control obesity and state obesity report cards

recess and physical education, and it has passed legislation to establish an obesity commission. But only the recess and physical education requirements are likely to have any near-term effect. West Virginia and Michigan have proposed legislation, but again, neither has successfully enacted any laws to control obesity. Overall, states have been slow to recognize the need for prompt actions that may have a more immediate effect. The absence of significant state efforts to address the epidemic is disturbing.

Since the awareness and response developments in relation to the obesity epidemic are strongly reminiscent of the battle against tobacco, we developed a second, childhood obesity report card for the states that focus on the first five of the eight types of legislation previously listed (which specifically address efforts to control increases in obesity prevalence among children). In the fight against tobacco addiction, efforts directed toward children were arguably the most influential.

In the control of childhood obesity, California is the only state to earn an 'A', as seen in Figure 8.5. Fifteen states earned a 'B'. The majority of states (21) earned a 'C'. More than a quarter of the states received a grade of 'D' or lower, with six states receiving an 'F'. Given the importance of establishing healthy habits early in life, the results are very disappointing.

Looking at the legislation that has already been enacted, the most frequently occurring category is legislation to establish an obesity commission to explore the issues. Altogether 21 states have such legislation. Obesity

Source: Schaefer Center for Public Policy, University of Baltimore. Copyright © A. Cotten, K. Stanton and Z. Acs.

Figure 8.5 *State efforts to control childhood obesity and state childhood obesity report cards*

programs and education, and recess/physical education requirements are the next two most common types of legislation to address obesity prevalence. Eight states have vending machine restrictions and seven states have nutrition standards for schools. Although the collection of data is an important part of finding the best solutions, only two states require that schools measure student BMIs. Only one state has legislation to establish support for obesity research.

Table 8.4 shows enacted and proposed legislation for the 50 states. Of these, 17 states, including some that have the most serious problems, have not enacted any legislation. For example West Virginia and Michigan, with the second and third highest obesity rates, have proposed legislation but neither has passed any into law.[11] Mississippi and Alabama, ranked first and seventh worst respectively, have established obesity commissions to evaluate the problem but have made little progress otherwise. Arkansas and California, with the sixteenth and twenty-first highest obesity rates, have been the most proactive states. Idaho, South Dakota, Utah and Wyoming are notable for the absence of any legislative response to the obesity problem.

Since the awareness and public policy responses in relation to obesity are reminiscent of the development of the battle against tobacco, the most effective policies may be designed to address childhood obesity.[12] The first five categories of legislation – mostly supply-side policies – listed previously are specifically directed at schoolchildren. Only California has passed laws in all five categories.

States were scored on whether or not they enacted or proposed legislation to address obesity. While many states made progress in enacting legislation, a look at the legislation that was introduced but not yet enacted provides a glimpse into future trends. As seen in Figure 8.6, there is great interest in establishing public policies that support the reduction of obesity in children. Legislation has been introduced in a majority of states (27) mandating time for recess and physical education. Controlling access to less healthful foods and beverages also generated great interest. In 23 states, legislation was introduced to establish nutrition standards. Legislation was initiated in 21 states to limit vending machine access or content. Numerous states (14) attempted the proactive response of assessing children's BMIs. Thirteen states attempted to mandate curricula to address nutrition education and obesity awareness.

One notable exception to the pattern of inaction is New Jersey. Effective in 2007, all soda, candy and foods listing sugar as the first or principal ingredient will be banned from school cafeterias from pre-kindergarten to high school. This success was due to a concerted effort on the part of officials from the Agriculture, Education and Health Departments who

Table 8.4   Legislative efforts to combat the 'infrastructure of obesity'

State	Nutrition standards	Vending machine usage	BMI measured	Recess/ physical education	Programs and education	Obesity research support	Obesity treatment in health insurance	Obesity commission	Obesity rate (BRFSS estimates)
Alabama					Proposed			Enacted	23.4
Alaska	Proposed	Proposed					Proposed	Proposed	21.0
Arizona	Enacted	Enacted	Enacted	Enacted				Enacted	17.9
Arkansas	Enacted	Enacted	Enacted	Enacted				Enacted	21.7
California	Proposed	Enacted		Enacted	Enacted		Proposed		20.9
Colorado	Proposed	Enacted		Proposed	Enacted		Proposed		14.4
Connecticut	Proposed	Enacted	Proposed	Proposed	Enacted		Proposed	Proposed	17.3
Delaware				Proposed	Enacted				20.0
Florida	Proposed	Proposed		Proposed				Enacted	18.4
Georgia			Proposed	Proposed	Enacted		Proposed	Enacted	22.1
Hawaii	Proposed		Proposed	Proposed	Proposed	Proposed	Proposed	Proposed	17.6
Idaho									20.0
Illinois	Proposed	Proposed		Proposed	Proposed			Enacted	20.5
Indiana	Proposed	Proposed		Proposed			Enacted		24.0
Iowa		Proposed	Proposed	Proposed				Proposed	21.8
Kansas		Proposed		Proposed	Proposed		Proposed	Proposed	21.0
Kentucky	Enacted	Enacted		Enacted				Enacted	24.2
Louisiana	Enacted	Enacted		Enacted				Enacted	23.3
Maine	Proposed	Proposed	Proposed	Proposed	Proposed			Enacted	19.0
Maryland	Proposed	Proposed		Proposed	Proposed	Proposed	Enacted	Proposed	19.8
Massachusetts	Proposed	Proposed		Proposed	Proposed			Enacted	16.1
Michigan	Proposed	Proposed		Proposed					24.4
Minnesota				Proposed				Proposed	19.2
Mississippi	Proposed	Proposed		Enacted	Proposed		Proposed	Enacted	25.9
Missouri	Proposed			Proposed	Proposed		Proposed	Proposed	22.5

151

Table 8.4 (continued)

State	Nutrition standards	Vending machine usage	BMI measured	Recess/ physical education	Programs and education	Obesity research support	Obesity treatment in health insurance	Obesity commission	Obesity rate (BRFSS estimates)
Montana		Proposed							18.2
Nebraska	Proposed	Proposed		Proposed					20.1
Nevada								Enacted	19.1
New Hampshire	Proposed	Proposed		Enacted	Enacted			Proposed	19.0
New Jersey	Proposed	Proposed	Proposed		Proposed		Proposed	Enacted	19.0
New Mexico	Proposed	Proposed		Proposed	Proposed			Proposed	18.8
New York	Proposed	Proposed	Proposed	Proposed	Enacted			Enacted	19.7
North Carolina	Enacted	Proposed	Proposed	Proposed		Proposed		Enacted	22.4
North Dakota	Proposed	Proposed		Proposed				Enacted	19.9
Ohio	Enacted	Proposed		Proposed		Enacted		Proposed	21.8
Oklahoma	Proposed	Proposed		Enacted	Enacted	Proposed		Enacted	20.7
Oregon	Proposed	Proposed	Proposed	Proposed				Proposed	20.7
Pennsylvania	Proposed	Proposed	Proposed	Proposed	Proposed			Proposed	21.4
Rhode Island	Proposed	Proposed		Enacted	Proposed			Proposed	17.3
South Carolina	Proposed	Proposed	Proposed	Proposed				Proposed	21.7
South Dakota									20.6
Tennessee	Proposed	Enacted	Proposed	Proposed	Enacted		Proposed	Enacted	22.6
Texas	Proposed	Proposed	Proposed	Proposed	Enacted			Enacted	23.8
Utah									18.4
Vermont					Proposed			Enacted	17.1
Virginia	Proposed	Proposed		Proposed	Proposed	Proposed		Proposed	20.0
Washington	Enacted	Enacted		Enacted	Enacted		Enacted	Enacted	18.9
West Virginia	Proposed	Proposed	Proposed	Proposed	Proposed			Proposed	24.6
Wisconsin					Enacted				21.9
Wyoming									19.2

152

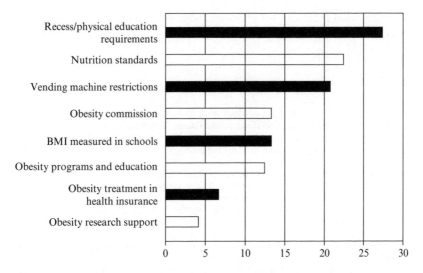

*Figure 8.6   Number of states proposing obesity control measures,
by category*

held hearings, conducted research and managed to operate largely outside
the political arena.[13]

CONCLUSIONS

The prevalence of obesity has increased in the USA and is spreading
around the world. If present trends continue, by 2010 74 percent of the
population may be overweight, 43 percent obese and medical expenses
associated with obesity could reach 15 percent of health care expenditures.
This chapter has suggested that an infrastructure exists that is the driver of
the rise in obesity and that public policy should focus on reversing this
trend.

Several difficulties are apparent in tackling the problem. From an economic perspective, there is a natural bias to favor of policies that tolerate
freedom of choice. This point has been one defense of the food lobby.
However, constraining individual choice and restricting access to certain
foods are precisely the policies that are likely to be most effective. Since
behavioral patterns are set early in life, addressing childhood obesity is particularly important. Consistent with that view, many state governments

have proposed measures for children such as setting nutritional standards and controls on vending machines in schools.

NOTES

1. We wish to thank David T. Levy and Alan Lyles for valuable comments on an earlier draft, and Robert Luke and Haitham Al-Foraih for valuable research assistance. The authors gratefully acknowledge the extraordinarily high-quality legal research provided by Mary W. Lovegrove, Joe Creed for collecting the data on state legislation, and Alex Acs for suggesting the title.
2. This has resulted in programs sponsored by the Department of Agriculture that have promoted fatty foods. For example, in the summer of 2003 the Department of Agriculture provided consumer research and support to Pizza Hut to create two of its most popular and cheesiest pizzas, the 'Stuffed Crust Pizza' and the 'Insider'. See Martin (2003).
3. Per capita consumption of high fructose corn syrup rose from 9.6 pounds in 1977 to 63.7 pounds in 1999, while consumption of all sweeteners increased from 122.8 pounds to 151.3 pounds over the same period (USDA 2005). The overall image from this is that more highly processed foods are providing a larger share of our growing caloric intake.
4. See Brownell and Horgen (2001). Also see Schlosser (2001). The term 'processed food' is broad enough to incorporate Chou et al.'s (2003) 'convenience foods', as well as more narrowly defined segments discussed by Brownell and Horgen (2004) and Cutler et al. (2003).
5. A second aspect of the infrastructure is that people find themselves increasingly in sprawling communities where physical activity is not a part of daily life. See Ewing et al. (2003).
6. For our purposes, rather than attempting to adjust the BRFSS data for all of the differences from the NHANES data, a simple approach is sufficient. Therefore, we incorporate an indicator variable to capture the net impact of all of the differences between the two data sets. The information added by the BRFSS data will improve our forecast over any model that uses only the NHANES data.
7. Purely for purposes of comparison, the second time-series in Figure 8.2 was created by artificially introducing a decay factor into the projected obesity growth rates.
8. Projections of the ratio beyond the year 2000 are constructed from our time-series forecasts of obesity and pre-obesity.
9. Because of differences in approaches and some rounding differences, our year 2000 cost estimate of $71.25 billion is lower than the Finkelstein et al. (2003) $78.5 billion estimate for 1998.
10. See www.ubalt.edu/experts/obesity/
11. West Virginia recently requested the assistance of the Centers for Disease Control to combat the epidemic (Kolata, 2005).
12. Unlike food, it was also feasible and effective to place heavy taxes and outright bans on tobacco products.
13. See www.state.nj.us/agriculture

REFERENCES

Austin, S.B., S.J. Melly, B.N. Sanchez, A. Patel, S. Buka and S.L. Gortmaker (2005), 'Clustering of fast-food restaurants around schools: a novel application of spatial statistics to the study of food environments', *American Journal of Public Health*, **95** (9), 1575–81.

Brown, E. (2003), 'Investing in obesity', accessed 7 October at www.forbes.com/2003/08/07/cz_eb_0807obesity_print.html

Brownell, K.D. and K.B. Horgen (2004), *Food Fight: The Inside Story of the Food Industry, America's Obesity Crisis, and What We Can Do About It*, New York: McGraw-Hill/Contemporary Books.

Chou, S.Y., M. Grossman and H. Saffer (2003), 'An economic analysis of adult obesity: results from the Behavioral Risk Factor Surveillance System', National Bureau of Economic Research working paper no. 9247.

Cutler, D.M., E.L. Glaeser and J.M. Shapiro (2003), 'Why have Americans become more obese?', *Journal of Economic Perspectives*, **17** (3), 93–118.

Ewing, R.S., T. Schmid, R. Killingsworth, A. Zlot and S. Raudenbush (2003), 'Relationship between urban sprawl and physical activity, obesity and morbidity', *American Journal of Health Promotion* (September) 47–57.

Finkelstein, E., I.C. Fiebelkorn and G. Wang (2003), 'National medical spending attributable to overweight and obesity: how much, and who's paying?', *Health Affairs*, (Millwood), January–June Supplement Web Exclusives: W3-219-26.

Flegal, K.M., M.D. Carroll, C.L. Ogden and C.L. Johnson (2002), 'Prevalence and trends in obesity among US adults, 1999–2000', *Journal of the American Medical Association* **288**, 1723–7.

Hannich, T. (2003), 'The (agri)cultural contradictions of obesity', *The New York Times Magazine*, 22 October, pp. 41–48.

Kellman, J.D. and E.T. Guarino (2000), *International Food Laws*, Norwich: Stationery Office.

Kolata, G. (2005), 'C.D.C. team to investigate an outbreak of obesity: West Virginia requests inquiry into crisis', *The New York Times*, 3 June, p. A12.

Martin, A. (2003), 'USDA role in food pyramid criticized: some see conflict of agency writing dietary guidelines', Washington Bureau: *Chicago Tribune*, 14 October, p. 8.

Naik, Y.N. and M.J. Moore (1996), 'Habit formation and intertemporal substitution in individual food consumption', *Review of Economics and Statistics*, (May), 321–8.

Philipson, T. (2001), 'The worldwide growth in obesity: an economic research agenda', *Health Economics*, **10** (1), 1–7.

Philipson, T. and R.A. Posner (1999), 'The long-run growth in obesity as a function of technological change', National Bureau of Economic Research working paper no. 7423.

Schlosser, E. (2001), *Fast Food Nation: The Dark Side of the All-American Meal*, Boston: Houghton Mifflin.

Schofield, W.N., C. Schofield and W.P.T. James (1985), 'Basal metabolic rate-review and prediction with annotated bibliography of source material', *Human Nutrition: Clinical Nutrition*, 39C, supplement 1, 5–96.

US Department of Agriculture (2000), 'Major trends in food supply, 1909–1999', *Food Review*, 1 January, p. 23.

US Department of Agriculture, Economic Research (2005), 'Food consumption (per capita) data system', accessed 19 July, 2006 at www.ers.usda.gov/Data/Food Consumption.

9. Federal communication about obesity in the *Dietary Guidelines* and checkoff programs

Parke E. Wilde[1,2]

INTRODUCTION

The most striking feature of the revised *Dietary Guidelines for Americans*, released January 2005, is the publication's increased emphasis on obesity prevention: 'To reverse the trend toward obesity, most Americans need to eat fewer calories, be more active, and make wiser food choices' (USDHHS and USDA, 2005). The *Dietary Guidelines*, which are released every five years, are intended as the federal government's most authoritative summary of the state of nutrition science and the basis for all federal communication with consumers on nutrition topics.

For most Americans, the new *Guidelines* recommend increased consumption of whole grains, fruits, vegetables, fish and low-fat dairy products within a balanced diet where total calories have been moderately reduced. By subtraction, the *Guidelines* clearly encourage a diet with lower average amounts of some combination of foods from other categories, such as added sugars, high-fat snacks and desserts, meat and high-fat dairy products.

Nevertheless, the best-known and best-funded federally sponsored consumer communications promote increased total consumption of beef, pork and dairy products, including calorically dense foods such as bacon cheeseburgers, barbeque pork ribs, pizza and butter. These communications are sponsored by the federal government's commodity promotion programs, known as 'checkoff' programs. The programs are established by Congress, approved by a majority of the commodity's producers, managed jointly by a producer board and the US Department of Agriculture (USDA) and funded through a tax on the producers. The federal government enforces the collection of hundreds of millions of dollars each year in mandatory assessments, approves the advertising and marketing programs, and defends checkoff communication as the federal government's own message – in legal jargon, as its own 'government speech' (Becker, 2004). Federal support for promoting fruit and vegetables is small by comparison (Produce for Better Health Foundation, 2004).

The leading checkoff advertising campaigns include: 'Beef. It's What's for Dinner', 'Ahh, the Power of Cheese', 'Pork. The Other White Meat', 'Got Milk?' and the 'Milk Mustache' campaign. These campaigns are so familiar that many readers will recognize the slogans immediately and be surprised only to hear that they are federally sponsored. They are.

This chapter compares the federal government's obesity prevention messages in the *Dietary Guidelines* and the commodity checkoff advertising. First, it describes the federal government's balanced healthy weight message, contained in the *Dietary Guidelines*. Second, it provides background on the commodity checkoff programs. Third, it reviews how consumer concerns about obesity are perceived in economic research sponsored by the checkoff programs, and how these perceptions have influenced weight-loss messages in checkoff advertising. For example, in addition to promoting increased food consumption in general, the checkoff boards encourage low-carb and high-calcium weight-loss diets, which emphasize particular nutrients at the expense of the balanced healthy weight message of the *Dietary Guidelines*.

FEDERAL DIETARY GUIDANCE ABOUT HEALTHY WEIGHT

To understand the importance of the federal government's consumer communication about healthy weight, it helps first to consider their competition. The private market for information about how to manage body weight is like a hurricane: ear-splittingly loud and chaotic. Far from converging on a coherent position, the economic dynamics of the book publishing trade and the food marketing trade both seem to ensure that each new year will bring a new, improved and different account of how to maintain a healthy weight.

Setting aside secondary food countercultures, and considering just recent mainstream books, one finds that *Dr Atkins's New Diet Revolution* recommends a high-meat, low-carbohydrate diet for weight loss (Atkins, 2004); *Eat More, Weigh Less: Dr Dean Ornish's Life Choice Program for Losing Weight Safely While Eating Abundantly* recommends a low-fat, plant-based diet (Ornish, 2001); *Eat, Drink, and Be Healthy*, by Harvard's Walter Willett, somewhat splits the difference by suggesting a heavily plant-based diet that nevertheless permits comparatively generous amounts of vegetable oils (Willett, 2001); *The Calcium Key*, by contrast, promises that a high-dairy diet boosts your metabolism and helps you lose 70 percent more weight than does calorie restriction alone (Zemel and Gottlieb, 2003). It would be nice if this cacophony of viewpoints were found only in popular culture and the commercial lay press. However, there is some scientific research in refereed journals that supports every one of the diametrically opposed popular approaches to weight loss. One sometimes hears the argument that public dietary guidance is unnecessary, because everybody knows how to maintain a healthy weight and it is just a matter of doing it. However, the wide diversity of popular weight loss strategies suggests otherwise.

In the face of these challenges, federal dietary guidance for obesity prevention offers an important contribution. For the current round of the *Dietary Guidelines for Americans*, USDA and the Department of Health and Human Services (DHHS) jointly appointed an external advisory committee to review and summarize the relevant scientific literature (Dietary Guidelines Advisory Committee, 2005). This committee drew on work by other authoritative bodies, such as the National Institutes of Health and the new Dietary Reference Intakes from the Institute of Medicine at the National Academies. In preparing its report, the advisory committee considered 435 written public comments and many oral presentations. Following the committee's report in August 2004, there was another period for public comment. Finally, based on the advisory committee's report and the additional comments, USDA and the DHHS released the new *Dietary Guidelines for Americans* in January 2005 (USDA and DHHS, 2005). Whatever flaws this process may have, the advantage of the *Dietary Guidelines* over the wild popular press on weight loss (discussed above), and over the industry-specific promotions (discussed below), is sharp.

While the message of the *Guidelines* may not be bluntly stated, it is sufficiently clear for specialists and interested lay readers alike. The guidelines most directly related to obesity prevention with a focus on calorie balance:

- To maintain body weight in a healthy range, balance calories from foods and beverages with calories expended.
- To prevent gradual weight gain over time, make small decreases in food and beverage calories and increase physical activity.

To somebody unfamiliar with the marketplace of weight-loss information, such advice might seem tautological, but it is not. These guidelines contrast sharply with food industry hopes that Americans might be able to solve the obesity problem through exercise alone and with the many weight-loss fads that encourage avoidance of or concentration on particular nutrients.

The Dietary Guidelines Advisory Committee was particularly concerned about popular low-carb weight-loss diets, due to multiple shortcomings: high saturated fat content; high cholesterol content; low fiber content; low intake of fruits, vegetable and grains; and unproven efficacy in the long term (Dietary Guidelines Advisory Committee, 2005). The Food and Drug Administration (FDA), which has oversight of food labeling issues, likewise emphasizes calorie balance (US FDA, 2004). With respect to fad diets, a 2002 article in *FDA Consumer* warned: 'The cabbage soup diet, the low-carbohydrate and high-protein diet, and other so-called "fad" diets are fundamentally different from federal nutrition dietary guidelines and are not recommended for losing weight'. For popular high-protein diets in particular, *FDA Consumer* quoted Robert Eckel, MD, Professor of Medicine at the University of Colorado Health Sciences Center in Denver: 'In general, quick weight-loss diets don't work for most people' (Bren, 2002). The Federal Trade Commission (FTC), which has oversight over food advertising, also supports the strong warning against fad diets. An FTC report by Harvard scientist George Blackburn argued, 'By promoting unrealistic expectations and false hopes, [fad diets] doom current weight loss efforts to failure, and make future attempts less likely to succeed' (Blackburn, 2002).

To evaluate the dairy promotions, it is important to understand that the *Dietary Guidelines* do not endorse the type of dairy weight-loss claim made in *The Calcium Key*. At the January 2004 meeting of the Dietary Guidelines Advisory Committee, Dr Greg Miller of the National Dairy Council suggested: 'Evidence indicates that three to four servings of dairy foods might play a role in weight management efforts, when coupled with a balanced, reduced-calorie diet'. However, the subcommittee that considered the dairy weight-loss claim declined to support it. According to the full committee's meeting summary for March 2004, 'Dr [Janet] King presented the Subcommittee's statement on this topic: "While the evidence is inconclusive that dairy foods help manage body weight, there is no evidence that consuming the recommended intakes of low-fat dairy foods increases body weight" '. The scientific literature is not yet of one mind on this question, but the advisory committee's skepticism of the dairy weight-loss claim has been reinforced by several recent articles and editorials (Barr, 2003; Gunther et al., 2005; Lanou, 2005; St Onge, 2005; Phillips et al., 2003; Berkey et al., 2005). The best consolation the committee could offer the National Dairy Council was to mention the absence of scientific grounds for shunning low-fat dairy foods.

Outside of the federally supported commodity promotions discussed in the following section, a review of federal communications found only rare divergence from the message espoused by the *Dietary Guidelines*.[3] The scientific completeness, clarity and steadiness of the federal government's consensus message is essential to the policy justification for federal dietary guidance in the first place. These qualities distinguish federal dietary guidance from the private sector information market.

THE COMMODITY CHECKOFF PROGRAMS

Congress has authorized mandatory generic commodity promotion – or checkoff – programs for 35 agricultural commodities. The largest food checkoffs are for meat and dairy products. In 2003, the checkoff assessments totaled $106 million for fluid milk, $86 million for other dairy products, $46 million for beef and $36 million for pork (see Figure 9.1). There is no checkoff for poultry or fish, and checkoff support for fruits, vegetables, and grains is minimal.

A common justification given for checkoff boards is that a free-rider problem prevents commodity producers from capturing the economic benefits from their own investments in advertising and promotion (Becker, 2004). A typical beef farmer cannot afford to advertise much on his or her own, because any market benefits will accrue to beef farmers in general. To a casual listener, this justification might sound like arguments that

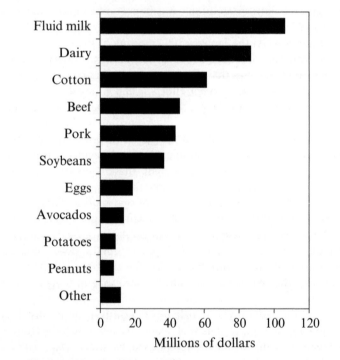

Source: Wilde (2004); data from Becker (2004).

Figure 9.1   Generic commodity promotion ('checkoff') program revenues, 2003

economists recognize as possible grounds for government intervention. One might think there is a free-rider problem in the provision of a public good, for which the solution is federal action to promote that good. However, increased meat and high-fat dairy consumption are not public goods in the usual sense. Indeed, food products are the archetypal private good, because one person's consumption unambiguously prevents another person's consumption of the same unit of food. A public interest justification would be compelling only with the addition of an argument that Americans consume too little hamburger and cheese, for example, or that they are exposed to too little advertising for their psychological health.

Instead, Congress's policy motivation for federal intervention to establish and oversee the commodity promotion boards was, without apology, to support the private-sector interests of the dairy, beef and pork producers. For example, the beef checkoff program's mission statement is: 'The Cattlemen's Beef Promotion and Research Board is dedicated to improving producer profitability, expanding consumer demand for beef, and strengthening beef's position in the marketplace'. The title of the board's annual report is, *It's About Demand* (Cattlemen's Beef Promotion and Research Board, 2005).

The checkoff programs have become more clearly identified as federal programs for three reasons. First, producer support for the dairy, beef and pork checkoff programs appears to have declined in recent years, so continuation of the programs relies more heavily on federal authority rather than voluntary producer endorsement. To take just one example, the pork checkoff program was supported by 77 percent of producers in a 1988 referendum. Then, a majority of producers voted to discontinue the pork checkoff in a 2000 referendum, and the Secretary of Agriculture directed the Agricultural Marketing Service (AMS) to shut down the program. However the National Pork Producers Council, a trade association, sued to continue the program. In 2001 USDA reached an agreement with the Council to continue the program. Despite the referendum showing opposition from more than half of pork producers, USDA enforces collection of the mandatory assessment from all of them (Becker, 2004).

Second, although USDA's oversight of the checkoff boards was fairly cursory in their early years, the department's involvement has intensified. In the late 1990s the USDA Inspector General strongly criticized the financial management and federal oversight of several checkoff boards, and federal involvement has been strengthened in response. For example in a 1998 report the Inspector General's office found 'serious problems' with the Fluid Milk Board: 'AMS provided little active oversight of the Board's activities . . . The Board entered into sole-source contracts without any competition to ensure the most cost-effective procurement and without obtaining AMS's approval prior to the effective date of the contracts' (USDA, 1998). The audit report recommended that USDA suspend the operations of the Fluid Milk Board and restructure its management. While the department declined to follow that recommendation, and asserts that Congress intended the programs to be largely producer-run, AMS reported that it has enhanced its oversight of financial management and now approves contracts for all of the Board's activities.

Third, to defend the checkoff programs against litigation, the federal government has declared that checkoff advertising is 'government speech'. In a series of lawsuits, dissident producers who disapproved of the mandatory checkoff payments have argued that the programs violated their First Amendment right to free speech by forcing them to support commercial speech with which they disagreed. This reasoning led federal appeals courts to rule in separate cases against the beef, pork and dairy checkoff programs on Constitutional grounds.

The US Supreme Court disagreed. The Court heard the beef case in December 2004, and in May 2005, and by a 6:3 margin decided in favor of USDA and the checkoff board. The federal government successfully argued that checkoff programs do not force producers to support private commercial speech with which they disagree. Rather, these programs force producers to support 'government speech', which is not subject to the same Constitutional objection. In his majority opinion in May, Justice Antonin Scalia, upholding the checkoff program, wrote: 'The message of the promotional campaigns is effectively controlled by the Federal Government itself. The message set out in the beef promotions is from beginning to end the message established by the Federal Government' (*Mike Johanns et al.* v. *Livestock Marketing Association et al.*, 2005).

In reaching this decision, the Supreme Court justices engaged in a fascinating debate over the relevant nutrition issues. Justice David Souter noted the inconsistencies between the beef advertising and the *Dietary Guidelines*. Justice Ruth Bader Ginsburg, although she ended up voting with the majority, likewise asked whether checkoff advertising and the *Dietary Guidelines* can both be government speech. In his majority opinion Scalia retorted, 'The beef promotions are perfectly compatible with the guidelines' message of moderate consumption – the ads do not insist that beef is also What's for Breakfast, Lunch, and Midnight Snack' (Wilde, 2005). A weakness of Scalia's retort is that the checkoff programs do not in fact just promote beef for dinner – they promote a wide variety of foods, making up a large share of the diet, for consumption at all times of day.

The government's stand in this matter is important, because federal communication about nutrition is supposed to be consistent with the *Dietary Guidelines for Americans*. Eric Hentges was a vice president of the pork checkoff program until his February 2003 appointment to lead USDA's Center for Nutrition Policy and Promotion, which is responsible for the *Dietary Guidelines*. He testified to Congress in September 2003: 'The *Dietary Guidelines* . . . serve as the vehicle for the Federal government to speak with "one voice" on nutrition issues for the health of the American public' (Wilde, 2004). The most recent *Dietary Guidelines* say in their introduction, 'Because of its focus on health promotion and risk reduction, the Dietary Guidelines form the basis of federal food, nutrition education, and information programs' (USDHHS and USDA, 2005).

WEIGHT-LOSS MESSAGES IN CHECKOFF ADVERTISING

To understand the origins of the weight-loss messages in checkoff advertising, it helps to consider how nutrition concerns are described in checkoff-sponsored research. The 1996 farm law requires each checkoff program to conduct a periodic independent evaluation of its effectiveness. For the fluid milk and dairy programs in particular, USDA/AMS makes an extensive annual report to Congress each summer, which includes a summary of the most recent independent evaluation. In addition to the formal evaluations, the checkoff programs have financed other relevant research, some of which has made it to the public domain.

In this literature, some nutrition concerns appear as constraints to the expansion of consumer demand, while other concerns appear to be harmless from an industry perspective. The most recent independent evaluation of the beef checkoff, by Ronald Ward of the University of Florida, employed econometric modeling to determine the impact of many factors on demand for beef (Ward, 2004). Overall, Ward found that the beef checkoff advertising and promotion was effective, in the sense of somewhat increasing overall beef demand compared to what it would be in the absence of the checkoff program. The increase in beef demand was found to be fairly modest, but more than enough repay the cost of the producer assessments. Consumer concerns about fat and cholesterol tended to reduce demand for beef but these concerns have been fading in recent years while concern about obesity has been increasing. Ironically, perhaps because of the popularity of high-protein weight-loss diets, consumer concern about obesity did not appear to harm demand for beef. 'Probably the most interesting result from this health measure,' Ward concluded, 'is that dieting has little impact on the whether or not you consume beef'.

For the pork checkoff, the econometric analysis in the most recent independent evaluation found several of the same patterns (Davis et al., 2001).

Specific indications of health awareness were associated with lower demand for pork but, paradoxically, neither having a high body mass index (BMI) nor being on a low-calorie diet caused any harm to pork demand.

More favorable attitudes toward fast food restaurants also encourage demand for beef and pork. Increased fast food restaurant consumption has been associated with increased risk of obesity, in cross-sectional and longitudinal non-experimental research (Binkley et al., 2000; Pereira et al., 2005), and has been cited in federal government publications as being associated with lower consumption of fruits and vegetables other than potatoes (Guthrie et al., 2002; Variyam, 2005). In his beef checkoff evaluation, Ward found that attitudes holding fast food in disfavor were one of the strongest covariates of lower beef demand. Indeed, as determinants of beef demand, these fast food attitudes were more influential than concerns about cholesterol or fat (Ward, 2004). Fast food consumption has increased by several multiples in recent decades, and continued increases would bode especially well for the products of the beef checkoff program.

For the dairy checkoff programs, increased restaurant use is a mixed blessing. Milk, for example, is more frequently consumed at home than in restaurants. Schmit and Kaiser (2004) found that the effectiveness of cheese advertising has increased over time but that it has been held back by increased restaurant consumption at the expense of food at home. The authors recommended that the dairy programs increase their cheese promotions targeted at the food-away-from-home market to compensate. A USDA report to Congress on the fluid milk and dairy checkoff programs was particularly upbeat about the promise of promoting cheese through fast food restaurants (Agricultural Marketing Service, 2004). The report found that each 10 percent increase in food away-from-home (as in restaurants) would contribute to a 1.1 percent increase in demand for cheese. 'The positive contribution to per capita [consumption] is largely captured by cheese usage in restaurants,' USDA's report said, 'particularly in fast-food businesses with burger, taco, and pizza products' (Agricultural Marketing Service, 2004, p. 38).

These conclusions from checkoff-sponsored research seem to be reflected in the nutrition and weight-loss messages of the checkoff boards' advertising campaigns. An important part of the Beef Board's marketing strategy is to promote restaurant and food service sales of beef sandwiches, such as steak sandwiches and cheeseburgers. According to a 2004 Beef Board analysis, sales of all these sandwiches are soaring (Cattlemen's Beef Promotion and Research Board, 2004). The very fastest growing sales were for steak sandwiches with cheese, with 18.9 percent growth in 2003.

In the fall of 2004, the Board collaborated with Quizno's sandwich shops on a special promotion of a Quizno's Steakhouse Beef Dip Sub, which 'features tender roast beef smothered in rich French onion sauce, and melted Swiss cheese, served in a toasted Quiznos roll, with a side of beefy, pan roasted au jus' (Cattlemen's Beef Promotion and Research Board and National Cattlemen's Beef Association, 2004). The sandwich is available on Low Carb Toasty™ Flatbread. Neither Quizno's nor USDA's Agricultural Marketing Service, which is supposed to have approved this promotion, provided nutritional information for this sandwich in response to requests from the author. However, a Quizno's restaurant in Boston provided a tally of 'net carbs' for most of the chain's sandwiches. The terminology 'net carbs', which has no FDA-approved legal definition, refers to the system for counting and limiting carbohydrate consumption in high-protein, low-carbohydrate diets. Like the reference to 'low carb' flatbread, the provision of 'net carb' information without other nutrition context endorses fad weight-loss strategies that are criticized in official federal communications about nutrition.

A website from the National Cattlemen's Beef Association, accompanied by the beef checkoff logo, offers very different advice from the weight control message of the *Dietary Guidelines*: 'Advice to reduce calories for weight control often focuses on reducing calories from fat and possibly limiting foods from the meat and dairy groups. The truth is, naturally nutrient-rich foods such as lean beef, can be part of the weight control solution' (National Cattlemen's Beef Association, 2004). The website suggests a link between higher beef consumption and reduced risk of overweight and obesity: 'In fact, as the incidence of obesity or being overweight has increased, meat consumption has decreased among the US population.' The website's conclusion is, 'Beef plays an important role in overall health, including a role in weight control.'

Similarly, the Pork Board promotes low-carb diets through a special motto and logo: 'Counting carbs? Pork's Perfect!' According to a Pork Board newsletter, 'The "Counting Carbs" initiative is part of ongoing checkoff promotions to highlight pork's role in a healthy diet and to encourage consumers to buy and consume more pork' (National Pork Board, 2004a). The Pork Board recently approved $750 000 for checkoff-funded efforts to increase consumer demand, 'particularly for people who are interested in low-carbohydrate, high-protein diets'. In additional to the 'Counting Carbs?' motto, these efforts use the slogans, 'Not all proteins are created equal' and the 'Power of Protein'.

There is a sharp contrast between the Pork Board's marketing to the nutrition community and its marketing to food services, including restaurants. The board's special website for nutritionists (www.porkandhealth.org) includes strong warnings against low carb diets: 'Unfortunately, these fad diets may have negative effects on your body' (National Pork Board,

2004b). Meanwhile, the Pork Board's website for food services (www. porkfoodservice.com) recommends low carb marketing: 'There's no denying that the low-carbohydrate/high-protein phenomena has taken the food world by storm. According to some reports, up to 50 million consumers have tried some type of low-carbohydrate diet plan' (National Pork Board, 2004c). The website favorably quotes a 'leading' chef, Marlin Kaplan, saying, 'There's no denying this diet. If you are a restaurant operator not offering high-protein, low-carb options on your menu, then you are not listening to your customer.'

According to USDA's report to Congress on the dairy and fluid milk checkoff programs, the Dairy Board's campaign with the motto 'Ahh, The Power of Cheese' is targeted at 'cheese lovers', with an emphasis on 'cheese enhancers' and 'cheese cravers'. The 'enhancers' use cheese in their cooking, while the 'cravers' eat cheese straight on its own (Agricultural Marketing Service, 2004). In April 2005 the Dairy Board began a collaboration with Pizza Hut to promote a three-cheese stuffed-crust pizza. This pizza features an exceptional amount of cheese. A single slice of the plain cheese version contains 35 percent of the federal government's recommended daily value for saturated fat and 39 percent of the daily value for salt, based on a 2000-calorie diet. The Dairy Board features this pizza on the front page of its website, with the address www.ilovecheese.com.

Recent Fluid Milk Board and Dairy Board promotions build on the high-dairy weight loss dietary message of Michael Zemel's research (Zemel et al., 2004) and book, *The Calcium Key* (Zemel and Gottlieb, 2003). According to a milk and weight-loss study prepared by the checkoff-funded Milk Processors Education Program, dairy weight-loss claims that consumers find scientifically plausible would be highly effective: 'Benefit claims simply stating that milk is good for you, or is an effective way to lose weight, show the most promise for inspiring consumption of 3–4 servings of milk a day' (Milk Processor Education Program, 2004). The need for scientific credibility creates pressure to publicize scientific positions that were not accepted by the *Dietary Guidelines*. For example, a 'milk mustache' advertisement features the slender actress Kelly Preston, with accompanying text that implies an association between higher milk consumption and lower body weight. USDA/AMS could not provide a breakdown of the funding level for promotions using the dairy weight-loss claim, but it appears to be substantial. Agency staff reported that, as of the fourth quarter of 2004, the weight-loss message was a key part of the '3 A Day of Dairy' campaign, whose total budget was $34 million in 2004 and will be $46 million in 2005. The program's new logo says: '3-a-Day. Milk–cheese–yogurt. Burn more fat, lose weight' (Figure 9.2).

**3 servings of dairy a day in a reduced-
calorie diet supports weight loss.**

Source: Dairy Board.

Figure 9.2   The dairy board's logo with the dairy weight-loss claim

CONCLUSIONS

It seems unlikely that any government-sponsored advertising strategy for all
of the foods supported by checkoff programs could be found consistent with
the *Dietary Guidelines*. One must ask whether it is possible to eat more beef,
more pork, more cheese and more eggs in answer to the checkoff advertising,
while simultaneously consuming more fruits and vegetables, whole grains
and low-fat dairy in answer to the *Dietary Guidelines*, and furthermore moderately reducing calorie intake overall.

Beyond the implications of raising food consumption in general, the
checkoff-sponsored research findings give the programs a strong incentive
to promote nutrition and obesity messages that are more specifically at
odds with the *Dietary Guidelines for Americans*. The mainstream of federal
dietary advice emphasizes calorie balance and warns against fad weight-
loss diets focusing on particular nutrients. The checkoff programs rely on

exactly such diets to counteract a major constraint they perceive in consumer concerns about nutrition and obesity.

These contradictions have not been reconciled, perhaps because the checkoff programs have only recently drifted into having a strong identity as federal programs. Whereas the checkoff programs once were portrayed as producer self-help institutions, they now rely on the federal government to enforce collection of the mandatory assessments in the face of considerable opposition from individual producers. Whereas the checkoff programs once operated with minimal USDA oversight, they now are monitored more closely. And whereas the federal government itself used to treat the programs as private sector sponsors of advertising messages, the government now claims the checkoff messages as its own 'government speech'.

Following the Supreme Court's recent endorsement of this government speech doctrine, the inconsistencies between the government's message in the *Dietary Guidelines* and in the checkoff promotions deserve renewed attention. These inconsistencies undermine the effectiveness of the *Dietary Guidelines* as an antidote to the wild private sector market for information about weight and obesity.

NOTES

1. This manuscript was improved by helpful comments from participants at a workshop on public policy and obesity organized by Zoltan J. Acs at the University of Baltimore, and from colleagues at a lunchtime seminar at the Friedman School of Nutrition Science and Policy at Tufts University, both of which took place in May 2005.
2. Material for this chapter appeared in the June 2006, issue of the journal *Obesity*, and is published here with permission.
3. Oddly, a recent exception was an offhand comment by the Secretary of Health and Human Services, Tommy Thompson, at the January 2005 press conference outlining the new guidelines. Thompson suggested that to look better and feel better, 'you lower your calorie intake, you lower your fats, your carbs, you eat more fruits and vegetables, more whole grain, and you exercise'. The encouragement to lower carbs does not appear in the *Dietary Guidelines*.

REFERENCES

Agricultural Marketing Service (2004), *Report to Congress on the National Dairy Promotion and Research Program and the National Fluid Milk Processor Promotion Program*, Washington, DC: USDA.

Atkins, R.C. (2001), *Dr. Atkins' New Diet Revolution*, (revised edn), New York: Avon Books.

Barr, S. (2003), 'Increased dairy product or calcium intake: is body weight or composition affected in humans?', *Journal of Nutrition*, **133**, 245S–8S.

Becker, G.S. (2004), *Federal Farm Promotion ('Checkoff') Programs*, Washington, DC: Congressional Research Service.

Berkey, C.S., H.R.H. Rockett, W.C. Willett and G.A. Colditz (2005), 'Milk, dairy fat, dietary calcium, and weight gain: a longitudinal study of adolescents', *Archive Pediatric Adolescent Medicine*, **159**, 543–50.

Binkley, J.K., J. Eales, and M. Jekanowski, (2000), 'The relation between dietary change and rising US obesity', *International Journal of Obesity*, **24**, 1032–9.

Blackburn, G. (2002), 'Introduction', *Weight-Loss Advertising: An Analysis of Current Trends*, Washington, DC: Federal Trade Commission.

Bren, L. (2002), 'Losing weight: more than counting calories', *FDA Consumer*, **36** (1), accessed at www.fda.gov/fdae/features/2002/102_fat.html

Cattlemen's Beef Promotion and Research Board (2004), 'Beef. It's what's news in foodservice' (PowerPoint presentation), accessed June 2005 at www.beeffoodservice.com/Facts/Download.aspx

Cattlemen's Beef Promotion and Research Board (2005), *It's About Demand: 2004 Beef Board Annual Report*, Centennial, CO: Cattlemen's Beef Promotion and Research Board.

Cattlemen's Beef Promotion and Research Board and National Cattlemen's Beef Association (2004), 'Beef Checkoff partners with Quiznos Sub to promote new steak sandwich' (press release), accessed May 2005 at www.beef.org/newsbeefcheckoffpartnerswithquiznossubtopromotenewsteaksandwich3519.aspx

Davis, G.C., O. Capps, D.A. Bessler, J.H. Leigh, J.P. Nichols and E. Goddard (2001), *An Economic Evaluation of the Pork Checkoff Program*, College Station, TX: Texas A&M University.

Dietary Guidelines Advisory Committee (2005), *2005 Dietary Guidelines Advisory Committee Report*, Washington, DC: US DHHS and USDA.

Food and Drug Administration (FDA) (2004), *Calories Count: Report of the Working Group on Obesity*, Washington, DC: US FDA.

Gunther, C.W., P.A. Legowski, R.M. Lyle, G.P. McCabe, M.S. Eagan, M. Peacock and D. Teegarden (2005), 'Dairy products do not lead to alterations in body weight or fat mass in young women in a 1-y intervention', *American Journal of Clinical Nutrition*, **81** (4), 751–6.

Guthrie, J.F., B.H. Lin and E. Frazao (2002), 'Role of food prepared away from home in the American diet, 1977–78 versus 1994–96: changes and consequences', *Journal of Nutrition Education & Behavior*, **34**, 140–15.

Lanou, A.J. (2005), Letters to the editor: data do not support recommending dairy products for weight loss', *Obesity Research* **13** (1) (January), 191.

Mike Johanns, Secretary of Agriculture, et al., Petitioners v. *Livestock Marketing Association et al.* Nos 03–1164 and 03–1165. S Ct (2005).

Milk Processor Education Program (2004), *Milk and Weight-Loss Study: Final Report*, Washington, DC: Milk Processor Education Program.

National Cattlemen's Beef Association (2004), *Cattle and Beef Handbook*. Centennial, CO: National Cattlemen's Beef Association, accessed at www.beef.org/ncbanutrition.aspx

National Pork Board (2004a), 'Counting carbs initiative draws attention', *Pork Leader*, **24** (18), 1, accessed at www.porkboard.org/publications/pubissues.asp?id=38, now on www.iowapork.org/pork_checkoff/consumer/locarb.html

National Pork Board (2004b), 'Eating well to stay healthy: the role of protein', accessed June 2005, at www.theotherwhitemeat.com/userdocs/theroleofprotein.pdf

National Pork Board (2004c), 'Promotional tools: pork's role in today's diets promotional materials' accessed, June 2005 at www.porkfoodservice.com/promotionalTools.asp

Ornish, D. (2001), *Eat More, Weigh Less: Dr. Dean Ornish's Life Choice Program for Losing Weight Safely While Eating Abundantly* (revised edn), New York: HarperCollins.

Pereira, M.A., A.I. Kartashov, C.B. Ebbeling, L. Van Horn, M.L. Slattery, D.R. Jacobs and D.S. Ludwig (2005), 'Fast-food habits, weight gain, and insulin resistance (the CARDIA study): 15-year prospective analysis'. *Lancet*, **365**, 36–42.

Phillips, S.M., L.G. Bandini, H. Cyr, S. Colclough-Douglas, E. Naumova and A. Must (2003), 'Dairy food consumption and body weight and fatness studied longitudinally over the adolescent period', *International Journal of Obesity*, **27** (9), 1106–13.

Produce for Better Health Foundation (2004), *2003 Annual Report*, Wilmington, DE: Produce for Better Health Foundation.

Schmit, T.M. and H.M. Kaiser (2004), 'Decomposing the variation in generic advertising response over time', *American Journal of Agricultural Economics*, **86** (1), 139–48.

St Onge, M.P. (2005), 'Dietary fats, teas, dairy, and nuts: potential functional foods for weight control?', *American Journal of Clinical Nutrition*, **81**, 7–15.

US Department of Agriculture (1998), Office of the Inspector General audit report 'National fluid milk processor promotion program', Washington, DC: USDA.

US Department of Health and Human Services and US Department of Agriculture (2005), *Dietary Guidelines for Americans, 2005, 6th edition*, Washington, DC: US DHHS and USDA.

Variyam, J. (2005), *Nutrition Labeling in the Food-Away-From-Home Sector: An Economic Assessment*, Washington, DC: USDA Economic Research Service.

Ward, R.W. (2004), *Beef Demand and the Rate-of-Return to the US Beef Checkoff: Two Independent Evaluation Approaches*, Centennial, CO: Cattlemen's Beef Promotion and Research Board.

Wilde, P.E. (2004), 'Message under revision: USDA speaks about beef, pork, cheese, and obesity', *Choices Magazine*, **19** (3), 47–51.

Wilde, P.E. (2005), 'What do Supreme Court Justices know about nutrition?', *US Food Policy Weblog*, http://usfoodpolicy.blogspot.com/2005/05/what-do-supreme-court-justices-know.html, June.

Willett, W.C. (2001), *Eat, Drink and Be Healthy*, New York: Free Press.

Zemel, M. and B. Gottlieb (2003), *The Calcium Key: The Revolutionary Diet Discovery That Will Help You Lose Weight Faster*, New York: Wiley.

Zemel, M.B., W. Thompson, A. Milstead and K. Morris (2004), 'Dietary calcium and dairy products accelerate weight and fat loss during energy restriction in obese adults', *Obesity Research*, **12** (4), 582–90.

10. Tax solutions to the external costs of obesity

Julie Ann Elston, Kenneth R. Stanton, David T. Levy and Zoltan J. Acs

INTRODUCTION

In previous and subsequent chapters the case has been made that the current obesity problem is a consequence of an infrastructure of obesity. That means that in order to solve the problem we need to think carefully about the parts of the infrastructure that can be controlled and which mechanisms are likely to be the most effective means of control. The roles of individuals, governments, business and legal structures are of critical importance in analysing the potential for success of any proposed policy solution. In this chapter we explain how tax mechanisms could be applied to the infrastructure to improve diet.

To aid in understanding the obesity problem and its potential solutions, it is useful to divide our view of the infrastructure into two parts – supply and demand. Some aspects of the infrastructure directly affect the availability or supply of foods or activities that contribute to obesity. Other portions of the infrastructure do not affect the supply but do restrict or alter the demand side, or use of such foods or activities. As an example, banning soda and snack machines from schools is a direct restriction on supply but educating the students in order to encourage healthier preferences is an attempt to alter demand. In some cases, this distinction between the supply side and demand side can be rather subtle, but as a broad tool for evaluating policy prescriptions it remains useful.

From an economic perspective, arguments in favor of allowing individuals freedom in choosing how to allocate their money and their time are generally difficult to argue against. That is, unless a case can be made for some form of market failure, society is best served by avoiding interventions in the markets for goods and services. Without intervention, the prices of resources generally rise as the resource becomes scarce, or as the demand for that particular resource increases. The pricing mechanism is a simple means of directing resources to their most highly valued use and interfering with this mechanism is not advisable unless a case can be made that the market solution will not generate the optimal outcome. We discuss this in greater detail in the following section, but in many cases the justification for interfering rests on market failures where individuals face prices that do not reflect society's value of the resource.

If circumstances justify intervention, then the next important step is to determine the best form of that intervention in terms of effectiveness, cost and feasibility. That decision will be driven by trade-offs between the ideal and the pragmatic. Interventionist policies are predominantly focused on the demand side. That is, typical approaches include educating consumers against socially undesirable products or activities, or employing taxes to influence demand. Supply-side approaches on the other hand are more likely to involve restrictions or outright bans on undesirable goods. Viewed in this way, demand-side approaches are more acceptable since the individual retains the right to make allocative choices.

Supply-side interventions tend to be used primarily when all else fails. However, if it is desirable to make rapid changes in behavior, supply-side policies can be attractive in terms of the immediacy of their impact. For those reasons such policies are likely to meet stiff resistance from both suppliers and consumers.

As a demand-side tool, a tax placed on a particular product leads to an increase in the end price of that product. According to the law of demand, price increases lead to a reduction in the quantity consumed. This occurs through some consumers stopping their purchase of the product and some cutting back on their purchases. Even on items where habits (and addiction) play an important role, such as alcohol and tobacco, taxes have been found to reduce consumption (Cook and Moore, 2002; Chaloupka et al., 2002; Jha and Chaloupka, 1999; Levy et al., 2004). Taxes may be levied on the food items that are most strongly associated with obesity and have previously been used in attempts to reduce the health related problems associated with alcohol and tobacco consumption. Before analysing the role of tax solutions, we first justify any proposed intervention in food markets.

EXTERNAL COSTS OF OBESITY

Obesity has roughly the same association with chronic health conditions as does 20 years of aging. But obese people only hurt themselves – right? If that is true, then from an economic standpoint people should be at liberty to make any diet and exercise choices they wish, including those which place them at greater risk of becoming obese. However, the costs of individual obesity are not purely an individual problem; the costs are substantial and widely shared.

One of the most obvious cost burdens arises from the health problems created by excess weight. According to Finkelstein et al. (2003) the combined prevalence of pre-obesity (having a body mass index (BMI) of 25 or greater but less than 30) and obesity (a BMI of 30 or more) averages 53.6 percent across all insurance categories and is the largest for those enrolled in Medicare, at 56.1 percent. A number of studies document the increase in costs associated with obesity including Sturm (2002) which analyses national data in the USA and finds that obesity is associated with a 36 percent increase in inpatient and outpatient spending and a 77 percent increase in medication costs, with an average premium of $395 in individual care costs over a non-obese person. Based on projected prevalence rates and adjusting for inflation, the total incremental direct health care cost for 2005 was estimated to be $119 billion (Stanton and Acs, 2005).

The existence of such large health care costs does not on its own justify interfering with the market. As long as the individual making the choice to become obese can do so freely, with full information as to the costs and consequences of their choice and without placing a burden on the rest of society, then they ought to be free to do so. That is, if an individual chooses to over-consume and they become obese, that is their right, provided they also absorb the additional costs that result from their obesity. But obesity-related health costs are more likely to be shared by others, including those who expend a great deal of effort to reduce their risk of becoming obese, through the pooling of health insurance risks.

At first glance it would seem that the solution to the problem is for insurers to adjust the premiums based on obesity-related risk (in the same way that smokers pay higher life insurance premiums and drivers with poor driving records pay higher automobile insurance). Seen in this way, individual decisions leading to obesity and all of its related costs and consequences are private and society has no justification for interfering. However, the problem is more complicated than it first appears.

The additional health care costs of obesity fall not only on private insurers who could adjust their rates in response to the individual risks, but also on public insurers. Publicly funded health programs such as Medicare, Medicaid and Veterans benefits disproportionately absorb the additional medical costs since obesity and poverty are correlated. Because of the health consequences of obesity, obese individuals are less likely to be adequately employed and consequently more likely to rely on publicly financed health care and other public support.

Using data from the National Health Interview Survey and the RAND Health Insurance Experiment, Keeler et al. (1989) estimated that healthy individuals generated a $1900 total subsidy over their lifetime to sedentary individuals through cost sharing in collectively financed programs such as health insurance, sick-leave coverage, disability insurance and group life insurance. Specifically private insurance, through risk pooling of both obese and non-obese people charge higher rates to both groups than would be the case in the absence of the obese group.

Other medical costs that are not represented in these studies include the costs of purchasing special equipment such as lifts, wider hospital beds and sturdier wheel chairs and gurneys, to accommodate increasing numbers of obese patients. Extending beyond medical costs, it is apparent that obesity lowers life expectancy and obesity-related health problems reduce efficiency through lost days at work. Weight-related factors reduce individual, family and national productivity levels and although these costs are difficult to isolate and measure they are likely to be substantial.

Obesity costs also arise in the form of expenditures made to accommodate greater numbers of obese people. These costs are passed to all consumers through higher prices, as in the cases of transportation and theater tickets where fewer larger seats replace higher numbers of smaller ones at higher average prices.

So far, two key points should be apparent. First, the combined costs of obesity are large, and second, society as a whole bears much of the costs of the decisions that result in individual obesity. Whatever the underlying reasons, left to freely choose consumption and exercise combinations more and more people are making choices that create large and growing social costs. The externalities associated with the individual decisions justify political interventions designed to control such choices. This notion of external costs is important enough to warrant further discussion.

Economists define an externality as an event that confers an appreciable damage (or benefit) on one or more individuals who were not fully consenting parties in reaching the decisions that led to the negative (or positive) event in question. In the classic example, a manufacturer that pollutes a stream in the manufacturing process will not take the costs of the pollution into mind when making production decisions. The affected people downstream will unwillingly absorb the pollution costs generated by each unit manufactured. Therefore, the manufacturer will produce more than the socially optimal output. The reason is that they will continue to produce one more unit of output as long as the incremental revenue from the additional unit exceeds the cost. Since they are not paying the people downstream for the environmental damage, the costs used in choosing the level of output will be too low. Consequently, the level of production will be too high because of the negative externality.

Thus obesity generates negative externalities. In other words, obesity does not just affect the obese but those who bear the costs of others' obesity through public programs, risk pooling, collectively financed programs and other sources. Whether we view obesity as an individual choice, or the consequence of consumers being manipulated by food manufacturers will not appreciably alter the solution. However for the moment, it is simplest to view obesity as the result of the individual choice of intake and output that involves a net calorie surplus. That is, eating too much and exercising too little.

At least one of the contributing factors to the problem is clear. The externality arises because the price that the individual faces for the excess calories they consume is lower than the social cost of those calories. Food and exercise choices that lead to obesity elevate health care and other costs for everyone, including those who make healthy choices. What is required is a reduction in the quantity of calories that can be obtained at any specific price, or alternatively the price must be increased in some manner such that it reflects all costs, including the external portion currently passed to society at large. Introducing a tax is one means of internalizing the cost.

THEORETICAL TAX SOLUTIONS TO THE OBESITY PROBLEM

Economists have long studied both the problem of externalities and possible solutions. Referring back to the example of the manufacturer polluting the stream, the problem is to force the manufacturer to internalize all of the costs of production, including the pollution costs. That can be accomplished by placing a tax on the manufacturer's products. If the socially optimal decision is to reduce the production where there is an external cost, then introducing a tax effectively increases the price, which reduces the demand.

Alternatively, there can be cases in which we wish to increase the output because of external benefits that are not captured by the decision-maker. For example, suppose that instead of polluting, the manufacturer's process improved water quality. The benefit from improving water quality would not turn up in the price of the product so the manufacturer would have no incentive to increase the quantity of the water-purifying side benefit. In that case, the recommendation would be a subsidy to encourage production because otherwise the manufacturer would produce less than the socially optimal quantity.

Problems of this type have been successfully addressed through tax policy. We know that consumers do respond behaviorally to tax increases and subsidies. In fact, this approach has worked even in challenging circumstances. For example, in order to reduce the externalities associated with cigarette smoking, taxes were applied to the purchase of cigarettes to successfully mitigate their consumption. Sumner and Wohlgenant (1985) found that both the demand and supply of cigarettes is highly price inelastic. That is, altering the price of cigarettes had little effect on the quantity of cigarettes sold, which suggests that an excise tax should have less effect. However, others have found that demand is more elastic, especially for those at younger ages when smoking is generally initiated (Jha and Chaloupka, 1999; Levy et al., 2004). For that reason, taxes are widely viewed as an effective way to reduce smoking externalities.

Although there are similarities to the smoking problem, addressing obesity is slightly more complicated. One of the concerns that that did not arise with tobacco is setting the tax too high. Unlike food, there is no minimum daily requirement of tobacco so problems associated with driving consumption to zero posed no concern in controlling tobacco use. For food, the objective is not to eliminate all caloric intake but only the calories that are in excess of daily requirements.

Adding a tax to specific foods may have a greater impact than is the case with inelastic goods such as tobacco. For example if we consider soda and high-fat snack foods, there are many substitutes, resulting in more elastic demand-and-supply schedules. The reason for the greater elasticity is that when there are substitutes for a product, consumers will switch to the substitute when prices rise. For that reason, the quantity of the original good demanded will be even more price sensitive. Wansink and Huckabee (2005) claim that people are genetically hardwired to prefer foods that contain fat, sugar and salt; consequently snack foods are likely to be much less sensitive to price increases. If true, this would suggest that a tax on such foods would have little effect. Although there may be some hardwired component to the development of tastes, it would be a mistake to conclude that any such predisposition is the only factor.

Experience and common knowledge indicate a much greater role of learning in the acquisition of taste preferences. There is evidence (Kuchler et al., 2005) supporting the assumption of inelastic demand for salty snack foods in particular. This does not rule out the potential for employing a tax to curb the consumption of high-fat and other less healthy foods. On the other hand, if consumption of snack foods is inelastic, then the potential tax revenue may be substantial. Kuchler et al. (2005) estimate that the tax revenue from a 1 percent tax on salty snack foods would generate revenue of $100 million, which could be directed to education and advertising programs designed to improve health and exercise choices or to treat the adverse health effects of obesity.

Among the potential dietary behaviors that contribute to excessive fat intake is the consumption of convenience foods, according to the US

Department of Agriculture (Biing-Hwan and Frazio, 1997), and vending machine snacks are a prime example of convenience foods that fill our worksites and secondary schools. In a recent study, French et al. (2001) found that reducing the prices of low-fat snacks in vending machines resulted in statistically significant increases in low-fat snack sales in both adolescent and adult populations. Further, the fact that average profits per machine were not affected by this pricing scheme is indicative that, first, people may be willing to substitute healthy for high-fat foods when the prices of the former are lowered, and second, the industry need not worry that profits will be forgone if the lower-priced healthy food alternatives are readily substituted for higher-priced, high-fat foods.

The French et al. study was recently augmented by an examination of the relationship between weight gain in schoolchildren and the real prices of fruits and vegetables. Sturm and Datar (2005) found that between kindergarten and third grade, the weight gain in excess of growth chart predictions was related to the prices of fruits and vegetables in the area, adjusted for the cost of living and other factors. In areas where fruits and vegetables were comparatively more expensive, the BMI increase was greater than in areas where the prices were lower. In the study Mobile, Alabama faced the highest prices and the average BMI of children there increased by 0.21 units more than the national average. The average BMI of children in Visalia, California, which had the least expensive fruit and vegetable prices, increased 0.28 units less than the national average.

Although Sturm and Datar did not directly explore the issue, their study lends credence to the idea that the prices of healthy foods relative to the prices of snack foods may be at least as important as the overall level of food prices in general, if not more so. In Chapter 8 it was argued that agricultural subsidies have favored the production of highly processed, calorically dense food. In particular, corn subsidies have led to overproduction of high-fructose corn syrup, which in turn has artificially reduced the price of a wide array of highly processed foods and snacks. In economic terms, the relative price of these highly processed foods (that is, the price compared to the price of other healthier foods) is too low, encouraging greater consumption of less healthy foods. The point to be made here is that not only do we need to raise the price of the unhealthy foods but the price increase that is required to be effective is likely to depend on the prices of healthy foods. The risks and consequences of over-consumption will be greater if the prices of calorically dense foods are too low, than the risks from low prices on less processed, lower caloric density foods. The key is to reduce caloric intake either through an overall reduction in food intake, or by encouraging a shift away from high caloric density foods to lower caloric density foods.

While taxation alone is unlikely to fully address the problem, several studies including Ippolito and Mathios (1995) and Hu et al. (1995) have shown that education alone is insufficient to tackle the weight problem, particularly when the industry reacts with advertising designed to counter government warnings. Bearing such concerns in mind, a tax solution has other benefits as well. In addition to changing poor consumer choices or behavior, the tax revenue can be used to further reduce the burden of the externality in terms of providing better education on the implications of being obese, providing low-cost exercise facilities for the public, and otherwise providing reimbursement to individuals who are making healthy choices and lowering the public costs of health care. A tax can in effect ensure that the private costs of the decision-maker are the same as the social costs to society as a whole.

From an efficiency or tax incidence perspective it does not matter whether the unhealthy foods are taxed resulting in a higher price or whether healthier foods are subsidized and offered at a discount. The result in either case will be a shift in consumption to healthy foods. In Figure 10.1 shows the relationship between the quantities supplied or demanded and the price. The upward sloping line is the supply curve. It shows that as production levels rise, the price that suppliers require also rises. This is reasonable if we assume for example that per unit costs eventually increase when we push production to higher output levels. The downward sloping line represents consumer demand. As prices fall, all else equal, consumers purchase greater quantities and as the price rises, they purchase less. Without any taxes or other interference, the point where the supply and demand curves

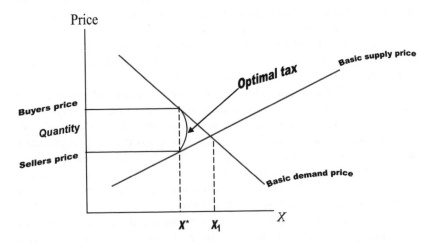

Figure 10.1   Symmetry of a tax on the buyer and seller of good X

intersect will dictate the equilibrium quantity X_1. The steeper the slope of the demand or supply curve, the smaller the effect on quantity of any given price change. For example, suppose that the demand curve was vertical. In that case, changes in price would not affect the quantity at all and it could be said that the demand was price inelastic. On the other hand if the curve was very flat, or elastic, minor changes in price would have a large impact on the quantity.

In a competitive market in equilibrium, as long as demand is not entirely inelastic, lower consumption will occur whether the buyer's price is increased by the tax or whether the seller is levied with the tax and passes on the tax in full to the consumer. The incidence of the tax – who ends up actually paying the tax – will depend on the elasticities of supply and demand. Intuitively, if demand is less elastic consumers will be less able to avoid the tax by reducing consumption levels and will bear more of the tax burden. Although estimating the elasticities is beyond the scope of this chapter, the results from French et al. (2002) discussed previously lend support to the view that convenience foods are relatively price responsive, although results from Kuchler et al. (2005) raise some doubts.

The source of market failure here is the fact that one person's consumption directly or indirectly affects others, rather than through the prices that he or she faces. If the obese person were faced with the true or full cost of their decisions, they would consume less high-fat foods. Thus the price system is only efficient in allocating resources when prices measure marginal opportunity costs. The externality can therefore only be addressed by internalizing the costs of obesity to make sure that individuals pay the full cost of their actions, or alternatively are paid for the full benefits of their actions. Efficiency demands that we equate the private costs of the individual with that of the marginal social cost. In other words, the price that the individual must pay for one more unit is equal to the cost to society of that next unit when all of the social costs are included.

In Figure 10.2 the marginal social cost (MSC), or the social cost of producing one more unit, increases as the level of output rises. At all positive output levels the marginal social cost exceeds the average private costs (AC). Without a tax the consumption level is X_1, but the social optimum is at the lower level of X^* where:

$$\text{Marginal Benefit} = \text{Marginal Social Cost} \qquad (1)$$

At that point, the individual would be willing to pay a price for the last unit consumed that equals the cost to society of that last unit. To induce the private behavior to arrive at the lower consumption level, X^*, we must

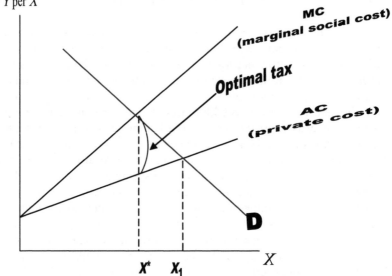

Figure 10.2   Optimal tax to reduce high-fat food consumption

make the private cost equal to the social cost by imposing a tax exactly equal to the marginal social cost minus the average private cost:

$$MC - AC = tax$$

Notice that what we have done here is simply add a tax that equals the extra cost to society that is ignored by the private costs. This will reduce the individual's consumption of X to the level that he or she would encounter if he or she were paying the true and full costs of his or her obesity. In some sense we would be forcing the obese to internalize the costs of their obesity, demanding that they pay the true and higher costs associated with it, which would result in incentives to make healthier choices.

Micro Analysis

To see why the social optimum is attainable we can view the problem from the perspective of the individual consumer. In Figure 10.1 we see that in a competitive market in equilibrium, lower consumption of high-fat foods will occur whether the buyer's price is increased by the tax or whether the seller is levied with the tax and passes on the tax in full to the consumer. (Pigouvian taxes and subsidies are an alternative approach for modeling an optimal solution.)

$$\text{Buyer's price} = \text{seller's price} + \text{tax} \qquad (2)$$

Who bears the burden of the tax (the tax incidence) depends on the elasticity of supply and demand for the good in question, but in any case any tax will involve some efficiency losses and alter the allocation of resources. Theoretically, a tax on one good only – like high-fat convenience foods – will have both a substitution and income effect on consumer behavior. The substitution effect in this case is such that consumers of convenience foods will substitute away from the higher-priced, high-fat goods towards the lower-priced, low-fat goods. The income effect is a consequence of reducing disposable income by the amount of the tax. Intuitively, with less income available to spend the individual must spend less on all goods. The combined substitution and income effects in this case are not positive, and will result in a negative substitution away from the higher-priced, high-fat foods.

Could a tax be used to control the supply side? If we were to select particular parts of the infrastructure of obesity then taxes could be applied to reduce them. Just as consumers look at the after-tax price of goods to make their decisions, suppliers must evaluate their net return. As an example, suppose that meals eaten outside the home are a major culprit in the obesity epidemic and a decision is made to target fast food franchises in particular. Rather than placing a tax on the foods that they sell to reduce demand for such foods, levying a tax on restaurant franchises would reduce the supply of the restaurants themselves. Placing the tax on top of the existing costs of supply would be equivalent to a leftward shift of the supply curve. Just as we saw with taxing food directly, the ability of the suppliers to pass the tax burden through to the purchaser, or the incidence of the tax, would depend on the elasticities of supply and demand. Similar taxes could be applied to snack vending machines, food advertisements directed at children, or any other parts of the infrastructure that were selected.

It may occur to the reader that another alternative would be to place subsidies on the energy-output side to encourage physical activity but the evidence to date points to reducing caloric intake as a more promising route to addressing obesity. It is also true that subsidizing exercise is a more challenging problem from a practical standpoint. For instance, subsidies to memberships in a health and fitness club may increase club memberships but there is no means of assuring that the new members will use the membership. The increase in memberships, if unused, would result in a pure wealth transfer from taxpayers to fitness club owners. These problems do not occur if the tax is placed on the input side of the equation since a reduction in food purchases necessarily results in reduced food consumption.

REAL-WORLD ISSUES IN IMPLEMENTING A FOOD TAX

The real-world problem of using a food tax to correct the obesity problem is admittedly more complex than our theoretical example, for many reasons. Unlike the example with one simple good, there are a vast number of types of foods, some of which may actually alleviate the obesity problem. The range of foods and determination of the foods taxed is critical to developing a successful taxing scheme. We consider the following potential tax solutions:

1. A single uniform tax applied to all foods.
2. A hedonic pricing form of tax that links to characteristics of foods that contribute to obesity. For example, the tax could be proportional to the content of high-fructose corn syrup (HFCS) or other components implicated as contributing to the obesity epidemic.
3. A differential tax applied to specific categories of foods, such as prepared foods, snack foods and soda. Categorization could also depend on food contents such as fat or sugar where the same tax is applied to all foods in the high-fat or high-sugar category.
4. A value-added tax applied at the production stage.

Each of these taxing schemes has advantages and disadvantages.

A Uniform Tax on all Foods

Applying one uniform tax to all foods would likely reduce food consumption overall. As long as consumers are to some extent price sensitive, the addition of the tax will discourage consumption. In economic terms, consumption expenditures will fall as long as the demand for food is price elastic. The tax rate can be adjusted such that the revenue is sufficient to cover the social costs of obesity. Tax revenues could even be directed to programs designed to further reduce the overeating problem. For example, educational programs could be offered, or some of the funds could be directed to counter advertising designed to promote healthier choices or reduce the consumption of unhealthy foods. The main advantage of this tax is its simplicity. With all foods treated the same, there is no need to monitor or assess individual food products, so the administrative costs are likely to be small.

The single uniform tax on all foods has some significant drawbacks as well. The most obvious is that it discourages all food consumption including foods that might have a positive role in reducing obesity. Since all foods are equally affected this tax does not necessarily induce any shift from unhealthy foods to healthier foods. Indeed, since the tax reduces disposable income, consumers might substitute toward less healthy, fatty foods. A related drawback is that at lower income levels food forms a larger percentage of household expenditure so a general tax on food is likely to be highly regressive. That is, lower income groups will bear a disproportionate share of the tax burden. Some might argue that, by creating more income disparity, obesity will be encouraged (Drewnowski and Darmon, 2005).

Mechanisms for Taxing Unhealthy Foods: a Hedonic Pricing Approach

Rather than tax all foods, a more efficient scheme might tax the foods contributing most to obesity. For simplicity, we refer to these foods as 'unhealthy', while recognizing (see below) the difficulty in making such distinctions. If the distinction between healthy and unhealthy foods is meaningful, then it is desirable to tax unhealthy foods more heavily. The problem lies in constructing a practical mechanism to categorize healthy and unhealthy foods. Ideally, the tax should target foods known to be more detrimental, which contribute the most to the obesity problem and have low or zero health benefits. There are various forms that such a tax could take.

A hedonic pricing approach provides a way of identifying unhealthy foods. Hedonic pricing mechanisms are most easily explained through a typical application in housing markets. Although we cannot pinpoint precisely what sets the price of a house, we can point to specific characteristics that affect the market price, such as location, size and amenities. It is then possible to measure the incremental effect or value that each characteristic has on the selling price. These incremental effects are the implicit prices of the characteristics. Adding together the implicit prices of the individual characteristics of a house provides a means of estimating the overall price. For instance, we may find that being on a cul-de-sac adds $5000 to the price, and having central air conditioning adds $3000. Other characteristics may either add or detract by measurable amounts. Taxes may be imposed on specific characteristics, such as size or the existence of air conditioning, instead of on houses as a whole. These taxes would then discourage those characteristics. For example, a tax on space in total square feet would likely encourage buyers to economize on size and substitute toward other amenities.

If we wish to tax the health-reducing aspects of foods we may be able to do so indirectly by placing taxes on individual ingredients or food components. In the same way that the price of housing can be estimated from the characteristics of the house, we could hedonically price the negative health aspects of foods. For example, food item i, (Food$_i$) might be thought of as a function of fat, sugar and other ingredients in that product, or

$$\text{Food}_i = f(\text{Fat}_i, \text{Sugar}_i, \text{Other}_i) \tag{3}$$

A tax might be levied on fat or sugar content, or both, which would raise the cost of items high in content of the taxed characteristic.

In this case we would need to estimate the implicit prices associated with specific ingredients. As an example of how this tax could be implemented, if there are different tax rates on the percentages of fat and sugar then the total tax on the food product is obtained by multiplying the tax rate for each of the three components by the amount contained in the product and adding together the results. With mechanisms that rely on categorizing foods, minor changes in content can generate jumps in tax treatment at points where the change causes a change in categorization. Using the hedonic approach, the tax is proportional to the quantity of specified ingredients. Minor changes in the contents generate similarly minor changes in the tax.

The effectiveness of such a tax scheme will depend on how consumers react. Consumers substitute away from items with taxes on specific characteristics based on their elasticity with respect to those characteristics. They would ultimately choose less of the taxed characteristic, both by buying specific types of food with lower sugar or fat and by buying food types that are generally low in those characteristics. In addition, consumers will increase their consumption of other foods. For example, with less fat consumers may substantially increase their consumption of carbohydrates. With large enough increases in these other foods, weight loss may be minimal or there might even be weight gain.

Another difficulty in implementing such differential taxes is that the mechanism may categorize some foods in higher tax groups than is desirable. For example milk, butter and many dairy products would fall into high tax categories if the tax was based on fat content. However, some of these products are simultaneously being recommended as part of a healthy diet. Recent research findings indicate that milk may be beneficial in controlling obesity. Similarly, efforts to reduce the use of butter may cause consumers to switch to butter substitutes that pose greater health risk.

Problems arise in implementing and administering this type of tax system. First, there would have to be agreement on characteristics to be taxed. A differential tax of this type could be structured with varying tax rates applied to each food category. Higher tax rates could be applied to the categories deemed to generate the most harm. Determining which food categories are the most harmful is a problem in terms of implementing such a tax. However, since fat and sugar can play an important role in diet, and their specific link to obesity is subject to debate, it would be difficult to agree on the characteristics. Once agreed upon, there would be considerable debate on how to define the categories. Intense lobbying by the different food manufacturers might be expected regarding both the foods to be taxed and how the categories are to be defined. Once the categories are defined, food manufacturers may attempt to evade being considered in the taxed categories. They may substitute ingredients that are not being taxed, which may be no healthier than the taxed ingredients. These problems raise the social costs of implementing and administering the tax system.

One variant of the differential tax treatment is to directly tax specific ingredients that are implicated as factors contributing to the obesity problem. As an example, HFCS has been considered a suspect in the search for the underlying causes of obesity. Its role in the problem remains controversial but it is a key ingredient in many of the snack foods and sodas that are often viewed as key contributors. Current labeling laws facilitate an ingredient-based tax because the ingredients must be listed in order of content. If for example sugar is listed first, then it is the primary ingredient and the product would be taxed.

Certainly HFCS is an inexpensive sweetener that facilitates the production of calorically dense snack foods and beverages. Without this low-cost sweetener the selling prices of snack foods would be higher and consumption would probably be lower. Therefore, a tax placed on HFCS would be passed through to consumers as higher prices for snack foods, sodas and similar products, which would likely achieve the desired result of lower consumption of these goods. However, there is still the potential problem of consumers substituting to alternative products that may be nearly as unhealthy, or producers substituting sweeteners that may be nearly as unhealthy. In addition, firms will still be lobbying against the tax, and the means of defining the ingredient, and they may attempt to evade the tax by substituting non-taxed ingredients that are equally or nearly as unhealthy.

A hedonic tax scheme is potentially quite complex, but an advantage is that the tax is proportional to the amount of the targeted characteristic or ingredient. Because minor changes in contents will have only minor tax consequences, the incentive for manufacturers to evade the tax by adjusting the ingredients or lobbying for preferential categorization of their products can be greatly reduced.

Mechanisms Using Differential Taxes on Specific Targeted Foods

To avoid the complexity and difficulties in implementing a broad-based taxing scheme on unhealthy foods, taxes could be levied on items for which there is general agreement that they are unhealthy and there exist adequate healthy substitutes. Specific food groups such as snack foods or soda could be targeted.

An alternative is to tax certain types of food purchases that might encourage overeating or eating particularly unhealthy foods. Some states exempt food purchases at stores from taxation, while taxing food eaten outside the home. If people eat more when they eat at restaurants, this policy might contribute to weight reduction. Special taxes might be levied on fast food or particular types of fast food to also help reduce unhealthy eating patterns.

Poor diet by specific population can be targeted by taxing products in locations frequented by particular populations. The most notable example would be to tax soft drinks at schools. Other snack foods might also be taxed, whether from vending machines or served in the cafeteria (French, 2003).

The effectiveness of this type of tax still depends on whether consumers are responsive to price increases, and how consumers substitute for the taxed good. If they substitute other unhealthy foods, then the overall effects may be small or even harmful. The advantage of a tax on sodas in specific locations such as schools is that the ability to substitute may be minimal.

Some forms of a differential tax may generate other effects that need to be addressed. If a manufacturer can adjust the ingredients of their product to place it in a more favorable tax category, they are likely to do so. Although it is unlikely to be a common problem, it is conceivable that products modified to avoid or reduce taxation could be more harmful than the original. Another problem in applying this type of tax is that the ingredients of some food products are changed from time to time for reasons that have nothing to do with taxes. Such routine adjustments could trigger changes to the tax treatment of the product. Therefore, depending on the mechanism used to categorize foods, the costs of monitoring products and altering the tax structure could be costly.

A Value-Added Tax Approach

As an alternative to basing the tax on specific components or placing foods into distinct tax categories, a value-added tax could also be employed. Such a tax would be placed at the manufacturing level where it would be based on the differential between the costs of the ingredients and the selling price of the finished product. On this basis, the foods that most closely resemble products sold at the farm gate would incur low taxes and highly processed foods would be more highly taxed.

Provided that less healthy foods tend to be more highly processed as well then the value-added tax is an attractive alternative. As a casual observation it seems that many snack items tend to be highly manufactured and heavily packaged, which would increase the value-added component on which the tax would be based. Milk, on the other hand, is not subject to much manufacturing and would face little tax in a value-added system. As with the hedonic tax system, the tax would be proportional rather than having jumps in taxation that occur with categorization-based approaches.

SUMMARY AND CONCLUSIONS

Taxes have been successfully applied to other social problems involving externalities and there is considerable potential for addressing the obesity problem with a tax approach. Applying a tax to foods is challenging since it may not be desirable or feasible to tax all foods. Attempts to tax only specific types of foods may be difficult in terms of selecting the targets, as well as being difficult to administer. Pragmatically, some forms of tax may also be difficult to implement due to responses from manufacturers and consumers. For example, a proposed snack food tax was scuttled in Maryland when Frito-Lay threatened to move a large distribution facility out of the state (Shelsby, 2004). Generally, consumers and producers can substitute away from eating or producing the taxed goods and these substitutions may not improve the overall eating patterns in a way that reduces obesity. In addition, most forms of taxes on foods are likely to have a larger impact on low income groups.

Still, a tax-based or incentive-based solution to obesity has several advantages. It can be used to generally discourage consumption and can target specific unhealthy foods or eating patterns (such as eating in fast food restaurants). It involves no direct budget cost and provides a source of revenue. The revenues generated in part or in total may be earmarked for other obesity programs, such as educational initiatives through schools or the media. Indeed, the publicity surrounding the taxes may reinforce the messages from educational programs. To avoid regressivity concerns, it can be combined with subsidies – either in cash or in kind. For example, extra food stamps might be given that can only be used for specific foods, or specific types of healthy foods may be subsidized.

In conclusion, the selection of a specific tax mechanism involves trade-offs between simplicity, administrative costs, the potential for unintended adverse effects and other market distortions. In the case of an obesity tax, these choices are particularly difficult due to the equity considerations and the difficulty in isolating the culprit products. However beginning with a tax on specific products, such as sodas or snack foods, will not only create some disincentive to purchase these foods but also send the message that these foods are not healthy and should be discouraged. As better knowledge is gained about the role of specific foods and eating habits, taxes might be broadened and some foods subsidized.

188 *Obesity and government*

REFERENCES

Biing-Hwan, I. and E. Frazio (1997), 'Nutritional quality of foods at and away from home', *FoodReview*, Washington, DC: US Department of Agriculture, pp. 33–40.
Chaloupka, F.J., M. Grossman and H. Saffer (2002), 'The effects of price on alcohol consumption and alcohol-related problems', *Alcohol Research and Health*, **26** (1), 22–34.
Cook, P.J. and M.J. Moore (2002), 'The economics of alcohol abuse and alcohol-control policies', *Health Affairs*, (Millwood), **21** (2) (Mar–Apr), 120–33.
Drewnowski, A. and N. Darmon (2005), 'The economics of obesity: dietary energy density and energy cost', *American Journal of Clinical Nutrition*, **82** (Jul) (1 Suppl), 265S–273S.
Finkelstein, E., I. Fiebelkorn, and G. Wang (2003), 'National medical spending attributable to overweight and obesity: how much and who's paying?', *Health Affairs Web Exclusive*, 14 May.
French, S.A. (2003), 'Pricing effects on food choices', *Journal of Nutrition*, **133** (3) (Mar), 841S–843S.
French, S.A., R.W. Jeffery, M. Story, K.K. Breitlow, J.S. Baxter, P. Hannan, and M.P. Snyder (2001), 'Pricing and promotion effects on low-fat vending snack purchases: the CHIPS study', *American Journal of Public Health*, **91**, 112–17.
Hu, T.W., H.Y. Sung, and T. Keeler (1995), 'The state antismoking campaign and the industry response: the effects of advertising on cigarette consumption in California', *American Economic Review*, papers and proceedings, **85** (May), 85–90.
Ippolito, P. and A. Mathios (1995), 'Information and advertising: the case of fat consumption in the United States', *American Economic Review*, papers and proceedings, **85** (2), 91–5.
Jha, P. and F.J. Chaloupka (1999), *Curbing the Epidemic: Governments and the Economics of Tobacco Control*, Washington, DC: World Bank.
Keeler, E.G., W.G. Manning, J.P. Newhouse, E.M. Sloss and J. Wasserman (1989), 'The external cost of a sedentary life style', *American Journal of Public Health*, **79** (8), 975–81.
Kuchler, F., A. Tegene and J.M. Harris (2005), 'Taxing snacks to reduce obesity', *Review of Agricultural Economics*, **27** (1) (Spring), 4–20.
Levy, D.T., F. Chaloupka and J. Gitchell (2004), 'The effects of tobacco control policies on smoking rates: a tobacco control scorecard', *Journal of Public Health Management and Practice*, **10** (4) (July–August), 338–53.
Shelsby, T. (2004), 'House committee abolishes 5% snack tax: Harford officials worried it was threat to Frito-Lay', *Baltimore Sun*, 24 March, p. B1.
Stanton, K.R. and Z.J. Acs (2005), 'The infrastructure of obesity and the obesity epidemic: implications for public policy', *The Journal of Applied Health Economics and Health Policy,* **4** (3), 139–46.
Sturm, R. (2002), 'The effects of obesity, smoking, and drinking on medical problems and costs', *Health Affairs*, **21** (2), 245–53.
Sturm, R. and A. Datar (2005), 'Body mass index in elementary school children, metropolitan area food prices and food outlet density', *Public Health*, **119** (12) (December), 1059–68.
Sumner, D.A. and M.K. Wohlgenant (1985), 'Effects of an increase in the federal excise tax on cigarettes', *American Journal of Agricultural Economics*, **5**, 235–42.
Wansink, Brian and Mike Huckabee (2005), 'De-marketing obesity', *California Management Review*, **47** (4), 6–18.

PART V

Lessons from the past

11. Tobacco control as a model for trimming the obesity problem

David T. Levy and Marilyn Oblak

INTRODUCTION

Smoking has long held the title as the 'leading preventable cause of death' (USDHHS, 2001). It still holds that title, but if trends continue it may not in the foreseeable future. The prevalence of smoking has been on a downward trend in the USA since the widely publicized *Surgeon General's Report* in 1964, which provided strong evidence of the risks of smoking. Smoking prevalence in the USA has declined from a peak of about 50 percent of the adult population to slightly above 20 percent in recent years, with some states nearing 15 percent (CDC, 2002). Obesity, on the other hand, is still growing and reaching 'epidemic' proportions. During the past decade, the obesity rate has risen by 74 percent, with at least one in five adults now classified as obese (Mokdad et al., 1999; Mokdad et al., 2000; Flegal et al., 2002; Baskin et al., 2005).

In light of the addictive nature of cigarettes, 'tobacco control' might be viewed as a contradiction in terms. Nevertheless, a large part of the decline in smoking rates is attributable to better information about its health risks. In addition, evidence presented in the *Surgeon General's Report* indicates that a large part of the decline in the number of smokers can be attributed to other public health policies. Numerous studies provide evidence for the effectiveness of population-based strategies, such as increases in cigarette taxes, clean air restrictions, and media campaigns (USDHHS, 2000; Levy et al., 2004). States such as Arizona, California, Massachusetts and Oregon have had documented success in reducing smoking rates through comprehensive anti-smoking programs.

Public policies to combat obesity are relatively new and little is known about effective policies (Faith et al., 2000; Campbell et al., 2002; Allison and Weber, 2003; Green et al., 2003; Summerbell et al., 2003). The current individual-based approaches to obesity, such as physician interventions and treatments, appear to have had limited success. Few population-based strategies have been attempted and even fewer have been evaluated. To combat the growing obesity epidemic, more comprehensive and innovative interventions are clearly needed, with children and high-risk adults as primary target groups.

This chapter will examine the lessons for obesity control that can be learned from tobacco control. We will consider the perspective of the individual, the role of public policy, the role of business and the interrelationship between the individual, business and society. First, we will discuss the similarities and differences between the two problems. Next, we will consider the different tobacco control policies both individually and combined, and how the lessons learned can be applied to obesity control. Next, the role of business in public policy toward obesity is considered. Finally, we conclude with a discussion of a need for a comprehensive approach.

THE INDIVIDUAL: TOBACCO VS. OBESITY

Habitual Nature

Regular tobacco use more clearly meets the definition of addictive, because the neurological pathways to the brain are well understood. Individuals can function without smoking, as they can without regular exercise. Food, however, is a necessity. Like eating and exercise, the choice of eating habits reflects patterns that often begin early in life. Obesity does not as closely fit most definitions of addiction, but like smoking, eating and exercise it influences the human body's homeostasis and can create habitual behaviors that are difficult to change (Roth et al., 2004).

When attempting to quit, smokers are often unsuccessful and have substantial rates of relapse (Hughes, 1999). Obesity control at the individual level also requires behavioral changes, such as an improved diet and sufficient exercise, which are difficult to implement and maintain. Relapse from diets and exercise routines are common, especially among those that are obese.

Health Risks

The disease risk from both tobacco use and obesity has been established through epidemiological, animal and biological studies (USDHHS, 1989; Burns et al., 1997; Allison et al., 1999; Must et al., 1999; Flegal et al., 2005). Both raise the risk of a wide variety of diseases; most importantly heart disease, but also cancer and other diseases.

Smoking in itself is the major risk factor and its effects, especially over the long-term, are more clearly defined. The role of the intensity and duration of cigarette use and the interactive effects of smoking with diet and other lifestyle influences have been well studied. With obesity, genetic predisposition probably plays a greater role on health impacts. In addition, obesity involves at least two behaviors: diet and physical activity. The relationship between eating and exercise and their interactive effects on obesity are less clearly defined than the risk factors for smoking. Further, the risks of specific foods by themselves and foods eaten in particular combinations are often subject to considerable uncertainty.

External Effects

While many of the effects of obesity and smoking are borne by the individual, the choice to engage in the associated behaviors may not be fully rational and may depend on others. Many of the habits are formed in youth, when it may be argued that the individual is less well informed. In addition, adult behaviors have ramifications for children. Parents that smoke are more likely to have children who smoke, both through their example as a role model and through genetic tendencies. In addition to the parents' position as role model and through genetic predisposition, over-weight parents, who eat foods that promote obesity, are likely to supply these same types of food to their children.

The effects of smoking and obesity-related behaviors have effects that are not fully borne by the individual engaging those behaviors. Smoking and obesity both lead to increased medical costs that are shared with others through the entanglements of the health care system. While the individual bears the physical burden of the disease, the actual costs of treatment for obesity- and tobacco-related diseases are borne by all citizens through shared expenditures for government-financed health care (for example, Medicare, Medicaid and Veterans Benefits). The costs covered through payments by private insurance are also shared (that is, risk-pooled within firms and by insurance companies) over groups of people.

Smoking, unlike obesity, has a direct effect on others through second-hand smoke. There is clear evidence that when an individual smokes at home, work or in a public place, others in the same room (and possibly other rooms due to poor ventilation) are affected. The link of tobacco smoke to both lung cancer and heart disease is well established, with suggestive evidence of a link to stroke, chronic obstructive pulmonary disease (COPD), and other cancers (National Cancer Institute, 1999). Overweight individuals, on the other hand, do not impose direct physical harm on others.

PUBLIC POLICIES TOWARD OBESITY: LESSONS FROM TOBACCO CONTROL

Smoking and obesity, along with alcohol and drug use, are among the leading public health concerns. Tobacco has received considerable attention since the 1950s. As a result, tobacco control policy has also been subject to study for a longer period of time than have obesity control policies. Broad-based educational, regulatory and economic policies to combat obesity are much more recent and there has been little evaluation of obesity control efforts either individually or in combination.

Tobacco policies are often classified as individual-oriented and environmental. Individual-based policies focus on changing individuals' behavior, such as educating individuals on health risks and providing the means to quit smoking. Environmental policies focus on changing aspects of the general surroundings, such as changing opportunities to smoke (by raising costs or prohibiting smoking in public places) or changing the attitudes of the general public towards smoking (for example, through media campaigns).

Health Care Interventions

Individual-based approaches have long been applied to both tobacco and obesity control through clinical intervention and management. Physicians and other health practitioners provide brief interventions that involve advising smokers and those overweight of the health dangers and ways to change their behaviors. Government policies, such as clinical guidelines, encourage health care providers to intervene and teach effective techniques to quit smoking. Similar policies are being adopted in attacking the nation's obesity problem.

Through the health care system, interventions have been made more effective by providing greater access to cessation treatments that aid smokers in quitting (Friend and Levy, 2001; Levy and Friend, 2002b). These treatments include both behavioral and pharmacological therapies. In addition to short-term and long-term counseling, government and privately financed telephone 'quit lines' provide guidance and help individuals deal with behavioral issues that surface while attempting to quit smoking. Generally, public policies can encourage greater availability of treatments by financing them in government-provided health care (such as through Medicare or Medicaid) and by mandating or encouraging (through financial subsidy) private insurance payers to provide these services. Some states have mandated that private insurers cover cessation treatments. While these policies have been an important part of tobacco control strategies, they appear to affect a small though important (such as the more 'hard core') segment of smokers (Levy and Friend, 2002a).

The effectiveness of treatments for obesity, including diet pills and stomach stapling, is more controversial but the government has encouraged evaluation of these treatments and has begun to consider financial coverage. For example, obesity has recently been categorized as a 'disease' under Medicare and, as such, the doors have been opened for greater coverage of treatments. The challenge in future years will be to better understand the application and effectiveness of treatments so that clear guidelines can be developed. With clearer guidelines, private insurers are more likely to provide coverage.

As in the tobacco control experience, government and pharmaceutical firms will be part of the efforts to develop and evaluate better treatments. Like smoking cessation treatment, behavioral therapy can play an important role in effective treatment, both by itself and in conjunction with pharmacotherapy and surgical treatments.

Media and Informational Campaigns

Campaigns conducted outside the traditional health care system have also been geared to changing individual behavior. These campaigns inform individuals of health risks and ways to reduce those risks. They can take the form of publicized reports (for example, the *Surgeon General's Reports*), media campaigns and educational programs in schools. Each of these approaches have been used in tobacco and obesity control, with increasing attention to obesity issues in recent years.

Warning labels on cigarette packages have also been found to be effective in some tobacco control studies (USDHHS, 2000; Levy et al., 2004). To be effective, however, warnings need to be bold and graphic. Analogous to this policy, the labeling of nutritional content can help promote healthy eating habits. While at least some consumers are more likely to find the information desirable, those who may be most in need of it may be least likely to pay attention to the labels. Bolder and, perhaps, graphic nutritional labels may be needed to increase the effectiveness of this policy with the problem population.

Informational strategies were important in the early stages of tobacco control policies, and appear to be important in the current obesity control strategies. Educational programs in schools focused on informing youth of the dangers of smoking and ways to cope with the pressures to smoke. Studies have found varying degrees of effectiveness, and the long-term effectiveness has been questioned (USDHHS, 2000; Levy et al., 2004). Early media campaigns were also directed at providing information, and information was disseminated in the *Surgeon General's Reports*. In the 1960s and 1970s, these programs were effective in changing trends in smoking prevalence (USDHHS, 2000; Levy et al., 2004).

Anti-tobacco media campaigns in the last 15 years have been focused more on changing general attitudes of the population (Levy and Friend, 2000a). For example, the California campaign and the nationally televised Legacy campaign (with the body bags and the mock Marlboro man) have attempted to expose the actions of tobacco manufacturers. By increasing awareness of their actions, the goal is to create anti-smoking sentiments. This approach is thought to be especially effective with the young, and is meant to create awareness of industry marketing tactics, especially regarding advertising. Campaigns have also been targeted to specific socio-demographic groups.

Experience from informational campaigns in tobacco control indicates that campaigns have been most effective when market tested (such as through focus groups) and when they reach a threshold level (Levy and Friend, 2001a; Friend and Levy, 2002). The same principles that apply to marketing by private firms also apply to social marketing. Nevertheless, the tobacco control experience tells us that information programs, along with other individually oriented policies, are likely to be only a part of the solution to the obesity epidemic.

Limits on Marketing

Tobacco control advocates have also attempted to limit the location and content of marketing by tobacco manufacturers. Restrictions on marketing, especially advertising, have been found to be effective in reducing smoking in some studies but others have found limited or no effect (USDHHS, 2000; Levy et al., 2003; Levy et al., 2004). Marketing restrictions are more effective when they are comprehensive, since, otherwise firms find alternative marketing channels. For example, the ban on TV advertisements has probably led to more magazine advertisements and in-store marketing.

While bans on TV advertisements for tobacco have been implemented in the USA, attempts to enact stronger bans have been stifled by concerns about freedom of speech. Attempts have been made to restrict advertisements to youth by limiting the content of them and the places where youth are likely to view them. However, it has been difficult to frame such restrictions in a way that is likely to be effective. Attempts to regulate the marketing of products that promote obesity are likely to face the same or worse stumbling blocks, because of a less well-defined link between food consumption and poor health than between smoking and poor health. The more effective approach may be to create an environment in which the food companies take a 'socially responsible' stance toward the marketing of their products.

Restricting Access to Youth

Media campaigns have also been directed at upholding laws that ban the sale of tobacco to youth. Youth access laws are enforced through government enforcement programs (sting operations). These policies, if properly enforced, appear to reduce youth smoking but their effect on overall tobacco use is less clear (Levy and Friend, 2000; Levy et al., 2001). Because youth obtain a significant proportion of their cigarettes from non-retail sources, they can substitute these sources (for example, through older peers or theft) for retail purchases. Consequently, youth access policies are more effective when combined with policies that reduce the smoking habits of these other sources, such as smoking parents and older peers. In addition, youth access policies affect only a small percentage of the potential problem population. Youth access policies delay, rather than eliminate, initiation unless policies continue to discourage smoking at later ages, particularly between the ages of 18 and 24 (Levy et al., 2000b).

While it is not likely that sales of unhealthy food to youth will be outlawed, youth access to unhealthy food can be restricted in certain places, such as in schools. For example, soda machines can be banned and serving certain unhealthy foods can be prohibited in school cafeterias (or perhaps just in before- and after-school programs). However, these youth policies are not a panacea and may lead to greater substitution of unhealthy food outside of school (although it could have the opposite effect; an empirical issue). The types and quantity of food eaten at home may prove to be more important.

Clean Air Laws and Social Norms

Tobacco control media campaigns have also been directed at increasing awareness about second-hand smoke risks. Besides informing non-smokers of the risks, these campaigns can lead to stricter clean air policies by promoting stronger anti-smoking attitudes. Clean air laws limit smoking in the work site and public places, such as restaurants and shopping areas. Besides creating anti-smoking norms, these policies reduce opportunities to smoke (for example, while at work). Thereby they reduce the quantity smoked and cause some smokers to quit (Levy and Friend, 2001b).

Since obesity does not have the same kind of direct ramifications as second-hand smoke, there is not a clearly analogous policy for obesity control. However, it is important to consider policies that create pro-health opportunities and social norms. For example, creating more parks and recreation areas increases the opportunities to exercise and encourages healthy attitudes. Physical activity in schools, such as required gym classes and after-school programs, if well executed, may play a similar role.

Taxes and Economic Incentives

From economics we know that, as price goes up, opportunities are restricted and consumption declines. This principle has been found to apply even for addictive goods. Taxes on cigarettes have been widely used and have proven an effective means to reduce smoking, especially by the young. Higher taxes have been found to reduce the likelihood of initiation and quantity smoked, as well as increase the likelihood of successful smoking cessation (Levy et al., 2000a). Higher taxes have been the starting point for most of the effective state and national tobacco control programs, with the resulting tax monies often earmarked to implement other tobacco control policies.

Because of the less well-defined linkage of health outcomes to 'unhealthy' (such as fatty, high-sugar) foods, it will be more difficult to establish criteria for taxing foods with poor health attributes. Although not implemented on a wide-scale basis, some states have taxed specific items (for example, soda), and school cafeterias can raise the price of specific unhealthy foods (French, 2003). While economic disincentives have the potential to have greatest effect on those with lower incomes, they also create the greatest economic burden to those groups. A more politically acceptable policy to implement might be to subsidize healthy foods, especially in nutritional programs aimed at schools or for the poor (for example, through food stamp programs). In addition, government agricultural programs can strive to avoid subsidizing unhealthy food products such as corn syrup.

Legal Challenges

While not systematically evaluated, legal challenges to tobacco manu-facturers, both through public and private suits, appear to have had a beneficial effect. They have raised the financial costs of tobacco manu-facturers, which has led to higher cigarette prices and consequently lower tobacco consumption. In addition, the tobacco lawsuits create pub-licity about the socially harmful practices of the firms and the risks of their products.

As discussed in Chapter 12, lawsuits may be less successful against food manufacturers than the tobacco manufacturers, due to the less well-defined relationship between use of specific foods and health risk, and because industry abuse is less blatant. However, the threat of lawsuits alone may encourage the firms to produce and advertise healthier products, as seems to have been the case for McDonald's (Daynard et al., 2002; Daynard et al., 2004). Firms will have strong incentives to avoid the publicity and costs of a potential lawsuit.

The Need for Comprehensive Policies

A final lesson learned from tobacco control is the need for multiple policies coordinated as part of a comprehensive strategy (USDHHS, 2000; Levy et al., 2004). Each of the policies described here have proven to be of limited effectiveness. The states with comprehensive tobacco policies such as Arizona, California, and Massachusetts have made important strides in reducing tobacco use. It appears that tobacco control policies individually need to reach threshold levels and after some point are subject to diminishing returns. A combination of different policies is then needed to further reduce the smoking habit. Similar tendencies might also be expected in obesity control, where strong habits must also be changed. As discussed above, policies like media initiatives or school education alone are likely to have limited effects. They will have stronger effects when reinforced by policies that affect the environment through promoting norms against unhealthy behaviors, promoting opportunities for healthy behaviors and creating economic disincentives for unhealthy behaviors.

BUSINESS, SMOKING AND OBESITY

In developing a coherent business strategy, it is important to recognize a strong public perception among much of the public and many in the public health community that 'big business' is a major culprit in the problem. However, business, especially the food industry but also other industries, can play a positive role in combating the epidemic.

Industries Whose Products Directly Affect Obesity

The food industry, like tobacco manufacturers, has borne the brunt of public disapproval. Marketing to children and the addition of unhealthy (and some claim addictive) ingredients by both the tobacco industry and the food industry is viewed as an important part of the problem from a public health perspective (Chopra and Darnton-Hill, 2004). However, there are important differences in the two industries.

Tobacco companies, in the USA, are a tight oligopoly (the 'big three'). Evidence indicates that the leading firms have acted in concert to raise prices and to actively lobby government. While we often hear of the large corporations, such as McDonald's, the food industry is much less concentrated and much more diverse. The industry includes large and small firms producing and distributing food prepared and eaten at home, and some large chains, but mostly relatively small restaurants, that serve food eaten outside the home. Many separate markets are involved, and, except in some market niches (such as cereals in the 1960s), there is little evidence of collusive behavior. The food industry is a less well-coordinated political lobby, with diverse interests.

To date, there are important differences in how tobacco companies and food companies have presented their products. Tobacco manufacturers have been denying (until recently) the health risks of smoking, denying the addictive nature of smoking (while adding ingredients to make it more addictive) and targeting youth in their marketing campaigns. While there has been some change in their behavior in recent years, it has been viewed by public health advocates as 'too little, too late'. There are claims that food manufacturers and fast food chains could have done more to improve the nutritional content of food and have targeted children in promoting unhealthy food (Chopra and Darnton-Hill, 2004), but they have clearly been less overt in their behaviors than the tobacco companies; the case for unethical behavior against firms in the food industries is less clear.

Firms in the food industry can play an important role in promoting public health. They can learn from the mistakes of firms in the tobacco industry, where ultimately their actions hurt their public image and large amounts are now being spent to improve that image. Food manufacturers and vendors, especially fast food restaurants, can adopt a more conciliatory and supportive approach to government public health policy. Marketing strategies promoting unhealthy foods to youth are likely to have consequences in creating a poor public image. Socially responsible policies can promote public image. Even supporting government policies that restrict certain types of marketing or that regulate the content of foods can be a profitable strategy. By limiting competition to promote and sell less healthy products, the image of the regulated firms improves without facing the prospects of lost sales to firms using less socially responsible policies.

Another set of businesses that can directly affect the obesity epidemic are the health care industries. In contrast to the tobacco industry, the pharmaceutical industry has generally attempted to take a public health stance and have supported tobacco control advocates. As an ally, their public image improved and they became a positive force in tobacco control. Physicians and health care workers have also generally been supportive of tobacco control, although they have sometimes been criticized for failing to take a more preventive-oriented approach through brief interventions. The difficulties in advocating behavioral change to patients and the lack of financial remuneration for their time have been recognized as drawbacks to their efforts.

Insurance firms affect the coverage and remuneration to health care workers as well as coverage for cessation treatments. In tobacco control, insurance has been slow to cover cessation treatments, due to the lifestyle element. The same concerns arise in obesity control. However, recent changes in government policy to recognize obesity as a disease, and movements toward greater coverage by Medicare and Medicaid, should help make the case for broader coverage. Nevertheless, much of the coverage provided by insurance is likely to depend on business, since they are the payers for most private insurance.

Efforts by the General Business Public in Dealing with the Obesity Epidemic

The ability of American industry to affect the smoking and obesity problem is limited, but there is still a potentially important role that firms can play. As in reducing smoking, firms have incentives to reduce obesity. Policies encouraging obesity control can have direct financial payoffs. High insurance costs have hurt firms in the USA, especially those facing foreign competitors who have lower insurance costs. Increasing physical activity and improving diet can reduce those costs. Besides reducing the insurance costs, smoking and obesity control policies can provide increased productivity and lower absenteeism; healthier employees are less likely to take sick days and will generally be more productive on the job. In addition, fewer sick days will be needed to care for the sick children of employees. The increased productivity with less obesity may be even greater than for smoking. In addition, while smoking policies affect primarily the declining percentage that smoke, obesity control policies have the potential to affect a larger percentage of workers. Physical activity and healthy eating potentially benefits all workers.

Indeed, the majority of employees that work indoors are subject to bans on smoking in the workplace (Shopland et al., 2001), and many firms have their own programs to help smokers quit (Glasgow et al., 1996). Company policies such as clean air restrictions in the work site and cessation treatment programs have been found to encourage smoking cessation. Increasingly, firms have elected to have insurance plans that provide coverage for smoking cessation treatments (Friend and Levy, 2001; McPhillips-Tangum et al., 2002).

Similar to programs directed at smoking, firms can provide physical activity programs or provide access to healthier foods in the workplace. They may also provide weight loss and counseling programs, and provide insurance coverage for obesity interventions. Interestingly, some evidence indicates that anti-smoking policies may have encouraged obesity (Cawley et al., 2004; Chou et al., 2004). Well-integrated programs that encourage healthy lifestyles could counteract any negative synergies. Encouraging exercise programs could reduce the likelihood of both smoking and weight problems. Industry might take a lead in developing programs that generally support healthy lifestyles.

Programs for employees are part of the larger system of public policies directed at obesity control. By publicly supporting government policies that help to reduce obesity and the associated health problems firms can cut these costs, and the productivity of their workforce can benefit. In addition, by supporting government obesity policies, the firm's public image may benefit.

CONCLUSIONS

As with tobacco control, a comprehensive strategy will be necessary to tame the obesity epidemic. Policies will need to be directed at children and high-risk adults, and a multiplicity of different policies will be needed. In addition to educational and informational programs, limits on marketing by the industry, improved opportunities for better diets and exercise, greater access to treatments and economic incentives can all play a role. Similar conclusions have been drawn in other reviews (Daynard, 2003; Mercer et al., 2003; Yach et al., 2003; Chopra and Darnton-Hill, 2004; Warner, 2005). In developing sound policies, it will be important to gain a better understanding of how diet and exercise affect obesity and, in turn, how public policies affect each of those behaviors.

Using the framework suggested in Chapter 2, both demand-side and supply-side policies are needed. Policies will be needed to affect demand through educating the consumer, providing treatments, putting limits on marketing and through economic incentives such as the use of taxes, subsides and insurance. However, important supply-side changes can be made that affect which foods are available to children at school, regulations and incentives for food manufacturers to provide healthier foods can be implemented, and areas where and times when physical activity can take place can be provided.

While the government will need to spearhead the fight against the obesity epidemic, American business can play a limited but important role. Support for public health programs by business is essential in terms of public and financial support. This is not only the 'right thing to do', but should also pay dividends at the bottom line. In tobacco, the conflict between business and public health advocates has proven destructive to business and to the public health of our nation. This state of affairs must be avoided in the tackling of obesity problems.

REFERENCES

Allison, D.B. and M.T. Weber (2003), 'Treatment and prevention of obesity: what works, what doesn't work, and what might work', *Lipids*, **38** (2), 147–55.

Allison, D.B., K.R. Fontaine, J.E. Manson, J. Stevens and T.B. VanItallie (1999), 'Annual deaths attributable to obesity in the United States', *Journal of the American Medical Association*, **282** (16), 1530–8.

Anderson, J.F. (2006), 'Perspectives on the economic and cultural effects of obesity litigation: lessons from *Pelman* v. *McDonalds*', Chapter 12, this volume.

Audretsch, David B. and D. DiOrio (2006), 'The spread of obesity', Chapter 2, this volume.

Baskin, M.L., J. Ard, F. Franklin and D.B. Allison (2005), 'Prevalence of obesity in the United States', *Obesity Review*, **6** (1), 5–7.

Burns, D., L. Garfinkel and J. Samet (eds) (1997), *Changes in Cigarette-Related Disease Risks and Their Implication for Prevention and Control*, smoking and tobacco control monograph 8, Bethesda, MD: National Institutes of Health, National Cancer Institute.

Campbell, K., E. Waters, S. Kelly and C. Summerbell (2002), 'Interventions for preventing obesity in children.' *Cochrane Database of Systematic Reviews*, **2**, CD001871.

Cawley, J., S. Markowitz, et al. (2004), 'Lighting up and slimming down: the effects of body weight and cigarette prices on adolescent smoking initiation', *Journal of Health Economics*, **23** (2), 293–311.

CDC (2002), accessed at www.cdc.gov/tobacco/research_data/adults_prev/ adstat3.htm and www.cdc.gov/tobacco/research_data/adults_prev/tab_3.htm.

Chopra, M. and I. Darnton-Hill (2004), 'Tobacco and obesity epidemics: not so different after all?', *British Medical Journal*, **328** (7455), 1558–60.

Daynard, R.A. (2003), 'Lessons from tobacco control for the obesity control movement', *Journal of Public Health Policy*, **24** (3–4), 291–5.

Daynard, R.A., L.E. Hash and A. Robbins (2002), 'Food litigation: lessons from the tobacco wars', *Journal of the American Medical Association*, **288** (17), 2179.

Daynard, R.A., P.T. Howard and K.L. Wilking (2004), 'Private enforcement: litigation as a tool to prevent obesity', *Journal of Public Health Policy*, **25** (3–4), 408–17.

Faith, M.S., K.R. Fontaine, L.J. Cheskin and D.B. Allison (2000), 'Behavioral approaches to the problems of obesity', *Behavior Modification*, **24** (4), 459–93.

Flegal, K.M., M.D. Carroll, C.L. Ogden and C.L. Johnson (2002), 'Prevalence and trends in obesity among US adults, 1999–2000', *Journal of the American Medical Association*, **288** (14), 1723–7.

Flegal, K.M., B.I. Graubard, D.F. Williamson and M.H. Gail (2005), 'Excess deaths associated with underweight, overweight, and obesity', *Journal of the American Medical Association*, **293** (15), 1861–7.

French, S.A. (2003), 'Pricing effects on food choices', *Journal of Nutrition*, **133** (3), 841S–43S.

Friend, K. and D. Levy (2001), 'Smoking cessation interventions and policies to promote their use: a critical review', *Nicotine and Tobacco Research*, **3** (November), 299–310.

Friend, K. and D. Levy (2002), 'Reductions in smoking prevalence and cigarette consumption associated with mass-media campaigns', *Health Education Research*, **17** (1), 85–98.

Glasgow, R.E., G. Sorenson, C. Giffen, R.H. Shipley, K. Corbett and W. Lynn (1996), 'Promoting worksite smoking control policies and actions: the Community Intervention Trial for Smoking Cessation (COMMIT) experience. The COMMIT Research Group', *Preventative Medicine*, **25** (2), 186–94.

Green, L.W., S.L. Mercer, A.C. Rosenthal, W.H. Dietz, C.G. Husten (2003), 'Possible lessons for physician counseling on obesity from the progress in smoking cessation in primary care', *Forum Nutr*, **56**, 191–4.

Hughes, J.R. (1999), 'Four beliefs that may impede progress in the treatment of smoking', *Tobacco Control*, **8** (3), 323–6.

Levy, D.T. and K.B. Friend (2000), 'A simulation model of tobacco youth access policies', *Journal of Health Politics, Policy and Law*, **25** (6), 1023–50.

Levy, D.T. and K. Friend (2001a), 'A computer simulation model of mass media interventions directed at tobacco use', *Preventive Medicine*, **32** (3), 284–94.

Levy, D.T. and K. Friend (2001b), 'A framework for evaluating and improving clean indoor air laws', *Journal of Public Health Management & Practice*, **7** (5), 87–96.

Levy, D.T. and K. Friend (2002a), 'Examining the effects of tobacco treatment policies on smoking rates and smoking related deaths using the SimSmoke computer simulation model', *Tobacco Control*, **11** (1), 47–54.

Levy, D.T. and K. Friend (2002b), 'A simulation model of policies directed at treating tobacco use and dependence', *Medical Decision Making*, **22** (1), 6–17.

Levy, D.T., K.M. Cummings and A. Hyland (2000a), 'Increasing taxes as a strategy to reduce cigarette use and deaths: results of a simulation model', *Preventive Medicine*, **31** (3), 279–86.

Levy, D.T., K.M. Cummings and A. Hyland (2000b), 'A simulation of the effects of youth initiation policies on overall cigarette use', *American Journal of Public Health*, **90** (8), 1311–4.

Levy, D.T., K. Friend and M. Carmona (2001), 'Effect of policies directed at youth access to smoking: results from the SimSmoke computer simulation model', *Tobacco Control*, **10** (2), 108–16.

Levy, D.T., J.G. Gitchell and F. Chaloupka (2004), 'The effects of tobacco control policies on smoking rates: a tobacco control scorecard', *Journal of Public Health Management & Practice*, **10** (4) (Jul–Aug), 338–53.

Levy, D.T., E. Mumford and B. Pesin (2003), 'Tobacco control policies, and reductions in smoking rates and smoking-related deaths: results from the SimSmoke model', *Expert Review of Pharmacoeconomics and Outcomes Research*, **3** (4), 457–68.

McPhillips-Tangum, C., A. Cahill, C. Bocchino and C.M. Cutler (2002), 'Addressing tobacco in managed care: results from the 2000 survey', *Preventive Medicine in Managed Care*, **3** (3), 85–95.

Mercer, S.L., L.W. Green, A.C. Rosenthal, C.G. Husten, L.K. Khan and

W.H. Dietz (2003), 'Possible lessons from the tobacco experience for obesity control', *American Journal of Clinical Nutrition*, **77** (4 Suppl), 1073S–1082S.

Mokdad, A.H., M.K. Serdula, W.H. Dietz, B.A. Bowman, J.S. Marks and J.P. Koplan (1999), 'The spread of the obesity epidemic in the United States, 1991–1998', *Journal of the American Medical Association*, **282** (16), 1519–22.

Mokdad, A.H., M.K. Serdula, W.H. Dietz, B.A. Bowman, J.S. Marks and J.P. Koplan (2000), 'The continuing epidemic of obesity in the United States', *Journal of the American Medical Association*, **284** (13), 1650–1.

Must, A., J. Spadano, E.H. Coakley, A.E. Field, G. Colditz and W.H. Dietz (1999), 'The disease burden associated with overweight and obesity', *Journal of the American Medical Association*, **282** (16), 1523–9.

National Cancer Institute (1999), *Health Effects of Exposure to Environmental Tobacco Smoke: The Report of the California Environmental Protection Agency*. Smoking and Tobacco Control Mongraph no. 10. USDHHS, National Institutes of Health, National Cancer Institute.

Roth, J., X. Qiang, S.L. Marban, H. Redelt and B.C. Lowell (2004), 'The obesity pandemic: where have we been and where are we going?', *Obesity Research*, **12** (suppl 2), 88S–101S.

Shopland, D.R., K.K. Gerlach, D.M. Burns, A.M. Hartman and J.T. Gibson (2001), 'State-specific trends in smoke-free workplace policy coverage: the current population survey tobacco use supplement, 1993 to 1999', *Journal of Occupational & Environmental Medicine*, **43** (8), 680–6.

Summerbell, C.D., V. Ashton, K.J. Campbell, L. Edmonds, S. Kelly and E. Waters (2003), 'Interventions for treating obesity in children', *Cochrane Database Systematic Review*, **3**, CD001872.

US Department of Health and Human Services (USDHHS) (1989), *Reducing the Health Consequences of Smoking: 25 Years of Progress: A Report of the Surgeon General*, Atlanta, GA: Centers for Disease Control and Prevention, National Center for Chronic Disease Prevention and Health Promotion, Office on Smoking and Health.

USDHHS (2000), 'Reducing tobacco use: a report of the Surgeon General', Atlanta, GA: Centers for Disease Control and Prevention, National Center for Chronic Disease Prevention and Health Promotion, Office on Smoking and Health.

USDHHS (2001), 'Women and smoking: a report of the Surgeon General', Rockville, MD: Centers for Disease Control and Prevention, National Center for Chronic Disease Prevention and Health Promotion, Office on Smoking and Health.

Warner, K.E. (2005), 'Tobacco policy in the United States: lessons learned for the obesity epidemic policy', *Policy Challenges in Modern Health Care*, (May), 99–114.

Yach, D., C. Hawkes, J.E. Epping-Jordan and S. Galbraith (2003), 'The World Health Organization's Framework Convention on Tobacco Control: implications for global epidemics of food-related deaths and disease', *Journal of Public Health Policy*, **24** (3–4), 274–90.

12. Perspectives on the economic and cultural effects of obesity litigation: lessons from *Pelman* v. *McDonald's*

José Felipé Anderson

INTRODUCTION

Most controversial public policy issues in the USA end up in its state or federal courtrooms for resolution. The recent national focus on health and obesity is no exception.

The controversial lawsuit by plaintiffs against the fast food giant McDonald's, for serving allegedly unhealthy food that contributes to obesity, has drawn sharp criticism and international media attention (*Pelman* v. *McDonald's*, 2003). Although in some quarters the lawyers bringing the suit were harshly attacked, noticeable changes in the menu of the entire fast food industry occurred shortly after the case was filed. Although it may be years before the legal aspects of this issue are worked out in the courts, it is clear that beyond the possible financial recovery for the individual plaintiffs in the case, there is a potential for lawsuits themselves to bringing about reform in this multi-billion-dollar industry. This chapter offers some practical perspectives on how tort law and class action litigation may work together to transform the fast food industry in the way that legislation or other political action could not. The McDonald's case may have the potential to result in decades-long reforms similar to those brought about by tobacco, asbestos and medical products class action litigation. These cases may offer the promise of improving the health conditions for at-risk, poor, minority and disenfranchised communities. These communities may not have the clout to meaningfully assert concerns in the political process to create positive change from businesses that service their communities, including those that serve fast food.

Some research indicates that the cost of obesity exceeds billions of dollars, which includes hospitalization and treatment for diabetes, coronary heart disease and hypertension. Some segments of society have sought to identify a source of blame for the spike in obesity and attention has centered on the products and marketing techniques of the fast food industry.

High-profile lawsuits have focused public attention on the balance between personal responsibility and corporate responsibility. One the one hand, the selection of food is seen as essentially voluntary choice. On the other hand, like tobacco, corporate choices about marketing to high-risk groups have caused relief to be given to some plaintiffs in the litigation process when legislatures have not responded to the need to address serious public health consequences.

The future success of such lawsuits is uncertain. The current trend in product liability litigation is to test the flexible outer limits of tort law. This process has been used to fix the boundaries on the responsibility of food and drug manufacturing companies to provide more complete information and detailed warnings for the known risks of their products. The cost of such efforts, along with concerns about First Amendment rights to commercial speech are implicated when the government seeks to control the content and target of messages a business chooses to offer.

The commercial freedom our country has enjoyed in marketing products to the public is an important business asset. The opportunity to fashion those commercial messages is at the heart of many of the nations major industries. In 1917 alone $13.4 billion was spent on radio advertising, and $44.5 billion on television (Federal Communications Commission, 1998). In no area is this advertising freedom more apparent than in the fast food industry that markets to families, and particularly children. With the inducement of special offers and collectable toys, children are drawn to national fast food chains at an early age.

Furthermore, the continuing public interest in effective weight loss approaches in a largely unregulated high-profit diet industry raises additional questions about the best public policy approach to the obesity problem in the USA. The problem will likely be resolved in the court system if policymakers do not reach agreement on the best approach to the problem through legislative action. Health care, food and insurance industries that will ultimately absorb the financial cost. Those costs will be passed on to consumers and may not be limited to product price but also product choice options and convenience.

Central to the debate is whether a jury should play any role in awarding damages for unhealthy products sold by fast food chains to a willing public. Much of the controversy over using the courtroom as a laboratory for business reform centers on the role of the jury, and whether so much power to shift wealth should be placed in its hands. Alexis de Tocqueville observed '. . . the main reason for the practical intelligence and political good sense of the Americans is their long experience with the juries in civil cases'

(Meyer, 1969, p. 269). Indeed, even prior to the founding of this nation the awarding of civil damages for punishment had been assigned as part of a jury's responsibility (*Wilkes* v. *Wood*, 1763). There have been critics of the jury's traditionally broad power to assign monetary damages. One federal judge vigorously asserted his concern that the jury had available to it 'a vast power to commit error and do mischief by loading it with technical burdens far beyond its ability to perform' (*Skidmore* v. *Baltimore & Ohio R.R. Co.*, 1948).

Although this debate will continue to divide the public on the use of the jury system to make important economic decisions in our culture, it is clear that allowing it to do so was a structural choice consciously made by the founding fathers. '[P]erhaps the central theme of the United States Constitution is the division of power. The involvement of the jury decentralizes the most devastating exercise of government power over its own citizens' (Attanasio, 2001, p. 1682). There is also some doubt as to whether the critics of the jury system can establish that a different system would lead to less controversial results. For example, one survey of Texas federal judges found that approximately 90 percent of them agreed with the jury's verdict most of the time (Attanasio, 2001).

Still, calls for tort reform have swept the nation. Often allegations are advanced that America's courts are filled with frivolous litigation that threatens our entire economic structure. Not all observers agree that the jury and the use of the courts as a tool of economic, legal and public policy reform is a crisis that constitutes a threat to the nation. Consumer advocate Ralph Nader describes the tort reform movement as 'one of the most unprincipled public relations scams in the history of American industry' (Nader, 1987, p. 18).

The threat of punitive damage awards also fuels the 'anti-lawsuit' fervor because such awards often receive a great deal of medical attention. However, at least one study has concluded that only about 1.5 percent of personal injury awards contain any punitive damages at all (Fried, 1998). Many states have set damage award limits precluding jurors from awarding amounts above the statutory maximum limits (*USA Today*, 3 March 2003). The process for such laws usually allows the jury to set the damages without knowing that they are limited as to the amount. Thereafter, the judge is legally required to reduce the amount to the legally imposed maximum. There is evidence that such legislation may not have even been necessary. One study indicates that jurors, when not informed of those legally imposed limits, only exceeded them in 7 percent of the cases (Baldus et al., 1995). One scholar has suggested that 'Tort reform advocates limiting the power of juries and expanding the power of judges or blue ribbon panels of jurors . . . [create] a significant imbalance in terms of race, gender, and ideology . . . In short, tort reform proposals that limit the power of the jury pose a real danger'(McClellan, 1996, p. 791).

Despite the critics who believe that the jury trial is not the proper venue to decide the responsibility of the fast food industry to its customers, lawyers are ready to attempt to litigate the issues in order to change the very culture of our nations, its eating habits and health condition.

THE MCDONALD'S OBESITY LAWSUIT

An important historical development in the obesity controversy are the McDonald's Corporation lawsuits that originated in New York in August 2002, and were first decided by a federal court the following year (*Pelman* v. *McDonald's*, 2003). The case involved several minor children who filed suit through their parents, alleging that the fast food chain was making and selling their product in a deceptive and negligent manner that was causing injury to the health of the children by making them obese. The multiple-count 'complaint' that initiated the lawsuit set forth several alternative theories suggesting why McDonald's had financial responsibility for the alleged harm cause by its food products. The plaintiffs filing the case had a strategy relying on several legal theories, as is typical of many tort lawsuits. Particularly, suits that introduce issues of 'first impression' in the nation proceed in this manner. Lawyers who pursue such strategies wisely anticipate that parts of their case will be rejected by a reviewing court, since there may be little or no legal precedent for the court to follow in addressing the issues in the case.

Like other controversial tort claims, the federal trial court dismissed the complaint, but allowed the plaintiffs to file modified, or 'amended', claims within 30 days. What was somewhat unusual about the McDonald's case was that US District Judge Robert W. Sweet laid out a roadmap to aid the plaintiffs in filing, at least potentially, a more viable lawsuit. Judge Sweet's detailed discussion of the issues raised by the plaintiffs demonstrated a thoughtful examination of an issue that could easily be misunderstood as mere 'ambulance chasing' or abuse of the tort litigation system.

The opinion is a complex piece of jurisprudence that contains several aspects beyond the scope of this chapter. However, it is useful to survey some of the opinion's most intriguing components. Newspaper accounts of the lawsuit either fail to explain or misunderstand the judge's approach to the lawsuit. The trial judge understood that taking the claims lightly would simply prolong the years-long journey that will ultimately lead to a settled balance between law and policy on claims against the fast food industry. Clearly, lawyers who are filing these suits, like their forerunners in the tobacco and asbestos litigation, intend to pursue their claims until they prevail or until no court will entertain any of their legal theories. Accordingly, the judge's comprehensive treatment of these issues in the lawsuit was a sound use of judicial resources since the claims against the fast food industry are unlikely to disappear overnight.

Describing the case as 'unique and challenging', the Judge's opinion probed legal and policy aspects of the dispute. Exploring both medical reality, corporate marketing and the procedural implications of such lawsuits against multi-state fast food chains, the court cautiously began the difficult task of establishing guidance for what likely will be the next great wave of class action lawsuits involving products of common and voluntary use.

The Judge started his opinion with the unavoidable acknowledgment that the claim involved the intake of a legal product that poses known health risks. Like cigarettes and the smoking-related claims of prior years, the plaintiff's free will choice to engage in the activity needed to be taken into account. Indeed, the Judge framed the controversy in this way: '[t]he issue of determining the breath of personal responsibility underlies much of the law: where should the line be drawn between an individual's own responsibility to take care of herself, and society's responsibility to ensure that others shield her?' (*Pelman* v. *McDonald's*, p. 516).

He explained that '[l]aws are created in those situations where society needs to provide a buffer between the individual and some other entity – whether herself, another individual or a behemoth corporation that spans the globe' (op. cit., p. 516). When analysing whether to hold McDonald's responsible in the litigation at all, the court said that its opinion was:

> 'guided by the principle that legal consequences should not attach to the consumption of hamburgers and other fast food fare unless consumers are unaware of the dangers of eating such food . . . they cannot blame McDonald's if they, nonetheless, choose to satiate their appetite with a surfeit of super-sized McDonald's products.' (op. cit., p. 516)

But the court cautioned, '[o]n the other hand, consumers cannot be expected to protect against a danger that was solely within McDonald's knowledge. Thus, one necessary element of any viable claim must be that "McDonald's" products involve a danger that is not within the common knowledge of the consumers'. The Judge noted that the plaintiffs made no such allegation in the case as it was presently filed. That failure was among the primary reasons that the lawsuit was dismissed but the judge continued to discuss the potential boundaries of the fast food lawsuit.

The Court later addressed in the opinion McDonald's concerns about the possibility that the suit against them in this case could potentially lead them into a host of other lawsuits, and noted that Americans spend more than $110 billion on fast food each year, and as much as 30 percent of the average household diet is composed of food prepared in fast-food-type operations. In light of such a profound effect on daily commerce, the court said that it was 'cognizant of its duty "(*Pelman* v. *McDonald's*, p. 518) to limit the legal consequences of wrongs to a controllable degree and to protect [McDonald's] against crushing exposure to liability".'

Reviewing the allegations of the specific facts in the pleadings the court identified the plaintiffs as infant consumers who purchased and consumed the defendant's product and had become overweight and developed diabetes, coronary heart disease, high blood pressure, elevated cholesterol intake and other adverse health effects. The Judge then turned his attention to the national problem of increased childhood obesity over the years. 'Today there are nearly twice as many overweight adolescents as there were in 1980. In 1999, an estimated 61 percent of US adults were overweight or obese and 13 percent of children aged 6 to 11 years and 14 percent of adolescents aged 12 to 19 were overweight. In 1980, those figures for children were 7 percent for children aged 6 to 11 years and 5 percent for adolescents aged 12 to 19 years' (*Pelman* v. *McDonald's*, p. 518).

The Judge then turned his attention to the societal cost of obesity:

> 'Obese individuals have a 50 to 100 percent increased risk of premature death from all causes. Approximately 300 000 deaths a year in the United States are currently associated with overweight and obesity. As indicated in the US *Surgeon General's Report on Overweight and Obesity*, "left unabated . . . [both] may soon cause as much preventable disease and death as cigarette smoking".' (*Pelman* v. *McDonald's*, p. 518)

Judge Sweet's opinion also cited the estimated financial costs of obesity: 'In 1995, the total cost estimates attributable to obesity amounted to an estimated $99 billion. In 2000, the cost of obesity was estimated to be $117 billion' (op. cit., p. 518). The detailed focus on the health consequences of obesity in the opinion is an interesting intervention into the public policy of health care. Once the judge included this discussion in his opinion he has all but concluded that he believes that potential damages for harm is a real possibility in an appropriate case. He could have easily omitted this level of detail in his discussion. It certainly was not necessary to the decision to dismiss the claims against McDonald's.

The plaintiff also pursued a legal theory making McDonald's responsible for encouraging that its food could be eaten 'every day' as part of a health diet. This claim is interesting, if for no other reason than the well-known strategy of fast food companies to focus their marketing on children. The company also commits a great deal of money to all forms of media promotion and centers most of its marketing push to its younger customers. The Court also dismissed the deceptive practices claims in the case noting that 'the complaint does not identify a single instance of deceptive acts . . .' To end the discussion at the failure to plead any facts to support deceptive acts or advertising would have been appropriate. However, in a detailed further explanation, bordering on a judicial advisory opinion, the court examined in great detail the advertising practices of the fast food industry in general and McDonald's in particular. Examining the website of the fast food giant, the court noted that indeed McDonald's had encouraged customers to eat McChicken and the Big N' Tasty sandwich 'everyday'. The court dismissed the plaintiff's emphasis on the advertising encouragements as mere 'puffery', 'exaggerated general statements that make no specific claims on which consumers could rely' (*Pelman* v. *McDonald's*, p. 518). The court then examined several examples from other fast food promotions that were designed to encourage the daily eating of fast food. This portion of the opinion strongly suggested that no amount of suggestive advertising could establish a cause of action for damages of any kind.

The court did, however, curiously note that McDonald's may be potentially open to liability on a 'deceptive omission' claim if it failed to provide product information on the contents of the food. Although the court did not believe the plaintiffs pleadings in this case alleged a 'deceptive omission', it suggested that such a case could be made if 'the information regarding the nutritional content of the McDonald's product was solely within McDonald's possession or that the consumer could not reasonably obtain such information' (op. cit., p. 518).

The claim with the most potential to destroy the fast food industry was the allegation that 'McDonald's products are inherently dangerous because of the inclusion of high levels of cholesterol, fat, salt and sugar' (*Pelman* v. *McDonald's*, p. 518). Although the trial court acknowledged that the plaintiffs had a high burden to establish this 'inherently dangerous food' claim, the judge made several analogies to the tobacco litigation cases in his explanation. Ultimately, the judge rejected the comparison to the tobacco cases because the cigarette 'companies had intentionally altered the nicotine levels of cigarettes to induce addiction' (op. cit., p. 518). The Judge also rejected comparisons to the asbestos class action litigation because the 'dangers of asbestos did not become apparent until years after exposure . . . Thus, any liability based on over consumption is doomed if the consequences of such over consumption are common knowledge' (op. cit., p. 518).

The most promising of all the arguments asserted by the plaintiffs was a claim that was not even in the original pleadings but raised in the opposition papers to McDonald's motion to dismiss. Those papers were filed by McDonald's' lawyers in an effort to have the case bounced from court before they were required to make any response to the allegations in the lawsuit at all. It was on the basis of those papers filed by McDonald's that the Judge conducted a hearing where both lawyers were questioned about the case and had an opportunity to further explain their positions. It was at those hearings that the plaintiffs claim expanded to focus on the processing of McDonald's' foods.

The plaintiffs lawyers further alleged that McDonald's had created an entirely different, more dangerous food than one would expect from an ordinary hamburger or piece of chicken prepared at home. The plaintiffs argued that:

> 'McDonald's products have been so altered that their unhealthy attributes are now outside the ken of the average reasonable consumer . . . For instance, Chicken McNuggets, rather than merely chicken fried in a pan, are a McFrankenstein creation of various elements not utilized by the home cook . . . Chicken McNuggets while seemingly a healthier option than McDonald's' hamburger because they have "chicken" in their names actually contain twice the fat per ounce as a hamburger' (*Pelman* v. *McDonald's*, p. 519).

The court explained that the average consumer would need to go to the company website to have any idea of the degree to which the foods have been altered. The Court reasoned that '[t]his argument comes closest to overcoming the hurdle presented to plaintiffs. If plaintiffs were able to flesh out this argument in an amended complaint, it may establish that the dangers of McDonald's' products were not commonly well known and thus McDonalds had a duty toward its customers' (op. cit., p. 519). The opinion spent a good deal of time identifying some of the extensive ingredients and chemical processes used to produce the menu offerings at McDonald's.

In what was clearly the trial judge's most far-reaching policy statement, he rejected McDonald's claims that a successful suit against them on the contents of their processed food would lead to lawsuits against 'pizza parlors, neighborhood diners, bakeries, grocery stores and literally anyone else in the food business . . .' (op. cit., p. 519). The judge noted that:

> '[m]ost of the above entities do not serve food that is processed to the extent that McDonald's' products are processed, nor food that is uniform to the extent that McDonald's' products are throughout the world. Rather they serve plain-jane hamburger, fries and shakes – meals that are high in cholesterol, fat, salt and sugar but about which there are no additional processes that could be alleged to make the product even more dangerous' (op. cit., p. 519).

After the discussion of product ingredients a most promising statement for the plaintiffs emerged in the lengthy opinion. The judge said:

> It was premature to speculate as to whether this argument will be successful as a matter of law, if the plaintiffs amend their complaint to include these allegations, as neither argument has been more than cursorily presented to the court and certainly is not before it. McDonalds' argument is insufficient, however, to convince this court that the plaintiffs should not have the opportunity to amend their complaints to include these allegations.

The Judge noted the extent to which McDonald's food has become a mainstay of the American diet. By information provided in the companies own legal papers it reported that the Corporation served over 99 billion customers, about 46 million each day, at 13 000 outlets in the USA and had a '43 percent share of the United States fast food market' (*Pelman* v. *McDonald's*, p. 519). The court then suggested another possible legal theory for the plaintiffs.

> A better argument based on over-consumption would involve a claim that McDonalds' products are unreasonably dangerous for their intended use. Their intended use of McDonald's' food is to be eaten, at some frequency, that presents a question of fact.

If plaintiffs can allege that McDonald's products' intended use is to be eaten for every meal of every day, and that McDonalds is or should be aware that eating McDonald's products for every meal of every day is unreasonably dangerous, they may be able to state a claim. (op. cit., p. 519)

Several aspects of Judge Sweet's opinion are noteworthy. First, although McDonald's succeeded in having the judge rule that the entire lawsuit should be dismissed, the opinion followed the unusual approach of explaining how the plaintiff's complaints could be more effectively crafted. Although judges often make occasional suggestions in written and oral opinions for the parties as they proceed in continuing litigation, the extent of Judge Sweet's suggestions to the plaintiffs both in kind and quality are unusually detailed. Some advocates of limiting the judicial role to concrete cases and controversies might be critical of his advisory role in this case. Clearly, the judge made a decision to thrust himself into this controversial policy debate. The Judge does not explain why he has offered so much detail in his explanation of the plaintiff's potential viable claims. One can only speculate as to his actual motives. Obviously if it was an indication that he was sympathetic to the plaintiff's cause, that motivation would be inappropriate. If however, the judge believed he was serving a function to advance this issue through the legal system more quickly so that years of legal wrangling could be reduced, he may be justified in attempting to provide notice of the potential issues looming for both plaintiffs, lawyers and the fast food industry.

The tradition of tort law forming from the common law evolving from precedent grounded in principles of negligence theory provides ample support for Judge Sweet's broad approach attempting to anticipate issues of suits against the fast food industries. The history of other product liability and fair warning tort cases suggest that eventually many aspects of policy and damages compensation will wind through the courts until a body of case precedents eventually emerge to guide affected industries and consumers. Such evolution often takes decades. Large industries can benefit from the certainty of these issues being decided sooner rather than later. In fact, the filing of a lawsuit and early rulings by one judge in one jurisdiction can result in industry changes immediately to minimize the risk of future expense to the business while waiting for the nation's courts to reach a consensus.

Legislative solutions are unlikely to occur until the courts have ruled on most of the outstanding legal issues. Large industries usually can prevent too much unfavorable legislation because of their resources to obtain access to the legislative process through lobbying (Wood, 2003). However, anti-consumer legislation or laws that remove protections from the average citizen often receive negative media attention and could lead to bad publicity for a business seeking to portray itself as safe and consumer friendly. Although McDonald's is properly concerned about this litigation from consumers and the threat on its profits (Olson, 1994), it may be a blessing for the company for it to be warned by a judge to identify potential areas of legal risk sooner rather than later. The company can make menu, processing and warning changes in a way that will help meaningfully avoid other potential legal consequences.

If juries are involved in deciding any of these disputes, the issues are not only legal but cultural. What is 'reasonable' or 'negligent' or 'deceptive' for the purposes of who is financially responsible for harm is to be decided by people who view the problem as one of actual behavior in daily life. For example, if we are eating at McDonald's three times a week with our children and it turns out that such a frequency will harm our children when they reach their 20s, some jurors will make McDonald's pay. Arguments about personal responsibility will be balanced against facts like who made the food, what was in the food and who was in the best position to know the outcome of eating it so often. A jury may ultimately make McDonald's or other fast food establishments accountable for failing to warn, or at least advise, its customers.

Suburban white jurors who might have more sophisticated health care (Ayanian, 1993) and greater access to a varied, healthier diet might see the issue differently than a black urban juror who primarily eats fast food because of access and convenience in the community (Johnston, 2003). It may be that McDonald's will ultimately fall prey to its best customers serving on the jury; the customers whose culture the company in some measure created may later judge its actions as a juror in a lawsuit.

Such possibilities might suggest that corporate players might seek legislative help to remove the possibility of such lawsuits from the courts and juries. Perhaps in the short term, this strategy might seem effective. In the long term the attention to the health consequences of obesity may suggest that the better approach for McDonald's would be to provide more health-conscious products. Perhaps if the industry leader would modify its approach to the marketing of food items and choices, it could avoid the potential harm that is the ironic consequence of its success in dominating the fast food market. Whatever choices McDonald's makes today, other lawsuits will be filed and attention will be turned to its actions in the future.

The lawsuit as a tool to reform corporate culture is here to stay (*Deposit Guaranty* v. *Roper*, 1980). Silencing it through legislative action is tricky business. A company that is so familiar to the average citizen as McDonald's cannot avoid running into its customers on juries or in the legislative process. Perhaps it should learn valuable lessons from the lawsuit so that it can avoid being subjected to its billions of customers when it may turn out that their health has been adversely effected by its products. Certainly, people should take responsibility for personal choices including occasional enjoyment of unhealthy food. However, McDonald's may need to modify the consequences of its own domination of the fast food market by taking steps to reduce the long-term harmful effects of its menu. Judge Sweet's opinion forecasting possible successful lawsuits may in the long run have been the best thing that could have happened to the fast food industry.

REFERENCES

Attanasio, John (2001), 'Foreword', *Juries Rule, SMU Law Review*, **54**, 1681, 1682.

Ayanian, John Z. (1993), 'Heart disease in black and white', *New England Journal of Medicine*, **329**, 656, (noting the differences in heart disease between black and white patients).

Baldus, David, John C. MacQueen, and George Woodworth (1995), 'Improving judicial oversight of jury damages assessments: a proposal for the comparative additur/remmittur review of awards for non-pecuniary harms and punitive damages', *Iowa Law Review*, **80**, 1109, 1122.

de Tocqueville, Alexis (1969), *Democracy in America*, J.P. Meyer (ed.), New York: Doubleday.

Deposit Guaranty National Bank v. *Roper*, 445 US 326, 338 (1980), (discussing the appeal of class action suits as 'offering substantial advantages for named plaintiff; it may motivate them to bring cases that for economic reasons might not otherwise be brought').

Federal Communications Commission (1998), 'Briefing notes on advertising study', 4–6.

Fried, Gil B. (1998), 'Punitive damages and corporate liability analysis in sports litigation, *Marquette Sports Law Journal*, **9** (45), 51–52.

Johnston, Jason Scott (2003), 'Paradoxes of the safe society: a rational actor approaches the reconceptualization of risk and the reformation of risk regulation', *University of Pennsylvania Law Review*, **151**, 747, 782.

McClellan, Frank M. (1996), 'The dark side of tort reform: searching for racial justice', *Rutgers Law Review*, **48**, 761, 791.

Nader, Ralph (1986–7), 'The corporate drive to restrict their victims' rights', *Gonzaga Law Review*, **22**, 15, 18.

Olson, Theodore B. (1994), 'The parasitic destruction of America's civil justice system', *SMU Law Review*, **47** (359), 360–62 (discussing several multi-million dollar verdicts that in the author's view effected the economy).

Pelman v. *McDonald's*, 237 F. Supp. 2d 512 (S.D.N.Y. 2003).

Skidmore v. *Baltimore & Ohio R.R. Co.*, 167 F.2d 54, 61 (2d. Cir. 1948).

USA Today (2003), 'Hype outraces facts in medical malpractice debate', Special Report, 3 March, p. A1.

Wilkes v. *Wood*, 98 Eng. Rep. 489 (C.P. 1763).

Wood, Seth W. (2003), 'The master settlement agreement as class action: an evaluative framework for settlements of publicly initiated litigation', *Virginia Law Review*, **89**, 597 (noting the lobbying strength of the fast food industry).

PART VI

Policy conclusions

13. A policy framework for confronting obesity

Zoltan J. Acs, Lenneal J. Henderson, David T. Levy, Alan Lyles and Kenneth R. Stanton

INTRODUCTION

In this book the issues of obesity have been considered by critically examining the choices and status of three broad groups: the individual, business and the government. Chapters describe and examine the health, consumer, tax, marketing, cultural, ethical and institutional dimensions of the obesity challenge in the USA. As a health policy challenge obesity affects all levels of society. Consumers are asked to rethink what 'quality' means in food choices. A raging debate about the impact of marketing on consumer health escalates. Consumers are psychologically and culturally caught between media images of 'thin is good' but 'food is good'! Obesity treatment and prevention continues to be challenged by clear cultural differences in America. And every American institution, whether public or corporate, faith or educational, cultural or professional, is either promoting or responding to shrill ethical messages about the outrage of increasing obesity among Americans of all ages, races and regions of the nation.

What American consumers buy, what we allow and disallow in the marketplace and what health costs, as well as its opportunity costs, place consumer policy in the core strategic complex of policy issues. As both a cause and consequence of consumer behavior, marketing can and does play a key role in structuring consumer consciousness and preferences. From health-conscious television, radio, Internet and print-level food and drug advertisements to dedicated weight control campaigns and promotions, marketing is an essential policy link to necessary changes in our understanding and response to the challenges posed by obesity. Business and government regulations directly affect the marketing mix through regulations, as well as the tax system.

Business, through the marketplace, determines the incomes that affect eating, work, activity and leisure choices. Businesses may also directly affect physical activity through the job tasks required and the provision of exercise facilities to their employees, and similarly affect diet at work via the vending machines and cafeterias commonly provided. In addition, when insurance is provided to employees' businesses affect the types of health care covered, including obesity prevention and treatment. Even entry to the workforce is affected by obesity.

Public policy, through government and public interest groups, strongly influences opportunities to address the obesity crisis. First, the government defines what is and is not obesity through the Centers for Disease Control (CDC), among other agencies, and even federal disability law (Tucker and Milani, 2004). Second, public policy can also directly affect diet and exercise activities through tax, infrastructure (such as the availability of sidewalks and bike paths) and consumer policy. Third, government directly influences the policies and programs of the educational system, as it provides food services and exercise facilities as well as education encouraging youth to make better choices. Notably, the government can sponsor or encourage programs made available through business, as well as those directly provided by government, such as wellness programs or particular insurance coverage.

For obesity policy to be effective, the complex circuits between obesity analysis and obesity advocacy, between market and policy, and between prevention and treatment must be rewired to maximize consumer and policy energy towards obesity reduction. Yet there is no single view of what, if anything, needs to be done. Instead, there are differing interests and their perspectives that exert divergent forces on initiatives for change. Public policy arises from and is shaped by these divergent interest groups.

In this chapter we provide a framework for considering the role of these three groups in treating and preventing obesity. We first consider the nature of the obesity epidemic. Second, we examine the causes of the obesity epidemic. Third, we examine the consequences of the obesity epidemic followed by an explanation of the need for public policy in the fight against it. In the following section, we discuss selected challenges in coordinating a coherent obesity strategy facing these groups. In the final section we synthesize the many observations and strategies for confronting obesity in both public policy and the marketplace and outline the case for making childhood obesity the intervention point in the policy agenda.

THE OBESITY EPIDEMIC

Looking through the news media you will find a plethora of statistics on weight and obesity over the past several decades. These will include different measures about who is obese and who is not, and various views of how to measure obesity. However, only one statistic really counts – the rising trend in obesity rates in the general public and in children in particular. During the past 20 years there has been a dramatic increase in the prevalence of obesity in the USA and in most other countries.

In 1985 only a few states participated in the CDC's Behavioral Risk Factors Surveillance System (BRFSS) survey and collected obesity data. Most of the reporting states had an obesity rate of less than 10 percent. Only a few states had obesity rates between 10 percent and 14 percent, including North Dakota, Michigan, Indiana, Ohio, Kentucky, West Virginia, Georgia and South Carolina. As shown in Figure 13.1, by 1990 the number of states having an obesity rate of between 10 percent and 14 percent had increased to over two-thirds of all states. By 1995 there had been a dramatic increase in obesity rates. Over half of the states then had obesity rates of between 15 percent and 19 percent, and almost all other states had an obesity rate of between 10 and 14 percent. By 2000 there was another quantum leap in prevalence, with half of the states registering over 20 percent obesity rates and the rest of the country in the 15–19 percent range. By 2004, the most recent year for which data is available, nine states had obesity rates of over 25 percent and the rest of the country was predominantly in the 20–24 percent range. The trend shows no sign of abating. In fact, projections in

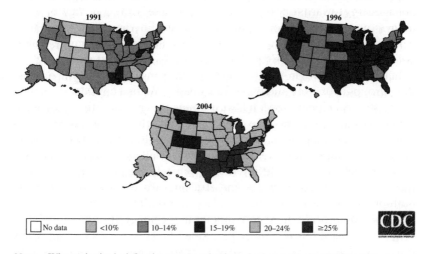

Note: Where obesity is defined as a person having a body mass index (BMI) of 30 or greater (or about 30 lb overweight for a 5 ft 4 in person).

Source: Behavioral Risk Factor Surveillance System, CDC.

Figure 13.1   Obesity trends among adults in the USA (BRFSS, 1991, 1996, 2004)

Stanton and Acs (2005) show that the rise in obesity prevalence may continue for quite some time and it is not going to disappear on its own.

There are three aspects of the obesity epidemic that are disturbing. The first aspect of concern is the rise in childhood obesity. Since the early 1970s, the prevalence of overweight (classed as having a BMI of 25 or greater) has more than doubled among children aged 2–5, almost quadrupled for children aged 6–11 years, and more than doubled among adolescents aged 12–19 years. During 1999–2000, the prevalence of overweight was 11.6 percent among children aged 6–23 months, 10.4 percent among those aged 2–5 years, 15.3 percent among those aged 6–11, and 15.5 percent among those aged 12–19. Childhood and adolescent overweight are likely to persist into adulthood, suggesting that the best way to prevent adult obesity in the future is to prevent childhood obesity today.

The second aspect of concern is that the incidence of obesity among minorities is much higher than in the general public. The National Health and Nutrition Examination Study 1999–2002 (NHANES III) found obesity rates of 36.5 percent for non-Hispanic Black women and 33.3 percent for Mexican American women. Adding in the prevalence of pre-obesity (having a BMI of between 25 and 30), the combined prevalence of those with BMIs of 25 or higher, were 77.3 percent among non-Hispanic Black women and 71.9 percent among Mexican American women. Similarly, the prevalence for Mexican American men was 74.7 percent, while the prevalence among non-Hispanic White men was 67.4 percent. Although this emphasizes that the problem is currently much more severe among minorities, it would be a mistake to conclude that the rest of the population won't reach equally high levels. These rates are a warning signal as to how serious and how costly the epidemic may become.

Finally, while weight is an issue for all income groups, obesity seems to be much more prevalent among the poor. The existence of a relationship between obesity and income is observable even through casual observation. On a recent visit to two graduations at affluent upper-income schools one co-author of this chapter observed that at a boys' school not one student was overweight, while at a girls' school only one student was noticeably overweight.

Two neighborhoods in New York City more concretely demonstrate the extremes of the problem. Upper East Side Manhattan is 84 percent white. It has a median household income of $74 446, a poverty rate of 6.2 percent and an obesity rate of 7 percent. East Harlem, right next door, has a 55 percent Hispanic population, a median household income of $20 111, with 38.2 percent living in poverty and an obesity rate of 31 percent. In terms of causality, it is not certain how much of the poverty problem is a consequence of obesity and other related health problems versus the effects of poverty driving obesity. However, combining serious health problems with poverty ensures that the costs will be borne by Medicare, Medicaid and other public assistance schemes.

THE CAUSES OF THE OBESITY EPIDEMIC

As we described above, the surge in obesity rates started some time in the late 1970s and has continued now for the better part of two decades. Moreover, this epidemic first spread across the USA in about a decade and now is spreading across most of the developed world.

There are many factors that have been suggested as contributing to the obesity increase, from environmental factors to changes in behavioral patterns, and it is likely that the current problem is the combined result of several of these. There is a remaining need to adequately identify the most important underlying causes since adjusting those factors first will produce the most rapid improvements. The tools of economics are well suited to this task and to addressing the long-term questions of how serious the future prevalence rates of obesity and overweight are, and how much it is likely to cost. Answering these key questions plays an important role in pinpointing the most promising policy options.

What is it that we do understand about the epidemic? With considerable certainty, we know that taken to its most elementary form, excess body weight results from individuals taking in more calories than they are expending. So the excess weight problem is either the result of a decrease in the amount of energy that Americans expend through work or leisure, or a general increase in caloric intake. This simple observation generates the following question: is the weight problem caused by less energy output from the shift toward more sedentary lifestyles, on the input side as a result of pouring in more energy than the human body requires, or both? One piece of evidence that may narrow the search for an answer is that the prevalence rates appear to have jumped upward near the end of the 1970s. That tells us that any theory offered in explanation of the causes of increased obesity has to explain not only the overall increase but also the characteristic time path of the increase.

Most would agree that there has been a shift away from manual labor-intensive work to more sedentary lifestyles. However, this does not satisfy our requirement of fitting in with the time path of changes in the weight problem. Philipson and Posner (1999) state that our energy output has not changed much since the 1980s. The evidence points more heavily toward increased caloric intake as the more important part of the explanation. In fact, the sheer magnitude of the increased caloric intake would be difficult, if not impossible, to counter by exercising or choosing more physically demanding work. However, this may not be the case with children, where there has been a marked decrease in physical activity. As TV and computer time have grown and physical activity has declined, schools scaled back physical education and recess. At the same time drug addiction, gang activities and associated violence caused the number of safe places to play and exercise to dwindle.

Technological and other supply-side changes have also contributed to the epidemic. Reductions in the cost of producing food due to technological improvements, in combination with reductions in the amount of time required for preparing and consuming food, are among the primary explanations for the weight problem (Philipson and Posner, 1999). As we expect, a reduction in the price of any good leads to greater quantity demanded. Food consumption has increased markedly over the past two decades and on the supply side improvements in food production technology have greatly reduced the costs of production (Philipson and Posner, 1999). A key reason for this can be found in policy changes in the early 1970s. In terms of kilocalories per person per day, there has been a very noticeable upswing in demand since the late 1970s. During the 1950s and 1960s the value is in the range of 3200 to 3300 kilocalories per day, but by 1999 it had increased to the 3700 mark. The upswing is not explained by increased wastage. Nor can the additional 300–400 kilocalories be easily expended by more strenuous work (USDA, 2000).

Exploring the changes in the types of foods consumed reveals another important aspect of the increase in caloric intake. Products with higher shares of value going to the farm have become less important in terms of calories consumed, while products that are more highly processed, with a lower farm share of value, have increased in terms of proportion of caloric intake. We have handed over the traditional preparation of meals from basic foodstuffs to outside sources that present us with highly processed, ready-to-eat meals.

The available data confirm that the pattern is one of an overall increase in calories per day from the late 1970s to the mid-1990s – an increase of 268 for men and 145 for women – even though the calories consumed in the home at dinnertime have been greatly reduced. The most notable increase in calories appears as snacks, with snacks consumed in the home almost fully offsetting the reduction in calories obtained from dinners at home. Men increased their intake of snacks by 242 calories, 160 of which are comprised of snacks in the home. Women followed with a snack increase of 162 calories with 112 calories from snacks at home.

It is not just a simple case of pointing the finger at the growth of fast food franchises. The causes are more complex. But increases in calories derived from fast food do show substantial increases, especially for men. Considering only lunch and dinner, men increased their fast food intake by 113 calories. The comparable increase for women was 48 calories.

High-fructose corn syrup has been the target of much criticism as a potential cause of the epidemic because of its widespread use in sodas and many highly processed snacks and other prepared foods. In truth, the increases in the production levels of high-fructose corn syrup closely match the time path of the changes in body weight measures. Furthermore, highly processed foods are providing a larger share of our growing caloric intake (Naik and Moore, 1996). What may be an important factor is that high-fructose corn syrup and the subsidies to corn that make the syrup cheap to produce also reduce the production costs of highly processed and sweetened foods relative to healthier foods.

The importance of relative prices extends to factors other than choices between different foods. The relative prices of leisure and food consumption that result in changes in lifestyle choices are also important factors affecting demand (Chou et al., 2003). In particular, the value that Americans place on their time has increased, especially for women (Chou et al., 2003), which helps explain that the price changes have caused people to work more, spend less time at home, and to shift away from home-prepared meals to foods that require less preparation time. These changes have been accompanied by an increase in the availability of fast food and other restaurant-prepared meals, at generally lower prices. Chou et al.'s (2003) regression analyses of the factors affecting obesity, overweight and BMI incorporated explanatory variables such as indicators of the availability and prices for fast food and full service restaurants, and the price of food prepared at home. Although the pattern of increase in the per capita numbers of restaurants is positively correlated with increases in obesity, overweight and increases in BMI, the direction of causality is not resolved by their study. In other words it does not tell us whether the increase in the number of restaurants is driven by the increased demand for their products, or if the increased supply of restaurants is causing our national weight problem.

Marketing and expanded food distribution networks may also be an important factor. Americans face a continuous barrage of marketing tricks to encourage excess consumption of unhealthy foods.[2] Not only have fast food restaurants dramatically increased in number, but so have enticements to purchase junk food, which run from the placement of candies, snacks and soda at every checkout counter to the increased availability of unneeded food even at gasoline stations.

Combining the results of the available studies provides some important insights. The trend of reduced food production costs is likely to continue, which encourages increased consumption of food in general and of more highly processed food in particular. More processed foods have a tendency to be less healthy overall. As the price of less healthy food falls, consumption is likely to increase. This is supported by the US Department of Agriculture consumption data that show that processed foods are rapidly gaining ground.

The evidence is sufficiently compelling that we can state that the most important cause of the increase in the rate of obesity over the past 20 years is increased caloric intake rather than reduced caloric expenditure (Cutler et al., 2003). While we cannot be certain that this explanation is right or that it is the entire explanation for the rise in obesity, it is the most plausible given trends in obesity rates and the available data.

At the individual level, if any part of the explanation lies in personal failures to make appropriate lifestyle choices then the situation is more likely to become worse than it currently is. Basically, if the price of eating falls and self-control is not adequate, then excess consumption resulting in increased body weight is the outcome. Unless the current situation is significantly altered, we can expect people to eat more of the types of food that increase their weight and associated health risks. Increasing exercise, although helpful, will not by itself eliminate the upward trend in body weight measures if the current rate of increase in caloric intake is not slowed.

The case we have tried to make in this section is that the 'infrastructure of obesity' fuels the epidemic and the prevalence of obesity continues to increase in the USA and around the world (Flegal et al., 2002). The nature of the infrastructure favors food processing over home production. This has tilted the balance, resulting in a rapid movement into the fast food industry, snack food industry and the consumption of large amounts of low nutritional processed food. So while people were eating more, they were getting more of the kinds of foods that are implicated in the obesity crisis as a share of their overall consumption. The fast food industry, vending machines and easy access to food all proliferated and eating became a national pastime. From movie theatres to sporting events to watching television, food was everywhere.

It is important to think about the consequences of these trends. First, food knowledge and an understanding of the costs of preparing food accompanied production. The transition of food production outside of the home created a generation that is dangerously ignorant of nutrition and food preparation. Fads from low-fat to low-carbohydrate diets spread all over the country as people stumbled about in search of a healthy diet. This void in our understanding of food is filled by multi-billion-dollar advertising campaigns that promote a large variety of foods that are high in sugar, salt and starches. Advertisers are also guilty of replacing traditional food knowledge with information about the new manufactured food industry. The assault to abolish our kitchens was predominantly led by the soda industry, the snack food industry and the fast food industry. As was made clear in Chapter 6, marketing can have more than one message about obesity, but the sheer magnitude of the information distorted the reality about a healthy diet.

THE CONSEQUENCES OF OBESITY

'L'obésité tue', reads a French poster meant to educate the general public about the dangers of obesity. As we saw in Chapter 7, obesity has become a worldwide phenomenon and even countries like France are taking the issue seriously. In a country with universal health care coverage the government is highly motivated to curb health care costs.

This raises a crucially important point. While it was not a part of this book, perhaps the most serious aspect of obesity is the relationship between being overweight and the burden of disease. Obesity is entwined with a host of other serious health problems that are increasing in prevalence with obesity. As shown in Figure 13.2, hormones, heredity, stress, diet and the lack of exercise all affect obesity and in turn affect the health of the individual. However, the *increase* in the rate of obesity can only be explained by diet and physical activity. In other words obesity is a condition that has been around for a long time and can be related to genetics, and the increase in the rate has to do with environmental factors – diet and exercise.

Excess weight is associated with an increased incidence of cardiovascular disease, type-2 diabetes mellitus (DM), hypertension, stroke, dyslipidemia, osteoarthritis and some cancers. Among people diagnosed with type-2 diabetes, 67 percent have a BMI greater than or equal to 27, and 46 percent have a BMI greater than 30. An additional 20 million have impaired glucose tolerance, sometimes called pre-diabetes, which is a strong risk factor for the development of diabetes later in life.

The age-adjusted prevalence of hypertension in overweight Americans is 22.1 percent for men with a BMI between 25 and 27, and 27 percent for men with a BMI between 27 and 30. The prevalence of hypertension in adults who are obese (that is, having a BMI greater than 30) is 41.9 percent for men and 37.8 percent for women. Hypertension is defined as mean systolic blood pressure greater than or equal to 140 mm Hg, mean diastolic greater than or equal to 90 mm Hg. While direct prevalence information is not available, a recent study found that people whose BMI was 40 or more had death rates from cancer that were 52 percent higher for men and 62 percent higher for women than the rates for normal-weight men and women. Overweight and obesity could account for 14 percent of cancer deaths

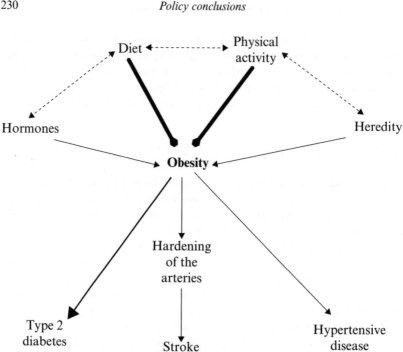

Source: Adapted from Stallones, R.A. (1966), *Public Health Monograph* **76**, 53.

Figure 13.2 Simplified web of causation applied to obesity and cardiovascular disease

among men and 20 percent among women in America. Most studies show an increase in mortality rate associated with obesity. Obese individuals have a 50–100 percent increased risk of death from all causes, compared with normal-weight individuals (those with a BMI of 20–25). Most of the increased risk is due to cardiovascular causes.

The level of mortality and health problems highlights the significance of research on obesity and sedentary lifestyles. According to McGinnis and Foege (1993) and Allison et al. (1999), obesity and sedentary lifestyles result in over 300 000 premature deaths per year in the USA. By comparison, the mortality associated with tobacco, alcohol and illicit drugs is about 400 000, 100 000 and 20 000 deaths per year respectively. The life expectancy of a moderately obese person could be shortened by 2–5 years.

While there is a large and growing literature on the relationship between obesity and health, the effect of obesity on medical costs is a rather new area of research. Recently, two influential studies have attempted to measure the cost of obesity relative to the health care cost of smoking and drinking and who pays for it. Sturm (2002) found that in terms of absolute changes in costs, obesity is associated with an average increase of $395 per year. Obesity was associated with a 36 percent increase in inpatient and outpatient spending and a 77 percent increase in medications, compared with a 21 percent increase in inpatient and outpatient spending and a 28 percent increase in medications for current smokers, and smaller effects for problem drinkers. Obesity appears to have a stronger association with the occurrence of chronic medical conditions, reduced health-related quality of life, and increased health care and medication spending than have smoking or problem drinking. Only 20 years of aging has effects of a similar proportion.

The above study was limited to people less than 65 years old and therefore grossly underestimates the cost of obesity since one-quarter of the obese population is over 65. Finkelstein et al. (2003) used the 1998 Medical Expenditure Panel Survey (MEPS) and the 1996/1997 National Health Interview Surveys (NHIS) to estimate national medical spending attributable to pre-obesity and obesity. The estimated increase associated with being pre-obese is 144.5 percent ($247). The average increase in annual medical expenditures associated with obesity is 37.4 percent ($732). For the adult population in the USA as a whole, 3.7 percent of medical expenditures are attributable to pre-obesity and 5.3 percent is attributable to obesity. Therefore, total medical expenditures attributable to pre-obesity and obesity are 9.1 percent of health care costs. Using National Health Association data for 1998, $47.5 billion is attributable to obesity and $78.5 is attributable to combined pre-obesity and obesity. The analysis has several limitations, however. First, NHIS relies on self-reported height and weight, and pre-obese and obese people tend to under-report their weight. As a result, pre-obesity and obesity prevalence and corresponding expenditures may be under-reported by as much as 30 percent compared to NHANES IV.

In a series of four articles, *The New York Times* documented the relationship between obesity and diabetes. Diabetes is an epidemic that has afflicted entire neighborhoods and threatens to bankrupt the health care system. In East Harlem, 14 percent of the population has been diagnosed as having diabetes. Aggravated by poverty, health care accessibility problems and other related factors, diabetes in East Harlem results in blindness, limb amputations and early death at an all-too-alarming rate. As the disease spreads it can overwhelm the health care system, creating a city where hospitals are swamped with patients and struggle to care for the sick. By itself, this is truly a horrifying prospect. But then there is the cost burden. According to *The New York Times* (5 February, 2006):

'The sheer cost of caring for diabetics, who often do not get help until they are in catastrophic need, will keep going up. The financial burden of attending to diabetes' with its many uninsured victims eventually lands on state and local governments. In New York City – where one in eight adults has diabetes, or nearly 150 percent more than just 10 years ago – that cost is about $200 million annually and growing.'

See Chapter 7 for a fuller discussion on how to deal with the consequences of obesity.

OBESITY AND PUBLIC POLICY

Is there a role for public policy in the fight against the obesity epidemic? Wansink and Huckabee (2005) advocate allowing the market to solve the obesity problem on its own. In their framework, food and leisure choices belong to the individual and profit motivations will direct the food industry to provide healthier products. Huckabee, Governor of Arkansas and chairman of the National Governors Association, knows the battle against obesity on a personal level having lost over 100 lb through diet and exercise. There are many success stories of obese individuals who have managed to lose weight but this does not direct us to a solution to the obesity epidemic. The reason is that the policy challenge arises at the macro-level.

In the current state, individual micro-level choices are resulting in ever-increasing obesity prevalence. Those who are gaining weight increasingly outnumber the few obese people who manage to lose weight as Huckabee did. If we accept the fact that the obesity epidemic is a result of market failure and therefore public policy intervention is needed, how do we get a handle on this complex issue?

In preventing addiction to tobacco products, the most effective strategy was preventing people from becoming smokers in the first place and the obesity challenge is parallel. Policy is necessary to counteract the individual tendency to make unhealthy diet and exercise choices and policy is needed to unravel the infrastructure that biases the food industry to market unhealthy products. Consider as an example that the taxes attached to discouraging tobacco use amounted to approximately $500 per smoker. What would it mean if we could apply the same tax treatment to obesity? At current obesity rates, the tax revenue would be $50 billion. Admittedly, the notion of directly taxing the obese is not a viable solution, but the tax revenue figure does indeed provide some perspective on the problem.

How do we move towards an implementable public policy solution to obesity? Public policy involves decisions and or actions of a polity (state or organized community), not individuals. It also involves the rules of the game of a particular society, including levels of compliance and enforcement. The process also includes the decision not to do anything. This choice to do nothing is in fact heavily favored by economists unless it can be demonstrated that the market will not on its own arrive at the optimal outcome. As we explain below, market failures do justify intervention in controlling obesity but the dynamics of reaching policy solutions are of interest and importance in the obesity issue. To explain the process, we use the life cycle concept of public policy as a simple guide.

The model has four stages. As shown in Figure 13.3, the first stage of the life cycle concept of public policy starts with *changing expectations*. The level of attention that a particular problem receives is small in this stage as select groups start to form changing expectations about the problem. It has three components: structural changes, social discussion and interest group attention. What were the structural changes that took place during the 1970s that might have contributed to changing expectations? First, changes in the technology of food processing largely moved food production from the house to the factory. Second, women moved into the workforce in large numbers which affected the responsibility of feeding the family. Third, the improvements in technology made the production of food much cheaper and more readily available. Finally, the shift of food production out of the home resulted in the loss of knowledge about food and nutrition that existed as a by-product of in-home food production.

Over the decades an infrastructure of obesity developed where millions of dollars were poured into the production of unhealthy junk foods and the marketing of these products made sure that a demand for them existed and continued. The marketing to children and the spread of childhood obesity is an important aspect of this debate. A second aspect is the inter-relationship between obesity and poverty. It was clear from early on that the obesity epidemic affected the poor and less educated much more than it affected the affluent. (See *The New York Times* on nutrition, obesity and diabetes in two boroughs.) Finally, even though we have estimates of the costs of obesity we have not fully answered the question, 'what is the impact of obesity on the productivity of the economy?' While we have some evidence in Chapter 5 on this issue the causation is not neatly defined.

The social discussion of the epidemic started in the 1990s. In this book, we add to the dialogue in our discussions of childhood obesity (Chapter 3), the issues of diversity, poverty and obesity (Chapter 4) and the labor market impact of obesity (Chapter 5). Interest groups also became interested in the obesity issue in the 1990s. First, the health insurance community became interested in treating obesity (Chapter 7). Second, the marketing industry as it represented the food processors, fast food restaurant industry and the beverage industry started to focus on obesity (Chapter 6). The federal

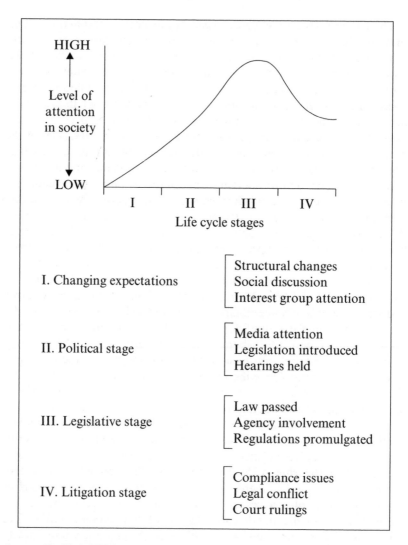

Source: Buchholz (1992), p. 511.

Figure 13.3   The life cycle concept

government was already a complex player in the obesity epidemic. Via the Department of Agriculture it not only played a large role in providing cheap food and in marketing commodities to the American public, but at the same time the Department of Agriculture was supposed to be the guardian of the American diet (Chapter 9).

The second stage of the life cycle concept focuses on the *political stage*. In the political stage the level of attention in society increases exponentially. It has three components: media attention, legislation introduced and hearings held. By the early 2000s the obesity rate had increased to epidemic proportions and media attention took off. In a relatively short period of time obesity, diet, weight loss and junk food were the topics of thousands of newspaper stories, hundreds of television programs and dozens of documentaries. The media attention galvanized a growing awareness of the problem and triggered the start of a search for a solution to the problem. This communication of the problem started a debate in the press about how to deal with it, the solution for which was not to be found in the free market. In other words there was a clearly felt need for a public policy solution, although it was not apparent whether that solution was going to be either an active or a passive one.

It took very little time before the media attention given to obesity started to draw parallels between obesity and smoking. The country has waged a 30-year war against tobacco, including a very successful effort against smoking among children. Tobacco control became a model for fighting obesity in the eyes of some. Chapter 11 examines this issue and draws out the similarities and the differences. Recall that in the introduction to this book, we drew the parallel between driving and obesity as yet another way to think about the problem. Each of these frameworks serves some useful role in advancing the discussion and focusing attention.

As public awareness about the obesity epidemic grew and people started to connect the dots, pressure from constituents began to stir the legislative process. The first area in which the process drew attention to itself was that of childhood obesity. Chapter 8 examines the rise of legislative actions in all 50 states and documents the introduction of legislation and the hearings held. One tool open to legislative action that has not been exploited to any significant extent is some form of tax or its counterpart, subsidy. In the fight against tobacco taxes played an important role in reducing demand. Tax solutions to the external costs of obesity are being examined along with other changes to relative prices (Chapter 10).

The third stage in the level of attention in society to a public policy process is in the *legislative stage*. The legislative stage also has three parts: law passed, agency involvement and regulations promulgated. If one were to date the level of attention in the fight against obesity this is where we are today. We are in the pre-legislative stage. All parties, all stakeholders, have a vested interest in finding a solution to the obesity epidemic. While all stakeholders do not have the same outcome in mind, all want to maximize their position with respect to the outcome.

The final stage in the life cycle concept of public policy is the *litigation stage*. The litigation stage also has three levels: compliance issues, legal conflict and court rulings. During this stage, however, the level of attention in society declines. Chapter 12 examines the perspectives on the economic and cultural effects of obesity litigation.

If one were to place the public policy of the obesity epidemic, we are between the political stage and the legislative stage. The process is now moving to the legislative stage at both the local and national level. However, before we move toward understanding the main legislative initiatives we need to outline the institutional infrastructure that any legislative action will have to navigate.

THE AGONY AND THE ECSTASY OF THE OBESITY POLICY CHALLENGE

Facing a growing national obesity crisis, what are the specific challenges and opportunities of both the marketplace and of public policy in addressing the legislative phase of it? First, we must face the fact that a single, coordinated public policy that addresses the obesity infrastructure is unlikely, largely due to four factors:

1. The social structures constituting the galaxy of households, families, communities, regions, states and indeed the national fabric are complex. Both industry and the policy system are challenged by the intricate and often perplexing ways in which individual, family, cultural and community forces structure consumer, dietary and lifestyle preferences.
2. Federalism in the Constitution of the USA assigns both express and implied health and welfare roles to states. The consequence is significant variation among the states and their constituent local governments in how they address obesity issues.
3. Political pluralism, reflected in the multiplicity of cultural perspectives, socioeconomic dynamics and market preferences is likely to frustrate a unitary policy or market approach to an obesity policy strategy.
4. Interest groups and lobbying at the federal, state and local levels by varied and disparate industry, consumer, health care, insurance, medical, agricultural, educational and other groups will not result in a single, coherent, feasible and effective policy or market strategy that will advance both obesity treatment or prevention imperatives.

Complex Social Structures

Any industry or policy strategy to treat or prevent obesity immediately confronts a complex web of individual, household, family, cultural, demographic and institutional dynamics in the USA. The varied and often intricate connections between individuals and their families and between families and retail, workplace, neighborhood, cultural, faith, media and governmental institutions are continually changing and are often difficult to decipher and characterize. Consequently, individual, family and household preferences, lifestyles and decisions represent a micro-level challenge to obesity prevention and treatment. At this level, we confront the economics and politics of personal and family choice and lifestyle. Depending upon the individual exposure to stress, poor health consciousness and information, and a lifetime of socialization in food and drink, individuals may descend into the abyss of obesity because of anxiety, depression or chemical imbalances.

Consumer dynamics often dangle precariously between want and need. Along with prices, marketing and the media, they cultivate individual and family choice on a thin want/need boundary. Simultaneously, they often fail to provide quality information about those choices and their consequences. Having allowed industrial food production to supplant our traditional, home-prepared foods, a large part of consumer choice has been delegated to food manufacturers.

While decisions are made at a micro-level, obesity is a macro-level policy challenge for the public, corporate, industrial, small business and non-profit sectors of our society. But what are the limits to the feasible, since profit-seeking firms may in their own self-interest encourage over-nutrition? What can these institutions do to raise consciousness, change lifestyles and preferences and alter the manufacture, testing, marketing and distribution of products and services that exacerbate micro-level obesity-related decisions? How well do these sectors work together as institutions ostensibly interested in the health, education and the welfare of American citizens? Are there best or promising practices that could serve to transform our policy orientation to obesity issues? What are the various kinds of policy issues and strategies that, individually or collectively, could constitute a new policy consciousness and regime?

Individual, household, and family nutritional preferences and choices at the micro-level are involved in a complex of interplay at the macro-level of market and policy choices. The twin challenge to both market and policy decision-makers is to both influence healthy preferences and choices at the individual, family and household levels and influence the interaction of these preferences with both intermediary institutions at the macro-level of

institutions such as industry, the media and the public sector at the point
of their interaction with individuals, families and households.

Federalism and Obesity

The distribution of policy authority among federal, state and local levels
of government animates and catalyzes much of the political pluralism and
varied interest group and lobbying activities around issues of obesity. State
authority for the regulation and provision of health care, coupled with the
limited federal role, have produced 50 natural experiments in public policy
approaches to the obesity infrastructure. To date, legislative responses have
been concentrated at the state level. Over time, there may be a degree of
convergence in the types of legislation that are passed as some policy
approaches are found to be more successful. However, states will continue
to differ in their specific priorities and in the political will of their electorate,
favoring either regulatory or market-oriented solutions.

The very existence of regulatory differences across states creates yet
another level of challenges since the potential target of any control measure
may either move across state lines or threaten to do so, as a means of arbi-
traging or otherwise influencing regulatory differences. Such a strategy
could prove particularly effective when used by companies with large
numbers of employees or large tax contributions against state governments
facing revenue or employment rate constraints. This sets the stage for an
ongoing regulatory dialectic between states and highlights the special role
that federal policy can provide.

Crucial to obesity policy are policies directed at the poor, who disproportionately add to the obesity epidemic. The health consequences of
public policies toward the poor are strongly felt in federal and state medical
assistance and insurance programs. Rapidly accelerating Medicare and
Medicaid budgets are in part an indicator of both the state of health of
needy Americans and the quality of access and affordability of health services. According to the American Obesity Association (AOA), state
Medicaid programs do not cover obesity-related health care costs. In 1990,
Congress enacted the Omnibus Budget Reconciliation Act (OBRA), which
provides pharmaceutical products to Medicaid recipients for most chronic
medical conditions except obesity.

Although the wide variation in market dynamics and policy preferences
among federal, state and local governments is a significant challenge to a
coherent unitary obesity policy strategy, a balanced and coordinated series
of obesity covenants, concordants and mutual aid agreements may be
possible through the variety of lobbies representing each level of government. The National Governors Association, the National Association of

Counties, the National League of Cities, the National Council of State Legislatures and the US Conference of Mayors are examples of nationwide organizations able to mobilize their members for a coordinated strategy of obesity prevention and treatment. Mobilizing these lobbies to concentrate legislative activities in specific directions could serve as a significant counterforce limiting the ability of influential constituencies to manipulate competing states.

Economic and Political Pluralism

Given the increasing significance of racial, ethnic, regional, age and socioeconomic diversity in the USA, business and public policies must take into account the relationship between 'culture' in all of its forms and the breadth and depth of the obesity issue. These cultural orientations project norms, mores and institutions that socialize the consumer, health and social orientations of many Americans and influence conceptions of the state and local government role in addressing obesity. It is difficult for a corporate or public policy to have any meaningful impact without attention to the profound role of thousands of intermediary cultural institutions who stand between the policy and people. Whether faith-based, community-based, educational, recreational, fraternal or professional, these cultural institutions are both a resource and a challenge to obesity policymaking and implementation. Part of the infrastructure of health, consumer and cultural frameworks that condition obesity prevention and treatment rests on the capacity of corporate, non-profit and public agencies to reflect a sensitivity to and skill with negotiating these complex institutional forms and varieties.

Those who produce foods, snacks and beverages and those who pay for the consequences of the resulting obesity in the form of rising health insurance premiums divide the private sector. Consequently, employer health insurance purchasing coalitions have arisen to exert market leverage to restrain costs and promote novel benefit options to encourage early intervention and wellness. The largest of these, the National Business Coalition on Health, established an Institute on the Costs and Health Effects of Obesity. Employers have a coherent interest and may, over time, exert influence on public policy and private practices.

As stewards of America's industries and protectors of consumers, the public sector has conflicting roles affecting the obesity infrastructure. One of the oldest government programs of significance for childhood nutrition and obesity is the National School Lunch Act of 1946 (NSLA) and its numerous amendments through to 2006 (Sims, 1998). Designed by Congress 'as a measure of national security, to safeguard the health and well being of the Nation's children and to encourage the domestic consumption of nutritious agricultural commodities', it supported children as well as the nation's agricultural industry (Sims, 1998, p. 451). Administered at the federal level by the US Department of Agriculture's Food and Consumer Service, the program is administered at the state level by state departments of education and usually at the local level by school district administration (Sims and Stillman, 2005). The NSLA is a splendid metaphor for the struggle in public policy to accommodate human need and support market dynamics, particularly the agricultural industries ranging from crops to beef.

Government regulation through the Food and Drug Administration and a plethora of state and local regulatory agencies contributes significantly to strategies for preventing and treating obesity, as well as pursuing massive changes in media imaging and messages to influence demand-side dynamics, and thereby changes in consumer behavior.

Obesity Interest Groups and Lobbies

Given the complex and varied marketplace and policy system, interest groups and lobbies are unlikely to reach a stable consensus on obesity policy. Some, like the American Medical Association, urge disciplined individual and household consumer behavior to prevent egregious health problems resulting from obesity. Others, like the Center for Science in the Public Interest and the Consumer Federation of America, believe that industry regulation at the federal, state and local level submits too often to industry preferences. The Center for Consumer Freedom, a coalition of restaurants, consumers and constituents from the food industry, argues that the entire issue should be one of personal responsibility and the freedom to make individual choices. Labor organizations have emphasized the importance of overall good health to their members while negotiating for sufficient health benefits. Other large food and drug lobbies argue that excessive regulation is costly to consumers both in dollars and in opportunity costs for better product development.

It may not always be obvious where resistance to policy proposals will be met. Even seemingly benign policies can come under attack, as was demonstrated in Maryland in early 2006, when state politicians proposed that schools provide parents with a health report card, including BMI measures for the students. The proposal met harsh resistance from a most unlikely alliance of objectors, consisting of snack food vendors hoping to defend their profits, medical practitioners claiming that this is an issue that should only occur as a discussion between doctors and patients, and psychiatrists concerned that the policy could elevate the societal focus on bodyweight to the point that it may generate a backlash in the form of an increase in eating disorders. Separating resistance driven by genuine concern from the resistance that arises from greed and self-interest is not always a trivial task and once identified, the nature of any political fallout may be unpredictable.

Central to advocacy for obesity reduction and policy is the AOA. It is a non-profit, tax-exempt educational and advocacy organization. Pharmaceutical research and development and weight-management companies such as Weight Watchers, Jenny Craig, Inc., and Slimfast Foods provide a substantial base of its support. AOA promotes the creation of a new National Institute of Obesity at the National Institutes of Health to coordinate obesity research, policy and treatment efforts. The AOA has also advocated an amendment of the Americans With Disabilities Act of 1990 to include obesity.

Other groups combining research, development, professional development and advocacy include the Hormone Foundation, the American Society for Bariatric Surgery, the American Heart Association, the American Cancer Association, the Congressional Heart and Stroke Coalition, the National Family Caregivers, the American Health Planning Association and the American Society for Bariatric Physicians.

Given the complex social, cultural and consumer dynamics in American society, the even more complex systems of economic and cultural pluralism in the nation, the noisy and delicate nature of federalism in the policy system and the frenetic and disparate activity of a plethora of interest groups, lobbies and professional groups, it is imperative that we locate points of policy consensus and convergence. These points of convergence reflect the intricacies of obesity policy issue networks at every level of American society. Numerous marketplace and public policy initiatives are underway or under advisement. They represent a synthesis of the substantial discourse and debates on obesity. They also represent promising and best practices around every dimension and aspect of obesity. Nonetheless, the conflicts of opinions across these groups and the resulting pressure to suppress all but the least contentious proposals may also rule out the very policy actions that have the greatest potential to reduce obesity.

Public policy, through government and public interest groups, strongly influences opportunities to address the obesity crisis. First, the government defines what is and is not obesity through the Centers for Disease Control (CDC) and even federal disability law (Tucker and Milani, 2004). Second, public policy can directly affect diet and exercise activities through tax and consumer policy. Third, government directly influences the policies and programs of the educational system as it provides food services and exercise facilities as well as educating youth to make better choices. Notably, the government can sponsor or encourage programs made available through business or other channels in addition to any more direct actions. The education system is one in which government has many points of interaction or exchange, and consequently many opportunities to take actions that could alleviate the epidemic.

THE CASE FOR INTERVENING TO PREVENT CHILDHOOD OBESITY

If we were to draw together the strands of understanding that we have gleaned so far, two salient points emerge. The first point is that a policy focus on childhood obesity is justified and sensible. The second is that the National Governors Association is appropriately positioned to play an important role in facilitating it.

Justification for the focus on childhood obesity follows from standard market failure arguments. The first market failure results from the externalities associated with the costs of obesity. The individual choices that lead to obesity and any ensuing health problems are largely paid for by society as a whole. Everyone pays for the health care costs through higher insurance premiums and higher taxes, and the lower productivity resulting from obesity also creates an economic loss that is fully shared. The macro-level external costs driven by the micro-level decisions sanction society's right to intervene.

The second market failure is an information failure in the sense that children do not have the capacity to evaluate and utilize nutrition or other health information on their own, even if it were properly available. The evidence of increasing childhood obesity rates undeniably indicates that their parents are not adequately taking up the task either. Far too many parents are now setting poor examples because of the habits that they developed in their childhood, setting the stage for a repeating cycle of obese children becoming obese parents.

The inertia inherent in the infrastructure is the other large factor in preventing an interruption of the obese parent–obese child cycle. As an example, schools are very reluctant to evict soda and snack vending machines because they have come to rely on the machines as a source of revenue to support other, often positive, activities. Adding to the problem, marketing continues to reinforce the entire obesity infrastructure and largely fails to provide anything but biased health and nutritional information. Although the government has a natural role in filling in the information gap, it also has conflicts of interest arising from its activities to support agriculture, food manufacturers and other businesses. Furthermore, even if the information shortage could be alleviated, the knowledge that a product or activity is unhealthy does not preclude its use. Poor choices are still made in the face of perfectly adequate information.

So what is the main message? Unhealthy children become unhealthy parents and each successively more obese generation costs society more than the one before. The case for focusing our attack on childhood obesity is practically self-evident. And, given that the knowledge needed to make appropriate health choices is lacking, there is a clear role for educators to improve food and exercise knowledge and training among students. Obviously schools' complicity via the selling of junk food and soda also needs to be addressed. We cannot hope to develop health sense in the children if we confuse our message by profiting from the encouragement of unhealthy choices.

The advantages afforded to unhealthy foods are pervasive and certainly do not end with school vending machines. An important key is that the relative prices of calorie-laden junk foods are lower than healthier foods. There are many reasons for this relative price advantage including agricultural subsidies that encourage overproduction of corn and high-fructose corn syrup; technological improvements in manufacturing; and the lengthy shelf life of junk foods. Typical junk foods are heavy on preservatives and packaging that accommodate cheap delivery systems such as vending machines.

Relative price differences are an important aspect in understanding why consumers will choose unhealthy foods even if they are armed with the knowledge to understand the health risks of their choices. Obesity is a greater problem for people in lower income levels. To some extent, it may be that people with weight-related health problems are more likely to be poor but this is not the entire story. Poor people tend to be less educated and that may very well extend to having less knowledge about food and nutrition too. The rest of the explanation is that the relative price of unhealthy food in comparison to healthy food becomes more important as disposable income decreases. With less income to spend, health choices are driven to a greater extent by comparative prices than by the prospect of poorer future health. Lower obesity rates among those with more education and among high-income groups is fully in keeping with this idea.

The State Level

It is increasingly clear that the key to winning the obesity battle is to rescue the children. Although not the only possible approaches, the most apparent actions are implementable through the school system. Schools are the appropriate avenue for implementing programs to improve knowledge about nutrition and to develop better exercise habits.

Table 13.1   A framework for obesity policies

Input/nutrition	Output/physical activity
Behavior	Behavior
• Improve nutrition education of physicians	• Communicate the advantages of physical activity
• 'Sin taxes' on snacks and beverages, lower taxes on vegetables	• Tax breaks for the purchase of exercise equipment or membership in health clubs
• Family diet counseling	
Environment	Environment
• Improve the availability of healthful foods in schools and workplaces	• Mandatory K-12 physical education
• Encourage supermarkets to open in disadvantaged areas	• Creation of bike paths and walking trails
• Limit sales of soft drinks in schools	• Incentives for the development of workplace fitness programs

Source: Anthony Wellever (2004).

Education falls within state control. Although only a few state governments have passed obesity control measures so far, most of the laws and proposed legislation have focused on the schools as a point of interaction, which is in keeping with our earlier statement that the education system affords many opportunities.

As a first step, we need to think about the question, how can we build a program for improvement into our school system? There are some starting points that show promise in this pursuit. Beginning with the work of Anthony Wellever, writing for the Kansas Health Institute, a simple four-cell matrix combining policies relating to food, exercise, behavior and environment is shown in Table 13.1.

Wellever's work generated a comprehensive policy strategy for obesity prevention and reduction based on the work of Raymond and Moon (2005). These policy options reflect the possibility of a range of coordinated activity not only across schools but also across work sites, communities, industry and the health care system. Not all of them pass the test of being implementable or effective. For example, providing tax incentives for health club memberships may result in a pure wealth transfer to health club owners without any net benefit – but the table does provide a starting point for the debate. For example, according to Andrew L. Yarrow:

The once-ubiquitous daily school gym class has become an endangered species. Only half of America's elementary schools require physical education (PE), and only 5 percent of high school seniors must take PE. The share of high school students attending daily PE class fell from 42 percent to 28 percent between 1991 and 2003. Although the national Association for Sport and Physical Education recommends daily recess through at least sixth grade, a stunning 29 percent of elementary schools schedule no recess. (2006, p. 17A)

At the current stage of the process a core set of policies have drawn media attention, agencies have debated the appropriate responses and hearings have been held. The policies that have made it to the legislative stage were discussed in Chapter 5 and have been tracked for the past three years by the William Donald Schaefer Center for Public Policy at the University of Baltimore. Acs et al. (2005) identified the following six main types of state legislation that focus predominantly on childhood obesity:

- Nutritional standards controlling the types of food and beverages offered during school hours.
- Vending machine usage prohibiting types of foods and beverages sold in school and prohibiting access to vending machines at certain times.
- BMIs measured in school and reported to school officials, parents and pediatricians.
- Additional time allocated in the school day for recess and physical education mandated by the state.
- Obesity programs and education established as an integral part of the curriculum.
- The establishment of commissions at the state level by the legislature or Governor, designed both to study the scope of the obesity issues in the state and to evaluate the efficacy of current obesity-related policies and programs.

As we have discussed in earlier sections, some of these legislative approaches remain controversial and in many states are bogged down in lobbying and political controversy between individuals, business and government. However, as Chapter 11 points out, firms in the food industry can play an important role in promoting the public health. They can learn from the mistakes of firms in the tobacco industry, where ultimately their actions hurt their public image and large amounts are now being spent to improve that image. Food manufacturers and vendors, especially fast food restaurants, can adopt a more conciliatory and supportive approach to government public health policy.

Marketing strategies promoting unhealthy foods to youth are likely to have consequences in creating a poor public image, while socially responsible policies can promote a more positive public image. Even supporting government policies that restrict certain types of marketing or that regulate the content of foods can be a profitable strategy. By limiting competition to promote and sell less healthy products, the image of the regulated firms improves without facing the prospects of lost sales to firms using less socially responsible policies.

There are some vehicles in the public milieu that can be particularly constructive and supportive in developing positive policies. The National Governors Association, for example, can and ought to provide leadership in encouraging greater participation and in sharing ideas to develop implementable legislation at the state level. As Chairman of the association, Arkansas's Governor Huckabee is making the case that obesity is the most serious problem currently facing state governments. He is motivated by the severity of the problem in his home state of Arkansas as well as by his own personal battle with obesity. Arkansas has led the country in developing obesity control measures at the state level. State governments, cognizant of their voters' perceptions, are sensitive to how they are perceived in relation to other states' responses and in many cases the legislation that is introduced is reactive to what has happened in other states; they do not want to be perceived as 'behind'. Of course, state governments are not the only route of response to deal with the epidemic.

The Federal Government

Some of the policy solutions are more appropriately implemented at the federal level. In some cases, the inability to arbitrage state regulations could be sufficiently severe that a federal approach is the only solution. In other cases the issue is one of jurisdiction, or simply the result of existing structures and policies.

There are two areas where the federal government has been asked to intervene: limiting the advertising of junk food to children and altering the relative price of healthy foods. The federal roles arise through the Federal Trade Commission (FTC) in regulating advertising and in large part through the Department of Agriculture in the effects of its policies on prices. Some have advocated that advertising to children should be regulated because children, being less than fully rational, are too vulnerable to marketing (Nestlé, 2002; Schlosser, 2001).

However, as John Cawley points out, Congress has historically tolerated very little regulation of commercial speech. A cautionary tale for those who urge greater regulation of food advertising to children is the 1979 'KidVid' episode in which the FTC sought to regulate the television advertising of sugary cereals to children under age 13 (interestingly, not because of obesity but because of tooth decay). Congress responded firmly to defend commercial speech and to limit the FTC's power; as a result, the FTC had to struggle just for reauthorization (Engle, 2003). Nevertheless, we believe that some limit on advertising to children is needed. The unprecedented need for this limit is predicated by the fact that as food production moved out of the home, knowledge about food, food nutrition and healthy eating has been lost.

Prior to the upward swing in obesity prevalence at the end of the 1970s, household preparation of traditional family meals was the mainstay of our food intake. Since that time, traditional meals have been heavily replaced by manufactured foods both within and outside of the home. What have we lost in the process? Most obviously, basic knowledge about nutrition and food preparation has been heavily delegated to the food manufacturing industry. Consumers have increasingly abandoned the kitchen for restaurants and vending machines and we are only beginning to discover that these industrial substitutes for home-prepared foods may be far less healthy than we ever imagined. It is no secret that the food manufacturing industry is very profitable. That feature will present serious challenges to any attempts to engineer a reduction in consumption of the unhealthy foods currently marketed or to encourage the industry to offer healthier foods.

Into this void has moved a $10 billion dollar per year industrial-strength marketing campaign of advertising on children's television. The commercials hawking sugary treats or 'empty' calories contribute to soaring rates of obesity and diabetes among the young. The Institute of Medicine, in a report in December 2005 sponsored by the federal Centers for Disease Control and Prevention, said that, 'Current food and beverage marketing practices put children's long term health at risk'.

Here again, we can learn from the tobacco industry. Tobacco manufacturers have been denying (until recently) the health risks of smoking, denying the addictive nature of smoking (while adding ingredients to make it more addictive) and targeting youth in their marketing campaigns. While there has been some change in their behavior in recent years, it has been viewed by public health advocates as 'too little, too late'. There are claims that food manufacturers and fast food chains could have done more to improve the nutritional content of food and that they have targeted children in promoting unhealthy food (Chopra and Darnton-Hill, 2004) but they have clearly been less overt in their behaviors than the tobacco companies. The case for unethical behavior against firms in the food industry is less clear.

The second factor that has a direct impact on childhood obesity is the relative price of healthy food. Sturm and Datar (2005) found that between kindergarten and third grade, the weight gain in excess of growth chart predictions was related to the prices of fruits and vegetables in the area, adjusted for the cost of living and other factors. In areas where fruits and vegetables were comparatively more expensive, the BMI increase was greater than in areas where the prices were lower. In the study Mobile, Alabama faced the highest prices and the average BMI of children there increased by 0.21 units more than the national average. The average BMI of children in Visalia, California, which had the least expensive fruit and vegetable prices, increased 0.28 less than the national average.

Although Sturm and Datar did not directly explore the issue, their study lends credence to the idea that the prices of healthy foods relative to the prices of snack foods may be at least as important as the overall level of food prices in general, if not more so.

In its role of improving the information available to consumers, the Department of Agriculture distributes basic information to guide healthier dietary choices. The new *Dietary Guidelines for Americans* focus on obesity prevention. They recommend increased consumption of whole grains, fruits, vegetables, fish and low-fat dairy products within a balanced diet in which total calories have been moderately reduced. On the other hand, the best-known and best-funded federally sponsored consumer communications promote increased total consumption of beef, pork and dairy products, including calorically dense foods such as bacon cheeseburgers, barbeque pork ribs, pizza and butter.

The federal government's commodity promotion programs, known as 'checkoff' programs, sponsor these communications. The programs are established by Congress, approved by a majority of the commodity's producers, managed jointly by a producer board and USDA, and funded through a tax on the producers. The federal government enforces the collection of hundreds of millions of dollars each year in mandatory assessments, approves the advertising and marketing programs and defends checkoff communication as the federal government's own message – in legal jargon, as its own 'government speech'. Federal support for promoting fruit and vegetables is small by comparison.

In Chapter 10, Elston et al. make the point that the tax system might be used to alter the obesity prevalence trajectory. They point out that rather than tax all foods, a more efficient scheme might tax the foods contributing the most to obesity. For simplicity, they refer to these foods as 'unhealthy', while recognizing the difficulty in making such distinctions. If the distinction between healthy and unhealthy foods is meaningful, then it is desirable to tax unhealthy foods more heavily. The problem lies in constructing a practical mechanism to categorize healthy and unhealthy foods. Ideally, the tax should target foods known to be more detrimental, that contribute the most to the obesity problem and have low or zero health benefits. There are various forms that such a tax could take.

A hedonic tax pricing approach provides another way of taxing unhealthy foods. If we wish to tax the health-reducing aspects of foods, we may be able to do so indirectly by placing taxes on individual ingredients or food components. A tax might be levied on fat or sugar content, or both, which would raise the cost of items high in content of the taxed characteristic. In this case, we would need to estimate the implicit prices associated with specific ingredients. As an example of how this tax could be implemented, if there are different tax rates on the percentages of fat and sugar, then the total tax on the food product is obtained by multiplying the tax rate for each of the three components by the amount contained in the product and adding together the results. With mechanisms that rely on categorizing foods, minor changes in content can generate jumps in tax treatment at points where the change causes a change in categorization. Using the hedonic approach, the tax is proportional to the quantity of specified ingredients. Therefore, minor changes in the contents generate similarly minor changes in the tax.

The effectiveness of such a tax scheme would depend on how consumers react. Consumers could substitute away from items with taxes on specific characteristics based on their elasticity with respect to those characteristics. They would ultimately choose less of the taxed characteristic, both by buying specific types of food with lower sugar or fat and by buying food types that are generally low in those characteristics. In addition, consumers will increase their consumption of other foods. For example, with less fat, consumers may substantially increase their consumption of carbohydrates. With large enough increases in these other foods, weight loss may be minimal or there might even be weight gain.

It is undeniable that obesity policy will evolve over time through the interactions of all of the participants – consumers, business and the various levels of government. However, the complexity of the dynamics may be problematic on its own.

SUMMARY

This chapter has provided a framework for thinking about confronting the obesity epidemic. Although we see the need for developing the mechanisms that can help in the fight to control the obesity epidemic, this may not come about overnight (Barrett et al., 1998). Long-term goals will be to unravel the pieces of the infrastructure that are fundamentally responsible for the epidemic, including targets as politically challenging as farm policy.[3] Taxes and other mechanisms can also be developed to divert consumers' preferences away from unhealthy foods. Meanwhile, there are common sense measures that ought to become priorities for immediate implementation because they are likely to have an impact and they can be established quickly.

We have stated in various places throughout the book that childhood obesity is the first front of the battle and that the most obvious point of attack is through the schools. First steps should focus on increasing physical education and banning junk foods and sodas from schools. Some states have already demonstrated that these are achievable policy goals. Schools must also incorporate nutritional education into the curriculum. Another important but probably more difficult step will be to place controls on any advertising that targets children.

It has taken most of three decades for the obesity crisis to get to today's level so it is unrealistic to assume that we can solve it overnight. However, the consequences of obesity are sufficiently severe that we must initiate the turnaround immediately.

NOTES

1. Naik and Moore point out that the annual per capita consumption of high-fructose corn syrup increased from 9.6 lb in 1977 to 63.1 lb in 1999. Over the same time period, the consumption of all sweeteners rose from 122 lb to 155 lb per person per year.
2. See Brownell and Horgen (2003). Also see Schlosser (2001). The term 'processed food' is broad enough to incorporate. Chou et al.'s (2003) 'convenience foods' as well as more narrowly defined segments discussed by Brownell and Horgen (2003) and Cutler et al.
3. This has historically been intractable but a recent *Wall Street Journal* article makes the case that even some farmers are willing to eliminate agricultural subsidies and are allying with other subsidy opponents (Kilman and Thurow, 2006).

REFERENCES

Acs, Zoltan, Ann Cotten and Kenneth R. Stanton (2005), *State Efforts to Control Obesity*, Baltimore, MD: William Donald Schaefer Center for Public Policy.

Allison, D.B. et al. (1999), 'Annual deaths attributable to obesity in the United States', *Journal of the American Medical Association*, **282**, 1530–38.

American Obesity Association (2005), *AOA Fact Sheets*, Washington, DC: AOA.

Barrett, Frank J., Gail Fann Thomas and Susan P. Hocevar (1998), 'The central role of discourse in large-scale change: a social construction perspective', *The Journal of Applied Behavioral Science*, **31** (3), 352–72.

Brownell, K.D. and K.B. Horgen (2003), *Food Fight: The Inside Story of the Food Industry: America's Obesity Crisis and what we can Do About It*, New York: McGraw Hill/Contemporary Books.

Buchholz R.A. (1992), *Business Environment and Public Policy Implications For Management and Strategy*, Englewood Cliffs, NJ: Prentice Hall.

Chopra, M. and I. Darnton-Hill (2004), 'Tobacco and obesity epidemics: not so different after all?', *British Medical Journal*, **328** (7455), 1558–60.

Chou, S.Y., H. Saffer and M. Grossman (2003), 'An economic analysis of adult obesity: results from the Behavioral Risk Factor Surveillance System', National Bureau of Economic Research working paper no. 9247.

Cutler, D.M., E.L. Glaeser and J.M. Shapiro (2003), 'Why have Americans become more obese?', Harvard Department of Economics working paper.

Engle, M.K. (2003), 'FTC regulation of marketing to children', presentation to the Institute of Medicine Workshop on the Prevention of Childhood Obesity: Understanding the Influences of Marketing, Media, and Family Dynamics, 9 December, Washington, DC, accessed 25 May, 2006 at www.iom.edu/?id=17215.

Finklestein, E., I.C. Fiebelkorn and G. Wang (2003), 'National medical spending attributable to overweight and obesity: how much and who's paying?', *Health Affairs*, (Millwood), January–June, Web Exclusives: W3-219-26.

Flegal, K., M.D. Carroll, C.L. Ogden and C.L. Johnson (2002), 'Prevalence and trends in obesity among US adults, 1999–2000', *Journal of the American Medical Association*, **288**, 1723–7.

Institute of Medicine (2005), meeting no. 4: Symposium Progress in Preventing Childhood Obesity: Focus on Industry, accessed at www.iom.edu/?ID=34010.

Kilman, Scott and Roger Thurow (2006), 'Pork chops: in fight against farm subsidies, even farmers are joining foes', *Wall Street Journal*, 14 March, p. A1.

McGinnis, J.M. and W.H. Foege (1993), 'Actual causes of death in the United States', *Journal of the American Medical Association*, **270**, 2207–12.

Naik, Y.N. and M.J. Moore (1996), 'Habit formation and intertemporal substitution in individual food consumption', *Review of Economics and Statistics*, **78** (2) (May), 321–8.

Nestle, M. (2002), *Food Politics: How the Food Industry Influences Nutrition and Health*, Berkley and Los Angeles: University of California Press.

New York Times (2006), 'Diabetes and its awful toll quietly emerges into a crisis', 9 January, p. 1.

New York Times (2006), 'Declare war on diabetes', East Coast edn, 5 February, p. 4.11.

Philipson, T. and R.A. Posner (1999), 'The long-run growth in obesity as a function of technological change', National Bureau of Economic Research, working paper No. 7423.

Raymond, B. and C. Moon (2005), 'Prevention and treatment of overweight and obesity: toward a roadmap for advocacy and action', *The Permanente Journal*, **7** (4) (Fall).

Schlosser, E. (2001), *Fast Food Nation: The Dark Side of the All-American Meal*, Boston: Houghton Mifflin.

Sims, Laura S. (1998), *The Politics of Fat: Food and Nutrition Policy in America*, Armonk, NY: M.E. Sharpe.

Sims, Laura S. (2005), 'Reinventing school lunch: transforming a food policy into a nutrition', in Richard J. Stillman (ed.), *Public Administration: Concepts and Cases*, New York: Houghton Mifflin.

Stanton, Kenneth R. and Acs, Zoltan (2005), 'The infrastructure of obesity and the obesity epidemic', *Journal of Applied Health Economics and Health Policy*, **4** (3), 139–46.

Sturm, R. (2002), 'The effects of obesity, smoking and drinking on medical problems and costs', *Health Affairs*, (21), 245–53.

Tucker, Bonnie Poitras and Adam A. Milani (2004), *Federal Disability Law in a Nutshell*, 3rd edn, St Paul, MN: Thomson-West Publishing Company.

US Department of Agriculture (USDA) (2000), 'Major trends in food supply, 1909–1999', *Food Review*, **23** (1), 21–8.

Wansink, B. and M. Huckabee (2005), 'De-marketing obesity', *California Management Review*, **47**, 6–18.

Wellever, Anthony (2004), *Obesity and Public Policy: A Public Policy Framework for Intervention*, Topeka, KS: Kansas Health Institute, p. 26.

Yarrow, Andrew L. (2006), 'Let's get children moving toward a healthier future', *Baltimore Sun*, 9 March, p. 17A.

Index

CRITERIA FOR QUALITY
OF PETROLEUM PRODUCTS

Criteria for Quality
of
Petroleum Products

Edited by

J. P. ALLINSON
Technical Secretary, Institute of Petroleum, London

A HALSTED PRESS BOOK

JOHN WILEY & SONS
New York—Toronto

PUBLISHED IN THE U.S.A. AND CANADA BY
HALSTED PRESS
A DIVISION OF JOHN WILEY & SONS, INC., NEW YORK

> *The symbol I.P. on this book means that the
> text has been officially accepted as authoritative
> by the Institute of Petroleum, Great Britain.*

Library of Congress Cataloging in Publication Data

Main entry under title:
Criteria for quality of petroleum products.
"A Halsted Press book."
1. Petroleum products—Analysis. 2. Petroleum
products—Testing. I. Allinson, J. P., ed.
TP691.C7   665'.538   73–7958
ISBN 0–470–02500–X

WITH 8 ILLUSTRATIONS AND 31 TABLES
© APPLIED SCIENCE PUBLISHERS LTD 1973

Printed in Great Britain by Galliard Limited, Great Yarmouth, Norfolk, England.

PREFACE

Most industrialised countries have established standard methods for testing petroleum products, and such methods are being increasingly adopted as international standards either on a regional (*e.g.* European) or world-wide (ISO) basis. The texts of these methods sometimes include a section on the 'significance' of the test. Of necessity this section is invariably brief and cannot provide much guidance on the correlation between the results of the test and the performance of the product in practice; in particular it cannot explain how the various characteristics of the product are interrelated so as to contribute both separately and collectively to its 'quality'. It is the purpose of this book to provide this information.

The tests are usually identified in terms of their IP or ASTM designations but the discussion is equally applicable to the corresponding tests standardised by other bodies.

Each section of the book deals with a group of products, and has been written in such a way as to be largely self-contained. Since some tests are applied to several products, this inevitably results in a certain amount of repetition; it was felt that this was preferable to elaborate cross-referencing.

Many of the sections represent the joint efforts of several people, those named as the authors being the primary contributors. The Council of the Institute wishes to record its indebtedness to the experts on both sides of the Atlantic who gave such valuable assistance in the writing and publication of this book.

INTRODUCTION

The March Hare found that the 'best' butter was in fact a very poor quality lubricant for his watch. This serves to illustrate the fact that it is absurd to refer to the quality of a product except in the context of the use for which it is intended: 'quality' can, therefore, be defined as 'fitness for purpose'.

Petroleum products are used for hundreds of different purposes with widely differing requirements; the criteria for quality are, therefore, numerous and complex. It is the purpose of this book to identify these criteria, to explain how they are met by suitable refining and to describe how the quality is controlled by appropriate analysis and testing.

The behaviour of any material in a given environment is, of course, a function of its chemical composition. It might be thought, therefore, that, given a complete analysis of a petroleum product, it should be possible to deduce its performance. This indeed is largely true in the case of the simplest products such as the gases. Some of the performance characteristics of the lighter distillates, such as gasoline, can also be derived from analytical data. For heavier products, such as lubricating oils, waxes and bitumens, the chemical composition becomes so complex and its relationship to performance so difficult to define that direct correlation is no longer possible. In any case, simpler tests are required for quality control purposes. Analysis is then confined to the determination of certain important elements and to 'characterisation' in terms of structural groups. Other aspects of 'quality' are assessed by measurement of physical properties such as relative density (specific gravity), refractive index or viscosity, or by empirical tests such as pour point or oxidation stability, which are intended to relate to behaviour in service. In some cases the evaluation may include tests in mechanical rigs and engines either in the laboratory or under actual operating conditions.

Having decided what characteristics are necessary, it then remains to describe them in terms of a specification: this entails selecting suitable test methods and setting appropriate limits. Many specifications in widespread use have evolved usually by the addition of extra clauses (rarely is a clause deleted). This has resulted in unnecessary restrictiveness which, in turn, results in increased cost of the products specified. Although not directly involved in the writing of specifications, the Institute of Petroleum is anxious to ensure that best use is being made of the methods available, and a chapter of this volume deals with this subject.

If this book helps towards a better understanding of the criteria for quality of petroleum products and so leads to the writing of better specifications, it will have served its purpose.

C. F. McCue
Chairman, Standardization Committee

CONTENTS

LIST OF CONTRIBUTORS

R. S. BARNES
Amoco Chemicals Corporation, Naperville, Illinois, USA.

J. B. BERKLEY
Manager, Research and Technical Service Department, Mobil Oil Company Ltd, Victoria Street, London, UK.

V. BISKE
Chief Chemist Quality Control, Burmah Oil Trading Ltd, Burmah Refinery, Ellesmere Port, Cheshire, UK.

KENNETH BOLDT
Research Associate Products Research, Union Oil Company of California, Union Research Center, Brea, California, USA.

D. C. BROOME
Lately Chief Technical Adviser, Limmer and Trinidad Group, UK.

E. A. GOODCHILD
Lately Products Research Manager, Hoffmann Manufacturing Co. Ltd, Chelmsford, Essex, UK.

A. J. GOODFELLOW
Technical Director, Carless, Capel and Leonard Ltd, Hepscott Road, London, UK.

R. I. GOTTSHALL
Technical Associate, Product Evaluation Division, Gulf Research and Development Company, Pittsburgh, Pennsylvania, USA.

S. T. GRIFFITHS
Senior Technical Adviser, Sales Department, The Associated Octel Co. Ltd, Berkeley Square, London, UK.

G. I. JENKINS
Central Developmental Planning Department, BP Trading Ltd, Britannic House, London, UK.

W. H. KITE, Jnr
Marketing Technical Services Coordinator, Esso Inter-America Inc., Coral Gables, Florida, USA.

D. T. McALLAN
Research Associate, Fuels Projects, BP Research Centre, Sunbury-on-Thames, Middlesex, UK.

C. F. McCUE
Senior Technical Adviser, Esso Research Centre, Abingdon, Berks., UK.

J. O'DONNELL
Petroleum Technologist, BP Research Centre, Sunbury-on-Thames, Middlesex, UK.

R. E. PEGG
Manager, Burner Fuels and Combustion Section, Esso Research Centre, Abingdon, Berks., UK.

D. RAWLINSON
Head of Management Advisory Unit, Shell UK Ltd, Shell Haven Refinery, Stanford-le-Hope, Essex, UK.

A. G. ROBERTSON
Head of Quality Control, Airfield Services Section, Shell International Petroleum Co. Ltd, Shell Centre, London, UK.

R. SEFTON
Lansdown Road, Stanmore, Middlesex, UK.

G. G. STEPHENS
Lately Head of Fuel Oil Group, Analytical Branch, Petroleum Division, BP Research Centre, Sunbury-on-Thames, Middlesex, UK.

F. A. WADELIN
Head of Bitumen Division, Egham Research Laboratories, Shell Research Ltd, Egham, Surrey, UK.

E. R. WARD
Gas Engineering Consultant, London, UK.

D. WYLLIE
Deputy Superintendent, Admiralty Oil Laboratory, Fairmile, Cobham, Surrey, UK.

Chapter 1

THE SPECIFICATION OF PRODUCT QUALITY— PRESENT PRACTICES AND FUTURE POSSIBILITIES

G. I. JENKINS

1. INTRODUCTION

An efficient specification may be defined as one that gives adequate control of product quality without being over restrictive, and at the same time involves the minimum of testing effort. This definition raises certain questions which are considered below.

In the first place what is meant by product quality and how is it measured? Ultimately quality is judged by the discriminating consumer who assesses the performance against the cost. The performance of the product in particular appliances is therefore the ultimate criterion of quality. However, performance tests are usually too costly and frequently lack the necessary precision to be used satisfactorily as quality control tests. It is therefore necessary to find other properties, the values of which can be established precisely and relatively simply by inspection tests in a control laboratory, and which correlate closely with the important performance properties. Sometimes the inspection tests attempt to measure these properties, for example the research octane number test which was devised to measure the antiknock performance of motor fuel. In other cases the significant property is obtained indirectly from the inspection test results as illustrated by the following example:

Performance property	*Property specified*	*Laboratory measurements* *(inspection tests)*
Ignition quality (of a diesel fuel)	Diesel index	(a) Aniline point (b) Specific gravity

A specification clause cannot control a performance property and at the same time avoid being over restrictive unless the property specified in the clause is correlated with the performance feature which it is intended to control. Where the specified property is not measured directly, it is important to ensure that a suitable combination of inspection tests is selected to give

1

a high degree of correlation with the specified property. Clauses in many present day specifications for petroleum products do not satisfy these conditions, for example the octane number by the motor method for motor gasolines.

An efficient specification will call for the minimum of test effort and expense compatible with the control desired. Technological advances in the design of user equipment have resulted in additional clauses to many specifications. Whilst each additional test may have been justified by a high correlation with some important performance property, control of which was desired, thought must also be given as to how the tests are inter-related. The properties measured by many of the frequently specified inspection tests are far from independent of each other and thus there can be a considerable redundancy of information. For example, vapour pressure is closely related to front end recovery in a distillation test, and flash point also bears some relationship to both these properties. Again the knock rating of a lead-free motor gasoline is closely connected with the molecular weight and with the hydrocarbon types as measured for example by chromatographic analysis.

Clearly for maximum efficiency the tests which are specified for any product should be as independent of each other as possible. In fact the efficiency of a specification should be judged by the extent to which the tests specified will:

(a) control the product quality;
(b) measure independent properties;
(c) measure these properties with adequate precision;
(d) be economical in manpower and equipment.

The following sections discuss in greater detail some of the work that has already been done in studying the inter-relationships between different tests. Although the tools used to make these studies are essentially statistical in nature and may appear complex to many readers, the qualitative concepts involved are simple and may readily be appreciated.

2.   RELATIONSHIPS BETWEEN TESTS

One of the easiest ways of finding out if there is a relationship between two measured properties is to plot one against the other. In Fig. 1 the aromatics content is plotted against the specific gravity for a set of 20 motor gasolines and clearly there is a close relationship between the two properties.

There is some scatter of the points around the line and in the set of data considered the largest deviation from the line (point A) corresponds to 8 per cent aromatics. The aromatics content calculated from the specific gravity would, however, generally be within a few per cent of the observed figures. Several such relationships are employed in the petroleum industry, for example between smoke point and luminometer number on aviation turbine fuels. In refineries, where the crude quality is known, the sulphur content is checked against the gravity of many products.

A more frequent occurrence is that a property is found to be related not to one, but to two or more other properties. To return to Fig. 1, suppose further examination of the gasoline analyses showed that the samples lying above the line had higher olefins contents than the average whilst those

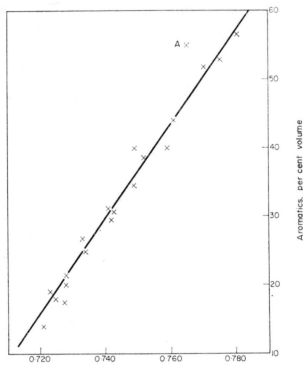

Specific gravity 60°F/60°F

FIG. 1. *The relationship between the specific gravity and aromatics in a series of motor gasolines.*

lying below the line had lower than average olefins contents. Using this knowledge it might be possible to improve the relationship between the gravity and the aromatics content and to obtain a more reliable prediction of any one of the three properties (specific gravity, aromatics content, olefins content) from the other two.

The graphical approach would not be appropriate for finding the relationship between more than two properties, but the well established statistical technique of regression analysis can be used to find the relation between one property and any number of other properties. There are many instances in which relationships of this sort enable properties to be predicted from other measured properties with as good precision as they can be measured by a single test. It would be possible to examine in this way the relationships between all the specified properties of a product and to establish certain key properties from which the remainder could be predicted, but this would be a tedious task.

An alternative approach to that of picking out the essential tests in a specification using regression analysis is to take a look at the specification as a whole, and extract the essential features. This is termed 'principal components analysis', which may be explained qualitatively in the following way.

The points in Fig. 1 form an elongated group in the specific gravity/aromatics plane. If three tests are now considered, *i.e.* by including an octane number of the gasolines (the octane number axis being at right angles to the specific gravity and aromatics axes), the points will form an elongated cloud. The shape of this cloud will depend on how well, in the set of gasolines considered, the octane number is related to the aromatics content and the specific gravity. If the three tests are well correlated, the cloud will be pencil shaped. If the deviations from the axis of the pencil are such as can be accounted for by the experimental errors, then the three tests are measuring a single property. Three uncorrelated tests would give a roughly spherical cloud as each test may be considered as measuring a different direction in space.

Principal components analysis examines a set of data as points in *n*-dimensional space (corresponding to *n* original tests) and finds first the direction that accounts for the biggest variability in the data. This is called the first principal component. The process is repeated until *n* principal components are evaluated, but not all of these are of practical importance since some may be attributable purely to experimental error. The number of significant principal components shows the number of independent properties being measured by the tests considered.

Having established the number of independent properties there exists a natural basis for making the specification more efficient. On a long-term approach it might be possible to obtain new tests of a fundamental nature to replace existing tests. In the short-term, selecting the best of the existing tests to define product quality will be beneficial. The procedures outlined also show the scope for critically examining new tests before they are accepted into general use or more particularly accepted as specification tests.

The Method Evaluation Sub-Committee of the IP Standardization Committee has been exploring ways of improving the specifications of some major products. A report of its work on the combustion properties of kerosine-type jet fuels has been published in the IP Journal (*J. Inst. Pet.*, 1969, **55**, 330–7). Another paper relating to gasoline specifications was published in the same journal in January 1972.

3. APPLICATION TO PRESENT DAY SPECIFICATIONS

(a) EXAMPLE 1. MOTOR GASOLINE

Consider the following two groups of clauses, some or all of which might be included in a motor gasoline specification (the approximate number of man hours involved in each test in Group A is shown in brackets).

Group A		Group B
Specific gravity	$(\frac{1}{4})$	Colour
		Odour
Distillation 10 per cent evaporated		Distillation, final boiling point
Distillation 50 per cent evaporated	(1)	Residue
Distillation 90 per cent evaporated		Total sulphur
Vapour pressure (Reid)	(1)	Corrosion test
Vapour/liquid ration at T_1 and T_2	(2)	Existent gum
Aromatics and olefins by		Potential gum
chromatography	(1)	Antioxidants
Research octane number	(2)	Detergents
Motor octane number	(2)	Metal deactivators
Research octane number on a		Upper cylinder lubricants
specified distillate fraction	(3)	Anti-icing additives
Lead alkyls	(2)	Deposit modifiers

The properties listed in Group A are generally concerned with the bulk of the product and those in Group B with minor constituents. In Group A the first eleven clauses are obtained from eight tests and the distillation test also contributes two clauses to Group B. The lead alkyls content shown in the last line, though strictly a minor component, is closely associated with three of the bulk properties and so is usefully included in this group.

The properties in Group A may be subdivided into three sections. The distillation, the vapour pressure (Reid), the vapour/liquid ratio are all concerned with the volatility of the gasoline. The specific gravity, chromatographic analysis and the lead alkyls are chemical characterisation factors. The three octane numbers are simulated performance properties of the most important characteristic of the fuel and sometimes all three octane numbers are included in a specification. Examination of the Group A properties of a wide range of motor gasolines using the technique of principal components analysis leads to the conclusion that there are probably only five independent properties being measured by the thirteen tests or clauses considered. Thus the analysis shows that approximately five properly selected independent properties would describe the quality of the gasoline as adequately as the thirteen tests in Group A. In the longer term is might be desirable to develop new tests to measure these properties, but in the shorter term it is desirable to select the more suitable of the present inspection tests and eliminate the remainder.

It is possible to show statistically that both the motor octane number and the research octane number on a distillation fraction can be calculated from the research octane number and other specification properties of the total gasoline nearly as well as they can be measured in a single test. A vapour/liquid ratio can be calculated from vapour pressure (Reid) and distillation data more precisely than it can be measured in a single test. By eliminating testing of these three redundant properties we can reduce the testing time in Group A by a half and simplify the specification.

(b)   EXAMPLE 2, AVIATION TURBINE FUEL

Consider the tests listed in Appendix 1 of ASTM specification D1655. The tests measuring bulk properties are contained in groups (ii) to (v) and are listed below.

  (i) *Performance characteristics*
 (ii) *Combustion properties*
      A. Luminometer number
      B. Smoke point
      C. Aromatics
      D. 16-hr Burning test
      E. Naphthalenes content
      F. Smoke volatility index
(iii) *Fuel metering and aircraft range*
      A. Gravity
      B. Net heat of combustion (calculated from aniline point)
 (iv) *Fuel atomisation*
      A. Distillation
      B. Vapour pressure
      C. Viscosity
  (v) *Fluidity at low temperature*
      A. Freezing point

Three other tests are also associated with bulk properties, the aniline point, the solid point and the pour point. It does not need a statistical examination of the tests listed above to show that there is a great deal of overlap in the testing. Some specifications utilise the inter-relationships by requiring certain tests to be experimentally determined only if other tests exceed limited values. It is instructive to consider principal components analyses on selected groups of the tests.

First consider a group comprising specific gravity, aniline point, aromatics content, smoke point and luminometer number. A principal components analysis of these five tests is shown in Table 1.

It may be seen that the first two independent properties account for most of the variance of the system, the remaining variability being due to test error. Thus the five tests considered measure only two distinct properties. This large redundancy of information was not surprising as it had previously been established that both the aniline point and the smoke point could be calculated from the gravity, aromatics content and freezing point, using data

TABLE 1

Principal components analysis of five tests associated with aromaticity on aviation fuels

Tests	Independent properties (principal components)				
	1	1	3	4	5
Specific gravity	0·22	0·86			
Aniline point	0·47	−0·41			
Aromatics content	−0·50	0·24			
Smoke point	0·54	0·13			
Luminometer number	0·43	0·11			
Relative importance[a] (%)	55·8	20·8	12·1	6·2	5·0

[a] Statistically the figures in this row are known as 'eigenvalues' and represent the percentage of the total variance that is accounted for by the particular principal component.

on unrefined kerosines from many different crudes. The luminometer number may be calculated in several ways from a variety of tests with a precision similar to that of the experimental determination so it was not anticipated that this test would significantly contribute to characterising the fuel.

Four tests are frequently employed to measure the flow properties of aviation fuel; the freezing point, pour point and kinematic viscosity at two temperatures, for example −30°F and 100°F (−34°C and 38°C). Principal components analysis suggests that these four tests are in fact measuring only one property.

(c) EXAMPLE 3, GAS OILS

The following tests are frequently employed on distillate oils:

gravity;
sulphur content;
viscosity 100°C (212°F);
aniline point;
pour point.

A set of data was obtained for 250 distillates with a fixed boiling range, 600–700°F (315–371°C), all the oils being of different crude oil origin.

Principal components analysis showed that these five tests were measuring only three independent properties. It was subsequently found that both the aniline point and the pour point could be predicted from the other three tests with a precision very similar to that with which they could be experimentally determined. These results show that the quality of the oil is governed by the gravity, sulphur and viscosity. If performance data suggest that the pour point and the aniline point are concepts which correlate well with actual performance there is no need to insist on experimental determination of these tests. Restrictions placed on calculated values of these tests will serve the same purpose. The aniline point is of course used in the calculation of the diesel index which is calculated from the aniline point and gravity. The cetane index, which is derived from the gravity and 50 per cent distillation point, is claimed to correlate better with the ignition quality of diesel fuel than the diesel index. Hence when the cetane index is included in a specification the need for an aniline point is eliminated.

4. FUTURE TRENDS

It is in the interests of the refiner, the marketer and the consumer to see that specifications are efficient. All three parties do not want to waste time with worthless specification tests and in addition the refiner might also find a worthless test restrictive to production.

Where a refiner is manufacturing a product in compliance with a number of different marketing specifications he can draft his manufacturing specification in such a way as to ensure that these are all satisfied in the most efficient manner. In the case of particular marketing specifications, however, very little improvement can be achieved without the full co-operation of supplier and consumer. It is to be hoped that such co-operation between the parties in rejecting the worthless tests will provide a sound foundation for the introduction of tests that are fundamental in nature and give the best possible control of product quality. Because of the difficulty of devising inspection tests which correlate sufficiently highly with the important performance properties of products, it is possible that there will be an increasing tendency for product quality to be specified in terms of suitably chosen indices which are not measured directly in the laboratory but are calculated from two or more measured properties. This approach should lead to fewer manufacturing restrictions, to closer control of quality and to economies in testing.

5. SUGGESTIONS FOR FURTHER READING ON STATISTICAL BACKGROUND

R. W. Cranston and J. Gammon (1963). A new slant on the construction of specification and testing, *J. Inst. Pet.*, **50**, 73.

R. W. Cranston and L. Downer (1964). 'Defining the properties requiring measurement', Conference on Automatic Control in the Process Industries, Society of Chemical Industry, Liverpool, April.

E. G. Duncan and E. S. Sellers (1964). 'Product quality from the point of view of the consumer, the refiner and the community', IP/AFTP Joint Summer Meeting, Gleneagles.

B. A. M. Thomas (1961). Some industrial applications of multivariate analysis, *Applied Statistics*, X, 1.

O. L. Davies (ed.) (1958). Multiple and curvilinear regression, in *Statistical Methods in Research and Production*, 3rd edn, Oliver and Boyd, London.

D. N. Lawley and A. E. Maxwell (1963). The method of principal components in *Factor Analysis as a Statistical Method*, Butterworth, London.

Chapter 2

CRUDE OILS

J. O'DONNELL

1. INTRODUCTION

Crude oils exhibit wide variations in composition and properties, and these occur not only in crudes from different fields but also in oils taken from different production depths in the same well. Even though there is available a wealth of data on crudes from oilfields throughout the world, no entirely satisfactory system for classifying these oils has been developed.

Elemental analyses of crude oils show that they contain mainly carbon and hydrogen in the approximate ratio of 6:1 by weight. Sulphur, nitrogen, and oxygen are present in smaller amounts and also trace elements such as vanadium, nickel etc; of these elements sulphur is the most important. The mixture of hydrocarbons is highly complex; paraffinic, naphthenic, and aromatic structures can occur in the same molecule and the complexity increases with boiling range. The attempted classification of crude oils in terms of these three main structural types has proved inadequate. However, the US Bureau of Mines method based on the determination of the properties of key fractions of specified boiling range provides a rough classification which is useful for comparison purposes, and to this end a vast library of analyses of world crude oils has now been accumulated by the US Bureau of Mines using this method.

The value of a particular crude to a refiner depends upon its quality and whether he can economically obtain a satisfactory product pattern which fits existing markets. In the main, he is not concerned with the actual chemical nature of the material but in methods of analysis which would provide information sufficient to assess the potential quality of the oil, to supply preliminary engineering data, and also to indicate whether any difficulties might arise in handling, refining, or transporting the oil or its products. Such information may be obtained in one of two ways:

1. preliminary assay—inspection data;
2. a full assay involving the preparation of a true boiling point curve and the analysis of fractions and product blends throughout the full range of the crude.

At the present time, the pressure of competition, the technological advances within the industry, and the continuous search, and need, for products of better quality, demand a knowledge of the detailed hydrocarbon type composition of a crude. The modern instrumental techniques of chromatography, ultra-violet and infra-red spectroscopy, together with mass spectrometry facilitate such an analysis. Their successful application is helping considerably to provide more detailed information on the identification and estimation of individual hydrocarbons and compound types present in petroleum. In conjunction with the data from the assays these techniques enable a superior evaluation of hydrocarbon quality to be obtained, as well as an assessment of the difficulties that might arise in normal bulk oil operations with a particular crude.

2. SAMPLING

The importance of the correct sampling of crude oil which usually contains light hydrocarbons cannot be overstressed. Properties like the specific gravity, distillation yields, vapour pressure, hydrogen sulphide content, and octane numbers of the gasolines are affected by the light hydrocarbon content so that suitable cooling or pressure sampling methods have to be used and care taken during the subsequent handling of the oil in order to avoid the loss of any volatile components. In addition, adequate records of the circumstances and conditions during sampling have to be made, for example, in sampling from oilfield separators, the temperatures and pressures of the separation plant and the atmospheric temperature would be noted.

Attention to factors such as these enables standardised comparisons to be made when subsequent samples are taken.

Crude oils which are very waxy, and in a solid state, may require judicious heating to dissolve the wax, and some crudes which are liable to precipitate wax on cooling have to be suitably heated or homogenised to ensure correct sampling.

Standard procedures to be followed are described in the ASTM *Manual on Measurement and Sampling* and in Part IV of IP *Standards for Petroleum and its Products*.

3. PRELIMINARY ASSAY—INSPECTION DATA

The preliminary assay provides general data on the oil and is based on simple tests such as distillation range, water content, specific gravity, sulphur content etc. which enable desirable or undesirable features to be noted. This form of assay requires only a small quantity of sample and is therefore particularly useful for the characterisation of oilfield samples produced from cores, drill stem tests or seepages. Many of these tests can also be easily converted to micro methods.

TABLE 1

Preliminary assay data for a range of crude oils

	North America USA West Texas	South America Venezuela Quiriquire	North America Sahara Hassi Messaoud	Middle East Kuwait Burgan	Far East Sumatra Minas
Specific gravity at 60°F/60°F	0·866	0·955	0·809	0·868 5	0·842 5
Distillation test					
IBP (°C)	55	162	40	44	60·5
Volume (per cent) at:					
50°C (122°F)	—	—	1·0	1·0	—
75°C (167°F)	2·0	—	5·0	3·5	1·0
100°C (212°F)	7·5	—	12·5	7·5	3·5
125°C (257°F)	13·0	—	20·0	12·0	7·5
150°C (302°F)	18·0	—	27·0	16·0	9·5
175°C (347°F)	23·5	1·5	34·5	20·5	13·0
200°C (392°F)	28·0	3·0	42·0	25·0	16·5
225°C (437°F)	32·5	7·0	48·5	29·0	21·0
250°C (482°F)	37·5	13·0	54·5	33·5	24·5
275°C (527°F)	43·0	18·5	60·0	37·5	29·5
300°C (572°F)	49·0	22·0	66·0	42·0	35·0
Total distillate (per cent)	49·6	22·6	67·1	43·5	36·0
Residue (per cent)	50·4	77·4	32·9	55·5	63·5
Loss (per cent)	—	—	—	1·0	0·5

Specific gravity at 60°F/60°F of distillate	0·789 0	0·866 5	0·764	0·762	0·773
Specific gravity at 60°F/60°F of residue	0·941[a]	0·981 5[a]	0·904[a]	0·955[a]	0·890[a]
Sulphur content (% wt)	1·78	1·27	0·13	2·50	0·10
Asphaltenes (% wt)	0·58	1·3	0·08	0·80	0·12
Carbon residue (Conradson) (% wt)	3·15	4·9	0·9	5·4	2·7
Wax content (% wt)	5·7	<0·5	3·3	5·4	32·0
Pour point (°F)	−15	−5	<−30	−20	95
Kinematic viscosity at 70°F (21°C) (cSt)	10·72	415	2·75	16·5	Waxy
Kinematic viscosity at 100°F (38°C) (cSt)	—	124	2·09	9·0	7·66
Salt content (lb/1 000 bbl)	138[b]	13·5[b]	8·5	4·0	Nil
Water content (% wt)	1·8[b]	0·7[b]	Nil	Nil	Nil
Water and sediment (% vol.)	—	—	—	<0·2	—
Vanadium content (ppm)	11	31	<1	28	<1
Nickel content (ppm)	4	6	<1	5	<1
Light hydrocarbon analysis (% wt)					
Ethane	0·03	—	0·05	0·07	0·03
Propane	0·25	—	0·59	0·55	0·31
i-Butane	0·18	Nil	0·27	0·27	0·20
n-Butane	0·76	Nil	1·85	1·09	0·55
i-Pentane	0·78	—	0·96	0·82	0·51
n-Pentane	0·89	—	2·35	1·40	0·60

[a] Converted from the value determined at 140°F (60°C) (uncorrected for hydrometer expansion) using the appropriate correction factor.

[b] Except for these tests the data refer to a dry sample.

Inspection data on these lines for a number of world crude oils are shown in Table 1 above.

(a) Specific Gravity, Carbon Residue, Asphaltenes

Specific gravity ASTM D1298–IP 160 although not strictly a criterion of quality for crude oil is always included in lists of inspection data mainly for its use in bulk oil measurement. This use is illustrated in the IP–ASTM Measurement Tables. The test is also used in field operations as a rough control test during stabilisation of a crude.

Tests for Conradson carbon residue ASTM D189–IP 13 and asphaltenes IP 143 are sometimes included in inspection data on crude oils. They give an indication of the amount of heavy or high boiling residue in a crude.

(b) Distillation Test

In the preliminary assay of crude oils the method of distillation described in IP 24 is often used in the United Kingdom to give a rough indication of the boiling range of the crude. The test is very similar to the well known method for gasoline distillation ASTM D86–IP 123 and like this is carried out at atmospheric pressure and under conditions of poor fractionation. With crude oils, the distillation is stopped at 300°C (572°C) to avoid excessive decomposition, and the distillate and residue can be further examined by tests such as specific gravity, sulphur content ASTM D129–IP 61 and viscosity ASTM D445–IP 71, etc. The tests give a rough indication of the quality of the products to be obtained from the crude and have been used to compare crude oils in respect of the quality of the 300°C (572°F) cut point residue. For example, the waxiness or viscosity gives a pointer to the type of residual fuels obtainable from the crude. The value of this distillation test is, however, strictly limited.

(c) Sulphur Content

The sulphur content of crude oils varies widely within the rough limits 0·3 to 3·0 per cent weight although some heavy crudes exist having values up to 7 per cent. Compounds containing this element are among the most undesirable constituents of crude oil since they can give rise to plant corrosion and atmospheric pollution. Certain crudes when distilled evolve hydrogen sulphide, low boiling sulphur compounds and also the decomposition products of heavy sulphur compounds, thus adding considerably to processing difficulties. Generally, however, the sulphur compounds concentrate in the distillation residue, the volatile sulphur compounds in the distillates being removed by such processes as hydrofining, soda washing etc. The sulphur content of the fuels obtained from the residue and the atmospheric pollution arising from the use of these fuels have become an important factor in the economics of crude oil utilisation, so that the increasing insistence on a low sulphur content fuel oil has increased the value of low sulphur crudes.

A large number of tests are available to estimate the sulphur in petroleum or to study its effect on various products. In crude oil itself it is normally estimated by combustion methods, as described in ASTM D129–IP 61 (Bomb Method) or IP 243 (Wickbold). Hydrogen sulphide dissolved in crude oil is normally determined by absorption of the hydrogen sulphide in a suitable solution which is subsequently analysed chemically.

(d) Viscosity and Pour Point

The viscosity and pour point of a crude oil are determined principally for use in pumping and pipeline design calculations. Difficulty occurs in these determinations with waxy crude oils which begin to exhibit irregular flow behaviour when wax begins to separate. These crudes possess viscosity relationships which are difficult to predict in pipeline operation. In addition, some waxy crude oils are sensitive to heat treatment which can also affect their viscosity characteristics. This complex behaviour limits the value of viscosity and pour point tests on waxy crude oils. At the present time, long crude oil pipelines and the increasing production of waxy crudes make an assessment of the pumpability of a wax-bearing crude through a given system a matter of some difficulty which can often only be resolved after field trials.

Consequently, considerable work is in progress to develop a suitable laboratory pumpability test, and one such test is described in IP 230 which gives an estimate of minimum handling temperature and minimum line or storage temperature.

(e) Light Hydrocarbons

The amount of the individual light hydrocarbons in a crude oil (methane to butane or pentane) is often included as part of the preliminary assay since modern techniques make such an analysis easy to perform. This analysis, however, is always included in the fuller examination of crude oil.

(f) Water and Sediment

Considerable importance attaches to the presence of water or sediment in crude oil for they lead to difficulties in the refinery, e.g. corrosion of equipment, uneven running on the distillation unit, blockages in heat exchangers and adverse effects on product quality.

The sediment consists of finely divided solids which may be dispersed in the oil or carried in water droplets. The solids may be drilling mud or sand or scale picked up during the transport of the oil, or may consist of chlorides derived from evaporation of brine droplets in the oil. In any event, the sediment can lead to serious plugging of the equipment, corrosion due to chloride decomposition, and a lowering of residual fuel quality.

Water may be found in the crude either in an emulsified form or in large droplets and can cause flooding of distillation units and excessive accumulation of sludge in tanks. The quantity is generally limited by refiners, and although steps are normally taken at the oilfield to reduce the water content as low as possible, water may be later introduced during shipment. In any form, water and sediment are highly undesirable in a refinery feedstock and the relevant tests (ASTM D95–IP 74, ASTM D1796–IP 75 and ASTM D96) are regarded as important in crude oil quality examinations. Prior to assay it is sometimes necessary to separate the water from a crude oil sample and this is usually carried out by one of the procedures described in IP 24 (Preliminary distillation of crude petroleum). Certain crude oils, notably heavy asphaltic types, often form persistent emulsions which are difficult to separate, whilst in testing wax-bearing crude oils for sediment and water care has to be taken to ensure that wax suspended in the sample is brought into solution prior to the test otherwise it will be recorded as sediment. Careful sampling of a crude oil is necessary when examination has to be made for suspended impurities of the type discussed.

(g) SALT CONTENT

There is a great variation in the salt content of crude oil depending mainly on the oilfield source, and possibly on the producing wells or zones within a field. In addition, at the refinery, salt water introduced during shipment by tanker may have contributed to this total salt content. These salts have adverse effects on refinery operations especially in increasing maintenance following corrosion in crude units and heat exchangers. It is common practice to monitor wells in a producing field for high salt content, and it is also general practice to desalt the crude at the refinery. The determination of the salt content of crude oil is often made, but as with water and sediment tests, careful sampling is necessary. It would appear that further tests to determine the corrosiveness due to the individual chemical components of the 'salt' and also a determination of the extent of evolution of hydrogen chloride on heating would be desirable.

(h) WAX CONTENT

Crude oils of high wax content present difficulties in handling and pumping. They produce distillate and residual fuels of high pour point and lubricating oils which are costly to dewax. Thus considerable study has been made of wax cracking or destruction processes.

All the standard methods for the determination of the wax are empirical. Such methods as that described by Holde and others involve precipitating the wax from solvents such as methylene chloride, acetone etc. under special conditions of solvent/oil ratio and temperature. Measurements such as these give comparative results which are often useful in characterising the wax content of crude oil, or for investigating factors involved in flow problems.

(i) METALLIC CONTAMINANTS IN CRUDE OIL

Certain classes of trace components other than sulphur and water which are also present in crude oils can produce adverse effects in refining either by causing corrosion, by affecting the quality of refined products, or by exerting a deleterious influence on the efficiency of various processing catalysts. This last has become of increasing importance due to modern developments in refinery processing. Examples of this class of compounds are those of vanadium, nickel, sodium and arsenic.

Vanadium compounds can cause refractory damage in furnaces and adverse effects in glass manufacture, steel failure in turbines, as well as catalyst poisoning when present in distillate feedstocks.

Arsenic and lead are also active catalyst poisons in reforming processes, whilst the presence of sodium in fuel oils causes failures in furnace brickwork. It is necessary, therefore, for crude oils and distillation unit feedstocks to be examined for the presence of these harmful contaminants, and some form of treatment devised for reducing their effect during or before processing.

The application of quick methods of instrumental analysis, *e.g.* by X-ray techniques, for these metals is often of considerable assistance to the petroleum refiner.

4. FULL ASSAY—BASED ON TRUE BOILING POINT DISTILLATION

The tests in the preliminary assay are relatively simple and can be completed in a short time and generally on a routine basis. This assay gives a useful general picture of the quality of a crude, but it does not cover the work necessary to provide adequate data, for example, for the design of refinery equipment, nor does it produce a sufficient quantity of the various products from the crude so that they can be examined for quality.

Owing to the wide variation in the types of crude oil and to the fact that most companies have evolved their own assay methods, it has proved difficult to devise a rigid procedure to be followed in all cases, although there are considerable advantages to be gained if this were possible.

The Standardisation Committee of the IP studied the possibility of evolving a standard method for the fuller assay of crude oil, and in a paper in the *Journal of the Institute of Petroleum* (1950), **36,** 693–704 set out the general principles involved in such an assay and put forward a general procedure. This procedure is, in essence, that followed by many companies.

The method is based on a true boiling point distillation of the crude, and sufficient data are obtained to assess the yields and properties of the straight run products, covering light hydrocarbons, light, middle and heavy distillates, lubricants, residual fuels and bitumens.

The method involves the distillation of the crude oil in one to five gallon quantities in a column equivalent to fourteen theoretical plates and with reflux adjusted to obtain a true boiling point versus yield relationship. Narrow fractions can be taken throughout the distillation and the still pressure can be reduced as necessary to avoid decomposition in the higher boiling ranges. The fractionating distillation is continued to a relatively high temperature *e.g.* 371°C (700°)F equivalent temperature at 760 mm of mercury absolute. (The actual operating pressure of the still at this stage would be in the region of 2 mm of mercury absolute.)

The distillate fractions up to this point cover the light and middle distillates, and after the analysis of the required fractions in this range, curves relating the various properties to yield on fraction or on crude oil can be drawn.

A series of residues can also be prepared by appropriate blending of distillates with the final residue, and after analysis, property relationships with yield can also be prepared for the residues.

From the true boiling point curve, the yields of products of a required boiling range can be deduced and fractions can be blended to match required products for further analysis or treatments.

The residue above 371°C (700°F) obtained from the true boiling point distillation quoted, contains the main lubricating oil stock, and by further distillation under high vacuum a series of distillates can be prepared to cover the various lubricating oil grades.

With waxy crudes, it is necessary to remove the wax from these distillates and further examine the wax-free lubricating oil distillates.

Such analyses give a preliminary assessment of the yields and properties of the lubricating oils from the crude as well as the yields of wax and an indication of the further refining requirements of the oils.

It is often useful in this type of crude oil assay to be able to extend the boiling point data to higher temperatures than are possible in the fractionating distillation method previously described, and for this purpose a vacuum distillation in a simple still, with no fractionating column, similar to the ASTM distillation method D1160, can be carried out. This distillation, which is done under fractionating conditions equivalent to one theoretical plate, allows the boiling point data to be extended to about 600°C (1112°F) (corrected to 760 mm of mercury absolute) with many crudes. Bearing in mind the limitations in accuracy of the temperature measurements in the high boiling ranges of crude it is possible to construct a wide range boiling point curve for the crude by combining the results of the simple distillation with those of the main distillation. This method gives useful comparative and reproducible results which are often accurate enough for engineering purposes.

It is advantageous in a petroleum organisation dealing with crude oil to collect information by the above methods on a standard series of distillates or residues from crude oils, so that valuable comparisons become available as the data accumulate. These distillates should be prepared as near as possible to the boiling ranges which are known to be suitable for marketable products. Typical fractions for this purpose are shown below and are illustrated in Fig. 1 together with a true boiling point yield curve:

Gas to   15·5°C (60°F)   Gas oil   232–343°C (450–650°F)
Gasoline 15·5–149°C (60–300°F)   Heavy gas oil 343–371°C (650–700°F)
Kerosine 149–232°C (300–450°F)   Residue   above 371°C (700°F)

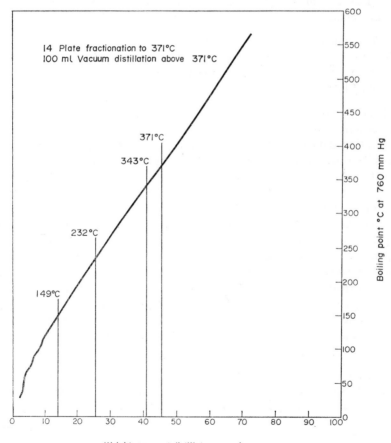

Weight per cent distillate on crude

FIG. 1.   *Typical Middle East crude oil TBP curve to 550°C weight per cent basis.*

The 371°C (700°F) residue can be further fractionated, if required, as described earlier using however a high vacuum still of sufficient capacity to give fractions in suitable quantity for subsequent analysis.

The test requirements for these fractions from the crude can vary to a considerable extent depending on the current quality requirements but are described in detail elsewhere in this volume.

5. APPLICATION OF INSTRUMENTAL TECHNIQUES

The common method of assay described above has been greatly augmented in recent years by applying a wide variety of instrumental techniques to studies of the hydrocarbon composition of crude oils and their products. Prior to this, hydrocarbon type analyses (per cent paraffins, naphthenes, olefins and aromatics) were derived from correlations based upon physical data. The advent of instrumental techniques has led to two major developments:

(a) individual component analysis;
(b) an extension to, and more detailed subdivision of, the various compound types that occur in the higher boiling ranges of petroleum distillates.

Of these instrumental techniques, gas/liquid chromatography (GLC) and mass spectrometry are the most important in providing the hydrocarbon composition data in crude oil assay work. By GLC it is now possible to determine routinely the individual C_1 to C_7 hydrocarbons and the individual aromatics that boil below 165°C (329°F) and also obtain a complete normal paraffin distribution up to C_{50}. In addition, by using a microcoulometric detector specific to sulphur, the sulphur compound distribution can be obtained throughout the normal distillate range. GLC can also be used to provide simulated True Boiling Point curves while recent developments in preparative scale GLC have made possible the preparation of fractions in quantities sufficient not only for extensive spectrometric analyses but also for the normal inspection type tests to be undertaken on them.

Mass spectrometry offers a very rapid method for obtaining hydrocarbon type analyses on a wide range of fractions up to and including heavy gas oils. The information obtained on a routine basis subdivides the hydrocarbons into the following groups:

paraffins, naphthenes according to the number of rings per molecule, alkyl benzenes, alkyl indanes/tetralines, indenes, alkyl naphthalenes, acenaphthenes/biphenyls, acenaphthylenes/fluorenes and anthracenes/ phenanthrenes.

The technique can also be used in conjunction with separation procedures such as GLC, molecular distillation, thermal diffusion or selective adsorption to provide more detailed analyses where necessary even on fractions in the lubricating oil range.

From such a knowledge of the chemical composition of petroleum distillates obtained using these instrumental techniques, and the information from the standard assays, the refiner is better able to predict and control crude oil operations and to assess the quality and performance of his products.

6. SUGGESTIONS FOR FURTHER READING

'The Bureau of Mines Routine Method for the Analysis of Petroleum', US Bureau of Mines Bulletin 490.

Nelson (1958). *Petroleum Refinery Engineering*, 4th edn, McGraw-Hill, New York.

Robinson and Gilliland (1950). *Elements of Frictional Distillation*, 4th edn, McGraw-Hill, New York.

'ASTM Manual on Hydrocarbon Analysis', First Edition 1933, ASTM Special Technical Publication No. 332.

'Symposium on Hydrocarbon Analysis', ASTM Special Technical Publication No. 389.

W. L. Nelson (1958). Metal contaminants in petroleum, *Oil Gas J.*, **56**, No, 51, 75.

E. W. Baker (1964). Vanadium and nickel in crudes of South American and Middle East origin, *Journal of Chemical Engineering Data*, **9,** No. 2, 307, April.

Chapter 3

PETROLEUM GASES

D. RAWLINSON and E. R. WARD

1. INTRODUCTION

The liquid products derived from crude petroleum can be very complex mixtures of hydrocarbons, but petroleum gases have a simpler composition. A study of the properties of these gases can therefore be based to a large extent on a determination of their exact composition and a knowledge of the characteristics of the constituents. Empirical procedures can be useful as supplementary tests in evaluating properties relating to application and performance.

2. NATURE AND COMPOSITION

The term 'petroleum gases' in the context of this book is used to describe the gaseous phase and liquid phase mixtures comprised mainly of C_1 to C_4 hydrocarbons described below.

(a) Natural Gases

The bulk of natural gas found is not associated with oil. The hydrocarbon content varies from mixtures of methane and ethane and little else—the 'dry' gases—to mixtures ranging from methane to pentane, sometimes associated with a substantial naphtha fraction—the 'wet' gases. In both cases some carbon dioxide and inert gases, including helium, are present together with hydrogen sulphide and a small quantity of organic sulphur.

Substantial natural gas production is associated with crude oil production and its stabilisation. These associated gases are comparable to the 'wet' gases described above.

(b) Refinery Gases

At source refinery gases vary from mixtures comparable to 'wet' natural gas, to mixtures of methane and hydrogen, or mixtures with high concentrations of C_2 to C_4 olefinic hydrocarbons. These gases are not always streamed. The term 'refinery gas' therefore potentially covers a wider range of gas compositions than commercial natural gas, and is characterised by the presence of hydrogen and unsaturated hydrocarbons.

(c) Liquefied Petroleum Gases (LPG)

LPG's are comprised of the fractions of the gaseous mixtures described under (a) and (b) which are liquefiable under pressure at ambient temperature. They are composed almost entirely of propane and butanes if derived from natural sources; derived from refinery operation substantial proportions of the corresponding olefins will be present unless separated.

Table 1 provides a list of molecular weights, boiling points and densities of the hydrocarbons which may be found in either natural or refinery gases. Tables 2 and 3 give the characteristics of examples of the various gases.

TABLE 1

Molecular weights, boiling points and densities of hydrocarbons normally found in natural and refinery gas

Gas	Molecular weight	Boiling point 1 atm[a,b]		Density at 60°F (15·6°C), 1 atm	
				Real gas	
		°C	(°F)	g/litre[c]	Relative to air = 1
Methane	16·043	−161·5	(−258·7)	0·678 6	0·554 7
Ethylene	28·054	−103·7	(−154·7)	1·194 9	0·976 8
Ethane	30·068	−88·6	(−127·5)	1·279 5	1·046 0
Propylene	42·081	−47·7	(−53·9)	1·805 2	1·475 7
Propane	44·097	−42·1	(−43·8)	1·891 7	1·546 4
1,2-Butadiene	54·088	10·9	(51·6)	2·345 1	1·917 2
1,3-Butadiene	54·088	−4·4	(24·1)	2·349 1	1·920 3
1-Butene	56·108	−6·3	(20·7)	2·444 2	1·998 1
cis-2-Butene	56·108	3·7	(38·7)	2·454 3	2·006 3
trans-2-Butene	56·108	0·9	(33·6)	2·454 3	2·006 3
iso-Butene	56·104	−6·9	(19·6)	2·444 2	1·998 1
n-Butane	58·124	−0·5	(31·1)	2·532 0	2·069 8
iso-Butane	58·124	−11·7	(10·9)	2·526 8	2·065 6

[a] Values taken from API Project 44 Data, Boiling Points of Hydrocarbons, Tables 1a (1952), 8a (1954) and 11a (1952).

[b] W. S. Hanna and R. Matteson (1947). Physical constants of low-boiling hydrocarbons and miscellaneous compounds, *Oil Gas J.*, **45**(36), 61.

[c] Calculated from ideal gas densities using the deviation factors given in 'Physical Constants of Hydrocarbons Boiling Below 350°F', ASTM Special Technical Publication No. 109 and California Natural Gasoline Bulletin TS-401, 1953.

TABLE 2

Characteristics of selected natural gases

	Examples of untreated gases			Examples of some of the major natural gases as marketed				
	Non-associated gas		'Associated gas'	UK	Holland	USA		
	of relatively older period	of geologically recent period						
	1	2	3	4	5	6	7	8
	France, Lacq	Salt Lake, Utah	Persian Gulf area, Aga Jari	North Sea, Leman Bank	Groningen	Monroe, Louisiana	Amarillo, Texas	Ashland, Kentucky
Composition % v/v								
Methane	69·1	96·0	66·0	94·7	81·2	94·7	72·9	75·0
Ethane	2·8	—	14·0	3·0	2·9	2·8	19·0	24·0
Propanes	0·8	—	10·5	0·5	0·4	—	—	—
Butanes	1·5	—	5·0	0·2	0·1	—	—	—
$C_5{}^+$	0·6	—	2·0	0·2	0·1	—	—	—
Hydrogen sulphide	15·4	—	—	—	—	—	—	—
Carbon dioxide	9·7	3·7	1·5	0·1	0·9	0·2	0·4	—
Nitrogen	—	0·3	1·0	1·3	14·4	2·3	7·7	1·0
Helium	—	—	—	<0·1	<0·1	—	—	—
Argon	—	—	—	—	—	—	—	—
Sp. gr. $\frac{\text{(dry gas)}}{\text{(dry air)}}$	0·75	0·59	0·87	0·59	0·64	0·58	0·68	0·67
C. V. Gross								
Btu/ft³ (stp dry)	910	952	1 403	1 037	843	988	1 054	1 161
MJ/m³ (st)	33·9	35·4	52·3	38·6	31·4	36·8	39·2	43·2

The gases shown in Cols 1 to 3 are untreated.
The gases shown in Cols 4 to 5 have been subjected to a minor adjustment of hydrocarbon dewpoint.
The gases shown in Cols 6 to 8 have been treated for the removal of LPG and higher hydrocarbons.

TABLE 3

Chemical and physical characteristics of examples of refinery gases and LPG

| | Refinery gases | | | Commercial propane | | Example of |
	Low cal. val.	Inter-mediate cal. val.	High cal. val.	For enriching	For gasmaking	commercial butane
Analysis (% mol)						
CH_4	12·0	21·4	17·2	Nil	Nil	0·1
C_2H_6	13·0	18·6	17·8	1·5	Nil	7·2
C_2H_4	Nil	2·5	4·0	Nil	Nil	Nil
C_3H_8	13·0	16·0	20·7	45·0	92·5	0·5
C_3H_6	2·0	5·4	14·9	52·0	5·0	4·2
C_4H_{10}	2·0	12·4	21·9	} 1·5	} 2·5	87·0
C_4H_8	1·0	Nil	Nil			1·0
CO_2	Nil	0·1	0·3	Nil	Nil	Nil
H_2	56·0	21·8	0·2	Nil	Nil	Nil
N_2	1·0	1·8	3·0	Nil	Nil	Nil
Total	100·0	100·0	100·0	100·0	100·0	100·0
Gross cal. val.						
(Btu/ft³)	1 000	1 620	2 181	2 386	2 476	3 052
MJ/m³	37·9	61·4	82·6	90·4	93·8	115·7
Sp. gr.						
(air = 1)	0·54	0·96	1·35	1·47	1·53	1·96
Characteristics as liquid						
Sp. gr.						
(H_2O = 1)	—	—	—	0·52	0·51	0·58
Gross cal.						
val. (Btu/lb)	—	—	—	21 440	21 250	21 350
MJ/kilo	—	—	—	49·9	49·4	49·7

3. UTILISATION

(a) NATURAL GAS AND LPG

Natural gas and LPG where available are the preferred fuels for high premium uses, *i.e.* for domestic, commercial, and small to moderate scale industrial applications where the greatest advantage accrues from their convenience, and since these are the low level waste gas emitters, the greatest advantage results from the low pollution arising from their use.

To a limited extent national shortages of natural gas can be met by imports in the liquid phase from overseas. LPG which is more versatile than natural gas or LNG since it can be transported in vehicles at ambient temperatures

Group 1
Uses in which the gas stock is transportable
Use on civil and other engineering sites
e.g. shipbuilding sites
Agricultural uses
Automotive uses, including aircraft

Group 2
Ferrous-metal treatments
Engineering and shipbuilding
Metal goods manufacture
Vehicle production
Fine chemicals and allied trades
Non-ferrous metal treatments
Food, drink and tobacco processing
Glassware manufacture and finishing
Electrical goods production
China and fine ceramics production
Textiles, leather and clothing production
Paper and printing—ancillary uses
Agricultural uses (static)
Various miscellaneous uses

Manufactured
gas
applications

Group 3
Steam raising—small scale
Power generation for use on site
Bricks, cement bricks and coarse ceramics
Chemical synthesis gases—feedstock
Ore reducing gases—feedstock
Town gas manufacture—feedstock
Power generation—extreme peak load
Iron and steel making—ancillary uses
Paper making
Glass making
Lime making
Sugar refining
Oil refining

Group 4
Power generation
Steam raising—large scale
Iron and steel making
Non-ferrous ore reduction
Cement

Natural gas   Liquefied
applications   petroleum
                gas
                applications

FIG. 1. *Potential range of industrial applications of fuel gases.*

(Gasmaking and natural gas, *British Petroleum*, 1972, 251)

can fulfil the need for a gaseous high premium fuel outside of the economic transmission range of gaseous or liquid phase natural gas.

In those areas, such as the USA, where the supply of natural gas and LPG even now, although decreasingly, exceeds the requirements of the high premium users, it overflows first into petrochemical uses, where it should obtain a premium over alternative process materials, and finally into bulk fuel uses where the premium value is at the minimum other than in special circumstances relating to atmospheric pollution.

In addition to domestic and industrial uses hydrocarbon gases have a limited role in automotive applications where the levels of pollutant emissions are currently in process of legal restriction. LNG or compressed natural gas (CNG) will be economical only in narrowly restricted circumstances, but LPG with the help of tax remission is nearest to being a substitute for petrol, although it could not be economically manufactured for the purpose.

In the interim between the present and the time when the petrol driven vehicles emissions are improved to an acceptable level, engine conversions to the use of LPG, or purpose built LPG vehicles, can make a marginal contribution to the prevention of atmospheric pollution. The most appropriate applications in this area are for the mechanical equipment used within factories and similar areas and for public transport fleets operating in congested cities.

A diagram comparing the potential range of natural gas and LPG applications with that of manufactured town gas is shown in Fig. 1.

(b) REFINERY GASES

The inevitable variations in the composition and availability of the gas produced from a refinery renders its reticulation in the manner of natural or manufactured gas impractical. It can be used with advantage however for the production of a lean gas for use either in chemical syntheses, or for hydrogen or town gas production. A preferred use would be as enriching medium for town gas manufacture.

In the main, however, refinery gas is put to bulk fuel uses mainly in the refinery.

Prior to the application of refinery gases to the uses referred to above they would be exploited to the economic limit as sources of LPG, of olefins for a whole range of petrochemical activities, or where applicable as a source of hydrogen-rich gas.

4. CHARACTERISTICS AND PERFORMANCE REQUIREMENTS

(a) NATURAL GASES

Raw natural gases vary greatly in composition (*see* Table 2), and the treatment required to prepare them for distribution by public utilities varies accordingly.

Carbon dioxide in excess of 3 per cent is normally removed for reasons of corrosion prevention and/or high pressure transmission cost reduction. Hydrogen sulphide in excess of from 1 to 15 ppm v/v, according to local statutory levels, is also removed. The organic sulphur content is normally acceptably low, and frequently so low that it needs augmenting by means of alkyl sulphides, mercaptans or thiophens in order to maintain an acceptable safe level of odour.[1]

The hydrocarbon dewpoint is reduced to such a level that retrograde condensation, i.e. condensation resulting from pressure drop, cannot occur under the worst conditions likely to be experienced in the gas transmission system. Similarly the water dewpoint is reduced to a level sufficient to preclude formation of C_1 to C_4 hydrates in the system.[2] In the case of the UK North Sea supplies the following dewpoints are required in order to achieve this.

	Summer	Winter
Water dewpoint	+4·5°C (40·1°F)	−9·0°C (15·8°F) at 1000 psig
Hydrocarbon dewpoint	+10·0°C (50°F)	−1·0°C (30·2°F) at 4000 psig

The natural gas after appropriate treatment for acid gas reduction, odorisation, and hydrocarbon and moisture dewpoint adjustment, would then be sold within prescribed limits of pressure, calorific value and possibly Wobbe Index [W1 = cv/(sp. gr.)$^{\frac{1}{2}}$].

(b) Refinery Gases

Residual refinery gases, usually in more than one stream, which allows a degree of quality control, are treated for hydrogen sulphide removal on streams where the content is excessive, otherwise the gases are used untreated. Bulk sales would be on a thermal basis preferably with scope for wide calorific value and hydrocarbon type variation.

(c) Liquefied Petroleum Gases for Gasmaking and Petrochemical Uses

The hydrocarbon type is relatively more important in the context of the gasmaking and petrochemical applications of LPG than in the fuel use.

For example, the presence of propylene and butylene above approx 10 per cent by volume inhibits the application of hydrodesulphurisation prior to steam reforming.

At the other extreme some petrochemical processes require the exclusion of the saturated paraffins. A very special case is the production by alkylation of iso-octane for automotive use, this demands the exclusion of all but iso-butane and butylene.

Other quality requirements, in particular those related to contaminants, would be comparable to those of LPG for fuel use detailed below, and the same or similar sampling and testing methods would apply.

(d) LPG for Fuel Uses

(i) General

LPG shares with LNG the facility of being stored and transported as a liquid and then vaporised and used as a gas. In order to achieve this the LPG must be maintained at a moderate pressure, say up to 14 atm max, but at ambient temperature. The LNG can be at ambient pressure but must be maintained at a temperature of roughly $-160°C$ ($-256°F$). On balance this favours the storage and transportation of LPG.

In some applications it is economical and convenient to use LPG in the liquid phase. Where this is done aspects of composition or quality, such as the ratio of C_3 to C_4 hydrocarbons, and the presence of traces of heavier hydrocarbons, water and other extraneous materials becomes irrelevant compared with their significance if the LPG is used in the vapour phase.

LPG, however, is used mainly in the vapour phase and this leads to the consideration and defining of certain characteristics regarding composition and the presence of contaminants as set out below.

(ii) Composition

If the conversion from liquid phase LPG to the vapour phase is to take place without the use of a vaporiser, as is the case with all domestic and some small industrial consumers, the contents of the bottle or tank should be of such quality that it will all evaporate at ambient temperature whilst exerting sufficient pressure to enable the LPG appliance to operate satisfactorily.

This involves the supply of propane in cold climates and either propane or butane in hot climates. In temperate climates there is a tendency to use propane/butane mixtures, in some cases with seasonal variation in the proportions, but this should be viewed critically in the light of the fact that the cylinder appears to be an effective separation column, and there is room for doubt regarding the need for propane in, for example, 50:50 mixtures since it is likely that as the cylinder becomes exhausted only butane will emerge, in which case the question arises as to whether the propane was needed.

The presence of propylene and butylenes in LPG used as fuel gas is not critical. The vapour pressures are slightly higher and the flame speeds substantially higher than those of propane and butane; but this latter quality is an advantage since the flame speeds of propane and butane are very slow. The only difficulty which could limit the olefins to a level of the order of

50 per cent is their sooting propensity, which would vary with the appliance. It will also be necessary to limit olefins in LPG used for automotive purposes owing to their low octane rating.

The large scale use of LPG involves the use of a vaporiser. The specific heats and latent heats of all the hydrocarbons involved are similar. The relatively higher vapour pressure of propane and propylene do, however, serve to render unnecessary the use of a pump between the storage tank and vaporiser. Such a pump is usually required for C_4 hydrocarbons.

(iii) Contaminants

The substances under this head are controlled at a level at which they do not corrode fittings and appliances or impede the flow of the LPG.

Sulphur

Hydrogen sulphide should be absent and carbonyl sulphide preferably so. Organic sulphur to the level required for adequate odorisation, or stenching, is a normal requirement in LPG, dimethyl sulphide and ethyl mercaptan are commonly used at 50 ppm w/w. Natural gas is similarly treated possibly with a wider range of volatile sulphur compounds including thiophen.[3]

Oily matter and gums

Heavier materials varying from middle distillates to lubricating oil may be picked up by LPG during handling. Good housekeeping should prevent their reaching unacceptable levels.

Olefins and especially diolefins are prone to polymerisation. The absence of carbonyl sulphide restricts this where olefins are concerned. The less stable diolefins are preferably absent.

Water

The presence of water in LPG is undesirable since it can produce hydrates which will cause a multistage pump, handling liquid-phase material, to seize up. In the vapour phase it can be responsible for blockages, due to the formation of hydrates in certain conditions if the water dewpoint is reached. LPG usually retains a trace of water and if this is exceeded and either of the above effects results, a small addition of methanol will counteract.

Trace metals

Adequate drying of LPG, required for the reasons set out in the foregoing paragraph, would reduce the risk of contamination by water soluble impurities such as sodium hydroxide. As an additional safeguard an allowance of 1 hour per ft depth of settling time with provision for separation of the underlying liquid normally suffices for separation.

Ammonia

LPG may be transported in vessels which have been used to carry liquid ammonia. Ammonia contamination can result which is highly corrosive to copper alloy fittings under pressure. Providing that the contamination is minimised and copper alloys are excluded from the bulk handling and high pressure fittings, no difficulty should be experienced at the domestic appliance end even if copper alloy fittings are used at this stage.

5. SAMPLING

The only special features characterising the sampling of petroleum gas are as follows.

With crude natural gas and refinery gas samples, liquid phase material may separate on change of conditions, this can be corrected by restoring the original conditions.

The sampling of LPG vapour, or liquid, from a given liquid storage system is complicated by the fact that the composition of the supernatant vapour phase material of mixtures differs from that of the liquid phase material, and that both vary as the bulk vaporises. To check delivered quality, therefore, samples must be taken during filling, or, failing that, from a fully charged tank.

6. ASSESSMENT OF QUALITY

Hydrocarbon gases, as described, are comprised of a narrow range of the simplest hydrocarbons in a form readily amenable to analytical techniques. More use therefore is made of these techniques for the determination of both main and trace constituents than is the case with the heavier hydrocarbons. Methods have been developed for the determination of physical characteristics such as calorific value specific gravity and enthalpy from the analyses of mixed hydrocarbon gases, although as yet not with the accuracy of direct determinations. Methods of calculating flame speed factors from gas analyses have been developed by Weaver[4] and Delbourg[5]; this will be referred to again later.

Despite the great value of analytical procedures, however, many empirical tests relating to chemical and physical characteristics are carried out, either because they are more convenient, or more accurate, than determinations dependent upon analysis. The tests referred to in the following text are incorporated in Appendix IV.

(a) ANALYTICAL METHODS FOR COMPOSITION

Currently the preferred method for the analysis of petroleum gases is gas chromatography. ASTM D2163–IP 264 is a typical technique, whilst capillary column gas chromatography is an even quicker and equally accurate alternative. This versatile and powerful analytical technique will identify and measure both main components and traces, but it should be noted that gas chromatography is not entirely satisfactory for determining traces of heavier hydrocarbons.

The technique of mass spectrometry ASTM D1137, is also suitable for analysis of petroleum gases, but is not likely to be used if the chromatographic apparatus is already available. Of the other spectroscopic techniques, infrared and ultra-violet absorption may be applied to petroleum gas analysis for some specialised applications. Gas chromatography has also largely supplanted chemical absorption methods of analysis but again these may have some limited specialised application.

A considerable amount of information about the technique of gas chromatography and its application to particular problems is available from the various equipment manufacturers and several standard methods written in fairly general terms, are available for petroleum gas analysis. Published methods (see Appendix IV) are written specifically for 'Natural Gas', 'LP Gases and Propylene Concentrates', 'Commercial Butane–Butylene Mixtures', and 'Petroleum Gases'.

(b) Assessment of Combustion Characteristics of Gaseous Phase Materials

Satisfactory combustion of hydrocarbon gases depends upon the matching of burner and appliance design with certain gas characteristics. The most important of these are the Wobbe Number [calorific value/(specific gravity)$^{\frac{1}{2}}$], and the flame speed, usually expressed as a factor or an arbitrary scale on which that of hydrogen is 100, as proposed by Weaver.[4] This factor can be calculated from the gas analysis.[6]

The Wobbe Number gives a measure of the heat input to an appliance through a given aperture at a given gas pressure. Using this as a vertical co-ordinate and the flame speed factor as the horizontal co-ordinate a combustion diagram can be constructed for an appliance, or a whole range of appliances, with the aid of appropriate test gases. This diagram shows the area within which variations in the WI and fsf of gases may occur for the given range of appliances without resulting in either incomplete combustion, flame lift, or the lighting back of pre-aerated flames.[6,7] This method of prediction of combustion characteristics is not sufficiently accurate to eliminate entirely the need for the practical testing of new gases.

Another important combustion criterion is the Gas Modulus, $M = P^{\frac{1}{2}}/W$ where P is the gas pressure and W the Wobbe Number of the gas. This must remain constant if a given degree of aeration is to be maintained in a pre-aerated burner using air at atmospheric pressure.

In practice the low flame speed of hydrocarbon gases has so far resulted in the virtual elimination of diffusion flames from domestic and commercial appliances.

The gas and/or air supply to industrial appliances is commonly endowed with considerable pressure above the ambient, this gives more scope for burner design, reduces the importance of flame speed, and renders the use of diffusion flames more practical.

TABLE 4

Typical emissivities of diffusion flames

Fuel	Emissivity (black body = 1·0)
Town gas ⎱ Natural gas ⎰	0·20 or less
LPG	0·40
Gas oil	0·60
Fuel oil	0·85
Pulverised coal	0·95

Characteristics which become of more importance in the industrial context are flammability limits, flame emissivity (*see* Table 4), and the carbon/hydrogen ratio.

The substitution of a gaseous fuel, for a fuel such as HFO which can produce a highly radiant flame, could result in the redesign of furnaces designed to take full advantage of flame radiation.

TABLE 5

Relative losses, owing to the latent heat of water vapour, of the potential heats of fuels burnt in heat transfer systems in which the waste gases retain the product water in the vapour phase

Fuel	Per cent difference gross and net calorific value
Town gas ⎱ Natural gas ⎰	10
Liquefied petroleum gas	8
Gas oil	6
Fuel oil	6
Coal (bituminous)	4
Anthracite	2

Carbon/hydrogen ratio is of importance since it is normally uneconomical to recover the latent heat of the water vapour resulting from combustion. This results in higher heat losses in waste gas from the combustion of gaseous hydrocarbons than from other fuels, as can be inferred from Table 5. This effect largely counteracts the higher combustion efficiency which would otherwise be obtainable from the use of hydrocarbon gases owing to their superior flexibility and controllability.

(c) ANALYTICAL METHODS FOR CONTAMINANTS

Analytical methods are available in standard form for determining volatile sulphur content and certain specific corrosive sulphur compounds which are likely to be present. Volatile sulphur determination is made by a combustion procedure. The 'Lamp Method ASTM D1266–IP 107 Sulphur in Petroleum Products and Liquefied Petroleum (LP) Gases' uses a modification of the standard wick-fed lamp. Many laboratories use rapid combustion techniques with an oxy-hydrogen flame in a Wickbold or Martin-Floret burner ASTM D2784 and IP 243. Absorption methods are suitable for determination of particular sulphur compounds—'Hydrogen Sulphide Content—Cadmium Sulphate Method' IP 103 and 'Mercaptan Sulphur Content—Silver Nitrate Method' IP 104. Other procedures have been developed in several laboratories in which the sulphur compounds are titrated electrometrically after absorption in alkaline solutions.

Trace hydrocarbons which may be regarded as contaminants may be determined by the gas chromatographic methods already discussed. Heavier hydrocarbons in small amounts may not be completely removed from the column. If accurate information is required about the nature and amount of heavy ends then temperature programming or a reconcentration procedure may be used.

The quantitative determination of water content is carried out by titration with Karl Fischer reagent and suitable procedures have been described in British Standard 2511: 1970.

Analytical methods for determining traces of various other impurities are known to be in use. No published methods are available but procedures based on standard analytical practice have been worked out for traces of ammonia, alkali, and alkali metals. The method for determination of inert gases in LPG based on absorption of the hydrocarbons in glacial acetic acid using an Orsat type apparatus has been superseded by gas chromatography.

(d) EMPIRICAL TESTS FOR COMPOSITION AND PHYSICAL CHARACTERISTICS

Once the composition of a mixture has been determined it is possible to calculate various properties. Values which can be derived in this way include specific gravity, vapour pressure, calorific value and dewpoint. Where it is necessary therefore to carry out the full analysis for some purpose, or where the facilities (gas chromatography) are available to do it, empirical tests are not necessary. However, because the composition of most commercial LPG is simple, and the number of components are few, the results of empirical tests do convey fairly precise information about composition.

One of the most widely used tests is vapour pressure ASTM D1267 and IP 161. Suitable procedures are described in ASTM, IP, and NGPA publications. These all set out instructions for the test at 100°F (38°C) and are technically equivalent, but in addition the IP method covers the determination at 113°F (45°C). An article in the IP Journal in 1955 describes the development of the test in this form and the reasons for the higher temperature.

Simple evaporation tests in conjunction with vapour pressure measurement give a further guide to composition. In these tests an LPG is allowed to evaporate naturally (to 'weather') from an open graduated vessel. Results are recorded on the basis of volume/temperature changes, *e.g.* temperature recorded when 95 per cent has evaporated, or volume left at a particular temperature. In one form of the test the temperature is taken as the freezing point of mercury. This is the 'NGPA Mercury Freeze Test for Residue in Propane'. Results are interpreted in relation to commercial butane or butane–propane mixtures. The presence of heavy ends will increase the temperature at the 95 per cent evaporation point. The method is described generally in the method for 'Volatility of Liquefied Petroleum (LP) Gases'. ASTM D1837.

Since dewpoint can be calculated from composition, direct determination of dewpoint for a particular LPG type is a measure of composition. It is, of course, of more direct practical value and if there are small quantities of higher molecular weight material present, it is preferable to use a direct measurement. The method is essentially a simple one of basic physics but skill and experience are necessary to detect the haze formation correctly and to distinguish between the required hydrocarbon dewpoint and a film due to moisture. Equipment is available for both manual measurement and automatic recording of the dewpoint.

Specific gravity again can be calculated, but if it is necessary to measure it several pieces of apparatus are available. For determining the specific gravity (or density) of LPG in its liquid state NGPA give two methods, using a metal pressure pyknometer. The latter is also described in an ASTM method (*see* Table 2). Various procedures, manual and recording, for specific gravity or density in the gaseous state are given in two methods—'Specific Gravity and Density' IP 59 and 'Specific Gravity of Gaseous Fuels' ASTM D1070.

Various types of calorimeter are available for the direct determination of calorific value. Suitable equipment is described in ASTM standard tests ASTM D900, ASTM D1826.

(e) Empirical Tests for Contaminants

Corrosive sulphur compounds can be detected by their effect on copper and the form in which the general copper strip corrosion test ASTM D1838 for petroleum products is applied to LPG is covered in 'Copper Strip Corrosion by Liquefied Petroleum (LP) Gases'. The procedure, which uses a stainless steel test cylinder is also described in NGPA 2140. Hydrogen sulphide can be detected by its action on moist lead acetate paper and a procedure is also used as a measure of sulphur compounds. The method follows the principle of the standard 'Doctor test'.

For traces of heavier hydrocarbons and oily matter a method is published for residue which involves a preliminary weathering. The residue after weathering is dissolved in a solvent and the solution applied to a filter paper. The presence of residue is indicated by the formation of an oil stain. The method in this form is published in NGPA 2140. The procedure is taken further in an ASTM method by combining the oil stain observation with other observed values to calculate an 'End Point Index', ASTM D2158 ('Residues in Liquefied Petroleum (LP) Gases End Point Index Method'). The method is not very precise and work is proceeding in several laboratories to develop a better method for the determination of residue in the form of oily matter.

In an LPG whose composition is such that the hydrocarbon dewpoint is known to be low, a dewpoint method will detect the presence of traces of water, NGPA describes a US Bureau of Mines apparatus ASTM D1142 for detecting the presence of moisture in essentially dry propane. For the same application NGPA give a method using the effect of water vapour on cobalt bromide. ASTM have proposed a method for detecting water in propane— the 'Valve Freeze Method'—in which the propane is allowed to flow through a cooled restrictive valve and the time noted for the valve to become blocked.

Odour of LPG has to be detectable to avoid the risk of explosion. Odour is a very subjective matter and no standard method is available. It is desirable to set up some system in which the concentration of gas can be measured in relation to its explosive limits and in which some variables can be standardised, *e.g.* flow-rate, orifice size, etc. This will ensure that in any one location the LPG is always being assessed under similar conditions from day to day.

7. SPECIFICATION DETAILS AND THEIR SIGNIFICANCE

(a) NATURAL GAS

The following summary of a bulk natural gas supply agreement covers the range of characteristics normally specified by public utilities with long distance transmission systems. Bulk supplies other than to utilities, where they can be made, are likely to be less rigorously specified. It states that the gas as delivered shall:

Purity
Be free from objectionable odours, solid or liquid particles and gum forming constituents. (An objectionable odour would be one which prevented the

purchaser from endowing the gas with the characteristic odour of town gas at an appropriate level.)

Water dewpoint
Have a dewpoint, at 1000 lbf/in² gauge, not exceeding those of a schedule showing a transition from 15°F (−9·4°C) in winter to 40°F (4·4°C) in summer. (The object is to prevent the formation of hydrates.)

Hydrocarbon dewpoint
Have a dewpoint, at any pressure less than delivery pressure, not exceeding those of a schedule showing a transition from 30°F (−1·1°C) in winter to 50°F (10°C) in summer. (The object is to prevent retrograde condensation.)

Total sulphur
Contain not more than 35 ppm v/v expressed as hydrogen sulphide. (At this level both appliance corrosion and atmospheric pollution will be negligible.)

Hydrogen sulphide
Conform to the statutory level as expressed in the regulations governing the purchaser. Currently 1 ppm v/v approx in the UK with possible future increase to 3·3 ppm v/v. (The latter level conforms more nearly to statutory levels outside of the UK. The object here is to render further gas treatment unnecessary.)

Carbon dioxide and oxygen
Contain not more than 2·0 per cent of carbon dioxide and 0·1 per cent of oxygen mol/mol. (A safeguard against corrosion at high pressure.)

Wobbe index
Be within 1246 and 1378 expressed in UK units. (This allows a ±5 per cent variation from the mean, the normal limit of tolerance for gas consuming appliances.)

Gross calorific value
Be within 970 and 1070 Btu/ft³ stp with a specified restriction on the speed of the change without prior consent of the purchaser.

Temperature
Have a temperature between 33°F (0·6°C) and 100°F (38°C) at any time.

(b) Refinery Gas

In contrast to the elaborate specification of natural gas for sale by public utilities, bulk supplies of refinery gas are more likely to be sold on a simple basis such as that set out below.

Refinery gas specification
Total sulphur
Not more than 15 grains per 100 ft^3 (2·8 m^3) expressed as hydrogen sulphide. (This would be equivalent to approx. 400 ppm w/w and would be mainly in the form of hydrogen sulphide. If unacceptable relative to the proposed use of the gas the purchaser would appropriately treat the gas.)

Water or hydrocarbon dewpoint
This shall be below ambient temperature at a pressure of 25 lbf/in^2 gauge.

Gas pressure
Not less than 25 lbf/in^2 gauge at point of delivery.

Gross calorific value
950 to 2200 Btu/f^3 stp.

Refinery gas specifications will vary according to the gas qualities available and the end use. For fuel uses, gas as specified above presents little difficulty used as supplied. Alternatively a gas of constant Wobbe Index, say for gas turbine use, could readily be produced by the user. Part of the combustion air would be diverted into the gas stream by an automatic Wobbe Index controller. This would be set to supply gas at the lowest Wobbe Index with which the undiluted gas will be endowed.

(c) LIQUEFIED PETROLEUM GASES

The quality requirements can be summarised thus: the LPG must vaporise completely and burn satisfactorily at the applicance without causing any corrosion or producing any deposits in the system.

LPG is usually available in four grades: Commercial Propane, Commercial Butane, Commercial Propane–Butane (P–B) Mixtures and Special Duty Propane.

Commercial Propane consists predominantly of propane and/or propylene while Commercial Butane is mainly composed of butanes and/or butylenes. Both must be free from harmful amounts of toxic or nauseating substances and free from mechanically entrained water. In the case of Commercial Propane, water content may be further limited by specific tests.

Commercial Propane–Butane mixtures are produced to meet particular requirements and find application as fuels in areas and at times where low ambient temperatures are less frequently encountered. Typical specifications (shown in Appendices I, II and III) contain clauses covering volatility, vapour pressure, specific gravity, hydrocarbon composition, sulphur and its compounds, corrosion of copper, residues and water content.

Special Duty Propane is intended for use in spark-ignition engines. In Europe this demand is often met by the commercial grades described above but in USA a tightly controlled C_3 mixture is specified. In addition to the usual clauses, the specification includes a minimum 'motor octane number' to ensure satisfactory antiknock performance.

Propylene has a significantly lower octane number than propane, so there is a limit to the amount of this component that can be tolerated in the mixture.

(i) Volatility, vapour pressure and relative density

The vaporisation and combustion characteristics of commercial liquefied gas products are completely defined for normal applications by volatility, vapour pressure, and to a lesser extent, specific gravity. The last by itself has little significance and can only give an indication of quality characteristics when combined with values for volatility and vapour pressure. It is important for stock quantity calculations and is used in connection with transport and storage. Volatility is expressed in terms of the temperature at which 95 per cent of the material is evaporated. It gives a measure of the least volatile component present. Vapour pressure is related to the more volatile components present. It therefore gives a measure of the most extreme low temperature conditions under which initial vaporisation can take place.

By setting limits to vapour pressure and volatility jointly the specification serves to ensure essentially single component products for the butane and propane grades. By combining vapour pressure/volatility limits with specific gravity for propane–butane mixtures, essentially two-component systems are ensured.

(ii) Hydrocarbon composition

Clauses are included to limit the amounts of minor constituents. These may relate to groups of hydrocarbons or to specific compounds. Thus limits are set to the total amount of C_2, C_4 or C_5 hydrocarbons, and to ethylene in particular, to total dienes and total acetylenes.

By limiting the amount of hydrocarbons lighter than the main component the vapour pressure control is reinforced. The limitation on the amount of heavier hydrocarbons supports the volatility clause. The vapour pressure and volatility specifications will often be met automatically if the hydrocarbon composition is correct.

The amount of ethylene is limited for two reasons. Firstly, it may be desirable to restrict the amount of unsaturated components so as to avoid the formation of polymerisation deposits. Secondly, the restriction constitutes an additional volatility clause. Ethylene is more volatile than ethane and therefore a product with all its C_2 hydrocarbons in the form of ethylene will have a higher vapour pressure and volatility than one in which the C_2's are entirely ethane. Both could, however, meet the relevant C_2 clause.

Acetylene is an undesirable constituent because of its corrosive action on copper. A further point, less significant because of the low concentration of acetylene, is that acetylene is more explosive than the other hydrocarbons present.

Butadiene is also undesirable because it may produce deposits which will cause blockages.

(iii) Sulphur, sulphur compounds and corrosion of copper

The following may be defined by a specification: total (volatile) sulphur, carbonyl sulphide, hydrogen sulphide, mercaptan and copper corrosion.

The manufacturing processes for LPG are such that most sulphur compounds are removed. The total sulphur level is therefore considerably lower than for other petroleum fuels. A maximum limit for sulphur content helps to define the product more completely. The sulphur compounds which are mainly responsible for corrosion are hydrogen sulphide, carbonyl sulphide and sometimes elemental sulphur. Hydrogen sulphide and mercaptans have distinctive unpleasant odours.

A control of the total sulphur content, hydrogen sulphide and mercaptans ensures that the product is not corrosive or nauseating.

The control of the corrosion is further ensured by stipulating a satisfactory copper strip test.

(iv) Residue

The presence of any component substantially less volatile than the main constituents of the LPG will give rise to unsatisfactory performance. It is difficult to set limits to the amount and nature of the 'residue' which will make a product unsatisfactory. Obviously small amounts of oily material can block regulators and valves. In liquid vaporiser feed systems even gasoline type material could cause difficulty.

The residue as determined by the End Point Index (EPI) endeavours to give a measure of the heavier hydrocarbons but the relationship between EPI, hydrocarbon range, and performance is not established.

Other methods are available which measure residue more directly and for particular applications it may be possible to relate the values obtained to the performance required and so set satisfactory limits.

(v) Moisture and water

It is a fundamental requirement that any LPG should not contain free water. Dissolved water may give trouble by forming hydrates and giving moisture vapour in the gas phase. Both of these will lead to blockages. It is therefore necessary to limit the amount of dissolved water also.

8. REFERENCES

1. *Gasmaking and Natural Gas*, British Petroleum (1972). 184.
2. D. L. Katz *et al.* (1969). *Handbook of Natural Gas Engineering*, McGraw-Hill, New York, 209.
3. A. B. Densham *et al. The odorisation of Natural Gas*, UK Gas Council Research Communication G C 178.
4. E. R. Weaver (1951). Formula and graphs for representing the interchangeability of fuel gases, *J. Nat. Bur. Stand.* **46,** 213.
5. P. Delbourg and H. Schrench (1956). 'Interchangeability of gases (improvement of methods)', Ass. Tech. de l'Ind. du Gaz en France Congress.
6. M. C. Gilbert and J. A. Prigg (1955/6). The prediction of the combustion characteristics of town gas, *JIGE* 530.
7. *Gasmaking and Natural Gas*, British Petroleum (1972). 10.

Appendices follow on next page

APPENDIX I

SUMMARY OF ASTM SPECIFICATIONS FOR LIQUEFIED PETROLEUM (LP) GASES

Product characteristic	Product designation				ASTM test methods
	Commercial propane	Commercial butane	Commercial PB mixtures	Special duty propane	
Vapour pressure at 100°F (37·8°C), psig (kPa), max	210 (1 447)	70	a	200 (1 379)	D1267 or D2598
Volatile residue: evaporated temperature, 95 per cent, °F (°C), max	−37 (−38·3)	36 (2·2)	36 (2·2)	−37 (−38·3)	D1837
or					
butane and heavier, per cent, max	2·5	—	—	2·5	D2163
pentane and heavier, per cent, max	—	2·0	2·0	—	D2163
Motor octane number, min	—	—	—	95	D2598 or D2623
Residual matter:					
residue on evaporation of 100 ml, ml, max	0·05	0·05	0·05	0·05	D2158
oil stain observation	Pass^b	Pass^b	Pass^b	Pass^b	D2158
Sulphur content, grains/100 ft³ (2·8 m³), max	15	15	15	10	D1266
grains/m³, max	—	—	—	2·832	
Specific gravity, 60°F/60°F	c	c	c	—	D1657 or D2598
Corrosion, copper strip, max	No. 1	No. 1	No. 1	No. 1	D1838
Hydrogen sulphide content	—	—	—	Pass^d	D2420
Moisture content	Pass	None	—	Pass	D1835
Free water content	—	None	None	—	D1835

^{a} The permissible vapour pressures of products classified as PB mixtures must not exceed 200 lb and additionally must not exceed that calculated from the following relationship between the observed vapour pressure and the observed specific gravity:

Vapour Pressure, max = 1 167 − 1 880 (sp gr 60°F/60°F)

^{b} An acceptable product shall not yield a persistent oil ring when 0·3 ml of solvent–residue mixture is added to a filter paper, in 0·1 ml increments and examined in daylight after two minutes.

^{c} Although not a specification requirement, the specific gravity should be reported.

^{d} An acceptable product shall not show a distinct coloration.

APPENDIX II

SUMMARY OF NGPA SPECIFICATIONS FOR LIQUEFIED PETROLEUM GAS

Product characteristics[a]	Product designation			
	Commercial propane	Commercial butane	Butane–propane mixtures[b]	Propane HD5
Description	Shall be a hydrocarbon product composed predominantly of propane and/or propylene	Shall be a hydrocarbon product composed predominantly of butane and/or butylenes	Shall be a hydrocarbon product composed predominantly of mixtures of butanes and/or butylenes with propane and/or propylene	Shall be special grade of propane for motor fuel and other uses.
Vapour pressure at 100°F psig max	200	70	200[b]	200
Evaporated temperature, 95 per cent, °F, max	−37	36	36	−37
Residue: oil stain observation	Pass	—	—	Pass
Residue on evaporation	Pass	—	—	Pass
Volatile sulphur, grains per 100 cu ft, max	15	15	15	10
Corrosion, copper strip, max	No. 1	No. 1	No. 1	No. 1
Dryness, cobalt bromide test	Dry	—	—	Dry
Free water by inspection	—	None	None	—
Propylene, per cent liquid, max	—	—	—	5
Propane, per cent liquid, min	—	—	—	90

[a] NPGA tests where applicable.

[b] Butane–propane mixtures shall be designated by the vapour pressure at 100°F in psig. To comply with the designation the vapour pressure of mixtures shall be within +0 lb −5lb of the vapour pressure specified.

APPENDIX III

BRITISH STANDARD SPECIFICATIONS FOR COMMERCIAL BUTANE AND PROPANE
BS 4250 : 1968

Product characteristics	Product designation		Test method
	Commercial butane	Commercial propane	
Scope	Suitable for general domestic and industrial purposes		
Description	Shall be a hydrocarbon mixture consisting predominantly of butanes and/or butylenes. It shall not contain harmful quantities of toxic or nauseating substances and shall be free from mechanically entrained water.	Shall be a hydrocarbon mixture consisting predominantly of propane and/or propylene. It shall not contain harmful quantities of toxic or nauseating substances and shall be free from mechanically entrained water.	—
Volatility	95 per cent v shall evaporate at 36°F (2.2°C) or lower		ASTM D1837
Vapour pressure at 45°C (113°F)	85 psig max (70 psig min for portable containers only)	255 psig max	BS 3324
Total sulphur	0·2 per cent w max		ASTM D1266 IP 107
Mercaptan sulphur (after stenching)	4·0 grains/100 cu ft max	(under review)	IP 104A
Hydrogen sulphide	not detectable		BS 3156
Odour	The odour of the gas shall be distinctive, unpleasant, and non-persistent and shall indicate the presence of gas down to concentrations in air of 1/5th of the lower limit of flammability		BS 4250 App. B
Oil residue			under development
Acetylenes	2 moles per cent max		
Dienes	10 moles per cent max		
C_2 hydrocarbons		5·0 moles per cent max	By gas chromatography mass spectrometry or infra-red spectrometry as appropriate.
Ethylene		1·0 moles per cent max	
C_4 and higher hydrocarbons		10 moles per cent max	
C_5 and higher hydrocarbons		2 moles per cent max	

APPENDIX IV

PUBLISHED METHODS RELATING TO PETROLEUM GASES

	ASTM	IP	NGPA
Sampling and Measurement			
Sampling liquefied petroleum (LP) gases	D1265-55 (1970)		2140-70
Sampling petroleum gases including liquefied petroleum gases		181/62[b]	
Sampling natural gas	D1145-53[a] (1970)		
Measurement of gaseous fuel samples	D1071-55[a] (1970)		
Physical Characteristics			
Specific gravity of gaseous fuels	D1070-67[a] (1970)		
Specific gravity of light hydrocarbons by pressure hydrometer	D1657-64 (1968)		2140-70
LPG specific gravity test (pressure pyknometer method)			2140-70
Specific gravity and density		59/72 A, B, C	
Method of test for interconversion of the analysis of C_5 and lighter hydrocarbons to gas-volume, liquid-volume, or weight basis	D2421-66 (1971)		
Vapour pressure of liquefied petroleum (LP) gases	D1267-67	161/69	2140-70
Calorific value of gaseous fuels by the water-flow calorimeter	D900-55[a] (1970)		
Calorific value of gases in natural gas range by continuous recording calorimeter	D1826-64[a] (1970)		
Volatility of liquefied petroleum (LP) gases	D1837-64 (1968)		2140-70
Proposed method of test for knock characteristics of liquefied petroleum (LP) gases by the motor (LP) method	D2623-68	238/69	
Tests for Contamination			
Propane dryness test (cobalt bromide method)			2140-70
Water vapour content of gaseous fuels by measurement of dewpoint temperature	D1142-63		2140-70
Proposed method of test for moisture in liquefied petroleum (LP) gases (valve freeze method)	D2713-70		
Copper strip corrosion by liquefied (LP) gases	D1838-64 (1968)		2140-70
Propane residue test (mercury freeze method)			2140-70
Residues in liquefied petroleum (LP) Gases (end point index method)	D2158-65 (1970)		
Hydrocarbon composition			
Analysis of commercial butane–butylene mixtures by gas chromatography	D1717-65		

[a] ASTM Committee D-3 on Gaseous Fuels.

[b] IP Standards, part IV.

APPENDIX IV—*continued*

	ASTM	IP	NGPA
Hydrocarbon composition—continued			
Analysis of liquefied petroleum (LP) gases and propylene concentrates by gas chromatography	D2163-71	264-72	
Analysis of natural gas by gas chromatography	D1945-64 (1968)		2261-64T
Analysis by gas chromatography petroleum gases		169/61T	
Alpha acetylenes in butadiene, butadiene concentrates and butane–butene mixtures	D1020-61 (1968)		
Unsaturated light hydrocarbons, silver mercuric nitrate method	D1268-55 (1968)		
Total sulphur and sulphur compounds			
Total sulphur in fuel gases	D1072-56^a (1970)		
Sulphur in petroleum products and liquefied petroleum (LP) gases (lamp method)	D1266-70	107/70T	
Sulphur in liquefied petroleum gases	D2784-70	243/70T	
Hydrogen sulphide in liquefied petroleum (LP) gases (lead acetate test)	D2420-66 (1971)		
Hydrogen sulphide content, cadmium sulphate method		103/70A	
Mercaptan sulphur content, silver nitrate method		104/53TA	
General and miscellaneous analytical methods			
Analysis of natural gases by the volumetric—chemical method	D1136-53T^a (1970)		
Analysis of natural gases and related types of gaseous mixtures by the mass spectrometer	D1137-53^a (1970)		
Oxygen in light hydrocarbon vapours	D1021-64 (1968)		
Proposed method of test for traces of volatile chlorides in butane–butene mixtures	D2384-68		
Method of determination of non-condensable gases in C$_3$ and lighter products by gas chromatography	D2504-67		

ASTM Methods appear in Part 18 of the Book of ASTM Standards under the jurisdiction of ASTM Committee D-2 unless otherwise stated.

IP Methods appear in Part 1 of the IP Standards for Petroleum and its Products unless otherwise stated.

NGPA Methods are approved as Recommended Procedures by the Natural Gas Processors Association.

^{a} ASTM Committee D-3 on Gaseous Fuels.

Chapter 4

PETROLEUM SOLVENTS

A. J. GOODFELLOW

1. INTRODUCTION

The term 'Petroleum Solvents' describes the special liquid hydrocarbon fractions obtained from petroleum and used in industrial processes and formulations. These fractions are also referred to as Industrial Naphthas. In recent years the range of petroleum solvents has been considerably extended following the development of processes designed primarily for the transformation of low knock rate feed stocks to high knock rate fuels, but which have also led to the production of certain important solvents and intermediates which were previously obtained only from the coal carbonising industry. By definition the solvents obtained from the petrochemical industry, the alcohols, ethers, etc., are outside the scope of this chapter.

The special value of petroleum solvents lies in their inherent stability and purity, and the wide use range is supported by the ready availability in large volume and the low cost relative to alternative solvents from other processes. In the United Kingdom legislation which allows draw back of duty on hydrocarbons used for approved industrial processes is an important factor when considering applications for the solvents, and is itself an indication of their growing importance in the modern economy.

A modern solvent refinery is capable of producing hydrocarbons of a high degree of purity and at the present time petroleum solvents are available covering a wide range of grades giving varying solvent properties and embracing both highly volatile and high boiling qualities. The various grades are often referred to by trade names and their properties and applications are described in the following.

2. USES

Before considering the specific characteristics required in petroleum solvents it is helpful to review their application. The industries employing solvents in their manufacturing processes comprise deposition industries, in which are included the paint, printing ink and polish manufacturers and the rubber and adhesive industries, and extraction industries which deal with the preparation of edible oils, perfumes, glues and fats. Further uses are found in the dry-cleaning, leather and fur industries and also in the pesticide field. These solvents, in highly purified condition, are also becoming increasingly important for use as reaction media in certain catalytic processes.

3. PRODUCT REQUIREMENTS

The variety of applications emphasises the versatility of petroleum solvents. The characteristics which determine the suitability of a petroleum fraction for a particular use are its volatility, its solvent properties, its purity and its odour.

Odour is particularly important since unlike most other petroleum liquids, many of the manufactured products containing petroleum solvents are used in confined spaces, in factory workshops, and in the home.

In order to meet the demands of industry certain basic grades are produced which are normally identified by boiling range. The actual ranges vary somewhat from country to country but all are fractions lying within the extremes of 30°C to 325°C (86° to 617°F) and possessing well defined solvent properties.

The complete range of hydrocarbon solvents may be divided into the following groups:

(a) Special boiling point spirits having overall distillation range within the limits 30–165°C (86–329°F);
(b) Pure aromatics, *e.g.* benzene, toluene, xylenes;
(c) White spirits, also known as mineral spirits and naphthas, usually boiling within 150–210°C (302–410°F);
(d) High boiling petroleum fractions boiling within limits 160–325°C (320–617°F).

Most grades are available in both high and low solvency categories. Since the end use dictates the required composition of a solvent it follows that test results may be significant in some applications and of negligible significance in others. Hence the application and significance of tests must be considered in the light of the proposed end use. The following table lists the salient features of the four chief categories of solvents.

4. PROPERTIES AND THEIR ASSESSMENT

A preliminary examination of a hydrocarbon solvent will assess the colour, freedom from visible impurities, odour and specific gravity of the material. The specific gravity determination ASTM D1298–IP 160 provides a means of

Typical properties of petroleum hydrocarbon solvents

Properties	Special boiling-point spirits								Pure aromatics		
Nominal boiling range, °C, or product type	62–68	35–115	70–95	100–120	40–150	90–105	140–160	100–160 Rubber Solvent	Benzene	Toluene	Xylene
Sp. gr, 60°F/60°F (IP 59)	0·680	0·681	0·705	0·738	0·702	0·720	0·770	0·750	0·883	0·870	0·868
Distillation (IP 123):											
Initial boiling point, °C	62	43	71	102	48	90	140	117	79·5	110·0	139·0
50% vol. boils at, °C	65	67	78	109	93	93	147	128	80·0	110·5	141·0
Final boiling, °C Point	68	102	94	120	150	104	163	158	80·5	111·0	143·0
Flash point, °F (IP 33)	<0	<0	<0	15	<0	<0	84	40	12	40	78
Aromatic content, % vol. (IP 128)	4	3	4	10	5	5	17	12	99·9	99·5	98·5
Kauri butanol No. (ASTM D1133)	31	30	33	35	32	31	35	37	112	105	98
Aniline point, °C (IP 2)	63	61	56	52	56	52	55	54	—	—	—

Product type	White spirits				Kerosines				
	Ordinary	115°F Flash	45% Aromatic	98% Aromatic	Odourless	Ordinary	Odourless	Distillate	Aromatic
Sp. gr, 60°F/60°F (IP 59)	0·780	0·784	0·817	0·877	0·761	0·799	0·784	0·795	0·985
Distillation (IP 123):									
Initial boiling point, °C	155	170	145	162	180	164	195	154	162
50% vol. boils at, °C	162	183	162	166	185	219	227	192	210
Final boiling point, °C	199	198	193	180	206	265	262	270	272
Flash point, °F (IP 33 or 34)	105	120	93	117	131	110	158	107	132
Aromatic content, % vol. (IP 128)	17	12	46	98	0	11	<1	13	87
Kauri butanol mo. (ASTM D1133)	35	34	55	90	26	31	28	—	81
Aniline point, °C (IP 2)	60	67	22 (Mixed Aniline Pt)	14	85	65	79	—	24 (Mixed AP)

rapid identification between grades but can only be used to evaluate product quality when considered in conjunction with other tests. The value obtained can be used to convert volumes to a weight basis, a requirement in many of the industries concerned. For the necessary temperature corrections and also for volume corrections the appropriate sections of the ASTM–IP petroleum measurement table ASTM D1250–IP 200 are used. Grades of hydrocarbon solvents are often referred to by boiling points, that is the defined temperature range in which the fraction distils. The ranges are determined by standard methods ASTM D86–IP 123 and ASTM D107–IP 195, it being especially necessary to use a recognised method since the initial and final boiling points which ensure conformity with volatility requirements and absence of 'heavy ends' are themselves affected by the testing procedure.

The nature of the uses found for the petroleum solvents demands compatibility with the many other materials employed in formulation, with waxes, pigments, resins, etc.; thus the solvent properties of a given fraction must be carefully measured and controlled. For most purposes volatility is important, and, because of the wide use of hydrocarbon solvents in industrial and recovery plants, information on some other fundamental characteristics is required for plant design.

(a) SAMPLING

Because of the high standards set for petroleum solvents it is essential to employ the correct techniques when taking samples for test; mishandling, or the slightest trace of contaminant can give rise to misleading results. Sampling methods are described in ASTM D270–IP 51. Special care is necessary to ensure that containers are scrupulously clean and free from odour. Samples should be taken with the minimum of disturbance so as to avoid loss of volatile components; in the case of the lightest solvents it may be necessary to chill the sample.

While awaiting examination samples should be kept in a cool dark place so as to ensure that they do not discolour or develop odours.

(b) VOLATILITY

The volatility of a petroleum solvent may be considered a measure of its drying time in use. The requirements of drying vary between very wide limits, e.g. for a solvent used in gravure printing on a modern rotary press with paper travelling at 1200 feet per minute, a high volatility and fast dry-off time are required in order to give clear definition and freedom from offsetting. The temperature of use obviously governs the choice of solvents; thus a high boiling close cut fraction of gas oil may be required for a heat set ink where the operating temperature may be as high as 600°F (316°C). Whilst pure hydrocarbons such as pentane, hexane, heptane, benzene, toluene and xylene which are now largely of petroleum origin may be characterised by a fixed boiling point, other petroleum solvents are mixtures of many hydrocarbons and cannot be so identified. The distillation test does however give a useful indication of their volatility. The data obtained should include the initial and final temperatures of distillation together with sufficient temperature and volume observations to permit a characteristic distillation curve to be drawn.

This information is especially important when a formulation includes other volatile liquids since the performance of the product as a whole will be affected by the relative volatility of the constituents. An illustration of the importance of this aspect is found in the use of a special boiling point spirit in cellulose lacquers, where a mixture with ester, alcohols, and other solvents may be employed. The petroleum spirit does not act as a solvent for the cellulose ester but is incorporated as a diluent to control the viscosity and flow properties of the mixture. If the diluent evaporates too rapidly blistering and pimpling of the surface coating may result, while if the solvents evaporate unevenly, leaving behind a higher proportion of the non-solvent petroleum hydrocarbon, precipitation of the cellulose may occur leading to a milky opaqueness known as blushing.

In the extraction processes, where high temperatures are to be avoided, low boiling fractions often known as petroleum ethers are used, but in the extraction of animal waste products where a controlled water removal is required a different choice is necessary.

Although much dependence is placed on the assessment of volatility by distillation methods, some specifications include measurement of drying time by evaporation from a filter paper or dish. Laboratory measurements are expressed as 'evaporation rate' either by reference to a pure compound evaporated under similar conditions as the sample under test or by constructing a time weight loss curve under standard conditions. Although the results obtained on the hydrocarbon solvent provide a useful guide it is, wherever possible, better to carry out a performance test on the final product when assessing formulations.

In choosing a petroleum solvent for a particular purpose it is necessary to relate volatility to the fire hazard associated with its use, storage and transport, and also with the handling of the products arising from the process. Legislation covering this aspect is found in most countries and is normally based on the characterisation of the solvent by flash point limits, ASTM D56–IP 170, or ASTM D93–IP 34.

(c) PURITY

Petroleum solvents, other than the simple hydrocarbons such as toluene, are mixtures of straight, branched-chain and cyclic paraffins, and aromatic hydrocarbons, with a possible trace of olefinic material. With this composition they are, in the refined state, inert substances and as such may be used in the preparation of surface coatings and adhesives and in a multitude of applications without risk of side effects due to reaction with other substances in the formulation or with the application surface.

Refinery treatment ensures freedom from alkalinity and acidity (ASTM D1613 or IP 1) and controls olefin content (ASTM D1319–IP 156) at a very low level. Special treatment also ensures the absence of corrosive or offensive sulphur compounds (ASTM D130–IP 154).

Apart from certain high boiling aromatic fractions, which may be pale yellow in colour, other petroleum solvents are normally water white. Measurement of colour (ASTM D156 or IP 17) provides a rapid method of checking the degree of freedom from contamination. Observation of the test for residue on evaporation (ASTM D381–IP 131) provides a further guard against adventitious contamination.

The degree of purity is of paramount importance with petroleum solvents and strict segregation of all distribution equipment is maintained in order to ensure strict and uniform specification for the product handled.

(d) SOLVENT PROPERTIES

In many applications petroleum solvents are used as a vehicle which is required to evaporate after an optimum time period to give the desired result; examples of this are their use in the printing ink, rubber coating and dipping, paint, lacquer and polish industries. The solvent properties will depend on the hydrocarbon types present, in general the aromatic hydrocarbons having the highest solvent power and the straight-chain aliphatics the lowest.

The methods used for assessing the solvent properties fall into two groups. The first estimates the proportion of the hydrocarbon types present and thus gives an indication of the solvent power, the second measures the performance of the fraction when used as a solvent under specified conditions.

Thus methods are available for the determination of saturates, non-aromatic olefins and aromatic compounds (ASTM D1319–IP 156). An indication of the composition may also be obtained from the determination of aniline point (ASTM D1012 or IP 2).

The second group of methods incorporates the use as solute of material similar to that envisaged in the final process, e.g. gum, wax, cellulose ester. These methods are often particular to the industry concerned but are exemplified by the Kauri Butanol test ASTM D1133, the measurement of dilution ratio and also viscosity reduction power. The results obtained depend upon factors other than just solvent power and have meaning only for the particular solute involved. The measurement of surface tension may be used to calculate the more fundamental solubility parameter which provides an indication of compatibility.

(e) Odour

Earlier mention has been made of the need for solvents to be refined to a low level of odour. This refers to the residual odour as well as to the immediate odour and a low level is necessary in order to meet the personal needs of the operators and consumers in the deposition industries and to ensure that the final product from an extraction process is unaffected by trace odours.

In general the paraffinic hydrocarbons possess the mildest odour and the aromatics the strongest, the odour level (ASTM D268–IP 89) being to some extent related to volatility. Marked and unpleasant odours due to sulphur compounds or high unsaturation are excluded by specification.

(f) Toxicity

In use the hydrocarbon fractions present few difficulties. Where a solvent is mainly paraffinic or naphthenic in composition there is very little toxic effect and the inhalation of small quantities of petroleum vapour is comparatively harmless. The aromatic hydrocarbons have greater toxicities and where benzene, the most volatile of the aromatic hydrocarbons, is present special regulations govern the handling and use of such materials. In those petroleum solvents which by their boiling range potentially contain benzene, a specification limit is usually laid down by the consuming industry. The method of estimation used, for example, by the rubber industry (Dolin Method, Industr. Engng Chem. (*Anal.*) (1943), **35**(4), 242) involves nitration of the mixed aromatics, extraction with ether, and development of characteristic colours with butanone and alkali. Physical methods may be used for the estimation of benzene content using spectrophotometric analysis ASTM D1017 and also gas–liquid chromatography ASTM D2267.

5. SUGGESTIONS FOR FURTHER READING

T. H. Durrans (1957). *Solvents,* Chapman & Hall, London.
I. Mellan (1950) *Industrial Solvents,* 2nd edn, Reinhold, New York.
I. Mellan (1957). *Handbook of Solvents*, Vol. 1, Reinhold, New York.
Cleaver-Hume (1963). *Solvents Guide*, 2nd edn, Marsden, London.
Modern Petroleum Technology (1973). 4th edn, Applied Science, London.
Guthrie (1960). *Petroleum Products Handbook*, McGraw-Hill, New York.
W. W. Reynolds (1963). *Physical Chemistry of Petroleum Solvents*, Reinhold, New York.
I. Mellan (1970). Industrial Solvents Handbook, Noyes Data Corporation, New Jersey.
Highly Flammable Liquids and Liquefied Gases Regulations (1972) (and appropriate guides) H. M. Stationery Office.

Appendix follows on next page

APPENDIX

BSI SPECIFICATIONS FOR SOLVENTS

(These are being revised and will be published in 1973)

BS 245: 1965	Specifications for White Spirit
BS 135: 1963	Specifications for Benzenes and Benzoles
BS 805: 1963	Specifications for Toluenes
BS 458: 1963	Specifications for Xylenes

ASTM SPECIFICATIONS

D1836	Commercial Hexanes
D235	Petroleum Spirit (Mineral Spirits)
D484	Stoddard Solvent
D361	Benzene Industrial 90
D362	Toluene Industrial Grade
D364	Xylene Industrial Grade
D838	Refined Solvent Naphtha

Chapter 5

MOTOR GASOLINE AND VAPORISING OIL

K. A. BOLDT and S. T. GRIFFITHS

1. INTRODUCTION

The primary requirement of a gasoline is that its combustion should be smooth, starting at the sparking plug and spreading evenly through the combustion chamber. Its hydrocarbon composition must be of a type that does not readily cause detonation or knocking in the engine. Both engine design and fuel quality are of equal importance. The features of engine design which affect the proper utilisation of the fuel are very complex and the main variables are concerned with the compression ratio, the shape of the combustion chamber, the cooling system and the timing of the spark.

The properties required of a satisfactory motor gasoline are quite diverse; for example, it must not have an odour offensive to the user and this entails, in general, freedom from certain evil smelling compounds, notably mercaptans. It must be non-corrosive to metals and other materials used in the construction of fuel systems and engines and must not deposit gum which is liable to clog fuel lines and cause sticking of valves and impaired operation of the carburettor. Furthermore, it must not form gum in storage and its volatility must be such that when mixed with air in the carburettor, it readily forms a combustible mixture. On the other hand, it must not evaporate to an extent that tank losses are excessive or that boiling occurs in the fuel system giving rise to the condition known as vapour lock.

In recent years, the introduction and proposed introduction of legislation designed to reduce, chiefly, the quantity of carbon monoxide and unburnt hydrocarbons emitted by the spark ignition engine has had the effect of focusing closer attention on to the cleanliness, volatility and composition of motor gasolines.

2. THE NATURE AND COMPOSITION OF GASOLINE

The hydrocarbons produced by modern refining techniques (distillation, polymerisation, isomerisation, alkylation, catalytic reforming and cracking) provide excellent blending components for motor gasoline production. Each component is refined according to a predetermined plan and the final blend has to meet the specification standards. It is usual to incorporate very small quantities of certain additives in order to inhibit knocking, pre-ignition, gum formation and icing of the carburettor.

The final blend will be stored, handled and transported in successively smaller quantities until it eventually enters the automobile tank. Subsequent movement and contact with air is liable to cause deterioration of the gasoline and the refining plan will have included steps to ensure good stability, *i.e.* minimal gum formation during storage over a reasonable period of time.

Apart from its physical characteristics and the effect of additives such as gum inhibitors and anti-knock compounds, the quality of a gasoline depends on its chemical composition, but, because a gasoline consists of a very large number of different hydrocarbons, its composition is usually expressed in terms of hydrocarbon types (saturates, olefins and aromatics) rather than in terms of individual hydrocarbons. This simplified method of describing gasoline composition enables important inferences to be made as to the general behaviour of the gasoline.

Several procedures have been devised for the determination of hydrocarbon type and of those which have been standardised, the method based on fluorescent indicator adsorption (ASTM D1319–IP 156) is the most widely employed.

Infra-red, ultra-violet, mass and X-ray spectroscopy, along with other highly sophisticated techniques such as nuclear magnetic resonance are in considerable use for elucidating the fundamental properties of gasoline, but the techniques involved do not lend themselves readily to routine testing.

3.   THE PROPERTIES OF GASOLINE

The principal properties affecting the performance of a gasoline in an engine are volatility and combustion characteristics. These properties are adjusted to some extent according to the topography and climate of the country in which the gasoline is to be used. Thus, mountainous regions will require gasolines with volatility and knock characteristics somewhat different from those which are satisfactory in flat or undulating country only a little above sea level. Similarly, extremes of temperatures will necessitate special consideration, particularly with regard to volatility.

(a) VOLATILITY

The volatility of a motor gasoline affects the performance of the engine in a number of ways, the chief of which are ease of starting, rate of warm-up, vapour lock, carburettor icing and crankcase dilution (the dilution of the engine lubricating oil with the higher boiling constituents of the gasoline). The fuel must be sufficiently volatile to give easy starting, rapid warm-up and adequate vaporisation for proper distribution between the cylinders. Conversely, it must not be so volatile that vapour losses from the fuel tank are excessive or that vapour is formed in the fuel line causing vapour lock which may impede the flow of fuel to the carburettor. To some extent these conflicting requirements can be met by using a more volatile gasoline in winter than in summer, but some degree of compromise is obviously necessary.

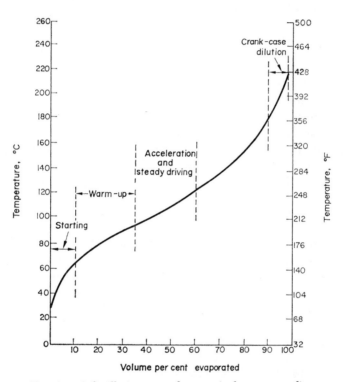

FIG. 1.   *A distillation curve for a typical motor gasoline.*

The volatility of gasolines is normally assessed by the joint distillation test (ASTM D86–IP 123) which provides data to enable a graph to be drawn relating the percentage evaporated to the boiling range of the gasoline. A typical graph is presented in Fig. 1 and the portions of the curve which influence certain performance features of the gasoline have been appropriately indicated.

The test is empirical. Furthermore, the apparatus employed provides little in the way of fractionation and although the thermometer is accurately standardised at total immersion, it is used at partial immersion and no temperature corrections are made for emergent stem. However, provision is made in the test for correcting the thermometer readings for variations in atmospheric pressure whenever the barometric reading is sufficiently far from standard atmospheric pressure to make corrections desirable. Therefore, whilst the temperatures are highly reproducible they are not true vapour temperatures. The boiling range of motor gasolines falls in the range 30°C to 210°C (86°F to 410°F) and through the judicious blending of the available refinery components a balance can be maintained between the different volatility requirements.

The determination of vapour pressure (ASTM D323 or IP 69) is another means for assessing the volatility of a gasoline, particularly its tendency towards vapour locking. The latter is caused by an excess of low-boiling components which under critical circumstances of temperature and pressure tend to boil off in the fuel supply system. The bubbles of vapour thus formed impede the flow of gasoline to the carburettor, thereby causing rough engine operation, reduction in power output and in severe cases stopping the engine. Vapour pressure is the force exerted on the walls of a closed container by the vaporised portion of a liquid. Conversely, it is the force which must be applied to the liquid to prevent it vaporising further. Vapour pressure increases with increase in temperature and is variously expressed in terms of millimetres of mercury, pounds per square inch or other equivalent units of pressure depending on common usage. Gasoline vapour pressure depends critically on its butane content, and in the refinery the final adjustment of vapour pressure of a gasoline to meet the specification is often made by butane injection. Vapour pressures of gasolines are normally measured by the Reid Method IP 69 or ASTM D323 at a temperature of 37·8°C (100°F) in a closed apparatus under a standard but arbitrary condition that the air volume above the liquid gasoline is four times the volume of the test sample.

However, due to the complicated make-up of gasoline, the Reid Method has proved inadequate as a criterion of vapour locking tendencies and various control methods based on a combination of distillation results with Reid vapour pressure measurements have been suggested. One of these, where the Reid vapour pressure is linked with certain distillation data has shown promise but the most reliable procedure is to measure at various temperatures the volume of vapour (V) in equilibrium with the volume of liquid fuel (L) and to express the vapour locking tendency as a value V/L at a suitable specified temperature.

(b) COMBUSTION CHARACTERISTICS

Combustion in the spark ignition engine depends chiefly on engine design and fuel quality. Under ideal conditions, the flame initiated at the sparking plug spreads evenly across the combustion space until all the gasoline has been burned. The increase in temperature caused by the spreading of the flame results in an increase in pressure in the end gas zone, which is that part of the gasoline–air mixture which the flame has not yet reached. The increase in temperature and pressure in the end gas zone causes the gasoline to undergo preflame reactions. Amongst the main preflame products are the highly temperature sensitive peroxides and if these exceed a certain critical threshold concentration, the end gas will spontaneously ignite before the arrival of the flame front emanating from the sparking plug: this causes detonation or 'knocking'. If, on the other hand, the flame front reaches the end gas zone before the build up of the critical threshold peroxide concentration, the combustion of the gasoline–air mixture will be without 'knock'.

The various types of hydrocarbons in gasoline behave differently in their preflame reactions and thus, their tendency to knock. It is difficult to find any precise relationship between chemical structure and anti-knock performance in an engine. Members of the same hydrocarbon series may show very different anti-knock effects; for example, normal heptane and normal pentane, both paraffins, have anti-knock ratings (octane numbers) of 0 and 62 respectively. Very broadly, however, it can be stated that aromatic hydrocarbons (*e.g.* benzene and toluene), highly branched iso-paraffins (*e.g.* iso-octane) and olefins (*e.g.* di-isobutylene) have high anti-knock values. In an intermediate position are iso-paraffins with little branching and naphthenic hydrocarbons (*e.g.* cyclohexane), while of low anti-knock value are the normal paraffins (*e.g.* normal heptane).

Engine design and operating conditions have a pronounced effect on the tendency of a fuel to knock. The knocking tendency of a gasoline is increased by increasing compression ratio, spark advance, engine loading, mixture temperature and atmospheric temperature and pressure. Conversely, the knocking tendency is decreased by increased engine speed, turbulence of the gasoline–air mixture and atmospheric humidity. At any given set of operating conditions, the tendency to knock is greatest at the chemically correct (stoichiometric) mixture strength (about 14·5 to 1 air–gasoline mixture ratio by weight); at weaker or richer mixtures the tendency to knock decreases.

Under any given set of conditions, the maximum performance of an engine can be realised only when the anti-knock quality of the fuel permits operation without the occurrence of knock. On the other hand, the use of a fuel with a knock rating above this minimum requirement will not of itself lead to any improvement in performance. It will, however, permit changes to be made in engine design of operating conditions, such as increase in compression ratio or use of wider throttle openings, which result in higher power output or improved fuel economy. The actual loss of power and damage to an automotive engine due to knocking is generally not significant until the knock intensity becomes severe. However, heavy and prolonged knocking will cause loss of power and possible damage to the engine due to the high rates of pressure rise occurring in the combustion chambers.

The knock rating of a gasoline is determined in the CFR engine developed by the Co-operative Fuel Research Committee of the USA and is expressed as 'Octane Number' (ON), this being the percentage by volume of iso-octane

(octane number 100 by definition) in admixture with normal heptane (octane number 0 by definition) which has the same knock characteristics as the fuel being assessed. Gasolines are normally rated in the CFR engine under two sets of conditions of differing severity. One, known as the Research Method (ASTM D2699–IP 237) gives a rating applicable to mild operating conditions, *i.e.* low inlet mixture temperature and relatively low engine loading such as would be experienced generally in passenger cars and light duty commercial vehicles. The other is the Motor Method (D2700–IP 236), which represents more severe operating conditions, *i.e.* relatively high inlet mixture temperature and high engine loading such as would be experienced during full throttle operation at high speed.

Research octane numbers are generally higher than those obtained by the Motor Method and the difference between the two ratings is known as the 'sensitivity' of the gasoline. The sensitivity of low octane number fuels is usually small, but with high octane fuels it varies greatly according to fuel composition and for most commercial blends it is between 7 and 12 in the 90 to 100 Research octane number range. The actual performance of a gasoline on the road, *i.e.* its 'road octane number' usually falls between the Research and Motor values, and depends on the engine used and also on the gasoline composition and choice of anti-knock compounds.

A road vehicle engine is said to be 'severe' if it rates a motor gasoline significantly lower than the corresponding research rating obtained in the CFR engine. Conversely, a 'mild' engine would rate a gasoline similar to the research octane number. However, 'severe' engines do not necessarily have a high 'octane requirement' and high requirement engines are often mild. There is no completely satisfactory way of translating Research and Motor octane numbers into terms of a rating for all vehicles on the road. Correlations of laboratory ratings with road ratings have been developed but at the best they only represent the average result obtained for a limited number of vehicles when operated under prescribed conditions. Changes in air humidity and in altitude may readily alter the tendency of a gasoline to knock by the equivalent of several octane numbers. The accumulation of combustion chamber deposits and other slow changes in engine condition can also alter the knocking tendencies.

New and modified laboratory knock test methods are being investigated with the object of improving test precision and of providing ratings of greater significance with respect to road anti-knock behaviour than is given by the Research and Motor Methods. The investigation has confirmed that a single laboratory test method cannot give ratings which adequately reflect the road anti-knock performance of all types of gasoline in all vehicles under a variety of operating conditions. In recent years, however, the development of CFR engine methods to determine the octane number of the front end of motor gasolines has led to a better prediction of road ratings. For example, road rating prediction equations based on the Research octane number of the whole gasoline and the Research octane number of the front end of the gasoline have yielded superior correlations than prediction equations based on Research and Motor octane ratings.

The production and use of motor gasolines of 100 octane number and above have made it necessary to extend the octane number scale. Ratings above 100 octane number are obtained in the CFR engine by determining the amount of tetraethyl lead (TEL, an anti-knock additive) in iso-octane which has the same knock characteristics as the gasoline being tested. This procedure has been used for many years when knock rating aviation gasolines and the ratings have been expressed as Performance Numbers (PN). This scale was based on the average increase in knock limited power obtained under rich mixture conditions in a variety of laboratory and full scale aero engines by adding increments of TEL to iso-octane.

To avoid the confusion arising from the use of two separate scales, one below and one above 100 ON, an arbitrary extension of the octane number scale was agreed by ASTM and IP. This was selected so that the value in terms of automotive engine performance of each unit between 100 and 103 ON was similar to those between 97 and 100 ON. The relationship between the Octane Number scale above 100 and the Performance Number scale is ON = 100 + (PN − 100)/3 and the relationship between TEL concentration in iso-octane and octane number is given in test methods ASTM D2699–IP 237 and ASTM D2700–IP 236.

(c) STABILITY

Gasolines manufactured by cracking processes contain unsaturated components which may oxidise during storage and form undesirable oxidation products. Motor gasolines are often stored for six months or even longer before use and thus it is essential that they should not undergo any deleterious change under storage conditions and should remain stable during their passage from the fuel tank of a vehicle to the cylinder of its engine so that no harmful deposits are built up in the tank and fuel lines and in the inlet system and on the valves. In storage, gasoline is exposed to the action of air at ambient temperature and in its path from vehicle tank to engine, it is mixed with air and also subjected to the effects of heat. An unstable gasoline will undergo oxidation and polymerisation under such conditions forming gum, a resinous material which in the early stages of formation may remain in solution in the gasoline but due to further chemical changes, may be precipitated. Gum formation appears to be the result of a chain reaction initiated by the formation of peroxides and catalysed by the presence of metals, particularly copper, which may have been picked up during refining and handling operations. The operation of an engine under constant heavy duty tends to form a gum lacquer in the inlet system but low duty operation lessens this tendency. Consequently, smaller engines are more liable to inlet system deposits than larger engines, since the former are usually operated at a higher proportion of their maximum power output.

Provided the gasoline has been properly refined, deterioration (*i.e.* gum formation) can be eliminated for a substantial period of time by the addition of small quantities of anti-oxidant additives known as inhibitors which retard the oxidation of the olefin constituents of the fuel. These inhibitors are normally phenols or amine compounds and quantities of between 0·001 and 0·02 per cent by weight are usually sufficient to ensure good storage stability. Another type of additive employed to ensure stability is the 'metal deactivator' which acts either by passivation of the metal surfaces, thus preventing the gasoline from dissolving copper, or by the deactivation of copper compounds already dissolved in the fuel. The chief disadvantage of all these additives is the ease with which they are liable to be leached out of the gasoline by alkaline solutions and water.

'Existent-gum' is the name given to the non-volatile residue present in the fuel as received for test and is estimated by ASTM D381–IP 131. In this test, the sample is evaporated from a beaker maintained at a temperature of 160–166°C (320–331°F) with the aid of a similarly heated jet of air. Because many gasolines contain traces of non-volatile oils and additives, the residue left in the beakers is washed with heptane before the gum-residue is dried and weighed. The existent gum test is useful as a refinery control but is to some extent unrealistic as a criterion of performance and therefore engine tests have been developed to determine the tendency towards inlet system deposits.

In order to assess the possibility of gum formation in storage, in other words, the gum stability of the gasoline, a test (ASTM D525–IP 40) is employed which determines, in a pressure vessel, the 'induction period' or time of heating at 100°C (212°F) with oxygen at an initial pressure of 100 pounds per square inch, which elapses before the oxygen pressure begins to fall, due to the oxidation of the sample and the formation of gum therein. The figure for oxidation stability, or 'break-down time' as it is sometimes called, is thus regarded as a measure of the stability of the gasoline. However, due to the multiplicity of types and conditions of storage, it is impossible to equate induction-period with safe storage time, but it has been found by long experience that a minimum figure of 240 minutes induction-period usually ensures a satisfactory level of gum stability for most normal marketing and distributing purposes. Induction period is also a useful control test for determining the amount of gum inhibitor required to be added to a gasoline, provided that the storage stability of the combination of the gasoline and inhibitor has been established by practical storage experiments.

(d) CORROSIVENESS

Because a gasoline would be unsuitable for use if it corroded the metallic parts of the fuel system or the engine, it must be substantially free from corrosive compounds both before and after combustion. Corrosiveness is usually due to the presence of free sulphur and sulphur compounds which burn to form sulphur dioxide; this combines with water vapour formed by the combustion of the fuel to produce sulphurous acid which may oxidise to a slight extent to sulphuric acid. Both acids are corrosive towards iron and steel and would attack the cooler parts of the engine's exhaust system and its cylinders as they cool off after the engine is shut down. The total sulphur content of most gasolines is very low and a knowledge of its magnitude is of chief interest to the refiner who must produce a product which conforms to a stringent specification. Various methods are available for the determination of total sulphur content. The one most frequently quoted in specifications is the Lamp Method (ASTM D1266–IP 107), in which the gasoline is burned in a small wick-fed lamp in an artificial atmosphere of carbon dioxide and oxygen; the oxides of sulphur are converted to sulphuric acid, which is then determined either volumetrically or gravimetrically. A more recent development is the Wickbold Method (IP 243 or ASTM D2785). This is basically similar to the Lamp Method except that the sample is burned in an oxy-hydrogen burner to give much more rapid combustion. An alternative technique, which has the advantage of being non-destructive, is X-ray spectrography as described in ASTM D2622.

An additional incentive to reduce sulphur in gasoline stems from the fact that all forms of organic sulphur compounds seriously impair the anti-knock effectiveness of the lead alkyl compounds that are added to motor gasolines.

Hydrogen sulphide and mercaptan sulphur are most undesirable contaminants because, apart from their corrosive nature, they possess an extremely unpleasant odour. Methods for their estimation are IP 103 and IP 104 or ASTM D1219, respectively; nevertheless, they should have been removed completely during refining and normally their presence and that of free sulphur can be detected by the 'Doctor Test' (IP 30). The action on copper of any 'free' or corrosive sulphur present in gasoline may be estimated by the procedure described in ASTM D130–IP 154. In this test, a strip of polished copper is immersed in the sample which is heated under specified conditions of temperature and time and any staining of the copper is subsequently compared with the stains on a set of reference copper strips and thus the degree of corrosivity of the test sample determined.

(e) ADDITIVES

Certain substances added to gasoline, notably the lead alkyls, have a profound effect on anti-knock properties and inhibit the precombustion oxidation chain which is known to promote knocking. For a considerable period, tetraethyl lead (TEL) was the preferred compound, but more recently tetramethyl lead (TML) has been shown to have advantages with certain modern types of gasolines because of its lower boiling point (110°C (230°F) as against 200°C (392°F) for TEL) and therefore its higher vapour pressure which enables it to be more evenly distributed among the engine cylinders with the more volatile components of the gasoline. Some gasolines contain a mixture of TML and TEL, whilst others contain compounds prepared by a chemical reaction between TML and TEL in the presence of a catalyst. These chemically reacted compounds contain various proportions of TML and TEL and their intermediates, trimethylethyl lead, dimethyldiethyl lead and methyltriethyl lead, and thus provide anti-knock compounds with a boiling range of 110°C to 200°C (230°F to 392°F). The lead compounds, if used alone, would cause an excessive accumulation of lead compounds in the combustion chambers of the engine and on sparking plugs and valves. Therefore 'scavengers' such as dibromoethane, alone or in admixture with dichloroethane, are added to the lead alkyl and combine with the lead during the combustion process to form volatile compounds which pass harmlessly from the engine.

The amount of lead alkyl compounds used in gasoline is normally expressed in terms of equivalent grams of metallic lead per gallon or per litre. The maximum concentration of lead permitted in gasoline varies from country to country according to governmental legislation or accepted commercial practice, and it is a subject which is currently under discussion in many countries due to the attention being paid to reduction of exhaust emissions from the spark ignition engine.

The total lead anti-knock compounds in gasoline may be determined gravimetrically using method ASTM D526–IP 96 or polarographically by means of ASTM D1269. When it is desired to estimate TEL only IP method 116 can be used, while for the separate determination of TEL and TML recourse can be made to ASTM D1949 or IP 188. Other methods which have been developed but not yet standardised, include X-ray absorption techniques for the determination of total lead in gasoline and a gas chromatographic procedure using an electron capture detector for the determination of the individual lead alkyls.

Other additives used in modern motor gasolines include anti-oxidants and metal deactivators for inhibiting gum formation, surface-active agents and freezing point depressants for preventing carburettor icing, deposit modifiers for reducing spark plug fouling and surface ignition, and rust inhibitors for preventing the rusting of steel tanks and pipework by the traces of water carried in gasoline. For their estimation specialised procedures involving chemical tests and physical techniques such as spectroscopy and chromatography have been used successfully.

4. VAPORISING OILS

Vaporising oil or 'power kerosine' is primarily intended as a fuel for agricultural tractors and is, in effect, a low volatility gasoline.

In tractor engines, the fuel, being much less volatile than motor gasoline, is vaporised in a preheater maintained by the exhaust gases at an overall temperature in the region of 200°C (392°F), although the temperature gradient through the preheater is approximately from 60°C to 280°C (140°F to 536°F). For steady operation the vaporiser needs to be free from deposits such as gum or carbon which would choke the vaporiser channels. The residue on evaporation (ASTM D381–IP 131) must, therefore, be at a low figure.

Although tractor type engines do not require fuel of as high a volatility as do gasoline engines, the boiling range of the vaporising oil must be such as to ensure the complete vaporisation of the fuel. As for gasoline, the volatility of vaporising oil is assessed by the distillation test (ASTM D86–IP 123) the requirement normally being controlled by the percentages boiling at 160°C and 200°C (320°F and 392°F).

The octane number is determined by the Motor Method (ASTM D2700– IP 236) to meet the specification requirements, whereas motor gasoline specifications usually require Research Method octane numbers.

Because of the lower volatility of vaporising oil compared with that of gasoline, a relatively high proportion of aromatics is necessary to maintain the octane number although cracked spirit containing unsaturated hydrocarbons may also be used in proportions compatible with stability requirements.

In view of the conditions of storage on farms and isolated locations it is necessary to limit the flash point of vaporising oil so that it does not present too great a fire hazard.

The tests normally carried out on vaporising oil are distillation, flash point (IP 33 or IP 170), sulphur content (ASTM D1266–IP 107), corrosion (ASTM D130–IP 154), octane number and residue on evaporation.

5. SUGGESTIONS FOR FURTHER READING

Science of Petroleum, Vol. V, part III, Oxford University Press.
H. Powell and W. H. Thomas (1958). Modern trends in petroleum analysis, *J. Inst. Petrol.*, **44**, 19–28.
E. M. Goodger (1953). *Petroleum Performance in Internal Combustion Engineering*, Butterworth, London.

Chapter 6

AVIATION FUELS

R. I. GOTTSHALL, D. T. McALLAN and A. G. ROBERTSON

INTRODUCTION

It is difficult to discuss the quality assessment of aviation fuels without reviewing the development history of the various types of aviation fuel and describing their quality requirements in terms of the official specifications which are produced by the co-operative efforts of engine manufacturers, airline operators, fuel suppliers and appropriate Government departments. These documents define the required fuel properties and specify the standard test methods to be used; their international validity and rigid enforcement ensure that fuels of uniform quality are available on a world-wide basis for all types of aero engine.

It is not feasible to include full details of all major international specifications in this survey and even summaries of the main requirements would be of little permanent value, since these specifications are frequently revised and up-dated to meet new aircraft needs or to reflect changing supply situations. The basic content of the various specifications covering similar grades of fuel do not, however, differ greatly, and with few exceptions the same fuel properties are controlled in each. Typical examples of current specifications covering the physical and chemical properties are included for each of the main aviation gasoline and jet fuel grades, but comprehensive and more up-to-date details of the main internationally used specifications can be found in the 'Specification Guides' issued and up-dated regularly by several major oil companies (*see* Bibliography).

Aviation gasolines for spark ignition engines reached their development peak in the 1939–45 war years. The advent of the gas turbine inhibited further piston engine development in this field and, although large quantities of gasoline will be required for many years ahead, the quality test requirements are unlikely to change significantly.

The first aviation gas turbine engines were regarded as having non-critical fuel requirements. Ordinary illuminating kerosine was the original development fuel and so the first British turbine fuel specification was largely written round the properties and test methods associated with this well-established product. However, with increased complexity in design of the engine and its control, fuel specification tests have inevitably become more complicated and numerous. Current demands for improved performance, economy and overhaul life will indirectly continue the trend towards additional tests; nevertheless, the optimum compromise between fuel quality and availability is largely achieved by the current list of fuel tests.

AVIATION GASOLINE

1. COMPOSITION AND MANUFACTURE

Aviation gasoline consists substantially of hydrocarbons; sulphur-containing and oxygen-containing impurities are strictly limited by specification and only certain additives are permitted (*see* Section on Additives). Straight run gasolines from crude oil, containing varying proportions of paraffins, naphthenes and aromatics, invariably lack the high proportion of branch chain paraffins (isoparaffins) required to produce the higher quality aviation fuels. No unsaturated hydrocarbons (olefins), as produced from petroleum cracking processes, can be included as they are relatively unstable and give rise to excessive gum formation. Only the lower grades of fuel can include a proportion of straight run gasoline and the higher grades (100/130 and 115/145) consist mainly of isoparaffins with a small amount of aromatic material to improve the rich mixture anti-knock performance. The main component of these high grade fuels is isooctane produced in the alkylation process by reaction of refinery butenes with isobutane over the acid catalysts. In order to meet the volatility requirements of the final blend, there is added a small proportion of isopentane, obtained by super-fractionation of light straight run gasoline. The aromatic component required to improve rich mixture rating is now usually a catalytic reformate and the amount added is indirectly limited by the gravimetric calorific value requirement.

Aviation gasoline is the most complex fuel produced in a refinery and very strict process control is required to ensure that the stringent and conflicting specification demands on volatility, calorific value and anti-knock ratings are met. In addition, great care has to be taken with housekeeping standards during storage and distribution of the product to avoid various forms of contamination which can affect such properties as volatility, gum values and the copper strip corrosion test.

2. SPECIFICATIONS

(a) Content

Aviation fuel specifications generally contain three main sections, covering Suitability, Composition and Chemical and Physical Requirements.

The Suitability Section is included as a safeguard against the possible failure in service of a fuel which meets the specification in respect of all the published physical and chemical tests; it throws the onus on the fuel producer to obey the spirit as well as the letter of the law. This philosophy is inherent in all aviation fuel specifications.

The Composition Section stipulates that the fuel must consist entirely of hydrocarbons except for trace amounts of approved additives (*see* Section on Additives) such as alkyl lead anti-knock additive, dyes and oxidation inhibitors. Its main importance is in listing the approved additives and indirectly in excluding any non-hydrocarbon material which might be used to improve a critical property of the fuel at the ultimate expense of other fuel properties.

The Chemical and Physical Requirements Section is the one most familiar to the users since it carefully defines both the allowable limits for many chemical and physical properties of the fuel and the standard test methods to be employed. The main tests for each basic type of aviation fuel are described separately below.

(b) Fuel grades

A number of different grades of aviation gasoline are available, identified generally by their weak and rich mixture anti-knock rating, and these are produced to meet the requirements of the various types of spark ignition piston engines in service world-wide. About six basic fuel grades have been in use since the 1939–45 war period, but during recent years diminishing demands for aviation gasoline have led to a reduction in the number of grades made generally available, which has helped to minimise manufacturing, storage and handling costs.

Specifications covering the various grades have been drawn up by a number of bodies, and these have been reissued from time to time as engine requirements have changed. No significant changes have now occurred in these specifications for a number of years, except for the gradual reduction in the number of grades covered.

The most commonly quoted aviation gasoline specifications are those issued by the American Department of Defense (US Military specifications) and by the British Ministry of Defence (D Eng RD specifications) but those drawn up by the ASTM (D910) and by some engine manufacturers are still quite widely used. Table 1 lists the main aviation gasoline specifications in current use and indicates the various grades covered, together with their identifying dye colours.

Due to the international nature of aviation activities, the technical requirements of all the Western specifications are virtually identical and only differences of a quite minor nature exist between the specifications issued in the various major countries. The Russian GOST specifications (and their East European equivalents) differ in the grades covered and also in respect of certain of the limits applied, but in general the same fuel properties are controlled and most test methods are basically similar to their Western equivalents (IP/ASTM standards). Russian Aviation Gasoline grades are summarised in Table 2.

TABLE 1

Aviation gasolines—main international specification grades

Identifying colour	NATO code number	D Eng RD 2485	MIL-G-5572	ASTM D910	Pratt & Whitney	Use
Colourless	F-13	73	—	—	—	Blending, etc.
Colourless	—	80 non-leaded	—	80/87	80/87	} Minor civil and military
Red	F-12	—	80/87	—	—	
Blue	F-15	91/96	—	—	91/98	Obsolete
Green	F-18	100/130	100/130	100/130	100/130	Main civil
Brown	—	—	—	—	108/135	Limited civil
Purple	F-22	115/145	115/145	115/145	115/145	Main military

Table 3 details the main technical requirements of the British D Eng RD 2485 specification, covering five grades of aviation gasoline. All other Western specifications include virtually identical technical requirements, differing only in the number of grades covered and in some cases by the amount of TEL permitted. It can be seen that the various grades differ fundamentally in only a few respects, albeit very vital ones, which are colour, anti-knock ratings and

TABLE 2

Russian aviation gasoline grades

Specification	Grade	Colour	Use
GOST-1012	B.70	Colourless	Current
GOST-1012	B.91/115	Green	Obsolete (?)
GOST-1012	B.95/130	Yellow	Obsolete (?)
GOST-1012	B.100/130	Bright orange	Current
GOST-5761	BA (115/160)	Varies	Obsolete (?)

TEL content. Except for very minor differences in the case of grade 115/145 (calorific value and aromatic content) the remaining general requirements are identical for all grades. This is a feature of all the Western aviation gasoline specifications, although the Russian GOST specification exhibits additional grade to grade variations in properties such as distillation range and vapour pressure.

With regard to the various Western grades of aviation gasoline, the limits specified were in most cases based originally on the requirements of various military aero engines. The performance requirements for both civil and military aero engines have changed very little over the years, but improved fuel manufacturing techniques and the reducing demand for certain grades has enabled fuel suppliers to produce modified fuel grades more suited to current civil market requirements. In some cases the objective has been to offer a technically superior fuel, in other cases the aim has been to reduce the fuel suppliers' production and handling costs by providing a fuel suitable for use in a wider range of aero engine types than was possible with the standard grades. Three examples of these 'grade variations' are worthy of mention:

(i) Whilst both the British and American Military specifications for grade 100/130 permit up to 4·6 ml/US gal of TEL (as for the 115/145 grade) airline experience showed that the overhaul life of certain engines could be improved significantly by using fuel with a lower TEL content (due to reduced valve and spark plug fouling) as specified by one engine manufacturer for the special 108/135 grade required by some of their engines. It has now for many years been accepted practice for civil supplies of the 100/130 grade to be produced in North America with a TEL limit of 4·0 ml/US gal and elsewhere with a limit of 3·0 ml/US gal.

British aviation gasoline grades: specification D Eng RD 2485
(Issue 6, Amendment 1, dated January 1969)

Grade	73	80	91/96	100/130	115/145
TEL content, ml/UK gal, max.	nil	nil	5·52	5·52	5·52
TEL content, ml/US gal, max.	nil	nil	4·60	4·60	4·60
Knock ratings					
Lean mixture—Motor Method (IP 44)	73 ON	80 ON	90 ON	99 ON	—
or Lean mixture—Aviation Method (IP 42)	—	—	91 ON	100 ON	115 PN
or Lean mixture—Extended Motor Method (IP 150)	—	—	—	—	116 PN
Rich mixture (IP 119)	—	—	96 ON	130 PN	145 PN
Colour (visual)	colourless	colourless	blue	green	purple
Heat of combustion (net), Btu/lb, min.	18 700	18 700	18 700	18 700	18 900
or Aniline gravity product, min.	7 500	7 500	7 500	7 500	9 000
Aromatics, per cent vol, min.	—	—	—	—	5·0
Specific gravity at 60°F/60°F	Not limited but shall be reported				
Distillation test					
Fuel evaporated (per cent) at 75°C (167°F)	10 min; 40 max.				
Fuel evaporated (per cent) at 105°C (221°F)	50 min.				
Fuel evaporated (per cent) at 135°C (275°F)	90 min.				
Final boiling point	170°C (338°F) max.				
Sum of 10 per cent and 50 per cent evaporated points	135°C (307°F) min.				
Freezing point	−60°C (−76°F) max.				
Gum existent, mg/100 ml	3 max.				
Gum accelerated (16 hr)					
Residue, mg/100 ml	6 max.				
Precipitate, mg/100 ml	2 max.				
Total sulphur, per cent wt	0·05 max.				
Corrosion test—copper strip	Classification 1 max. (slight stain only)				
Reid vapour pressure, psi/100°F (38°C)	5·5 min.–7·0 max.				
Water reaction—volume change, ml	2 max.				
Water reaction—interface rating	2 max. with sharp separation				

Note: The corresponding US specification MIL-G-5572 differs only in two respects.
1. The 73 and 80 grades of fuel are replaced by an 80/87 grade with a TEL content of 0·6 ml/UK gal max and dyed red.
2. The aniline gravity product for the 115/145 grade is 10 000 min.

(ii) Among the lower grades of aviation gasoline, limited requirements exist for a non-leaded grade (73 octane) for use in certain aero engines (chiefly of pre-war European design) and also for blending and special test purposes, whilst many newer and slightly higher rated engines require an 80/87 grade fuel, in which a maximum TEL content of 0·5 ml/US gal is specified. With diminishing demand for both these grades, a need arose for a fuel which was unleaded but would also meet the 80/87 rating requirements, so that it could be used satisfactorily in both types of engine. This led to the introduction of a new non-leaded grade in the British Military specification, known as 80NL or 80 Clear; this was marketed in selected areas, particularly the UK and Western Europe where demand for the 73 grade still remained significant.

The 80NL grade (unleaded and colourless) was not, however, introduced into the corresponding US Military specification, which retains the requirement for a leaded 80/87 grade (coloured red), as do several other major specifications. It was found that the complete absence of TEL from the fuel could have an adverse effect on the valves in certain aero engines normally operated on the leaded grade (causing excessive valve seat wear or valve sink) and this has mitigated against the more widespread use of the unleaded material. One engine manufacturer in fact recommends the addition of 1 part in 6 of grade 100/130 to any stocks of 80NL used, to re-establish the previous TEL content in order to alleviate this problem.

(iii) With the continuing fall in demand for all aviation gasolines a further step has recently been taken towards simplifying the range available. By careful choice of blending components a satisfactory 100/130 grade can now be manufactured with a TEL content of only 2·0 ml/US gal with little or no cost penalty. This Low Lead 100/130 grade offers valuable benefits to normal users of 100/130 (improved plug life, etc.). In the case of aero engines normally operated on Avgas 80/87 (0·5 ml/US gal of TEL) most engine manufacturers have now given unlimited approval for alternative use of the Low Lead 100/130 grade.

3.   CHARACTERISTICS AND REQUIREMENTS

(a) Anti-knock properties
The various fuel grades are classified by their 'anti-knock' quality characteristics as determined in single cylinder laboratory engines. Knock, or detonation, in an engine is a form of abnormal combustion where the air/fuel charge in the cylinder ignites spontaneously in a localised area instead of being consumed progressively by the spark-initiated flame front. Such knocking combustion can damage the engine and give serious power loss if allowed to persist and the various grades are designed to guarantee knock-free operation for a

range of engines from those used in light aircraft up to high powered transport and military types.

The anti-knock ratings of aviation gasolines are determined in standard ASTM–CFR laboratory engines by matching their performance against reference blends of pure isooctane and n-heptane. Fuel rating is expressed as an octane number (ON) which is defined as the percentage of isooctane in the matching reference blend. Fuels of higher performance than isooctane (100 ON) are tested against blends of isooctane with various amounts of anti-knock additive. The rating of such fuel is expressed as a Performance Number (PN), defined as the maximum knock-free power output obtained from the fuel expressed as a percentage of the power obtainable on isooctane.

The anti-knock rating of fuel varies according to the air/fuel mixture strength employed and this fact is used in defining the performance requirements of the higher grade aviation fuels. As mixture strength is increased (richened), the additional fuel acts as an internal coolant and suppresses knocking combustion thus permitting a higher power rating to be obtained. Since maximum power output is the prime requirement of an engine under rich take-off conditions, the 'rich mixture performance' of a fuel is determined in a special supercharged single cylinder engine (ASTM D909 or IP 119).

TABLE 4

Knock characteristics of gasolines—Test methods

Knock Rating Methods	Standard Methods		New Joint Methods
	IP	ASTM	
Research Method (F-1)	126	D908	} ASTM D2699–IP 237
Extended Research Method	172	D1656	
Motor Method (F-2)	44	D357	} ASTM D2700–IP 236
Extended Motor Method	150	D1948	
Aviation Method (F-3)	42	D614	—
Supercharge Method (rich mixture F-4)	119	D909	—

Similarly, economic cruising operation of an engine is obtainable on weak mixture strengths and, therefore, the 'weak mixture performance' of the fuel is also determined under standard conditions which vary slightly between alternative test methods. Depending on the fuel grade, three methods may be used; the Motor Method, the Extended Motor Method and the Aviation Lean Method. All the various methods for determining anti-knock ratings are summarised in Table 4 and for completeness the Research Methods are included, but it should be noted that these are only used on motor gasolines and are not acceptable methods for rating aviation fuels. Some of the test procedures have recently been combined into new Joint ASTM–IP methods, but as the main aviation gasoline specifications have not been revised for several years most still specify the rating requirements against the older standard methods. The higher grades of fuel are thus classified by their specified anti-knock ratings under both sets of test conditions. For example, 100/130 grade fuel has an anti-knock quality of 100 minimum by the weak mixture test procedure and 130 minimum by the rich mixture procedure. Octane numbers are used to specify ratings of 100 and below while perform-ance numbers are used above 100. The lower grades of fuel, designed for light aircraft engines with little or no supercharge, are only critical in respect of weak mixture performance and are, therefore, defined by this rating alone.

The use of limited amounts of alkyl lead compound (tetraethyl lead— TEL) is permitted to enable very high anti-knock ratings to be achieved economically (*see* also Section on Additives). An adverse side-effect of this additive is the deposition in the engine of solid lead compounds formed in the combustion process which promote spark plug fouling and corrosion of cylinders, valves etc. A scavenging chemical—ethylene dibromide—is mixed with the compound and largely converts the lead oxides, etc., into volatile lead bromide which is then expelled with the exhaust gases. As a compromise between economic considerations and the avoidance of these side-effects, the maximum addition of TEL is carefully controlled by specifica-tion using Method D526–IP 96.

(b) Volatility

All internal combustion engine fuels must be easily convertible from storage in the liquid form to the vapour phase in the engine to allow formation of the combustible air/fuel vapour mixture. If gasoline fuel volatility were too low, liquid fuel would enter the cylinder and wash lubricating oil from the walls and pistons and so lead to increased engine wear; a further effect would be to cause dilution of the crankcase oil; poor volatility can also give rise to critical maldistribution of mixture strength between cylinders. Conversely, if volatility is too high, fuel can vaporise in the fuel tank and supply lines giving undue venting losses and the possibility of fuel starvation through 'vapour lock' in the fuel lines. The cooling effect due to rapid vaporisation of excessive amounts of highly volatile materials can also cause ice formation in the carburettor under certain conditions of humidity and air temperature. Many modern aircraft have anti-icing devices on the engines, including the provision of carburettor heating, but not all light aircraft are so equipped and carburettor icing can be a serious problem if care is not exercised.

A suitable fuel must therefore have a balanced volatility which is deter-mined by a laboratory distillation test procedure (ASTM D86–IP 123) whereby a standard quantity of fuel is boiled and the temperatures noted at which certain proportions of the fuel distil over. The specification distillation points for aviation gasoline are designed to control volatility in the following ways. The 10 per cent minimum and 40 per cent maximum boiling to 75°C

(167°F) control front end volatility, the minimum value ensuring that volatility is adequate for normal cold starting. The maximum value is a safeguard against vapour lock, fuel system vent losses and carburettor icing.

The 50 per cent minimum boiling to 105°C (221°F) ensures that the fuel has even distillation properties and does not consist of low boiling and high boiling components only. Control is thereby provided over the rate of engine warm-up and stabilisation of slow-running conditions.

The minimum of 135°C (307°F) for the sum of the 10 per cent and 50 per cent evaporated temperatures also controls the overall volatility and indirectly places a lower limit on the 50 per cent point. The clause is an additional safeguard against excessive fuel volatility. (Note: temperatures must be converted independently before addition to obtain sum.)

The 90 per cent minimum to 135°C (275°F) controls the proportion of less volatile fuel components and, therefore, the amount of unvaporised fuel passing through the engine manifold into the cylinders. The limit represents a compromise between ideal fuel distribution characteristics and commercial considerations of fuel availability, which could be adversely affected by further restriction of this limit.

The final boiling point of 170°C (338°F) excludes any undesirable heavy material which could cause fuel maldistribution and also dilution of the crankcase oil.

All spark ignition engine fuels have a vapour pressure which is a measure of the tendency of the more volatile components to escape from the fuel tank in the form of vapour. When an aircraft climbs rapidly to a high altitude the atmospheric pressure over the fuel is reduced and may drop to the vapour pressure of the fuel at its prevailing temperature. When this occurs the fuel will 'boil' and considerable quantities of the more volatile components will escape as vapour through the tank vents. Fuel vapour pressure is, therefore, controlled and measured by the Reid Vapour Pressure test (ASTM D323–IP 69) as the pressure exerted by the vapour from a fixed volume of the fuel when heated at 37·8°C (100°F) in a bomb which has a vapour expansion chamber volume four times that of the liquid chamber volume. The limits for aviation gasoline are between 5·5 and 7·0 pounds per square inch (psi); the lower limit is an additional check on adequate volatility for engine starting while the upper limit guards against excessive vapour formation during high altitude flight and 'weathering' losses in storage.

(c) Density (specific gravity)
The density of a fuel is a measure of the mass per unit volume and is read directly using calibrated glass hydrometers. It is used in fuel load calculations, since weight or volume fuel limitations (or both) may be necessary according to the type of aircraft and flight pattern involved. In most cases the volume of fuel which can be carried is limited by tank capacity and to achieve maximum range a high density fuel is preferred, as this will provide the greatest heating value per gallon (litre) of fuel. The heating value per pound

(kilogramme) of fuel, however, falls slightly with increasing density, so that on occasions where the weight of fuel which can be carried is limited (*e.g.* to achieve maximum payload) it can be advantageous to use a lower density fuel, provided adequate tank volume capacity is available.

As fuel density varies with temperature it must be specified under standard conditions and the most usual are 60°F or 15°C. Most British and other European specifications define the fuel density in terms of the Specific Gravity under standard conditions (ASTM D1298–IP 160); this is a measure of the mass of a given volume of fuel related to the same volume of water (under specified temperature conditions) and is directly equivalent to the density at 15°C in grammes/millilitres or kilogrammes/litre (and is related by a factor of ten to the density in pounds/UK gallon).

In the USA it is more common to specify fuel density in terms of the API Gravity. (ASTM D287.) The gravity in degrees API (°API) is calculated from the Specific Gravity 60°/60°F by the following formula:

$$\text{API gravity, degrees} = \frac{141 \cdot 5}{\text{S.G. } 60°/60°\text{F}} - 131 \cdot 5$$

No reference temperature is required, since 60°F is included in the definition.

(d) Heat of combustion (calorific value)

Heat of combustion (ASTM D240–IP 12 or ASTM D2382) is a direct measure of fuel energy content and is determined as the quantity of heat liberated by the combustion of a unit quantity of fuel with oxygen in a standard bomb calorimeter. This fuel property affects the economics of engine performance and the specified minimum value is a compromise between the conflicting requirements of maximum fuel availability and good fuel consumption characteristics. An alternative criterion of energy content is the 'Aniline Gravity Product' (AGP) which is fairly accurately related to calorific value but more easily determined. It is the product of the gravity at 60°F (expressed in degrees API) and the aniline point of the fuel in °F (ASTM D611 or IP 2). The aniline point is the lowest temperature at which the fuel is miscible with an equal volume of aniline and is inversely proportional to the aromatic content. The relationship between AGP and calorific value is given in method ASTM D1405–IP 193.

No great variation in either density or heat of combustion occurs in modern aviation gasolines since they depend on hydrocarbon composition which is already closely controlled by other specification properties. Both factors have relatively greater importance with jet fuels, which is discussed later.

(e) Freezing point

Maximum freezing point values are laid down for all types of aviation fuel as a guide to the lowest temperature at which the fuel can be used without risk of separation of solidified hydrocarbons at low operational temperatures.

Such separation could lead to fuel starvation through clogging of fuel lines or filters and loss in available fuel load due to retention of solidified fuel in the tanks. The standard test involves cooling the fuel slowly until a slurry of crystals forms throughout the fuel and noting the temperature at which all crystals disappear on re-warming the fuel (ASTM D2836–IP 16).

The freezing point of aviation gasoline is controlled to below −60°C (−76°F) and was originally designed to limit the amount of benzene (freezing point +5·4°C) added to the fuel as a high anti-knock value component. It is retained as a specification property in order to safeguard high altitude performance.

(f) Storage stability

Aviation fuel must retain its required properties for long periods of storage in all kinds of climates. Unstable fuels will oxidise and form polymeric oxidation products which will remain as a resinous solid or 'gum' on induction manifolds, carburettors, valves, etc. as the gasoline is evaporated. Formation of this undesirable gum must be strictly limited and is assessed by the existent and accelerated (or potential) gum tests. The existent gum value (ASTM D381–IP 131) is that actually present in the fuel at the time of test and is measured as the weight of residue obtained after controlled evaporation of a standard volume of fuel. The accelerated gum test (ASTM D873–IP 138) is a safeguard of storage stability and predicts the possibility of gum forming during protracted storage and decomposition of the anti-knock additive. The fuel is heated for 16 hours with oxygen under pressure in a bomb at 100°C (212°F) and then both the gum content and amount of precipitate are measured.

To ensure that the strict limits of the stability specification clauses are met, aviation gasoline components are given special refining treatments to remove the trace impurities responsible for instability. In addition, limited quantities of approved oxidation inhibitors are added and little trouble is experienced nowadays with gum formation or degradation of anti-knock additive.

(g) Sulphur content

The total sulphur content of aviation gasoline is limited to the low level of 0·05 per cent weight maximum because most sulphur compounds have a marked deleterious effect on the anti-knock efficiency of alkyl lead compounds. If sulphur content was not limited in this way, the highly leaded grades of aviation fuel would not reach the specified anti-knock values. Sulphur content (ASTM D1266–IP 107) is estimated by burning a sample of the fuel in a simple lamp device and determining the quantity of gaseous oxides of sulphur so formed.

Some sulphur compounds can also have a corroding action on the various metals of the engine system, varying according to the chemical type of sulphur compound present. Fuel corrosivity is assessed by its action on copper and is controlled by the copper strip test (ASTM D130–IP 154) which specifies that not more than a slight stain shall be observed when the polished strip is immersed in fuel heated for 2 hours in a bomb at 100°C (212°F).

(h) Water reaction

The original aim of the water reaction test was to prevent the addition of high octane, water soluble components such as ethyl alcohol to aviation gasoline. The test method involves shaking 80 ml of fuel with 20 ml of water under standard conditions and observing phase volume changes and interface condition.

It is specified that phase volume change shall not exceed 2 ml and that the interface shall be substantially free from bubbles or scum, with sharp separation of the phases without emulsion or precipitate within or upon either layer. The long-established standard test methods for water reaction (Federal method 3251–ASTM D1096) cover only the volume change and the interface condition, and special clauses have been included in most specifications to cover the phase separation requirements. An improved method (IP 289) has now been introduced which rates all three of the test criteria in detail and the older methods are likely to be similarly updated shortly.

AVIATION TURBINE FUELS (JET FUELS)

1. Introduction

Aircraft gas turbine engines require a fuel with quite different properties from those outlined above for aviation gasoline. Probably the greatest difference is that anti-knock value is of no importance and is replaced by the need for a heating fuel of good combustion characteristics and high energy content. Illuminating kerosine was chosen as the fuel for the first generation of engines largely because of its ready availability, low fire hazard, good combustion properties and, not least, the war-time need to conserve gasoline supplies. As engine and fuel system designs have become more complicated so, unfortunately, have the fuel specifications become more varied and restrictive; however, the fuel must still have the properties outlined above as well as a ready availability in times of military emergency.

Jet fuel quality worldwide is dictated largely by the British Ministry of Defence (D Eng RD) specifications and by the US Department of Defense (US—MIL) specifications, although a number of other closely related specifications are widely quoted, including those issued by the ASTM, the International Air Transport Association (IATA) and by various engine manufacturers, airlines and national governments. Almost without exception these other specifications cover grades having virtually identical basic properties to the major British and American Military jet fuel grades and differ only in the types of additives permitted. The only significant exception is in the case of the fuel types used in Russia and most East European countries; these grades are based on USSR State Standards (GOST specifications) and differ in several major respects from their nearest 'Western' equivalents.

Only two basic types of jet fuel are in general use world wide, the kerosine type and the wide-cut gasoline type. The former is a much modified development of the illuminating kerosine originally used in gas turbine engines, whilst the latter is a wider boiling range material including some gasoline fractions, developed primarily in the USA to improve on availability from crude oil. In addition a number of specialised fuel grades are required for limited military use, as referee fuels and particularly in supersonic aircraft.

2. Fuel Developments

Jet fuel development has differed somewhat in Europe and America, but in recent years the British and US specification requirements have gradually been brought into line, in the interests of military (NATO) standardisation. Because of the differences in early development philosophy, a brief historical review of the way the quality requirements have developed in different countries is a necessary preamble to a discussion of the test requirements and their significance.

(a) British jet fuels

The British Jet Fuel specification D Eng RD 2482 issued shortly after World War II was based on the experience gained from operations on illuminating kerosine. It was rather restrictive on aromatics (12 per cent maximum) sulphur content (0·1 per cent maximum) and calorific value (18 500 Btu/lb minimum) but contained no burning quality requirements. Although further experience permitted relaxation of some of the early requirements it also became necessary to introduce additional tests as new service problems were encountered, and to amend some existing test limits. For example, the progressive development of more powerful turbine engined aircraft with greater range and altitude performance made the $-40°C$ ($-40°F$) freezing point limit of the D Eng RD 2482 type fuel inadequate to ensure that hydrocarbon wax would not separate from fuel during prolonged cold soaking at altitude. A new D Eng RD 2494 specification was then issued with a maximum freezing point of $-50°C$ ($-58°F$) and this fuel quality still remains the optimum compromise between engine development requirements, fuel cost and a strategic availability: a flashpoint of 100°F minimum is specified, more for fiscal than for technical reasons.

Whilst D Eng RD 2494 (Avtur) is now the standard British Civil Jet fuel, a new D Eng RD 2453 specification (Avtur/FSII) was issued in 1967 incorporating anti-icing and corrosion inhibitor additives, in line with the latest US military and NATO requirements.

A less volatile kerosine fuel for use in naval carrier-borne aircraft with a higher flashpoint of 140°F minimum was defined originally by the D Eng

RD 2488 specification. In line with the need for improved low temperature performance, a later specification D Eng RD 2498 (Avcat) introduced a modified freezing point requirement of −48°C (−55°F) maximum, as compared with the 40°C (−40°F) for former D Eng RD 2488 specification.

In the UK wide range turbine fuel has never been in such wide-spread military usage as in the USA (*see* below), due among other reasons to the fact that crude oils giving high gasoline yields are not in such abundant supply. However, the D Eng RD 2486 (Avtag) specification was introduced in 1951 to cover a fuel grade basically identical to the American wide-cut JP-4 grade (MIL-T-5624) and this fuel grade has been quite widely used, particularly under NATO arrangements. More recently the grade has been brought completely into line with the American equivalent with the issue in 1967 of the D Eng RD 2454 specification (Avtag/FSII), incorporating anti-icing and corrosion inhibitor additives.

A feature of all the above D Eng RD specifications not at present included in their US Military equivalents is that static dissipator additive is permitted by user agreement and in the case particularly of civil supplies to D Eng RD 2494 this additive is now nearly always present.

Table 5 lists the British D Eng RD specifications for aviation fuels and related products.

(b) American military jet fuels

In America, jet fuel development followed a different pattern to the UK with the early US specification for JP-1 (MIL-F-5616) covering a paraffinic kerosine with a freeze point of −60°C (−76°F); this naturally restricted its availability and the grade soon became obsolete (although the term JP-1 is still widely used, quite incorrectly, to describe current kerosine type jet fuel) and was superseded by a series of military wide-cut fuels. The wide range distillate type of turbine fuel originated in the USA where it was realised that in times of military emergency the fuel supply could be increased considerably if more of the readily available gasoline fractions were incorporated into jet fuel to supplement the basic kerosine component. This philosophy is the converse of the war-time choice of kerosine for the early jet engines, in order to conserve gasoline stocks for the then predominant piston type aero-engines.

The first wide-cut grade (JP-2) allowed a Reid Vapour Pressure of 2 lb maximum to increase availability through the inclusion of heavy gasoline fractions. Experience suggested that a further increase in volatility might be tolerated to give an advantage in engine starting and the specification for JP-3 was, therefore, introduced, with vapour pressure limits of 5·0 to 7·0 lb. However, operational problems due to high venting losses at altitude led finally to the formulation of the JP-4 specification in 1950 and, with slight modifications to the specific gravity and distillation requirements plus the inclusion of certain additives, this MIL-T-5624 (JP-4) material remains the main military fuel for jet aircraft in the USA and many other countries. The British D Eng RD 2454, wide-cut fuel is its direct equivalent.

TABLE 5

British military specifications for aviation fuels and related products

D Eng RD specification	British joint services designation	NATO code number	Type	Use
2451	AL-31	S-748	Ethylene glycol monomethyl ether	Fuel system icing inhibitor
2453	Avtur/FS11	F-34	Kerosine, with FS11	Military
2454	Avtag/FS11	F-40	Wide-cut, with FS11	Military
2482	Avtur/40	F-30	Kerosine, −40°C (−40°F) freezing point	Obsolete
2485	Avgas	*a*	Aviation gasoline (several grades)	General
2486	Avtag	F-45	Wide-cut	Civil
2488	Avcat/40	F-42	High flash kerosine, −40°C (−40°F) freezing point	Obsolete
2491	AL-9/24/28	—	Methanol and Water/methanol mixtures	Thrust augmentation fluids
2492	Avpin	S-746	Isopropyl nitrate	Turbine engine starter fuel
2494	Avtur (50)	F-35	Kerosine, −50°C (−58°F) freezing point	Civil
2495	—	—	Kerosine rocket fuel	Obsolete
2496	Avcos	—	Cold starting fuel for piston engines	Obsolete
2498	Avcat (48)	F-44	High flash kerosine, −48°C (−24°F) freezing point	Naval carrier aircraft

a See Table 1.

Kerosine type jet fuels have not in fact achieved any very significant military usage in the USA although fuels of this type are included among some of the specialised jet fuels used in limited quantities for particular applications. The most common of these is JP-5 (covered also by the MIL-T-5624 specification) being a special low volatility kerosine used in naval carrier borne aircraft and identical to the British D Eng RD 2498 grade (*see* above). JP-6 (MIL-T-25656) is a fairly light kerosine type fuel, having improved thermal stability properties and intended for use in certain supersonic aircraft. JP-7 (MIL-T-38219) is another low volatility high flashpoint kerosine, but having very enhanced combustion and thermal stability properties and developed specially for use in very high performance (Mach 3) aircraft.

More recently, concern over the combat hazards when using wide-cut fuels has lead the US military authorities to reconsider the use of a standard kerosine type fuel and service trials have been undertaken to evaluate a proposed new JP-8 (MIL-T-83133) differing only in minor respects from the British D Eng RD 2453 grade. However, it now seems very doubtful whether JP-8 will in fact be widely adopted by the US Military, as apart from the technical considerations, a change from a wide-cut fuel to a kerosine type by such a major international user could have a very serious effect on the world wide supply position for jet fuels.

Table 6 lists the US Military specifications for jet fuels and related products.

(c) American civil jet fuels

The basic civil jet fuel specification used in the USA is ASTM D1655, covering three types of fuel: Jet A, a nominal −40°C (−40°F) freeze point kerosine; Jet A-1, a nominal −50°C (−58°F) freeze point kerosine (basically similar to the British D Eng RD 2494 specification) and Jet B, a wide-cut gasoline grade (similar to JP-4 but without certain additives). Jet A is used internally within the USA by all domestic operators, whilst Jet A-1 is the standard grade used for international flights. To differentiate from the military fuel grades (which often contain special additives not commonly used in civil fuels) the terms Jet A-1 and Jet B have now achieved world wide usage to describe the basic kerosine and wide cut gasoline types of civil jet fuel, although the latter is only in fairly limited civil usage at present.

A number of jet fuel specifications are also issued by the major US aero engine manufacturers and by certain airlines, but these are either basically similar to the equivalent ASTM grades or are less restrictive versions of one or more ASTM grades.

(d) Russian jet fuels

A wide range of jet fuels covered by various Russian GOST specifications are manufactured for both civil and military use. The main grades are also covered by similar specifications issued by a number of other East European countries. Whilst the fuel characteristics in some cases differ considerably from those of jet fuels used elsewhere, the main properties are controlled by

TABLE 6
US military jet fuels and related specifications

Specification	First issued	Grade	Type	Use
AN-F-32	1944	JP-1	Very low freeze kerosine	Obsolete
MIL-F-5616	1950	JP-2	Wide-cut (RVP max. 2 lb)	Obsolete
AN-F-34	1945	JP-3	Wide-cut (RVP 5–7 lb)	Obsolete
AN-F-58	1947			
MIL-F-5624	1950	JP-4	Wide-cut (RVP 2–3 lb)	Air force standard
MIL-T-5624	1950	JP-5	High flash kerosine	Naval carrier aircraft
MIL-T-5624	1950	JP-6	Light kerosine (thermally stable)	Supersonic bombers (Obs)
MIL-F-25656	1956	JP-7	Low volatility kerosine (special properties)	Very high performance A/C
MIL-T-38219	1965	JP-8	Kerosine	Proposed 'safety' fuel
MIL-T-83133	1968			
Related specifications				
MIL-F-5161		—	Referee JP-4 and JP-5	Ground test fuels
MIL-F-5572		Avgas	Aviation gasoline (several grades)	Military standard
MIL-I-25017		—	Chemical materials	Fuel soluble corrosion inhibitor
MIL-F-25524		—	Thermally stable kerosine	Flight test fuel
MIL-F-25558		RJ-1	High density kerosine	Air force ramjet fuel
MIL-P-25576		RP-1	Narrow cut kerosine	Rocket fuel
MIL-J-27275		—	Referee JP-6	Ground test fuel
MIL-I-27686		FSII	Ethylene glycol monomethyl ether	Fuel system icing inhibitor
MIL-F-82522		RJ-4	T-H Dimer	Navy ramjet fuel

test methods very similar to their ASTM–IP equivalents. A few additional test methods *e.g.* iodine number (related to olefin content), hydrogen sulphide content, free sulphur content and filtration rate, are sometimes included and thermal stability is also usually specified by a completely different test procedure.

Only limited information is available on some of these fuel grades and only a few of them are in regular civil use. Brief details are shown in Table 7. T-1, TS-1 and more recently T-7 (plus their East European equivalents) are the only grades normally offered to international airlines at civil airports and in practice these are usually found to meet the equivalent 'Western' kerosine specifications with the exception of having a lower flash point (often about 85/95°F: 29/35°C) and sometimes having a poor odour and rather high mercaptan sulphur content.

TABLE 7

Russian jet fuel specifications

Specification	Grade	Type	Use
GOST-10227	T-1	Kerosine from low sulphur crude (SR)	General
GOST-10227	TS-1	Kerosine from high sulphur crude (SR)	Most common civil
GOST-10227	T-2	Wide cut fuel (SR)	Military (?)
—	T-4	Wide cut, high in aromatics	Unknown
GOST-9145	T-5	Heavy kerosine	Unknown
GOST-12308	T-6	Heavy paraffinic kerosine (HT)	Unknown
GOST-12308	T-7	Very low sulphur TS-1 (HT)	Replacing TS-1
—	T-8	Low volatility kerosine (HT)	Supersonic civil

SR = Straight Run   HT = Hydro-treated.
Note: TS-1 appears as TC-1 in Russian Alphabet.
     T-8 is close equivalent to Western Jet A-1 in all respects.

(e) Other foreign jet fuels
A number of other countries also issue jet fuel specifications and the most important of these are indicated in Table 8. In most cases these specifications are virtually identical with their American or British equivalents, particularly in the case of countries committed to multi-national military agreements (*e.g.* NATO or SEATO). Even in this case, however, some countries incorporate special national requirements (*e.g.* the Canadian specifications normally require the mandatory addition of a static dissipator additive and some Australian specifications include a microbiological test requirement). Since withdrawing from NATO the French specifications have been modified in some respects from their earlier content.

(f) International standard specifications
Modern civil aviation recognises few frontiers and there is, therefore, a need for aviation fuels having similar characteristics to be available in all parts of

the world. This is especially important in the case of jet fuels used by international airlines and to provide a suitable basis 'guidance material' has been prepared by the International Air Transport Association and issued in the form of two specifications, for a kerosine and a wide-cut gasoline type jet fuel. The fundamental requirements of these two IATA grades are identical to those covered by the main British and American Military specifications,

TABLE 8

Minor national aviation fuel specifications

Grade Country	Jet fuels			Aviation gasolines		
	Kerosine (Avtur)	Wide-cut (JP-4)	High flash kerosine	80/87	100/130	115/145
Australia DEF (Aust)	208	—	207	215	215	215
Belgium Ba-PF-	3	2	—	5	5	5
Brazil CNP-08	QAV-1	QAV-4	—	—	—	—
Canada 3-GP-	23	22	24	25	25	25
France AIR	3405 (TRO)	3407 (TR4)	3404 (TR5)	3401	3401	3401
Germany VTL-9130-	—	006	010	001	003	004
Italy AM-C-	—	142	143	102	104	105
Sweden FSD-MO-754-	375	277	—	236	255	259

but a number of options are left to user choice, particularly in respect of additives requirements, and the specifications are not quite so restrictive in some respects. A number of major airlines have now adopted the IATA guidance material and some issue it under their own company designation.

Despite the standardising action taken by IATA and by certain military organisations, there are still a number of differences between the minimum quality standards established by the main internationally used specifications, those issued by the British and American military, by ASTM and by IATA. Jet fuels are normally manufactured for eventual supply to a number of different customers, both civil and military and of various nationalities, who may define their requirements in terms of any of these main international specifications. It is also regular practice for fuel produced at a given refinery to be shipped overseas and delivered over great distances to customers in different countries, and at certain stages of the distribution system stocks from various refinery sources may be comingled in storage tanks or hydrant fuelling systems before eventual delivery to customers. In addition, it is becoming quite usual for fuel suppliers to draw locally from common refinery sources and to operate a variety of 'borrow and loan' arrangements where economic advantages result. Such arrangements are still fairly rare within North America but are becoming increasingly common in the rest of the world.

Military authorities normally purchase their fuel requirements against their own national specifications or else against the appropriate British or American military specifications and compliance raises few problems. In the case of civil airlines, however, who often purchase more fuel 'offshore' than they use domestically, difficulties often arise due to the variety of names, definitions and specifications chosen to describe their international require- ments. Out of date issues of specifications are frequently quoted and partic- ularly in the case of kerosine type jet fuel (Jet A-1) grade names of doubtful significance have often been used, such as kerosine, Avtur and JP-1. Most airlines now quote their Jet A-1 requirements against either the D Eng RD 2494, ASTM D1655 or IATA specifications and their (limited) requirements for Jet B against the D Eng RD 2486, US MIL-T-5624, ASTM D 1655 or IATA specifications, but permitted additive contents are frequently ill- defined, particularly where only simple reference to military specifications is made.

For the above reasons, a need has arisen for basic fuel specifications which define the quality requirements precisely and in such a manner that the most stringent requirements of each of the many international specifications are included. This will ensure that aviation fuels meeting these specified require- ments will automatically be in full compliance with any or all of the commonly quoted official specifications relating to that particular grade and will there- fore be acceptable to the widest possible range of users. Suitable specifica- tions have now been drawn up by a working party representative of all major international oil companies supplying aviation fuels outside North America and have been issued as the 'Aviation Fuel Quality Requirements for Jointly Operated Systems'. Whilst two aviation gasoline grades are included (100/130 and 115/145), the main content of this document is two detailed 'check lists' giving the requirements for a Jet A-1 kerosine and Jet B wide-cut gasoline type jet fuel. Full details are included in Appendix II.

3. SPECIFICATION REQUIREMENTS

The requirements for jet fuels lay stress on a different combination of prop- erties and tests than those required for aviation gasoline. The same basic controls are needed for such properties as storage stability and corrosivity but the gasoline anti-knock tests are replaced by a combination of tests directly and indirectly controlling energy content and combustion characteristics. It is, therefore, more convenient to deal with the chemical properties (and composition) separately from the physical properties of jet fuel. In many cases, the information on test methods, etc. given in the Aviation Gasoline Sections above applies also to jet fuels.

(a) Chemical properties and composition

Jet fuels consist entirely of hydrocarbons except for trace quantities of sulphur compounds and approved additives (see Section on Additives). Since they are usually produced by blending straight run distillate components they contain virtually no olefins, which in any case are limited by specification (ASTM D1319–IP 156); a few specifications allow an alternative method of control by the bromine number (ASTM D1159–IP 130). The amounts of aromatics are also directly limited (ASTM D1319–IP 156) because they are not so clean burning as the other hydrocarbon types and can cause smokiness and carbon deposition in the engine. They also increase the luminosity of the combustion flame, which can adversely affect the life of certain designs of combustion chamber, and also degrade elastomers used in the fuel system.

The principal non-hydrocarbon components permitted are the sulphur compounds present in the fuel as produced. The amount and type of sulphur compound varies with crude source, but, generally speaking, no difficulty is met in meeting the specified total sulphur content (ASTM D1266 or IP 107) which ranges in level between 0·2 and 0·4 per cent weight maximum. Experimental evidence indicates that high sulphur levels may adversely affect the carbon forming tendency in combustion chambers and the presence of large amounts of oxides of sulphur in the combustion gases is undesirable because of possible corrosion.

Direct corrosivity of sulphur compounds is controlled by the copper strip test (ASTM D130–IP 154) although this particular method is not always capable of reflecting fuel corrosivity towards other fuel system metals. For example, service experience with corrosion of silver components in certain engine fuel systems led to the development of a silver corrosion test (IP 227) which now appears in the British military specifications for kerosine type turbine fuels. The mercaptan sulphur content (ASTM D1219–IP 104) of jet fuels is specifically limited to a maximum in the range 0·001–0·005 per cent weight because of objectionable odour, adverse effect on certain fuel system elastomers and corrosiveness towards fuel system metals. As an alternative to determining the mercaptan content, a negative result by the Doctor Test Method (ASTM D484 or IP 30) is usually acceptable.

Mercaptan removal from fuel blends can be effected by sweetening processes which convert them to less objectionable, non-volatile disulphides and most of the processes use a chemical reagent which does not effect any reduction in total sulphur content. The more common hydrofining procedure, however, catalytically converts all sulphur compounds to gaseous hydrogen sulphide which is then stripped from the refined fuel. It must be mentioned here that improper control of any sweetening process can produce trace materials which will subsequently cause service trouble even though the fuel meets all the specified physical and chemical tests.

No direct limit is placed on the presence of oxygenated materials but if they are present as acidic compounds such as phenols and naphthenic acids, they are controlled in different specifications by a variety of acidity tests. The total acidity (ASTM D974–IP 139) is still widely used but has been found to be insufficiently sensitive to detect trace acidic materials which can adversely affect the water separating properties of fuel. The ASTM D974 method has, therefore, been modified for use in some US military specifications and the latest British specifications call for a more precise acidity test method (IP 273). The acidity limits specified normally vary with the test method required. Oxygen-containing impurities in the form of gum are limited by the existent gum (ASTM D381–IP 131) and potential gum (ASTM D873–IP 138) but the limits are less restrictive than for aviation gasoline. In practice, the current refined, straight run fuels have gum values very much lower than the specification limits.

The various approved additives for jet fuels include oxidation inhibitors to improve storage stability, copper deactivators to neutralise the known adverse effect of copper on fuel stability, and corrosion inhibitors intended for the protection of storage tanks and pipelines. An anti-icing additive (fuel system icing inhibitor) is called for in many military fuels and a static dissipator additive (anti-static additive) may be required to minimise fire and explosion risks due to electrostatic discharges in installations and equipment during pumping operations. Details of the various approved additives (mandatory or optional) are included in every specification (*see* Section on Additives).

(b) Physical properties—contaminants

Jet fuels are subjected to considerable changes in temperature and pressure in service and their physical properties must be closely controlled (*see* below). Apart from these requirements the fine clearances and precision mechanisms of the modern fuel system demand that the fuel be delivered free from water, dirt and other foreign contaminants; this has necessitated the establishment of stringent storage and handling procedures to cover what is simply referred to in some specifications as 'appearance' or 'workmanship'. In fact, fine particle filtration and water separation facilities are generally provided to ensure that dirt and free water contents are very much lower than the maximum levels of 1 mg/litre and 30 ppm respectively, proposed by the International Air Transport Association (IATA) and applied generally to supplies of civil jet fuel. Certain US military specifications and some civil airline specifications do, however, now call for more stringent limits, such as 1·0 mg/gallon for dirt and 15–20 ppm for free water.

Field quality control of dirt content is by a membrane filtration method (ASTM D2276–IP 216) in which the dirt retained by filtration of a sample through a cellulose membrane is expressed as weight per unit volume of the fuel; this can be supplemented by a visual assessment of the membrane appearance after test against ASTM colour standards.

Another contamination problem is that of microbiological growth activity which can give rise to service troubles of various types. This problem can generally be avoided by the adoption of good housekeeping techniques by all concerned, but major incidents in recent years have led to the development of several microbiological monitoring tests for aviation fuel. In one of these fuel is filtered through a sterile membrane which is subsequently cultured for microbiological growths; other tests employ various techniques to detect the presence of viable microbiological matter but none of the tests have yet been standardised.

Free water in jet fuels can be detected by the use of a variety of field test kits developed over the years by major oil companies and which generally rely on colour changes produced when chemicals go into aqueous solution. The most commonly used of these simple test kits are the Esso Hydro-Kit, the Mobil Moisture Indicator and the Shell Water Detector; these kits provide only a qualitative indication or at best a low precision quantitative result and none have been covered by standard test methods. A further test device, the Aquaglow, appears capable of more precise quantitative results (whilst sacrificing test simplicity) and is under evaluation by ASTM as a possible standard test method. The total water content of aviation fuels (free and dissolved water) can be determined by means of the Karl Fischer titration method (ASTM D1744) but the basic method has inadequate precision and various improvements have been proposed by the individual users to obtain more useful results.

These contamination control tests are not yet directly covered in most specifications except by the broad 'Suitability' clause and represent areas where the spirit, rather than the letter, of the specification prevails.

(c) Density and heat of combustion

These are very important properties when applied to jet fuel as they control the total energy content of a fuel uplift on a weight and/or volume basis. Variation in specific gravity is controlled within broad limits because it dictates the setting and calibration of engine fuel metering equipment and hence proper engine control. Both fuel specific gravity and calorific value vary somewhat according to crude source, paraffinic fuels having a slightly lower specific gravity but higher gravimetric calorific value than those from naphthenic crudes. On a volume basis (Btu/gallon), naphthenic fuels have, however, superior calorific values. The relative importance of energy content on a weight or volume basis depends on the design and flight pattern of an aircraft, which may be weight or volume limited in its fuel load.

Certain civil specifications include a volumetric calorific value clause but the specified value must be chosen carefully if the fuel is to be procured on a world-wide basis from various crude sources. (*See* also Section on Aviation Gasoline, 3 (c) and (d).)

(d) Volatility

Volatility is one of the more obvious differences between kerosine and wide-cut jet fuels which have typical boiling ranges of 150–250°C (300–480°F) and 50–250°C (120–480°F) respectively. The low volatility requirements for kerosine are controlled by flash point and by a small number of distillation test points (ASTM D86–IP 123). The wide-cut fuels have a volatility intermediate between aviation gasoline and kerosine, and are controlled by distillation tests and Reid vapour pressure (ASTM D323 or IP 69). The overall effect of the volatility tests is to give a reasonable compromise between safety, combustion efficiency and fuel availability.

The 10, 20, 50 and 90 per cent distillation points are specified in various ways to ensure that a properly balanced fuel is produced with no undue proportion of light or heavy fractions. The distillation end point excludes any heavy material which would give poor fuel vaporisation and ultimately affect engine combustion performance.

The flashpoint test is a guide to the fire hazard associated with the fuel and in a number of countries is (or was) also used as a basis for defining the revenue duty or taxation class of the fuel (e.g. to differentiate between high tax gasolines and low tax diesel fuels or kerosine). It can be determined by several test methods and the results are not always strictly comparable. The minimum flash point in British military specifications is usually defined by the Abel method (IP 170), except for high flash kerosine, where the Pensky–Martens method (ASTM D93–IP 34) is specified. The ASTM and IATA specifications use the TAG method (ASTM D56) for both the minimum and maximum limits, whilst certain US military specifications also give minimum limits by the Pensky–Martens method (ASTM D93–IP 34). As indicated above, the various methods can yield different numerical results and in the case of the two most commonly used methods (Abel and TAG) it has been found that the former (IP 170) can give results up to 3–5°F (2–3°C) lower than the latter method (ASTM D56). Recently, increasing interest has centred on the use of the Setaflash tester (originally intended as a go–no go field tester, but apparently capable of equal or even better precision than certain of the standard methods) and this is now covered by a proposed IP method. Another proposed IP method covers flash point tests using any standard closed cup apparatus (Abel, Pensky–Martens or TAG) and these new methods may eventually replace the existing standards.

(e) Low temperature properties

Jet fuels must have acceptable freezing point and low temperature pumpability characteristics so that adequate fuel flow to the engine is maintained during long cruise periods at high altitude. The freezing point test (ASTM D2386–IP 16) and its associated specification limits guard against the possibility of solidified hydrocarbons (wax) separating from chilled fuel and blocking fuel lines, filters, nozzles, etc. An alternative method of defining the low temperature pumpability limits of jet fuel (cold flow test IP 217) has been considered in recent years but it will probably not replace the freezing point criterion which gives an adequate safety margin in practice.

The viscosity (ASTM D445–IP 71) of fuels at low temperature is limited to ensure that adequate fuel flow and pressure are maintained under all operating conditions and that fuel injection nozzles and system controls will operate down to design temperature conditions. Viscosity can significantly affect the lubricating property of the fuel and can have an influence on fuel pump service life.

(f) Combustion quality

Jet fuels of the same class can vary widely in their burning quality as measured by carbon deposition, smoke formation and flame radiation. This quality aspect is largely a function of hydrocarbon composition since paraffins have excellent burning properties in contrast to those of the aromatics (particularly the heavy polynuclear types); naphthenes have intermediate combustion characteristics nearer to those of the paraffins. As a control measure the smoke point test (ASTM D1322 or IP 57) for illuminating kerosine was written into the British kerosine specifications and gives the maximum smokeless flame height in millimetres at which the fuel will burn in a wick-fed lamp under prescribed conditions. The combustion performance of wide-cut fuels correlates well with smoke point when a fuel volatility factor is included, since carbon formation tends to increase with boiling point. A minimum smoke volatility index (SVI) value is specified and is defined as SVI = Smoke Point + 0·42 (per cent distilled below 204°C: 400°F).

The smoke point test is not universally accepted as a completely reliable criterion of combustion performance and various alternative laboratory test methods have previously been specified such as the lamp burning test (ASTM D187 or IP 10) and a limit on the polynuclear aromatic content (ASTM D1840). However, the alternative test now generally accepted is the lumino-meter number (ASTM D1740) which was developed because certain designs of jet engine may experience a shortened combustion chamber life due to high liner temperatures caused by the radiant heat from luminous flames from certain qualities of fuel. The test apparatus is essentially a smoke point lamp modified to include a photoelectric cell for flame radiation measurement and a thermocouple arrangement to measure temperature rise across the flame. Fuel luminometer number (LN) is expressed on an arbitrary scale on which values of 0 to 100 are given to reference fuels tetralin and isooctane respectively.

(g) Water retention and separating properties

Because of their higher density and viscosity, jet fuels tend to retain fine particulate matter and water droplets in suspension for a much longer time than aviation gasoline.

Jet fuels can also vary considerably in their tendency to pick up and retain water droplets or to hold fine water hazes in suspension depending on the presence of trace surface active impurities (surfactants). Some of these materials (such as sulphonic and naphthenic acids and their sodium salts) may originate from the crude source or from certain refinery treating processes, whilst others may be picked up by contact with other products during transportation to the airfield, particularly in multi-product pipelines. These latter materials may be natural contaminants from other less highly refined products (*e.g.* burning oils) or may consist of additives from motor gasolines (such as glycol type anti-icing agents). It should be noted that some of the additives specified for jet fuel use (*e.g.* corrosion inhibitors and static dissipator additive) also have surface active properties.

The presence of surfactants can also impair the performance of the water separating equipment (filter/separators) widely used throughout fuel handling systems to remove the traces of free (undissolved) water, particularly at the later stages prior to delivery to aircraft. Very small traces of free water can adversely affect jet engine and aircraft operations in several ways, and the water retention and separating properties of jet fuels have become a critical quality consideration in recent years.

The standard water reaction test (ASTM D1094 or IP 289) is the same as for aviation gasolines, but the interface and separation ratings are more critically defined. Test assessment is by subjective visual observation and, whilst quite precise when made by an experienced operator, the test can cause rating difficulties under border-line conditions. As a consequence a more objective test is now included in many specifications, known as the Water Separometer Test (ASTM D2550).

In this test, fuel is mechanically mixed with a small quantity of water and the resulting emulsion is passed through a miniature water coalescing pad and then through a settling chamber followed by a photo-electric device which measures the clarity of the effluent fuel. A good fuel, which has shed easily the entrained water, has a high rating or Water Separometer Index-Modified (WSIM) on a numerical scale directly related to the percentage of light transmission. This test has already undergone several changes (hence the inclusion of 'modified' in the title) and is widely recognised as being far from ideal for a number of reasons, but at present represents the only available standard method for controlling this particular fuel property. A new test apparatus known as the Mini-Sonic Separometer has recently been developed which incorporates all the fundamental features of the standard water separometer but is greatly simplified and 'miniaturised' and is in fact portable for field use. This apparatus, which produces a satisfactory test result much quicker and on a much smaller fuel sample, is now under evaluation by ASTM as a possible replacement for the standard WSIM test.

The portable nature of this 'Mini-WSIM' makes it particularly attractive, as surfactant problems often arise at airfield locations remote from major laboratory test facilities and there is often a real need for an on-the-spot diagnostic tool which can be used for check-testing in the field to help locate a source of contamination, etc. A number of other tests have been developed over the years, both as refinery control tests and as field tests, to help combat recurring surfactant problems. Among these have been various Interfacial Tension (IFT) Methods, the Kerosine Surfactant Test and the Haze Light Transmission Test, both developed in the USA, and the Water Retention Test developed by a European oil company. A commercially developed apparatus, the Millipore Surfactometer, has also been widely used, but as with all these tests it has proved very difficult to achieve a high degree of precision or to establish reliable correlations between the different test methods. More recently growing interest has been shown in the Constant Volume Drop Time Test (CVDT) developed by a US oil company, which is a basic IFT technique (pendant drop method) taking into account the time variable nature of surfactant effects at an interface and capable of automatic and semi-continuous use on flowing pipeline streams.

(h) Thermal stability

Although the conventional (storage) stability of aviation fuel has long been defined and controlled by the existent and accelerated gum tests, another test is required to measure the stability of a fuel to the thermal stresses which can arise during sustained supersonic flight and in some high-subsonic applications. In high speed flight, the fuel is subjected to considerable heat input due to kinetic heating of the airframe and also to the use of the bulk fuel as a coolant for engine oil, hydraulic and air conditioning equipment etc. Consequently, fuel for supersonic flight must perform satisfactorily at temperatures up to about 250°C (480°F) without formation of lacquer and deposits which can adversely affect the efficiency of heat exchangers, metering devices, fuel filters and injector nozzles. The initial problem was that of reduced overhaul life in military engines due to high fuel system temperatures upstream of the injector nozzles giving rise to deposit formation.

Research on the problem led to the development of the ASTM–CRC Fuel Coker (ASTM D1660–IP 197) as a laboratory test apparatus for assessing the tendency of jet fuels to deposit thermal decomposition products in fuel systems. Fuel is pumped through a preheater tube assembly representing fuel/oil heat exchange systems and then through a sintered stainless steel filter representing nozzles and fine orifices where fuel degradation products could become trapped. Fuel degradation is assessed in terms of pressure drop across the filter and visual preheater tube deposit condition (rated numerically in accordance with ASTM colour standards).

A research fuel coker has also been developed, which has provision for the test fuel to be thermally soaked (simulating bulk fuel stored during sustained supersonic flight) prior to passage through a standard fuel coker test section. So far this modified test has not been standardised by ASTM, but a test of this nature could come into increasing use in the future. Table 9 summarises the test temperatures specified for various US military jet fuel grades and illustrates how these have gradually become more stringent to meet the fuel requirements of new very high performance aircraft. In most cases the test limits (*e.g.* tube rating 3 maximum and filter pressure drop maximum 3 in Hg) are the same, although some civil specifications are currently less restrictive. However, among the disadvantages of the ASTM–CFR fuel coker are the need for a large fuel sample and the relatively poor precision of the test. A study was recently carried out to evaluate possible replacement tests and the new Alcor JFTOT apparatus (jet fuel thermal oxidation tester) has now been selected. This uses less than 1 litre of fuel (5 US gallons previously

TABLE 9

Thermal stability test conditions

Fuel coker conditions (5 hr at 6 lb/hr fuel flow)		US Military grade applicability
Preheater (T°F) (°C)	Filter (T°F) (°C)	
300 (149)	400 (204)	JP-4, JP-5, JP-8[a]
400 (204)	500 (260)	MIL-F-25524A ⎱
450 (232)	550 (288)	MIL-T-25524B ⎰ thermally stable kerosine
425 (221)	525 (276)	JP-6
500 (260)	600 (316)	JP-7 (research coker, with fuel reservoir temperature 300°F (149°C)

[a] Also applies to British and other international specifications for standard jet fuel grades.

required) and initial indications are that the precision (repeatability/reproducibility) is at least twice as good as with the CFR fuel coker. The fundamental principles of the test apparatus remain unchanged, but a number of new features have been introduced to help achieve the desired improvement. A standard test method written around the new JFTOT apparatus is now being finalised for early publication by ASTM and will be introduced progressively into US military jet fuel specifications and eventually into most others.

(i) Miscellaneous properties
A few specifications for some of the lesser used fuel grades call for special tests not generally applied to aviation fuels (*e.g.* the Explosiveness Test for JP-5 jet fuel—Federal Test Method 1151) but these tests have a very limited application. The colour of jet fuels is another property which is now rarely specified by test method. It is usually required to be 'colourless' or 'water white', but a few specifications require it to meet colour limits by the Saybolt Method (ASTM D156). In the past jet fuel colour has also been specified by the Lovibond Method (IP 17), as currently used for the colour of dyed aviation gasolines (although colour 'by inspection' is generally considered adequate in most cases).

Test methods are also included in some specifications for electrical conductivity (ASTM D2624 or IP 274) and for the content of some additives (*see* Section on Additives below).

AVIATION FUEL ADDITIVES

1. GENERAL

Only a limited number of additives are permitted in aviation fuels and for each fuel grade the type and concentration are closely controlled by the appropriate fuel specifications. Additives may be included for a variety of reasons, but in every case the specifications define the requirements as follows:

Mandatory: Must be present between given minimum and maximum limits.

Permitted: May be added by fuel manufacturer choice up to a maximum limit.

Optional: May be added only with agreement of user/purchaser, within specified limits.

Not allowed: Additives not listed in specifications are not permitted.

In the case of aviation gasolines there is little significant variation in the types and concentrations of additives normally present in each standard grade, but considerable variations occur in the additive content of jet fuels, depending on whether they are for civil or military use and on the country of origin. Table 10 summarises the most usual additive content of aviation fuels on a world-wide basis (except for Russian grades) but many exceptions occur and reference to the appropriate specifications should be made to establish the precise requirements.

TABLE 10

Summary of usual additive requirements for British and US aviation fuels

Additive	Aviation gasoline	Civil jet fuels	Military jet fuels
Colour dyes	Mandatory	None	None
Tetraethyl lead	Permitted	None	None
Anti-oxidant	Mandatory	Permitted[a]	Permitted[a]
Metal-deactivator	None	Permitted	Permitted
Corrosion inhibitor	Normally none[b]	None	Mandatory
Fuel system icing inhibitor	None	By special request only	Mandatory
Static dissipator	None[c]	Optional (by user)[d]	Optional (by user)[d]

[a] Mandatory in British jet fuels produced by hydrogen treating processes.

[b] Not allowed by British gasoline specification. Permitted at user option in US military gasoline specification, not by civil gasoline specifications.

[c] Permitted in Canadian aviation gasoline.

[d] Usually included in civil jet fuels outside of USA and in British military jet fuels. Not permitted in US military jet fuels.

2. Additive Types

The following Sections describe the aviation fuel additives in current use, but no attempt is made to list fully all the various chemical and trade names of the approved materials as these are all detailed in the appropriate specifications.

(a) Tetraethyl lead (TEL)

This material is used widely to improve the anti-knock characteristics of aviation gasolines (*see* Section on Aviation Gasoline 3(a)) and maximum specification limits are established for each grade of fuel. TEL is not permitted in jet fuels.

The additive is incorporated into gasoline fuels by the addition of Ethyl Fluid ('Octel' Anti-knock Compound) which incorporates both TEL and an appropriate amount of ethylene dibromide lead scavenger. Aviation Compound also includes a blue dye, plus a small amount of kerosine and impurities. The maximum amount of TEL permitted in any aviation gasoline grade is 4·6 ml/US gal, but most grades have much lower limits.

TEL is also available as Motor Compound, identified by an orange dye and incorporating both ethylene dibromide and ethylene dichloride lead scavengers; Motor Compound is not permitted in aviation gasolines. During recent years the use of TEL in motor gasoline has been supplemented by the use of TML (tetramethyl lead) but this material is not currently permitted in aviation gasolines.

(b) Colour dyes

Dyes are used to identify the different grades of leaded aviation gasoline (*see* Table 1) and the required colours are achieved by the addition of various combinations of up to three special anthraquinone-based and azo dyes (blue, yellow and red). The amounts permitted are controlled between closely specified limits to obtain the desired fuel colours (ASTM D2392 or IP 17).

Dyes are not permitted in jet fuels.

(c) Anti-oxidant (gum inhibitor)

Anti-oxidant additive is mandatory in aviation gasolines to prevent the formation of gum and the precipitation of lead compounds. The additive concentration is closely controlled by specification, usually between 19·1 and 24·0 mg/litre.

Jet fuels are inherently more stable than gasolines and the use of anti-oxidants is permitted but not mandatory in most cases. However, it was established some years ago that jet fuels which are hydrogen treated (or produced by a 'hydrogen process') tend to generate a high peroxide content, which can cause rapid deterioration of nitrile rubber fuel system components. This is due to the removal of most of the naturally occurring inhibiting materials (trace sulphur compounds) by the very effective hydrogen-desulphur-ising treatment, and to combat this problem the British military specifications make the use of anti-oxidant mandatory in the case of these hydrogen treated jet fuels. A maximum permitted limit of 24·0 mg/litre usually applies for all jet fuels, with a minimum of 8·6 mg/litre when the additive is made mandatory.

A wide range of anti-oxidants or gum inhibitors are approved, although the chemical types permitted vary under different specifications. These additives are generally phenolic or nitrogen-containing materials and most approved types are manufactured under several trade names, such as Topanol. It should be noted that the British specifications do not approve certain of the phenylene diamine type additives allowed by US Military specifications.

(d) Metal deactivator
The use of one approved metal deactivator (N,N′-disalicylidene-1,2-propane diamine) is permitted in jet fuels but not in aviation gasoline. The purpose of this additive is to passify certain metallic materials which may be present in jet fuels, some of which can degrade by catalytic action the storage stability (gum forming tendency) or thermal stability of the fuel. Metallic copper is the worst of these materials and metal deactivator is normally only used in fuels on which a copper sweetening process has been used to remove mer-captans etc. in order to convert any trace metal carry over to inert copper chelates. In British specifications the copper content of such fuels (IP 225) is strictly limited by specification.

Trace iron compounds can also degrade the thermal stability of jet fuels to a minor degree and the use of metal deactivator as a thermal stability improver is now under consideration, to combat the possible adverse effects of handling jet fuels through unlined steel pipelines, etc.

(e) Corrosion inhibitors
Corrosion inhibitors are intended basically to minimise corrosive rusting of steel pipelines, tanks, etc., in contact with fuels and traces of water often unavoidably present from time to time. A direct consequence of their use is a reduction in the amount of scale and fine rust shed into the fuel as particulate contaminant.

Whilst fuel soluble corrosion inhibitors have been used in some specification fuels for many years, it has been established more recently that certain of these additives can improve significantly the 'lubricity' properties of jet fuels, i.e. can help to overcome problems involving excessive friction, rapid component wear or seizure sometimes encountered in certain fuel pumps and other fuel system components. These problems, which are far from fully understood, are largely of a metallurgical nature and can often be avoided by a change of component materials, but appear to be aggravated by the use of fuels having poor lubricating, anti-friction or load carrying properties (defined loosely as 'lubricity'). No single reliable test for measuring this property has yet been devised. Experimental studies indicate that poorer lubricity is generally exhibited by the lower viscosity fuels (*e.g.* wide-cut jet fuel) and in many cases by hydrotreated fuels (due to removal of certain polar compounds during the treating process), but some 'wet treated' kerosine type jet fuels also exhibit poor lubricity.

In view of the foregoing the specification requirements for fuel soluble corrosion inhibitors have varied considerably during recent years, with the additive being introduced for quite different reasons in different specifications and with fuel users often superimposing their own special requirements or restrictions on the basic specification content. As a general guide, it can be taken that US military jet fuels always require the addition of an approved corrosion inhibitor (*see* below) and that British military jet fuels also generally have to include this additive, primarily as a lubricity improver. Civil jet fuels, wide-cut or kerosine type (even when quoted against a basic military specification), normally must not contain corrosion inhibitor although occasional special user requests are made for inclusion of the additive as a lubricity improver.

A number of proprietary fuel soluble corrosion inhibitors are available, mostly of American manufacture, and the basic approval list is presented as a Qualified Products List (QPL-25017) of materials satisfying the requirements of the US military specification MIL-I-25017. This document includes for each approved additive, the minimum and relative effective concentrations together with the maximum allowable concentration (different for each additive type). However, most of these additives can exhibit some undesirable side effects under certain circumstances (including effects on the water separating properties (WSIM), electrical conductivity and thermal stability, particularly in the presence of other additive types) and there is a general reluctance by both manufacturers and fuel consumers to permit the use of additive types which have not been thoroughly proved in service, despite their type test laboratory approval.

In practice, the most commonly used fuel soluble corrosion inhibitor is Santolene C (now known as Hitec E-515) which is specifically called for by most US military purchasing authorities on the basis of long term experience and is the only type approved in the appropriate British military specifications, since it is the only additive type known to be an effective lubricity improver, for which purpose some civil fuel users also request it. Both Santolene C and a more concentrated version Santolene CM (Hitec E-534) contain linoleic acid and phosphate materials, and it is the undesirable presence of the latter (due to possible corrosive effects on hot engine parts) which has led to a lower addition level being given in the British military specifications (and by British aero engine manufacturers) than that permitted by the US military QPL (*e.g.* maximum about 12 mg/litre against 45 mg/litre). In fact the additive content of US military fuels is often limited in much the same way, depending on circumstances.

There are other additives on the QPL list, but none of these is very widely used in jet fuels; currently the most important of these others are probably

Du Pont AFA-1 (also a phosphate based material) and Tretolite Tolad 244/245 (carboxylic acid based), although Apollo PRI-19 (an acid ester) is now attracting some attention on a cost effectiveness basis. All the approved fuel soluble corrosion inhibitors are chemically similar to the above.

Some mention must also be made of water soluble corrosion inhibitors. To overcome corrosion problems in long distance pipelines, often carrying a variety of 'white' petroleum products as well as aviation fuels, the use of a corrosion inhibitor is generally desirable. Where the use of a fuel soluble corrosion inhibitor is not permitted in the aviation fuel shipments it is often possible to achieve adequate overall pipeline protection by including such an additive in some of the less stringently controlled non-aviation products (*e.g.* motor gasoline or domestic kerosine) provided additive pick-up by the aviation fuels can be kept to a negligible level. In other cases, it has been found more convenient to use a water soluble corrosion inhibitor, which will eventually settle or be separated from the fuels without conflicting in any way with the specification quality requirements. A material known as SCIP (Shell Corrosion Inhibitor for Pipelines) consisting of an aqueous solution of sodium nitrite and caustic soda added at about 1 gallon to 100 000 gallons of fuel, has been quite widely used for this purpose, usually with injection only into non-aviation fuels but in some cases in jet fuels also. However, the use of SCIP and similar water soluble materials is now becoming much less common due to its tendency to promote surfactant type water separating problems.

(f) Fuel system icing inhibitor (anti-icing additive)

This additive was introduced originally to overcome fuel system icing problems encountered by US military aircraft. Unlike most commercial aircraft and many British military aircraft, which have their main fuel filters heated to prevent blockage by ice formed from water precipitated from fuels in flight, USAF aircraft have no such protection and icing of filters and other fuel system components caused a number of accidents prior to 1960. Fuel system icing inhibitor (FSII) prevents these problems by lowering the freezing point of any water present in the fuel to such a degree that no ice formation can occur. The additive has only a limited solubility in fuel and has a much greater affinity for water; with the normally specified concentration of 0·10–0·15 per cent present in fuel, the additive partitions rapidly into any water present to give concentrations of up to 40 per cent in the water phase, depending on the temperature and relative amounts of fuel and water present (the lower the temperature and the less water present, the higher the additive concentration and the greater the anti-freeze protection).

FSII is a mandatory requirement in most US military fuels and has become standard also in most fuels used by British military aircraft and by many other military users, especially those covered by NATO or SEATO standardisation agreements. FSII now consists of a pure material ethylene glycol monomethyl ether (EGME), known also as methyl cellosolve, methyl oxitol, methyl glycol and 2-methoxyethanol by various chemical manufacturers. It is covered by the British military specification D Eng RD 2451 and the US military specification MIL-I-27686; when first developed (as 'Prist' or Phillips fuel additive PFA 55MB) a percentage of glycerol was included to prevent the deterioration of certain types of fuel tank linings, but this component caused solubility problems and was finally found to be unnecessary, so the glycerol has been deleted from the latest issues of both specifications.

Shortly after introducing the wide-spread use of FSII to combat icing problems, the USAF experienced a great reduction in the number of microbiological contamination problems being encountered in bolt aircraft tanks and in ground handling facilities; studies subsequently confirmed that this improvement was due primarily to the biocidal nature of the new additive. It is now generally accepted that the EGME component of the original additive is a very effective biostat if used continuously in jet fuels and a number of aircraft manufacturers now recommend the use of EGME (methyl cellosolve) in fuel supplies to combat microbiological contamination and resultant corrosion problems. The eventual use of FSII in British military jet fuels was in fact introduced more to help combat certain microbiological problems than to conform to NATO standardisation, since many RAF aircraft still have fuel heaters fitted and therefore do not really need an anti-icing additive.

Commercial aircraft are with minor exceptions provided with fuel heaters and have no requirement for an anti-icing additive, particularly in view of the relatively high cost which would be involved. A few turbine powered helicopters and corporate aircraft are not provided with fuel heaters, to save weight, but in most cases the operators make their own arrangements to inject EGME into the aircraft fuel supplies when necessary. Several Russian manufactured jet airliners are also not fitted with fuel heaters and special arrangements have sometimes to be made to provide fuel containing an anti-icing additive for these aircraft, particularly on long-haul flights. Domestically these aircraft use fuels containing a Russian anti-icing additive (believed to be ethyl cellosolve) but elsewhere the standard methyl cellosolve (EGME) material is generally accepted if supplies can be arranged.

Operators of some types of civil aircraft in certain tropical areas may also occasionally require fuel containing FSII purely for its biocidal properties and local arrangements are then made to inject the additive at the airfield prior to fuelling the aircraft. Whilst special situations such as those mentioned above may arise, there is no normal requirement for civil jet fuels to contain FSII, either as an anti-icing or as a biocide additive.

(g) Static dissipator (anti-static additive)
Static dissipator additives can be used to increase the electrical conductivity of hydrocarbon fuels in order to promote a more rapid relaxation of any static charges built up during movement of the fuel. The hazards of static

generation leading to high energy spark discharges capable of igniting flammable fuel/air mixtures are greatly enhanced in the case of modern jet fuels due to their extreme purity (and hence very low natural conductivity), the high pumping velocities employed and the wide-spread use of micro-filtration equipment, capable of producing a high rate of electrical charge separation and static build-up in the flowing fuel.

British military jet fuel specifications permit the optional use of a static dissipator additive, by agreement between supplier and user, but US military specifications do not at present permit its use. The additive is also optional in the IATA and ASTM D1655 specifications for civil jet fuels and in some other national specifications; in Canada it is mandatory in jet fuels and is permitted even in aviation gasoline, since the hazards of static discharges have been found to be particularly severe under very low ambient temperature conditions.

Only one additive type is currently approved for use in aviation fuels, Shell Anti-static additive ASA-3, which comprises a mixture of equal parts of the chromium salt of an alkylated salicylic acid (chromium AC), calcium didecyl sulpho succinate (calcium aerosol) and a vinyl/methacrylate copolymer (Alkadine). In non-aviation fuels, other additives such as Ethyl DCA 48 (Mobil RT 748C) are sometimes used. When required, a maximum add rate of 1 mg/litre of ASA-3 is permitted in jet fuels, but a strict control is placed upon the resulting conductivity of the fuel (ASTM D2624 or IP 274). The limits generally applied are 50 to 300 pico-siemens/metre at the prevailing temperature and only about 0·6 mg/litre (ppm) of additive is usually required to produce a target conductivity of about 200 pico-siemens/metre (or 200 CU—conductivity units) in a base fuel with a natural conductivity of about 1–5 CU. In the case of British military jet fuels containing also Hitec E-515 (Santolene C) corrosion inhibitor it has been found that due to a synergetic effect higher conductivities can result from the use of both additive types in some base fuels and a higher maximum conductivity limit of 500 CU is then specified. Since both of these additives are of a surface active nature (weak surfactants) the specified water separatometer (WSIM) limits are also relaxed when either or both additives are present.

Static Dissipator Additive (ASA-3) is normally added to the majority of civil jet fuels produced by major international oil companies outside of the USA, although there are a number of exceptions to this situation; it is also present in most supplies of British military jet fuels. The additive is not permitted in jet fuels for use by the US military and is presently only used on a limited and experimental basis in civil jet fuels at a few locations within the USA, although this situation could well change in the future.

(h) Non-specification additives

Whilst no additives except those mentioned above are approved under any current fuel specifications, there are a few other additive materials which are sometimes used for special purposes by individual arrangements. Only one of these (Biobor JF biocide additive) has any significant usage in commercially operated aircraft, but several merit mention.

(i) *Biobor JF*
This additive consisting of mixed dioxaborinanes is intended to prevent microbiological growth in hydrocarbon fuels. After extensive use in railway diesel fuels, etc. had established its effectiveness and lack of troublesome side effects, several major airlines and other jet fuel users adopted use of the additive to help control microbiological contamination problems arising in certain locations. As a result of further satisfactory experience, use of Biobor JF has during recent years become increasingly common and most engine and airframe manufacturers have now given it limited approval on an intermittent or non-continuous use basis up to a concentration of 270 ppm (20 ppm elemental boron). These approvals are covered by manufacturer's Service Bulletins or Notices to Operators and do not appear in standard fuel specifications, since they relate only to the fuel and additive use in specific types of aircraft and aero-engines and generally impose special operating restrictions.

Biobor JF is normally used at the 270 ppm level to 'disinfect' aircraft during a period of several days standing filled or partially filled with doped fuel; the fuel is then used in the normal manner, although in some cases it may be drained off or diluted with undoped fuel before being burnt through the engines. This treatment is only permitted at infrequent intervals to minimise the possible deposition of boron compounds in the engines.

The continuous or routine use of Biobor JF at a maximum concentration of 135 ppm is permitted in some aero engines, but this practice is almost never adopted.

Biobor JF may be considered as a competitor to Fuel System Icing Inhibitor (EGME) in respect of its biocidal properties (*see* above) and some anti-icing properties are also claimed for Biobor JF, but these have not been substantiated. Military jet fuels normally contain FSII as a dual purpose additive and there is therefore little military interest in the use of Biobor JF, but it offers a very convenient and effective form of 'Shock Treatment' to combat microbiological contamination arising in commercial aircraft pending more long term action to eradicate the problem.

(ii) *Anti-smoke additives*
Whilst the generation of excessive exhaust smoke by jet engines is primarily an engine combustion chamber design problem some reduction in smoke density on some engines may be possible by the use of certain additives. Among these are Ethyl CI2 and Lubrizol 565; the former is approved by one major engine manufacturer for post overhaul test cell operation of engines for up to 3 hours, but neither is approved for flight use. Limited military flight trials have however been carried out on several anti-smoke additives and they have also been used with some success in special prototype aircraft.

(iii) *Ignition control additive* (*gasoline engines*)
To minimise the adverse effects of spark plug deposits in gasoline engines several phosphorus containing additives have been developed and these are widely used in motor gasoline fuels. Typical of these are tricresyl phosphate (TCP) or tritolyl phosphate (TTP) which act by modifying the lead deposits so that they do not cause pre-ignition. Certain older types of aircraft piston engines suffered badly from spark plug fouling and the use of TCP/TTP was introduced by some users to help overcome the problem (concentrate usually added direct to the aircraft fuel tanks) and manufacturers' approval was given for this practice where appropriate. This problem, however, diminished as these engines were withdrawn from wide-spread service and also as the permitted alkyl lead (TEL) content of aviation gasoline was gradually reduced over the years. It is now very doubtful whether this additive is still in use in any piston type aero-engines.

3. ADDITIVE TEST METHODS

Whilst the type and amount of each additive permitted in aviation fuels are strictly limited, test methods for checking the concentration present are not specified in every case. In some cases tests to determine the additive content (or its effect) are called for, but in other cases a written statement of its original addition (*e.g.* at the refinery) is accepted as adequate evidence of its presence. The following relates to the various approved additives discussed above.

In aviation gasolines, the tetraethyl lead (TEL) content has such a critical influence on the anti-knock properties (Octane Rating) and also on the deposit forming tendency of the fuel that a test for TEL content (ASTM D526–IP 96 or IP 116) is included in all routine laboratory tests. After the specified amounts of colour dyes have been added to aviation gasolines the colour is normally only checked visually (by inspection), although the Lovibond method (IP 17) and Federal Test Method 103 are quoted in specifications.

After the required amounts of anti-oxidant, metal deactivator or corrosion inhibitor have been added to aviation fuels it is not normal to carry out any checks on the concentrations and no test methods are included in specifications for this purpose. Occasionally a need arises to determine the amount of corrosion inhibitor remaining in a fuel (it can be consumed in providing the corrosion inhibiting action in pipelines, etc.) and several analytical methods have been developed, none of which has yet been standardised.

Fuel system icing inhibitor used in jet fuels can be lost by evaporation and is also lost rapidly into any water which may contact the fuel during transportation. Routine checks have therefore to be made on the FSII content of the fuel, right up to the point of delivery to aircraft in some instances. The usual 'referee' test for FSII content is an iodometric titration method applied to a water extract (IP 277 Method C or Federal Test Method 5327) but for routine test purposes a simpler colorimetric version of this test is commonly used (IP 277 method D or Federal Test Method 5330). Some specifications also permit use of a refractometer method (Federal Test Method 5340), also applied to a water extract. Several other methods are available although not yet incorporated into specifications, including an infra-red spectrophotometric method (IP 277 method A) carried out on the fuel and a gas chromatographic method (IP 277 Method B) carried out on a water extract. Other methods have also been proposed, including alternative titration and refractive index methods and freeze point measurements on water extracts.

As static dissipator additive (ASA-3) is used in such small concentrations (less than 1 ppm) it is extremely difficult to detect by any standard analytical technique and its presence is therefore controlled by measuring the resulting electrical conductivity of the fuel. The standard methods (ASTM D2624 or IP 274) are basically 'field' tests employing an immersible conductivity cell and field meter (Maihak meter or similar type) intended for measuring the conductivity of fuel at rest in storage tanks, etc.; it can also be used in a laboratory on fuel samples, but errors can result if the samples are drawn or stored in unsuitable containers. The Conductivity Meter Method is intended primarily for use on fuels containing static dissipator additive and therefore of relatively high conductivity; more precise laboratory methods capable of measuring accurately the very low conductivity levels of undoped fuels are under development and should soon be standardised.

APPENDIX I

AUTOMOTIVE (MOTOR) GASOLINE —UNSUITABILITY FOR AVIATION USE

Differences in the properties and composition of motor gasoline and aviation gasoline makes the former unsafe for use in aircraft. The main differences between automotive and aircraft gasoline fuels are as follows:

(a) automotive fuels have a wider distillation range than aircraft fuels and this promotes poor distribution of the high anti-knock components of the fuel. Further, the octane ratings of automotive and aircraft fuel are not comparable due to the different test methods used to rate the two types of fuel. This would result in an appreciable difference in actual anti-knock performance for two fuels which have the same apparent octane number. This difference could lead to destructive pre-ignition or detonation;

(b) automotive fuels are more volatile and have higher vapour pressures which can lead to vapour lock. This greater volatility can also increase the fire hazard;

(c) the anti-knock compound (tetraethyl lead) used in automotive fuels contains an excess of chlorine and bromine whereas for aviation fuels it contains only the chemically correct amount of bromine. Chlorine compounds are very corrosive and under severe conditions can lead to exhaust valve failures.

(d) automotive fuels do not have as high a long term stability as aviation gasoline and can form gum deposits, which can result in valve sticking and poor mixture distribution;

(e) automotive fuels have solvent characteristics which are not suitable for aircraft engines. Seals, gaskets and flexible fuel lines may be attacked;

(f) the testing and quality protection measures applied to automotive gasoline are far less stringent than those for aviation fuels, so that there is a much greater possibility of contamination occurring and less possibility of it being detected.

Appendices II and III follow

APPENDIX II

AVIATION FUEL QUALITY REQUIREMENTS FOR JOINTLY OPERATED SYSTEMS

A.   INTERNATIONAL AVIATION FUEL SPECIFICATIONS

Almost all supplies of aviation fuel used internationally by both civil and military aircraft outside of Eastern Europe, the Soviet Union and China have to meet minimum quality standards detailed in specifications issued by one or more of the following bodies:

1. American Society for Testing and Materials (ASTM Specifications, published annually in Part 17 of the Book of ASTM Standards).
2. International Air Transport Association (IATA Guidance Material, prepared by the Aviation Fuel Sub-Committee of the IATA Technical Committee);
3. Ministry of Defence (D Eng RD specifications issued by the Procurement Executive of the British Ministry of Defence);
4. United States Military Authorities (MIL Specifications, issued by the US Department of Defense).

These bodies issue specifications covering various types of aviation fuels for use in piston engines and/or turbine (jet) engines. In the case of aviation turbine engine fuels, only two of the jet fuel types covered are in wide-spread international use by both civil and military operators and in each case the various specifications covering the two basic types detail almost identical technical requirements (as a result of international co-operation and agreement over many years). A similar situation exists with aviation gasoline fuels for use in piston engines, although in this case a larger number of basic grades are in current use.

Aviation fuel specifications are also issued by a number of aero-engine manufacturers and by many national government authorities, but most of these are based on those prepared by one or other of the above international bodies (with very minor variations), or are virtually identical specifications issued merely under a national designation. The national government specifications of a few countries incorporate special requirements not covered by the four main standardisation bodies, but these specifications have only limited international application and their requirements can be met easily by the addition of a few appropriate tests, etc. in the local areas concerned.

In the case of countries in the Soviet zone of influence, aviation fuel specifications are generally based on the USSR State Standards (GOST specifications). The various fuel grades covered differ quite significantly from the nearest Western equivalents and they cannot be considered as common grades. Aircraft operators from these countries, however, normally accept uplifts of Jet A-1 and some Western grades of aviation gasoline and in most cases specify their fuel requirements in Western countries against one of the above international standards.

B.   PURPOSE

As indicated above, only a small number of basic aviation fuel types exist, although they are covered by numerous fuel specifications issued by various national and international bodies. In the case of jet fuels, only two basic grades are of international significance, the kerosine type and the wide-cut gasoline type, typified by the ASTM designations Jet A-1 and Jet B respectively. In the case of aviation gasolines, about five basic grades exist, but only two of these, Avgas 100/130 and grade 115/145, are widely used by major international operators.

The purpose of the attached document is to define the quality requirements for these four basic grades of aviation fuel, in such a manner that the most stringent requirements of each of the main international specifications are included. This will ensure that aviation fuels meeting these specified requirements will automatically be in full compliance with any or all of the commonly quoted official specifications relating to that particular grade (with any minor local exceptions necessary).

The four basic aviation fuel grades covered are as follows:

Jet Fuel: Jet A-1
Jet B
Aviation Gasoline: Grade 100/130
Grade 115/145

C. APPLICATION

The contents of the attached document may be used to define the quality requirements for aviation fuel grades to be delivered from one party to another under a variety of contractual arrangements. They may be used in particular to define fuel grade quality for the following purposes:

(a) for refinery manufacture, where local production is delivered to several independent marketing companies;
(b) for exchanges between independent oil companies;
(c) for deliveries made by independent suppliers into jointly operated airfield fuel storage facilities.

In the case of the jet fuel grades, these may for convenience be referred to as meeting 'Check List Quality' (*see* below).

D. FUEL QUALITY REQUIREMENTS

The detailed technical requirements for each of the four basic grades are presented in the attachments. The 'Aviation Fuel Quality Requirements for Jointly Operated Systems' attachment explains how the quality requirements are related to those included in the relevant international specifications. In particular, it shows what exceptions, if any, are necessary (to promote maximum international acceptability by civil aircraft operators) and also makes mandatory certain items (*e.g.* additive content) left optional in the standard specifications.

In the case of the two jet fuel grades, detailed 'Check Lists' are included which itemise fully the quality requirements for each grade, so that cross reference to the standard specifications (in particular the D Eng RD equivalents) is only necessary to obtain minor guidance on the use of test methods, etc. In the case of the two aviation gasoline grades covered, the basic British and American specifications are so similar that no separate 'Check List' is considered necessary.

The term 'Check List' is used as its purpose is to provide the receiving party with a document against which they can 'check off' the properties included in the delivery party's specification test report or certificate of quality, to ensure full compliance with the requirements.

AVIATION FUEL QUALITY REQUIREMENTS FOR JOINTLY OPERATED SYSTEMS*

1. JET FUEL—JET A-1, MEETING

(a) British Ministry of Defence Specification D Eng RD 2494 (Issue 7) of August, 1971 with the following exceptions:
Items 2 and 3 below;
(b) International Air Transport Association Guidance Material for Aviation Turbine Fuels, Kerosine Type Fuel, November, 1969 with the following exceptions:
Items 1, 2 and 3 below;
(c) ASTM Specification for Aviation Turbine Fuels D1655-70 Kerosine Type Jet A-1, with the following exceptions:
Items 1, 2, 3 and 4 below.

2. JET FUEL—JET B, MEETING

(a) British Ministry of Defence Specification D Eng RD 2486 (Issue 8) of August, 1971 with the following exceptions:
Items 2 and 3 below;
(b) American Military Specification for Wide-Cut Turbine Fuel JP-4 MIL-T-5264H of 30 October, 1970 and Amendment 1, 30 July, 1971, with the following exceptions:
Items 1, 2, 3, 5 and 6 below;
(c) International Air Transport Association Guidance Material for Aviation Turbine Fuels, Wide-Cut Type, November, 1969 with the following exceptions:
Items 1, 2 and 3 below.
(d) ASTM Specification for Aviation Turbine Fuels D1655-70, Jet B with the following exceptions:
Items 1, 2 and 3 below.

3. AVIATION GASOLINES, MEETING

(a) American Military Specification MIL-G-5572E of 24 July, 1969 grades 100/130 and 115/145 with the following exceptions:
Items 3 and 7 below;
(b) British Ministry of Technology Specification D Eng RD 2485 (Issue 6) of May, 1966 grades 100/130 and 115/145 with the following exceptions:
Item 7 below.

*Issue 5—September, 1971 Superseding Issue 4 of February, 1969.

EXCEPTIONS

1. Anti-oxidants, will be mandatory in hydrotreated fuels.
2. The use of anti-static additive will be permitted only by agreement of all Participants. Where it is used the WSIM limit is reduced to 70 min.
3. Corrosion inhibitor, will not be permitted, unless agreed by all Participants.
4. Flash point.
5. Fuel System Icing Inhibitor, will not be permitted.
6. Particulate matter clause.
7. TEL content will be limited to 3·0 ml/US gal (max.) for 100/130 grade, except where otherwise agreed by Participants.

Appendix II continues on next page

JOINT FUELLING SYSTEM CHECK LIST JET A—1*

Embodying the most stringent requirements of the following specifications:

(a) D Eng RD 2494 Issue 7 of August, 1971.
(b) IATA Guidance Material—Kerosine Type Fuel November, 1969.
(c) ASTM D1655-70. Kerosine Type Jet A-1

Test	Limits	Test method		Remarks
		IP	ASTM	
Specific gravity at 60°/60°F min. max.	0·775 0·830	160	D1298	—
Gravity API min. max.	39 51	—	D287	—
Distillation: Initial boiling point °C.	To be reported	123	D86	See note
Fuel recovered per cent vol. at 200°C (392°F) min.	20			
Fuel recovered				
10 per cent vol. at °C (°F) max.	204 (399)			
20 per cent vol. at °C	To be reported			
50 per cent vol. at °C (°F) max.	232 (450)			
90 per cent vol. at °C	To be reported			
End point °C (°F) max.	288 (550)			
Residue per cent vol. max.	1·5			
Loss per cent vol. max.	1·5			
Flash point °F (°C) min. max.	100 (38) 150 (66)	170 Method C	(D56) D56	—

* Issue 5—September 1971 Supersedes Issue 4—February, 1969.

Property	Value		Method	Note
Total sulphur per cent wt max.	0·20	107	D1266	—
Mercaptan sulphur per cent wt max.	0·001	104	D1219 or D1323	—
or Doctor Test max.	Negative	30	D484	—
Corrosion (copper) (2 hours at 100°C) (212°F) max.	Classification 1	154	D130	—
Corrosion (silver) max.	1	227	—	—
Smoke point mm min.	20	57	D1322	See note
Luminometer number min.	45	—	D1740	—
or Smoke point mm min.	25	—	D1322	—
or Smoke point mm max.	20 and Naphthalene of 3 per cent max. vol.	—	D1332 D1840	—
Net heat of combustion Btu/lb min.	18 400	12	D240	See note
or Aniline gravity product min.	5 250	193	D1405	See note
Existent gum mg/100 ml max.	7	131	D381	—
Total potential residue 16 hour mg/100 ml max.	14	138	D873	—
Freezing point °C (°F) max.	−50 (−58)	16	D2386	—
Total acidity mg KOH/g max.	0·012	273	—	—

continues

JOINT FUELLING SYSTEM CHECK LIST JET A—1—*continued*

Olefin content per cent vol. max.	5	156	D1319	—
Aromatics per cent vol. max.	20	156	D1319	—
Water reaction:			D1094	
Volume change ml max.	1			
Interface rating max.	1b			See note
Separation rating max.	2			
Water separometer index modified min.	85	—	D2550	See note
Viscosity at −30°F (34°C) cST max.	15·0	71	D445	—
Thermal stability:		197	D1660	Preheater temp 300°F (149°C) Filter temp 400°F(204°C) Fuel flow 6 lb/hr Duration 300 min
Change in pressure drop in 5 hours inches Hg max.	3			
Preheater deposit rating max.	Less than 3			
Copper content μg/kg max.	150	225		See note
Additives:			—	The type and concentration of all additives used including all additions to be shown in the quality documents.
Anti-oxidant mg/litre (mandatory in hydro treated fuels min. 8·6)	8·6–24·0			
Metal deactivator mg/litre (optional) max.	5·7			
ASA-3 mg/litre max. (can be permitted only by unanimous agreement of all participants),	1·0			
The electrical conductivity of the fuel shall be within the range of 50 to 300 pS/metre at point, time and temp. of delivery to purchaser if ASA-3 present.		274	D2624	

Note: Reference should be made to the appropriate notes in the British Ministry of Defence Specification D Eng RD 2494 Issue 7 of August, 1971.

JOINT FUELLING SYSTEM CHECK LIST JET B*

Embodying the most stringent requirements of the following specifications:

(a) D Eng RD 2486 Issue 8 of August, 1971.
(b) MIL-T-5624H (Grade JP4) of 30th October, 1970, and Amendment 1, 30th July, 1971.
(c) IATA Guidance Material—Wide-Cut Type, November, 1969.
(d) ASTM D1655-70. Jet B.

Test	Limits	Test method		Remarks
		IP	ASTM	
Distillation:				
Initial boiling point	To be reported			
Fuel recovered 10 per cent vol.	To be reported			
Fuel recovered 20 per cent vol. at °F (°C) max.	290 (143·3)			
Fuel recovered 50 per cent vol. at °F (°C) max.	370 (187·8)			
Fuel recovered 90 per cent vol. at °F (°C) max.	470 (243·3)	123	D86	—
End point	To be reported			
Per cent recovered at 400°F (204·4°C)	To be reported			
Residue per cent vol. max.	1·5			
Loss per cent vol. max.	1·5			
Specific gravity at 60/60°F min.	0·751	160	D1298	—
max.	0·802			
Gravity API min.	45		D287	—
max.	57			

continues

* Issue 5—September, 1971 Supersedes Issue 4—February, 1969.

JOINT FUELLING SYSTEM CHECK LIST JET B—continued

Property	Value			
Existent gum mg/100 ml max.	7	131	D381	—
Total potential residue 16 hour mg/100 ml max.	14	138	D873	—
Sulphur, total per cent weight max.	0·2	107B	D1266	—
Mercaptan sulphur per cent weight max.	0·001	104	D1219/D1323	—
or			or	
Doctor Test	Negative	30	D484	—
Reid vapour pressure at 100°F psi min. / max.	2·0 / 3·0	69 / 171	D323 / D2551	See note
Freezing point °F (°C) max.	−72 (−58)	16	D2386	—
Net heat of combustion Btu/lb min.	18 400	12	D240/D2382	See note
or				
Aniline gravity product min.	5 250	193	D1405	See note
Aromatics per cent vol. max.	20	156	D1319	—
Olefin content per cent vol. max.	5	156	D1319	—
Smoke volatility index min.	54	57	D1322	See note
Copper corrosion (2 hr at 212°F) (100°C) max.	No. 1	154	D130	—

		IP	ASTM	Note
Water separometer index modified min.	85		D2550	See note
Water reaction: Volume change ml max. Interface rating max. Separation rating max.	1 1b 2		D1094	See note
Thermal stability: Change in pressure drop in 5 hours inches Hg max. Preheater deposit rating max.	3 Less than 3	197	D1660	Preheater temp. 300°F (149°C) Filter temp 400°F (204°C) Fuel flow 6 lb/hr Duration 300 min.
Copper content, µg/kg max.	150	225		See note
Total acidity mg KOH/g max.	0·012	273		—
Additives Anti-oxidants mg/litre (mandatory in hydro treated fuels min. 8·6) Metal deactivator mg/litre (optional) max. ASA-3 mg/litre max. (can be permitted only by unanimous agreement of all participants)	8·6–24·0 5·7 1·0 The electrical conductivity of the fuel shall be within the range 50 to 300 pS/metre at point, time and temp. of delivery to purchaser if ASA-3 present.	274	D2624	The type of concentration of all additives used including nil additions to be shown in the quality documents.

Note: Reference should be made to the appropriate notes in the British Ministry of Defence Specification D Eng RD 2486 Issue 8 of August, 1971.

APPENDIX III

QUALITY CONTROL TESTING OF AVIATION FUELS

1. SPECIFICATION PROPERTIES

All aviation fuels are required to meet stringent specifications which list a large number of properties and corresponding test methods. Some of the fuel properties can easily change if adequate precautions are not taken during the handling and transportation of the fuel, but others are of a more basic nature inherent to the type of petroleum product and unlikely to be changed, either by deterioration or normal contamination. Moreover, very wide variations are permitted in some properties whilst others are much more critical and must be maintained unchanged to ensure satisfactory performance.

Over the years, companies manufacturing and handling aviation fuels, as well as military and some civil airline users have developed a pattern of testing which is applied to the aviation fuels at various stages of distribution between refinery and aircraft to safeguard the fuel quality at every point in the supply system. The test requirements are detailed in Quality Control or Quality Protection regulations drawn up by the various companies and military authorities and strict compliance with these regulations is an inherent part of a fuel supplier's commitment to deliver on-specification aviation fuels to consumer customers.

Common experience and a need for international standardisation has led to the development of testing procedures which differ only slightly between companies and which are identical in all essential features affecting specification quality. The pattern of testing applied almost universally is outlined below.

2. REFINERY TESTING

All aviation fuels are allocated Batch Numbers on manufacture, normally related to the contents of individual refinery run-down tanks or shipping tanks. Each batch, which may comprise several thousand tons of fuel, is sampled and tested before release. The fuel may be manufactured to meet a single standard specification or (more commonly) may be produced against a special manufacturing specification devised to cover the requirements of several marketing specifications. In either case, the batch is tested fully against every specification item and the values obtained are recorded on a Certificate of Quality, which also includes details of the type and concentration of all additives incorporated. A copy of this document will normally accompany the fuel batch along the distribution system and comparisons between the manufactured values and the results of subsequent quality control tests (*see* below) may be made to establish whether significant deterioration or contamination has occurred during shipment, etc.

In the case of non-aviation fuels it is common practice to test at the refinery only the more critical properties on every batch and to check the remaining properties only on occasional batches or to estimate the values from other available data. Provided the crude oil used and the processing treatments applied remain unchanged this is a perfectly satisfactory procedure for non-aviation products, but is unacceptable in principle for aviation fuels. However, in the case of certain refineries supplying aviation fuels to a limited local market it has been found that some relaxation in the refinery test requirements can be permitted under special circumstances. This practice is now being adopted by some fuel manufacturing companies in respect of certain non-critical properties of jet fuels, such as viscosity, sulphur content, aromatic hydrocarbons, etc. The results shown on Certificates of Quality are then clearly annotated to show that they are only typical values and have actually not been obtained on that batch.

Where aviation fuels are exported or supplied to certain military customers (which in fact covers the great majority of aviation fuel batches produced world-wide) then no such relaxations are permitted and every fuel property must be individually batch tested.

3. QUALITY CONTROL TESTING

Every time that stocks of aviation fuel are transferred (whether by ocean tanker, barge, pipeline, rail or road vehicle) precautions are taken to avoid contamination and tests are made to check that contamination has not occurred. Aviation fuels may become contaminated by dirt and water or by other petroleum products; in some forms of transportation it is virtually impossible to avoid a degree of con-tamination by dirt (rust, etc.) or water and tests for the presence of these con-taminants are made at every stage of the supply system between refinery and aircraft. In some cases visual checks on fuel samples from selected points are ade-quate, but particularly as the fuel moves closer to the airfield and to the aircraft so the checks become more frequent and more stringent, with wide-spread use of the test techniques described earlier.

To combat contamination by other petroleum products, aviation fuels are handled as far as possible through segregated or 'dedicated' systems and grade selective couplings are also employed, particularly on airfields, to minimise the possibility of the wrong fuel being supplied (the delivery to aircraft of an incorrect fuel grade could have far more serious consequences than the delivery of a slightly contaminated fuel). Ocean tankers and some pipelines have however to carry a variety of petroleum fuels and the use of other non-dedicated transportation or storage facilities is sometimes unavoidable, and in these cases tests have to be carried out to confirm that the specification fuel properties have not been affected by contamination from other products.

These tests are required routinely at ocean terminals or intermediate depots on all stocks of aviation fuel received by tanker or multi-product pipeline; stocks received into storage tanks are sampled and tested (*see* below), issued with new batch or sub-batch numbers and a test certificate is issued. This procedure may be necessary several times between refinery and airfield and detailed batch records are main-tained so that the batch identity of all aviation fuel supplies is maintained and can be related to test results obtained at each stage of distribution. No further laboratory property tests are required once the fuel reaches the fully grade-segregated sections of the distribution system, *e.g.* at airfields.

Tests may however be required at airfields (or elsewhere) whenever aviation fuel is put into a storage tank which has just been cleaned or has for operational reasons been converted from use on another fuel grade; these tests are to ensure that traces of the previous grade or of cleaning materials (although no chemicals are normally permitted for cleaning aviation fuel tanks) have not affected the properties of the new fuel.

If aviation fuels are stored for long periods it is possible for deterioration to occur and for certain of the properties to move outside the specification limits. Few difficulties are encountered with jet fuels, but if aviation gasoline is stored for long periods, particularly in part-filled tanks in hot climates, evaporation losses (weathering) can lead to a serious reduction in the Reid Vapour Pressure and to an increase in the TEL concentration, making the fuel unsuitable for use. Excessive storage times can also lead to gum formation in all fuels and to the fuel becoming corrosive, particularly if traces of water are present in the tankage (due to the action of sulphate-reducing bacteria). Other forms of microbiological growth are also possible in jet fuels. To safeguard against fuel deterioration 'Ageing' or 'Periodic' tests are required after set intervals of static storage and in some cases at a specified regularity irrespective of the rate of 'turnover' of the stock.

4. SHORT TESTS

For the purposes outlined in the above section on Quality Control Testing it is not necessary to carry out the full range of specification tests. Instead special 'Short Tests' are carried out to check only those fuel properties most relevant to the purpose of the test. This also enables the testing to be carried out in smaller local laboratories, which usually do not have the facilities necessary for a full specification test as carried out by refinery laboratories.

These Short Tests are known also as 'Recertification Tests' or 'Acceptance Tests' for obvious reasons and vary slightly in content between users and depending on their exact purpose. The tests to be included are selected either as being very critical to any form of contamination (*e.g.* the knock rating of aviation gasoline) or else as providing a good indication of one particular type of inter-grade contamination (*e.g.* the flash point of kerosine type jet fuel, which is reduced severely by even trace contamination by gasolines or wide-cut turbine fuel). Where a Short Test is used as a periodic ageing test it generally covers only those properties easily influenced by ageing or weathering effects and in some cases a Short Test for contamination may cover only one or two properties where it is known that contamination by only one other product is feasible (*e.g.* on a two grade pipeline).

The following tests are the critical ones most commonly included in the Short Tests applied internationally for quality control purposes:

Aviation gasoline	*Jet A-1*	*Jet B*
Appearance	Appearance	Appearance
Density	Density	Density
Distillation	Distillation*	Distillation*
Existent gum	Existent gum	Existent gum
Colour (by inspection)	Colour (Lovibond/	Colour (Lovibond/
Reid vapour pressure	Saybolt)	Saybolt)
Copper corrosion	Flash point*	Reid vapour pressure
Knock rating–Lean	Copper corrosion	Copper corrosion
mixture*	Freeze point*	Water reaction
TEL content	Water reaction	(TEL content)
	(WSIM)	(WSIM)
	(Silver corrosion)	(Smoke volatility index)
	(Smoke point)	

TABLE 11

Significance of property tests included in 'short tests'

Test	Aviation gasoline	Jet A-1	Jet B
Appearance	Dirt and water	Dirt and water	Dirt and water
Density (sp gr)	Gross contamination by other products	Gross contamination by other products	Gross contamination by other products
Distillation	Contamination by kerosine, jet fuel or diesel/gasoil[a]	Contamination by gasoline, Jet B or luboil	Gross contamination by diesel/gasoil or luboil
Existent gum	Contamination by diesel/gasoil or luboil and check against ageing	Contamination by diesel/gasoil or luboil and check against ageing	Contamination by diesel/gasoil or luboil and check against ageing
Colour	Gross contamination by other gasoline grades	Contamination by gasoline or luboil	Contamination by gasoline or luboil
Reid vapour pressure	Insensitive to contamination (except possibly by motor gasoline) check against weathering/deterioration	NOT APPLICABLE	Gross contamination by gasoline and check against weathering/deterioration
Flash point	NOT APPLICABLE	Contamination by gasoline or jet B[a]	NOT APPLICABLE
Copper corrosion	Check against corrosive deterioration	Check against corrosive deterioration	Check against corrosive deterioration
Knock rating (weak)	Contamination by any product except higher octane gasoline[a]	NOT APPLICABLE	NOT APPLICABLE
TEL content	Contamination by higher lead gasoline and check against weathering/deterioration	NOT APPLICABLE	Contamination by gasoline[a]
Freeze point	NOT APPLICABLE	Contamination by diesel/gasoil or luboil[a]	NOT APPLICABLE
Water reaction or WSIM	NOT APPLICABLE	Contamination by diesel/gasoline or luboil or pick-up of surfactant materials[a]	Contamination by diesel/gasoil or luboil or pick-up of surfactant materials[a]

[a] Tests most sensitive to likely contaminants.

The tests shown in parentheses are not universally considered necessary in Recertification Tests and those asterisked are usually omitted from periodic ageing tests as the property does not deteriorate significantly.

In Table 11 an indication is given of the primary purpose served by the critical property checks usually included in Short Tests applied to the three main aviation fuel types. If contamination is indicated by a significant change in any of the fuel properties (when compared with earlier test reports) a careful appraisal of the changes will usually give an indication of the likely nature and source of the contaminating product.

It should be noted that even when the limited properties tested are all found to be on-specification it is still possible for significant contamination to have occurred. For example, a Jet A-1 kerosine type fuel originally manufactured with a very high flash point say 120°F (49°C), could have the flash point reduced to say 102°F (39°C) by contamination with motor gasoline yet still meet the specification limit of minimum 100°F (38°C), the fuel could, however, then contain a significant amount of TEL, corrosive chlorine compounds or unstable gum forming components capable of impairing its performance in an aircraft engine. It is therefore important always to check the results of Short Tests against earlier test data on the batch and if significant changes are observed, more detailed investigation should be made of the situation before the fuel is released for use.

BIBLIOGRAPHY AND SUGGESTIONS FOR FURTHER READING

Modern Petroleum Technology (1973). 4th edn, Applied Science, London.

Ya. M. Paushkin (1962). *The Chemical Composition and Properties of Fuels for Jet Propulsion*, Pergamon Press, Oxford.

G. Geoffrey Smith (1955). *Gas Turbines and Jet Propulsion*, Iliffe Books Ltd, London.

Maxwell Smith (1970). *Aviation Fuels*, G. T. Foulis and Co. Ltd, Henley.

FUEL SPECIFICATION GUIDES

Handbook of Products (Air BP), British Petroleum Co. Ltd, Britannic House, London, EC2.

Jet Fuel Specifications: Airlines, Military, Standards. Esso Research and Engineering Co., Linden, New Jersey, USA.

Specifications: Aviation Fuels and Engine Oils. Shell International Petroleum Co. Ltd, Shell Centre, London, SE1.

Chapter 7

DIESEL FUELS

W. H. KITE, Jr and R. E. PEGG

1. INTRODUCTION

The diesel engine is a high compression, self-ignition engine. The fuel is ignited by the heat of the high compression and no spark plug is used. The diesel cycle consists of charging the combustion chamber with air; compressing the air; injecting the fuel, which ignites spontaneously; expanding the burned gases; and expelling the products of combustion.

Diesel engines vary greatly in size, power output, and operating speeds. While some small, single cylinder units develop only a few brake horsepower, at the other extreme there are engines having cylinder diameters as large as 1050 millimetres (41·34 inches), developing several thousand horsepower per cylinder. Designed sizes and output continue to increase. Operating speeds are almost as diverse, ranging from below 100 revolutions per minute for some larger engines to 4000 rpm and above for those used in automotive and other vehicle prime mover service. Diesel engines now are fully established in all forms of surface transportation as well as for a wide range of power generation and pumping applications.

The entire range of diesel engines can be divided into the three broad classification groups indicated in the following table:

Classification	Speed range	Conditions	Typical applications
Low speed	Below 300 rpm	Sustained heavy load, constant speed	Marine main propulsion; electric power generation
Medium speed	300–1000 rpm	Fairly high load and relatively constant speed	Marine auxiliaries; stationary power generators; pumping units
High speed	1000 rpm or above	Frequent and wide variation in load and speed	Road transport vehicles; diesel locomotives

It should not be surprising that diesel engines also vary extensively in their requirements for fuel characteristics. Selection of the proper fuel is not a simple procedure but depends upon many variables, the most important of which are:

engine size and design;
operating speed and load ranges;
frequency of speed and load changes;
maintenance considerations;
atmospheric conditions;
fuel price and availability.

Each of the foregoing factors plays a part in dictating the fuel to be chosen, the relative influence of each being determined by the specific application and installation involved.

2.   THE DIESEL COMBUSTION PROCESS

When used in a diesel engine, a fuel passes through the following processes:

storage, pumping and handling;
filtering;
heating (if necessary);
atomisation and mixing with air;
combustion;
power extraction;
heat exchange and exhaust.

The fuel properties control performance in these processes and particularly influence combustion and resultant energy extraction.

In any combustion process, there are at least three basic requirements:

formation of a mixture of fuel and air;
ignition of the fuel/air mixture;
completion of combustion of the fuel/air mixture.

In the diesel engine, these requirements are met as indicated diagram matically in Fig. 1. Figure 2 shows a typical pressure *vs* crank angle diagram for a diesel engine combustion chamber.

Prior to the injection of the fuel, air alone is compressed and raised to a high temperature during the compression stroke. The final compression pressure and resultant air temperature will vary with such factors as compression ratio, speed, and engine design; but a pressure of 450 psi (31·6 kg/sq cm) and a temperature of 1000°F (538°C) are representative values. Shortly before the end of compression, at a point controlled by the fuel injection timing system, one or more jets of fuel are introduced into the combustion chamber.

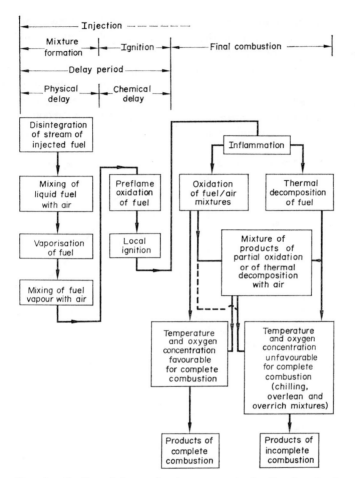

FIG. 1. *Outline of the combustion process in the diesel engine.[a]*

Ignition does not occur immediately on injection. The fuel droplets absorb heat from the compressed air. This is necessary for vaporisation and for increased efficiency. The duration of the delay period between injection and ignition is controlled by engine design, fuel and air inlet temperatures, degree of atomisation of the fuel, and fuel composition. This delay period is commonly known as 'ignition delay'.

The fuel/air mixture finally reaches a temperature at which self-ignition occurs and the flame begins to spread. Injection of fuel continues during this time. Therefore, the ignition delay period must be short in order to avoid 'diesel knock' which is caused by very rapid burning or detonation of relatively large amounts of fuel gathered in the cylinder before combustion begins. Once the flame has been initiated completely, the only fuel in the cylinder is

[a] M. A. Elliot (July 1949). Combustion of diesel fuel, SAE Transactions, Vol. 3, No. 3: 492.

that being injected into the burning mixture. This fuel burns almost instantaneously. The final part of the combustion cycle is the completion of burning after injection has ceased.

The quantity of fuel, the rate at which it is injected into the engine, and the timing and duration of the injection period are all accurately controlled by a cam-driven injection pump. The pump delivers the fuel to the injectors at a pressure at the time of injection varying from 1800 to 30 000 psi (130 to 2100 kg/sq cm), depending upon the design of the injection equipment.

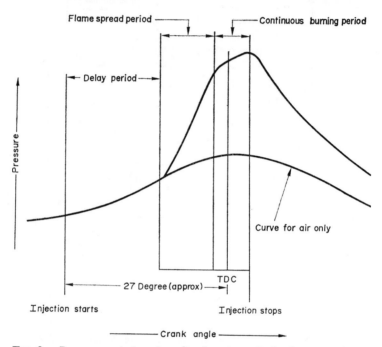

FIG. 2.   *Pressure variations in a diesel engine cylinder during combustion.*

Variation in the fuel quantity to conform to different speed and/or load conditions usually is by means of a governor, which admits fuel to the combustion chamber at a preset maximum rate until the new conditions are attained. The governor is set to avoid the onset of black smoke caused by an excessive amount of fuel.

The air that can be delivered to an engine is determined by design considerations. The amount of this air that is sufficiently utilised determines the optimum injection rate of fuel and hence the maximum power output of the engine. Below this maximum, the output of the engine is controlled solely by the amount of fuel supplied.

Pressure charging frequently is used as a means of increasing the amount of air delivered to an engine without increasing its size. A compressor, either directly coupled to the crankshaft (a supercharger) or driven by a turbine using the heat energy in the exhaust gases (a turbocharger), is used to increase the amount of combustion air available. Consequently, the engine is able to burn a greater quantity of fuel, and power increases in the order of 50 per cent are possible without exceeding the normal level of exhaust smoke. The amount of fuel ultimately is limited by the thermal and mechanical stresses that can be tolerated by engine components.

3. GENERAL CHARACTERISTICS OF DIESEL FUELS

The basic requirement of a diesel fuel is that it must ignite spontaneously and burn satisfactorily under the conditions existing in the combustion chamber; it must be suitable for handling by the injection equipment and must be adaptable to convenient handling at all stages from the refinery to the engine fuel tank, without suffering degradation and without harming any surface which it may normally contact.

Diesel fuels originally were straight-run products obtained from the distillation of crude oil. Today, with the various refinery cracking processes, diesel fuels also may contain varying amounts of selected cracked distillates to increase the volume available for meeting the growing demand, while still maintaining cost at a minimum. Care is taken to select the cracked stocks in such a manner that specifications are met as simply as possible. The boiling range of distillate fuels is approximately 150°C to 400°C (300°F to 755°F). The relative merits of the diesel fuel types to be considered will depend upon the refining practices employed, the nature of the crude oils from which they are produced, and the additive package (if any) used.

Under the broad definition of diesel fuel, there exist many possible combinations of various characteristics such as volatility, ignition quality, viscosity, gravity, stability, and other properties. To characterise diesel fuels and thereby establish a framework of definition and reference, various classifications are used in different countries. One of the most widely used is ASTM D975 'Classification of Diesel Fuel Oils'. This classification, shown in Table 1, covers three grades of diesel fuel oils, No. 1-D, No. 2-D and No. 4-D. It should be emphasised that ASTM D975 is a classification and not a complete set of quality specifications. In general, it presents certain minimum requirements necessary to assure reasonable operation under the conditions described.

In ASTM D975, Grades No. 1-D and 2-D are distillate fuels, the types most commonly used in high speed engines of the mobile type, in medium speed stationary engines, and in railroad engines. Grade 4-D covers the class of more viscous distillates and, at times, blends of these distillates with residual fuel oils. No. 4-D fuels are applicable for use in low and medium speed engines employed in services involving sustained load and predominantly constant speed.

TABLE 1

ASTM D975—Limiting requirements for diesel fuel oils[a]

Grade of diesel fuel oil	Flash point, °F (°C) Min.	Pour point, °F (°C) Max.	Water and sediment, per cent by volume Max.	Carbon residue on 10 per cent residuum, per cent Max.	Ash, per cent by weight Max.	Distillation temperatures, °F (°C) 90 per cent point Min.	Distillation temperatures, °F (°C) 90 per cent point Max.	Viscosity at 100°F (37.8°C) Kinematic, centistokes (or Saybolt Universal, sec) Min.	Viscosity at 100°F (37.8°C) Kinematic, centistokes (or Saybolt Universal, sec) Max.	Sulphur, per cent by weight Max.	Copper strip corrosion Max.	Cetane number[e] Min.
No. 1-D—A volatile distillate fuel oil for engines in service requiring frequent speed and load changes	100 or legal (37.8)	[b]	Trace	0.15	0.01	—	550 (287.8)	1.4	2.5 (34.4)	0.50	No. 3	40[f]
No. 2-D—A distillate fuel oil of lower volatility for engines in industrial and heavy mobile service	125 or legal (51.7)	[b]	0.05	0.35	0.01	540[c] (282.2)	640 (338)	2.0[c] (32.6)	4.3 (40.1)	0.50[d]	No. 3	40[f]
No. 4-D—A fuel oil for low and medium speed engines	130 or legal (54.4)		0.50	—	0.10	—	—	5.8 (45)	26.4 (125)	2.0	—	30[f]

[a] To meet special operating conditions, modifications of individual limiting requirements may be agreed upon between purchaser, seller and supplier.

[b] For cold weather operation, the pour point should be specified 10°F (5.6°C) below the ambient temperature at which the engine is to be operated except where fuel oil heating facilities are provided.

[c] When pour point less than 0°F (−17.8°C) is specified, the minimum viscosity shall be 1.8 cST (32.0 sec, Saybolt Universal) and the minimum 90 per cent point shall be waived.

[d] For all products outside the USA the maximum sulphur limit shall be 1.0 per cent by weight.

[e] Where cetane number by Method D613, Test for Ignition Quality of Diesel Fuels by the Cetane Method, is not available, ASTM Method D976, Calculated Cetane Index of Distillate Fuels may be used as an approximation. Where there is disagreement, Method D613 shall be the referee method.

[f] Low-atmospheric temperatures as well as engine operation at high altitudes may require use of fuels with higher cetane ratings.

TABLE 2

Requirements for No. 6, 'Bunker C' Fuel oil*

Fuel oil grade	Flash point, °F (°C)	Water & sediment, vol. per cent	Saybolt viscosity, secs				Kinematic viscosity, centistokes, 122°F (50°C)	
			Universal, 100°F (38°C)		Furol, 122°F (50°C)			
	Min.	Max.	Max.	Min.	Max.	Min.	Max.	Min.
No. 6 Preheating required for burning and handling	150 (66)	2·00^a	(9000) ^{b}	(900) ^{b}	300	45	(638) ^{b}	(92) ^{b}

* These data taken from ASTM D396 Table 1. *Detailed Requirements for Fuel Oils.*

^{a} The amount of water by distillation plus the sediment by extraction shall not exceed 2·00 per cent. The amount of sediment by extraction shall not exceed 0·50 per cent. A deduction in quantity shall be made for all water and sediment in excess of 1·0 per cent.

^{b} Viscosity values in parentheses are for information only and not necessarily limiting.

Equivalent fuel standards similar to those presented in Table 1 exist in European countries, *e.g.* DIN 51601, 'Fuels for High Speed Diesels' in Germany and BS 2869, 'Petroleum Fuels for Oil Engines and Burners' in the United Kingdom. Data for the latter are given in Table 4.

The BS specification covers four classes of fuels marketed specifically as engine fuels. Class A1 is of high quality and is designed primarily as an automotive diesel fuel; Class A2 is intended as a general purpose diesel fuel; Classes B1 and B2 are for larger engines, such as those used in marine practice. Class B2 allows for the inclusion of small amounts of residuum.

While the foregoing classifications deal principally with distillate fuels, residual fuels are used extensively in large, slow speed, marine main propulsion engines and in stationary land based engines, principally because of lower fuel cost. More recently, the lower cost aspect has promoted the increasing popularity of residual fuels in some smaller, medium speed auxiliary engines. Mixtures of residual and distillate fuels are used in installations where a compromise is sought between the more desirable properties of the latter and the lower cost of the former.

A typical heavy residual fuel is illustrated by the specifications established by ASTM Committee D-2 to define No. 6 Fuel Oil, often referred to as 'Bunker C'. These specifications, relatively few in number and broad in their limits, are shown in Table 2. Some diesel engines are operated on fuels of even lower quality than No. 6 Fuel Oil. However, it must be remembered that lower quality fuels, while having the advantage of lower fuel cost, usually require special equipment and special lubricating oils to achieve satisfactory performance.

TABLE 3

Typical inspections of diesel fuels

Fuel property	Fuel type			
	Kerosine	Premium diesel	Railroad diesel	Marine distillate diesel
Cetane number	50	47	40	38
Boiling range, °F (°C)	325–550 (163–288)	360–675 (182–357)	350–675 (176–357)	350–500 (176–250) (90 per cent)
Viscosity, SSU at 100°F (38°C)	33	35	36	47
Gravity, °API	42	37	34	26
Sulphur, wt per cent	0·12	0·30	0·50	1·2
Uses	High speed city buses	High speed Buses Trucks Tractors Light marine engines	Medium speed R. R. engines Marine engines Stationary engines	Low speed Heavy marine engines Large stationary engines

TABLE 4

Requirements for engine fuels British Standard 2869

Test	A1	A2	B1	B2[a]	ASTM D	IP
Viscosity at 37·8°C (100°F):						
min., cSt	1·6	1·6	—	—	445	71
max., cSt	6·0	6·0	14	14		
Cetane number, min.	50	45	35		—	41
Carbon residue:						
(Conradson), max., per cent by wt	—	—	0·2	1·5	189	13
On 10 per cent residue, max., per cent by wt	0·2	0·2	—	—		
Distillation:						
Recovery at 357°C (675°F), min., per cent by vol.	90	90	—	—	86	123
Flash point:						
Pensky Martens closed cup, min.	55°C (130°F)	55°C (130°F)	66°C (150°F)	66°C (150°F)	93	34
Water content, max., per cent by vol.	0·05	0·05	0·1	0·25	—	74
Sediment content, max., per cent by wt	0·01	0·01	0·02	0·05	473	53
Ash content, max., per cent by wt	0·01	0·01	0·01	0·02	482	4
Sulphur content, max., per cent by wt	0·5	1·0	1·5	1·8	—	63
Copper corrosion, max.	1	1	—	—	130	154
Cloud point, max.[b]	—	—	—	—	2 500	219
Pour point, max.	−7°C (20°F)	−7°C (20°F)	0°C (32°F)	3°C (35°F)	97	15

[a] In the UK available for ocean bunkers only.

[b] For summer (March/November) maximum Cloud Point 0°C (32°F).

Additives may be used to improve the fuel performance. Cetane improvers such as alkyl nitrates and nitrites can improve ignition quality; pour point depressants can improve low temperature performance; anti-smoke additives may reduce exhaust smoke, which is of growing concern as more and more attention is paid to atmospheric pollution; anti-oxidant and sludge dispersants may also be used, particularly with fuels formulated with cracked components, in order to prevent the formation of insoluble compounds that could cause line and filter plugging.

4. DIESEL FUEL PROPERTIES AND TESTS

(a) CETANE NUMBER

In the majority of diesel engines, the ignition delay period is shorter than the duration of injection. Under such circumstances, the total combustion period can be considered to be divided into the following four stages:

ignition delay;
rapid pressure rise;
constant pressure or controlled pressure rise;
burning on the expansion stroke.

The rapid pressure rise results from the large number of ignition points and the accumulation of fuel during the ignition delay period. Following this stage, the rate of combustion can be controlled to a much greater degree by controlling the injection rate, since the fuel is being injected into flame. Because the rapid pressure rise represents uncontrolled and inefficient combustion resulting from the burning of fuel accumulated during the ignition delay period, it is desirable to limit ignition delay to a minimum. This limitation can be accomplished mechanically by the development and selection of a spray pattern configuration properly tailored to the combustion chamber. Ignition delay can be reduced by the use of high fuel injection pressures and high fuel/air turbulence to promote rapid fuel jet break-up and thorough fuel distribution.

Although the reduction of ignition delay by mechanical means is important, the nature of the fuel is the primary factor in reducing the time consumed by ignition delay. Physical characteristics, such as viscosity, gravity, and mid-boiling point are influential. On the other hand, hydrocarbon type is important only as it affects the physical characteristics of the fuel. Since the ignition delay characteristics of diesel fuels directly influence the interval of uncontrolled combustion during injection and, as a result, the overall engine performance, this property is of primary importance. It thus becomes desirable to have a numerical basis for evaluating the fuel ignition delay and for measuring and predicting this property.

The cetane number of a diesel fuel is the numerical result of an engine test designed to evaluate fuel ignition delay. To establish the cetane number scale, two reference fuels were selected. One, normal cetane, has excellent ignition qualities and, consequently, a very short ignition delay. A cetane number 100 was arbitrarily assigned to this fuel. The second fuel, alpha-methylnaphthalene, has poor ignition qualities and was assigned a cetane number of 0. In 1962, alphamethylnaphthalene was replaced as a primary reference fuel by heptamethylnonane, which has a cetane number of 15 as determined by use of the two original primary reference fuels.

To determine the cetane number of any fuel, its ignition delay is compared in a standard test engine with a blend of reference fuels. This engine and the prescribed test method are described in ASTM D613 or IP 41.

The cetane number of a diesel fuel is defined as 'the whole number nearest to the value determined by calculation from the percentage by volume of normal cetane (Cetane No. = 100) in a blend with heptamethylnonane (Cetane No. = 15) which matches the ignition quality of the test fuel when compared by this method'. The matching blend percentages to the first decimal are inserted in the following equation to obtain the cetane number:

Cetane No. = per cent n-cetane + 0·15 (per cent heptamethylnonane)

The shorter the ignition delay period the higher the cetane number of the fuel and the smaller the amount of fuel in the combustion chamber when the fuel ignites. Consequently, high cetane number fuels generally cause lower rates of pressure rise and lower peak pressures, both of which tend to lessen combustion noise and to permit improved control of combustion, resulting in increased engine efficiency and power output.

In addition to the above, higher cetane number fuels tend to result in easier starting, particularly in cold weather, and faster warm-up. The higher cetane number fuels also usually form softer and hence more readily purged combustion chamber deposits and result in reduced exhaust smoke and odour.

High speed diesel engines normally are supplied with fuels in the range of 45 to 55 cetane number. Table 3 summarises the typical inspections of various diesel fuels characterised primarily on the basis of use. As can be seen, the cetane number ranges from 50 for kerosine to 38 for marine distillate fuel.

(b) CETANE INDEX

Since the determination of cetane number by engine testing requires special equipment, as well as being time consuming and costly, alternative methods have been developed for calculating estimates of cetane number. The calculations are based upon equations involving values of other known characteristics of the fuel.

One of the most widely used methods is based on the Calculated Cetane Index formula. This formula represents a method for estimating the cetane number of distillate fuels from API gravity and mid-boiling point. The index value as computed from the formula is designated as a Calculated Cetane Index (ASTM D976–IP 218). Since the formula is complicated in its manipulation, a nomograph based on the equation has been developed for its solution.

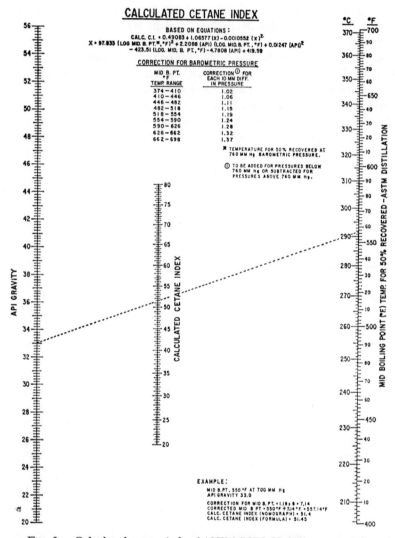

FIG. 3.   Calculated cetane index (ASTM D976–IP 218) nomograph.

This nomograph, together with the equation, are shown in Fig. 3. An example illustrating the use of the chart is also presented. It must be recognised that the calculation of Cetane Index is not an optional method for expressing cetane number. Rather, it is a supplementary tool for predicting cetane number with considerable accuracy when used with due regard for its limitations. Among the limitations of Calculated Cetane Index are the following:

it is not applicable to fuels containing additives for raising cetane number;
it is not applicable to pure hydrocarbons, synthetic fuels, alkylates, or coal tar products;
correlation is fair for a given type of fuel but breaks down if fuels of widely different compositions are compared;
appreciable inaccuracy in correlation may occur when used for crude oils, residuals, or products having end points below 500°F (260°C).

(c) DIESEL INDEX

The Diesel Index is derived from the API Gravity and Aniline Point (ASTM D611 or IP 2), the lowest temperature at which the fuel is completely miscible with an equal volume of aniline. The formula for Diesel Index is as follows:

$$\text{Diesel Index} = \frac{\text{Aniline Point (°F) API Gravity}}{100}$$

The above equation is seldom used because the results can be misleading, especially when applied to blended fuels.

(d) GRAVITY

Gravity is an indication of the density or weight per unit volume of the diesel fuel. The principal use of specific gravity (ASTM D1298–IP 160) is to convert weights of oil to volumes or volumes to weights. Specific gravity also is required when calculating the volume of oil at a temperature different from that at which the original volume was measured. Although specific gravity by itself is not a significant measure of quality, it may give useful information when considered with other tests. For a given volatility range, high specific gravity is associated with aromatic or naphthenic hydrocarbons and low specific gravity with paraffinic hydrocarbons. The heat energy potentially available from the fuel decreases with an increase in density, or specific gravity.

API Gravity (ASTM D1298–IP 160) is an arbitrary figure related to the specific gravity in accordance with the following formula:

$$°\text{API Gravity} = \frac{141{\cdot}5}{\text{Specific Gravity at } 60/60°\text{F}} - 131{\cdot}5$$

As can be noted, API Gravity decreases with an increase in specific gravity.

(e) DISTILLATION

Distillation (or volatility) characteristics of a diesel fuel exert a great influence on its performance, particularly in medium and high speed engines. Distillation characteristics are measured using a procedure (ASTM D86–IP 123) in which a sample of the fuel is distilled and the vapour temperatures are recorded for the percentages of evaporation or distillation throughout the range.

The average volatility requirements of diesel fuels vary with engine speed, size and design. However, fuels having too low volatility tend to reduce power output and fuel economy through poor atomisation, while those having too high volatility may reduce power output and fuel economy through vapour lock in the fuel system or inadequate droplet penetration from the nozzle. In general the distillation range should be as low as possible without adversely affecting the flash point, burning quality, heat content, or viscosity of the fuel. If the 10 per cent point is too high, poor starting may result. An excessive boiling range from 10 per cent to 50 per cent evaporated may increase warm-up time. A low 50 per cent point is desirable in preventing smoke and odour. Low 90 per cent and end points tend to ensure low carbon residuals and minimum crankcase dilution.

The temperature for 50 per cent evaporated, known as the mid-boiling point, usually is taken as an overall indication of the fuel distillation characteristics where a single numerical value is used alone. For example, in high speed engines, a 50 per cent point above 575°F (302°C) probably would cause smoke formation, give rise to objectionable odour, cause lubricating oil contamination, and promote engine deposits. At the other extreme, a fuel with excessively low 50 per cent point would have too low a viscosity and too low a heat content per unit volume. Thus, a 50 per cent point in the range of 450–535°F (232–280°C) is most desirable for the majority of automotive type diesel engines. This average range usually is raised to a higher temperature spread for larger, slower speed engines.

(f) VISCOSITY

Viscosity (ASTM D445–IP 71) may be described as a measure of a liquid's resistance to flow and usually is measured by recording the time required for a given volume of fuel at a constant temperature to flow through a small orifice of standard dimensions. The viscosity of diesel fuel is important primarily because of its effect on the handling of the fuel by the pump and injector system.

Fuel viscosity also exerts a strong influence on the shape of the fuel spray. High viscosities can cause poor atomisation, large droplets, and high spray jet penetration. The jet tends to be almost a solid stream instead of forming a spray pattern of small droplets. As a result, the fuel is not distributed in, or mixed with the air required for burning. Poor combustion is a result, accompanied by loss of power and economy. Moreover, and particularly in the smaller engines, the overly penetrating fuel stream can impinge upon the cylinder walls, thereby washing away the lubricating oil film and causing dilution of the crankcase oil. Such a condition contributes to excessive wear.

Low fuel viscosities result in a spray which is too soft and, thus, does not penetrate sufficiently. Combustion is impaired and power output and economy are decreased. Low viscosity can lead to excessive leakage past the injection pump plunger. Under this condition, fuel metering becomes inaccurate and engine efficiency is reduced. Wear of the fuel system components may increase because lubricating properties of fuels tend to decrease with viscosity.

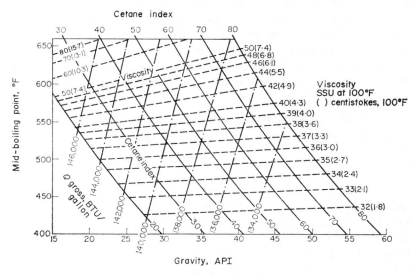

FIG. 4.   *Related properties of distillate diesel fuels.*

Fuel viscosities for high speed engines range from 32 SUS to 45 SUS (1·8 cSt to 5·8 cSt) at 100°F (37·78°C). Usually the lower viscosity limit is established to prevent leakage in worn fuel injection equipment as well as to supply lubrication for injection system components in certain types of engines. During operation at low atmospheric temperature, the viscosity limit sometimes is reduced to 30 SUS (1·4 cSt) at 100°F to obtain increased volatility and sufficiently low pour point. Fuels having viscosities greater than 45 SUS (5·8 cSt) usually are limited in application to the slower speed engines. The very viscous fuels, such as are often used in large stationary and marine engines, usually require preheating for proper pumping, injection, and atomisation.

A chart showing the relationships between distillation, API Gravity, Cetane Index, distillation and viscosity is presented in Fig. 4.

(g) HEAT OF COMBUSTION

The heat of combustion of a fuel (ASTM D240 or IP 12) is the amount of heat produced when the fuel is burned completely. There are two heats of combustion, or calorific values, for every petroleum fuel: gross and net. When hydrocarbons are burned, one of the products of combustion is water vapour and the difference between the two calorific values is that the gross includes the heat given by the water vapour in condensing, while the net value does not include this heat.

The power available from an engine under constant running conditions and with a constant rate of fuel supply is governed by the calorific value of the fuel. A fuel of low calorific value yields less heat on combustion and, therefore, less power than the same amount of a fuel with higher calorific value. To maintain power output with the low calorific value fuel, more of it would have to be used. Thus, the importance of this quality depends on whether the user purchases fuel on a weight or volume basis.

Calorific values can be calculated with an accuracy sufficient for normal purposes from the specific gravity of the product. One relationship which can be used is:

$$\text{Calorific Value (Gross Btu/lb)} = (12\,400 - 2100d^2) \times 1\cdot 8$$

where d is the specific gravity at 60/60°F (15·6/15·6°C).

(h) CLOUD POINT

Under low temperature conditions, paraffinic constituents of a diesel fuel may be precipitated as a wax. This settles out and blocks the fuel system lines and filters, causing malfunctioning or stalling of the engine. The temperature at which the precipitation occurs depends upon the origin, type, and boiling range of the fuel. The more paraffinic the fuel, the higher the precipitation temperature and the less suitable the fuel for low temperature operation.

The temperature at which wax is first precipitated from solution can be measured by the cloud point test (ASTM D2500–IP 219). The cloud point of a diesel fuel is a guide to the temperature at which it may clog filter systems and restrict flow. Cloud point is becoming increasingly important for fuels used in high speed diesel engines, especially because of the tendency to equip such engines with finer filters. The finer the filter, the more readily it will become clogged by small quantities of precipitated wax. Larger fuel lines and filters of greater capacity reduce the effect of deposits from the fuel and therefore widen the cloud point range of fuels which can be used.

(i) POUR POINT

The pour point (ASTM D97–IP 15) of a fuel is an indication of the lowest temperature at which the fuel can be pumped. Pour points often occur 8°F to 10°F below the cloud points and differences of 15°F to 20°F are not uncommon. Fuels, and in particular waxy fuels, will in some circumstances flow below their tested pour point. However, pour point does give a useful guide to the lowest temperature to which a fuel can be cooled without setting.

No wax precipitation problems are encountered at temperatures above the cloud point and satisfactory operation is unlikely at temperatures below the pour point. The level between these two temperatures at which trouble-free operation is just possible will depend upon the design and layout of the fuel system. A system that contains small, exposed lines and small area fine filters in cold locations will be more prone to early failure than one where the lines are unrestricted and sheltered and where any fine filters are located so that they readily pick up engine heat.

Sometimes additives are used to improve the low temperature fluidity of diesel fuels. Such additives usually work by modifying the wax crystals so that they are less likely to form a rigid structure. Thus, although there is no alteration of the cloud point, the pour point may be lowered dramatically. Unfortunately, the improvement in engine performance as a rule is less than the improvement in pour point. Consequently, the cloud and pour point temperatures cannot be used to indicate engine performance with any accuracy.

Attempts to develop suitable flow tests have to date been only moderately successful, primarily due to the limited amount of firm field operability data on which to base the work. Consequently, there has been a great reluctance to depart from the known and accepted cloud and pour point tests as the major low temperature performance criteria. Nevertheless, low temperature operability tests based on the plugging of cold filters have now been accepted by France (AFNOR-549), Germany (DIN 00 51 770) and Sweden (SIS 155 122), and moves to develop an agreed European standard are in progress.

(j) FLASH POINT

The flash point of a diesel fuel is the temperature to which the fuel must be heated to produce an ignitable vapour–air mixture above the liquid fuel when exposed to an open flame. Standard methods are available for measuring flash point, the most common one applied to fuels being the Pensky–Martens Closed Cup Flash (ASTM D93–IP 34).

In practice, flash point is important primarily from a fuel handling standpoint. Too low a flash point will cause fuel to be a fire hazard, subject to flashing and possible continued ignition and explosion. In addition, a low flash point may indicate contamination by more volatile and explosive fuels, such as gasoline. Insurance companies, government agencies and private users set mandatory minimum limits on flash point because of fire hazard considerations. These limits must be taken into account when establishing fuel specifications. In spite of its importance from a safety standpoint, the flash point of a fuel has no significance to its performance in an engine. Auto-ignition temperature is not generally influenced by variations in flash point nor are other properties, such as fuel injection and combustion performance.

(k) SULPHUR

Sulphur can cause wear, resulting from the corrosive nature of its combustion by-products and from an increase in the amount of deposits in the combustion chamber and on the pistons. The sulphur content of a diesel fuel (ASTM D129–IP 61 and ASTM D1551 or IP 63) depends on the origin of the crude oil from which it is made and on the refining methods. Sulphur can be present in a number of forms, e.g. as mercaptans, sulphides, disulphides, or heterocyclic compounds such as thiophens, all of which will affect wear and deposits.

Fuel sulphur tolerance by a diesel engine depends largely upon whether the engine is of the low or high speed type and what operating conditions prevail. Low speed engines can tolerate more sulphur than their high speed counter-parts. This is due primarily to the fact that the low speed engines are of the large size, high power output type, which are utilised primarily in such services as stationary power plants and marine main propulsion. These services are typified by operation under relatively constant speed and load conditions. Hence, operating temperatures of the lubricating oil and cooling water, as well as combustion zone temperatures, tend to remain at an equilibrium level rather than to fluctuate between high and low values.

High sulphur fuels are undesirable from a purely technical standpoint regardless of engine type, but less harm will occur from fuel sulphur when engines are operated at high power outputs and consequent increased operating temperatures. Under the lower temperature conditions resulting from stopping and starting or decrease of load and/or speed, moisture condensation is apt to occur within the engine. The sulphur in the fuel then combines with the water to form acid solutions which corrode metal components and increase wear of moving parts. Active sulphur in the fuel tends to attack and corrode injection system components. Sulphur compounds also contribute to combustion chamber and injection system deposits.

Fuel sulphur is measured both on the basis of quantity and potential corrosivity. The quantitative measurements can be made by means of a combustion bomb using a procedure such as described in ASTM D129–IP 61. The measurement of potential corrosivity can be determined by means of a copper strip procedure described in ASTM D130–IP 154. The quantita-tive determination is an indication of the corrosive tendencies of the fuel combustion products, while the potential corrosivity indicates the extent of corrosion to be anticipated from the unburned fuel, particularly in the fuel injection system.

It is not unusual for residual type fuels used in the larger, slower speed engines to have a sulphur content of 3·0 per cent by weight or even higher. On the other hand, fuel for high speed automotive use generally has a sulphur content of 0·4 per cent by weight or less to avoid excessive wear. Recommended practices are to maintain the sulphur content as low as practicable.

Modern heavy duty engine oils of high detergency and those containing reserve alkalinity properties have successfully minimised the effects of diesel fuel sulphur to a large extent. Before the use of a lower cost, higher sulphur content fuel is agreed upon, several factors must be considered carefully:

increased cost of higher quality lubricating oil required;

increased frequency of oil filter changes;

possible increased engine and fuel system wear;

probable fuel system modifications required if a residual type fuel is to be considered.

(l) CARBON RESIDUE

The Conradson Carbon Residue Test (ASTM 189–IP 13) is widely quoted in diesel fuel specifications. At one time, there was believed to be a definite correlation between Conradson Carbon results and deposit formation on injector nozzles, but this view now is thought to be an over-simplification. The type of carbon formed is as important as the amount. Small quantities of hard, abrasive deposits can do more harm than larger amounts of soft, fluffy deposits. The latter largely can be eliminated through the exhaust system. Distillate diesel fuels which are satisfactory in other respects do not have high Conradson Carbon values, and the test is chiefly used on residual fuels.Even for the residual type, the tendency to form deposits may be better measured in other ways.

The significance of the Conradson Carbon test results also depends on the type of engine in which the fuel is being used. Fuels with up to 12 per cent weight Conradson Carbon residue have been used successfully in slow speed engines.

Because of the considerable difference in Conradson Carbon residue results between distillate and residual fuels, the test can be used to indicate if there is any substantial contamination of the first with the second.

(m) ASH

Small amounts of non-burnable material are found in diesel fuels in the form of soluble metallic soaps and solids. These materials are designated as ash. The quantitative determination is made by standard procedure (ASTM D482–IP 4). In this test, a small sample of fuel is burned in a weighed container until all of the combustible matter has been consumed, indicated by the residue and container attaining a constant weight. The amount of unburn-able residue is the ash content, and is reported as per cent by weight of the fuel.

Since diesel fuel injection components are made with great precision to extremely close fits and tolerances, they are very sensitive to any abrasive material in the fuel. In addition, such abrasive material, such as ash, can cause wear within the engine itself by increasing the overall deposit level and by adversely affecting the nature of the deposits.

(n) Neutralisation Number

Neutralisation Number (ASTM D974–IP 139; IP 182) is a measure of the inorganic and total acidity of the unused fuel and indicates its tendency to corrode metals with which it may come into contact.

(o) Stability

On leaving the refinery, the fuel will inevitably come into contact with air and water. If the fuel includes unstable components, which may be the case with fuels containing cracked products, storage in the presence of air can lead to the formation of gums and sediments. Instability can cause filter plugging, combustion chamber deposit formation, and gumming or lacquering of injection system components with resultant sticking and wear.

An accelerated stability test (ASTM D2274) often is applied to fuels to measure their stability. A sample of fuel is heated for a fixed period at a given temperature, sometimes in the presence of a catalyst metal, and the amount of sediment and gum formed is taken as a measure of the stability.

(p) Water and Sediment

One of the most important characteristics of a diesel fuel, the water and sediment content (ASTM D1796–IP 75), is the result of handling and storage practices from the time the fuel leaves the refinery until the time it is delivered to the engine injection system.

Water can easily find its way into fuels. This form of contamination can occur as a result of breathing in moisture laden air in storage facilities when sudden changes of atmospheric temperature take place; condensation of moisture occurring when the temperature drops. Also, leakage of rain into fuel transportation and storage facilities, leakage of water during shipment by tanker, and the presence of water accumulated in tanks used for storage and handling can cause water contamination.

Sediment generally consists of carbonaceous material, metals, or other inorganic matter. There are several causes of this type of contamination:

rust or dirt present in tanks and lines;
dirt introduced through careless handling practices;
dirt present in the air breathed into the storage facilities with fluctuating atmospheric temperature.

Instability and resultant degradation of the fuel in contact with air contribute to the formation of organic sediment, particularly during storage and handling at elevated temperatures.

Water can contribute to filter blocking and cause corrosion of the injection system components. In addition to clogging of the filters, sediment can cause wear and create deposits both in the injection system and in the engine itself.

(q) COMPOSITION

The chemical composition of a typical diesel fuel is extremely complex, with an enormous number of compounds normally present. For this reason, it usually is neither practicable nor profitable to perform individual compound analyses. However, it is sometimes helpful to define the compounds present in a diesel fuel under broad classifications, such as aromatics, paraffins, naphthenes and olefins. A variety of test methods have been proposed. These include ASTM D1319–IP 156, which is for fuels boiling below 606°F (315°C).

(r) APPEARANCE AND ODOUR

The general appearance, colour and clarity of a distillate fuel are useful controls against contamination by residuals, water or fine solid particles. Although the small amount of water or solids required to produce an unsatisfactory hazy fuel is usually insufficient to affect the performance of the fuel, customer acceptance is important. Therefore, it is prudent to check by visual inspection that clear fuel is being delivered.

Similarly, customer acceptance is important with regard to odour and it is usually politic to ensure the fuel is reasonably free of contaminants, such as mercaptans, which impart unpleasant odours to the fuel.

5. SUGGESTIONS FOR FURTHER READING

Diesel Fuel Oils—Production, Characteristics and Combustion (1947). American Society of Mechanical Engineers.
Modern Petroleum Technology (1973). 4th edn, Applied Science, London.
C. C. Pounder (ed.) (1962). *Diesel Engine Principles and Practice*, Newnes, London.

E. Wright and H. P. F. Purday (1950). *Diesel Engine Fuels and Lubricants*, Constable, London.

F. Schmidt (1965). *The Internal Combustion Engine*, Chapman and Hall, London.

Low Temperature Problems with Diesel Vehicle Fuel Systems (1964). Applied Science, London.

Diesel engine problems at zero °F and below (1963). SAE Paper No. 719C, Montreal, June 10–14.

P. J. Agius *et al.* (1971). Current trends in fuel additives, 8th World Petroleum Congress, Moscow, June 13–19.

Chapter 8

BURNING OIL—KEROSINE

R. SEFTON

1. INTRODUCTION

Burning oil is the term generally applied to kerosine used for illuminating or heating purposes. It also includes the somewhat heavier products, used only to a limited extent, in railway signal and certain other lamps for long-time burning operation.

In the early years of the petroleum industry kerosine was its largest and most important selling product. The demand was such that many refiners, using a variety of crude oils, made as wide a distillation cut as possible in order to increase its availability, thereby causing the product to have a dangerously low flash point and to include undesirable higher boiling fractions.

Nowadays, burning oils are manufactured from carefully selected crudes or by the use of special refining procedures, to give products of the requisite volatility and high burning quality.

Before discussing the properties required in burning oils, it is necessary to consider the main kinds of equipment in which they are used.

2. TYPES OF EQUIPMENT

The appliances in which burning oils are used vary widely in design and efficiency; they are of three main types.

(a) WICK-FED—YELLOW FLAME TYPE

The use of simple forms of this type of lamp for illuminating purposes dates back to early times, when various fatty oils were often used. The use of kerosine appliances of this type is still widespread.

The lamp consists essentially of a reservoir containing oil, into which one end of a wick, usually woven of cotton, is immersed. The other end of the wick passes through a wick guide and projects upwards from this. A draught deflector and a chimney with air inlet are provided. Oil flows by capillarity

143

up to the top of the wick, where it is burned. A luminous yellow flame is produced, the light emission coming from incandescent particles. In design these lamps vary greatly in respect of oil reservoir, chimney, wick, and air supply.

Apart from its domestic use, the wick type of lamp in simple form is still much used in brooders and incubators in the poultry industry. Other uses of this type are in hurricane lamps, and certain railway signal lamps.

(b) WICK-FED, OR KINDLER—BLUE FLAME TYPE

Appliances of this type are mainly used for heating and cooking purposes. Blue flame wick-fed lamps are also used with incandescent mantles for lighting. The design is such that more intimate mixing of air and oil vapour takes place, resulting in more complete combustion, and the oil burns with a practically non-luminous blue flame.

In one kind a long drum or chimney is mounted over the burner to induce the air for combustion. It has a circular wick and a flame spreader.

In another, the perforated burner type, there are two (or more) concentric shells containing a large number of holes. At the bottom of the annulus there is an asbestos wick or kindler to which the oil is fed. On lighting, the shells are heated, the oil vaporises, and the air is drawn in through the holes, producing complete blue-flame combustion.

(c) PRESSURE BURNER TYPE

In this type the oil reservoir is fitted with a pump which enables pressure to be maintained above the oil. This forces the oil up a central tube, through a previously-heated vaporising coil, and out through a jet. The issuing oil vapour then mixes with air drawn in from the outside and the mixture passes to the burner, where complete blue-flame combustion takes place.

This principle is employed in the well-known Primus stove, various kinds of blow-lamps, certain pressure burners fitted with mantles for illumination, and also for a variety of minor industrial applications.

3. REQUIREMENTS OF EQUIPMENT

Burning oil should be reasonably safe in respect of flammability both in normal handling and in use.

In the wick-fed yellow flame type of lamp the oil should be capable of burning with a flame of high illuminating value without smoking, and of burning steadily without appreciable diminution in candlepower for a reasonable period without attention. This means that there should be a minimum tendency for clogging of the wick and formation of opaque deposits on the chimney glass. There should not be unpleasant odour or harmful fumes during burning. In such applications as signal lamps, the oil should burn with a steady flame for quite long periods without attention.

The same general considerations of uniform burning, absence of deposits on wicks or jets, and absence of harmful fumes apply to the other types of appliances and with any kind there should be no corrosive effect on metal components at the temperatures involved.

4. THE NATURE AND PROPERTIES OF BURNING OIL

Kerosines used as burning oils are refined petroleum distillates boiling within the range of approximately 150–300°C (302–572°F). The somewhat heavier products, still used to a small and diminishing extent in certain railway signal and other lamps have higher boiling ranges, approximately 250–350°C (482–662°F) or higher.

Kerosine is colourless when produced. However, burning oil kerosines marketed in this country contain trace proportions of identifiable dyes or marker compounds, furfuraldehyde and quinizarin, as required by Customs regulations designed to prevent the misuse of the product.

Burning oil kerosine contains three main types of hydrocarbons—paraffinic, naphthenic, and aromatic, with a preponderance of the paraffinic type. This is in contrast to 'power kerosine', or tractor vaporising oil, which has a comparatively high content of aromatics and naphthenes favourable for high octane rating. It may also contain slight amounts of sulphur in the form of a variety of organic compounds.

The quality of a kerosine as a burning oil is related to its burning characteristics and is dependent on such factors as its composition, volatility, viscosity, calorific value, sulphur content, and freedom from corrosive substances or contaminants.

Two grades of kerosine are specified in British Standard 2869: 1970, based on the above-named properties—Class C1, covering fuels suitable for free-standing flueless domestic burners, and Class C2, covering fuels of less stringent specification requirements, for appliances connected to flues.

5. ASSESSMENT OF QUALITY

(a) BURNING CHARACTERISTICS

While the performance of a particular burning oil is connected with its inherent properties, it can be greatly affected by changes in the design and operating conditions of the lamp or equipment in which it is used. With normal commercial burning oils of similar grade, differences in performance are more dependent on burner design than on hydrocarbon type composition.

However, the effect of hydrocarbon type composition is greater with wick-fed yellow flame burners than with wick-fed blue flame burners. With the former, kerosines which are mainly paraffinic burn well in lamps with a poor draught, whilst under the same conditions kerosines containing high proportions of aromatics and naphthenes burn with a reddish or even smoky flame.

With regard to wick-fed blue flame burners, since combustion is more complete than in yellow flame burners, the former show less differentiation between kerosine types. Even less differentiation between oil types is exhibited with pressure burners, which can operate satisfactorily with a wide range of kerosines.

Since kerosine type and quality are more critical with simple wick-fed yellow flame burners than with the other types, it is usual to assess the burning quality of an oil on the basis of performance in the former type of lamp.

(i) Flame height—smoke point

When the wick of a yellow flame type of lamp is turned up, a point is reached when smoking occurs. Thus, the degree of illumination possible depends mainly on the maximum height of non-smoking flame obtainable. This varies according to the hydrocarbon type composition of the oil. The maximum height of flame obtainable without smoking, termed the smoke point, is greatest with paraffins, considerably lower with naphthenes, and much lower still with aromatics.

The standard Smoke Point Test (IP 57) enables this property to be measured. In this test the oil is burned in a standard wick-fed lamp in which flame height can be varied against a background of a graduated scale. The maximum flame height in millimetres at which the oil burns without smoking under the standard conditions is termed the smoke point.

Even if full advantage is not taken to utilise maximum non-smoking flame height, the property of high smoke point ensures that in the event of sudden draught causing extension in flame height, there will be less tendency for smoking to occur in such circumstances.

The smoke point test is also used in the assessment of the burning characteristics of certain aviation turbine fuels.

In BS 2869: 1970, the minimum smoke point values specified for Class C1 and Class C2 kerosines are 35 mm and 25 mm respectively.

While a low smoke point is undesirable in that it may not give a satisfactory range of smokeless performance, a high smoke point alone is no guarantee that a kerosine has generally satisfactory burning characteristics.

(ii) Constancy of feed to wick

The maintenance of the initial degree of illumination in a lamp depends on the constancy of kerosine flow to the wick, as well as the condition of the wick.

The quantity of oil flowing up a wick is related to the height of the top of the wick above the level of oil in the container and the viscosity and surface tension of the oil. Viscosity is more significant in this respect than surface tension, since it varies more in magnitude than the latter with different kerosines and with change of temperature.

When an oil warms up in the initial burning period, flame size tends to increase slightly, due to increased evaporation rate and to decrease in viscosity. Again, in the case of lamps not provided with constant-level feed, as the height of unimmersed wick increases as oil is consumed, the viscosity becomes significant and, if it is too high, the feed of oil and, consequently, flame height and stability, can be seriously reduced. (With these lamps, the use of a wide, shallow, rather than a narrow, deep oil reservoir, is of advantage in that comparatively little change in the height of wick above the oil surface occurs during burning.)

The viscosity may be determined by ASTM D445–IP 71.

The presence of moisture in a wick also hinders the upward flow of oil and causes a drop in flame height and oil consumption.

(iii) Formation of char on wick

The exposed wick of a lamp, after an oil has been burning for some time, begins to be affected by the formation of a carbonaceous incrustation or char. This is not significant unless it affects the flame or the mechanism for adjusting the wick.

The incrustation may be either hard and brittle or soft, the amount and appearance varying according to the nature and properties of the oil burned. It may be of irregular formation, producing localised deposits known as 'mushrooms' on the surface of the wick, causing flame distortion, or be formed in such an amount and manner as to restrict the size of the flame or, in serious cases, to extinguish it.

The formation of char depends mainly on the chemical composition and purity of the oil and can be affected by the nature of the wick and the design and operating conditions of the lamp.

Possible causes of high char formation may be:

(a) insufficient refining, resulting in the presence of deleterious impurities in the oil;

(b) the presence on the tip of the wick of high-boiling residues which do not vaporise easily, causing decomposition and carbonisation. Contamination with even minute amounts of heavier products, such as lubricants or fuel oil, can cause seriously high char formation.

(iv) Formation of lamp glass deposits

In normal operating conditions there should not be any appreciable formation of deposits or 'bloom' on the lamp glass chimney during burning. Such bloom, when it does appear, may be either white, grey, brown, or blue in colour and should not be confused with the brownish-black or black deposits which are caused by a smoky flame.

Certain factors, such as the design, composition and temperature of the glass chimney and the purity of the atmosphere, can have a bearing on bloom formation; but it is mainly due to the deposition of sulphur compounds derived from the sulphur content of the oil.

(v) Evaluation by standard burning tests

IP 10—Burning Test—24 hour

IP method 10 provides an assessment of the burning characteristics discussed in the foregoing and is generally employed for kerosine used as an illuminant and as fuel for space heaters, cookers, incubators, etc.

In this method the simple flat wick yellow flame type of lamp with no constant feed device is used. As has been indicated, this kind of lamp has an advantage for test purposes over other more efficient types of appliances in that defects in burning quality can be shown which might not be detected with the others.

In the test, the oil is burned for 24 hours in the standard lamp with a flame initially adjusted to specified dimensions.

The details of operation are carefully specified and involve the test room conditions, volume of sample, wick nature, pre-treatment of wick and glass chimney, method of wick trimming, and the procedure for removal of the char.

At the conclusion of the test, the oil consumption and the amount of char formed on the wick are determined and the char value calculated as milligrams per kilogram of oil consumed. A qualitative assessment of the appearance of the glass chimney is also made.

In BS 2869: 1970, the maximum char value requirements specified for Class C1 and Class C2 kerosines are 10 mg/kg and 20 mg/kg, respectively.

Besides the intrinsic significance of char value in respect of oil quality, real differences in such values in a series of kerosines enable a relative comparison to be made of burning quality.

The considerable effect on char-forming tendency of even traces of high-boiling contaminants is demonstrated by the fact that the addition of 0·01 per cent of a heavy lubricating oil to a kerosine of a char value of 10 mg/kg (0·001 per cent), can result in doubling that char value.

The corresponding ASTM method is D187, in which the burning period is also 24 hours and for which the use of the IP lamp is permitted. The average oil consumption, change in flame dimensions, and final appearance of wick and chimney are noted; but the essential difference from IP 10 is that no quantitative determination of char value is made.

IP 11—Burning Test—seven day

This method is used to evaluate the burning properties of oil for use in railway signal lamps and similar kinds of lamps in which long periods of uninterrupted and unattended burning may be necessary.

The oil is burned for seven days in a specified lamp under strictly controlled conditions. Every 24 hours during the test the flame height is measured and, at the end of the test, the condition of the wick and burner is also recorded.

The corresponding ASTM method is D219, in which a standard semaphore lamp is used. The test is continued until 650 ml of oil are burned, which usually takes about five to six days. At the end of the test, the change in the height of the flame and the condition of the wick and chimney are recorded.

(b) Other Properties

The burning and smoke point tests have been shown to provide means of assessing burning characteristics.

The smoke point test adequately reflects the essential feature of hydrocarbon type composition in relation to burning characteristics, as already indicated, and consequently no analysis for composition is necessary in the normal evaluation of burning oils. It may be noted, however, that ASTM D1319–IP 156 is used for determination of aromatics content in the kerosine type products used as aviation turbine fuel.

Apart from burning characteristics, however, a knowledge of the other properties to which reference has already been made is useful in general evaluation of the quality of burning oils.

(i) Flammability

For safety reasons, mainly in view of the fire danger which is incurred in the use of oils of low flash point in lamps, the law demands that the closed flash point of kerosine marketed in the UK should not be below 73°F (23°C) as determined by the Abel instrument (IP 33). The flash points of modern burning oils are considerably higher, being well over 100°F (38°C), due to production as well as safety considerations.

(ii) Volatility

The nature of the distillation range (ASTM D86–IP 123) is of significance with regard to burning characteristics. It can control the flash point and viscosity, the effect of which has already been mentioned. The initial boiling point and the 10 per cent point chiefly affect the flash point and ease of ignition, while the mid-boiling point is more relevant to the viscosity.

It has been found that tendency to flare up in oil heaters can be controlled by regulating the volume percentage recovery at 200°C (392°F) in the distillation test. BS 2869: 1970 specifies for Class C1 kerosines that the percentage recovery figure at 200°C must not exceed 60. A minimum percentage recovery at 200°C of 15 per cent is also specified, to ensure adequate volatility.

An abnormally high final boiling point and percentage residue of a kerosine may indicate contamination with higher boiling constituents, although the presence of trace quantities of very heavy oils sufficient to cause high char values might not necessarily be revealed by these features.

Contamination of a kerosine with heavy oil may also be revealed by the residue on evaporation test (ASTM D381–IP 131), although this depends on the relative volatility of the contaminant.

(iii) Sulphur compounds

Only slight amounts of sulphur compounds remain in kerosine after refining. Refining treatment includes among its objects the removal of such undesirable products as hydrogen sulphide, mercaptan sulphur, and 'free' or corrosive sulphur.

Hydrogen sulphide and mercaptans cause objectionable odours and the former is particularly corrosive. Their presence can be detected by the Doctor Test (IP 30).

'Free' or corrosive sulphur in appreciable amount could result in corrosive action on the metallic components of an appliance. Corrosive action is of particular significance in the case of pressure burner vaporising tubes which operate at high temperatures. The usual test applied in this connection is the Corrosion (Copper Strip) Test (ASTM D130–IP 154).

It is important that the total sulphur content of a burning oil should be low. All the sulphur compounds present in an oil are converted to oxides of sulphur during burning. These oxides of sulphur should not be present to a harmful extent in the immediate atmosphere and this applies particularly to indoor burning appliances which are not provided with a flue. Also it has been indicated in the foregoing that a high total sulphur content of an oil can contribute to the formation of lamp chimney deposits. The total sulphur content of a burning oil may be determined by ASTM D1266–IP 107.

(iv) Freedom from impurities

As indicated earlier, it is important, particularly for use in wick-fed appliances, that the burning oil should be free from any form of contamination. The absence of significant amounts of water or insoluble matter can readily be checked by visual inspection.

The absence of unstable material which could cause deposit formation on heating, possibly tending to clog wicks, can be checked by means of the Flock Test (BS 2869: 1970). This involves maintaining the sample at 240°F (116°C) for six hours and observing any flocculent precipitate.

(v) Calorific value

A high calorific value is obviously desirable in an oil used for heating purposes. Calorific value does not, however, vary greatly in the range of paraffinic type kerosines. It may be determined by IP 12 or ASTM D240.

(vi) Specific gravity (relative density)

Specific gravity has no relation to burning quality but is a useful aid in checking consistency of production of a particular grade. The specific gravity of burning oils may be determined by the hydrometer method, ASTM D1298–IP 160.

6. SUGGESTIONS FOR FURTHER READING

J. Kewley and C. L. Gilbert. *Kerosine. 'The Science of Petroleum'*, Oxford University Press.

F. W. H. Mathews and W. H. Thomas (1946). The char value of kerosine, *J. Inst. Petrol.*, **32**, 269–88.

A. R. Javes and C. Liddell (1954). A rapid method for determining the char value of kerosine, *J. Inst. Petrol.*, **40**, 170–4.

D. G. Tompkins and G. F. J. Murray (1956). Petroleum fuels for domestic heating and lighting, *J. Inst. Petrol.*, **42**, 129–47.

Chapter 9

FUEL OILS, INCLUDING DOMESTIC HEATING OILS

W. H. KITE, Jr and G. G. STEPHENS

1. INTRODUCTION

While it can be said that most petroleum products can be utilised as fuels, the term 'fuel oil', if used without qualification, may be interpreted differently in different countries. The conventional European and United Kingdom conception of a fuel oil is generally associated with the black, viscous, residual material remaining as the result of refinery distillation of crude oil either alone or in blend with light components, and which is used for steam raising, marine diesel engine operation and various industrial processes. The term is sometimes used to refer to the light, amber coloured middle distillates or gas oils also used as fuels which, in the United Kingdom and Europe, are usually distinguished from the residual type fuels by being characterised as distillate fuels, domestic or diesel fuel oil etc. The use of kerosine type fuels in vaporising pot-type burners or in 'Wallflame' burners for domestic heating brings this material within the category of a 'fuel oil' as well. The subject of kerosine has been discussed in Chapter 8.

In the United States the term 'fuel oil' while being applied to the residual type materials is also used to refer to the distillate products, gas oil and kerosine, without qualification as instanced in the ASTM D396 Specification for Fuel Oils. In this specification the No. 1 grade fuel oil is a kerosine type used in vaporising pot-type burners while the No. 2 fuel is a distillate oil (gas oil) used for general purpose domestic heating.

To the unwary these designations can be confusing.

Fuel oil, therefore, in its various categories has a range of application which is quite extensive and the choice of a standard procedure to be used for assessing or controlling product quality must, of necessity, depend both upon the type of fuel and its ultimate use.

2. NATURE AND USES OF FUEL OILS

(a) DOMESTIC HEATING OILS

The term 'domestic heating oil' in the present context is applicable to the middle distillate or gas oil type product used principally with atomising burner heating equipment. In the UK this material normally consists of the straight run gas oil from the distillation of the crude oil and which boils within the approximate temperature range of 160–370°C (320–700°F). In the USA the straight run gas oil fraction is usually blended with the appropriate boiling range material from catalytic cracking processing. The components are suitably treated prior to final blending and additives may also be added to further assist in the stabilisation of the finished product. Because of fiscal regulations in some countries, particularly in Belgium, France and Germany, the gas oil grades are used in pot-type vaporising heating appliances as well as in atomising burner equipment. It may not be inappropriate at this stage to describe briefly the functioning of the atomising and vaporising type burners.

Before gas oil and residual fuel will burn readily and satisfactorily it is necessary that they be broken up into very fine particles or droplets and mixed with the requisite amount of air to provide a combustible mixture. In the vaporising pot-type burner, the fuel runs into the base of a metal container and is heated by radiation from the flame and by conduction down the wall of the container to the base. The fuel vaporises from the surface and as the vapours rise up the pot they mix with the air drawn through the perforated wall to burn.

In atomising burners, vaporisation is rapidly achieved by breaking the liquid fuel stream into a large number of very small droplets. This is accomplished, in the pressure jet burner, by forcing the fuel, under pressure, through a specially shaped orifice such that it emerges as a fine spray into the combustion chamber. With blast or twin-fluid atomisers, a high velocity stream of air, steam or gas impinges on the fuel tearing it into small droplets. In the third type of atomising burner, the Rotary Cup burner, the oil is fed through a central pipe onto the inner surface of a rapidly rotating, tapered, hollow-cup. By centrifugal action the oil is forced up into the wide end of the cup and is distintegrated from the edge of the cup. The finely divided oil is mixed with the necessary combustion air and burnt.

With most types of atomising burners the fuel cannot be metered into the system at a rate much less than half a gallon per hour which in terms of boiler output represents about 50 000Btu/h thus setting the lower limit for atomising burners. The maximum output of vaporising pot-type burners is of the order of 50 000 Btu/h. Hence in the smaller domestic heating installation in the UK and Europe vaporising burner equipment, installed in the house, is employed. Atomising burners, if used in such installations, tend to produce a noise level unacceptable in the house. In the USA, since the burner equipment is generally sited in the house basement, the noise level presents little problem.

This practice is becoming more popular in Europe where at present the number of atomising burners in domestic heating equipment is appreciably fewer than is the case in the USA where these burners are in use in the majority of such installations.

In all applications, except some room heaters, there is a decided requirement for unattended heating installations and to meet this a large number of automatic burners are available.

(b) RESIDUAL FUEL OILS

In the early days of the petroleum industry residual fuel oils consisted virtually of the residue remaining after removal of the lighter components, *e.g.* gasoline, kerosine and gas oil, during the processing of crude oil in the atmospheric distillation unit.

With the increasing demand for gasoline (petrol) grew the need for more and more lighter components than could normally be obtained by atmospheric distillation of the crude oil. Consequently, refining processes were developed, *e.g.* thermal cracking for conversion of more of the atmospheric residue into lighter materials suitable as components in gasoline blending. The continued increase over the years in the demand for all petroleum products and particularly for gasoline of improved quality, has seen the introduction of refining processes (*e.g.* catalytic cracking) aimed at maximising the yield of lighter components from the crude oil which could satisfactorily be employed in modern gasolines. As a consequence of these various developments the composition of the residual fuel oils gradually changed. The yield of residual material available for fuel oil decreased and various products from the refinery processes which were surplus to requirements (*e.g.* straight run gas oil, cracked gas oil) or waste by-products of these operations tended, in the earlier days, to be channelled rather indiscriminately to fuel oil and utilised as fuel oil blending components. The lighter of these components, the naphthas, straight run and cracked gas oils, the extracts from the production of kerosine and lubricating oils used as diluents for viscosity reduction are for this reason often referred to as 'cutter stocks'.

Today the residual fuel oils from the modern refinery, instead of simply being the residue remaining after removal of the lighter products, are the result of selective blending of the various residues and distillate cutter stocks to produce a variety of fuels which are suitable for a wide range of industrial applications. The characteristics of the fuels thus produced will depend largely upon the crude oil sources and the composition of the fuel oil blends.

3. SPECIFICATIONS

To ensure that fuels give trouble-free performance with the minimum of equipment servicing, the refiner applies specifications to his various fuel

TABLE 1
Specification for fuel oils
ASTM D396-69ª

Grade of fuel oil	Flash point, °F (°C) Min.	Pour point, °F (°C) Max.	Water and sediment, per cent by volume Max.	Carbon residue on 10 per cent bottoms, per cent Max.	Ash, per cent by weight Max.	Distillation temperatures °F (°C) 10 per cent point Max.	90 per cent point Min.	90 per cent point Max.	Saybolt viscosity, sec Universal at 100°F (38°C) Min.	Universal at 100°F (38°C) Max.	Furol at 122°F (50°C) Min.	Furol at 122°F (50°C) Max.	Kinematic viscosity, cSt At 100°F (38°C) Min.	At 100°F (38°C) Max.	At 122°F (50°C) Min.	At 122°F (50°C) Max.	Gravity, deg API Min.	Copper strip corrosion Max.	Sulphur, per cent Max.
No. 1—A distillate oil intended for vaporising pot-type burners and other burners requiring this grade of fuel	100 or legal (38)	0ᵈ (−18)	trace	0·15	—	420 (215)	—	550 (288)	—	—	—	—	1·4	2·2	—	—	35	No. 3	0·5 or legal
No. 2—A distillate oil for general purpose domestic heating for use in burners not requiring No. 1 fuel oil	100 or legal (38)	20ᵈ (−7)	0·05	0·35	—	ᵉ	540ᵈ (282)	640 (338)	(32·6)ᶠ	(37·93)	—	—	2·0ᵈ	3·6	—	—	30	—	0·5ᵇ or legal
No. 4—Preheating not usually required for handling or burning	130 or legal (55)	20 (−7)	0·50	—	0·10	—	—	—	45	125	—	—	(5·8)	(26·4)	—	—	—	—	c
No. 5 (Light)—Preheating may be required depending on climate and equipment	130 or legal (55)	—	1·00	—	0·10	—	—	—	150	300	—	—	(32)	(65)	—	—	—	—	c
No. 5 (Heavy)—Preheating may be required for burning and, in cold climates, may be required for handling	130 or legal (55)	—	1·00	—	0·10	—	—	—	350	750	(23)	(40)	(75)	(162)	(42)	(81)	—	—	c
No. 6—Preheating required for burning and handling	150 (65)	—	2·00ᵍ	—	—	—	—	—	(900)	(9 000)	45	300	(92)	(638)	—	—	—	—	c

ª It is the intent of these classifications that failure to meet any requirement of a given grade does not automatically place an oil in the next lower grade unless in fact it meets all requirements of the lower grade.

ᵇ Outside USA the sulphur limit for No. 2 shall be 1·0 per cent.

ᶜ Legal requirements to be met.

ᵈ Lower or higher pour points may be specified whenever required by conditions of storage or use. When pour point less than 0°F is specified, the minimum viscosity shall be 1·8 cSt (32·0 sec, Saybolt Universal) and the minimum 90 per cent point shall be waived.

ᵉ The 10 per cent distillation temperature point may be specified at 440°F (226°C) maximum for use in other than atomising burners.

ᶠ Viscosity values in parentheses are for information only and not necessarily limiting.

ᵍ The amount of water by distillation plus the sediment by extraction shall not exceed 2·00 per cent. The amount of sediment by extraction shall not exceed 0·50 per cent. A deduction quantity shall be made for all water and sediment in excess of 1·0 per cent.

TABLE 2
British Standard specification 2869: 1970
Requirements for burner fuels

	Class D	Class E	Class F	Class G	Class H	Test method BS reference	Technically identical with
Viscosity, kinematic at 37·8°C (100°F), cSt, min.	1·6	—	—	—	—	BS^a	ASTM D445–
max.	6·0	—	—	—	—		IP 71
Viscosity, kinematic at 82·2°C (180°F), cSt, max.	—	12·5	30	70	115		
Carbon residue, Conradson on 10 per cent residue, per cent by mass, max.	0·2	—	—	—	—	BS 4380	ASTM D189– IP 13
Distillation							
Recovery at 200°C (392°F), per cent by volume, min.	—					BS 4349	ASTM D86– IP 123
Recovery at 200°C (392°F), per cent by volume, max.	—	—	—	—	—		
Recovery at 357°C or 675°F, per cent by volume, min.	90	—	—	—	—		
Final boiling point, max.	—	—	—	—	—		

	55°C or 130°F[b]	66°C or 150°F[b]	66°C or 150°F[b]	66°C or 150°F[b]	66°C or 150°F[b]	BS	ASTM
Flash point, closed, Pensky–Martens, min.	55°C or 130°F[b]	66°C or 150°F[b]	66°C or 150°F[b]	66°C or 150°F[b]	66°C or 150°F[b]	BS 2839	ASTM D93–IP 34
Water content, per cent by volume, max.	0·05	0·5	0·75	1·0	1·0	BS 4385	IP 74
Sediment, per cent by mass, max.	0·01	0·15	0·25	0·25	0·25	BS 4382	ASTM D473–IP 53
Ash, per cent by mass, max.	0·01	0·1	0·15	0·2	0·2	BS 4450	ASTM D482–IP 4
Sulphur content, per cent by weight, max.	1·0	3·5	4·0	4·5	5·0	BS 4350	D1266–IP 107
Copper corrosion test, max.	1	—	—	—	—	BS 4384 BS 4351	IP 63 ASTM D130–IP 154
Cloud point, max. Summer	0°C (32°F) Mar./Sept. inclusive					} BS 4458	ASTM D2500–IP 219
Winter	−7°C or 20°F[b] Oct./Feb. inclusive						

[a] Pending publication of the appropriate British Standard method, the technically identical method listed in the table is to be used for testing against the requirements of this British Standard.

[b] The alternative Celsius and Fahrenheit temperatures shown in this table are in some cases not exactly equivalent, but are the closest whole number equivalents compatible with the test procedures. Such cases are indicated by the use of the term 'or' between the two values.

grades. These normally include a number of control tests which aim at evaluating the significant and important properties of the fuel, which reflect the fuel composition, the crude oil and refinery treatment. The tests may be physical or chemical in character and in very many cases are empirical procedures, and as such are designed to provide an indication of certain characteristics of the fuel. Consequently they are strictly standardised in the petroleum industry by such bodies as the Institute of Petroleum (IP) and the American Society for Testing and Materials (ASTM). Provided the test procedures are strictly followed the results obtained are normally repeatable within the limits laid down in the appropriate standard methods. Both the ASTM and the British Standards Institution issue specifications for fuels which are widely accepted. The relevant details of these two specifications are given in Tables 1 and 2.

The primary object of a specification is to guarantee that the consumer receives a product of consistent and satisfactory quality for the purpose intended. It should not contain unnecessarily restrictive clauses which may seriously limit manufacture and the control tests included, whether basic, empirical or arbitrary should relate to the fuel performance in transit, storage and in use. Thus an understanding of the test methods and their significance is necessary when applied to specification work. Various test procedures which are normally specified or used for the assessment of quality control of domestic heating oils and residual fuel oils are briefly described and their significance discussed. Full details of the procedures will be found in the appropriate ASTM or IP Standard Methods.

4.   PROPERTIES AND THEIR ASSESSMENT

(a) DOMESTIC HEATING OILS

Of the various properties of domestic heating oils those which are associated with the burning characteristics of the fuel may be considered of primary importance since the customer will be more aware of them.

Ignition troubles can occur if the fuel is not sufficiently volatile; burner efficiency is impaired if the fuel smokes badly and the tendency for the formation of carbonaceous deposits, which can block burner nozzles or vaporising devices, will result in too frequent need for cleaning and possible ignition difficulty. Manufacturers, therefore, during refining operations ensure that these various burning qualities are carefully controlled by the use of the various tests described below. These include standard procedures used for evaluating such properties as volatility, calorific value, viscosity, sulphur which can affect the burning quality characteristics of heating oils. Other test procedures aimed at assessing handling and transportation problems and freedom from contamination and corrosion are also discussed.

No standard procedures for evaluating the performance of heating oils in domestic heating equipment were available until 1963 when the ASTM issued two tentative methods for assessing the tendency of fuels used in such equipment towards smoke formation and deposition. Both methods may be used either as laboratory or field procedures and a comparison of heating appliances as well as an assessment of the burning characteristics of heating oils may be made by these means. In method ASTM D2156 (Smoke Density in Flue Gases from Distillate Fuels) the procedure is used as a means of controlling the production of smoke emitted to an acceptable level when burning heating oils in domestic heating installations. Efficient operation of the equipment can be adversely affected if smoke density becomes excessive.

The second method ASTM D2157 (Effect of Air Supply on Smoke Density in Burning Distillate fuels) is applicable only to equipment incorporating pressure atomising and rotary wallflame burners. In this method, efficiency of operation is related to clean burning of the fuel and the extent to which combustion air can be reduced without producing an unacceptable level of smoke is indicative of the maximum efficiency for a particular installation at any acceptable smoke level.

(i) Calorific value

Since the function of a fuel is to produce heat the calorific or heating value (ASTM D240 or IP 12) is one of the important fuel properties and a knowledge of this is necessary in obtaining information regarding the combustion efficiency and performance of all types of oil burning equipment.

The determination is made in a bomb calorimeter under specified conditions, the oxygen in the bomb being saturated with water vapour prior to the ignition of the fuel so that the water formed during combustion is condensed. The calorific value so determined will include the latent heat of water at the test temperature and is known as the Gross Calorific Value at constant volume. The corresponding Net Calorific Value at constant pressure is obtained by deducting the latent heat of water formed during the burning of the hydrogen present in the fuel to produce water. The calorific value is usually expressed in British Thermal Units per pound (Btu/lb) or in calories per gram (cal/g). In Europe the net calorific value is more often called for in calculations on burner efficiency since the water formed during combustion passes out as water vapour with the flue gases and hence its latent heat of condensation is not realised as useful heat. In the UK the gross calorific value is normally used for this purpose.

The variation in calorific value within a particular fuel grade is small and the value can be calculated with sufficient accuracy for normal purposes from other known data. This property is not always quoted in specifications as it is not controllable in the manufacture of the fuel other than indirectly by the inclusion of other tests in the fuel specification.

The specific gravity (ASTM D1298–IP 160) normally included in heating oil specifications is of use mainly in volume–weight relationships and in the calculation of calorific value.

(ii) Sulphur

Organic sulphur compounds (*e.g.* mercaptans, sulphides, polysulphides, thiophens etc.) are present in petroleum products to a greater or lesser extent depending upon the crude oil origin and the refinery treatment. Corrosion of heating equipment can occur if the sulphur oxides formed on combustion of the fuel are allowed to condense in the presence of moisture on the cooler parts of the flue system. Corrosion of metal parts of the fuel system may also reflect the presence of corrosive sulphur components in the fuel. The corrosive tendencies of the fuel may be detected by the Copper Strip test (ASTM D130–IP 154), the effect of these sulphur compounds being indicated by discoloration of the copper strip. Specifications include a limiting clause on the degree of staining tolerated in these fuels.

It is, therefore, necessary that the sulphur content in these fuels should be kept as low as possible. Most marketed fuels within the gas oil boiling range contain amounts of sulphur of less than one per cent although some specifications permit somewhat higher maximum values. BS 2869 Class D quotes a maximum of one per cent.

Various standard procedures are available for the determination of the sulphur content of distillate fuels. In the lamp method (ASTM D1266–IP 107), which is widely used, the product is burned completely in a small wick-fed lamp, the gases formed by combustion are absorbed in hydrogen peroxide solution and the sulphur is subsequently determined as sulphate. Several rapid methods, including X-ray absorption and high temperature combustion, for the determination of sulphur are also available.

(iii) Carbon residue

The use of oil fuel for heating has resulted in the availability of a variety of burner types which are classified according to the manner in which they prepare the fuel for combustion. In the vaporising pot-type burner, extensively used for domestic heating purposes, the oil is brought into contact with a hot surface and the oil vapour subsequently mixed with combustion air. This type of burner has the disadvantage that any carbonaceous residue formed by the decomposition of the oil or any incomplete vaporisation is deposited in, or near, the inlet surface, thus reducing fuel flow, particularly if copper unions are used, with resultant loss in burner efficiency. The burner can, therefore, only be operated satisfactorily on distillate fuels having low carbon forming tendencies. With such fuels used in atomising type burners, where the fuel is broken up into fine particles which are then mixed with the necessary combustion air, any carbon formed during this process is in a more favourable state for complete combustion.

For the purpose of assessing the carbon forming tendencies of the gas oil type heating oil used in domestic heating installations a carbon residue test is normally used. Two standard procedures are available, the Conradson Test (ASTM D189–IP 13) used principally for distillate and residual fuel oils and the Ramsbottom Test (ASTM D524–IP 14) specified mainly for lubricating oils. With light distillate oils forming only small amounts of carbonaceous deposits, the carbon residue value by both methods is obtained on the ten per cent residue obtained by means of an adaptation of the standard distillation procedure for gas oil (ASTM D86–IP 123) and similar distillates, in order that the accuracy of the determination may be improved.

The carbon residue test is, therefore, a useful means for indicating the carbon forming tendencies of gas oil type fuel oils (*e.g.* ASTM No. 2) used in vaporising burner installations. For this purpose, maximum values for the Conradson carbon residues (on 10 per cent residue) of the fuel should be of the order of 0·05 per cent weight. As already mentioned, little difficulty is normally encountered in burning the gas oil or ASTM No. 2 type fuel in atomising burner appliances. However, since excessive carbon deposition can foul burner nozzles, with consequent unsatisfactory combustion, limits are included in fuel specifications for the ten per cent residue Conradson value. For heating oils containing a small percentage of residual fuel limits of the order of 0·5 per cent weight are specified for this value.

Because of their empirical nature and the differences in apparatus and procedure, there is no precise correlation existing between the Conradson and Ramsbottom carbon residue tests. While a graph is given in the text of the standard method showing the approximate relationship between the procedures it is suggested that with low carbon residue values it should be used with caution. It should also be noted that the relationship is not suitable for use with fuels containing additives.

(iv) Viscosity

In heating installations, viscosity is significant in that it regulates the flow of fuel and so influences the heat output of the system. With pressure jet atomising burners fed by a pump, the fuel flow may fall with low viscosity fuels due to leak-back past the working parts of the pump. This tendency may be accentuated since low viscosity fuels generally have lower lubricating properties and thus pump wear may increase. The discharge coefficient of pressure jet burner nozzles is also affected by fuel viscosity and for a given pressure the fuel delivered to the combustion chamber will decrease as the fuel viscosity decreases. With vaporising and wallflame burners where the fuel flow is controlled by a float operated needle valve, a change in viscosity can markedly affect the fuel flow for a given head of fuel. In these appliances a decrease in viscosity will lead to an increase in fuel flow at the same control setting. Fuel viscosity could also affect the combustion process in a pressure jet burner as it will influence the size of fuel droplets from a given nozzle. In extreme conditions where atomisation is severely affected, flame instability, poor combustion or ignition failure may result.

For the determination of the viscosity of petroleum products various procedures, *e.g.* Saybolt (ASTM D88) and Engler, are available and have been in use for many years, all being of an empirical nature, measuring the time taken in seconds for a given volume of fuel to flow through an orifice of specified dimensions. The use of these empirical procedures is being super-seded by the more precise kinematic viscosity method (ASTM D445–IP 71) in which a fixed volume of fuel flows through the capillary of a calibrated glass capillary viscometer under an accurately reproducible head and at a closely controlled temperature. The result is obtained from the product of the time taken for the fuel to flow between two etched marks on the capillary tube and the calibration factor of the viscometer and is reported in centistokes. Since the viscosity decreases with increasing temperature the temperature of test must also be reported if the viscosity value is to have any significance. For distillate fuel oils the usual test temperature is 100°F (38°C) in the US and UK and 20°C (68°F) on the European continent.

(v) Volatility

When operating heating installations using vaporising or atomising burner systems with distillate fuel oils it is essential that the fuel can be readily ignited and a stable flame maintained. The fuel must contain sufficient volatile components to ensure that this can be done easily even with the atomising burners which are less sensitive to volatility than the vaporising burners. The volatility of the fuel must be uniform, from batch to batch, if too frequent resetting of burner controls is to be avoided and if maximum performance and efficiency is to be maintained. Information regarding the volatility and the proportion of fuel vaporised at any one temperature may be obtained from the standard distillation procedure (ASTM D86–IP 123).

Specifications for domestic heating oils generally include limits on the temperatures at which ten per cent and ninety per cent of the fuel are distilled by the standard procedure. For the kerosine type fuel (ASTM No. 1) these values control the volatility at both ends of the distillation range while for the gas oil (ASTM No. 2), where the front end volatility is not so critical, only the ninety per cent distillation temperature is normally specified. This ensures that high boiling point components which are less likely to burn, and which can cause carbon deposition, are excluded from the fuel.

To enable calculation of the Cetane Index to be made and to check normality of the fuel the fifty per cent distillation temperature is sometimes included in some fuel specifications.

(vi) Stability

Heating oils must be capable of storage for many months without significant change. They should not break down to form gummy material and insoluble sediments or change or darken in colour. In other words they must be stable.

Instability in heating oils can be a serious problem since the deposition of organic sediments in storage tanks can result in blocked filters, malfunctioning and even complete ignition failure if the burner nozzle becomes blocked with these degradation products. From the standpoint of customer acceptance it is essential that the fuel supplied should not exhibit these peculiarities. The use of inhibitor additives to reduce the amount and size of the sediment has been found useful in this respect.

The storage stability of these fuels may also be influenced by the crude oil origin, the hydrocarbon composition and the refinery treatment. Heating oils containing unsaturated hydrocarbons and catalytically cracked components have been shown to be inherently less stable chemically and to have a greater tendency to form sediment on ageing than the straight run fuel oils. The presence of reactive compounds of sulphur (*e.g.* thiophens), nitrogen (pyrroles) and oxygen is also considered to contribute to fuel instability.

To ensure a product of satisfactory stability, test procedures are necessary to predict this aspect of quality control. For this purpose the ASTM D2274 procedure (Stability of Distillate Fuel Oil–Accelerated Method) and the British Ministry of Defence Specification DEF 2000 Methods 16 and 17 are the procedures (of the many available) which are now widely used in the USA and the UK respectively. ASTM D2274 and DEF Method 16 are short term/high temperature procedures which are generally preferred to the long term/lower temperature Method 17 test. While the accuracy of these empirical tests leaves much to be desired they do provide, with some background knowledge of the fuel, useful data relating to the fuel's storage stability characteristics.

(vii) Low temperature properties—cloud and pour point

Distillate fuels in oil fired heating installations in some countries are normally stored in outside tankage and a knowledge of the lowest temperature at which the fuel can be transferred from tank to burner, thus avoiding line and filter blockage difficulties, is necessary. An indication of this temperature may be obtained from the Cloud (ASTM D2500–IP 219) and Pour Point (ASTM D97–IP 15) tests which under standard conditions give, respectively, the temperature at which wax begins to crystallise out of the fuel and when the wax structure has built up sufficiently to prevent the flow of oil. In these installations, a coarse filter is normally sited in the system near to the tank outlet to remove large particles of extraneous matter; a fine filter is positioned near the burner to protect the pump. Provided the outside temperature does not drop below the cloud point temperature it is unlikely that filter blockage will occur and the fuel will thus perform satisfactorily down to the temperature at which gelling takes place. This may occur at, or close to, the pour point and certainly below the cloud point temperature. Hence, limits on pour and cloud point levels are included in most heating oil specifications.

The cloud point test has been criticised in recent times for lack of precision and consequent product 'give-away' and the need for a more dynamic test for predicting the low temperature operability limit of distillate fuels has been expressed. Of the various procedures being used within various organisations, based either upon a pour type test or screen type tests—where the fuel is passed through a mesh screen by pressure or suction at low temperatures, the screen type test approach seems to be gaining favour, particularly on the Continent. Both ASTM and IP are currently studying this problem.

(viii) Cleanliness, etc.

In addition to the various test procedures concerned with the storage, handling and burning characteristics of heating oils, other tests are invariably called for in assessing or controlling the cleanliness, freedom from contamination and safety aspects involved. Contamination by water and sediment can lead to filter and burner clogging problems, and to the production of emulsions which are removable only with difficulty. The corrosion of storage tanks may also be associated with water bottoms which accumulate from atmospheric condensation and water contamination. This particular problem can be partially alleviated by the use of anti-rust additives.

Water content may be determined by a distillation procedure (ASTM D95–IP 74) and sediment (ASTM D473–IP 53) can be estimated by toluene extraction of the oil through a refractory thimble, the insoluble sediment being retained in the thimble. Total water and sediment may be determined together by a centrifuge procedure (ASTM D96 or IP 75) but separate determinations of water and sediment are generally more accurate.

Alkaline compounds resulting from entrainment during distillation, rust and sand present as filterable sediment and abrasive solids in fuels contribute to the ash (ASTM D482–IP 4) which remains after incineration of the fuel at relatively high temperatures. The presence of such materials in excess in distillate fuels can lead to wear troubles in burner nozzles, pumps and other mechanical parts in the installation. Hence, in gas oils and diesel fuels of high quality, ash contents of low values only (ca. 0·01 per cent or less) are tolerated.

Nowadays the presence of inorganic acids in distillate fuels, resulting from refinery treatment, is unlikely. However, specifications for these fuels still include limiting clauses for acidity, both total and inorganic, as a check against possible corrosion of metal equipment in contact with the fuel. Inorganic acidity should in any case be entirely absent. Test methods include potentiometric (ASTM D664–IP 177) and colour-indicator titration (ASTM D974–IP 139) procedures in addition to inorganic acidity (IP 182) and total acidity (IP 1) methods.

While necessary limits are placed on these various contamination or 'housekeeping' tests to ensure that the customer receives a satisfactory product, it is also essential that the fuel is safe to transport and store. For this purpose a flash point procedure is used to indicate the temperature at which the fuel gives off sufficient hydrocarbon vapours to form an explosive mixture with air. The Pensky-Martens closed cup procedure (ASTM D93–IP 34) is normally employed for testing heating oils since it approaches the conditions of storage of the fuel in storage tanks. Limits are placed on the flash points for legal, insurance and fire regulation requirements. ASTM fuels 1 and 2 specify the legal minimum value of 38°C (100°F). The BS specification for Class D domestic fuel calls for a minimum of 55°C (130°F) but recognises that there are circumstances where a minimum flash point of 66°C (150°F) is permitted as is the case in many other heating oil specifications. It should be noted that the use of 'go–no go' flash point procedures is gaining popularity. Two such procedures are published in the 1972 edition of IP Standards as 'Proposed Methods'.

As flash point is associated with volatility, contamination of the fuel by a more volatile product, whereby a fire hazard could exist, may be indicated by a reduction in the normal flash point of the fuel.

Degradation by heavier residual products can affect fuel performance by increasing the fuel's carbon-forming tendencies. A knowledge of the colour of the fuel can therefore provide a useful check on contamination. While the colour of distillate heating oils (including those which, for fiscal reasons, contain a trace of residue) can vary within wide limits without affecting performance, customer acceptance is associated with the colour and appearance of the fuel normally supplied. A significant difference in colour or haziness due to presence of moisture may result in the customer presupposing he is receiving a fuel of different and/or inferior performance. Hence the colour, as determined by ASTM D1500–IP 196 of these heating oils can constitute a useful feature of quality control.

(b) RESIDUAL FUEL OILS

As with the domestic heating oils contamination in residual fuel oils may be indicated by the presence of excessive amounts of water, emulsions and inorganic material such as sand and rust. Blockage of fuel filters, erosion of burner tips and other mechanical parts may also result. This aspect of fuel quality control may be dealt with by placing restrictions on the water (ASTM D95–IP 74), sediment by extraction (ASTM D473–IP 53), or water and sediment (ASTM D96 or IP 75) values obtained on the fuel. Similarly considerations of safety in storage and transportation and, more particularly, contamination by more volatile products may be handled by the Pensky-Martens flash point test (ASTM D93–IP 34). For the heavier fuels a minimum flash point of 130°F or 150°F (55°C or 66°C) is included in most specifications.

The significance of other properties of fuel oils may, however, depend largely upon the ultimate uses of the fuels. These will include steam raising for process purposes, marine propulsion, electrical power generation, and oil fired locomotives; central heating; diesel engines; industrial applications such as steel, glass, ceramic manufacture; the cement and allied processes; gas turbines; gas enrichment and oil gas manufacture. Problems of corrosion, ash deposition, atmospheric pollution, product contamination, can result from the combustion of fuel oils used in these various applications and in particular cases properties such as vanadium, sodium and sulphur contents may become significant. The possibility of corrosion of tanks and pipelines by acidic constituents of the fuel will be covered by the limiting acidity clauses included in most fuel oil specifications.

Problems of handling and storage may also arise unless recommended practices such as are detailed in the British Standards Code of Practice 3002 and BS 799 are observed, particularly with the heavier fuel oils, since at ambient temperatures these fuels may be quite viscous or even semi-solid. Although they will normally be kept in heated tankage details of their low temperature characteristics will be necessary. In addition, since the fuels will need to be preheated in order to obtain the correct atomising conditions for efficient combustion, information regarding viscosity limits will also be necessary.

Of the remaining properties the specific gravity (ASTM D1298–IP 160), as far as the combustion characteristics of residual fuels are concerned, is probably of least importance. It has its uses, however, in refinery product control, in weight–volume relationships and, in conjunction with other fuel properties, in the calculation of calorific value. In this connection fuels of higher specific gravity will have higher calorific values if these are reported on a volume basis. The significance of calorific value (ASTM D240 or IP 12) in relation to domestic heating oils has already been discussed and will be similar for the residual fuel oils. The calorific value of these fuels will be somewhat lower due largely to their higher carbon/hydrogen ratio and the incidence of greater amounts of less combustible material, e.g. water, sediment and generally higher levels of sulphur whose calorific value is only about 4000 Btu/lb. Since for most residual fuel oils the range of calorific value is relatively narrow, limits are not normally included in fuel specifications. When precise determinations are not essential, values of sufficient accuracy may be derived from calculations based upon specific gravity and sulphur as given in the US Bureau of Standards Miscellaneous Publication No. 97.

(i) Viscosity
This is one of the more important properties of residual fuel oils since, as for domestic fuel oils, it provides information on the ease (or otherwise) with which a fuel can be transferred, under the prevailing temperature and pressure conditions, from storage tank to burner system. It also indicates the degree to which a fuel oil needs to be preheated to obtain the correct atomising temperature for efficient combustion. Most residual fuel oils function best when the burner input viscosity lies within a certain specified range. A knowledge of the viscosity is therefore necessary for the efficient utilisation of the fuel and so specifications include a viscosity clause.

Reference has already been made to the various empirical procedures in use for viscosity determinations. The Saybolt Universal and Saybolt Furol viscometers are widely used in the USA and the Engler in Europe. In the USA, viscosities on the lighter fuel grades are determined using the Saybolt Universal instrument at 38°C (100°F); for the heaviest fuels the Saybolt Furol viscometer is used at 50°C (122°F). Similarly, in Europe, the Engler viscometer is used at temperatures of 20°C (68°F), 50°C (122°F) and in some instances at 100°C (212°F). The use of these empirical procedures for fuel oils is being superseded by the kinematic system which is included in both the BS 2869 and ASTM D396 specifications for fuel oils.

The determination of residual fuel oil viscosities is complicated by the fact that some fuel oils containing significant quantities of wax, do not behave as simple Newtonian liquids in which the rate of shear is directly proportional to the shearing stress applied. At temperatures in the region of 38°C (100°F) these fuels tend to deposit wax from solution with a resulting adverse effect on the accuracy of the viscosity result unless the test temperature is raised sufficiently high for all wax to remain in solution. While the present reference test temperature of 50°C (122°F) is adequate for use with the majority of residual fuel oils there is a growing trend of opinion in favour of a higher temperature (e.g. 82·2°C; 180°F) particularly in view of the increasing availability of waxier fuel oils from the newer crude oils from North Africa. The 1970 revision of BS 2869 supports this viewpoint in specifying 180°F as the viscosity test temperature for fuels of Class E to H. A number of difficulties related to anomalous viscosities would also be obviated.

Anomalous viscosity in residual fuel oils is best shown by plotting the kinematic viscosity determined at the normal test temperature and at two or three higher temperatures on ASTM D341 viscosity–temperature charts. These charts are constructed so that, for a Newtonian fuel oil, the temperature–viscosity relationship is linear. Non-linearity at the lower end of the applicable temperature range is normally considered evidence of non-Newtonian behaviour.

These ASTM charts are also useful for the estimation of the viscosity of a fuel oil blend from a knowledge of the component viscosities and for calculation of the correct preheat temperature necessary to obtain the required viscosity for efficient atomisation of the fuel oil in the burner.

While it is considered a technical advantage to specify kinematic viscosity, the conventional viscometers are still in wide use and it may be convenient, or even necessary, to be able to convert viscosities from one system to another. Provision is made in ASTM D2161 for the conversion of kinematic viscosity to Saybolt Universal and Furol and in IP Standards for conversion to Redwood viscosity.*

The following table gives an approximate indication of these conversions.

Kinematic viscosity at 122°F (50°C) cSt	36	125	370	690
Kinematic viscosity at 100°F (38°C) cSt	61	—	—	—
Redwood No. 1 viscosity at 122°F s	148	510	1500	2800
Redwood No. 1 viscosity at 100°F s	250	1000	3500	7000
Saybolt Universal viscosity at 100°F s	285	1150	4000	8000
Saybolt Furol viscosity at 122°F s	—	60	175	325
Engler degrees at 122°F	4·8	16·5	48·7	91·0

* IP 70—Redwood viscosity was withdrawn in 1973.

(ii) Pour point and pumpability
Whilst one of the attributes of liquid fuels is the relative ease with which they can be transferred from one place to another, it is still necessary to have some indication of the lowest temperature at which this may be achieved. The pour point procedure (ASTM D97–IP 15) defined as the lowest temperature at which, under prescribed conditions, an oil will flow is generally used for this purpose. Depending upon the storage conditions and application of the fuel, limits are placed upon the pour point. Storage of the heavier viscosity fuel oils in heated tankage will permit of higher pour points than would otherwise be possible. While the failure to flow can generally be attributed to the separation of wax from the fuel it can also, in the case of very viscous fuels, be due to the effect of viscosity.

The pour points of residual fuels may be much influenced by the previous thermal history of the fuels and the fact that any loosely knit wax structure built up on cooling the fuel can, generally, be readily broken up by the application of a little pressure—thus allowing fuels to be pumped at temperatures below their pour point temperatures. The usefulness of the pour point test in relation to residual fuel oils is, therefore, open to question and the tendency to regard it as the limiting temperature at which a fuel will flow can be misleading unless correlated with low temperature viscosity.

While the pour point test is still included in many specifications (but not, however, in BS 2869 or in ASTM D396 for the heavier fuel oils) its technical limitations have necessitated much effort to devise a satisfactory alternative or replacement procedure to the pour point test for assessing the low temperature pumpability characteristics of residual fuel oils. Pour point procedures involving various preheat treatments prior to the pour point determination and the use of viscosity at low temperatures have been proposed. The ASTM version of the P and O fluidity test ASTM D1659 (Maximum Fluidity Temperature of Residual Fuel Oil) is one such procedure used as a 'go–no go' method in the USA. Another test, based upon viscosity measurements, recently published by the IP is the Pumpability Test for Industrial Fuels (IP 230), and is currently being assessed by the oil companies and by ASTM.

All these alternative methods tend to be time consuming and as such do not find ready acceptance as routine control tests for assessing low temperature pumpability.

(iii) Conradson carbon residue and asphaltenes
The propensity of residual fuel towards carbon deposition in use may be indicated by the Conradson carbon residue test (ASTM D189–IP 13).

Pressure jet and blast atomising type burners are not very sensitive to the carbon residue of the fuel used. In well designed installations incorporating such burners, and where combustion efficiency is maintained at a high level, it is unlikely that difficulties would normally arise in burning residual fuel oils. It is debatable, in these circumstances, whether the Conradson test is of any real significance relative to the combustion characteristics of the fuel.

The Conradson carbon residue test can also provide an indication of the extent of carbon deposition arising out of the thermal decomposition of residual fuel oils used in oil gasification and carburetted water gas processes. The significance of the test depends to a large extent on the particular process under consideration. In some processes residual fuels of fairly high Conradson carbon residue (above six per cent weight) are required while in others, fuels of both low and high carbon residue are used. For the carburetted water gas process a gas oil of low carbon residue is normally employed, but by suitable modification such plants can operate on residual fuels of higher carbon residue.

The test for asphaltenes content (IP 143), in which the fuel is treated with solvent to precipitate the brown/black solid asphaltenes which are then recovered from a benzene solution, is sometimes associated with the Conradson test in that results by the two procedures appear, on occasion, to run in parallel. High values for both Conradson and Asphaltenes tests may be obtained with some of the heavier residual fuel oils. For such fuels used in efficient boiler systems operating under correct conditions, this merely indicates that the fuels contain asphaltic residue which, in these conditions, will burn without difficulty.

It is generally considered that asphaltenes are more difficult to burn than the remainder of the fuel and it has been suggested that this might be reflected in the carbon residue result of fuels of high or low asphaltenes content. However, so many factors, including crude oil origin and refining treatment, can influence the asphaltenes value that any relationship which may exist between the two procedures is evidently not straightforward.

Many manufacturers' specifications include a minimum clause for asphaltenes (usually about 0·5 per cent weight) principally to comply with UK customs definition of a fuel oil destined for the UK market.

(iv) Ash content

The ash content (ASTM D482–IP 4) may be defined as the small amount of residue, free from carbonaceous matter, remaining after ignition in air of the residual fuel oil at fairly high temperatures.

Most fuel oils contain varying amounts of ash (but seldom more than 0·2 per cent by weight) which may originate from organometallic complexes soluble or inherent in the crude oil; from oil bearing strata; from contact of the crude oil or fuel oil with water, pipelines and storage tanks or during transportation and subsequent handling. Additives used to improve particular fuel properties and carry-over from refining processes may also contribute to the ash.

These ashes will contain small amounts of many metallic compounds of which those of sodium, vanadium, nickel, iron and silica are generally present in significant quantities. While the total amounts of ash in different fuel oils may be similar, their compositions will depend on the crude oil origin of the respective fuel oils. These constituents ultimately concentrate in the distillation residue and so their presence will be reflected in the fuel oil ash. Distillate fuel oils, therefore, should contain only negligible amounts of ash. While a knowledge of the total amount of ash is also important there is a greater awareness, nowadays, of the deposit forming tendency and corrosive effect of certain ash constituents when very high temperatures are employed in power station, gas turbine and marine propulsion equipment.

The sodium and vanadium compounds are, undoubtedly, the principal sources of these difficulties. The vanadium, present in the crude oil as an oil-soluble complex, is neither water soluble nor is it removable by centrifuging or filtration techniques. Sodium may be introduced into the crude or fuel oil by sea water contamination or by the refinery practice of alkali injection into distillation equipment to combat corrosion. The water soluble sodium salts may be partially removed by water washing operations. In this connection information regarding the water solubility of fuel oil ashes can often be useful.

The presence of sodium and vanadium complexes in the fuel oil ash can, under certain plant operating conditions, result in considerable harm to the equipment. Spalling and fluxing of refractory linings is associated with the presence of sodium in the fuel. Above a certain threshold temperature, which will vary from fuel to fuel, the oil ash will adhere to boiler superheater tubes and gas turbine bladings thus reducing the thermal efficiency of the plant. At higher temperatures, molten complexes of vanadium, sodium and sulphur are produced which will corrode all currently available metals used in the construction of these parts of the plant. The presence of trace amounts of vanadium in fuel used in glass manufacture can affect the colour of the finished product. Standard procedures for the determination of vanadium (ASTM 1548, IP 285 or IP 286) and sodium (ASTM D1318) are available.

Additives which act either by reacting with the corrosive materials to form innocuous compounds or by raising the fusion temperature of the ash have been used with varying degrees of success in combating this particular problem.

(v) Sulphur

Residual fuel oils are variable products whose sulphur contents depend not only on their crude oil sources but also on the extent of the refinery processing received by the fuel oil blending components. Sulphur, present in these fuel oils in varying amounts up to 4 or 5 per cent by weight, is generally regarded as an undesirable constituent.

In boiler systems, kilns etc. fired by residual fuel oils, the conversion of a small fraction of the sulphur to sulphur trioxide during combustion of the fuel can give rise to low temperature corrosion problems if this gas is allowed to condense and form corrosive sulphuric acid on cool metal surfaces of the equipment. Sulphur from the fuel, in combination with sodium and vanadium complexes, contributes to the formation of deposits on external surfaces of superheater tubes, economisers and oil heaters resulting in corrosion of equipment and loss of thermal efficiency.

Maintaining the cooler metal surfaces of the equipment above the acid dew point temperature may minimise the low temperature corrosion problem but will result in reduced thermal efficiency. Desulphurisation of fuels for combating this problem alone is, at present, considered an uneconomic proposition and efforts have been directed towards other means of reducing the effects of acid condensation. Operation with a minimum of excess air has been found to be of considerable value. The injection of ammonia into the flue gases or the addition of metallic compounds, although costly in the required concentrations, are also used for this purpose.

BS 2869 gives upper limits for the sulphur contents of residual fuel oils, otherwise, where sulphur is considered critical, agreement on limits is generally made between supplier and the consumer. This is the case with many manufacturing processes utilising fuel oil where the sulphur may adversely affect the product obtained. For example, in the steel industry, fuel oils having low sulphur contents (in the range 0·5 to 1·5 per cent by weight) are preferred for open hearth furnace operation. Using higher sulphur fuels the refining time needs to be prolonged if the deep drawing properties of the steel are not to be affected.

Sulphur may also contribute to the increasing problem of atmospheric pollution when sulphur oxides, produced on combustion of high sulphur fuel oils, are emitted into the surrounding atmosphere of densely populated industrial areas or large towns. In specific applications fuel oil desulphurisation may have to be employed in order to comply with air pollution legislation.

For the determination of sulphur contents of residual fuels a variety of procedures are available. The bomb (ASTM D129–IP 61) and quartz tube (ASTM D1551 or IP 63) combustion methods have long been established. Other more rapid techniques are becoming increasingly available which include high temperature combustion (ASTM D1552) X-ray absorption and fluorescence methods and the Schoniger oxygen flask procedure.

It may be said that of all the elements present in a normal residual fuel oil, vanadium, sodium and sulphur contribute most to difficulties and problems which may arise in the industrial application of fuel oils.

(vi) Stability

The problem of instability in residual fuel oils may manifest itself either as waxy sludge deposited at the bottom of an unheated storage tank, or as fouling of preheaters on heating the fuel to elevated temperatures.

Much speculation exists regarding the mechanism of sludge deposition. It may be a consequence of the effects of such factors as oxidation, polymerisation and the method of production of the fuel, which can result in the formation of insoluble compounds which eventually settle to the tank bottom and form sludge. The incidence of such deposition in light residual fuel oils (*e.g.* BS 2869 Class E fuels) used in large heating installations may be reflected in the clogging of external or cold filters, blocking or restriction of pipelines and combustion difficulties.

While no standard procedures are published by ASTM, or IP, various empirical procedures are available within oil company organisations for assessing the tendency of fuel oils towards deposition in storage. Details of one such procedure, the filtration ratio of fuel oils, are given in the *IP Journal* (1963, **49**, 259–72). This method consists of forcing the fuel, by means of air at constant pressure, through a filtration element into a twin bulb receiver and recording the ratio of the times taken to fill the first bulb and both bulbs. A fuel is considered to be of satisfactory quality if it has a filtration ratio less than a specified value when passed through a filter of given mesh size.

Problems of thermal stability and incompatibility in residual fuel oils are associated with those fuels used in oil fired naval or marine vessels—where the fuel is usually passed through a preheater before being fed to the burner system. In earlier days this preheating, with some fuels, could result in the deposition of asphaltic matter culminating, in the extreme case, in blockage of preheaters, pipelines and even complete combustion failure. Nowadays with the increased 'know-how' in refinery techniques in producing fuel oils of stable characteristics this position is unlikely to occur.

Asphaltic deposition may, however, result from the mixing of fuels of different origin and treatment, each of which may be perfectly satisfactory when used alone. This could be the case when a vessel replenishes its bunkers at another, probably distant, port. Such fuels are said to be incompatible. Straight run fuels from the same crude oil source are normally stable and mutually compatible. Fuels produced from thermal cracking and visbreaking operations which may, themselves, be stable can be unstable or incompatible if blended with straight run fuels and vice versa.

Many empirical procedures, including filtration techniques have been employed to ensure that a residual fuel, particularly if supplied for naval purposes, is unlikely to deposit asphaltic matter. Of these, the NBTL Heater Test (Federal Test Method 3461.1) has been widely used for many years. In this test the fuel is circulated over an internally heated steel tube for twenty hours at an oil temperature of 93·3°C (200°F). The tube is then examined for asphaltic deposition and the fuel rated stable, borderline or unstable accordingly. To assess the compatibility characteristics of the fuel it is blended in 50/50 properties with each of two reference fuels (one paraffinic, the other asphaltic or thermally cracked in nature) and each blend is subjected to the NBTL heater test. For the fuel to be satisfactory in service it must be stable and the blended fuel must be of borderline quality or better when assessed by this procedure.

As this method is time consuming and rather cumbersome, a simpler more rapid version using glass apparatus and less sample has been standardised by the ASTM (D1661—Thermal Stability of US Navy Special Fuel). This procedure, generally known as the Tidewater small scale heater test, assesses the fuel in the same way as the NBTL test and can be completed in about six hours. The Tidewater test is now included in naval boiler fuel specifications as a replacement or alternative procedure for the NBTL test.

Another procedure for predicting the compatibility of residual stocks and distillate fuels which are used to produce intermediate marine diesel fuels made under in-line or custom blending conditions is the Compatibility of Fuel Oil Blends by Spot Test (ASTM D2781). The method covers two spot test procedures for rating a residual fuel with respect to its compatibility with a specific distillate fuel. Procedure A indicates the degree of asphaltenes deposition that may be expected in blending the components. This procedure is used when wax deposition is not considered a fuel application problem. Procedure B indicates the degree of wax and asphalt deposition in the mixture at room temperature.

(c) SAMPLING

In the analysis and testing of these fuel oils the importance of correct sampling cannot be over emphasised, because no proper assessment of quality may be made unless the data are obtained on truly representative samples.

Details of sampling procedures are given in both the ASTM (D270) and IP (IP 51) handbooks.

5. SUGGESTIONS FOR FURTHER READING

Modern Petroleum Technology (1973). 4th edition, Applied Science, London.
Guthrie (ed). (1960). *Petroleum Products Handbook*, McGraw-Hill, New York.
Francis (1965). *Fuels and Fuel Technology*, Vols I and II, Pergamon Press, Oxford.

Chapter 10

LUBRICATING OILS

J. B. BERKLEY

1. INTRODUCTION

The major function of lubricating oils is the separation of metallic surfaces which are moving with respect to each other, thereby reducing friction and wear. They can also act as carriers for corrosion inhibitors, anti-wear agents, friction modifiers and other additives. Performance requirements can also include cooling, and the dispersion and neutralisation of combustion products from fuels. The high quality and improved properties of present-day lubricants have enabled engineers to design machines with higher power to weight ratios which generally have higher stresses, loads, and operating temperatures than before. Thus, it has been possible to develop automobile engines capable of higher rotational speeds and higher specific power output per unit cubic capacity. In a very different field lubricants have been developed for nuclear power stations with increased resistance to the effects of radiation.

Improvements in base oil refining methods have resulted in the production of stock oils which are more responsive to additive treatment. Research in the field of additives has, for example, enabled lubricants to be formulated which can operate under the higher piston-ring belt temperatures of supercharged automotive diesel engines and provide the dispersancy required to prevent the formation of low temperature sludges in petrol engines for stop–start, short distance motoring.

In spite of the increasing temperatures, loads and other requirements imposed on lubricants, mineral oils are likely to continue to be employed in the foreseeable future for the majority of automotive, industrial and marine applications. However, in the aviation field, synthetic lubricants are extensively used and there are a growing number of critical automotive, industrial and marine applications where the use of synthetic lubricants can be justified on a cost/performance basis.

New uses and new formulation technology for lubricating oils necessitate a constant review of the methods for assessing the quality of both new and used lubricating oils. The traditional physical and chemical tests are still applied, but these are being supplemented and, in some cases replaced, by instrumental techniques based on physico-chemical methods which include infra-red, ultra-violet and emission spectroscopy and X-ray absorption and fluorescence methods. It is convenient to consider these tests in five categories. The first three determine the characteristics and compositions, and the last two the effects on the lubricants of simulated service conditions in the laboratory.

(a) PHYSICAL TESTS

These include comparatively simple laboratory tests which define the nature of the product by measuring physical properties. Examples are viscosity, flash point, specific gravity, colour and appearance.

(b) CHEMICAL TESTS

These tests define the composition of the lubricating oil by determining the presence of such elements as sulphur, chlorine, phosphorus and metals.

(c) PHYSICO-CHEMICAL TESTS

Tests in this classification are either (i) those which determine the presence of elements using instrumented physical procedures, or (ii) those which give information on the molecular structure of the components of the lubricant.

These first three groups of tests are used to characterise products for specific applications, to provide quality control at blending plants and to check the suitability of used lubricants for further service.

(d) LABORATORY BENCH TESTS

This category includes tests which subject the lubricating oil to individual environmental conditions which are normally designed to exceed the appropriate service requirements. These include such glassware tests as thermal stability, oxidation and corrosion which are frequently used for screening formulations during the development of a new product.

(e) ENGINE AND RIG TESTS

In order to evaluate lubricants under the practical environment provided, for example, by engines and transmissions, mechanical tests are used to assess their effect on the various properties of the oil. The equipment is set up in a pre-scribed manner on laboratory stands and extended tests are carried out under carefully controlled conditions. Such tests are generally designed to correlate as far as is possible with actual service, but for new products, laboratory mechanical testing is usually followed by field evaluation.

2. COMPOSITION AND MANUFACTURE

Petroleum base lubricating oils are present in the residue boiling above 370°C (698°F) from the atmospheric distillation of selected crude oils of both paraffinic and naphthenic types. This residue is further distilled under con-ditions of high vacuum into a series of fractions to provide light to heavy lubricating oil stocks. The number of fractions depends on the type of crude oil and the requirements of the refiner, but four to five is a typical number. These basic stock oils are further refined, usually by solvent extraction, to produce de-asphalted and de-waxed oils suitable for incorporating into finished lubricants. The individual refined stock oils from one or more crude sources are blended in various proportions to provide lubricating oils suitable for a wide range of applications. The blending process can be by mechanical or air agitation, and can be either by a batch or a continuous in-line method.

Only for the less severe uses is it possible to employ straight mineral oils. In the majority of cases chemical additives are used to enhance the properties of base oils to enable specific applicational requirements to be met. These additives are used to improve such characteristics as the oxidation resistance, change in viscosity with temperature, low temperature flow properties, emulsi-fying ability, extreme pressure, anti-wear and frictional properties, corrosion and radiation resistance. Lubricants frequently contain a number of additives to achieve a balance of properties suitable for the intended application. These must be compatible with the base oil, and with the other additives present. Thus the proper selection of the components for the lubricating oil formula-tion requires knowledge of the most suitable crude sources for the base oils, the type of refining required, the types of additive necessary and the possible interactions of these components on the properties of the finished lubricating oil.

Control of product quality at the blending plant is usually based on suppliers' own internal standards. The number of tests applied varies with the complexity of the product and the nature of the application. The more important tests, such as the viscosity, flash point, colour, etc., are usually performed on every batch. Other tests may be on a statistical basis dependent on data developed at the individual blending plant. Newer methods of control testing include infra-red spectroscopic analysis, which can be presented in the graphical form of a 'fingerprint' which is specific for the blend of mineral oils and additives in a particular formulation. Comparison of the 'fingerprint' with a known standard can be used as a check on the composition.

3. GENERAL PROPERTIES

Before describing the quality criteria applicable to lubricating oils for some of the more important types of application, the properties which are common to most lubricating oil products are first discussed.

(a) VISCOSITY

The viscosity of a lubricating oil is a measure of its flow characteristics. It is generally the most important controlling property for manufacture and for selection to meet a particular application. The viscosity of a mineral oil changes with temperature, but not normally with shear rate, unless specific additives which may not be shear stable are included to modify the viscosity/temperature characteristics—an aspect that is discussed more fully in the section on Automotive Engine Oils. Thus for base oils, the rate of flow of the oil through a pipe or capillary tube is directly proportional to the pressure applied. This property is measured for most practical purposes by timing the flow of a fixed amount of oil through a calibrated glass capillary tube under gravitational force at a standard temperature, and is known as the kinematic viscosity of the oil (ASTM D445–IP 71). The unit of viscosity used in conjunction with this method is the centistoke, but this may be converted into the other viscosity systems (Saybolt, Redwood, Engler) by means of tables. At very high pressures, the viscosity of mineral oils increases considerably with increase in pressure, the extent depending on the crude source of the oil and on the molecular weight of the constituent components.

Because the main objective of lubrication is to provide a film between load bearing surfaces, the selection of the correct viscosity for the oil is aimed at a balance between a viscosity high enough to prevent the lubricated surfaces from contacting and low enough to minimise energy losses through excessive heat generation caused by having too viscous a lubricant.

The 'classical' hydrodynamic theory for moderately loaded bearings predicts complete separation between metallic surfaces with a comparatively thick layer of fluid oil, whilst highly loaded gears are considered to be in a state of boundary lubrication in which opposing surface irregularities cause metal-to-metal contact to occur. Modern elastohydrodynamic theory for lubricated surfaces takes into account that owing to the high pressure generated, the viscosity of the oil increases considerably and that elastic deformation of the surfaces occurs. Under these conditions it has been shown that the lubricant film under 'boundary' conditions is thicker than was previously supposed.

Because the viscosity is an important property, it is used for the identification of individual grades of oil and for following the changes caused in the oil in service. Viscosity increase usually indicates that a used oil has deteriorated by oxidation or by contamination, whilst a decrease usually indicates dilution by a lower viscosity oil or by a fuel. The extent of the viscosity change permitted before corrective action is required differs in various applications, but is generally determined from experience.

The standard viscosity temperature charts of ASTM D341 are useful for estimating the viscosity of an oil at the various temperatures which are likely to be encountered in service.

(b) Viscosity Index

The viscosity of petroleum base oils decreases with a rise in temperature, but this rate of change depends on the composition of the oil. The viscosity index is an empirical number which indicates the effect of change of temperature on the viscosity of an oil. It compares the rate of change of viscosity of the sample with the rates of change of two types of oil having the highest and lowest viscosity indices at the time (1929) when the viscosity index scale was first introduced. A high viscosity index denotes a low rate of change of viscosity with temperature. Paraffinic oils were found to have the lowest rate of change of viscosity with temperature (highest viscosity index), while the naphthenic/aromatic oils had the highest rate of change (lowest viscosity index).

A standard paraffinic oil was given a viscosity index (VI) of 100 and a standard naphthenic oil a VI of 0. Equations were evolved connecting the viscosity and temperature for these two types of oil, and from these equations tables were prepared showing the relationship between viscosities at 100°F and 210°F (38°C and 99°C) for oils with a VI between 0 and 100. With these tables and the viscosities at 100°F and 210°F of an oil, the viscosity index can be calculated. Improvements in refining, and the use of additives known as viscosity index improvers, have produced oils with viscosity indices in excess of 100. Initially this problem was solved by simply extrapolating the original tables, but as VI's rose even higher this gave rise to anomalies. In 1964 ASTM adopted an extension based on an equation developed for the purpose. Values derived from this equation are designated VI_E to distinguish them from the original VI. This method has since been adopted by IP under the joint designation ASTM D2270–IP 226 which replaces the former method ASTM D567–IP 73. It should be noted that viscosity indices below 100 have not been affected by this revision.

The viscosity index of an oil is of importance in applications where an appreciable change in temperature of the lubricating oil could affect the operating characteristics of the equipment. Automatic transmissions for passenger vehicles are an example of this where high viscosity index oils using VI improvers are used to minimise differences between a viscosity low enough to permit a sufficiently rapid gear shift when starting under cold conditions and a viscosity adequate at the higher temperatures encountered in normal running.

(c) Cloud and Pour Points

Petroleum oils contain components with a wide range of molecular sizes and configurations and thus do not have a sharp freezing point. They become more or less plastic solids when cooled to sufficiently low temperatures.

The cloud point (ASTM D2500–IP 219) of a lubricating oil is the temperature at which paraffinic wax and other readily solidifiable components begin to crystallise out and separate from the oil under prescribed test conditions. It is of importance when narrow clearances might be restricted by accumulation of solid material (for example oil feed lines or filters).

The pour point (ASTM D97–IP 15) is the lowest temperature at which the oil will just flow under specified test conditions and is roughly equivalent to the tendency of an oil to cease to flow from a gravity-fed system or from a container. However, since in practice the size and shape of the container, the head of oil and the physical structure of the solidified oil all influence the tendency of the oil to flow, the pour point of the oil is a guide to, and not an exact measure of, the temperature at which flow ceases under the service conditions of a specific system. The pour point of wax-containing oils can be reduced by the use of special additives known as pour-point depressants which inhibit the growth of wax crystals, thus preventing the formation of a solid structure. It is a recognised property of oil of this type that previous thermal history may affect the measured pour point. The test procedure (ASTM D97–IP 15) includes a section which permits some measurement of this thermal effect on waxy oils.

The importance of the pour point to the user of lubricants is limited to applications where low temperatures are likely to influence oil flow. Examples are refrigerator lubricants and automotive engine oils in colder climates.

(d) Flash and Fire Points

The flash point test gives an indication of the presence of volatile components in an oil and is the temperature to which the oil must be heated under specified test conditions to give off sufficient vapour to form a flammable mixture with air.

The fire point is the temperature to which the product must be heated under the prescribed test conditions to cause the vapour/air mixture to burn continuously on ignition. The Cleveland open cup method (ASTM D92–IP 36) can be used to determine both flash and fire points of lubricating oils and is the most generally used method for this purpose in the USA. In the UK the Pensky–Martens closed (ASTM D93–IP 34) and open (IP 35) flash points are more widely used.

The flash and fire points are significant in cases where high temperature operations are encountered, not only for the hazard of fire, but also as an indication of the volatility of an oil. In the case of used oils, the flash point is employed to indicate the extent of contamination with a more volatile oil or with fuels. The flash point can also be used to assist in the identification of different types of base oil blend.

(e) Relative Density (Specific Gravity) and API Gravity

These are alternative but related means of expressing the weight of a measured volume of a product. Relative Density (also known as specific gravity) is used widely outside the United States whereas the API gravity used throughout the petroleum industry in the United States is based on an arbitrary hydrometer scale which is related to the relative density.

Both types of gravity measurements are used as manufacturing control tests and, in conjunction with other tests, are also used for characterising unknown oils since they correlate approximately with hydrocarbon composition and, therefore, with the nature of the crude source of the oil. The method ASTM D1298–IP 160 is widely used in the UK.

(f) Colour

The colour (ASTM D1500–IP 196) of a sample of lubricating oil is measured in a standard glass container by comparing the colour of the transmitted light with that transmitted by a series of numbered glass standards, and the best match noted. The test is used for manufacturing control purposes, and is important since the colour is readily observed by the customer. The colour of a lubricating oil is not, however, always a reliable guide to product quality and should not be used indiscriminately in specifications. Where the colour range of a grade is known, a variation outside the established range indicates possible contamination with another product.

4. STEAM TURBINE OILS

Lubricating oils for steam turbine circulating systems need to provide satisfactory lubrication and cooling of the bearings and gears. The viscosity of the oil is important for both of these functions, but the loading of the gear is the major factor in the choice of lubricant. A sufficiently thick film of oil must be maintained between the load-bearing surfaces and thus the higher the load on the gears, the higher the viscosity required. However, as the circulated oil also acts as a coolant for the bearings, it is necessary to have as low a viscosity as possible consistent with the lubrication requirements.

Since steam turbine oils are generally required to function at elevated temperatures, it is most important that the oxidation stability of the oil is satisfactory, otherwise the service life of the oil will be unduly short. Oxidation inhibitors are added to the base oil to improve this characteristic. Lack of oxidation stability results in the development of acidic products which can lead to corrosion and can also affect the ability of the oil to separate from water. Oxidation can also lead to an increase in viscosity and the formation of sludges which can restrict oilways, thus impairing circulation of the oil and interfering with the function of governors and oil relays. Correctly formulated turbine oils have excellent resistance to oxidation and will function satisfactorily for long periods without changing the system charge. Oxidation stability can be assessed by IP 114, or by IP 157–ASTM D943 (Turbine Oil Stability Test—TOST), which is a more elaborate test using copper as well as iron as catalysts in the presence of water to simulate metals present in service conditions.

Turbine oil systems usually contain some free water as a result of steam leaking through glands and then condensing. Marine systems may also have salt water present due to leakage from coolers. Because of this, rust inhibitors are usually incorporated. The rust-preventing properties of turbine oils are measured by ASTM D665–IP 135 which employs synthetic sea water or distilled water in the presence of steel. The oil should also be non-corrosive to copper and this property is measured by ASTM D130–IP 154.

The presence of water in turbine systems tends to lead to the formation of emulsions and sludges containing water, oil, oil oxidation products, rust particles and other solid contaminants which can seriously impair lubrication. The lubricating oil, therefore, should have the ability to separate from water readily and to resist emulsification. This property of the oil can be measured by IP 19, in which steam is passed into the oil until a pre-determined volume has condensed, and the time required for separation measured. Alternatively, ASTM D1401 measures the rate of separation of oil which has been stirred with an equal volume of water. These test methods are only approximate guides to the water-separating characteristics of modern inhibited turbine oils and the results should be used in conjunction with experience gained of the particular service conditions encountered.

Although systems are usually designed to avoid entrainment of air in the oil, it is not always possible to prevent this. The formation of a stable foam increases the surface area of the oil which is exposed to small bubbles of air, thus assisting oxidation. The foam can also cause loss of oil from the system by overflow. Defoamants are usually incorporated in turbine oils to decrease their foaming tendency and this can be measured by ASTM D892–IP 146. Air release is also an important property and a careful choice of type and amount of defoamant is necessary to provide the correct balance of foam protection and air release properties.

Marine turbine gearing design has advanced to the stage where increased loading has permitted a decreased size of the gear train. This saving in space is very desirable, particularly in naval vessels, but turbine oils for such applications may also require extreme pressure characteristics. IP 166 measures the load-carrying properties of oils by the IAE gear rig whereas ASTM D1947 uses the Ryder gear rig. Specifications for oils using these gear rigs are in use for naval requirements where gas turbines are coupled through a common gear box to steam turbines for an additional power boost.

5. AUTOMOTIVE ENGINE OILS

(a) Properties

The crankcase oil of automotive petrol and diesel engines is used to lubricate the pistons, cylinders, bearings and valve train mechanism. Also, in some automobiles, notably those European cars with transverse engines, the engine and gearbox or automatic transmission may be served by a common lubricant. Thus, the duty performed by an automotive engine oil is highly complex and needs to be matched by an appropriate formulation. For example, the oil must contain sufficient high temperature anti-oxidant and detergent to enable the piston assembly to function satisfactorily. This entails keeping the rings free from carbon deposits and lacquer under the very high temperatures encountered in the ring belt area. Unburnt carbon from incomplete combustion of the fuel may tend to form undesirable sludges, particularly in the presence of water which condenses during short-distance motoring. Low temperature dispersants are used to prevent the formation of such sludge which otherwise could clog oilways and cause lubrication failure. In the case of engines using diesel fuel, the lubricating oil must possess sufficient reserve alkalinity to neutralise acidic products formed as a result of burning the sulphur present in the fuel for the life of the engine oil charge. Modern high performance petrol-engined cars have dynamic tappet loadings which generally require special anti-wear additives in the lubricating oil.

The compatibility of the various additives employed to provide all of the properties required in a satisfactory automotive engine oil is an important aspect of the formulation. A wide range of laboratory bench, rig and engine tests is employed to check the quality of both gasoline and diesel engine oils.

The viscosity of the engine oil is the main controlling property for manufacture and for selection to meet the particular service condition. Engine oils are generally recommended by automotive builders according to the American Society of Automotive Engineers (SAE) viscosity classification. The higher viscosity oils are standardised at 210°F (99°C), and the lighter oils, which are intended for use in cold weather conditions, are standardised at 0°F (−18°C).

The introduction of multigrade engine oils for all-the-year-round service enables oils to be purchased which are sufficiently fluid at low temperatures to permit easy starting of the engine in winter conditions, but which maintain the required viscosity at their operating temperature. The viscosity index of multigrade oils is typically in the range 130 to 190, whilst monograde oils are usually between 85 and 105. The improved viscosity/temperature characteristics of multigrade oils enables, for example, an SAE 20W/50 oil to be formulated which spans SAE 20W viscosity characteristics at low temperatures, and SAE 40 to 50 characteristics at the working temperature. Multigrade oils, however, do not behave as Newtonian fluids and this is primarily due to the presence of polymeric viscosity index improvers. The result is that the viscosity of multigrade oils is generally higher at 0°F than is predicted by extrapolation from 210°F and 100°F values, the extent of the deviation varies with the type and amount of the viscosity index improver used. To overcome this, the SAE classification is based on a measured viscosity at 0°F using a laboratory test apparatus known as a Cold Cranking Simulator (ASTM D2602).

A further property of a multigrade engine oil is that its viscosity is not stable to mechanical shearing action. The extent of this is dependent mainly on the type of VI improver used since the base oil is shear stable. There are a number of methods of evaluating the shear stability of a multigrade oil, one of which is to observe the viscosity reduction as a result of pumping the oil through a diesel injector orifice under high shear conditions. The viscosity of automotive engine oils in service may also be decreased by fuel dilution, but increased by oxidation and combustion products. Detergent/dispersant oils can keep these contaminants in suspension, but undesirable sludges can be deposited within the engine if oil drain periods are indiscriminately extended. Recommendations for oil-change intervals are usually made by the engine builder, or in the case of commercial vehicle fleets with known patterns of operation, the user may establish his own optimum change periods, dependent on the level of quality of the lubricating oil employed.

(b) Engine Test Specifications and Procedures

Engine test methods used in the development of new formulations, and for purchase specifications have originated from the following sources:

1. API/ASTM/SAE engine service classifications;
2. Institute of Petroleum tests;
3. Co-ordinating European Council (CEC) tests;
4. Caterpillar Tractor Company heavy-duty, supercharged engine tests;
5. Military specifications (US Army and Navy, British Ministry of Defence, NATO, etc.).

The original API classifications aimed to define the type of service which an engine oil was designed to meet and the 'MS' test sequence has been widely used for this purpose. ('MS' denoted a service condition which was most severe for gasoline engines.) A new joint API/ASTM/SAE system of nomenclature has been agreed as a guide to the selection of engine oils for different service conditions.

Petrol engine service conditions are designated by the letters SA, SB, SC, SD and SE in increasing order of severity. Diesel engine oils are designated by CA, CB, CC and CD, also in increasing order of severity of service condition. Performance criteria have been established for each designation using published engine tests known as Sequences IIA, IIB, IIIA, IIIB, IIIC, IV, V, VB and VC, and other procedures which include the Caterpillar Tractor Company tests. (The designation and the performance criteria are fully described in the SAE Technical Report J 183a and were published in the 1972 SAE Handbook.) Caterpillar Series 3 (*see* note added in proof, p. 197) performance level oils were widely accepted for superior heavy-duty supercharged diesel engines using comparatively high sulphur fuels.

Important US Army specifications include the MIL-L-2104B and the succeeding MIL-L-2104C specifications which are also used as performance references for commercial automotive engine oils. Two US automotive manufacturers specifying engine oils required during their warranty periods for cars and trucks are Ford (ESE-M 2C 101C) and General Motors (GM 6041M for cars and light trucks and GM 6042M for heavily loaded petrol and diesel engines).

Engine tests for the evaluation of lubricants are being developed in Europe through the Institute of Petroleum (IP) and the Co-ordinating European Council (CEC).

Methods in current use include:

Engine	Performance Aspect Evaluated	Designation
Caterpillar 1G	Engine cleanliness	IP 231/69T
Petter AV-1	Engine cleanliness	IP 175/69, CEC L-01-A-69
Petter W-1	Oil oxidation and bearing corrosion	IP 176/69, CEC L-02-A-69
Ford Cortina	High temperature test	IP 246/69T, CEC L-03-T-69

The assessment of the various quality aspects of oils by these standard engine tests is widely accepted. For example, in method IP 175 the detergent properties of an automotive engine oil can be evaluated in the laboratory by using a single cylinder compression ignition engine run under specific operating conditions and with a specified reference fuel. The quality of the oil is determined by a rating procedure which assesses the presence of deposits on the piston crown, skirt, undercrown and ring zone, the condition and amount of wear on the piston rings and on the liner, and the degree of ring sticking.

The oxidation resistance and ability of the oil to prevent corrosion of the bearings is determined in IP 176 by running the oil under specified conditions in a single-cylinder spark ignition engine. The weight loss of copper/lead bearing shells is measured and the extent of the varnish deposits on the piston skirt is assessed. The oil is also examined for viscosity increase at the end of the test.

The most frequently used UK specification for automotive engine oils is the Ministry of Defence DEF-2101-D Specification. This was published in

November, 1965 and utilises the Petter AV-1 single cylinder laboratory diesel engine with 1 per cent sulphur fuel as a qualification test for detergency (modified IP 175) and the Petter W-1 single cylinder laboratory petrol engine for the oxidation and bearing corrosion test (modified IP 176).

Although military specifications are widely used for civilian purchasing specifications, it should be recognised that the two uses are by no means identical. Formulations developed by reputable suppliers usually have quality levels in excess of the minimum standards required by military specifications and have a more satisfactory all-round balance of properties for mixed fleet, all-duty service.

(c) EXAMINATION OF USED OILS

Diesel fuel dilution, resulting from low temperature or short distance stop/start operation, can be approximately estimated from measurements of the flash point of the oil (ASTM D92–IP 36) which is appreciably lowered by small quantities of fuel. Petrol dilution can be measured by the distillation procedure ASTM D322–IP 23, or by an infra-red spectroscopic method.

Low temperature service conditions may also result in water vapour from combustion products condensing in the crankcase. This can be measured by ASTM D95–IP 74.

The extent and nature of the contamination of a used automotive engine oil by oxidation and combustion products can be ascertained by determining the amounts of materials present in the lubricating oil which are insoluble in normal pentane and benzene by ASTM D893. A solution of the used lubricating oil in pentane is centrifuged, the oil solution is decanted and the precipitate washed, dried and weighed. 'Insolubles' (precipitate) are expressed as a percentage by weight of the original amount of used oil taken and include the resinous material resulting from the oxidation of the oil in service, together with the benzene insolubles. The latter are determined on a separate portion of sample which is weighed, mixed with pentane and centrifuged. The precipitate is washed twice with pentane, once with benzene–alcohol solution and once with benzene. The insoluble material is then dried and weighed to give the percentage of benzene insolubles which contain wear debris, dirt, carbonaceous matter from the combustion products and decomposition products of the oil, additives and fuel.

Where highly detergent/dispersant oils are under test, coagulated pentane insolubles and coagulated benzene insolubles may be determined, using methods similar to those just described, but employing a coagulant to precipitate the very finely divided materials which may otherwise be kept in suspension by the detergent/dispersant additives.

Size discrimination of insoluble matter may be made to distinguish between finely dispersed relatively harmless matter and the larger potentially harmful particles in an oil. The method employs filtration through membranes of known pore size. Membrane filtration techniques are being increasingly used and are expected to be published shortly as standard test procedures.

The constituent elements (barium, calcium, magnesium, tin, silica, zinc, aluminium, sodium or potassium) of new and used lubricating oils can be determined by a comprehensive system of chemical analysis described in ASTM D811. Corresponding methods for barium, calcium and zinc in unused oils are available under the designations IP 110, IP 111 and IP 117 respectively. For new lubricating oils ASTM D874–IP 163 can be employed to check the concentration of metallic additives present by measuring the ash residue after ignition. This latter method is useful to check the quality of new oils at blending plants or against specifications. These standard chemical procedures are time-consuming to carry out and where the volume of samples justifies the purchase of such equipment, emission spectrographs, X-ray fluorescence spectrometers, atomic absorption and other instruments are available which are very much more rapid.

The amount of reserve alkalinity remaining in the used oil can be determined by measuring the Total Base Number of the oil (ASTM D664–IP 177, or IP 276). Essentially, these are titration methods where, because of the nature of the used oil, an electrometric instead of a colour end-point is used.

6. MARINE DIESEL ENGINE OILS

Marine diesel engines are of two principal types from the lubrication viewpoint. These are trunk-piston engines, in which the crankcase oil also lubricates the cylinders, and crosshead engines in which the cylinders and bearings are separately lubricated. Marine diesel engines can also be classified into low, medium and high speed types with speeds of 0–50 rev/min, 250–1000 rev/min and over 1000 rev/min respectively. The lower speed engines are less sensitive to fuel quality and can operate satisfactorily on residual fuels with high sulphur contents, whilst the higher speed engines are generally more similar in design to automotive engines and use distillate fuels. Medium speed engines vary in their fuel requirements according to the design.

The oil used in trunk-piston engines must have a viscosity suitable for lubricating the bearings and the cylinders. The trend in marine diesel engine design is towards smaller and lighter engines of higher specific output so that proportionally less space in a ship is required for the propulsion unit. Turbocharging is becoming more frequently used as a means of increasing the amount of power obtained from a given size of engine. This increases the heat input, and oils with comparatively high levels of detergents and antioxidants are required to maintain satisfactory engine cleanliness. The oxidation stability of trunk-piston engine oils can be measured by the single cylinder CRC L-38 and the Petter W-1 (IP 176) tests, and the level of detergency by one of the single-cylinder Caterpillar procedures.

Alkaline additives are required in the formulation of marine engine oils to neutralise potentially corrosive acids formed as a result of sulphurous blow-by gases entering the crankcase. These additives must be capable of maintaining the alkalinity of the oil throughout the life of the charge. This is particularly important when high sulphur residual fuels are used. Samples of oil drawn from the crankcase can be tested to assess the reserve of alkalinity remaining by determining the Total Base Number of the oil by ASTM D664–IP 177, or by IP 276. Other tests performed on the used engine oil, which serve as a guide to the suitability of the oil for further service, are the viscosity, flash point, pentane and benzene insolubles and sulphated ash. These methods are described in the section on automotive engine oils.

In the crosshead type engines, the crankcase oil lubricates the bearings and may also be used to cool the pistons. As well as having the appropriate viscosity, the oil must also have satisfactory oxidation resistance, good anti-foam and anti-corrosion properties. Small amounts of acidic contaminants entering the crankcase oil from the cylinders can be neutralised by using crankcase oils with a low level of alkalinity.

The cylinders of crosshead diesel engines are lubricated separately on an all-loss basis. The oil is injected into the cylinders through feed points around the cylinder and is distributed by the scraping action of the piston rings. Excess oil collects in a scavenge space and is run off to the exterior of the engine. The oil used for this purpose is exposed to particularly high temperatures. As crosshead engines usually operate on residual fuels which frequently contain relatively high levels of sulphur, it is important that the cylinder oil has a sufficiently high level of alkalinity to neutralise acidic combustion products formed and thus to minimise the occurrence of corrosive wear. Some low specific output engines are prone to exhaust-port blocking with carbonaceous combustion products and may require special lubricating oils to reduce this tendency. Crosshead cylinder oils may be single phase, in which the additives are dissolved in the oil, or they may contain finely divided solid additives suspended in the oil.

The deposit-forming tendencies due to thermal instability can be assessed by the Panel Coking Test when used in conjunction with other tests and the available alkalinity of these oils can be measured by ASTM D664–IP 177 or by IP 276.

An indication of the overall performance of marine crosshead engine oils can be made in a laboratory version of the Bolnes 2L marine diesel engine. This is a relatively small two-cylinder engine with separately lubricated cylinders and crankcase. However, although laboratory engines give a guide to performance, the variety of sizes and types of marine diesel engines necessitates the final evaluation of these oils in carefully controlled ship trials.

The high speed engines for fishing vessels, or for auxiliaries in larger vessels, require lubricating oils of a similar type to the higher detergency level automotive diesel engine lubricants. In some cases, automotive grades are recommended for use in these marine engines. However, since the sulphur contents of the fuels normally used in marine applications are higher than those of the fuels normally used for automotive purposes, it is important to ensure that the reserve of alkalinity is sufficient to neutralise the additional amounts of corrosive acids which may be formed.

7. INDUSTRIAL AND RAILWAY ENGINE OILS

A wide range of sizes and designs are employed for industrial engines, but the types of lubricant used and their related test procedures are similar to those described under the sections on automotive and marine engines. Crankcase systems for land based engines may be larger in capacity than for marine purposes and the oil charge in these cases would be expected to be satisfactory for longer periods of operation.

Engines with larger cylinder bores usually have higher cylinder wall temperatures and require oils with higher viscosities. Intermediate size engines generally use SAE 30 and 40 grade oils, whilst for the largest engines SAE 50 oils may be recommended.

Since space is more limited in locomotives, their engines tend to have high specific ratings and thus bearing and cylinder temperatures are also relatively high. Long idling periods can be followed by rapidly increased speed and load and this makes the lubricant performance criteria relatively severe. The importance of keeping railway locomotives in service for as long as possible before overhaul has led to the use of the regular checking of oil samples for the presence of wear metals. Sudden increase in the amount of a particular metallic element present in the oil could well be due to an incipient bearing failure and indicate the need for overhaul. Direct reading spectrographs requiring a minimum of operator time have been developed to monitor used oil samples for this purpose.

8. GAS TURBINE LUBRICANTS

Gas turbine engines, originally developed for aviation use, are now being employed increasingly for industrial, marine and automotive applications. The electricity generation industry, for example, uses a considerable number of gas turbines for stand-by and peak-lopping purposes.

From the lubrication viewpoint, the most important features of gas turbines are the large volumes of high temperature combustion gases which flow through the engine and the comparatively high loading on the gearing resulting from the need to reduce weight to a minimum. Thus high thermal and oxidative stability combined with good load-carrying properties are essential. The latter property is particularly important where the engine oil also has to lubricate gearboxes used for turbo-propeller or helicopter transmissions.

For aviation purposes, British and US Military specifications have had a strong influence in establishing quality criteria and performance levels for gas turbine lubricants. The continuous development of engines for military and commercial use has resulted in increasingly high bearing temperatures requiring the adoption of synthetic rather than mineral oils. The wide temperature ranges over which gas turbine lubricants must function satisfactorily are reflected in the following table of current British defence specification viscosities and pour points.

Specification	*DERD* 2487	*DERD* 2497
Type	*Type I Ester*	*Type II Ester*
Viscosity 210°F (98·9°C)	7·5 cSt min.	5·5 cSt max.
100°F (37·8°C)	39·0 cSt max.	25·0 cSt min.
−40°F (−40°C)	13 000 cSt max.	13 000 cSt max.
Pour point °F	not specified	−65 max.

These specifications also include requirements for resistance to oxidation and corrosion and for load-carrying properties defined by the IAE Gear Test. Other important properties of aviation gas turbine lubricants are low volatility, foam resistance and seal compatability.

The Type I synthetic lubricants were produced to meet the requirements of engines in the 1950s, but with further advances in engine design, together with the demand for increased periods between engine overhauls, the more thermally and oxidative stable Type II lubricants were developed. Certain engine manufacturers have developed their own laboratory test procedures and Rolls-Royce, for example, have a series of methods for synthetic oil evaluation.

The Rolls-Royce thermal and oxidative bulk oil stability tests assess lubricant deterioration over a period of time in terms of volatility loss, viscosity increase, acidity increase and build-up of insoluble material at a range of temperatures. This enables the temperature at which a specified level of deterioration is reached to be determined. A typical temperature range for Type I Esters is 150–180°C (320–374°F) while advanced Type II Esters are stable up to 200–215°C (392–419°F). Compatability with advanced types of constructional and sealing materials at elevated temperatures is assessed by immersion in the lubricant for a specified time. Also included are tests for evaluation for hydrolytic stability, coking propensity and load carrying performance.

Because of the safety aspect and the need to prolong periods between engine overhauls, the in-service condition of aviation lubricants is usually monitored by drawing regular samples for analysis. Metals analysis by emission spectroscopy can check whether or not any particular metal shows a sudden change in concentration in the used oil. This can indicate increased wear of a particular engine component and a possible need for replacement.

Industrial and marine gas turbine installations vary in their severity of operating condition and may run satisfactorily on high quality steam turbine mineral oils or may need synthetic oils according to the particular service requirements. Automotive gas turbine engines are being developed with the objective of using mineral oils, but in most cases high bearing temperatures, particularly immediately after stopping the engine due to heat soak back along the drive shaft, have necessitated the use of either synthetic oils or mineral oil/synthetic oil blends.

9. GAS ENGINE OILS

In areas where natural or liquefied petroleum gas (LPG) is available at an economic price level, these gases are finding increasing use as fuels for industrial engines. Gas engines range from large, relatively low output, low temperature engines to small, high speed, supercharged engines. Lubricant requirements vary with the engine design and operating conditions from un-inhibited mineral oil, through mildly alkaline oxidation-inhibited detergent oils, to ashless highly detergent oils. Combustion in the large, low output engines using natural gas or LPG fuels is relatively clean and as crankcases for these engines usually contain large quantities of oil, the operating conditions for the lubricant tend to be comparatively mild. For example, under certain conditions, an oil change life of several years may be achieved.

Tqe principal difference between the requirements of gas and other internal combustion engine oils is the necessity to withstand the degradation that can occur from accumulation of oxides of nitrogen in the oil which are formed by combustion. The condition of gas engine oils in large engines can be followed by measuring oil viscosity increase and by using ASTM D664–IP 177 or ASTM D974–IP 139 to determine changes in the neutralisation value resulting from oxidation. In addition, analytical techniques such as infra-red spectroscopy and membrane filtration can be used to check for nitration of the oil and the build-up of suspended carbonaceous material.

The small gas engines generally operate at higher temperatures than the larger types and lubricant degradation in these engines can be traced by the usual methods of viscosity, neutralisation number and insolubles determinations described under automotive engine oils.

In general, the comparatively high fuel cost for gas engines dictates that they operate at their maximum efficiency. In the case of two-stroke cycle gas engines relatively small amounts of port plugging (*i.e.* about 5 per cent) can increase fuel costs to such an extent that engine overhaul becomes necessary. In these engines, port plugging can be caused by carbonaceous lubricant deposits and solid impurities in the combustion air. The lubricant should minimise port plugging from either of these causes and thus help to increase operation time between overhauls.

10. GEAR OILS

The range of uses for gear oils is extremely wide and includes industrial, automotive, marine and aviation applications. Gears can vary from large open types used in quarrying to very small instrument gears used for the control of aircraft. However, the primary requirement is that the lubricant shall prevent wear and other forms of damage by maintaining a lubricants film between the moving surfaces 'in contact'.

Although gears are of many types including spur, helical, worm, bevel, hypoid, etc., they all function with a combination of rolling and sliding motion. The contact between the mating surfaces may be either along a line (as in the case of spur gears), or at a point (as for non-parallel, non-intersecting helical gear shafts). Although deformation of the metal will broaden these lines or points to areas of contact under service conditions, these areas are small in relation to the load on them. Thus, the unit loadings of gear-tooth surfaces are relatively high compared with ordinary bearing surfaces.

Where the gear loadings are comparatively light, straight mineral oils may be used as the lubricant, but with increased unit loading, it is necessary to incorporate anti-wear additives. For very highly loaded conditions in which shock is also experienced, special anti-weld compounds are included in gear oil formulations. It is necessary for a satisfactory balance to be maintained between the properties desired in the lubricant and the components used. For example, over-active chemical additives may promote undesirable wear by chemical attack. This type of wear is known as corrosive wear and results from the progressive removal of chemical compounds formed at the elevated temperatures on the tooth surface. Other types of gear wear are caused by fatigue, abrasion and welding. In the case of metal fatigue, contact between the surfaces is not necessary for its occurrence. If the gear surfaces are subjected to stresses that are above the fatigue endurance limit of the metal, sub-surface cracks can develop which may eventually lead to surface failure. Abrasion of the gear surface is caused either by the harder surface of the two cutting into the other, or a hard contaminant or wear particle acting as the abrasive medium. Welding occurs when the severity of the load is high enough to cause complete breakdown of the lubricant film and metal to metal contact occurs, resulting in transfer of metal between the surfaces. The correct choice of lubricant and satisfactory standards of cleanliness will minimise these wear effects.

Various methods are used to apply gear lubricants. Application may be by drip feed, splash, spray or by a lubricant bath. For large open gears, the lubricant must possess a sufficiently high viscosity and good adhesive properties to remain on the metal surface. This is particularly the case for applications such as open-cast coal mining and in the cement industry where gears may have to operate under wet and dirty conditions. In such cases, bitumen or grease soaps may be blended into the oil formulation.

Large industrial gear sets using spur or helical gears operating under moderate loads are usually lubricated by circulating systems. The heavier viscosity turbine oils are generally suitable for this application. In enclosed systems the temperatures reached may be high enough to necessitate the use of oils of good oxidation resistance. The oils should also possess satisfactory anti-foam properties, and, if water is present, good anti-rust and good demulsibility properties. Where higher loadings are encountered in industrial gears, lead, sulphur and phosphorus compounds are commonly used to improve the load-carrying capacity of the lubricant.

For highly-loaded spiral bevel, worm or hypoid gears, where sliding contact predominates over rolling contact between gear teeth, lubricating oils with special extreme pressure additives are used. Sulphur, chlorine, lead and phosphorus compounds are widely used for this purpose.

Analytical techniques are available for identifying and determining the amount of active elements in these load-carrying compounds. The total quantity of sulphur in a gear oil due to the base oil and to the additives present can be determined by a Bomb Method, ASTM D129–IP 61, in which the sulphur is assessed gravimetrically as barium sulphate. The copper strip test, ASTM D130–IP 154, is used to simulate the tendency of the oil to attack copper, brass or bronze. Since active sulphur is desirable for some extreme-pressure applications, a positive copper strip result can indicate that the formulation is satisfactory but care is necessary in the interpretation of copper strip results because formulations of different chemical compositions may give different results and yet have similar performance in the intended application. The copper strip test is widely used for the quality control of gear oils at blending plants.

The lead content of new and used gear oils can be determined by the chemical separation method IP 120. However, there are a number of instrumental techniques which enable the results to be obtained very much more rapidly, amongst these being polarographic, flame photometric and X-ray fluorescence methods. Chlorine can be determined by a chemical method as silver chloride by ASTM D808 or by a titration method ASTM D1317–IP 118. Phosphorus can be determined by a photometric procedure IP 148 or by the similar method ASTM D1091.

The analytical techniques described for measuring the elements associated with the load-carrying compounds present in gear oils do not identify the specific additives used, nevertheless they are useful for controlling the quality of the finished products at blending plants. Similarly, they can be used for determining the same elements in used oils, but they do not differentiate between the additives and contaminants which may be present.

Mechanical tests are used for assessing the extreme pressure, friction and anti-wear properties of gear oils in the laboratory. Examples of these are the IAE (IP 166) and Ryder gear rigs, the Timken Lubricant Tester, the SAE, David Brown and Caterpillar Disc (or Roller), 4-Ball, Falex, Almen and FZG machines. The selection of the appropriate test machine depends on the application being considered, but in spite of the variety of equipment available, the correlation of laboratory tests with practice is not precise and hence the final evaluation of the lubricant needs to be under controlled field conditions.

A number of industry and military specifications exist for automotive extreme pressure gear lubricants. Examples of these are the US Military MIL-L-2105 and 2105 B specifications. The MIL-L-2105 specification is still used to indicate the performance level of oils although the specification is now obsolete. The MIL-L-2105 B specification describes an axle oil with a higher EP performance level which is measured in the CRC L-42 car axle high speed shock test, and the CRC L-37 truck axle high torque test. Also included in this specification are a thermal and oxidation stability test (TOST), the CRC L-33 axle moisture corrosion test, a copper corrosion test ASTM D130–IP 154, and a Channel Point test to assess the low temperature flow properties of the oil. The British Ministry of Defence Specification CS 3000B is based on the performance of a blended oil in full scale axle tests as well as a comprehensive series of laboratory bench tests including oxidation, foam and storage stabilities. The axle tests specified are the IP 232 High Torque Test and a modified IP 234 High Speed Shock Test.

In the case of farm tractor and highway construction equipment transmission lubricants, the fluid may be required to perform more than one function. For example, several tractor manufacturers recommend oils for use as both hydraulic and transmission fluids. 'Universal' tractor oils are also available which are suitable for the engine, transmission, hydraulics and some types of final drive.

Several larger tractor models are now fitted with oil immersed 'wet' brakes. The oil used for this purpose may require special frictional characteristics to avoid the occurrence of severe vibration or 'chatter' when braking is applied. Special additives are incorporated in oil formulations to meet this requirement.

11. AUTOMATIC TRANSMISSION FLUIDS

The fluids used to lubricate automatic transmissions for passenger cars should facilitate the satisfactory operation of such components as the torque converter, planetary or differential gearing, wet clutches, servo-mechanisms and control valves. The viscosity characteristics of the oil are extremely important and because the viscosity must not change unduly with temperature (for example, from $-20°C$ ($-4°F$) on starting in cold climates to operating temperatures as high as $150°C$ ($302°F$)), viscosity index improvers are incorporated. Low viscosity improves the efficiency of the torque converter, but the lower limit is dictated by the viscosity required to protect the gearing. It is usual to employ fluids in the range of SAE 5W to 20W for automatic transmissions.

The shearing forces exerted by the automatic transmission components such as the pumps and clutches tend to reduce the viscosity of the polymeric viscosity improvers incorporated in these fluids. It is important, therefore, that these fluids have adequate resistance to mechanical breakdown and for this purpose full scale road, dynamometer or laboratory bench tests may be used with the viscosity compared before and after shearing. Because of the comparatively high temperatures reached in service, oils with very good oxidation and thermal stability are necessary.

The two most important specifications for automatic transmission fluids in the US are the Ford M2C 33G and the General Motors 'Dexron II'. In Europe, transmissions of US design generally use fluids to US specifications.

A number of constant speed and cycling full scale transmission tests are used to evaluate the thermal and oxidation resistance of automatic transmission fluids. Amongst these are the Powerglide oxidation test (which is part of the General Motors 'Dexron' specification requirement), the Ford Mercomatic Oxidation Test, and the Powerglide AT-12 Oxidation and AT-13 Durability Tests. Load-carrying additives are usually necessary to protect the gearing and the thrust washers. With most automatic transmissions, the static and dynamic frictional properties are important for satisfactory operation of the clutches and brake bands and specific additives may be included to control the frictional properties. These properties are measured by bench tests (for example, the Low Velocity Friction Apparatus), rig tests (for example the SAE No. 2 machine) or car tests for torque capacity and 'shift feel'. Also, since many seals are used in these transmission units, the fluid must be compatible with these seal materials. Because of the complex range of functions performed, automatic transmission fluids tend to be highly complex products and additive compatibility is an important factor in the development of their formulations.

12. HYDRAULIC OILS

The operation of many types of industrial machines can be conveniently controlled by means of hydraulic systems, which consist essentially of an oil reservoir, a motor driven pump, control valves, piping and an actuator. The wide range of hydraulic applications encountered necessitates the use of a variety of pump designs including gear, vane, axial and radial piston types which, in turn, utilise various metallurgical combinations. Thus the hydraulic fluid is required to transmit pressure and energy, minimise friction and wear in pumps, valves and cylinders, minimise leakage between moving components and protect the metal surfaces against corrosion.

To obtain optimum efficiency of machine operation and control, the viscosity of the oil should be low enough to minimise frictional losses and pressure loss in piping, particularly when starting up from cold. However, it is also necessary to have a sufficiently high viscosity to provide satisfactory wear protection and to minimise leakage of the fluid. High viscosity index fluids help to maintain a satisfactory viscosity over a wide temperature range. The anti-wear properties of high quality hydraulic oils are usually improved by the incorporation of suitable additives in the formulations.

Since the clearances in pumps and valves tend to be critical, it is important to maintain the system in as clean a condition as possible. The oil should have good oxidation stability to avoid the formation of insoluble gums or sludges, it should have good water separation properties, and because air may be entrained in the system, the oil should have good resistance to foaming and air release properties. Similarly, good rust protection properties will assist in keeping the oil in a satisfactory condition. Most of the tests used to assess the quality of hydraulic oils are described in the earlier section on 'Steam Turbine Oils'. The anti-wear properties may be determined by several of the tests described under 'Gear Oils' or by laboratory procedures using hydraulic pumps operating under specified conditions and observing the final condition of the components.

13. OTHER LUBRICATING OILS

Whilst many of the properties which have been discussed earlier apply to other types of lubricating oils, there are a number of industrial applications for which special performance requirements are demanded. The following examples illustrate this.

(a) AIR COMPRESSOR OILS

In addition to possessing the correct viscosity for satisfactory bearing and cylinder lubrication, very good oxidation resistance is required to avoid degradation of the lubricant in the presence of heated air. This is particularly important where discharge temperatures are high, since hard deposits originating from oxidised oil should be avoided. Condensed moisture is frequently present and the oil rather than water should wet the metal surfaces. Also, the water should separate out rather than forming an emulsion.

(b) REFRIGERATOR COMPRESSOR OILS

The efficiency of compression–refrigeration systems can be directly influenced by the properties of the lubricant. This is because the oil used for cylinder lubrication tends to be carried over into the system where it can have a detrimental effect on the efficiency of the evaporator and associated equipment. The lubricating oil, therefore, must not only effectively minimise friction and wear in the compressor and prevent the formation of undesirable deposits, but it must also not adversely affect the operation of the condenser, expansion valve or evaporator. The low temperature viscosity must be balanced against the need to protect the head end of the cylinder against wear. Adequate oxidation resistance and adequate thermal stability to resist the high temperatures encountered at the compressor discharge are also necessary. In ammonia systems, it is important that the pour point of the oil is below the evaporator temperatures to avoid the congealing of the oil on evaporator heat-transfer surfaces. With Freon systems, a low Freon floc point of the oil indicates freedom from the likelihood of waxy deposits which could otherwise interfere with the satisfactory operation of the expansion valve and lower the rate of heat transfer.

(c) STEAM CYLINDER OILS

Steam engines, pumps, forging hammers and pile drivers are amongst the equipment using steam cylinders. The performance of this type of machinery is directly affected by the efficiency of the lubrication of the valves, piston rings, cylinder walls and rods. The selection of the lubricating oil is influenced by the steam temperatures encountered, by the moisture content of the steam, by the cleanliness of the steam (*i.e.* possible contamination by solids) and by the necessity for the oil to separate from the exhaust steam or condensate. Excessive oxidation of the oil in service could cause a build-up of deposits in the stem and rod packings and result in shut-down of the equipment for cleaning. High quality oils will resist deterioration and minimise the formation of deposits.

(d) MACHINE TOOL TABLEWAY LUBRICATING OILS

Satisfactory lubrication of the ways and slides of machine tools is important in maintaining the precision of equipment designed to work to close tolerances. The movement of work tables, work heads, tool holders and carriages should be facilitated by the lubricant so that the control is smooth and precise. The characteristics required for these oils include a suitable viscosity to enable ready distribution of the oil to the sliding surfaces, but ensuring that the necessary oil films are formed at traverse speeds under high load conditions. Static friction must be minimised and the oil should prevent the alternate sticking and slipping of moving parts, particularly at very low speeds. Good adhesive properties are also required to maintain an adequate film on intermittently lubricated surfaces, especially when the position of these surfaces is in the vertical plane.

   A more detailed study of lubricating oils and their applications may be made by reference to the literature suggested for further reading.

14. SUGGESTIONS FOR FURTHER READING

O'Connor and Boyd (1963). *Standard Handbook of Lubrication Engineering*, McGraw-Hill, New York.

Boner (1964). *Gear and Transmission Lubricants,* Reinhold, New York.

Boner and Gruse (1967). *Motor Oils—Performance and Evaluation*, Reinhold, New York.

Schilling (1968). *Motor Oils and Engine Lubrication,* Scientific Publications (GB) Ltd.

Schilling (1972). *Motor Oils and Engine Lubrication, Vol. II. Automobile Engine Lubrication*, Scientific Publications (GB) Ltd.

Papers on specific subjects will be found in appropriate sections of Proceedings of the Seventh and Eighth World Petroleum Congress.

NOTE ADDED IN PROOF

Since October 1972 Caterpillar have recommended the use of oils meeting SAE engine service classification CD performance requirements in place of Series 3 oils. These are the same as in MIL-L-2104C.

Chapter 11

LUBRICATING GREASES

R. S. BARNES, E. A. GOODCHILD and D. WYLLIE

1. INTRODUCTION

Grease has been defined as 'a solid to semi-solid product in which a thickening agent is dispersed in a liquid lubricant'. Greases vary in texture from soft to hard and in colour from light amber to dark brown. Their particular value lies in the fact that unlike liquid lubricants and because of their semi-solid nature they will stay in place in a bearing assembly with comparatively elementary mechanical seals. Furthermore, they assist in sealing against extraneous material and in contrast to oil will lubricate without constant replenishment.

Until comparatively recently, individual greases were required for specific purposes but with the advent of new types of formulations, a wider range of applications is now covered. This has resulted in the emergence of multi-purpose industrial and automotive greases which are replacing the very numerous specialised materials formerly required.

2. COMPOSITION

Although most fluid lubricants can be 'gelled' into greases, mineral oil is the normal base material. The choice of oil depends on the intended application and may extend from light spindle oil to heavy steam-cylinder oil but in general a light or medium machine oil is preferred. For wide and/or very high temperature use synthetic diesters, silicones and other special fluids are used in place of oil.

The earlier greases were thickened with metallic soaps. Soap-type thickeners used to form the grease 'gels' are usually calcium, sodium or lithium salts of fatty acids and are produced by the saponification of the fat or fatty acid with the appropriate alkali in the presence of the oil. Sometimes pre-formed soaps are used, for example, aluminium stearate.

In most soap-based greases the soap is dispersed in the grease as fibres or ribbons varying in size from about 1 to 100 microns in length with a length diameter/ratio of about 10 to 100.

The fatty materials used for soap formation are usually of animal origin but they may be vegetable oils or fats; hydrogenated fats, particularly fish oil and castor oil, are also used. The type of fatty material affects the melting point of the soap and texture. Special properties are obtained in some greases by using more than one type of acid at the same time and forming complex soaps.

Non-soap thickeners are also used. These may consist of silica or clay or may be organic materials of high melting point including some dyes; their oleophilic character can be improved either by the inclusion of long-chain hydrocarbons or by coating the particles with organic cations. Inorganic thickeners, coated and dried, need dispersion aids such as polar organic compounds of low molecular weight (methanol, acetone and propylene carbonate).

As with lubricating oil, various additives are incorporated into greases in order to confer or enhance certain properties such as rust prevention, resistance to oxidation and extreme pressure properties and to improve stability, resistance to 'bleeding', water resistance etc.

3. TYPES

CALCIUM-SOAP GREASES

These are resistant to water, they have a smooth texture and their chief use is for plain bearings and low-speed rolling bearings. Their water content varies usually between 0·4 to 1·0 per cent, is present in the form of water of crystallisation and has a stabilising effect. High temperatures cause a loss of water and a consequent weakening of soap structure and therefore the use of these greases is limited to a maximum temperature of about 60°C (140°F). Other stabilisers and structure modifiers can now be used in place of or as well as water and the water content no longer has its former importance, e.g. in calcium hydroxystearate greases some of which can be used up to 120°C (248°F).

SODIUM-SOAP GREASES

These are fibrous in structure, they are resistant to moderately high temperature but are not resistant to water. They are used for rolling bearings at higher temperatures and speeds than normal conventional calcium soap-greases.

LITHIUM-SOAP GREASES

These were developed during the 1939–45 war. They are normally smooth in appearance but sometimes exhibit a grain structure. They are resistant to water and to the highest normal service temperatures and because of their variety of types, their versatility and extensive scope they are frequently employed as multi-purpose greases.

ALUMINIUM-SOAP GREASES

These are invariably translucent. They are made with oils of high viscosity, they often contain polymers and although water resistant and adhesive, they possess poor mechanical stability and so are not suitable for rolling bearings.

MIXED-SOAP GREASES

(For example, the sodium/calcium soap greases.) These are made by some manufacturers for uses which include high speed rolling bearings.

COMPLEX-SOAP GREASES

These contain calcium, calcium/lead or other metallic complexes with fatty acids and acetate, benzoate or other salts. These have high melting points and are competing for a share of the market for high quality multi-purpose greases.

OTHER GREASES

Examples of these are non-soap types with high water resistance and mechanical stability and some from selected organic compounds; they are now being further developed for multi-purpose use. Treated clays or organic dyes of high temperature resistance along with synthetic heat resisting fluids are used for extreme temperatures. Non-soap greases are also used in nuclear power plants. Solid additives such as graphite and molybdenum disulphide are included in some formulations intended to function under conditions of exceptionally heavy loading or high temperature.

4. PROPERTIES AND THEIR ASSESSMENT

(a) PENETRATION

The standard method of measuring grease consistency is the penetration test ASTM D217–IP 50. In this, a doubled angled cone is allowed to fall freely into the grease under controlled conditions and the depth of penetration measured in tenths of a millimetre is taken as the penetration value. The harder the grease the lower the penetration value. The penetration varies according to the amount of shearing to which the grease has been subjected. It may be measured on the grease as received in its original container (undisturbed penetration), after transfer with minimum disturbance to a standard container (unworked penetration), after a standard amount of shearing (worked penetration), and after a prolonged period of shearing in a mechanical worker. The worked penetration is normally used for classification and the National Lubricating Grease Institute has classified greases into universally accepted grades according to penetration ranges running from very soft grease at Grade 000 to very stiff grease at Grade 6.

For very soft or semi-fluid greases the penetration is measured by a special penetration cone IP 167, as the normal cone would sink right into the grease.

The penetration can be measured on samples insufficient for IP 50 using $\frac{1}{4}$ scale or $\frac{1}{2}$ scale cones as described in ASTM D1403.

In all the above tests the grease is brought to a temperature of 25°C (77°F) before carrying out the determination.

(b) Drop Point

The drop point is an indication of the temperature at which a grease passes from a semi-solid to a liquid state. The tests consist of heating the grease under prescribed conditions in a cup supported at the end of a thermometer. As the grease is heated it will gradually extrude through the orifice in the cup. The temperature at which the first drop of material falls from this orifice is called the drop point.

There are three test methods in current use and these do not give identical results. Therefore drop point should be quoted in terms of the method used. IP 31 has now been largely superseded by the joint method ASTM D566–IP 132. More recently the ASTM have published D2265 which heats the apparatus through an aluminium block in place of the more usual bath of hot oil.

It should not be considered that the drop point indicates the maximum service temperature the grease will withstand, since other factors such as mechanical stability, loss of water, oxidation and thermal changes and base oil volatility are also important. It does, however, indicate the approximate temperature above which the grease cannot be used. The drop point is normally used for quality control and identification purposes.

(c) Flow Properties

Grease is non-Newtonian in behaviour and, unlike oils, an initial shear stress (yield value) must be applied before it will deform and commence to flow. It is this non-flowing characteristic that enables grease to offer certain advantages over lubricating oils and results in their extensive use for the lubrication of rolling bearings.

The yield value of a grease will determine whether the grease will tend to slump and churn in rolling bearings, as well as its feeding characteristics to the inlet ports of dispensing pumps. No standardised method is published for determining the yield value of a grease, although various ways have been suggested. The best known is the Cone Resistance Value (ref. Lubn. Eng. 1957, Vol. 13, No. 6, pp. 341–6) which can be measured up to the maximum temperature at which the grease may have to operate. It will be more reliable to perform a churning test in a bearing if there is little experience with the type of grease involved.

The exact study of flow properties requires the study of shear stresses and shear rates in narrow clearances between concentric cylinders or between shallow cones and plates. Specialised equipment is marketed by some manufacturers for this purpose but none has yet been standardised. The only standard test is ASTM D1092 for the Apparent Viscosity of Lubricating Greases in the apparatus often known as the SOD Viscometer. Grease is forced through short steel capillary tubes and the apparent viscosity calculated as if the grease was in fact a Newtonian fluid. The test can be carried out over a range of temperatures. It has been used as a low temperature test of grease pumpability and in the USA the NLGI have worked out a procedure for giving empirical data on flow rates, pipe sizes etc. for handling grease in long line dispensing systems.

(d) Low Temperature Torque

Greases become harder and more viscous as the temperature drops and in extreme cases can become so rigid that excessive torque occurs within the bearing. Measurement of low temperature torque is described in IP 186 and ASTM D1478. In both tests the pre-greased ball bearing is cooled to the desired temperature and the starting and running torques determined at 1 rev/min.

These tests indicate the ability to start up rather than the lubricating ability of a grease at sub-zero temperatures.

(e) Mechanical Stability

The ability of a grease to withstand a large degree of mechanical working without changing its consistency unduly can be important during the initial clearing stages in a bearing, or in certain applications, for example in a bearing assembly under vibrating conditions. The effects of mechanical instability can lead in some cases to the grease becoming fluid and losing its sealing properties. Leakage from the assembly and inadequate lubrication can then follow.

The two tests most widely used to assess mechanical stability are the prolonged worked penetration test (ASTM D217–IP 50) and the ASTM Roll Test (D1831). In the former the grease is subjected to a large number of strokes (usually 100 000) in a motorised version of the worker pot used for the penetration test, at room temperature. In the Roll Test a measured amount of grease is placed in a horizontally mounted drum in which a steel roller rotates. The drum is turned about its axis, thereby subjecting the grease to a milling action similar to that occurring in rolling bearings. In both tests the difference in penetration of the grease, before and after, is a measure of the grease breakdown.

(f) OIL SEPARATION

It has been shown that greases can be treated as permeable structures and fluid can be squeezed out at varying rates, depending on the grease structure and the nature and viscosity of the lubricating fluid, as well as on the applied pressure.

Greases differ very markedly in their tendency to liberate oil, and although opinions differ on whether or not lubrication is dependent on oil bleeding, liberation of free oil during storage or in feed lines to a bearing is to be avoided.

The IP and ASTM have developed standard methods for predicting the amount of oil liberated by greases when stored in containers. In both methods the grease is supported by a wire mesh screen; a weight (IP) or air pressure (ASTM) is applied to the top surface of the grease to accelerate oil separation. The test duration is 24 hours for the ASTM method (D1742) and 7 days for the IP method (IP 121) but it may be possible to shorten the duration of the IP test as a result of work now in hand.

In those tests aimed at storage conditions only small pressures are applied. In some spring loaded grease cups and some centralised feed systems, greases may be exposed to differential pressures across an interface at which oil can separate and escape. No standard test has been published but various workers have used the ASTM test for prolonged periods and/or with higher pressures or other apparatus to assess oil separation under these conditions. Appreciable oil separation leaves hard residues which block feed pipes, therefore such studies often include penetration measurements on the grease cakes produced.

(g) VOLATILITY

The effective life of a grease, especially under high temperature conditions, is dependent on such factors as oxidation, retentive properties and evaporation of the base oil. Evaporation of the oil can result in the grease becoming stiffer and drier and ultimately lead to bearing failure.

The volatility of a grease can be determined by IP 183 and the corresponding ASTM D972 test method. In this test air is passed at a known flow rate over a weighed amount of grease in a standard cell which is immersed in an oil bath at a required temperature. Since air is used some oxidation of the grease will occur, but nevertheless a comparative rating for evaporation loss can be obtained by measuring the loss in weight of the grease sample.

(h) Oxidation Stability (shelf storage)

The storage stability of a grease when packed into bearings is assuming considerable importance as more prepacked sealed-for-life bearings are adopted in industry. In these bearings the grease acts as a protective until the bearings are put into operation. Under such conditions thin films of grease in contact with steel or steel and bronze are exposed to air and moisture which promotes oxidation of the grease, the products of which can cause corrosion of the bearing surfaces.

The standard test to evaluate storage properties under these conditions is described in the joint ASTM D942–IP 142 method. In this method oxidation of a thin film of grease is accelerated by heating the grease at 99°C (210°F) in oxygen at a pressure of 110 pounds per square inch. The amount of oxygen absorbed by the grease is recorded in terms of pressure drop over a period of 100 hours and in some cases up to 500 hours. Greases showing high oxygen absorption become fluid, increase in acidity and are generally considered unsatisfactory.

The oxidation stability as assessed in this test determines the shelf storage life of greases in stored bearings; it is not intended for predicting the performance of a grease under dynamic service conditions, neither is it intended for predicting stability of grease stored in commercial containers.

(i) Water Resistance

The resistance of a grease to water contamination is an important property since greases have to lubricate mechanisms where water will be present to a greater or lesser extent. The presence of water can cause changes in grease consistency, emulsification with water soluble soap base greases and a reduction in mechanical stability. The effects of such changes can lead to grease being washed out of the mechanisms, resulting in inadequate lubrication and poor protection against rusting. Most greases classed as water resistant greases are able to take up large amounts of water without suffering the serious changes mentioned above. It does not, however, follow that a grease with high water resistance will afford adequate protection against rusting unless rust preventives are incorporated in the grease.

The most commonly used test for measuring water resistance is the 'Water Wash-out Test' described in IP 215 and the corresponding ASTM D1264 method. In this test a greased ball bearing is rotated at 600 rev/min in an assembly with specified clearances in the covers to allow entry of water from a water jet which impinges on the face of one cover. The loss in grease pack after one hour of operation is a measure of the resistance to water. Such tests are not capable of distinguishing between greases of similar performance.

(j) ANTI-CORROSION PROPERTIES

Water resistance alone does not ensure that a grease will protect bearings or other mechanisms against moisture corrosion. Methods for assessing rust prevention by grease are described in IP 220 and ASTM D1743.

In the ASTM method a taper roller bearing is packed with grease and following a short running-in period is dipped and stored above distilled water. The bearing is then cleaned and examined for corrosion.

In IP 220 the grease is tested in a ball bearing under dynamic conditions. The bearing is run intermittently in the presence of distilled water and at the end of the test is rated for corrosion. Although not part of the standard test some workers replace the distilled water by salt water where this is likely to come in contact with bearings in use.

It is also important that greases themselves should not be corrosive to metals with which they come in contact, neither should they develop corrosion tendencies with ageing or oxidation. In IP 112 a polished copper strip (other metals can also be used) is immersed in the grease which is stored at a temperature relevant to the use of the grease. The metal strip is then examined for etching, pitting or discoloration. The ASTM method D1261 is similar in principle but is an accelerated test in that the grease/copper strip is stored in an oxygen bomb under pressure.

(k) EXTREME PRESSURE PROPERTIES

The use of additives in greases to confer high load bearing properties is demanded in certain applications, where shock loading or unit loading and sliding are very high.

A variety of test machines have been developed to assess load carrying ability, the two most commonly used being the Timken Extreme Pressure Tester and the Four-Ball machine. Each employs one type of contact conditions and as these are likely to differ from those met in any particular machine care should be taken in the interpretation of results. The methods are, however, useful for quality control, development work and research.

In the Timken test method standardised as IP 240 a steel ring is rotated against a steel test block under load. The 'OK Value' which is frequently quoted is the maximum load the lubricant film will withstand without rupturing and causing scoring in the contact zone after 10 min running. A wear test may be carried out at loads below the OK value, the ring and block being weighed before and after test to determine weight loss, or the friction loss may be measured.

The Four-Ball test, IP 239 or ASTM D2266, is operated with one steel ball rotating under load, and sliding against three similar steel balls which are held stationary in a cup holding the lubricant. Several types of test procedures can be employed to indicate the suitability of the grease to prevent wear. The Mean Hertz Load is frequently called for, it is a number derived from the overall wear diagram over a range of loads. The welding load may also be quoted.

(l) ANALYSIS FOR COMPOSITION, CONTAMINATION ETC.

ASTM D128 describes a detailed and complex analytical procedure for the separation of grease into its component parts and their measurement. Spectrographic methods may also be used to determine the metal present as soaps or the wear elements in used greases, in conjunction with separation techniques to measure and identify the various types of fats, lubricating fluids or additives present. The simpler tests which are more likely to be quoted are ash content, acidity and alkalinity, water and dirt content.

The ash on ignition is a measure of the amount of metals as oxides present in the soaps and will include the bulk of clay type non-soap thickeners. IP 5 includes a rapid rout ne method and a procedure similar to one section of ASTM D128, in which sulphuric acid is added to avoid loss of the more volatile oxides, and the result is reported as sulphated ash.

Water is determined by ASTM D95–IP 74. Some greases may contain traces of water. In conventional calcium base greases this is present as a stabiliser except in certain so-called heat stable greases whose heat stability is assessed by IP 180, Heat Stability of Calcium Greases.

Greases may contain small amounts of free organic acids but should not contain strong acids. (In some conventional lime base greases small amounts of free organic acids are intended as an aid to stability.) They may also contain small amounts of free alkalinity. IP 37 and ASTM D128 describe methods for their measurement for quality control or in the examination of used products for excessive acidity derived from oxidation. These methods are not applicable when lead, zinc or aluminium soaps are present or in presence of some additives, e.g. sodium nitrite.

Microscopic methods are used in the examination of used greases for wear particles. Wear is likely to be increased by the presence of abrasive dirt in grease. In IP 134 foreign particles are counted and graded for size under the microscope. It does not attempt to measure their abrasiveness. ASTM D1404 estimates deleterious particles by the extent to which they scratch plates of polished acrylic plastic. This may not indicate whether they would scratch metals. Other workers have tried non-standard tests with brass or other metals.

(m) PERFORMANCE TESTS

Performance tests are an essential part of the development and selection of greases for long term operation and/or operation under severe conditions. In this context these consist of running bearings of selected types and sizes that are grease lubricated under conditions intended to simulate the conditions which occur in practice. At one time there was little standardisation in this field, the major rolling bearing manufacturers and others having developed their own test procedures.

There are two philosophies behind rig testing. Some, mainly in the USA, have taken bearings, run them under standard conditions and expressed the results in terms of hours to failure. This type of test is to be found in various aircraft grease specifications. Rig tests in the UK have more often been run for definite periods, *e.g.* 500 hours, after which the conditions of the bearing and of the grease are rated. Performance testing is always time consuming, repeat tests being required because the repeatability and reproducibility of results is not high.

The first rig test to be standardised by the Institute of Petroleum was IP 168 Rolling Bearing Performance Test for Lubricating Greases. This uses a 40 mm ball bearing with a steel cage which is run under selected conditions of applied radial load, applied heat and speed for 500 hours. The performance of the grease is evaluated by assessing bearing and cage wear and the physical changes of the grease. This rig has been assessed by co-operative testing at 60°C, 121°C, 150°C and 177°C (140°F, 250°F, 320°F and 350°F). It is not difficult to pass the test at 60°C. At 150°C and 177°C it is very discriminating.

IP 168 will not necessarily predict whether greases will slump or churn and overheat in large bearings. IP 266 is a method of assessing the churning tendencies of greases operating in large ball and cylindrical roller bearings. The test was originally developed by the Ransome and Marles Bearing Company (now part of the RHP Group) as a test for grease churning and general grease performance. It was the subject of co-operative study by a Navy Department Advisory Panel and is used in a Navy Department grease specification. Part of this procedure has been standardised by the Institute as a 50 hour Rolling Bearing Grease Churning Test.

Other rigs used by the bearing manufacturers are aimed at severe thrust loading, vertically mounted bearings or spherical roller bearings. So far none has been standardised in the United Kingdom. SKF Gothenburg and SKF Luton have developed the R2 Rig using a heavily loaded 40 mm spherical roller bearing which is widely used and is the basis of the German Standard Method DIN 51806.

ASTM D1741 Functional Life of Ball Bearing Greases uses 30 mm deep groove ball bearings either for a short leakage test with fully packed bearings or a prolonged life test with partially packed bearings. The life test described in the US Federal Test Methods Standard No. 791, Methods 330 and 331, is probably better known in the United Kingdom as it is used in specifications for aircraft greases. It is frequently known as the Annapolis rig as it was developed at Annapolis by the US Navy laboratory there. A 20 mm ball bearing is rotated under light load at 10 000 rev/min at temperatures which vary from 121°C (250°F) up to 250°C (482°F) or over according to the specification.

ASTM D1263 Leakage Tendencies of Automotive Wheel Bearing Greases is a specialised test. It simulates conditions in a motor car wheel hub and is a good leakage test of short duration.

Fretting corrosion tests have been called for in a few government specifications but none have yet been standardised.

It will be seen that performance testing of grease is a lengthy procedure, especially if successive tests have to be carried out in the same rig, because the demand does not justify the expense of installing several rigs of any one type. Skill and experience are required in selecting the appropriate rig and conditions. Performance tests are therefore not suited for use as routine control tests. It is usual to establish the performance of a grease formulation and use simpler and cheaper chemical and physical tests to control and maintain quality during manufacture. Specifications for high quality greases may call for type approval with performance tests followed by inspection tests on batches of grease.

5. SUGGESTIONS FOR FURTHER READING

J. H. Harris (1967). *The Lubrication of Rolling Bearings*, Shell-Mex and BP.

C. J. Boner (1954). *Manufacture and Application of Lubricating Greases*, Reinhold Publishing Corporation, New York.

F. G. Bollo and A. A. Woods (1962). Modern grease technology *in Advances in Petroleum Chemistry and Refining*, Vol. VI, Chapter 5, Interscience, New York.

B. W. Hotten (1964). Formation and structure of lubricating grease, *in Advances in Petroleum Chemistry and Refining*, Vol. IX, Chapter 3, Interscience, New York.

Symposium on the use of grease as an engineering component (1970). Institution of Mechanical Engineers.

C. J. Boner (1960). Lubricating grease, *in Petroleum Products Handbook*, (ed. V. B. Guthrie), Section 9, Part 3, McGraw-Hill, New York.

S. Dawtrey (1973). Grease, *in Modern Petroleum Technology*, 4th edn, Applied Science, London.

Chapter 12

PETROLEUM WAXES, INCLUDING PETROLATUMS

R. I. GOTTSHALL and C. F. McCUE

1. INTRODUCTION

For many years the waxy materials recovered during the refining of crude oils were regarded as waste, with no commercial value. More recently products were recovered from this waste which, with additional refining, could replace natural waxes for most applications. The many grades of wax now available were developed because of the increased market demand.

Industrial uses of wax are more varied than those of any other petroleum product because of the unique properties and high performance required in specialised applications. The demand for tacky, high-melting point waxes was first met by the extraction of microcystalline waxes from the heavier fractions and residua of petroleum. Today complex blends, such as hot melts, which contain wax, polymers, resins and other additives, are becoming increasingly important to the packaging industry.

2. OCCURRENCE AND REFINING OF PETROLEUM WAXES

Wax is found in varying amounts in most crude oils. Paraffin base crudes (those rich in paraffin hydrocarbons) and mixed base crudes (containing both paraffins and naphthenes) usually have greater wax contents than aromatic base crudes. The type of wax recovered is dependent on the source and type of crude.

During the refining of waxy crudes, the wax becomes concentrated in the higher-boiling fractions used primarily for making lubricating oils. This wax is removed in order to improve the low-temperature performance of the lubricating oils. The highest molecular weight waxes are recovered from the residual fraction of the crude.

Paraffin waxes are obtained from the low-boiling and medium-boiling range lubricating oil fractions or from a special 'wax distillate' fraction.

Microcrystalline waxes are derived from the distillation residues or high-boiling lubricating oil fractions.

The refining of lubricating oil fractions to obtain a desirable low pour point, usually requires the removal of most of the waxy components. The dewaxing step is generally performed by the chilling and filter pressing method, centrifuge dewaxing, or the more modern and preferred method of filtering a chilled solution of waxy lubricating oil in a specific solvent. The waxy material thus removed is designated as 'slack wax' and contains 20 per cent or more oil which must be removed to make the wax suitable for most applications.

Processes generally used for deoiling slack waxes are 'sweating' and 'solvent deoiling'. Sweating involves raising the temperature of slack wax and allowing the oil and low melting fractions to drain from the wax cake. The pressing–sweating method is not suitable for microcrystalline slack wax because the oil is held so tenaciously by this type of wax that it will not press or sweat satisfactorily. Both paraffin and microcrystalline slack waxes are deoiled by dissolving them in solvent (usually a methyl ethyl ketone–toluene mixture) and then chilling the solution and filtering out the crystallised wax. Various grades of wax are obtained via both methods by repeating the deoiling step at successively lower temperatures. Some deoiled slack wax which is sold as crude scale wax contains about 2 per cent oil. The waxy oil removed from the slack wax is known as 'soft wax' and it is used chiefly as cracking stock.

The final stages of wax refining are usually standard, regardless of the process used in dewaxing and deoiling. Trace impurities of olefinic and aromatic hydrocarbons are removed by either hydrogenation or sulphuric acid treatment. The wax is decolorised and deodorised by clay filtration to produce a fully refined wax containing less than 0·5 per cent oil.

3. DEFINITIONS FOR PETROLEUM WAXES

When discussing the properties of petroleum waxes it is necessary to differentiate between the various types currently available. The classification of waxes has become intricate because of the wide variety of waxes made available through the expansion of refining technology.

A scheme for classifying waxes as either paraffin, semi-microcrystalline or microcrystalline was proposed in 1963 by an ASTM–TAPPI task force. This proposal was not adopted by ASTM–TAPPI as a standard, but it does serve as a useful means of characterising waxes. The basis of this classification is the equation

$$n_D^{210°F} = 0·000\ 194\ 3t + 1·3994$$

where 't' is the ASTM D938–IP 76 Congealing Point temperature in °F. Viscosity is included as an additional parameter, as explained later.

Paraffin wax is petroleum wax consisting mainly of normal alkanes characterised by a refractive index less than that obtained by the above equation. Paraffin waxes contain, in addition to normal alkanes, varying amounts of condensed and non-condensed cycloalkanes, isoalkanes and occasionally a very low percentage of aromatic material. Molecular weights are usually less than 450 and the viscosity at 210°F (99°C) will usually be less than six centistokes. Either needle or plate type crystal structures are common. Paraffin waxes also exhibit pronounced latent heats of crystallisation and possibly transition points, temperatures at which crystal structure modification occurs below the apparent solidification point of the wax.

Semi-microcrystalline wax and microcrystalline wax are petroleum waxes containing substantial portions of hydrocarbons other than normal alkanes. They are characterised by refractive indices greater than those given by the above equation, and by viscosities at 210°F of less than 10 centistokes for semi-microcrystalline waxes, or greater than 10 centistokes for microcrystalline waxes. Microcrystalline waxes have higher molecular weights, smaller crystal structures and greater affinities for oil than paraffin waxes. Microcrystalline waxes usually melt between 150°F (66°C) and 220°F (104°C) and have viscosities between 10 and 20 centistokes at 210°F.

Petrolatums are usually soft, unctuous products containing approximately 20 per cent oil and melting between 100°F (38°C) and 140°F (60°C). Petrolatum or petroleum jelly is essentially a mixture of microcrystalline wax and oil. It is produced as an intermediate product in the refining of microcrystalline wax or compounded by blending appropriate waxy products and oils. Petrolatum colours range from the almost black crude form to the highly refined yellow and white pharmaceutical grades.

Hot melts are blends of wax, polymers, resins or other additives. Total additive content is generally greater than 25 per cent. The additives usually increase strength, gloss, scuff resistance and viscosity. Of particular benefit to the packaging industry is the improved flexibility imparted by polymeric materials to wax coatings for paper and paper board. Increased flexibility improves coating fracture resistance at fold and crease areas of the package, thereby maintaining the good barrier properties of the coating.

4. APPLICATIONS FOR PETROLEUM WAX

Wax has been called the most versatile product of the oil industry. It was first used as a source of light and heat in such applications as candles, tapers, matches, flares, etc., but exploitation of its unique properties has led to many other uses.

Wax provides improved strength, moisture proofing, appearance and low cost for the food packaging industry, the largest consumer of waxes today. The coating of corrugated board with hot melts is of increasing importance to the wax industry.

Other uses include the coating of fruit and cheese, the lining of cans and barrels and the manufacture of anti-corrosives. Because of its thermoplastic nature, wax lends itself to modelling and the making of replicas; blends of waxes are used by dentists when making dentures and by engineers when mass-producing precision castings such as those used for gas turbine blades. The high gloss characteristic of some petroleum waxes makes them suitable ingredients for polishes, particularly for the 'paste' type which is commonly used on floors, furniture, cars and footwear. The highly refined waxes have excellent electrical properties and so find application in the insulation of low-voltage cables, small transformers, coils, capacitors and similar electronic components.

Wax is also used as a feedstock for the production of numerous petro-chemicals.

There are many other uses for petroleum wax, but these examples adequately illustrate its versatility.

5. QUALITY CRITERIA

Criteria for judging the quality of a wax must be specific for the type of wax and its intended application.

There are three general categories used in assessing the quality of waxes: (a) physical properties (used by producers for quality control); (b) functional properties (empirical evaluations under simulated consumer conditions); (c) chemical properties and composition (indicative of the other characteristics).

(a) CRITERIA FOR JUDGING PHYSICAL PROPERTIES

(i) Melting point
The melting point is one of the tests most widely used to determine the quality and type of wax. Petroleum waxes do not melt at sharply defined temperatures because they are mixtures of hydrocarbons with different melting points. Paraffin waxes, relatively simple mixtures, usually have a narrow melting range. Microcrystalline waxes and petrolatums are more complex and therefore melt over a much wider temperature range.

The melting point of a wax has both direct and indirect significance in most applications. Paraffin waxes are usually marketed on the basis of melting point—either English melting point (EMP) based on the ASTM–IP cooling curve, or the American melting point (AMP) which by definition is 3°F above the EMP—expressed as a range of either 2°F or 5°F. Thus, the designation 130/132 AMP indicates that the wax has an American melting point between 130°F (55°C) and 132°F (56°C), (and hence an English melting point between 127°F (53°C) and 129°F (54°C)).

Often it is necessary to compromise on the melting point specification because of its conflicting effects on functional properties important to the intended application. For example, in the waxing of paper, some high-melting waxes fracture readily when the paper is creased but have good gloss and blocking characteristics; low-melting waxes have a tendency to stick together or 'block' but may have good fracture resistance. Thus melting point is often of secondary importance when compared with hardness, tackiness or flexibility.

Some waxes (especially narrow-cut, highly paraffinic types) undergo a phase change or transition point in the solid state, usually about 25°F to 40°F (14°C to 22°C) below the melting point. This change of crystalline form is in some respects similar to the liquid–solid phase change at the melting point. Similar and significant changes of properties occur at both temperatures. Refractive index, density, flexibility, hardness, coefficients of expansion and friction, tensile strength, sealing strength, gloss and opacity change considerably over the transition temperature range. For applications requiring consistency of properties over a specific temperature range, a special effort should be made to select a wax that does not have a transition point in this range.

(ii) Oil content

It should be emphasised that there is no clear-cut division between oil and wax. The individual components of a commercial wax have melting points covering a wide temperature range. Components which may be liquid at room temperature are referred to as 'oil'.

It is necessary to distinguish clearly between paraffin wax, microcrystalline wax and petrolatums when discussing the significance of oil content because of the different degree of affinity that each of these wax types have for oil.

The oil content of paraffin waxes may be taken as a degree of refinement. Fully-refined wax usually has an oil content of less than 0·5 per cent. Waxes containing more than this amount of oil are referred to as 'scale wax', although an intermediate grade known as 'semi-refined wax' is sometimes recognised for waxes having an oil content of about 1 per cent.

Excess oil tends to exude from paraffin wax, giving it a dull appearance and a greasy feel. Such a wax would obviously be unsuitable for many applications, particularly the manufacture of food wrappings. A high oil content tends to plasticise the wax and has an adverse effect on sealing strength, tensile strength, hardness, odour, taste, colour and particularly colour stability.

Microcrystalline waxes have a greater affinity for oil than paraffin waxes because of their smaller crystal structure. The permissible amount depends on the type of wax and its intended use.

The oil content of microcrystalline wax is, in general, much greater than that of paraffin wax and could be as high as 20 per cent. Waxes containing more than 20 per cent oil would usually be classed as petrolatums, but the demarcation is by no means precise.

(iii) Fluid properties

Viscosity of molten wax is of importance in applications involving coating or dipping processes since it influences the quality of coating obtained. Examples of such applications are paper converting, hot-dip anti-corrosion coatings and taper manufacturing.

Paraffin waxes do not differ much in viscosity; a typical viscosity being 3 ± 0.5 cSt at 210°F (99°C). Microcrystalline waxes are considerably more viscous and vary over a wide range; 10 to 20 cSt at 210°F (99°C). Some hot melt viscosities exceed 20 000 cP at 350°F (177°C), although 100 to 2000 cP is the more common range currently found.

(iv) Hardness

Measurement of the depth of penetration of a needle or cone into a wax specimen is the usual method for determining hardness. Techniques for measuring hardness (cone penetration for softer waxes, and needle penetration for the harder waxes) have been standardised by ASTM and IP.

Hardness is a measure of resistance to deformation or damage; hence it is an important criterion for many wax applications. It is indirectly related to blocking tendency and gloss. Hard, narrow-cut waxes have higher blocking points and better gloss than waxes of the same average molecular weight but wider molecular weight range.

(v) Strength of wax

Another popular test for wax is tensile strength. Some manufacturers and consumers find this to be a useful guide in controlling the quality of the wax, although the actual significance of the results obtained is not clear.

The modulus of rupture is also an indication of strength or toughness of wax. It is claimed to correlate with the sealing strength and blocking tendency of waxed papers, although it would appear to be an indirect relationship.

(b) CRITERIA FOR JUDGING FUNCTIONAL PROPERTIES

Functional properties are empirical in nature and are based on the simulated conditions of use. The results of such tests are intended to correlate with practice, and are used to determine the suitability of a wax for a particular application.

The properties of waxed paper or board depend not only on the individual characteristics of the two components, but also on the manner in which they interact when they are combined in the waxing process. It is therefore necessary to conduct certain tests on the finished paper.

According to the method of application, the wax may be either impregnated into the pores and fibres of the paper or coated on one or both surfaces.

(i) Wax content of substrates

Many of the functional properties of coated board or waxed paper are dependent on the amounts of wax present either on the surface or internally.

Surface wax on each side or both sides of a weighed specimen can be determined by scraping each side and weighing the specimen after each operation. Internal wax is the difference between total wax content and total surface wax. Total wax content can be determined by solvent extraction or by finding the difference between average weight per unit area of waxed and unwaxed specimens.

(ii) Barrier properties

The ability of wax to prevent the transfer of moisture vapour is of primary concern in the food packaging industry. To maintain the freshness of dry foods, moisture must be kept out of the product, but to maintain the quality of frozen foods and baked goods the moisture must be kept in the product. This results in two criteria for barrier properties: moisture vapour transmission rates (A) at elevated temperatures and high relative humidity and (B) at low temperatures and low relative humidity, for frozen foods.

To have good barrier properties a wax must be applied in a smooth, continuous film and be somewhat flexible to prevent cracking and peeling of the film.

(iii) Surface disruption

A major problem in the paper coating industry is the relatively low temperatures at which waxed surfaces stick together or block. If the surfaces of waxed paper block, the surface appearance, gloss and barrier properties are destroyed when the papers are separated. The blocking and picking points indicate the temperature range at which waxed film surfaces are damaged if contact is made.

(iv) Adhesion

The thermoplastic properties of wax are used to good effect in the heat sealing of waxed paper packages. The strength of the seal is a function not only of the physical properties but also of the chemical properties and composition of the wax.

(v) Appearance

Waxed coatings provide protection for packaged goods and the high gloss characteristics provide improved appearance. Both the nature of the wax and the coating process contribute to the final gloss characteristics.

(vi) Slip properties

Friction is an indication of the resistance to sliding exhibited by two surfaces in contact with one another. The intended application determines the degree of slip desired. Coatings for packages that require stacking should have a high coefficient of friction to prevent slippage in the stacks. Folding box coatings should have a low coefficient of friction to allow the boxes to slide easily from a stack of blanks being fed to the forming and filling equipment.

(c) CRITERIA FOR JUDGING CHEMICAL PROPERTIES

Chemical properties and the composition of wax give a good indication of its degree of refinement.

(i) Odour and taste
Freedom from odour and taste is of importance in applications where the wax is likely to contact foodstuffs; e.g. in the manufacture of wrapping paper, the defeathering of poultry, or the waxing of cheese.

Poor wax odour and taste may be due to (1) inadequate refining; (2) contamination during transport or storage; or (3) deterioration in use. Odours due to inadequate refining are usually associated with a high oil content or, less frequently, with residual solvent. The most common odour acquired during storage is that absorbed from the material in which the wax slabs are usually packed. Wax also readily absorbs the odours of products such as cheese or soap if stored in proximity under conditions of poor ventilation. Wax that has been overheated in use tends to oxidise and develop an odour similar to rancid coconut oil, which is very penetrating.

Subjective evaluations such as odour and taste are difficult to standardise. There is, however, a technique which ensures reasonable concordance within a group whose members have agreed about odour level. Difficulties arise when there is a difference of opinion (e.g. as between purchaser and vendor) as to what constitutes an acceptable odour or taste.

(ii) Colour
Paraffin waxes are generally white in colour, whereas microcrystalline waxes and petrolatums range from white to almost black. A fully refined wax should be virtually colourless ('water-white') when examined in the molten state; paraffin scale wax usually exhibits a slight yellow or 'straw' tint. Absence of colour is of particular importance in waxes used for pharmaceutical purposes or for the manufacture of food wrappings.

The significance of the colour of microcrystalline waxes and petrolatums depends on the use for which they are intended. In some applications (e.g. the manufacture of corrosion preventives) colour may be of little importance, but in others it may be vital. For pharmaceutical purposes the colour of petrolatum is taken as an index of its purity; two grades are recognised in the British Pharmacopoeia: paraffinum molle flavum (yellow) and paraffinum molle album (white).

Colours in the solid state are normally expressed in descriptive terms such as white, offwhite, yellow, amber, brown, etc., there being no generally accepted standard method for measuring this characteristic.

(iii) Carbonisable material

Waxes and petrolatums intended for certain pharmaceutical purposes are required both by the British Pharmacopoeia and the United States Pharmacopoeia to pass the test for carbonisable matter. The degree of unsaturation (carbonisable material) is determined by reacting the wax with concentrated sulphuric acid. The resultant colour of the acid layer must be lighter than the reference colour if the wax is to qualify as a BP or USP grade.

(iv) Criteria for food grade wax

The UK Ministry of Agriculture, Fisheries and Food and the US Food & Drug Administration have imposed stringent ultra-violet absorbance limits on petroleum waxes used in the food industry. In particular it is necessary to ensure the absence of carcinogenic polynuclear aromatic hydrocarbons. A low absorbance value in the 280–400 millimicron region is necessary to meet the requirements.

(v) Storage stability

The presence of peroxides or similar oxy-compounds is usually the result of oxidation and deterioration of waxes either in use or storage. Antioxidants, such as butylated hydroxyanisole, may be used to retard oxidation.

(vi) Chemical composition

Paraffin wax consists almost entirely of n-paraffins containing 20–30 carbon atoms per molecule. Microcrystalline waxes and petrolatums are usually much more complex, with considerable branching of the molecules, which may contain 50 or more carbon atoms.

Almost all physical and functional properties of the wax are affected by: (1) its molecular weight range; (2) distribution of its individual components and the degree of branching. For a given melting point, a narrow-cut wax consisting almost entirely of straight chain paraffins will be harder, more brittle and have a higher gloss and blocking point than one of broader cut, or one containing a higher proportion of branched molecules.

6. ASSESSMENT

(a) PHYSICAL PROPERTIES OF WAX

(i) ASTM D87–IP 55 Melting Point of Petroleum Wax (Cooling Curve)

A sample of molten wax in a test tube, with thermometer, is placed in an air bath which is inserted into a room temperature water bath. The latent heat of crystallisation released during the solidification of a paraffin wax is sufficient to temporarily arrest the rate of cooling. This results in a plateau in the time/temperature relationship. The temperature at which the plateau occurs is the melting point. This procedure is not suitable for microcrystalline wax, petrolatums or waxes containing large amounts of non-normal hydrocarbons (the plateau rarely occurs in cooling curves of such waxes).

(ii) ASTM D127–IP 133 Drop Melting Point of Petroleum Wax, Including Petrolatum

This method can be used for most petroleum waxes and wax-resin blends. A chilled thermometer bulb is coated with the molten wax (which is allowed to solidify), placed in a test tube and heated at a specified rate in a water bath. The melting point is the temperature at which the first drop of liquid falls from the thermometer.

(iii) ASTM D938–IP 76—Congealing Point of Petroleum Wax, Including Petrolatum

This procedure can be used for almost all types of petroleum waxes and wax–resin blends. A thermometer bulb is dipped in the melted wax and placed in a heated vial. The thermometer is held horizontally and slowly rotated on its axis. As long as the wax remains liquid, it will hang from the bulb as a pendant drop. The temperature at which the drop rotates with the thermometer is the congealing point.

   The congealing point of a microcrystalline wax or petrolatum is invariably lower than its drop melting point.

(iv) Saybolt Melting Point of Paraffin Wax

This method is somewhat outdated but may be found occasionally in paraffin wax specifications. This procedure is also dependent on the latent heat of crystallisation and yields results very similar to the ASTM/IP Cooling Curve method. The distinctive feature of the Saybolt method is that the sample is contained in a shallow tray which is moved back and forth while the thermometer is held stationary, thus giving a stirring action.

(v) ASTM D721–IP 158—Oil Content of Petroleum Waxes

The fact that oil is much more soluble than wax in methyl ethyl ketone at low temperatures is utilised in this procedure. A weighed sample of wax is dissolved in warm methyl ethyl ketone in a test tube and chilled to $-25°F$ ($-32°C$) to precipitate the wax. The solvent–oil solution is separated from the wax by pressure filtration through a sintered glass filter stick. The solvent is evaporated and the residue weighed.

(vi) ASTM D445–IP 71—Viscosity of Transparent and Opaque Liquids

Kinematic viscosity is measured by timing the flow of a fixed volume of material through a calibrated capillary at a selected temperature. The unit of kinematic viscosity is the stokes and kinematic viscosities of waxes are usually reported in centistokes. Centistokes can be converted to Saybolt Universal Seconds by using ASTM D2161.

(vii) ASTM D2669—Apparent Viscosity of Petroleum Waxes With Additives

This method is suitable for blends of wax and additives having apparent viscosities up to 20 000 centipoises at 350°F (177°C). Apparent viscosity is the measurement of drag produced on a rotating spindle immersed in the test liquid. A suitable viscometer is equipped to use interchangeable spindles and adjustable rates of rotation. The wax blend is heated by means of a heating mantle in an 800 ml beaker and continuously stirred, until the test temperature is slightly exceeded. The sample is cooled to the test temperature, the stirring is discontinued and the viscosity is measured. Viscosities over a range of temperatures are recorded and plotted on semi-log paper to determine the apparent viscosity at any temperature in the particular region of interest.

(viii) ASTM D1321—Needle Penetration of Petroleum Waxes

The hardness or consistency of wax is measured with a penetrometer applying a load of 100 grams for 5 seconds to a standard needle having a truncated cone tip. The sample is heated to 30°F (17°C) above its congealing point, poured into a small brass cylinder, cooled and placed in a water bath at the test temperature for 1 hour. The sample is then positioned under the penetrometer needle which when released penetrates into the sample. The depth of penetration in tenths of millimetres is reported as the test value. This method is not applicable to oily materials or petrolatums which have penetrations greater than 250.

(ix) ASTM D937–IP 179—Cone Penetration of Petrolatums

This method is for soft waxes and petrolatums. It is similar to D1321 Needle Penetration except a much larger sample mould is used and a cone replaces the needle. The method requires that a 150 g load be applied for 5 seconds at the desired temperature.

A number of other methods are used to determine hardness, using equipment employed in other industries, such as the Shore Durometer for rubber or the Brinell test for metals. The Abraham Consistometer consists of a plunger which is pushed into the wax at a specified rate; the hardness is measured by the force required to do this.

(x) ASTM D1320—Tensile Strength of Paraffin Wax

This test is an empirical evaluation of the tensile strength of waxes which do not elongate more han $\frac{1}{8}$ of an inch under the test conditions. Six dumbell shaped specimens, with a cross-sectional area of $\frac{1}{4}$ of a square inch, are cast. The specimens are broken on a testing machine under a load which increases at the rate of 20 pounds/second along the longitudinal axis of the sample. Values are reported as pounds per square inch.

(xi) ASTM D2004—Modulus of Rupture of Petroleum Waxes

A wax slab, 8 × 4 × 0·15 inches, is cast over hot water. Small strips, about 3 × ½ in, are cut from the centre of the slab. The strips are placed lengthwise on the support beams of the apparatus and a breaking beam is placed across the specimen parallel to the support beams. A steadily increasing load is applied by water delivered to a bucket suspended from the breaking beam. The Modulus of Rupture (breaking force in pounds per square inch) is calculated from an equation relating thickness and width of test specimen with total weight required to break it.

(b) FUNCTIONAL PROPERTIES OF WAX COATED SUBSTRATES

The following methods are for the evaluation of wax coated papers. Suitable wax coatings can be obtained by many different methods of application. Therefore, the common starting point of having a standard paper properly coated with the wax under investigation is assumed.

(i) ASTM D2423—Weight of Surface Wax on Waxed Paper

This method determines the amount of wax present on the surface of a substrate, but not the absorbed wax. A waxed paper sample is cut to size and weighed. Wax is carefully scraped from one surface with a razor blade, then the sample is reweighed to determine the amount of wax removed. The process is repeated on the reverse side if total surface wax is desired.

(ii) TAPPI 464—Water Permeability of Sheet Materials at High Temperature and Relative Humidity

A desiccant is placed in a shallow test dish and the coated paper, either flat or creased, is sealed to the shoulder of the dish above the desiccant. The dishes are weighed and placed in a controlled environment of 100°F (38°C) and 90 per cent relative humidity. The dishes are reweighed at 24, 48 and 72 hour intervals to determine the rate of water passage through the waxed paper and into the desiccant. Water vapour permeability is reported as grams of water/square metre/24 hours.

(iii) ASTM D1465—Blocking Point of Petroleum Wax

Two strips of wax coated paper, 1 inch wide, are placed face to face between two uncoated strips of paper on a calibrated temperature–gradient blocking plate. The specimens are covered with foam rubber strips and steel bars and are subjected to the gradient heat of the blocking plate for 17 hours. They are removed, cooled and peeled apart. The picking point is the lowest tempera-ture at which the surface film shows disruption. The 50 per cent blocking point is the lowest temperature causing disruption of surface film over an area of 50 per cent of the strip width.

(iv) ASTM D2618 Pressure Blocking Point of Petroleum Wax and Wax Blends

This test is essentially the same as D1465 (above) except that the specimen is subjected to pressures of 20 to 100 psi (138 to 689 kN/m^2).

(v) ASTM D2005—Sealing Strength of Petroleum Wax

Two paper specimens, 5 × 10 inches, are cut and sealed together by passing them over a heated bar. The sealed papers are conditioned at 73°F (23°C) and 50 per cent relative humidity for 17 to 24 hours. Test specimens, 10 × 15 cm, are cut from the sealed paper and delaminated at the rate of 5 inches per minute. The open ends of the seal are in the same plane, with a 180 degree angle between the ends. The unseparated portion is perpendicular to this plane. Sealing strength is the force measured in grams/cm required to separate the sealed strips.

(vi) ASTM D1834—20-deg. Specular Gloss of Waxed Paper

Specular gloss is the capacity of a surface to simulate a mirror in its ability to reflect an incident light beam. The glossimeter used to measure gloss consists of a lamp and lens set to focus an incident light beam 20 degrees from a line drawn perpendicular to the specimen. A receptor lens and photocell are centred on the angle of reflectance, also 20 degrees from a line perpendicular to the specimen. A black, polished glass surface with a refractive index of 1·54 is used for instrument standardisation at 100 gloss units. A wax coated paper is held by a vacuum plate over the sample opening. The light beam is reflected from the sample surface into the photocell and measured with a null point microammeter.

(vii) ASTM D2895—Gloss Retention of Waxed Paper and Paperboard after Storage at 104°F (40°C)

The gloss is measured by method D1834 (above) before and after aging the sample for 1 and 7 days in an oven at 104°F (40°C). The specified aging conditions are intended to correlate with the conditions likely to occur in the handling and storage of waxed paper and paperboard.

(viii) ASTM D2534—Coefficient of Kinetic Friction for Wax Coatings

A wax coated paper is fastened to a horizontal plate attached to the lower, movable cross arm of an electronic load-cell-type tensile tester. A second paper is taped to a 180 gram sled which is placed on the first sample. The sled is attached to the load cell by a nylon monofilament passing around a frictionless pulley. The kinematic coefficient of friction is calculated from the average force required to move the sled at 35 in/minute, divided by the sled weight.

(c) CHEMICAL PROPERTIES OF WAX

(i) ASTM D1833–IP 185—Odour of Petroleum Wax

The odour of petroleum wax is determined by a pre-selected panel. Ten grams of wax are shaved and placed in an odour free glass bottle and capped. After 15 minutes the sample is evaluated in an odour free room by removing the cap and sniffing lightly. A rating of 0 (no odour) to 4 (very strong odour) is given by each member of the panel. The reported value is the average of the individual ratings.

(ii) ASTM D156—Saybolt Colour of Petroleum Products

Saybolt colour is determined on nearly colourless waxes by putting the melted sample in a heated vertical tube mounted alongside a second tube containing standard colour discs. An optical viewer allows simultaneous viewing of both tubes. Light is reflected by a mirror up into the tubes and viewer. The level of the sample is decreased until its colour is lighter than that of the standard. The colour number above this level is reported.

(iii) ASTM D1500–IP 196—ASTM–IP Colour of Petroleum Products

This procedure is for waxes and petrolatums which are too dark for the Saybolt colorimeter. A liquid sample is placed in the test container, a glass cylinder of 30–35 mm ID, and compared with coloured glass discs ranging in value from 0·5 to 8·0, using a standard light source. If an exact match is not found, and the sample colour falls between two standard colours, the higher of the two colours is reported.

(iv) IP 17—Colour by the Lovibond Tintometer

The Lovibond Tintometer measures the tint and depth of colour by comparison with a series of red, yellow and blue standard glasses. Waxes and petrolatums are tested in the molten state and a wide range of cell sizes ($\frac{1}{16}$ in to 18 in) is available for the different types.

(v) ASTM D612—Carbonizable Substances in Paraffin Wax

Five millilitres of concentrated sulphuric acid are placed in a graduated test tube and 5 ml of the melted wax are added. The sample is heated for 10 minutes at 158°F (70°C). During the last 5 minutes the tube is shaken periodically. The acid layer is compared to a standard reference solution and the wax sample passes if the colour is not darker than the standard colour.

(vi) ASTM D1832—Peroxide Number of Petroleum Wax

In this test a sample is dissolved in carbon tetrachloride, acidified with acetic acid and a solution of potassium iodide is added; any peroxides present will react with the potassium iodide to liberate iodine, which is then titrated with sodium thiosulphate.

(vii) Ultra-violet Absorbance of Petroleum Waxes: Code of Federal Regulations 121.1156—UK Mineral Hydrocarbons in Food Regulations 1966 (SI 1966 No. 1073)

The polynuclear aromatic content of waxes can be estimated by the ultra-violet absorbance of an extract of the sample when scanned in the 280–400 millimicron range. The sample is first extracted with a dimethylsulphoxide–phosphoric acid solution to concentrate the aromatic material. If the absorbance of the concentrate exceeds the allowable limits, the extracted material is passed through a chromatographic column to separate and recover the polynuclear aromatic fraction which is again evaluated for absorbance in the 280–400 millimicron region.

(viii) Determination of Chemical Composition of Waxes

Many methods are employed in the determination of the chemical composition and structural configuration of waxes. Mass spectrometry, X-ray diffraction, chromatography, sieve analysis, electron microscopy and urea adduction are a few of the currently used techniques. Very few of the procedures are published as ASTM–IP standards.

7. SUGGESTIONS FOR FURTHER READING

Petroleum Waxes: Characterisation, Performance and Additives, Technical Association of the Pulp and Paper Industry, Special Technical Association Publication, No. 2 (1963).

H. Bennet (1963). *Industrial Waxes*, Vols. I, II, Chemical Publishing Company Inc., New York.

A. H. Warth (1956). *Chemistry and Technology of Waxes*, Reinhold Publishing Corp., New York.

Appendix follows

APPENDIX

INSPECTIONS OF TYPICAL PETROLEUM WAXES

Wax grade	127/129 AMP Paraffin	156/158 AMP Semi-microcrystalline	150 Micro-crystalline	175 Micro-crystalline	USP Pet-rolatum
Appearance	Translucent White solid	Translucent White solid	Opaque White solid	Yellow solid	White semi-solid
Gravity, °API: (Calculated)	43·4	38·7	36·8	34·5	32·4
Melting Point, ASTM D87-IP 55: °F	125·2	154·0	—	—	—
Melting Point, ASTM D127-IP 133: °F	128	156	149	176	125
Congealing Point, ASTM D938-IP 76: °F	125	152	145	166	117
Penetration, ASTM D1321: 77°F (25°C): 100 g, 5 s	14	15	29	17	—
Penetration, ASTM D937-IP 179: 77°F (25°C): 150 g, 5 sec	—	—	—	—	155
Colour, Saybolt, ASTM D 156	30+	30+	14	—	8
Colour, ASTM D1500-IP 196	—	—	—	L 1·0	L 1·0
Viscosity, ASTM D445–IP 71: cSt at 210°F (99°C)	3·18	7·36	10·56	16·64	10·53
Refractive Index, ASTM D1747: n_D^{80}	1·432	1·444	1·450	1·456	1·45
Odour, ASTM D1833-IP 185	1·0	1·0	1·5	2·0	1·5

Carbonizable Substance, ASTM D612	pass	—	—	pass
Oil Content, ASTM D721-IP 158: wt per cent	0·2	0·1	2·4	0·1
Specular Gloss, ASTM D1834	35	39	44	38
Blocking Point, ASTM D1465: °F	95	117	120	127
Water Vapour Permeability, TAPPI 464:				
Grams Water/24 hr/m²				
Flat, 2·5 g/sq ft Deposition	6·5	8·0	—	4·2
Creased, 3 g/sq ft Deposition	9·7	36	—	12
Sealing Strength, ASTM D2005: g/cm				
(2·5 g/sq ft Deposition)	15	7	16	16
Coefficient of Friction, ASTM D2534	0·26	1·0	0·92	0·64
Tensile Strength, ASTM D1320: psi	290	360	385	385
Chemical Analysis: Volume per cent				
Alkanes	95	55	47	42
Non-condensed Cycloalkanes	5	40	45	48
Condensed Cycloalkanes	—	3	6	8
Benzenes	—	2	2	1
Naphthalenes	—	—	—	1

ᵃ Methyl isobutyl ketone used in place of methyl ethyl ketone for determination of oil content.

Note: These inspections are presented for information only; they must not be regarded as specifications. Data for other waxes of the same nominal grades may differ significantly from those quoted.

Chapter 13

BITUMEN (ASPHALT)

D. C. BROOME and F. A. WADELIN

1. INTRODUCTION

'Bitumen' is defined by the British Standards Institution as: 'A viscous liquid or a solid, consisting essentially of hydrocarbons and their derivatives, which is soluble in carbon disulphide; it is substantially non-volatile and softens gradually when heated. It is black or brown in colour and possesses waterproofing and adhesive properties. It is obtained by refinery processes from petroleum and is also found as a natural deposit or as a component of naturally occurring asphalt, in which it is associated with mineral matter.'

In the UK 'asphalt' means a mixture of bitumen with mineral matter. This can be either a mechanical mixture such as asphaltic concrete or hot rolled asphalt, or a natural material such as Trinidad Lake asphalt or natural rock asphalt, a form of limestone impregnated with bitumen. The soluble portion of these materials is known in the UK and generally in Europe as bitumen; in the USA however it is usually known as asphalt or asphaltic cement.

2. COMPOSITION

The chemical composition of bitumen is complex and varies considerably dependent upon feedstock and method of manufacture.

As indicated above, bitumen is essentially of a hydrocarbon nature. A great variety of hydrocarbons is present, mostly of high molecular weight, together with complex molecules including a certain proportion of nitrogen, oxygen and sulphur. Many of the hydrocarbons are of an aliphatic nature.

The most widely accepted concept of the constitution is that bitumen is made up of three major components. The first is described as a mixture of asphaltenes, which are high molecular weight complex molecules usually black in colour, insoluble in paraffinic hydrocarbons such as n-heptane and soluble in aromatic hydrocarbons such as benzene. A method for their estimation is given in IP 143. The second component is described as a mixture of resins, and the third is mineral oil. Together these components comprise a colloidal system in which the disperse phase is the mixture of asphaltenes suspended as micelles in the oil which acts as the continuous phase, and stability is provided by the resins.

The consistency of bitumens can vary almost infinitely owing to the scope provided by variations within each of the three components and by the variations in the proportions of the components. In general, the higher the asphaltenes component, the more non-Newtonian is the bitumen in its rheological properties.

The chemical composition of the bitumen is often of considerable importance in asphalt mixtures for building work. For example, the proportion of asphaltenes present will have a material effect on the flow properties, a relatively high asphaltenes content being generally desirable. The absence of sufficient asphaltenes tends to result in a bitumen of oily character and generally poor quality. The reactivity of bitumens to acids, alkalis, oils, fats, etc. is of importance in the manufacture of specialist grades of mastic asphalt for use as flooring or tank linings in chemical factories. Oxidation is also important in such work. Some oxidation, as in the preparation of blown bitumens, may be useful, but if a bitumen is severely oxidised it will become 'denatured' and serious failure may result. Coloured grades of mastic asphalt may also call for some measure of the colour of the bitumens employed, as the lighter the colour of the bitumen the more readily can it be pigmented.

3. MANUFACTURE

Bitumen is usually manufactured by straight distillation of asphaltic-base crude petroleum, bitumen being the residue left after removal of the more volatile oils. By this system the consistency and other properties of the bitumen may be controlled according to the stage at which the distillation is stopped.

In modern petroleum refineries, however, it is usual to exercise greater control over both the distillates and the residue by techniques which include the use of partial vacuum and controlled air flow through the residue. In general, the more air that is used, the higher is the asphaltenes component and the lower is the mineral oil fraction. The effect of the air-blowing process is to impart more 'elasticity' to the bitumens and to reduce their temperature susceptibility.

All the bitumens produced by these techniques are broadly known as refinery bitumens. Molecular cracking may also be employed but the products from this process are normally used for special purposes only.

The soluble portions of natural bitumens and asphalts are basically similar to the refinery products, although, in detail, they may possess special characteristics which are much valued for certain types of asphalt work, especially in Europe.

Refinery bitumens are marketed in a range of grades, primarily classified according to consistency in accordance with specifications* laid down for *e.g.* road bitumens. Alternatively they are manufactured to conform to specifications for a wide variety of asphalt road surfacing and other mixtures which include detailed technical requirements for the 'binder' to be employed.

All of the above bitumens have to be used hot in order to reduce their viscosity to a degree low enough to facilitate mixing with and coating mineral aggregates. An alternative type of bitumen suitable for use at lower working temperatures is also made and is commonly known as 'cutback' bitumen. This is made by blending a normal type of refinery bitumen with kerosine or other volatile solvent; the proportion of solvent, and its precise grade, are selected so as to provide a product suitable for any particular use over a wide range.

For use at ambient temperatures, bitumen can also be used in the form of emulsions which are prepared by breaking down bitumen into small droplets which are suspended in water with the aid of emulsifying agents. According to whether basic or acidic agents are used, the final product is known as an anionic or a cationic emulsion.

The problem with both cutbacks and emulsions is to control not only the properties of the basic bitumen, but also the rate at which the solvent or water will evaporate to leave behind an appropriate film of bitumen.

4. USES

All over the world modern highways are being constructed at an ever increasing rate. The vast majority are built either with cement concrete or with 'black-top' mixtures of bitumen (asphalt) and mineral aggregates.

Sometimes the two types of material are used in conjunction; for example, a layer of low cement content (lean cement) concrete may be laid as a base, upon which an asphaltic concrete, hot rolled asphalt, or bitumen macadam may be superimposed as the wearing course. The first two mixtures are dense, heavy-duty pavings in which a carefully graded mixture of stone, sand and mineral filler is coated with bitumen. The last of the three types is a coated stone mixture with a higher void content and generally more suitable for moderate traffic conditions. In all these types, the bitumen used as a binder must possess good properties of adhesion to the (possibly damp) mineral aggregates concerned and must also possess appropriate flow properties so as to ensure on the one hand that the bitumen will flow readily through pumps and pipes on the plant and on the other hand that the material will not suffer such defects on the road as bleeding, marking, pushing, rutting and cracking.

Apart from road construction of all types, bitumen has many other uses. In airfield runway construction, bitumen is being used increasingly in place of cement concrete. Also about 20 per cent of the world's production is used in processes for keeping water in, such as in the construction of reservoirs, and

* *See* Appendix.

irrigation channels, or for keeping water out, such as in materials for use in damp-proof courses and roofing materials. Pipelines are protected with wrappings impregnated with bitumen. The electrical industry uses bitumen for insulation and cable protection, although here plastics are fairly rapidly replacing bitumen, particularly on the smaller diameter cables.

For the surfacing of roofs, for damp coursing and for flooring and other building purposes, it is common in Europe to use a mixture of specially selected bitumens with carefully graded mineral matter which is not nearly so coarse as the aggregates normally employed for hot rolled asphalt and allied materials. These special mixtures are known as mastic asphalt and are hand-applied hot with the aid of special wooden trowels or floats. Somewhat similar mixtures are used in the USA under the name 'poured asphalt'. Mixtures of the mastic asphalt type, reinforced with grit or stone chippings, are employed for special work on roads as, for example, for dock traffic, bus halts, pedestrian crossings and the like.

Mastic asphalts and poured asphalts require bitumen—or a blend of bitumen—which may be assessed in very much the same way as bitumen for rolled asphalt, etc. The flow properties and the temperature susceptibility are however frequently more critical owing to the greater necessity to ensure absolute impermeability to water and complete absence of fracture when, for example, slight structural movements of the building may occur. It may incidentally be noted that mastic asphalt frequently has to withstand loads applied over relatively small bearing areas so that such loads may, in effect, be considerably in excess of those encountered in road construction and in consequence harder (lower penetration) bitumens are often employed.

Significant quantities of bitumen are employed for the manufacture and bedding of roofing felt and for a variety of purposes other than those referred to above. For roofing felt or roofing paper impregnation and bedding it is necessary to consider such properties as surface tension and weathering in addition to the regular characteristics. For the electrical industry a series of compounds is required where special attention must be paid to the electric strength and the pouring point. Occasionally, compounds are required with a low electrical resistivity in place of the normal high resistance. This can be achieved by special blending and the compounds are generally tested by the use of special test methods.

A wide variety of compounds is prepared from bitumen in conjunction with mineral fillers, sometimes with a proportion of natural or synthetic rubber as, for example, for such purposes as the filling and sealing of joints, e.g. between concrete slabs for paving. These compounds require special tests for assessing such properties as adhesion and grit retention.

5. ASSESSMENT OF BITUMENS

To characterise the effects of the manufacturing processes on the resultant bitumens and to control production, two tests are mainly used. These are penetration and softening point. They do not of course completely describe the properties of the bitumen. Other tests such as viscosity at various temperatures, brittleness at low temperatures, volatility and durability, also give information which assists in the selection of the right bitumen for any particular application. The significance of each of the above tests, and many others, will now be outlined.

(a) Penetration (ASTM D5–IP 49)

Under carefully controlled conditions, the depth to which a standard steel needle with a truncated cone penetrates into a bitumen sample, is directly related to the hardness or consistency of the material. Bitumens vary in penetration (Pen) at 25°C (77°F) from 0 to about 500.

Although this method of measuring consistency is empirical, it has been discovered during the past few years that penetration values are fairly closely related to more fundamental measurements such as dynamic viscosity. A value of 100 Pen is roughly equivalent to one million poises for a vacuum distilled bitumen.

(b) Softening Point (ASTM D2398–IP 198; IP 58; ASTM D36)

Again under carefully controlled conditions a disc of bitumen, with a steel ball placed on top, is heated until it softens. At a given point in the softening process the temperature is recorded. This corresponds to a change in the consistency of the bitumen, such that at the measured temperature, the penetration of the bitumen has increased to about 800 Pen. Such a temperature for the 100 Pen vacuum distilled bitumen is about 45°C (113°F).

(c) Viscosity

At ambient temperatures bitumens vary from highly viscous liquids (500 Pen) to apparently solid materials (10 Pen or less). For viscosity measurements under these conditions a Sliding Plate viscometer can be used. The procedure is described in ASTM Standards Part 11, 1970 Edition, p. 929. At high ambient temperatures (60°C: 140°F) such as could be expected in road or roofing surfaces in sunlight, viscosity can be measured by the procedure given in ASTM D2171–IP 222. Both procedures measure the viscosity in dynamic units (poises).

At elevated temperatures such as those required for applying bitumen to road aggregates or to felts for roofing, viscosity can be measured by conventional reverse flow glass capillary instruments as described in IP 71 or in ASTM D2170. Here the viscosity is provided in kinematic units (Stokes).

The relationship between Stokes and Poises is given by:

$$\text{Stokes} \times \text{density} = \text{Poises}$$

where density is measured in grams per cubic centimetre at the temperature of viscosity measurement. There are other empirical methods for viscosity measurement and until they disappear from specifications such instruments as the Saybolt Furol viscometer (ASTM D88) will still be required.

(d) BRITTLENESS

The weather-proofing properties of bitumens depend upon the maintenance of a continuous film under all conditions of stress and strain. When bitumen is cooled it becomes harder and eventually at a low enough temperature it will crack under the prevailing stress or strain. This means that bitumens which are likely to be used in cold conditions should have sufficient flexibility to withstand the lowest temperature involved.

There is only one test published for assessing this property. It is the Fraass Method (IP 80) in which a thin film of bitumen on a steel plate is cooled under controlled conditions and flexed at fixed intervals. The temperature at which the film cracks is described as the breaking point of the bitumen. In general both roofing felt bitumens and road bitumens have breaking points at about minus 20°C (-4°F).

(e) VOLATILITY

The volatility of bitumens is generally very low indeed, but it has been found necessary to measure this property in order to guard against undue loss of volatile material which would cause excessive hardening of the bitumen. Two tests are at present available. These are, the Loss on Heating Test and the Thin-Film Oven Test.

(i) Loss on heating (IP 45; ASTM D6)
The two versions of this method are virtually identical and will, it is hoped, be combined in a joint ASTM/IP method very soon. The procedure involves the heating of a 50 g bulk of bitumen at 163°C (325°F) for five hours under standard conditions and measuring the loss in weight. The test simulates hot bulk storage conditions. Most bitumens under the test conditions lose less than 1 per cent by weight and their penetrations rarely fall by more than 20 per cent.

(ii) Thin-film oven test (ASTM D1754; ASTM D2872)
This test assesses the effect of heat and air on bitumens when exposed in 3 mm films in flat-bottomed dishes at 163°C (325°F) for five hours. This is a more

severe test than ASTM D6 because there is a much greater surface area. It is designed to provide guidance on the effect of heat on films of bitumen when spread for example on hot aggregates, and then stored in bulk for the transport time from mixer to laying site. Usually the loss in weight in this test for comparable bitumens is about three times greater than that in ASTM D6. The penetration of the bitumen is measured after the heating period and is compared with that of the original bitumen.

More recently a further test has been developed for simulating the effect of mixing hot aggregates with binders. This is the Rolling Thin-Film Oven Test (ASTM D2872) in which a film of bitumen is rotated on the walls of a jar at 163°C for 75 minutes. Hardening is assessed by the change in physical properties.

(f) DURABILITY (ASTM D529; ASTM D1669; ASTM D1670)

The effect of weather, particularly direct sunlight, has been of considerable concern to roofing felt manufacturers, particularly in the USA where vast quantities of bituminous constructions are used. The problem has been to devise meaningful accelerated tests, which can adequately represent a period of about twenty years or more of the usual climatic weathering over wide geographical areas. The best that can be done is to compromise on standard laboratory conditions, which involve the exposure of films of bitumen to cycles of ultra-violet light and water sprays. Weatherometers designed for this purpose are described in ASTM E42 and specific methods for bituminous materials are described in ASTM D529, D1669 and D1670. Bituminous materials which survive a prescribed number of cycles under the test conditions are found to be satisfactory in practice.

(g) ELECTRIC STRENGTH TEST (IP 101)

Bitumen is a completely effective insulator but must be free of adventitious matter for such uses. A method of test is available in which an increasing alternating voltage is applied to the sample under standard conditions, either until breakdown occurs, or until a specified voltage is reached.

(h) FLASH POINT (ASTM D92–IP 36)

Bitumen is flammable if heated to temperatures of 200°C (392°F) and higher. For applicational purposes it must be heated to a temperature at which its viscosity is reduced to about 200 centipoises. This is usually safely below 200°C. However, most specifications quote a flash point below which the bitumen in unacceptable. The method most commonly used is the Cleveland

Open Cup in which a portion of the bitumen is heated in a cup under carefully controlled conditions until a temperature is reached at which, on applying a small flame to the surface of the bitumen, the flame extends across the area. New and very much more rapid tests are being developed for measuring this important property.

(i) SOLUBILITY (IP 47; ASTM D4)

To determine whether or not the bitumen has been contaminated with adventitious matter, solubility in solvents such as carbon disulphide, to comply with the definition of bitumen, has been determined for over half a century. Nowadays, however, carbon disulphide and other solvents such as benzene are unpopular mainly because of their toxic nature, so methylene chloride, trichloroethylene, carbon tetrachloride and cyclohexane all appear in specifications somewhere in the world. Most bitumens give solubility values in excess of 99 per cent by weight. The only exception is highly cracked bitumen which is made specifically for briquetting purposes or for a substitute for coal tar pitch. With the latter type of bitumen, solubility values in carbon tetrachloride and cyclohexane may be significantly lower than those obtained with the other solvents. Solubility is determined by dissolving the bitumen in the appropriate solvent and the solution is then filtered through a tared fine gooch or sintered crucible.

This property becomes significant when dealing with mixtures of bitumen and inorganic materials, because it provides a simple means of determining the bitumen or binder content of the mixture. Appropriate methods have been devised for every form of material containing bitumen. They all use the principle of refluxing or agitating the sample with an appropriate solvent which dissolves away the bitumen, leaving the aggregate, the paper, the felt, or the filler in a suitable condition for drying and weighing.

Methods for road materials analysis are described in ASTM D2172 and IP 162.

When the identification of the bitumen used in the mixture is required, special methods are used in which the solvent containing the bitumen extracted from the mixture can be evaporated off, leaving the bitumen with properties substantially the same as those it possessed in the mixture. Such methods are described in ASTM D1856 and IP 105.

(j) ASH (ASTM D482–IP 4)

There are usually only traces of organo-metallic compounds in bitumen, so that the ash content is equivalent to 100 minus the solubility value. High values, which are rare, are usually associated with iron oxide or other adventitious material.

(k) RELATIVE DENSITY (SPECIFIC GRAVITY) (IP 190; ASTM D70)

At 25°C (77°F) the relative density (specific gravity) of the whole range of petroleum refined bitumens is spanned by 0·95 to 1·15. The methods employ pyknometers of various types in which the weights of equal volumes of bitumen and water are compared. If the bitumen is sufficiently hard to be weighed directly in air and water ASTM D71 can be used.

(l) DUCTILITY (IP 32; ASTM D113)

This property has been used for many years to provide information upon the flexibility of bitumen. A specially prepared test specimen is drawn out at a constant speed at a selected temperature until the stretched bitumen breaks. A typical 100 Pen vacuum distilled bitumen at 25°C (77°F) under the pre-scribed test conditions will stretch for over 100 cm without breaking. The test is affected by particulate contaminants, even dust in the atmosphere during specimen preparation can be sufficient, so that three or more specimens have to be stretched to be certain that the result obtained has not been interfered with by extraneous matter.

(m) ACIDITY (IP 213)

Some bitumens contain organic acids usually described as 'naphthenic acids'. These acids are beneficial in some applications such as mastic asphalts and anionic emulsions. In the former the acids appear to lubricate or peptise the particles of limestone filler and considerably improve mixing during manu-facture and also ease the re-melting and the spreading during the application of the hot mastic.

The soaps of the acids are good emulsifiers for bitumen emulsions. Some manufacturers emulsify bitumens containing such acids by using only sodium or potassium hydroxide in the aqueous phase.

Acidity is measured by the direct titration of a solution of the bitumen with alkali, using either potentiometric or colorimetric methods for the detection of the end-point.

(n) COMPATIBILITY (ASTM D1370)

In some roofing felts, the saturant bitumen, usually of 200 penetration at 25°C (77°F) and the coating bitumen, usually an oxidised bitumen, are in surface contact with each other throughout the life of the felt. It is important therefore to know whether or not there is any interaction between them. For example, if the oils in the coating bitumen migrate into the saturant the coating bitumen becomes brittle and cracks. If the oils in the saturant bitumen migrate to the coating, the latter will soften and oily spots ('bleeding') will appear on the surface. This reactivity or lack of it can be measured by the Oliensis test described in ASTM D1370. In this test a drop of molten saturant is placed on the talced surface of the coating bitumen and compatibility is judged by the extent to which an oily ring develops in the talc surrounding the saturant.

6. CUTBACK BITUMENS

Bitumen for most applications requires to be heated to about 75–100°C (135–180°F) above its softening point in order to reduce its viscosity to that required for applicational purposes. There are uses for bitumen where lower application temperatures are desirable, so a range of products is manufactured in which the bitumen is fluxed or cut back with a volatile solvent such as white spirit. Alternative fluxes are kerosine, creosote or gas oil. These provide materials which range from rapid curing to slow curing types. The increased fire hazard is countered by the reduced working temperature. The solvent evaporates from the applied cutback bitumen until the penetration of the residual material approaches that of the original bitumen. In the case of white spirit, and dependent upon ambient conditions, this may take from a few hours to some weeks. With gas oil the cutback may never completely revert to the original bitumen.

Cutback bitumens can be manufactured very simply by mixing cold flux into the molten bitumen. For road surfacing the bitumen most commonly used has a penetration value at 25°C (77°F) of about 100 Pen. In hot climates a slightly harder grade may be used and in cold areas a softer grade such as 200 Pen bitumen is suitable.

For new installations in-line blending can be used provided that metering devices are sufficiently precise.

The major use for cutback bitumen is for road surface dressing, in which a film of the cutback is sprayed onto the existing surface, and is then covered with stone chippings or other aggregates. Some cutbacks are used for mixing with stone aggregates for open-textured surfacings which allow the volatile components to evaporate slowly away. There are also many other cutbacks or fluxed bitumens which are made for specific applications.

(a) ASSESSMENT OF CUTBACK BITUMENS

When the applied films of cutbacks are fully cured they possess the properties, for all practical purposes, of the bitumens from which they have been made. For controlling them for application, however, there are test procedures for ensuring that the appropriate fluxes and bitumen have been chosen and blended together in the correct proportions. These are viscosity, distillation and properties of the residue, flashpoint, solubility, and finally, for commercial purposes, relative density (specific gravity).

(i) Viscosity (ASTM D88; ASTM D2170; IP 71; IP 72)

The Saybolt Furol (ASTM D88) and the Standard Tar Viscometer (IP 72) have been used for many years to control the flow properties of cutback bitumens, and specifications still appear in which these methods are quoted. Kinematic reverse-flow glass capillary instruments are now available in which viscosity is measured in fundamental units. The procedure is described in ASTM D2170 and ASTM D445–IP 71. The viscosity varies with the proportion of flux incorporated in the bitumen so this measurement acts as an indirect control of flux content.

(ii) Distillation (ASTM D402; IP 27)

In this test the volatile material boiling up to 360°C (680°F) is distilled out of the cutback under empirical conditions with very little attempt to fractionate. The volumes of distillate collected up to selected temperatures are recorded. The residue in the flask can be examined for properties such as penetration (ASTM D5 and IP 49), solubility in carbon disulphide (ASTM D4 and IP 47) and float test (ASTM D139).

The relative density (specific gravity) of the distillate can be measured which, together with its distillation characteristics and odour, provides enough information to identify the flux used in the cutback.

(iii) Flash point (ASTM D1310; IP 113)

The procedure for measuring the flash point of cutback bitumen involves slow heating of the sample (2°F (1·1°C) per minute) in specified apparatus, either the Tag Open-Cup (ASTM D1310) or the Abel Modified (IP 113). When the pilot flame spreads out across the surface of the sample the flash point is reached. The Abel instrument has been modified to include a stirrer because the cutbacks used in the UK are so viscous at ambient temperatures that accurate flash points cannot be obtained without stirring. More rapid flash point methods are being developed and these are likely to replace the present procedures.

(iv) Solubility (ASTM D4; IP 47)

The solubility of cutback bitumen is determined in a similar manner to that for bitumen.

(v) Float test (ASTM D139)

This test is used to assess the consistency of the distillation residue at a selected temperature. A plug of bitumen in a metal collar is screwed into a metal float such that when the assembly is floated on water the collar is immersed in the water, usually at a temperature of 50°C (122°F). The time for the cutback residue to soften and allow sufficient water to enter the float and sink it, is measured. This time can be related to the consistency of the residue.

The use of this test is almost exclusively confined to the USA and South Africa.

7. BITUMEN EMULSIONS

There are applications for bitumen where it is not practicable to use heated material. For these situations bitumen can be applied at ambient temperatures, provided that they are above freezing point, in the form of a bitumen in water emulsion. The emulsion is usually manufactured from 200 or 300 penetration (at 25°C: 77°F) grades of bitumen. The bitumen at about 130–140°C (226–284°F), is emulsified in a colloid mill with 40–50 per cent by weight of water containing between 0·5 and 1·5 per cent by weight of an emulsifier. If the bitumen contains sufficient naphthenic acids, the aqueous phase need only contain caustic soda or potash for effective emulsification. Provided that the emulsification process is sufficiently effective to produce bitumen particles of about 2–3 microns in diameter, and the emulsifying agent provides sufficient stability, the emulsion should have a suitable consistency for spray application. Storage prior to use must be at temperatures above freezing point. When applied to road surfaces the water evaporates leaving the droplets of bitumen to coagulate and form a continuous film on the road. Chippings or other aggregates can be spread on the emulsion film before all the water has gone, but traffic must be restricted until coagulation has occurred.

There are numerous combinations of bitumen, emulsifying processes, and emulsifiers, capable of producing emulsions having specific properties for each application.

For road surfacing purposes, for example, a rapid-breaking emulsion is required. On the other hand, for mixing with aggregates, sands or natural earth, a much more stable emulsion is necessary for effective coating and waterproofing.

(a) ASSESSMENT OF BITUMEN EMULSIONS

For all practical purposes, when the emulsion has lost its water phase, the residual bitumen has the properties of the bitumen from which it has been manufactured. In some cases the coagulated bitumen may, by virtue of the emulsifier used in its emulsification, have better adhesion properties than the original bitumen, when in contact with certain types of aggregate. An example is that of residual bitumen from a cationic emulsion which will adhere to acidic type aggregates such as granite better than both the original bitumen and also residual bitumen from anionic emulsions. Thus any surface dressing work with granite aggregate is more safely carried out with cationic emulsions in damp climates.

From the above it can be seen that this usage of bitumen poses many more technical questions than the use of bitumen or cutback bitumen. For those interested further reading is strongly advised (*see* bibliography).

For the control of the properties of emulsions so that they can be applied correctly, there are a few simple tests available. These are water, viscosity, residue on sieving, storage stability, coating ability, and more recently, particle charge test. Many more *ad hoc* tests to assess the performance of emulsions have been developed, but none has gained more than localised acceptance. The reason for this is that an emulsion which is entirely satisfactory in one geographical and geological situation could be useless in another. By re-formulation, however, another equally satisfactory emulsion could be produced to meet the new requirement. Emulsion users are therefore best served by asking emulsion manufacturers to produce an emulsion to meet their specific needs in any given area and for any selected applications.

Provided that the water phase can evaporate, or remove itself by any other means from the bitumen after application, there are very few uses of bitumen for which emulsions cannot be used.

(i) Water (ASTM D244 paras 2–6; BS 434)
Accurate measurement of the water content of emulsions gives an indirect measurement of the amount of bitumen plus emulsifier in the sample. Because water is the continuous phase in the emulsion, it controls to a large extent the viscosity, and consequently the thickness of the applied residual film of bitumen. Water contents vary from 40–70 per cent by weight dependent upon the particular use of the emulsion.

The water content is determined by the Dean and Stark method in which the sample is heated under reflux with an organic solvent which is immiscible with water and of lower specific gravity. The solvent distils together with the water and is condensed in a trap so that the water separates to form the lower layer. The excess solvent overflows from the trap and is returned to the still.

Another method for the direct determination of bitumen plus emulsifier is to remove the water either by distillation or evaporation. Suitable procedures are described in ASTM D244, paras: 7 to 16.

(ii) Particle charge (ASTM D244 paras 18–20; BS 434)
The test is designed to identify the emulsion. If the bitumen particles are shown to be positively charged then the emulsion is cationic. The procedure is to immerse two stainless steel plate electrodes in the emulsion, parallel to each other and 12·5 mm apart. A direct current is passed through the electrodes for about half an hour. The current is then switched off and the electrodes are washed with water. A cationic emulsion will deposit a layer of bitumen on the negative electrode (cathode) and the positive electrode will

remain relatively clean. Anionic emulsions show the reverse behaviour and those emulsions made with very weakly acidic emulsifiers or non-ionic emulsifiers will deposit only minor amounts of bitumen. This test should be carried out first when analysing unknown emulsions because a knowledge of the type of emulsion is essential in order to choose suitable reagents for other tests.

(iii) Viscosity (ASTM D88; IP 212; BS 434)
The largest use of bitumen emulsions is in surface dressing of roads. In this application, rapid breaking emulsions are required so emulsions of low stability (labile) are supplied. This inherent instability causes difficulty in the measurement of viscosity, because in any instrument that is used a mono-molecular layer (at least) of bitumen is deposited on contact with any surface. For this reason it has not yet been possible to use capillary glass viscometers and only empirical measurement is possible with viscometers of fairly wide aperture to minimise the deposition effect. The Saybolt Furol viscosity method (ASTM D88) and that of the Engler (IP 212) are most frequently quoted in specifications.

(iv) Residue on sieving (ASTM D244 paras 37–40; IP 91)
This test indicates the effectiveness of the emulsification process. A few coarse particles may be produced during manufacture, particularly during the initial start-up period, but any marketable emulsion should deposit less than 0·1 per cent by weight on a sieve of 840 microns mesh size. Even on a 75 micron mesh, deposits of less than 0·5 per cent by weight are usual.

After having determined whether the emulsion is cationic or not, a weighed amount is poured through a weighed sieve prepared beforehand by moistening with an appropriate washing fluid. The sieve is washed free of emulsion with more of the washing fluid followed by distilled water and is then dried and reweighed.

(v) Storage stability (ASTM D244 paras 60–66; BS 434)
Provided that emulsions are stored at temperatures above 0°C and very gentle mixing is applied immediately before use, even labile emulsions should be satisfactory. After storage for fairly lengthy periods, such as three months, drums of emulsion should be inverted and left for a few minutes before further mixing, in order to provide the best conditions for dispersal without coagulation, of particles of bitumen packed together by sedimentation. Any form of more violent shearing can ruin perfectly satisfactory emulsions.

The ASTM procedure measures the bitumen content of portions of an emulsion taken from the top and bottom of a 500 ml sample stored in a glass cylinder for 24 hours. Any difference between the top and bottom samples is a measure of instability. The BS procedure measures the change in water content of a 40 gallon drum of emulsion during storage for three months.

(vi) Other stability tests (coating ability) (ASTM D244 paras 49–54)
Some emulsions are used for mixing with aggregates and with fillers. For such purposes there are a number of tests designed to ensure that the emulsion has sufficient stability to coat these materials before breaking. A selection of such tests are given in ASTM D244. Many other tests are agreed between the manufacturer of the emulsion and the user.

8. CONCLUSION

This chapter has been confined to providing information on the significance of tests usually carried out on bitumen, cutback bitumen and bitumen emulsions. For specific uses of bitumen many more methods have been developed in attempts to predict performance. When it is realised that the life of many of the bitumen applications is more than twenty years, some workers will never really know whether their *ad hoc* tests have been meaningful. Durability tests on bituminous roofing and on asphaltic concrete are typical examples. It is hoped that adequate records are being made so that future generations of bitumen chemists and engineers may indeed be able to interpret their findings in the light of sound documentary evidence.

9. SUGGESTIONS FOR FURTHER READING

ASTM Book of Standards, part 11, Bituminous Materials for Highway Construction, Waterproofing and Roofing; Soils; Skid Resistance.
IP Standards for Petroleum and its Products, part 1, Applied Science, London.
J. P. Pfeiffer (1950). *The Properties of Asphaltic Bitumen*, Elsevier, Amsterdam.
H. Abraham (1960-63). *Asphalts and Allied Substances*, 5 vols, D. van Nostrand, Princeton, N.J.
J. R. Martin and H. A. Wallace (1967). *Asphalt Pavement Engineering*. McGraw-Hill, New York.
D. C. Broome (1949). *The Testing of Bituminous Mixtures*, Edward Arnold, London.
DSIR/RRL (1963). *Bituminous Materials in Road Construction*, HMSO, London.
R. N. Traxler (1961). *Asphalt, Its Composition, Properties and Uses*, Reinhold Publishing Corporation, New York.
A. J. Hoiberg (1964/5/6). *Bituminous Materials: Asphalts, Tars and Pitches*, Vol. I, II, III, Interscience, New York.
C. G. Sumner (1954). *The Theory of Emulsions and Their Technical Treatment*, J. and A. Churchill, London.
L. W. Hatherly and P. C. Leaver (1967). *Asphaltic Road Materials*, Edward Arnold, London.
E. J. Barth (1962). *Asphalt Science and Technology*, Gordon and Breach, New York.

APPENDIX

BSI SPECIFICATIONS

BS	3690	Bitumens for Road Purposes
	594	Hot Rolled Asphalt
	1621 & 2040	Bitumen Macadam
	1690	Fine Cold Asphalt
	988 & 1162	Mastic Asphalt Roofings
	1076, 1410 & 1451	Mastic Asphalt Flooring
	1097 & 1418	Mastic Asphalt
	434	Bitumen Emulsions
	598	Testing of Bituminous Mixtures
	3712	Tests for Building Mastics
	743	Materials for Damp-proof Courses
	747	Roofing Felts
	1324	Asphalt Tiles
	2499	Joint Sealing Compounds
	2832	Damp Resisting Coatings for Solums
	1858	Bitumen Filling Compounds for Electrical Purposes

British Standard Codes of Practice

CP	144	Bitumen Felt Roof Coverings
	201	Mastic Asphalt Roofing
	204	*In situ* Floorings

Chapter 14

WHITE OILS AND ELECTRICAL INSULATING OILS

V. BISKE

A. WHITE OILS

1. INTRODUCTION

In the present context the term 'white oils' refers to colourless or very pale oils within the lubricating oil class as regards viscosity and boiling range. White oils belong to two main groups, pharmaceutical (medicinal) and technical, the chief difference being degree of refining; the former represent the most drastically refined petroleum products of the conventional type, *i.e.* materials which cannot be classed as pure chemical compounds.

The main use of medicinal oil has hitherto been as a laxative and in various pharmaceutical preparations such as ointments; whilst such use is continuing, this quality of oil is finding increasing utilisation as a lubricant for food processing machinery and in plastics manufacture. This is in consequence of legislative changes both in the UK and USA whereby control over traces of mineral oil which may find their way into food from contact of the latter with lubricated surfaces or packaging materials has been intensified. Hence not only the maximum permissible quantity of such oil traces is prescribed but also the purity of the oil.

The legal requirements in both countries are virtually the same as those of the respective national pharmacopoeias; these are substantially similar in the UK and USA although the ultra-violet absorbance test differs in the two countries; the UK test being direct absorbance whilst the USA procedure (closely similar to ASTM D2269) requires that the absorbance be measured on a dimethyl sulphoxide extract of the oil.

Whilst the British Pharmacopoeia (BP) has discontinued inclusion of the test for sulphur compounds (*see* below) this test is still called for by the regulations specifying the purity of the traces of mineral oil which may be permitted in food (*see* SI 1966 No. 1073).

Specifications for pharmaceutical grade oils are laid down in most countries by the national pharmacopoeia concerned or by semi-official publications such as the US National Formulary (USANF); pharmaceutical grades currently specified in UK and USA are shown below.

The principal aim of specifications for pharmaceutical oils is to ensure that the product is as inert as possible and that it should not contain any materials known, or suspected, to be in the slightest degree toxic.

TABLE 1

Pharmaceutical grades of white oils

	Liquid paraffin BP 1968	Mineral oil USP XVIII 1970	Light mineral oil NF 13th edn 1970 USA
Density at 20°C (68°F)	0·870–0·890	0·847–0·907[a]	0·820–0·882[b]
Viscosity, cSt at 37·8°C (100°F)	64 min.	38·1 min.	37 max.
Solid paraffins	←—Stipulated maximum opalescence at 0°C (32°F)—→		
Acidity/alkalinity	←——————————— Nil ——————————→		
Sulphur compounds	—	Negative to sodium plumbite test	
Carbonisable substances	Stipulated maximum colour development in acid layer		
Ultra-violet characteristics			
$E_{1\ cm}^{1\ per\ cent}$ 240–280 nm	0·05 max.	—	—
absorbance 260–350 nm[c]	—	0·1 max.	—

[a] Specified as spec grav at 25°C (77°F) 0·845–0·905.

[b] Specified as spec grav at 25°C (77°F) 0·818–0·880

[c] On dimethyl sulphoxide extract (essentially ASTM D 2269).

At one time the lighter grades of medicinal oils were used as components of nasal sprays; such use has now fallen into disfavour as there is evidence that oil used in this way can reach the lungs, with consequent risk of lipoid pneumonia. Such lighter medicinal grade has been withdrawn from the BP.

For technical white oils, requirements are much less stringent; such oils are largely used in cosmetic preparations, such as hair creams and the like; they are also employed in the plastics industry, in textiles processing, and numerous other applications. There is however an increasing tendency for the cosmetics industry and some branches of the plastics industry to turn to medicinal (or 'food-grade') quality in place of the technical oils.

In the UK there is only one official legally enforceable specification, that laid down under the Factories Act for oil to be used in lubrication of mule spindles.

In the USA certain oils which may be present in animal feed and for manufacture of food packages are controlled by specifications issued by the

Food and Drugs Administration.* Requirements for these technical grades of white oil are as follows:

TABLE 2

Technical grades of white oils

	Mule spindle oil[a]	Technical white mineral oil[b]
Viscosity, cSt at 60°C (140°F)	16–21	—
Colour, IP 17B, max.	0·5	1·75
Ultra-violet absorbance,[d] max.		
280–289 nm	—	4·0
290–299 nm	—	3·3
300–329 nm	—	2·3
330–350 nm	—	0·8

[a] Complying with SI 1953 No. 1545, must be 'drastically refined with sulphuric acid'.

[b] As stipulated by F & DA (USA). *Federal Register*, 2 Dec 1964, **29**, 16079, Section 121.2589.

[c] Specified as Saybolt 20 min.

[d] On dimethyl sulphoxide extract; test closely similar to ASTM D2269.

2. ASSESSMENT OF WHITE OILS

(a) Tests for physical characteristics

(i) *Appearance, odour, taste*

Probably the most self-evident requirement of white oils is that they should be colourless but although this can be assessed by eye, it is usual to determine colour by instrument. On the IP colour scale (IP Method 17B) a colour of 1·0 or under is considered water-white, medicinal oils will normally be 0·5 or less. On the Saybolt colour scale (ASTM Method D156), a figure of +25 corresponds to water-white, whilst the minimum colour intensity reading on this scale is expressed by +30, a value normally attained by white oils.

Another colour scale was developed before the war by the White Oil Manufacturers' Association (WOMA). Tests are done, as for IP method 17B, in an 18 in cell against colour slides on a scale for which WOMA 2 corresponds approximately to IP 17B 0·5, whilst the limit (*i.e.* IP 17B 1·0) of the water-white range is attained at around WOMA 4. The scale extends to a WOMA colour of 13, approximately equivalent to IP 17B 4·0.

* Loose reference is frequently made to 'FDA' oils. It is important to appreciate that oil specifications issued by this body cover several types, *viz.*:

White mineral oil to 121.1146 (medicinal and food grade oil)
Technical white mineral oil to 121.2589(b)
Mineral oil to 121.2589(c) (an oil which is not a white oil and hence is outside the scope of this chapter).

Absence or virtual absence of taste and odour is another requirement but this is, at present, only assessable organoleptically, although developments in gas chromatographic techniques give hope that these tests will become objective rather than subjective.

(ii) *Density*

The stipulation of density or specific gravity (relative density) (ASTM D1298–IP 160) which is found in almost all pharmacopoeias is one which it is difficult to justify, although for the manufacture of emulsions there is some validity in the view that a high density, which decreases the differential between the densities of the oil and water, can be helpful.

(iii) *Viscosity*

This (ASTM D445–IP 71) is defined to ensure that, in the case of oils for internal use as laxatives, unduly fluid material, which could increase risk of leakage through the anal sphincter, is not employed. The minimum viscosity laid down in the USP is far too low and normal practice is to employ oils that are even above the BP minimum, a value around 75 cSt at 37·8°C (100°F) being common. The temperature of viscosity measurement is a normal one employed for this purpose and happens, in the case of medicinal oils, to be virtually that of the human body. Thus the viscosity of these oils is measured at their working temperature.

(iv) *Solid paraffins*

The test for solid paraffins (*i.e.* for traces of wax) would be better replaced by the standard cloud point test (ASTM D2500–IP 219) known to the oil industry.

The degree of opalescence permitted to pharmaceutical oils by both BP and USP corresponds to a cloud point of about 4°C (40°F). Both pharmacopoeias use the same test, keeping the oil at 0°C (32°F) for 4 hours, when a 0·5 mm black line must be 'easily seen' through an oil layer 25 mm thick. The setting of a value as low as this is dictated largely by considerations of appearance of the oil; a much higher temperature could well be tolerated if only practical considerations applied, moreover the n-paraffins which are responsible for cloudiness (for the pharmacopoeia tests the oil is dried, hence the opalescence observed is not due to moisture) are among the more inert of the hydrocarbon groups of which these white oils are composed.

In the case of technical white oils that are used for dipping eggs, for preservation, it is usual to specify a minimum pour point, usually around 10°C (50°F) to ensure that a solid layer is formed over the shell at storage temperatures.

(v) *Aniline point*

This is not normally a test applied to medicinal oils but some users of technical grades specify a minimum value. Views have been expressed that the higher the aniline point (ASTM D611 or IP 2) the greater the stability of the oil. High aniline point only indicates more extensive refining if comparisons are made on fractions of the same boiling range from the same crude. For oils of same viscosity but of differing origins, variations in aniline point could reflect changes in depth of refining or differences in hydrocarbon group composition. Since for oils of similar purity and viscosity a high aniline point denotes a more paraffinic, and hence less dense, oil than a lower aniline point, the desire for a high aniline point runs counter to the view that the higher the density the more preferable the oil if it is desired to make emulsions (*e.g.* hair cream) therefrom.

(vi) *Flash point*
This test (ASTM D93–IP 34) is sometimes to be found in a white oil specification but the value is not usually of much significance and is merely laid down as some assurance against undue fire-risk. Typical values will be from 150°C (302°F) upwards, depending on viscosity.

(b) Tests for chemical characteristics
(i) *Carbonisable substances* (*'acid test'*)
All pharmacopoeias prescribe some form of test whereby the reaction of the oil to hot strong sulphuric acid is assessed, usually by keeping equal volumes of acid and oil in a boiling water bath for ten minutes, with frequent agitation. This is an important criterion for oils of pharmaceutical quality and in order to obtain reliable results the conditions have to be closely stipulated. This is done by both BP and USP although the tests differ somewhat; in BP the acid strength is slightly higher (95·5–96·0 per cent), shaking conditions are slightly different and permitted intensity of acid layer colour is a little paler. The USP test for carbonisable substances is virtually identical with the ASTM procedure (ASTM D565) which however prescribes the shaking conditions in slightly greater detail. In all cases, the purity (principally freedom from nitrogen) of the sulphuric acid is stipulated as well as its strength. The BP describes the permissible colour of the acid layer in terms of colour glasses defined in CIE terms, whereas the USP lays down a colour standard made up of a mixture of aqueous solutions of coloured inorganic salts. Careful comparison of the two procedures shows the BP test to be marginally the more severe.

The background of this test is that the recognised procedure for the refining of white oils was, and still is to a considerable extent, the use of strong sulphuric acid (oleum) as refining agent. In order to ensure that the refined oil only contains a very small amount of material still reactive to sulphuric acid, the 'carbonisable substances' type of test was introduced. The test is a fairly rapid and simple one, not calling for elaborate equipment and so it is unlikely to disappear from pharmaceutical specifications. However, with the introduction of ultra-violet absorption procedures (ASTM D2008 and D2269) discussed below, it is of less value than formerly although it still provides a useful safeguard against possible contamination of an oil with impurities transparent to both visible and ultra-violet light and hence not detectable by colour or by ultra-violet absorption measurements.

For technical white oils the test for unsulphonatable residue (ASTM D483) is sometimes applied and normally a reading of 97 per cent or more is obtained. The test is of little significance for oils refined to medicinal standard since the other quality criteria, already discussed, are much more stringent and the unsulphonatable residue procedure is, for such oils, much too coarse a method and will always show about 99 per cent.

(ii) *Polynuclear aromatics*
In recent years there has been considerable concern over the possible presence in white oils of traces of carcinogenic polynuclear aromatic hydrocarbons and much work has gone towards devising test methods which would detect the smallest traces of these. As a result, tests for the ultra-violet absorbance of white oils have been developed. Such measurement can either be directly on the oil itself (or on oil diluted with inert solvent as required by the BP), or else on a solvent extract of the oil, the solvent chosen being one which will concentrate therein the polynuclear aromatics. It is this form of test, with dimethyl sulphoxide as the extraction solvent, which has been chosen in the USA for evaluation of white mineral oils by ultra-violet absorption (ASTM D2269).

The sensitivity of this test to the presence of polynuclear aromatics is stated to be as high as 0·3 parts per million; even more sensitive tests for these materials (down to a concentration of around 10^{-9}) have been developed but the techniques involved make the procedures cumbersome for specification purposes. A guide to the absence of undesirable aromatics can be quickly obtained by observing fluorescence under ultra-violet light. Although both BP and USP require absence of fluorescence in daylight, fluorescence under ultra-violet light is not mentioned. Nevertheless this test is normally used by manufacturers and only a very slight degree of such fluorescence is considered permissible. Whilst it is possible to obtain fluorescent oils that are free from polynuclear aromatics, oils that do not fluoresce are virtually certain to be free of such compounds, although verification by one of the above-mentioned ultra-violet absorption methods is required.

The ultra-violet absorption level laid down by F & DA for technical white oil and given in Table 2 corresponds, approximately, to a maximum poly-nuclear aromatics content of about 5 parts per million.

(iii) *Sulphur compounds*
Whilst the total sulphur content of medicinal oil is not limited as such, it is in effect restricted (usually to well below 100 parts per million) by the necessity of severe refining to meet the other clauses of the specification. Many pharmacopoeias (but no longer the BP) do however lay down a test for sulphur compounds; the procedure is somewhat similar to the doctor test (IP 30)

used in the petroleum industry but the pharmacopoeia test would appear to be very much less sensitive than the petroleum industry version.

As laid down (USP) for medicinal oils the procedure is that two volumes of oil and one of absolute ethyl alcohol have added thereto 2 drops of a saturated solution of lead monoxide in 20 per cent aqueous sodium hydroxide. The mixture is heated to 70°C (158°F) for 10 minutes and should remain colourless.

It seems doubtful whether, especially in view of its lack of sensitivity, this test is of much significance; an oil to which butyl mercaptan was added sufficiently to give a strong odour still passes this test, although of course it would fail the 'odourless' clause of the specification.

(iv) *Acidity or alkalinity*

In this case also the pharmacopoeia has laid down a test procedure which departs from that used in the petroleum industry for the same characteristic. The pharmacopoeia method consists of boiling together the oil and ethyl alcohol (one volume of oil to two volumes of alcohol in the BP, equal volumes in the USP) and noting the reaction of the alcohol layer to litmus solution. For an oil to fail this test the acidity need only be in excess of 0·01 mg KOH/g; hence this test is more sensitive than the IP and ASTM methods for determining the acidity of petroleum products (ASTM D974, IP 1 and 139).

The test is largely a relic of earlier times when it was thought that detectable amounts of chemicals used in refining could remain in the finished product. With present day refining techniques this is virtually impossible but here again, as for the carbonisable substances clause, the test is considered as a further safeguard against trace contaminants.

(v) *Peroxide value*

This test is occasionally called for although it does not appear in either BP or USP. In its usual form it consists in heating the oil for a prescribed time, say 3 hours at 140°C (284°F), after which the content of peroxides (as determined by titration with sodium thiosulphate) must not exceed the small permissible limit.

Its purpose is to ensure that when medicinal oils are heated in sterilising equipment they do not deteriorate unduly. It is usually found that uninhibited oils will not pass this test, although oils containing the small amount of inhibitor permitted by BP (a maximum of 10 ppm of either tocopherol or butylated hydroxytoluene) will usually comply. Inhibitors are also permitted in oil to USP, although the quantity and identity of the inhibitor are not prescribed; these are however limited by USA (F and DA) regulations as to what is permissible in materials for human consumption.

(vi) *Iodine value*

This test (IP 84) is sometimes included in older white oil specifications and is a measure of unsaturation either as olefins and/or aromatics. The former are very unlikely to be present in any oil that has undergone sufficient refining to make it colourless, whilst the aromatic content can be controlled by setting a suitable value for the ultra-violet absorption. Moreover the precision of the iodine value procedure, when applied to mineral oils, is poor. To assure an adequately low level of the undesired constituents only a very small iodine value can be permitted and this will be at the limit of test sensitivity. There is thus little reason to retain this clause in the few specifications in which it still appears.

B. ELECTRICAL INSULATING OILS

1. INTRODUCTION

These can be divided into two main groups: (a) oils for transformers and switchgear and (b) oils for power cables; this latter group can be further sub-divided into thin oils, for use in oil-filled ('hollow core') cables and more viscous oils, sometimes used as such in cable insulation but more commonly as components of cable-impregnation compounds. Oils for capacitors form a lesser but not negligible group.

(a) Transformer oils
The main requirement of a transformer oil is that it should act as a heat transfer medium to ensure that the operating temperature of a transformer does not exceed acceptable limits; these are steadily rising with increasing loading of transformers and whilst temperatures around 60–70°C (140–158°F) have been considered usual, higher temperatures are becoming more common and values in the 90–100°C (194–212°F) region are envisaged. The present day view is that the limit on the upper operating temperature of a transformer is set more by other insulation components, especially the paper, than by the oil.

Transformer oils are expected to remain in service for many years, 15 or even more being common, hence a high degree of stability is required; moreover as the transformers operate at high voltages, the oil must be a good insulant.

This long service life calls for supervision of oil condition and many official guides to oil surveillance have been published. In the United Kingdom this aspect is covered by BSI CP1009 (1959, but currently under revision) and there is also an IEC document in preparation on this topic.

In many countries these oils are the subject of a specification issued by the national standardisation authority; in the United Kingdom this is the British Standards Institution (BSI) and transformer oils are covered by British Standard (BS) 148 'Insulating oil for transformers and switchgear'; a new edition has recently (1972) been issued. Characteristics of the oil are listed in Table 3.

In the United States there is no national specification for transformer oil. However, various users have set their own specifications and the American Society for Testing and Materials (ASTM) has published a recommended practice for the purchase of uninhibited mineral oil for use in transformers and circuit breakers. (D1040), a similar specification, covers inhibited oil.

TABLE 3

Requirements for transformer oil

	UK[a]	USA[bc]
Density at 20°C (68°F)	0·895 max.	0·84–0·91
Flash point °C (°F) min.	140 (284) closed	146 (295) open
Viscosity cSt max. at −15°C (5°F)	800	—
0°C (32°F)	—	69
20°C (68°F)	40	—
37·8°C (100°F)	—	12
Pour point °C max.	−30	−40
Oxidation		
Sludge per cent max.	IEC 74 {0·10	ASTM D2440 {0·7
Acidity mg KOH/g max.	{0·40	164h {2·6
Acidity mg KOH/g max.	0·03	0·05
Interfacial tension mN/m min.	—	40
Corrosive sulphur ASTM D1275	non-corrosive	non-corrosive
Electric strength kV min.	IEC 156 30	ASTM D877 30
Loss tangent max.	0·005 (90°C: 194°F)	0·005 (100°C: 212°F)
Water ppm max.	35	35
Colour ASTM D1500 max.	—	1

[a] British Standard 148: 1972 (technically equivalent to International Specification, IEC publication 296, 1969).

[b] American Society for Testing and Materials, D-1040-69.

[c] The requirements of the ASTM specification for oxidation inhibited oil are identical except for the oxidation test, which is D2112, with a minimum stability of 195 minutes.

The International specification (IEC 296) is gaining increasing acceptance and it is to be hoped that in consequence differences between national specifications will tend to decrease.

(b) Oils for power cables

Here the oil acts almost entirely as a dielectric (*i.e.* as an insulant). In solid type cables there is no cooling function and even in the oil-filled ('hollow core') type of cable, where there is free oil flow along the oil duct and into the frequently spaced oil reservoirs, the cooling function of the oil is only slight. Hence, because of their dielectric function (achieved by impregnating the paper with which the cable is covered in very many layers), the electric properties of cable oils are much more important than for transformer and switch oils. Chemical stability is also very significant not so much because of

TABLE 4

Requirements for cable and capacitor oils

	Oil for low-pressure cable systems ASTM D1818	Oil for high-pressure cable systems ASTM D1819	Oil for capacitors and cable accessories ASTM D2297
Rel. d. at 15·6°C (60°F)	0·890–0·905	0·917–0·930	0·922–0·934
Flash point °C (°F) min. open	149 (300)	193 (379)	235 (455)
Viscosity cSt at 37·8°C (100°F)	21·1–22·4	162–173	432–561
at 98·9°C (210°F)	2·6–4·2	9·7–11·1	20·4–22·5
Pour point °C (°F) max.	−40 (−40)	−21 (−5)	−5 (23)
Sulphur, total per cent max.	0·25	0·35	0·35
Sulphur, corrosive ASTM D1275	non-corrosive	non-corrosive	non-corrosive
Acidity mg KOH/g max.	0·014	0·05	0·04
Colour ASTM D1500 max.	1	2	2·5
Loss tangent at 100°C (212°F) max.	0·002	0·006	0·005
Resistivity gigaohm-m at 100°C (212°F) min.	500	25	10
Oxidation ASTM D1934 (uncatalysed)			
Acidity mg KOH/g max.	0·02	0·1	0·06
Colour ASTM D1500 max.	2	4	5
Loss tangent at 100°C (212°F) max.	0·007	0·028	0·02
Resistivity gigaohm-m at 100°C (212°F) min.	20	5	1
Electric strength kV ASTM D877 min.	30	30	30
Water ppm max.	45	45	35
Specific optical dispersion at 25°C (77°F) min.	113 × 10^{-4}	110 × 10^{-4}	113 × 10^{-4}

the risk of sludge deposition, as in transformer oil, with consequent interference with cooling function, but because an unstable cable oil will, on
aging, rapidly develop poor dielectric characteristics. This causes increased
heat loss in the cable, consequent increased oil deterioration, and may lead to
breakdown.

Capacitor oils can resemble either of the sub-divisions of group (b). Thin
oils similar to transformer oils in viscosity but electrically akin to oils for oil-
filled cables are most commonly used but some equipment employs oils of
viscosity similar to that of heavy cable oils. In capacitors the oil is again
mainly a dielectric and hence its electrical characteristics are of primary
importance, although in some types of capacitors the oil also acts as a
coolant. Operating stresses can be severe, as in a power cable, and it is therefore sometimes necessary for a capacitor oil to have high stability, like a cable
oil.

No national specification has been published in the United Kingdom for
either cable or capacitor oils but in the United States, ASTM has issued
specifications covering both low and high viscosity cable oils and also a
viscous type of capacitor oil. Details of these are given in Table 4.

The IEC is planning to issue a set of recommended values for oils for
oil-filled cables.

2.   ASSESSMENT OF INSULATING OILS

(a) Tests for physical characteristics
(i) *Density*
This test (IP 160) is frequently included as a specification requirement; apart
from its usual indication of the broad type of crude from which the oil has
been derived, density can be important when transformers operate in cold
climates. This is because water, however undesirable in electrical equipment,
does collect therein and if an oil is of too high a density it could occur that
as the oil density rises with decreasing temperature any ice present would
float on the oil, instead of remaining at the bottom of the oil container. It is
difficult to set a precise upper limit for oil density so as completely to exclude
this possibility because various ice forms differ in density and there is also
the complication arising from air entrainment, both in the ice and in the oil.
The upper limit of 0·895 at 20°C (68°F) set in the IEC specification however
ensures that ice should not float on oil till the temperature drops to below
about $-20°C$ $(-4°F)$.

For heavier insulating oils the purpose of limiting density range is as a check
on oil composition. Density, in conjunction with viscosity, does give a clue
to the preponderating hydrocarbon groups that are present and for these oils,
a minimum density is some assurance of adequate solvency for use in cable
impregnating compounds, as well as guarding against excessive paraffinicity.

In this respect the density clause to some extent duplicates the aniline point (IP 2) requirement which occurs in some specifications.

(ii) *Flash point*

In the UK the closed test (IP 34) is commonly used and a minimum value of 140°C (284°F) is required for transformer oil in order to limit fire risk. The stipulation of a suitable flash point also automatically limits the volatility of the oil and for this reason the old loss on heating test (IP 46) was omitted from BS 148 some years ago. In the case however of oils for oil-filled cables and the thinner capacitor oils, it is important to restrict excessive volatility and this can be adequately guarded against by setting a suitable minimum flash point, say 125°C (257°F). Some users also specify a loss on heating test and the otherwise obsolete IP test for this property is hence still sometimes used.

Fewer volatility problems arise with the heavier cable oils or oil-based cable impregnating compounds, although here also a minimum flash point, say around 230°C (446°F), is frequently specified as a precaution against the presence of lighter (and hence undesirably volatile) components which could be troublesome at impregnating conditions of over 100°C (213°F) and high vacuum.

(iii) *Viscosity*

It is essential for transformer oil to circulate freely in the equipment in order adequately to fulfil its function as coolant. A maximum viscosity (IP 71) at ambient temperature hence has to be stipulated. BS 148 requires not more than 40 centistokes at 20°C (68°F) but in fact oils delivered to this standard are usually appreciably more fluid and seldom exceed about 35 centistokes. There is in fact a tendency to call for lower viscosities and the IEC specification (296) includes a Class II oil with a maximum viscosity of 25 cSt at 20°C (68°F).

Oils for oil-filled cables are of a low viscosity similar to that of transformer oil or even less in order to facilitate impregnation and also to enable the oil to flow freely through the cable ducts, but a lower limit to viscosity is set by the need to avoid excessive volatility. Oil-filled cables are impregnated at elevated temperatures under vacuum and the oil is also degassed under such conditions prior to impregnation. It is necessary to avoid excessive loss of low-boiling constituents of the oil, both on economic grounds and also because such fractionation of the oil in degassing impregnating equipment could alter its chemical constitution and hence affect its properties.

Heavy cable oils are very much more viscous materials and typical viscosity values can be as high as about 200 centistokes at 60°C (140°F). Such oils are probably the only petroleum products for which a maximum viscosity index (ASTM D2270–IP 226) is sometimes specified, in order to ensure that whilst the oil will be as fluid as possible at impregnating temperatures (say 100°C (212°F) or more) it will be sufficiently viscous to prevent draining at ambient temperatures in cases where cables are laid on a steep gradient.

This can however alternatively be ensured by suitably blended 'non-draining' compounds, containing materials such as high-melting waxes. Low viscosity index is also associated with oils of a naphthenic/aromatic character which have greater solvency for the rosin frequently used in cable compounds.

It is of interest to note that if the minimum viscosity index for the last cable oil shown in Table 4 is calculated, the value is only 4; the maximum permissible value is 65.

(iv) *Pour point*

For pour point (ASTM D97–IP 15) of transformer oils a value below the lowest ambient temperature to be expected must be set. British requirements call for a maximum of $-30°C$ ($-22°F$) although most marketed oils have a pour point considerably lower, a typical figure being in the region of $-40°C$ ($-40°F$); adequate low temperature fluidity is also ensured by the maximum viscosity permitted at the sub-zero temperature. The thinner capacitor and cable oils have pour point requirements similar to those of transformer oil. These oils are normally prepared from wax-free crudes and the pour point is in effect a 'viscosity set'. That is to say, the pour point temperature does not denote, for wax-free oils, wax separation to such an extent as to cause the oil to gel but represents the temperature at which, under conditions of the pour test, the oil will no longer flow. Such a viscosity is of the order of 1200 stokes and an approximation of the pour point of a wax-free oil can in fact be obtained by extrapolating a viscosity/temperature graph so as to estimate at what temperature a viscosity of this magnitude is attained.

Heavier cable oils naturally have higher pour points, either due to the viscosity effect just mentioned or else because wax may sometimes be present or even deliberately added to cable compounds when the conditions under which the cable is designed to operate do not contra-indicate this. The presence of wax in insulating oils must be however carefully considered since in addition to the adverse effect on low temperature flow properties, the presence of wax in an insulating oil could affect the power factor/temperature curve by causing a discontinuity at the temperature of phase separation. The presence of wax (largely n-paraffins) would also tend to increase the tendency to gas evolution under electric stress, discussed later.

(v) *Colour*

Although sometimes to be found in insulating oil specifications, this characteristic is of no technical significance. Whilst pale oils are, as a broad rule, more severely refined than dark oils of the same viscosity, colour (IP 17) is not a guide to stability, and the evils of 'over-refining' are well recognised in the insulating oil field. Deterioration of colour after submission of the oil to some form of aging test is sometimes limited but here again extent of oil deterioration can be much better measured by some other property such as acidity development or change in electrical conductivity. About the only point that can be made in favour of colour measurement on new oil is that it can give an immediate guide to a change in supply continuity.

It is important to distinguish colour from 'appearance'; the latter can often give a guide to oil condition, especially for used oils. Thus dirt can be seen, cloudiness may indicate moisture and a green colour cause the presence of dissolved copper compounds to be suspected.

(vi) *Interfacial tension*
The measurement of interfacial tension (ASTM D971 or 2285) between oil and water, is a sensitive method for determining traces of polar contaminants, including products of oil oxidation, and minimum values will sometimes be found in insulating oil specifications. The test has found more favour in the United States than in Europe. It is also frequently employed to assess transformer oil deterioration and thus to maintain a check on the quality of oil in electrical equipment.

(vii) *Aniline point*
Aniline point (IP 2) gives an indication of the hydrocarbon group composition of an oil; aniline point rises with molecular weight, also for a given viscosity, the higher the aniline point the more paraffinic the oil. For electrical oils it is sometimes desired to control the aromatic content because too high a value could give rise to oxidation instability and too low a value to inadequate gassing characteristics under electric stress. For these reasons an aniline point, usually in the form of a range of permitted values, is sometimes included in specifications. Since however it can be considered more logical to control oxidation stability and gassing by tests specifically designed for these purposes, rather than indirectly, the justification for inclusion of aniline point is doubtful. Rise of aniline point after extraction with sulphuric acid is perhaps a better indication of aromatic content than aniline point per se.

Aniline point is also sometimes included as an indication of paraffin/naphthene ratio because in the blending of heavy cable oils with rosin for the preparation of cable impregnants, too high a proportion of paraffins could lead to inadequate solvency for the rosin.

(viii) *Specific optical dispersion*
This is a test (ASTM D1807) used mainly in the United States and serves as an indication of aromatic content. The difference in refractive index of the oil as measured at two wave lengths is determined, divided by the relative density (all measurements are at the same temperature) and multiplied by 10^4; values above around 97 are stated to bear a direct relationship to the aromatic content of the oil.

If however there is reason to be particularly interested in the aromatic content, it is preferable to assess this by one of the more direct methods.

(b) Tests for chemical characteristics

(i) *Oxidation stability of transformer oils*

Very many oxidation tests for transformer oils have at one time or another been used. Most of these tests are of a similar pattern, the oil is heated and subjected to oxidation by either air or oxygen and usually in the presence of a metallic catalyst, almost invariably copper, which is the main active metal in transformer construction. Temperatures and duration have varied within wide limits, from 95°C to 150°C (203°F to 302°F) and from 14 to 672 hours.

As all these tests were intended to assess similar oils performing a similar function the benefits of international standardisation were evident and, after discussions lasting many years, an international test for uninhibited transformer and switch oils has now been agreed and is being adopted by an increasing number of countries. In its essentials this test consists in keeping oil at 100°C (212°F) for just under a week (164 h) and during this period passing oxygen through the oil, in which metallic copper is immersed. At the end of the oxidation period the amount of solid deterioration products (*i.e.* sludge) is measured, after such sludge has been precipitated by dilution of the aged oil with n-heptane, and the soluble (*i.e.* acidity) decomposition products are also measured by determination of the neutralisation value of the aged oil.

Limit values (*see* Table 3) have been set, these have been selected on the basis of wide international experience indicating that on the whole oils complying therewith give satisfactory performance. Although this test has been selected to ensure that an oil will have a reasonably long life it is by no means certain that correlation exists between the results of this (or other) oxidation test and the service performance of the oil.

As has been mentioned the life of an oil in a transformer may be 15 or more years but laboratory tests have to be completed within a reasonable time, hence the problem of accelerating oil aging to such an extent that its long term behaviour may be predicted from a short laboratory test is not easy. In fact the view has been expressed that none of the present standardised aging tests does correlate with service life under the varying conditions applicable to the latter.

For production control and similar purposes the above-mentioned IEC test can be considerably accelerated by increasing the temperature to 110°C (230°F) and decreasing the duration to 48 h, there being normally close agreement between the results of the standard and accelerated tests.

The testing of inhibited oils presents a special problem since owing to their enhanced stability laboratory test conditions must be made more arduous than in the standard test if a meaningful result is to be obtained in a reasonable time.

The IEC test has been varied for application to inhibited oils and such modified test is expected to be published shortly; it is intended as a 'continuity' test, *i.e.* for checking known oils, rather than as an acceptance test for unknown oils.

In essence the variation from the standard test is that the temperature is increased to 120°C (248°F), the area of copper catalyst is trebled, and deterioration is assessed by recovering volatile oxidation products and determining the time required (induction period) for the neutralisation value of these to attain 0·28 mg KOH/g; such time is, typically, in the region of 100–200 h. The maximum test duration is limited to 236 h and at the end of the induction period the sludge content (as precipitated with n-heptane) of the aged oil may be determined as an optional characteristic.

In the early days of the development of the IEC test a considerable amount of work was done with soluble catalysts (copper and iron naphthenates). Whilst the majority view was that this did not present a suitable route for a standardised oxidation test, especially for uninhibited oils, the use of soluble catalysts has persisted in Sweden. In that country only inhibited oils are used and oxidation (at 100°C) is carried out using 20 ppm (as metal) of each of the above mentioned soluble catalysts till the curve of the development of oxidation products with time shows a definite break ('induction period').

Although the international test is now written into the national specifications of many countries (e.g. Belgium, France, Italy, Netherlands, United Kingdom) there are a number of other tests which warrant comment.

First we must mention the British test (IP 56) which has only just been superseded in BS 148. This was carried out at the rather high temperature of 150°C (302°F), for 45 h, and employed a water-cooled reflux condenser so that nearly all volatile oxidation products were returned to the reaction flask, unlike the IEC test in which there is no condenser and hence the extent of reflux is much less.

The IEC test was derived from the now obsolete ASTM sludge accumulation test (D1314) which as a result of the IEC work was subsequently revised in the USA to include the IEC apparatus and general conditions of test except that the temperature was increased to 110°C and two durations, of 72 and 164 hours, were specified (ASTM D2440).

As has already been indicated, one of the difficulties about oxidation tests for transformer oils is the time required. To shorten this, a test for sludge formation in transformer oil by high pressure oxidation bomb has been evolved by ASTM (D1313). Oxidation is carried out at 140°C (284°F) under 17·2 bar oxygen pressure for 24 hours and the precipitable sludge formed during the test period is weighed. One criticism of the test is that sludge precipitation is carried out with a 'precipitation naphtha'. Although the characteristics of this are defined, it is a complex hydrocarbon mixture whose composition can vary widely even within the range of prescribed properties. This could give rise to varying precipitation capabilities in various batches of such naphtha, a disadvantage that cannot occur when a pure chemical such as n-heptane as in the IEC test is used as precipitant.

A somewhat similar test, designed for inhibited oils, operates at the same temperature but lower pressure (6·2 bar), employs a copper catalyst and determines time to a specified pressure drop (ASTM D2112).

It has already been mentioned that the interpretation of oxidation tests for transformer oils is not free from controversy. In recent years the view has been expressed that, because large modern transformers are sealed and protected from air, *i.e.* oxygen, by means of nitrogen blanketing, the behaviour of the oil when artificially oxidised is becoming less relevant. Such views obtain support from extended trials that have shown that there is little difference between the long-term behaviour of uninhibited and inhibited oils operated in closed transformers, although the picture is very different if there is free air access. For these reasons proposals have been made that tests to determine the stability of oil under long-term anaerobic heating conditions be developed, but no generally recognised procedure has yet been evolved.

(ii) *Oxidation stability of cable oils*

In general, oxidation stability tests for cable oils are much less well defined than those for transformer oils. None of the IP oxidation test procedures is specifically designed for application to cable oils and whilst the transformer oil oxidation test could be used for the thinner type of cable oil, it is difficult to see what information could be gained thereby, in the absence (contrary to the position with transformer oil) of years of experience indicating that oil to a certain oxidation level is acceptable for service.

In view of the much greater importance of electrical characteristics for cable oils, as compared with transformer oils, most tests for oxidation stability of cable oils involve, after the oil has been oxidised, the determination of the electrical conductivity either with alternating current (ac) (*i.e.* loss tangent) or with direct current (dc) (*i.e.* resistivity) or both.

Acidity (ASTM D974, IP 1 or 139) after oxidation is another criterion by which the extent of deterioration is judged.

Whilst most transformer oil oxidation tests are of the air or oxygen blowing type, many methods of assessing cable oil deterioration depend on static oxidation, *i.e.* the oil and air are in contact but such contact is not stimulated. A catalyst is sometimes, but not invariably, used. Thus in the ASTM open beaker oxidative aging test (ASTM D1934) the oil is exposed to moving air at 115°C (239°F) for 96 hours but a metallic catalyst is optional. The metal is not specified although copper is the one most frequently used in oxidation tests on insulating oils. Characteristics to be determined after aging are again left open in the test description, although acidity and electrical conductivity (both ac and dc) are the commonest. Colour is sometimes included but the limited amount of information that this conveys has already been commented upon.

A variant on this procedure, not an official test but frequently used, is to heat the oil in an oven, with no forced circulation, for 50 hours at 100°C (212°F) in presence of copper wire, subsequently determining acidity and loss tangent. This rather low temperature test can be accelerated by mild temperature increase and results after 24 hours at 110°C (230°F) are very close to those obtained for 50 hours at 100°C.

Blowing tests are sometimes used for the heavier oils, for example, passing four litres of air per hour through oil for six hours without catalyst, at 125°C (257°F) and then determining the loss tangent. It is difficult to give generally applicable figures for limits since these vary with the type of test and the oil quality specified. However, broadly speaking it may be said that conditions for cable oil oxidation tests are usually chosen so that the values shown by a satisfactory oil for solid type cables will be in the region of an acidity of about 0·1 and a loss tangent (at 90°C: 194°F) of about 0·01. Somewhat lower limits are specified for the lighter type of cable oils and these are in the region of 0·05 for the acidity and 0·005 for the loss tangent.

Unlike transformer oils, which may be subject to oxidising conditions during their service life, cable oils are only exposed to these during manufacture of the cable. Their operating conditions are generally anaerobic, hence the different type of stability test which is applied to them.

Before concluding this review of oxidation tests for insulating oils, mention should be made of the generally poor precision of these tests. Those who have not had occasion frequently to interpret such figures must not be tempted to read more into variations between tests on different oils than is really justified.

As an example, the IP oxidation test (IP 56, previously laid down in BS 148) has a repeatability of 20 per cent and a reproducibility of 35 per cent (*i.e.* these are percentages of the mean by more than which results should not differ in 19 cases out of 20). No precision clause of the standard type is included in the IEC test but the somewhat similar ASTM procedure (D2440) has precision akin to IP 56.

(iii) *Acidity*

Total absence of organic acidity is never feasible but a very low limit has to be set if corrosion of copper and other components is to be avoided; moreover, more than a trace of some organic acids can adversely affect the response of the oil to amine inhibitors.

A figure of 0·03 mg KOH/g can be taken as the nominal maximum but in effect the value found in new transformer and light cable oils is normally at the lowest limit of detection, say 0·01 or 0·02. Any figure higher than this is to be viewed with suspicion except in the case of some additive-containing oils, where certain accepted additives do impart measurable organic acidity to new oils. For the more viscous cable oils, acidity tends to be slightly higher, around 0·05, moreover as such oils are usually darker, the determination of acidity below this level is not easy.

(iv) *Saponification value*

This has sometimes been inserted in specifications; it has now been generally dropped as a requirement for new oil but the German oxidation test (Baader) uses saponification value of the aged oil as a measure of its deterioration.

(v) *Sulphur*

Total sulphur content of insulating oils (IP 61) is not as important as the form in which the sulphur is present. Opinion is divided as to whether any limit on total sulphur is required. Maximum sulphur content is sometimes restricted to around 0·2 or 0·3 per cent and the main reason for this is probably a fear, for which there is not a very definite foundation, that as the oil deteriorates the innocuous sulphur compounds it contains may change to a corrosive form. Although most specifications (*e.g.* BS 148) place no limit on total sulphur, some do and an example is the Swedish limit of 0·2 per cent.

(vi) *Copper corrosion, corrosive sulphur*

In view of the wide use of copper in electrical equipment, it is essential to ensure that the oil does not corrode this metal. Adequacy in this respect can be verified by a test wherein the oil is heated in the presence of a metallic copper strip for 3 hours at 100°C (212°F); the strip must be not more than slightly discoloured. This test, whilst still recognised in some specifications, has now been replaced in the IEC specification and hence in BS 148 by the ASTM D1275 method for detection of corrosive sulphur in insulating oils. This is performed at a considerably higher temperature (140°C: 284°F) and for a longer period (19 h) the oil being in a nitrogen atmosphere, but the accepted darkening of the copper strip is rather more than by the older test at 100°C; however the ASTM test is almost certainly the more severe of the two.

Corrosiveness towards silver is becoming increasingly important and some users require a test for this, which is closely similar to the older copper corrosion test. A silver corrosion test is not at present standardised either in the UK or the USA, although it is specified in some national transformer oil specifications such as those of Germany and Switzerland.

(vii) *Water*

Water is obviously undesirable in electrical equipment and the water content of transformer and other insulating oils is frequently limited to a low maximum value.

Quantitative determination may be made by one of the many modifications of the well known Karl Fischer method (ASTM D1533). With careful application of this technique, using electrical methods of determining the end point and operating in a sealed system, water can be determined down to about 2 ppm or even less. Such sensitivity is however rather greater than is normally required and a water content of 35 ppm and preferably less than say 25 ppm is usually considered satisfactory. The solubility level of water in oil at 'room' temperature (say 20°C: 68°F) will vary with the type of oil but is around 40 ppm. Amounts of water down to about 5 ppm in addition to being measurable chemically can also be determined by removing the water from the oil by a combination of heat and vacuum and absorbing the freed moisture in a suitable weighed P_2O_5 trap.

A simple method for checking for water in oil is the 'crackle' test, which consists in heating the oil to well above 100°C and listening for crepitations. This method although only qualitative and which may appear primitive, is in fact fairly sensitive; it should give a positive indication at around 100 ppm and may detect water somewhat below this figure.

(viii) *Carbon-type composition*
This is one of the criteria which will provide an indication of aromatic content. The method standardised by ASTM D2140 is derived from the well known n-d-M analysis and involves the measurement of refractive index, density and viscosity, for all of which standard procedures are available. From the chart given it is possible to ascertain how the carbon in the oil is distributed between paraffin chains, naphthenic rings and aromatic rings. It is however important to bear in mind that the last of these, 'per cent C_A', merely indicates the proportion of carbon atoms in an aromatic ring structure. It does not correspond to 'aromatics' as determined by other procedures (*e.g.* adsorption analysis). This is well illustrated if a pure compound, such as dodecylbenzene, is considered. This only has 33 per cent C_A although it may be regarded as 100 per cent 'aromatic'; in other words, the n-d-M type of analysis gives no information as to side-chains in aromatic compounds.

(ix) *Infra-red absorption*
A technique for applying infra-red measurements to insulating oils has been standardised by ASTM D2144 and whilst the main purpose of issuing this standard is to provide a procedure for rapid oil identification and comparison with previous deliveries, considerable information as to oil composition can be gained from its infra-red spectrum. Oxygenated bodies formed when oil deteriorates can be recognised and hence this procedure can be employed for surveillance of oils in service. An infra-red spectrum can also give information as to the aromaticity of an oil and can detect anti-oxidants such as 2,6 ditertiary butyl paracresol. A chemical test for the latter is however available and is preferable for quantitative purposes (ASTM D1473).

(x) *Ultra-violet absorption*
Although this technique is not yet standardised for insulating oils, it has been applied to white oils (*q.v.*) and is certainly applicable for indicating the amount of aromatics in insulating oils. The test is used by some manufacturers for production control purposes, especially for the thinner type of cable oil in which aromatic content and type of aromatics can be critical in connection with the gassing behaviour of these oils under electric stress (*see* below).

(c) Tests for electrical characteristics
(*i*) *Sampling*
Whilst the importance of the careful sampling of any product which is to undergo testing is self-evident, very special precautions have to

be taken in the case of insulating oils (ASTM D923 or IP 51) for which special techniques are recommended; an IEC procedure for the sampling of insulating liquids is in draft.

Precautions which are stipulated are mainly concerned with the avoidance of contamination that would affect electrical tests.

The main contaminant which must be avoided is moisture; traces which would not influence the general run of petroleum product tests could have a very significant effect on properties such as electric strength.

Other electrical tests which are very contaminant-sensitive are loss tangent and especially resistivity. The presence of as little as 10^{-6} of certain materials such as petroleum sulphonates can exert a marked influence on the results of such tests. When samples of insulating oils have been taken they should, till required for testing, be stored in the dark. Light can affect electrical tests, such as resistivity and also some chemical tests, for example an oil which has an adverse copper corrosion test may show a satisfactory test after a period of exposure to light.

(ii) Electric strength

This property is included in virtually all specifications for insulating oils. It is however necessary to realise both its limitations and the importance of stating precisely at what point in the manufacturing/delivery sequence of the oil the sample for this test has been taken. The electric strength or breakdown test is essentially a method of indicating the freedom of the oil from certain types of impurity, principally free or suspended water and adventitious matter such as fibres. A high electric strength gives no indication of the 'purity' of an oil in the sense of degree of refinement or the absence of most types of oil-soluble contaminants. It is perfectly possible to get a carefully filtered distillate oil which, by its stability (or rather lack of it) and other characteristics would be totally unsuitable as an insulating oil, to show adequate electric strength.

This test is of some assistance, when applied to an otherwise satisfactory oil, to indicate that the oil is free of contaminants of the type indicated above; in practice this assures that the oil is dry. The point has often been made that such assurance would be more logically obtainable by a determination of water content. However, from the electrical industry viewpoint, the testing of an oil for electric strength is a somewhat simpler procedure than a water determination at the parts per million level. Moreover the fact that an oil has a good electric strength does satisfy the electrical engineer that, from this aspect, it is fit for filling into electrical equipment.

The test is of more significance when applied to oils in service as one of the methods of controlling the maintenance of an adequate quality level in such oils.

Whilst all types of electric strength test are broadly similar, being the measurement of the voltage at which breakdown occurs between electrodes immersed in the test oil and separated by a specified distance, there are important variations in the shape of electrodes and matters such as voltage rise and whether the test is of the 'hold' type, *i.e.* maintenance of a set voltage for a fixed period, usually one minute, without breakdown, or whether the voltage is increased continuously at the specified rate till breakdown occurs. The former type of test (IP 20) was till recently included in the British national specification for transformer oil (BS 148) which has however now, to conform to international requirements, changed to the latter, *i.e.* breakdown test (BS 148: 1972 Appendix C).

Electrode shape is another important factor and flat disc electrodes, such as are used in ASTM D877, are less sensitive to traces of contaminants than hemispherical VDE type (ASTM D1816) or spherical electrodes; the latter two types are those prescribed in the British and IEC test. Results by various test methods are not convertible but, broadly speaking, a satisfactory oil tested between rounded electrodes should show a breakdown strength of not less than around 120 kV/cm and a well-filtered dry oil will attain nearly twice this value. Standard tests are all with ac of industrial frequency; for special purposes dc tests are sometimes used.

(iii) Permittivity (dielectric constant)

This is a fundamental physical property and is the ratio of the capacity of a capacitor in which the oil is the dielectric to the capacity when air is the dielectric. Permittivity of mineral oils lies within a fairly narrow range, say 2·1 to 2·3, with about 2·2 as a fair average; it decreases with temperature and rises with density. Aromatic oils have higher permittivities than those which are preponderantly naphthenic or paraffinic in composition.

(iv) Loss Tangent*

This characteristic is a measure of the energy loss in a capacitor placed in an alternating current circuit and in which the dielectric is the test oil. In the case of transformer oils, its importance, though increasing, is not as great as for oils that are to be used in capacitors and cables. Hence whilst it has not always been included in transformer oil specifications, it does generally appear in specifications for cable and capacitor oils. In addition to limiting the value of loss tangent permissible in new oils of the latter type it is also usual to require that this property be measured after the oil has undergone some form of aging test and to specify a maximum allowable figure for such aged oil.

Loss tangent is very temperature dependent, increasing with rise of temperature; to avoid undue diversity in measurement, standard temperatures of 20°C, 60°C and 90°C (68°F, 140°F and 194°F) have been agreed for international acceptance. A good cable oil will have a value of around 0·001 (*i.e.* 0·1 per cent) at the highest of these temperatures.

---

* This property has many synonyms, such as: power factor, dielectric dissipation factor, loss angle, dielectric loss angle, tan δ.

Whilst loss tangent can be measured at any ac frequency, it is usual, in control tests, to use the normal frequency of current supply, *i.e.* 50 Hz in Europe and 60 Hz in the USA; although loss tangent is frequency-dependent (inverse proportionality) at this small frequency difference results are comparable.

(v) Resistivity

This (expressed in ohm-m) is a measure of the electrical resistance in ohms to direct current between opposite faces of a 1 m cube of the test material. Like loss tangent it is very temperature dependent, falling with increasing temperature. The test temperatures recommended for resistivity measurements on oils are the same as those for loss tangent readings. Both characteristics are often measured but if, as is usually the case, this is done on the same sample of fresh or aged oil, it is important to make the alternating current measurement first, to avoid 'dc clean-up', *i.e.* the attraction of polar impurities to the electrodes, which can occur if the resistivity is determined first. Resistivity values for mineral oils can be very high, around 10^{12} ohm-m or even more (at 90°C: 194°F) being attainable.

A method for determining both loss tangent and resistivity is given in BS 148: 1972, Appendix F.

In theory, as the product of loss tangent and resistivity is a constant (about $1 \cdot 6 \times 10^8$) it should be possible to calculate the loss tangent from the resistivity measurement, which latter is a somewhat simpler test to perform.

However there are interfering factors and such calculation cannot always be relied upon to give a reliable result; hence it is usual to determine both characteristics. If the product of these (measured of course at the same temperature) is in excess of the above-mentioned constant, not much can be deduced from this, but if it is below this is a useful indication that, almost certainly, one of the measurements is in error. Both loss tangent and resistivity give an indication of contaminants in the oil; these are frequently materials of a polar character and oils which show poor results in these tests can frequently be brought on grade by a supplementary 'polishing' treatment with a small amount of bleaching earth.

(vi) Gassing under electric stress

This behaviour of an insulating oil is of especial importance in cable, and to a lesser extent capacitor, oils, which are subject to high electric stresses. Under such conditions some types of oils can evolve gas (mainly hydrogen) which can lead to void formation and eventual breakdown. Several types of laboratory test have been developed for measuring this property. The general pattern of these tests is to subject the oil, usually in a hydrogen atmosphere, to stress (of the order of 4 kV/mm) for a given time and then to determine whether gas absorption or evolution has taken place.

A good cable oil should show definite gas absorption and, since cables operate at high temperatures, such absorption should be maintained at temperatures up to 100°C or over. Behaviour in this test reflects the hydro-carbon constitution of the oil and, in order to have adequate gas absorbing power, the oil should contain enough unsaturated components (aromatics and/or olefins) without however such components being present in sufficient amount adversely to affect the oil's oxidation resistance. This type of test (ASTM D2300) is based on a method originally developed by the Pirelli company. Another type of test is also laid down by ASTM (Merrell test, ASTM D2298) which whilst assessing a similar property exposes the degassed oil to electric stress, in a vacuum and at room temperature, the amount of gas evolved at the end of 1000 minutes being measured. Whilst, as in the case of loss tangent, gas stability tests may be carried out at various frequencies, it is usual to do them at the applicable industrial frequency; there is good evi-dence that gas evolution rises proportionately with frequency and hence suggestions have been made to accelerate the test by increasing the cycle frequency.

The test for stability (gas evolution) under electric stress must not be confused with tests for the gas content of insulating oil (ASTM D831; 1827; 2945). These tests are largely factory control tests to ensure that oils intended for filling into equipment have been adequately degassed (since dissolved gas, like gas evolved under stress, could cause void formation). Determination of inherent gas content gives no clue as to whether the oil has been suitably refined; it merely checks efficacy of one of the final preparation stages, nor-mally carried out by the oil user. Two types of gas content test can be used, one measures all dissolved gas, the other relies on alkali as the absorbent and hence excludes carbon dioxide. As this gas is frequently used for forming an inert atmosphere, and is extremely soluble in oil (about 10 times as soluble as air) the gas content test confined to non-acidic gases can only be used with a knowledge of the past history of the oil.

The determination of gas content of transformer oil is increasing in import-ance as there is a growing demand for such oil to have very low (2 per cent or less) air content when it is filled into equipment.

The analysis of gases obtained from transformer oil in service is a valuable method of transformer fault diagnosis and development of a standardised method for obtaining and analysing such gases is in hand by IEC.

C. SUGGESTIONS FOR FURTHER READING

White Oils Section

Modern Petroleum Technology (1973), 4th edn, Ch 24, Applied Science, London.
C. G. Scott. *Gas Chromatography* 1960, New approach to the study and assessment of medicinal white oil stability, 372–86, Butterworth, London.
E. O. Haenni *et al.* (1962). More sensitive and selective ultra-violet absorption criterion for mineral oil, *J. Assoc. Offic. Agric. Chem.* **45**, 59–66 (IP Abstr. 1963, No. 1447).

H. Böhme and W. Huhnermann (1966). Zur Untersuchung der Mineralölprodukte in Deutschen Arzneibuch, 7 Ausgabe, *Arch. Pharm.*, **299**, 368–80 (IP Abstr. 1966, No. 759).

White mineral oil (1967), *J. Inst. Petrol*, **53**, 121–8.

E. Meyer (1967). *White Mineral Oil, Petrolatum and Related Products*, 2nd edn, Chemical Publishing Co., New York (*J. Inst. Petrol*, 1968, 87A).

Insulating Oils Section

Modern Petroleum Technology (1973), 4th edn, Ch. 24, Applied Science, London.

Standard methods of testing insulating oils. ASTM method D117 (ASTM Standards, 1972, part 29, 37–46).

R. B. Blodgett (1960). Why and how of cable oil tests, ASTM Special Technical Publication No. 253, 15–31 (IP Abstr. 1960, No. 612).

G. H. von Fuchs (1963). High voltage dielectrics of petroleum origin: their manufacture and evaluation, AIEE, Electrical Insulation Conference, 126–30.

V. Biske (1965). Insulating oils: recent ERA/IEC work, *Proc. IEE*, **112**, 574–9 (IP Abstr. 1964, No. 1146).

H. D. Held (1966). Bewertung von Transformatorenöle, Vulkan Verlag W. Classen, Essen (*J. Inst. Petrol*. 1966, 122A).

R. A. Lipshtein and M. I. Shakhnovich (1968). *Transformer Oil*, 2nd edn, Moscow. Engl. trans. Israel programme for scientific translations, Jerusalem, 1970.

IEEE guide for acceptance and maintenance of insulating oil. IEEE No. 64, New York, 1972.

H. Hautzenberg (1971). Die Überprufung der Betriebstauglichkeit von Isolierölen, Elektrotechn. u. Maschinenbau., **88**, 312–17 (IP Abstr. 1972, No. 221).

INDEX